P9-DFD-655

GREAT RIVER

The Rio Grande
in North American History

VOLUME TWO

Mexico and the United States

GREAT

The Rio

VOLUME TWO

Mexico and the United States

RIVER

Grande

in

North American

History

by PAUL HORGAN

RINEHART & COMPANY, INC. *New York*
1954   *Toronto*

Published simultaneously in Canada by
Clarke, Irwin & Company, Ltd., Toronto

Library of Congress Catalog Card Number: 54-9867

Contents

Book Four: The United States Rio Grande

BOOK THREE

The Mexican Rio Grande

NEW MEXICO

LLANO ESTACADO

PECOS RIVER

COMANCHE TRAIL

T E

DEVIL'S RIVER

Fort Davis

Dryden

Camp Hudson

COMANCHE TRAIL

Fort Leaton

Presidio del Norte

Del Rio
Fort Clark

Ojinaga

Lajitas

Boquillas

RIO GRANDE

Fort Inge

Eagle Pass

CHIHUAHUA

Fort Rio Grande
Presidio
del Rio Grande

Fort Duncan

Morelos

France Way

San Juan
Bautista

RIO GRANDE

COAHUILA

Laredo
Nuevo Laredo

BOLSÓN DE
MAPIMÍ

ALCANTRO CR.

Monclova

NUEVO LEÓN

DURANGO

MILES
0   25   50

Monterrey

palacios

Nacogdoches

TRINITY RIVER

BRAZOS RIVER

NECHES RIVER

SAN JACINTO R.

Austin

Washington on the Brazos

COLORADO RIVER

BUFFALO BAYOU

LYNCH'S FERRY

San Felipe de Austin

Harrisburg

Anáhuac

GALVESTON BAY

The Alamo

Gonzáles

▼ *Fort Sam Houston*

San Antonio de Béxar

GUADALUPE R.

T E X A S

N E W   S A N T A N D E R

SAN ANTONIO RIVER

Velasco

Brazoria

Victoria

Matagorda

MATAGORDA BAY

Goliad

FRÍO RIVER

La Bahía

✝

NUECES R.

Refugio

Copano

San Patricio

(GULF of MEXICO)

M E X I C O   B A Y

PADRE ISLAND

LAGUNA MADRE

...ntosh

Mier
Roma
Rio Grande City
Fort Ringgold

Camargo

McAllen

Reynosa

Matamoros

Fort Texas

Brownsville

Bagdad

TAMAULIPAS

Inset map

LAGUNA MADRE

PADRE ISLAND

M E X I C O

ARMS OF ST. JAMES (BRAZOS DE SANTIAGO)

POINT ISABEL

✕ *Palo Alto*

Fort Polk

Boca Chica

✕ *Resaca de la Palma*

Brownsville

▼ *Ft. Texas (Ft. Brown)*

RIO GRANDE

Bagdad

Mata-moros

Gulf of

MILES

0   5   10

I.

A Colony for Mexico

THE DISTANCE WAS GREAT—twelve hundred miles—and overland travel from the middle Gulf Coast of Texas to the Mexican capital was toilsome and dangerous. The roads were appalling. Robbers abounded along the way. As the southbound traveller drew closer to the Rio Grande two dangers became intensified. One was the lack of support and habitation for him in the countryside, which became a wilderness of mesquite and chaparral where water and fodder were hard to find. The other was the roving presence of mounted Indians from the North American prairies. Beyond the river, provincial capitals lay on the way to Mexico City, but their comforts were meagre, their garrisons concerned with guarding governors rather than voyagers, and their societies exiled from great affairs by rocky and sandy distance. The mails were irregular, and a letter dispatched from the river crossings at Laredo or St. John Baptist or Reynosa might well have to be entrusted to a private traveller going its way. Any such place was "as poor as sand bank, or drought, and indolence can make it," in the words of a letter that went from Laredo to the Texas Gulf Coast in March, 1822. It was the first of a stream of papers that Stephen Austin wrote to his people while on the mission that took him to the Mexican capital for the first time.

He had left the early settlers of his colony on the Brazos and Colorado rivers of coastal Texas. Eight families were there. A hundred fifty-one men were already at work making houses out of what they could find, and planting fields for the time when they could send for their families out of Louisiana. They had come in good faith, under permission granted by provincial administrators of the Spanish Crown. But by the time they arrived, Mexico was independent, and the colonial

453

grants made to the Austins were meaningless without confirmation by the nascent Mexican government. It was to obtain this that Stephen F. Austin went to the capital.

There would, he felt certain, be little difficulty over the matter. A few interviews, an exchange of papers, some signatures—and the trick was done. His case was clear. Anyone with the smallest sense should be able to see it. The grand sweeps of Texas could only mean anything to Mexico if they were populated and developed, loyally, ably and at once. Austin and his people were ready to swear allegiance to the new Emperor Agustín I, and renounce altogether their United States citizenship. There was work in the new homes to be done, and in his dedicated zeal Austin counted on starting for Texas ten or twelve days after his appearance in Mexico City.

But if there were delays, he was patient. The Mexicans, absorbed with the thousand details of making a new government, were preoccupied with the Emperor's accession. Austin wandered observantly about the streets. The city was "magnificent," though most of the population lived in misery. He lived frugally. With him he had brought four hundred dollars in doubloons that had to last him. He was earnest and polite, and Mexicans formed an agreeable impression of him. He studied their language—his own new national tongue. He launched his petition on its way in various offices. There he heard hints of further delays. It appeared that while the government was glad to hear him, his enterprise, great as it might look to him, was but one of a number of applications already received from other colonizers; and all these together were only details of a much greater question—the whole question of Mexico's colonial policy under her new empire. There were indications that the large policy must be framed before any of its parts could be approved. It was encouraging that the Mexican Congress was at work in committee. It was time to be reasonable, and wait in calm for the new fathers of the empire to act. The Emperor was, he felt, "a very good man as well as a great one," who had the happiness of the nation much at heart.

Though how slowly moved the Congress; and what unsettling rivalries began to show plain. The Emperor had enemies who began to be heard. July passed, and the colonial question waited until in August the old patriot from the Rio Grande, José Antonio Gutierrez de Lara, spoke in Congress for the colonial bill. He let himself go, saying that, based on North American patterns, the bill with its enlightened provisions would call to settlers who would pour into the new Empire, bringing prosperity and civilization to outlands presently owned by animals and savages. The great isthmus of Mexico, connecting two continents and standing across the path between Europe and Asia, would become the center of the world's commerce. The bill in its details even embraced Austin's humble case, and he had every hope of seeing it passed and himself on his way home within the month, at last free to get on with his foundation, officially confirmed by the law of Mexico.

But the proud new machinery that would make this possible suffered a violent shock toward the end of August, when the Emperor's soldiery seized fifteen deputies of the Congress under a charge of treason. The nation was outraged, and the colonial question was lost in tumult over the government's condition. The new Empire was economically prostrate. The Emperor's court style was already a great burden financially. The Congress was paralyzed. A military tyranny was being born under the Crown, and swept along in the current of patriotic opposition to it were other energies less disinterested; for the unrest of the moment released the ambitions of men who strove to turn the new freedom of Mexico to their own advantage. In the largest sense the constitutional crisis was a legacy from Spain. For by centuries of rigid paternalism, the fatherland had denied the colonial Mexicans any fair share in their own government, had failed to educate them in public affairs, and had so deeply bred in them the hunger for freedom that a man's personal fate—human life itself—seemed trifles to spend recklessly if they could buy a share, whether just or not, of Mexico for a Mexican. All governments were ponderous, all were drugged with the petty satisfactions of daily policy making, all knew inner conflict, and divided opinion, and the centrifugal tendency to fly apart through partisan loyalties to opposed individuals or beliefs. But the Mexican government at its birth knew these tendencies to extremity and faced almost a century of effort to overcome them.

There were sharp differences in form, style and motive between the Spanish and Mexican concepts of government. The Austins, in founding their colony, were prepared to deal with Spain's colonial government. Tenuous as it may have become, it was yet experienced and established in its own elaborate authority. Its systems could be studied. Its principles were known and plain and rigid. And then Mexico broke free of Spain, and the official relationship of settler to government had to be redefined and newly approved. At first it might seem that the Mexicans, with their new empire, would merely change the actors and keep the old play. There would be a new set of bureaus, titles, insignia, but surely all would otherwise be the same. But what was profoundly different was what determined all—the Mexican character. Under the Castilian forms that the colonial society had for so long been trained to perpetuate, the Mexican character was not the same thing at all as the Spanish character.

For the people of Mexico, when they found themselves in possession of their own nation, brought with them to power all the qualities of temperament and inheritance that for centuries had been subordinate under the Spanish Crown. These were now dominant over the land, and even where refined in a fragment of the population by Spanish training, were greatly modified by the buried Indian past of Mexico. Between two lost disciplines—the ancient Indian and the formal Spanish—the Mexican character given freedom to express itself did so intemperately. The politics of the new nation seemed to care little for the individual human life. Such indifference was deeply rooted in the sacrificial rites of the ancient sun priests, and in pagan identification with pitiless earth deities, and in savage hunting ways, and in untold Indian centuries of inert impersonality for the mass of people, under which the individual was crushed into conformity with nature's pattern that wasted him in order out of decay to perpetuate the type, all heedless of his human capacities of mind and soul. Spain brought the individual to society in the New World, though she did not bring for him even the modest degree of freedom in representative government that Spaniards knew at home. Independent Mexico looked to the United States for a new pattern of government. A new dimension of freedom had come into the world with the creation of the young and amazingly dynamic nation in North America—it was barely fifty years old—whose constitution and laws and westward expansion Mexico's new statesmen examined with mixed longing and alarm.

But constitutional forms were not absolute, and what a citizen of the United States meant by independence and its methods and what a Mexican meant were not altogether the same thing. The difference in understanding that lay there was another of the difficulties that Stephen Austin began to encounter, along with the paralysis of Mexico's congress, and the stalling of the Texan petition in one after another bureau, and the furies that swept the capital at the Emperor's absolutism. Austin could only redouble his patience, and examine his purse.

His four hundred dollars' worth of doubloons was melting away. Unable to abandon his purpose in Mexico, he drew a draft on one of

his colonists, and filled his time with sober enterprises that would both
demonstrate his serious intention to enter into Mexican national life,
and, he hoped, prove useful to the struggling government. Writing for
hours, he produced memorials to the Congress that proposed organization plans for legislatures and law courts and colonies. He was invariably
polite when he called upon officials to invest them with his greater
political experience as a former citizen of a free country. His progress
in the Spanish language gratified them. Earnestly he exhorted his
younger brother John by letter to study, study, and prove progress by
writing him back in Spanish, the language, he was certain, of their
whole future in Texas.

Stephen Austin was a small, fastidious man, with a head rather
large for his body. His clean-shaven face was full, crowned with dis-
arrayed dark curls. Below the intense scowl of his domed brow gazed
his great eyes—the right, level and calm; the left, alight and piercing.
He had a large nose that inclined a trifle to the left, and a full mouth,
sensitively modelled. It was a visionary countenance, with something of
the facile good looks of an actor, through which his intensity could
flare in calculated animation. In his dress he courted a sober elegance.
His skirted dark coat sat on his narrow shoulders and lifted its rolled
collar up beside his smooth cheeks, and higher yet rose the white points
of his shirt collar, enclosing his chin above his white stock and bow
cravat. He wore a light waistcoat and tapering trousers and squared-toed
boots. If there was general fashion in all this, there was also much of
his nature—modest, decent and without any touch of personal style that
suggested humor or lightness of spirit. For of these traits he showed
no sign. In all the thousands of pages of his preserved letters there was
hardly a smile, or a revealed love—except for the establishment of the
colony that was his life's trouble and necessity. In Mexico waiting upon
the distracted government he was a bachelor thirty years old.

By November the Emperor's autocratic actions seemed on the way
to acceptance, and the general colonies law once again moved in channels.
Austin heard that it would soon go to the Emperor for signature, and
on the twenty-second, he wrote to Texas that "in less than ten days I
shall be dispatched with everything freely arranged." A quill, a flourish,
"Agustín" and a rubric— But suddenly in the ancient coastal city of
Veracruz on December 2, 1822, a republic was proclaimed and once
again the Emperor turned aside from the colonies bill. It appeared that,
as Austin wrote, the Veracruz revolutionary leader was a "General

Santana"—a name he was fated to spell, though no more correctly, for years to come in the struggles that would flow back and forth over the Rio Grande between Mexico and Texas.

The uprising at Veracruz was not a mere provincial disturbance. As December passed, the republicans of Veracruz won the ear of other Mexicans; and though the Emperor sent forces against them at Jalapa that defeated Santa Anna there, the nation had heard with eagerness of the uprising, and as fast as they had swept to the support of Iturbide a year ago, they now turned their support to his opponents. A fight for the crown was looming. The Emperor was preoccupied with it. Austin wrote to John on Christmas Day that Agustín had not yet approved the colonies bill, and held out little hope of action for "at least three weeks more." But at the New Year, word came from the Moncada Palace that the Emperor had read the bill, was returning it to the Congress with minor revisions, and by January fourth the bill was law. Austin took pride in the fact. "I am certain," he wrote, "that if I had not remained at the capital to agitate this subject . . . the law would never have been passed." But one heavy task led only to another. The bill provided the legal terms under which Austin's petition might be approved, but the petition itself now must be acted upon separately. Once again all hung upon the Emperor's attention. This was a restless faculty. Abroad in the nation, provinces and garrisons fell to the rebels, whether in terms of armed allegiance or vehement pronouncement. While the empire crumbled, Austin, again delayed, was obliged to sell his watch for one hundred dollars. His clothes were giving out. His privations were honorable, but tiresome. They contrasted soberly with the talk that was going around concerning the imperial court.

The Emperor—it was said—was drunk every day. The cost of his household was unreasonable—the Empress Ana María ordered chocolate in the amount of 480 pesos, and the Emperor spent too much on his wardrobe. There was a matter of a saddle fashioned from bearskin, green velvet, tooled leather and gold. Debts running to over two millions of pesos were already contracted by the imperial government. There were more officers and bandsmen in the imperial army than there were soldiers. Think of it: the Emperor might destroy his reign in one final burst of folly, such as a "murderous, bacchanalian orgy. . . ." Austin's purpose seemed lost in such confusions surrounding the "very good man as well as a great one" whom he had courted at the beginning with so much hope. Nevertheless he pressed his petition until with certain revisions it was signed by the Emperor on February 18, 1823. By then the

Emperor's dominion had shrunk until he controlled only the capital of Mexico and its environs. What if the government fell? Would its acts in behalf of the colony be valid? Austin saw too clearly what must follow upon Agustín's "violations" and "usurpations" not to know how these would affect his plans for Texas. The inevitable came to pass on March nineteenth, when the Emperor abdicated, and a delegate in the abused Congress cried, "Agustín! Agustín! you gave us independence but deprived us of liberty!"

At once the Congress passed a resolution declaring that "all governmental measures resulting from the coronation were . . . illegal," and orders went to the provinces that henceforth anyone was a traitor who acknowledged Agustín as Emperor of Mexico. The decree went to the outlandish Rio Grande towns, while the central government moved to establish a republic, and Austin wrote to Congress, who must now once more act upon his colonial grant, "I have already witnessed, with the greatest pleasure, the . . . entire change of the government . . . ," and asked once again for a ratification of his claim. He was rewarded at last. On April fourteenth, the Congress, though suspending the general colonies law, approved Austin's establishment. The way was open to the settlement of Texas by immigrants from the United States. It was the most fateful single act of the Mexican nation in the nineteenth century, for by it were released forces that must clash in always increasing energy until in the end they would meet in bloody battle along all but the whole course of the Rio Grande.

The deposed Emperor and the provisional government made certain arrangements for the future. He was to be known as Don Agustín de Iturbide, with the style of "Excellency." He was required to agree that he would depart for Italy, where he was to spend the rest of his life. So long as he lived, he was to receive a pension of 25,000 pesos annually. At his death, his widow would receive a pension of 8,000 pesos during her lifetime. In a matter of a few weeks the exiled family sailed from Veracruz on the British armed merchantman *Rawlins,* Captain Quelch. Their luggage indicated both imperial nostalgia and anxiety for the future. It contained paintings by old masters, personal jewels, hampers of silverware—and the ermine and embroidered velvet, the batons, stars and crosses of the imperial state regalia. In addition to their Excellencies Don Agustín and Doña Ana, the party included their eight children, and a number of chaplains, secretaries and servants. The *Rawlins* set out under sail to cross the Atlantic for Leghorn (it was not far from Elba) and once ashore, the exiles hoped to make their way to Rome, where—surely?—they would live, looking westward, forever after.

2.

A Wild Strain

The mountain system of the northern Rio Grande was a vast, secret world. Wandering Indians there made shrines of twig and feather and bone, and went their ways. Close to the high clouds that made their rivers, the inhuman peaks doubled the roar of thunder, or hissed with sheets of rain, or abided in massive silence. Below them lay every variation of park and meadow and lost lake; gashed canyon and rocky room-like penetralia in the stupendous temples of the high wilderness. Along hidden watercourses and in little cupped lakes lived and worked the family of a small creature destined to be the first cause of great change in the human life of the river during the early nineteenth century. It was the beaver.

In still pool or mild current the beaver made his house of mud and twig. Its doorway was under water. The occupants dived to enter it and came up beyond into the dry shelter of their lodge that they had built of sticks and mud, where their food was stored and where they were safe from animal predators. The backwater before the den had to be three feet deep, and if this did not exist naturally, the beavers built dams to collect it. They chose a tree by the edge. Sitting upright, they chewed away bark in a belt, eating of it now and then from their paws. Down to bare wood, they gnawed away until the tree was ready to fall. Often it fell into water where it would make a stout beginning for a dam. Working in concert they brought from near-by woods bundles of stick and bush and starting out from the bank began to shore up their barrier. They dived to the bottom of the water and brought up loads of mud. This was plaster. With their broad tails they trowelled mud over the laid timbers, layer upon layer, always extending the reach of the dam until it touched the opposite limit of the course or cove where they worked. At times they paused to play, racing each other in the water, diving, and loudly slapping the water with their tails.

When house and dam were finished, it was time to lay up provisions within against winter when there would be no green sprouts of willow and cottonwood and fresh grass to eat in season. The beaver clan went foraging, often far inland from their water, in search of bark. The best bark was on the smaller branches high out of reach. The beavers brought down the tree, and then stripped the tender young bark off the branches laid low. They cut the bark into three-foot strips, pulled them to their water, and there floated them to the lodge. They made little signs to guide them as they went—mounds of twig and earth which they impregnated with castorum, a musk secreted by the animal itself, that attracted their sense of smell and reassuringly meant *beaver* and told them where the road lay. Once in the lodge and eating, they were neat and fastidious. They took out through the water doorway all the refuse of a meal and threw it into the current. Drifting away, it lodged downcurrent out of their way—bits of gnawed stick and knotty branch and hard root.

In the spring came the young. Leaving the mother during gestation, the male went travelling, often far away to other water, where he swam and frolicked, ate tender greens at the bank, and did not return home until the offspring were born. Then he took them in charge, trained them in work, and in the late summer led them out to forage before the sharp frosts and the thickening of their fur against the cold. Everywhere in the secret lakes and along the tributaries and in the quieter passages of the main river this lively cycle was continued by beavers in incalculable thousands, and wherever mountain and water met, evidences of it were scattered and lodged undisturbed—until the last Spanish and the first Mexican years of the Rio Grande.

For by then the beaver's fur was in great demand for the making of men's hats. The hatters of London and Paris, New York, Boston and Philadelphia consumed great cargoes of beaver pelt, and the fur trade moved westward out of St. Louis over the American continent to Astoria and the northern Rockies. While Stephen Austin was completing his organized arrangements with the new government of Mexico to bring new settlers from the east nearer to the lower Rio Grande, the river's upper reaches knew another sort of growing infiltration by men who whether they came alone, or with a few companions, or many, still came without formal approval by the Mexican government, and with no resounding program of colonial loyalty or pious hope.

They came to take beaver in the mountain waters, in spring and autumn up north, or all through the winter in New Mexico if the season was mild. Many of them were French Canadians; the rest were from anywhere in the United States, though mostly from the frontier settlements. They outfitted themselves at St. Louis, and remembering what was commonly known out of Pike's reports, crossed the plains and entered the mountains by the hundreds in the 1820s. Among their number were men who made the first trails beyond the prairies, that led overland so early as 1826, to the Pacific. Jedediah Smith, Charles Beaubien, the Roubidoux brothers, Céran St. Vrain, Bill Williams, the youthful runaway Kit Carson for whose return a reward of one cent was posted by the employer to whom he was apprenticed—such men went to the mountains after beaver skins to sell for a few dollars a pound, and all unwitting showed the way across the continent.

The movement had already had its pioneer in James Pursley, the Kentuckian, who had been detained at Santa Fe in 1805 under the Spanish governor. Others entering New Mexico from the plains were arrested, to be marched down the Rio Grande to El Paso and the prisons of Chihuahua in 1812, after confiscation of their goods, and were not released until the freeing of Mexico in 1821. Another party of trappers were taken by the provincial Spanish government in 1817, jailed in irons for forty-eight days at Santa Fe, and were finally released after being stripped of thirty thousand dollars' worth of furs and supplies. Such actions by the government were meant to protect the trapping industry already worked on a small scale by the Mexicans of the valley. Regulations declared that only permanent residents might hunt beaver. They were required to buy a hunting license, their number in any party was carefully fixed and recorded, and so were the length of time to be spent in the hunt and the weapons to be used—traps, firearms, or snares. If the early American trappers could not buy official licenses, they soon found a way to get around the law. "The North Americans began to corrupt the New Mexicans," noted a Santa Fe lawyer, "by purchasing their licenses from them," and so risked arrest.

But still the trappers came, and against other hazards. The greatest of these were the roving Indians on the prairies and the eastern upsweeps of the Rocky Mountains. For an Indian hunter could read the menace that came with the white hunter; and he moved with every savagery to defend his hunting grounds. The trapper retaliated. He fought the Indian with Indian ways, and took scalps, and burned tepee villages, and abducted women, and pressed westward. He fought distance, hunger, and thirst, and if he was unwary enough to be bitten by a rattlesnake, he cauterized the wound by burning a thick pinch of gunpowder in it. Once in the mountains he met his second greatest adversary in great numbers. This was the great grizzly bear, who was curious, fearless and gifted with a massive ursine intelligence. With lumbering speed the grizzlies could travel forty miles between dawn and dark through mountains. It was not unusual for trappers to kill five or six in a day, or to see fifty or sixty, and one hunter declared that one day he saw two hundred and twenty of them. The grizzly towered above a man. His forepaws were eight or nine inches wide, and his claws six inches long. He weighed from fifteen-to-eighteen hundred pounds. His embrace was certain death. So steadily did he smell and find the trappers that in a few decades by their guns his kind was made almost extinct.

The earthen village of Ranchos de Taos near the Rio Grande was the northern town nearest the beaver waters of the mountains, and there came the mountain men to organize their supplies for the trapping seasons. They found that some men of the Ranchos de Taos already, though to a limited degree, followed the trapper's life. Seeing how swarthy they were, the newcomers thought they must be of mixed Negro and Indian blood. It was astonishing how primitive were the ways of life in Taos—the farmers used only oxen in cultivating their fields, and a miserable plow made of a Y-shaped branch from a tree, with an iron head to its end that turned the earth. Hoes, axes and other tools were all old-fashioned. There were no sawmills; no mechanical ingenuities to speed up work; and—what was oddest to the squinting and raring trappers from the East—the people seemed to have no desire for such means to change their slow, simple ways.

The mountain men encountered at Taos their first experience of the Mexican government. Taos was the seat of the northernmost customs house of Mexico. As the trappers brought little to declare in goods for sale, they were evidently allowed to go about their preparations for departure into the mountains. They bought what flour and produce they could, and recruited an occasional Taoseño to join their parties, and made ready their equipment. In the far northern Rockies the trapping parties were often large, numbering from fifty to a hundred men. Most of these were camp personnel who maintained a base for the trappers and hunters who went forward into the wilderness. The "Frenchmen" from Canada sometimes kept Indian wives, and established in the mountains a semipermanent household with rude domestic amenities. Other parties were smaller, and instead of working for the great fur companies as contract employees, went their ways alone, as "free" trappers. Those who descended to the Rio Grande's northern reaches were more often than not in small units of a dozen, or three or four, or even a single man, who meant to take their furs and sell them to the highest bidder at the season's end. But all the trappers shared aspects of costume, equipment and even character, many of which grew from the tradition of the forest frontiersman of the late eighteenth century.

The mountain man was almost Indian-colored from exposure to the weather. His hair hung upon his shoulders. He was bearded. Next to his skin he wore a red flannel loincloth. His outer clothes were of buckskin, fringed at all the seams. The jacket sometimes reached to the knee over tight, wrinkled leggings. His feet were covered by moccasins made of deer or buffalo leather. Around his waist was a leather belt into which he thrust his flintlock pistols, his knife for skinning or scalping, and his shingling hatchet. Over one shoulder hung his bullet pouch, and over the other his powder horn. To their baldrics were attached his bullet mould, ball screw, wiper and an awl for working leather. When he moved he shimmered with fringe and rang and clacked with accoutrements of metal and wood. The most important of these were his traps, of which he carried five or six, and his firearm with its slender separate crutch of hardwood. It was always a rifle—never a shotgun, which he scorned as an effete fowling piece. Made in the gun works of the brothers Jacob and Samuel Hawken, of St. Louis, the rifle had two locks for which he kept about him a hundred flints, twenty-five pounds of powder and several pounds of lead. The barrel, thirty-six inches long, was made by hand of soft iron. The recoil of its blast shocked into a hardwood stock beautifully turned and slender. Peering vividly out from under his low-crowned hat of rough wool, he was an American original, as hard as the hardest thing that could happen to him.

Alone, or with a companion or a small party, he packed his supplies on two horses and, riding a third, left Taos for the mountains in the autumn. He was wary of roaming Indians, dangerous animals— and other trapper parties. For nobody could stake a claim on hunting country, and every trapper party competed against every other. He did his best to keep his movement and direction secret, to throw others off the trail, and find the wildest country where he would be most free from rivalry. Following the groins of the foothills, the mountain men came among high slopes and rocky screens. If two worked as a pair, they sought for a concealed place where they could make camp and tether their horses, near beaver water. There they built a shelter, and if their goal was a mountain lake, or a slow passage of stream, they set to work hacking out a cottonwood canoe. In natural forest paths they looked for the little musky mounds that marked beaver trails. They searched currents for the drift of gnawed beaver sticks. Every such sign took them closer to their prey. When they were sure they had found its little world, at evening under the pure suspended light of mountain skies they silently coasted along the shores of quiet water to set their traps.

They laid each trap two or three inches underwater on the slope of the shore, and, a little removed, they fixed a pole in deep mud and chained the trap to it. They stripped a twig of its bark and dipped one end into a supply of castorum, the beaver's own secretion that would be his bait. They fastened the twig between the open jaws of the trap leaving the musky end four inches above water. The beaver in the night-time was drawn to it by scent. He raised his muzzle to inhale, his hind quarters went lower in the water, and the trap seized him. He threw himself into deeper water; but the trap held him, and the pole held the trap, and presently he sank to drown. In the high, still daybreak, the trappers coasted by their traps again in the canoe, and took up their catch.

Working a rocky stream from the bank the trappers lodged the trap and its chained pole in the current, where the beaver found the scent. In his struggles he might drag the trap and pole to the shore, where his burden became entangled in "thickets of brook willows," and held him till found. Sometimes he struggled to deeper midstream water, where the pole floated as a marker; and then the trappers putting off their buckskins that if saturated would dry slowly and then be hard as wood, went naked and shivering into the cold mountain stream to swim for their take. And some parties rafted down the whole length of the river in New Mexico, all the way to El Paso. Their method astonished the New Mexicans, to whom it seemed suspect because it was new. Was it proper to use a new kind of trap, and float noiselessly to a beaver site taking their catch by surprise, and spend the night in midstream with the raft moored to trees on each bank to be out of the reach of wild animals? And at the end of the journey, to sell the timbers of the raft for a good price at El Paso where wood was so scarce, take up the catch and vanish overland eastward without reporting to the government? The New Mexicans frowned at such ingenuity, energy and novelty.

When in the mountains they had exhausted a beaver site the trappers moved on to another. With their traps over their shoulders they forded streams amidst floating ice; or with their traps hanging down their backs, they scaled and descended the hard ridges between watercourses where the harder the country the better the chance that no others had come there before them. The trap weighed about five pounds, and its chain was about five feet long. A full-grown beaver weighed between thirty and forty pounds. The catch was an awkward burden to carry back to camp for skinning. Removing the pelt from the animal, the trappers stretched it on a frame of sprung willow withes to dry. The flesh they cooked by hanging it before a fire from a thong. The carcass turned by its own weight, roasting evenly. The broad, flat tail they liked best of all. They cut it off, skinned it, toasted it at the end of a stick, and ate it with relish, as a relief from the usual hunter's diet of deer, elk, antelope, bear, lynx, or buffalo meat, or buffalo marrowbones, or buffalo blood drunk spurting and warm from the throat of a newly killed specimen.

All through the winter-fast months the mountain men worked, obedient to animal laws and themselves almost animal in their isolation, freedom and harmony with the wilderness. Their peltries were cached and the piles grew, in the end to be baled with rawhide thongs. A trapper took in a good season about four hundred pounds of beaver skins. Sometimes his cache was invaded and destroyed by prowling animals, or stolen by mountain Indians; and then his months of hardship went for nothing. But if he kept his pile, he was ready to come out of the boxed mountains whose cool winds brushing all day over high-tilted meadows carried the scent of wild flowers down the open slopes where he descended with his haul. At five dollars a pound it would bring him two thousand dollars in the market.

But once again in Taos, he might then meet trouble with the Mexican authorities. Now that he had his cargo, they showed an interest in him. If he was unlucky, they questioned him, examined his bales, and invoking regulations that nobody mentioned when he started out months before, confiscated his whole catch. If he resisted he was taken to Santa Fe and jailed, with official talk about the Mexican decree of 1824 that prohibited trapping by foreigners in Mexican territory. Since there were no public warehouses hunters could only store their catches in towns by making deals with local citizens for storage space on private premises. If a Mexican citizen gave protection to a foreign trapper he was in danger from his own government. At Peña Blanca on the Rio

Grande in 1827 one Luís María Cabeza de Vaca hid in his house the "contraband" of beaver skins left there for safe keeping by a trapper named Young. From Santa Fe a corporal and eight soldiers of the presidial company came to seize it. Cabeza de Vaca resisted them, firing upon them in protection of his home. The soldiers returned the fire and killed him. The official report of the affair stated that "the deceased died while defending a violation of the . . . rights of the Nation," and asked exoneration for the corporal and his squad.

But local officials might be bribed, and a license trumped up, and the catch restored to the trapper. In any case, after his mountain months, he was ready to burst his bonds of solitude, and he did so with raw delight. All his general passion and violence that his mountain work required him to suppress while moving lithe and crafty after watchful creatures he now broke free in the clay village where he returned among men and women. He had a frosty look of filth over him. His hair was knotted and his beard was a catch-all for the refuse of months. His clothes reeked like his body. His mouth was dry with one kind of thirst and his flesh on fire with another. If the one tavern in the town was full, he went to a house and asked for a corner of the packed mud floor where he could throw his gear, and was granted it. The family knew what he came to seek with his comrades. The women took kettles out of doors and built fires around them to heat water. When it was hot they brought it in, and found him waiting in his crusted skin sitting in a wooden tub. The women poured the water over him. He thrashed. He was as hairy as an animal and as unmindedly lustful. The water hit him and he gave the recognized cry of the mountain man—"Wagh!"—a grunt, a warning, and a boast. Bathing as violently as he did all other acts, he began again to know forgotten satisfactions. As he emerged with wet light running on his skin, white everywhere but on face and hands whose weather would not wash off, he was a new man.

The whiskey of Taos—they called it "lightning"—now warmed him within. He drank until he had fire under his scowl. The women did what they could to improve his clothes. He rattled his money and they made him a supper that burned him inside with chilis and spices. Early in the evening he stamped his way to the tavern in the plaza where a fandango was about to start. All benches and tables were pushed back against the walls of the large room. Tin lanterns pierced with little nail holes in a design hung from the raw beams of the ceiling. Two fiddlers, a guitarist and a flutist began to make up the music together. They played popular ballads—the same ones that at slower tempos also served

for accompaniments to the Mass and to processions. As the crowd grew
the room was hazed with blue cigarette smoke from the mouths of men
and women alike. The women were powdered till their faces looked
pale lavender. They clustered together at one side of the room. From
the other the men came and took them somewhat as cocks took hens—a
dusty pounce met by a bridling glare, and then an impassive harmony
between the sexes suggesting absent-minded enjoyment. Lacking milled
lumber the floor was a hard and polished cake of earth. The couples
moved with expressionless faces—all but the mountain man. In his face
there glared a starved animation. His heels made muffled thunder on
the ground. The Mexican dances were set pieces, with evolutions and
patterns. He did not heed them. He threw himself in baleful joy through
whatever movements occurred to him, "Wagh!" The lightning jug went
around. The music scratched and squealed. The windows of the tavern
hall were like lanterns in the pure darkness below Taos Mountain.
When the fandango was over, all went home. The mountain man took
a woman from the ball to her house. At rut like a big, fanged mountain
cat—"Wa-a-a-g-h!"—he spent the night with her to nobody's surprise or
censure; and, as one such man said, he had no reason afterward to bring
"charges of severity" against her.

Presently he travelled to a trading post on the prairies, or to St.
Louis, to sell his catch. In the frontier cities of the United States he
was a prodigal spender, uneasy in their relatively ordered society, loose
as it was compared to life in older and more easterly places. When the
season rolled around again, he was off again to his lost lakes and rivers
where obscurely content he felt most like the self he imagined until it
came true.

For over three decades the trapping trade flourished. At its height
the annual shipment of beaver skins from Abiquiu on the Chama and
Taos on the Rio Grande was worth two hundred thousand dollars. But
in the 1830s the market for beaver began to break, for the China trade
out of England and New England was growing, and the clipper ships
were bringing silk in great quantities to the manufacturing cities of the
world. Fashion changed. Silk was offered for hats instead of fur; and
the change brought the decline and finally the almost virtual abolishment of the Rocky Mountain fur trade. The trapper was cast adrift to
find new work. He could abide it only in the land of his hardy prowess,
and there he found it, whether he joined the overland commercial caravans as a wagon hand, or the American Army's later surveying expeditions as a guide, or amazingly settled on river land as a farmer. He knew

the craft of the wilderness and he made its first trails for the westering white man. Some of the earliest venturers in the Mexico trade were trappers; and as the trade continued to grow and establish its bases ever farther west, the trappers met it with their wares; and what had been a memorized path became a visible road; and along it moved another of the unofficial invasions of the Mexican Rio Grande that could only end by changing nations. The first sustained effort toward that end was made by the individual trapper. His greatest power to achieve it lay in his individualism. Where the Mexican was hedged by governmental authority, the trapper made his own. Where the Mexican was formal, he was wild. Where the one was indolent, the other was consumed by a fanatical driving impulse. The invasion, unorganized as it was, commercial in purpose, wild and free in its individuals, seemed to express some secret personal motive beyond the material. The trappers forecast a new, a wild, strain of human society to come to the northern river.

3.

The Twin Sisters

Stephen Austin, after three hundred and fifty-five days in Mexico, left for Texas on April 18, 1823, having "determined to fulfill rigidly all the duties and obligations of a Mexican citizen." But these he saw as a nineteenth century rationalist, not as a Mexican. Nothing could better illustrate the difference than the subject of religion. One of the conditions of obtaining his grant imposed upon Austin the preservation of Roman Catholicism as the official religion of the colony, as it was of all Mexico. All colonists were to be "Roman Apostolic Catholics." Having ostensibly bowed to this requirement in order to obtain his charter, Austin's real views of the matter stung his thoughts as he travelled homeward. Finally at Monterey, his spite could no longer be contained. In a letter from there he wrote of the clergy—the "Fryers"—that

they were "miserable drones" and "the enemies of liberty." His bias
turned toward the Mexicans. "There never was a people so dreadfully
priestridden and enslaved by superstition and fanaticism as the great
part of this nation. The clergy literally [sic] suck the blood of the unfortunate people. . . ." And in another letter he poured out contempt upon
his new countrymen to whom he had sworn to be loyal: ". . . to be candid
the majority of the people of the whole nation as far as I have seen
them want nothing but tails to be more brutes than the Apes. . . . but
keep this to yourself, it wont do to tell them so—thank God there are
no fryars near the Colorado and if they come there to distress me I
shall hang them to a certainty. . . ."

As these were bigoted sentiments, he concealed them under
the better part of valor when he arrived at Matamoros on the Rio
Grande. He showed his grants to the local authorities, who did not
question them, and went on his way to the colony. Once home, he
addressed his colonists, and after assuring them that his mission to
Mexico had been entirely successful, and that "the titles to your land
is indisputable . . . perfect and complete for ever, and each settler may
sell his land the same as he could do in the United States," he touched
upon the subject that so inflamed his private letters. "I wish," he stated,
now for publication, "I wish the settlers to remember that the Roman
Catholic is the religion of this nation . . . we must all be particular on
this subject and respect the Catholic religion with all that attention due
to its sacredness and to the laws of the Church. . . ."

Was this conflict of views, private and public, to be taken as a
sign of cynical expediency, of vulgar contempt for the other party to
a bargain, whom it was proper in mean selfishness to outwit at any
cost, including honor? There was nothing to indicate that any of the
settlers were, or became, Catholics; and later advertisements in the East
calling for additional emigrants to Texas failed to set forth plainly the
full conditions of the Mexican law in respect to the religious requirement. From the beginning, the equivocal attitude of the settlers toward
their hosts foreboded much for the future ownership and character of
Texas. Austin was empowered to establish and administer his own civil
government, pending final extension of the Mexican authority over
the northeastern provinces. When this came, with San Antonio de Béxar
confirmed as the provincial seat and a Mexican administrator established there, government in Texas took form in the odd mixed image
of remembered Spain, Mexico, New England and the prairie frontier. It
was a mixture among whose strains conflict was ordained from the

beginning; for government could only be the expression of human character in the aggregate, and where that character arose from hopelessly different traditions, one must eventually triumph, by whatever means, until conflict should give way to peace under the stronger. The individualism of the trapper in the north had its counterpart on the great empty littoral of Mexico Bay at the river's end.

News of the work of the Mexican congress came slowly to the lower Rio Grande towns; they were hardly more in the stream of things in 1823 than when they were founded by the Count of Sierra Gorda in the 1750s. The river frontier was still thought of at times by the official mind as a place of exile. Far upstream, near Ojinaga, a penal colony called Vado Piedra—Rocky Ford—was established. It was peopled by criminals in a Condemned Regiment. Under a soldiery hardly superior to themselves in record and type, they guarded the cattle and horse plains of northern Chihuahua against raiding Apaches and Comanches, and worked the prison farms with water from the river, and marched by armed guards went out in hunting parties to take game in the empty plain of San Esteban north of the river. On one such hunt they found a herd of buffalo and looked forward to a supply of good fresh meat. They made the surround, the drive began, and the slaughter followed. Busy at the jobs of skinning and butchering their supply, they did not know what watched them from the hills that bounded the plain. It was a band of Comanches, who when the meat was ready flowed at full gallop down upon the Mexicans, killed them, scalped them, and made off with the supply. Such an episode was but one of countless examples of how the central government was without power, resources, or even imagination, to protect its far marches. In the summer of 1823, a group of northwestern provinces moved to acquire statehood for themselves, under the federal system even then coming to pass under debate in the Mexican congress.

Coahuila, Nuevo León, Tamaulipas and Texas sent delegates to Monterrey to draw up their claims and argue their cases for local government under the federal union. They hoped to reproduce the autonomous system of the United States. A measure of the autonomy enjoyed by the States was indicated in the general American usage of the plural verb in state papers and correspondence with reference to the several states. "The United States are," they said, over and over again—never "the United States is." The concept of the sovereign state dwelling in harmony with her sister states, but with proud local rights, internal powers and traditional if young privileges, was the chief element in the

design of federal union. It was a design that was to meet an early test
in relations between Texas and Mexico, and Mexico and the United
States.

The Mexican congress adopted the federal system; and in January,
1824, the northern states were granted what they asked for, with Nuevo
León, Texas and Coahuila as one vast state. The constitution provided
that each of the three units might petition for separate statehood if its
condition appeared to justify further separate incorporation. In May
Nuevo León was divided from the others under its own state government,
leaving Texas and Coahuila under a common governor. A precedent
had been established, and almost from the first the "Twin Sisters," as
Texas and Coahuila were called, listened to talk of their own separation,
and people wondered where the dividing line between them lay. Was
it the Mesina River? The Nueces? Or was the clumsy make-up of the
state separated naturally by the Rio Grande that so often before was
claimed as a boundary between nations? Saltillo was the capital of the
Twin Sisters. Much travel was required between Texas and Coahuila
on the state's business. The arrangement was awkward. Certain Texas
officers even found it hard to spell the name of their commonwealth. On
a legal paper offered in Texas court, it was given as "State of Cowehey
and Taxus." If the unembarrassed phonetics of the frontier owed something to illiteracy—for few of the Texan settlers, by the evidence of their
papers, had more than the simplest schooling—there seemed to be also a
touch of exasperation with the outlandish words and names with which
the Mexicans affronted their new citizens from the American prairies.
Again much explosive power lay buried under primitive attitudes.

And certain self-protective acts of the Mexican government were
ominous for the colony above the Rio Grande. In 1824, Mexico was
troubled with sectional uprisings and gatherings that threatened the
authority of the new government. A decree was published by the Congress forbidding assemblies or juntas of citizens. What sort of republic
was this that denied its people the right of free assembly? It was—whatever the current phrase would have been—un-American. But the point
was, it was not un-Mexican, and the new Texans did not grasp the fact.
It was more easily understood and accepted in the Rio Grande towns—
the same Mexican towns where the Gutierrez de Laras had lighted the
brands of revolt for Hidalgo—and life along the river continued to turn
itself to older interests and dangers. In 1824 a mission of the Oblate
Fathers established a chapel on the north bank across from Reynosa,
where the missioners set out in their cloister a grove of orange trees that

flourished prophetically, the first citrus plantation in the lower river meadows. And a few months later word went to Texas from across the river that Comanches were on the rampage, stealing horses and mules, killing soldiery, and committing "excesses against some poor women" who were alone on a ranch far removed from the last upriver fort of Saint John Baptist.

4.

Last Return

At the Mexican east coast port of Soto la Marina on July 17, 1824, the British ship *Spring* put in with passengers whose arrival created excitement, and brought swift action by the government. The passengers were the ex-Emperor Agustín I, his wife, and their two youngest children. After thirteen months of exile, Don Agustín was ready to resume his throne. On board the *Spring* was a printing press that had been turning out manifestoes during the Atlantic crossing. In the ship's hold were guns and munitions, and in the personal hampers of the travellers were the imperial state robes. "My return," recorded the exile, "has been solicited by different parts of the country, which considers me necessary to the establishment of unanimity there and to consolidation of the government." He also feared that Ferdinand VII of Spain, supported by the Holy Alliance, intended to reconquer Mexico. The months in Europe had been unsatisfactory. The College of Cardinals had denied him permission to settle in Rome. In England, where he had gone to place the ex-Crown Prince in school, Don Agustín had conferred with San Martín, the liberator of Peru, who was skeptical of an imperial return to Mexico. It seemed to him, he said drily, that the Mexicans "had made known their opinion when they banished" Iturbide. To this Iturbide replied, "This exile was a work of violence, and the wish of only four persons. . . ." He proceeded with his intrigues. He was watched. A Dominican friar who followed him to Europe reported his movements to the Mexican government; and by the time he was ready to return, they were ready for him. The Congress had passed a decree denouncing him as a traitor if he should ever again appear on Mexican soil, and a sentence of death lay over him and all Mexicans who might in any way assist him.

Leaving his wife and children on the *Spring,* Iturbide landed from a small boat, and was immediately arrested by General Garza. The legislature of Tamaulipas was sitting at the time, and he was taken before it. The presiding officer was a famous priest who in his own time had preached the revolution of Hidalgo along the Rio Grande. It was Father José Bernardo Gutierrez de Lara. He permitted Iturbide to speak to the legislators, who immediately voted under the Congressional decree to carry out the death sentence on the designated traitor. Father Gutierrez de Lara served not only as judge but also as confessor. He heard Iturbide's confession three times, and on July nineteenth, the rifle squad came, and took the prisoner away, and shot him to death under an act of Congress of which he had not heard until his return. On the twentieth, burial was held in the cemetery of the parish church of Padilla. Accompanied by her children, Doña Ana María was disembarked and her future discussed. In the end, on the pension of 8,000 pesos guaranteed to the Emperor's widow, she agreed to live out of Mexico, and left for Philadelphia to spend the rest of her days.

5.

The Spark

In March, 1825, another and more abiding threat to Mexico from without her boundaries made talk. A citizen wrote to Stephen Austin from the States concerning the outcome of the recent presidential election. "Mr. John Q. Adams had been Duly Elected . . . thare is great hopes of the United States becoming Peaceable possession of the

Province of Texas as far as the Rio Grande. . . ." Texas suddenly took on new promise for the North Americans. A father in New Orleans advised "his son to not sell his land claims in Texas," for the talk in New Orleans was that "our Minister to Mexico is about to conclude a Trety with the Mexican Republic for the Province of Texas—the Rio grande to be the line between the two governments. . . ." The writer ended by asking Austin to reserve him some good land on the Brazos or the Colorado. It was a sudden revival of Henry Clay's old demand for Texas all the way to the river, and now it was pressed by John Quincy Adams, who had opposed it during the debates of 1819 on the Florida Treaty.

There was more than frontier rumor to the report that the United States hankered after Texas and the Rio Grande. It seemed expedient to examine again, this time with Mexico instead of Spain, the terms of the Florida Treaty that had defined the Sabine as the western limits of Louisiana. United States policy desired to see the whole eastern drainage of the Rocky Mountains above the Rio Grande as American territory. Mexico would be asked to redefine the northeastern limits of her country. Discussions would take place in Mexico between the government and Mr. Joel Poinsett, the United States minister, who was empowered to offer certain reassurances such as a guarantee that in territory newly ceded by Mexico the States would provide measures to overcome the Comanche warfare that harassed the Rio Grande provinces. But rumors were not only current in Louisiana—they swept through Mexico; and the very suggestion by itself that the United States wanted to discuss boundaries, after she had in 1819 renounced forever "all rights, claims and pretensions" to Texas and the Rio Grande, created an atmosphere in which Poinsett found it difficult even to raise the question. For the time being he let it lie, and so did Mexico, while in Texas the colony toiled away in hardship and remoteness at the job of establishing a fragment of the only life they knew—that of the United States—under the Mexican flag.

Eighteen twenty-five was a wet year along the lower river. Commercial and official communications between the colony and the state capital at Saltillo were more difficult than usual. From Reynosa a colonist wrote to Austin, "All the water courses are up so that mules with Cargo cannot proceed . . . there has been a great deal of Rain in this Country . . . the Rio Grande is very high. . . ." Another wrote later, from Camargo, ". . . from what I can learn there are a grate many goods in this part of the Country,—the Indians are still doing Mischief . . . they Stole forty Horses from here a few days before we arrived here." He added a warning that a certain Nixon, also a colonist, was busying himself up and down the river in efforts to do harm to Austin, "writing against" him to the Mexican government. "My nearves," concluded the uprooted American, "are very weeke."

Such news was only an added discouragement to Austin in his labors, and at times he broke out in his letters with bitter denunciations of those whom he led, and gloomy predictions for the future. "You always," wrote his brother James to him, "you always put the worst construction on things and thereby render yourself fretful and melancholy." But colonial stresses were continuous, both from within and without. A Choctaw informant alarmed Austin in 1826 with word that "Comanches are going to make a grand effort, next Fall, against Bexar and the Rio Grande frontier," and he forwarded the warning to Saucedo, the Mexican administrator at San Antonio. The remorseless Nixon persisted in his defamations, even though a Mexican friend assured Austin that his protestations were "falso y falsisimo." But every whisper of ill will only increased the mistrust with which the central government viewed affairs above the river, and in December, 1826, a crisis came.

It arose between the Mexican government and the settlement made near Nacogdoches by American immigrants under Benjamin Edwards, who had obtained a Mexican grant after Austin had received his own. The two colonies were far apart, but, in the scale of Texan distances, they were still neighbors, and both groups of newcomers were American. The trouble was that Edwards and his followers settled on lands already occupied by a scattering of Mexicans. From the first, there were two factions—one American, one Mexican, in outlook and sympathy—in the Edwards colony. Disagreements were frequent and bitter. The local alcalde, Samuel Norris, favored the Mexican population, and upheld the Mexican claims to previous land grants. American settlers saw their hard work of establishment about to go for nothing. Mexicans seized their property, had them arrested on false charges, jailed and fined. Edwards appealed to Austin for advice on how to proceed. Austin counseled him to write Governor Blanco, at Saltillo, setting forth his complaints, and appealing for justice. This he did in September.

A few weeks later came the governor's reply. It annulled Edwards's contract, and expelled him from Mexican territory, even if he desired to appeal his case to the central government in Mexico City. It was too much for the settlers to accept. Edwards proclaimed freedom in a series of fiery broadsides and letters, alluding to the ills suffered by his followers. "Our properties daily seized by violence and injustice, our persons violated, our liberties trampled underfoot, and ourselves the destined and immediate victims of Spanish or Mexican bayonets; we have sprung to arms for our safety" from the works of "this imbecile, this faithless and perfidious government. Great God!" he cried, "can you any longer hesitate, fellow citizens, what to do?" He announced the founding of Fredonia, a new republic, and he called for aid from the United States, from Austin and his colonies, and from a coalition of Indian tribes. Of all these, only the Indians responded. "Twenty-three Nations of Indians," he announced, "exclusive of the Comanches, are now sacredly *pledged* to aid us in our *Independence—*". The price was great, and it was promised on a basis of no real authority. The Indians were to be given ownership of a vast area of the prairies, for Edwards had designated "a line North of this, running westwardly to the Rio Grande; securing all individual rights within their territory" to the Indians.

Austin saw it all with regret. He had worked hard enough to convince the Mexican government that he and his people intended to be loyal and were in fact so. He saw the Fredonians as the "Nacogdoches madmen," and he could only believe that they were inviting Indians to rise and sweep the frontiers with a reign of terror. Far from helping the Edwards movement, Austin called his militia to arms, and proclaimed that one hundred of his men would march to support the government against Nacogdoches. "I know nothing," he wrote icily to a correspondent in East Texas, "I know nothing positive as to the particular acts of oppression or injustice which you complain of against the local authorities of Nacogdoches. If report is to be believed you have cause to complain against the local authorities, but my Dr Sir the local authorities of Nacogdoches is not the whole Govt. What would you say in the U. S. if a party were to rebel against the Govt. because a Justice of the peace, had done wrong—"

Within a month Fredonia collapsed. The Mexican army sent troops. Austin's colony abided firmly loyal to their Mexican allegiance. Austin was commended by the government for his stand. New settlers entered East Texas to replace those cast out with Edwards. The Indian coalition was broken up, and the "twenty-three Nations" once more agreed to subsist under Mexican rule. The crisis was over; but a demonstration had been made of how difficult it was to hold together in peace two opposing national temperaments; and once again the cry of "to the Rio Grande" had been raised by men from the United States. It had hardly subsided when from a higher quarter the general idea was raised again, for later in 1827, Henry Clay as Secretary of State authorized Poinsett to offer Mexico $1,000,000 if she would permit the extension of the North American boundary to the Rio Grande. Poinsett, in the prevailing atmosphere in Mexico City, did not submit the offer. But its terms were known even in the colony, and J. E. B. Austin wrote to his sister that if the United States were to buy Texas, the family "would not take less than $500,000" for their "interest in the Country. . . ." in any settlement by the United States of individual claims following such a purchase.

On a more personal level, relations were at times touch and go. A colonist travelling through Matamoros wrote back to the Brazos: "We remain as usual with now and then a little difficulty, as hapened at a Ball the other evening, but since we have had fine dancing. . . . You know I am not in favor Spanish (except the Women of this Country they do verry well when that is said all is said) for the men are the damdest rascals in the world. . . . We had a frolick on the 8 January and got a little foxy."

Mexicans in their turn had their own views. In 1828 a certain José María Sánchez saw the Austin settlement. It was a scattered little town of about two thousand people, and its forms were new in Texas. The Rio Grande frontier had towns built of earth and rock, tinted plaster, and rocky streets laid out at right angles to a square central plaza dominated by a church. They were towns that rose from the river landscape like parts of it. At San Felipe de Austin on the Brazos, Sánchez saw forty or fifty little wooden houses. They were built in the image of the forest and cabin life of the North American frontier, out of logs interlocked at the corners, and chinked with mud plaster. Rock chimneys rose at the end of each house. Many houses had only one room. Those that had two displayed a new mannerism of the American forest primitive style, for the two rooms were separated by an open breezeway under the same roof that covered the rooms. Such a dwelling was called a dog-run house. Later it would know modifications in rock construction and stucco, and remain characteristic of Texas living. Austin's own bachelor quarters were of this design. Sánchez remarked "two wretched little stores" where the settlers bought their goods. One sold "only whiskey, rum, sugar, and coffee; the other rice, flour, lard and cheap cloth." There was no coherent plan to the village. The houses lay scattered at random on the low rolling land. Sánchez observed Austin at his labors, and learned something of the views and temperaments of the colonists. He shook his head over the whole spectacle, and wrote that

Austin "in all his action, has, as one may say, lulled the authorities into a sense of security, while he works diligently for his own ends." There was something in the air, and Sánchez felt it. "In my judgment," he concluded, "the spark that will start the conflagration that will deprive us of Texas, will start from this colony."

What was it that promised such trouble? Was it the energetic impatience of the Americans? They were accustomed to acting for themselves. They did not wait, anywhere, for central authority to justify them in what they sought and how they sought it. When men came together on the frontier to make a common life, they *were* the government, at once, and energetically. The colony saw only its own wants and problems. Austin could not help feeling exasperation at the miserable, poor, confused doings of the Mexicans. The Mexican government, he told a distinguished American who was considering a move to Texas—it was Commodore David Porter—"may easily make Texas a very flourishing and advantageous member of the confederation it is now a dead weight —Texas once settled and the whole of the frontier of the Rio Grande from New Mexico to Matamoros would be effectually protected from the indians which would be an incalcutable advantage. . . ."

But if he and his work suffered by the very remoteness of Texas from the heart of government, he was unable to comprehend the furies that swept through Mexico periodically. In the eight years since gaining independence from Spain, Mexico knew three revolutions and a shuttling of presidents by force of arms, from old General Guadalupe Victoria, the first—"one of Plutarch's Romans," as he was gloriously called in the usual elation that swept new officers into the Moncada Palace— to General Guerrero, while Santa Anna alternated between discreet obscurity on his ranch and armed uprisings in the posture of a hero. And in the summer of 1829, as Texas struggled to establish laws, and justify her growing sentiment for separate statehood, and resist discriminatory customs regulations at Mexican ports of entry, Mexico faced a preposterous threat from over the Atlantic.

For Ferdinand VII, bearing out the dead Iturbide's prediction, undertook to reconquer Mexico with thirty-five hundred troops who were embarked from Havana in July. It was the year's worst season in Mexico Bay, with hurricanes and rain. If Cortés had managed with fewer invaders, he did not have seven millions of inhabitants to face who could meet him with his own weapons. The Spanish fleet steered clear of San Juan de Ulloa and Veracruz. Instead, the miserable army was put ashore at Tampico, after which the ships sailed away for Cuba. The incredible monarch at Madrid was confident that once in Mexico, his forces would be met with legions of Mexicans who eager to throw off the disorders of self-government would spring loyally to the Crown and help put down the upstart republic overnight. The royal calculations were inexact. Seizing the opportunity for one of his emergences, Santa Anna rallied troops about him without help from the republican government and led the campaign against the Spaniards, who without reinforcement or support, and riddled by fever, surrendered to him on September 11, 1829. The invasion was over. Fewer than two thousand Spaniards survived to be shipped back to Cuba. Santa Anna was a national hero. Biding his time, he modestly retired to the country, and a few weeks later a revolution broke out in army garrisons in Yucatán and elsewhere, and the national government was overthrown. The new president was Anastasio Bustamante who after attending to the spoils of victory looked north to the colonies with new plans.

During that same summer the coastwise shipping of the gulf, plying between New Orleans and the Mexican east coast ports, put in and out of the anchorage at the mouth of the Rio Grande, carrying passengers, money and merchandise. Matamoros was the first considerable town upriver. Gulf vessels could not come to her riverbanks, for the river's last reaches were shallow, full of difficult bends and bars. Cargo had to be landed on the beaches of the estuary and hauled overland to the customs houses, and to the start of the long desert journey to the interior in wagons and on pack mules. Other towns farther upriver—Reynosa, Camargo, even Saint John Baptist, now called Presidio del Rio Grande—were terminal points for better roads to the interior than the one from Matamoros. But to reach them by water had never been tried, and the only boating upriver consisted of a ferry crossing here and there at the most populous routes, where a brown ferryman, who worked naked in readiness to jump into the water to push if his skiff went aground, poled his fares over the muddy current unchallenged—until August, 1829.

6.

The "Ariel"

On the third of that month, a letter was handed at Matamoros to an overland traveller leaving for San Felipe de Austin on the Brazos. It was addressed to Stephen Austin, and it said "I am here with a Steamboat and some goods for the purpose of ascending the River del norte to open a commercial intercourse with the interior if practicable and taking up land for future benefit— It is extreemly doubtfull whether the enterprise will result in success. I shall however give some months attention to it . . . It will be some weeks before I can get ready to start from this and Should the opportunity offer I should be pleased to hear from you. Your council after so much painfull experience would be valuable. . . ." In its calm determination and tractable realism the letter carried a certain familiar tone. It had the Austin touch, and in fact, it was signed by Captain Henry Austin, Stephen's cousin. Characteristically, it was obliged to add, in the North American obsession with a familiar topic, "before leaving the US I laid before the Govt a Memoir on the western boundary pointing out the advantages of an exchange of the territory west of the Rocky Mountains for the land between the Del norte and the US giving the Mexican Govt one or two millions to enduce the exchange—" If President Andrew Jackson, newly elected, had anticipated him by already sending an emissary to Mexico with an offer of five millions for the territory to the Rio Grande, Henry Austin nevertheless was thinking continentally, like a man of his time, and of his family; and he now proceeded with his venture as master of the first Rio Grande steamboat.

She was called the *Ariel* and was, so her captain said, "a boat of great speed and power," and perhaps could run as fast as seven knots an hour. She carried one hundred thousand pounds of freight. She burned wood in her great furnaces that made her bulge amidships, where she bulged again at each side with the paddle wheels that looked as if they

had been taken from a millstream. According to her type, the *Ariel*
carried a single tall black smokestack directly above her boilers and
engines. Her decks were wide, her hull narrow below them, taking a
draft of between three and four feet of water. The pilothouse forward,
and the cabin amidships, were high and narrow, with upright wooden
ribbing through which gaunt little windows looked out darkly. Against
her white paint two small brass cannon sparkled at bow and stern. These
were on guard against pirates in the Gulf or robbers on land. She pad-
dled along bustily like a heavy, changeling swan that could never leave
the water, though giving to the sky from her tall black neck a proud and
billowing banner of dense smoke shot through with huge sparks of
burning wood that crackled upward when the boilers were stocked
anew. Her fuel she took on board anywhere along the banks where
enough wood grew, and piles of it were stacked at the engine-room
door. She brought new sounds to the river. Her paddle wheels hissed
and foamed when she backed water, and chopped along sweetly dripping
when she was on a clear run. Blowing off steam she split the brilliant
air, and sounding her steam whistle with a let of white plume she made
travelling music, and with her brass bell atop the pilothouse she commanded in marine propriety her changes of speed and the passing of
hours. Around the endless loops and bends of the lower river she
searched in caution for enough water to bear her and above the flood-
cut banks her stack moved slowly by to be marvelled at from the few
cultivated fields, the pastures, the grazing land of the brush, until she
put in at a little town of stone and clay, where all swarmed to see her
in the beating heat of a Rio Grande summer.

The Captain's letter took twenty-four days to be delivered, and
Stephen Austin answered it at once, and with measured pessimism. He
feared that his cousin's doubts about the enterprise were "but too well
founded." He had been working on a map of Texas, and was full of his
subject. The Rio Grande and its country were "entirely unfit for steam
navigation." Captain Austin had asked for "council" and it came dutifully. "As regards the country on the Rio Grande, so far as my information extends it is calculated entirely for pastoral purposes and can never
be valuable as an agricultural section The soil is rich and fertile, but
the seasons are dry and so very iregular as to destroy every thing like
certainty in crops, unless where there are facilities for irrigation, and
those can only be obtained by means of machinery for raising the water
out of the river—an expedient which would be expensive and I think
inadequate—tho many have had it on contemplation, as I have been

told, to use steam for this purpose—" A thought occurred to him. Perhaps, if the climate and soil were suitable, a coffee plantation might be tried somewhere on the river, and he left it politely with Captain Austin, who was much travelled, adding, "Your observation in all quarters of the world, will enable you to form a much more correct opinion as to this, than any one who has ever visited there." Still, he would say one thing. "As regards lands for future benefit, I am decidedly of opinion that one league of land well situated in Texas will be worth more than ten on the Rio Grande— The Sun and moon are not more dissimilar than the two countries. . . ." He had really given it much thought, while making notes for his map. Texas teemed with natural products— beef, dairy fats, grain, garden crops, cotton, sugar, tobacco, timber, and lumber; and industries could readily be set up to turn out cotton and woollen fabrics, distilled liquors; and the horse and mule trade could be developed. What was needed was more immigration by civilized persons, and the establishment of Texas as a separate state under Mexico. Given these, the "citizens of Texas would deal with the Indians, and protect the whole Rio Grande frontier at no cost to the government." One vision led to another, and to his cousin he added that he had "in contemplation to open a road direct from here"—the Brazos—"to *Passo del Norte* and Santa Fe." The idea was to turn, in one sweeping gesture, the Missouri-New Mexico trade southward to Texas, where between a city which he might found at Galveston and the ancient pass into northern Mexico a new highway could be stretched across all of Texas. If this could be managed, and if Henry's "views incline this way," wrote Stephen, "I would join with you on equal terms—"

But Henry Austin, occupied with the poor realities of the river, was learning them fast. He had been "induced to embark in this operation by the hope of retrieving my ruined fortune and of laying a foundation for an estate for my family by Securing a large tract of land." His contract with the Mexican political authority empowered him to colonize "any of the vacant lands on this river but there are none vacant that are worth having or that can be got at conveniently." By September he had been upriver nearly as far as Revilla, where he found "the river so dangerous in low water" that he "did not think it prudent to proceed up at this late season." Only in wet season could the *Ariel* go above Mier, (by which he really meant Roma), and below Mier all the good land was already taken. He had to decide to spend the winter plying between Camargo and Matamoros, making two or three trips a month, depending upon how much business was to be had. The outlook was not encouraging. If it came to failure, he said, "I should only be able to save my self from ruin by taking the boat to some place where She could be Sold or employed to advantage." Could Stephen tell him whether there might be enough wealth, travel and shipping from the Brazos to justify taking the *Ariel* there?

Even when there was enough water, the *Ariel* knew misfortune. In late September a great flood came down the river, and Captain Austin remarked that it "would have enabled him to go quite to Santa Fe," but for one thing. The very flood that would float the *Ariel* far upriver brought with it "a pestilence which prostrated everybody." He was the only member of the *Ariel's* crew to escape the epidemic. For nearly three months, during which the high water would have taken the *Ariel* most profitably up and down the river, his men were all incapacitated, and she lay idle at Matamoros, while salaries continued, and expenses of upkeep. Morosely he discussed with a group of local merchants the idea of selling them a half interest in the steamboat, to keep it running between the river's mouth and Matamoros. But he found it a sore trial to negotiate with the Matamorans. "There is such an inveterate jealousy of strangers," he said, "and so much perfidy in the Mexican people that nothing conducted by a stranger can succeed if they can prevent it." All he could do was make plans for withdrawal from the river without too great a loss. Even that would take months more of steaming up and down the restricted river to earn freighting fees. If he could not in the end sell the *Ariel* and leave her behind, he would have to run to New Orleans and sell her there. It would be as well to dispose of some of her original cargo in any case. He asked his cousin about an item of that. "I have a printing press, and types. is it wanted in Texas. It will not sell here as the people cannot read. the value is 1500$." There was something absurdly valiant in taking a steamboat where there was no water, a printing press where none could read. . . .

Though business improved early in 1830, and for three months the *Ariel* "more than paid her expences," until the merchants of Matamoros were convinced that "a Steamboat to facilitate the transportation of goods is all important to the prosperity of the place," Captain Austin was firm in his resolve to depart as soon as he could "quit with credit. . . . Nothing," he said, "nothing but my pride and the censure to which I should expose myself by abandoning a project of my own proposing has induced me to continue here so long— At all events I shall extricate myself with a few months—"

7.

Slavery

Meanwhile affairs in Mexico were producing high feelings in Texas, and the effects of these were increasingly to be met with on the Rio Grande. Captain Henry Austin kept abreast of issues that developed in the utmost gravity for the future of Texas—both immediate and ultimate.

Chief among them was the issue of slavery.

From Matamoros at the end of January, 1830, Captain Austin wrote to his cousin, ". . . We have many rumors here of a revolutionary disposition in the people of Texas on account of the decree freeing all slaves in the Republic." He referred to an action taken by President Guerrero in September, 1829, abolishing slavery throughout Mexico, excepting the Isthmus of Tehuantepec. The president acted under dictatorial powers that the Congress had granted him during the attempted invasion by troops of Ferdinand VII. The decree was seen in Texas by Austin and all his people, and by members of the several colonies scattered to the east, as a mortal blow to their existence; for the economy of the settlements rested upon slave labor, and ever since their foundation they had had to resist Mexican attempts to abolish slavery by law. What could be done now? Austin counseled moderation. "There ought to be no vociferous and visionary excitement or noise about this matter. Our course is a very plain one—calm, deliberate, dispationate, inflexible firmness; and not windy and ridiculous blowing and wild threats, and much less anything like opposition to the Mexican Constitution, nothing of this kind will do any good. . . ."

What he warned against revealed what was already the temper of the settlers. There was time for reflection, for the Mexican political chief of the Department of Texas had already, on his own authority, suspended the execution of Guerrero's edict in Texas, and had appealed to the President that Texas be added to Tehuantepec as exempt from the new law. Let the government have time to reconsider. Austin himself was sternly resolved to fight for the right to hold slaves, for though he owned only one, "an old, decreped woman, not worth much" whom he had bought the year before for $350, he declared the whole thing was a matter of principle, and he intended to protect his constitutional rights in the matter so far as he was able. He was not at once obliged to do so, for in December came word that the President "has been pleased . . . to declare the department of Texas excepted. . . ." Slavery was secure for the time being in the settlements.

Its presence there was legal under the Mexican grants originally given to Austin in 1822. One of his continuing troubles in Mexico City during the trying months of pressing his petition through government channels had been a disagreement about the terms under which settlers could introduce slaves into Mexico and keep them. The new government's feeling was that slavery should be done away with, and prescribed accordingly, under a gradual process. Austin wrote in 1822, that his "principal difficulty is slavery, this they will not admit—as the law is all slaves are to be free in ten years. . . ." He was working for arrangements more to the advantage of his colonists. ". . . I am trying to have it amended so as to make them slaves for life and their children free at 21 years. . . ." He was afraid that he would not succeed in his efforts, but in the turmoil of Mexico City politics, he came off better than he had dared hope. The colonies law finally provided that "After the promulgation of this law there shall be neither sale nor purchase of slaves who are brought to the empire; their children born in the empire shall be free at the age of fourteen." The slave trade, of course, was prohibited by these terms, and the children would be lost just as they reached a useful age; but the parents until their death were secured to their owners as economic machinery. It seemed like a piece of good business, and after all, laws could be modified. For the next decade Stephen Austin never stopped trying to modify them—though his attitude toward slavery at times wavered oddly, and for curious reasons.

In 1824 the colonists were alarmed by talk that all slaves were to be freed in Mexico. Austin headed a committee that filed a protest, pointing out how ruin would befall the colony if the original three hundred families could no longer rely on their slaves for farming, defense and propagation of involuntary labor. The committee went further than a request that the current regulations be undisturbed; they asked that these be revised to declare that "the slaves and their descendants of the 300 families . . . shall be slaves for life. . . ." The provisions freeing children at fourteen were thus to be abolished, to insure unending generations of slave labor from which there was to be no escape in perpetuity. Commercial traffic in slaves, however, the committee did not ask for, but courteously bowed to the current provision banning it. Austin was busy all year with letters and petitions to hold fast to the institution that provided property holders with human chattels.

Not that he would have Mexican officials think he approved of slavery—perish the thought. ". . . por me parte," he declared to one of them, "no soy en favor de la esclavitud en ninguna manera qe. sea. . . ." But if he was not in favor of slavery in any possible form, he was able to go on to say that slavery, having been legally recognized by the central government in the colonies law, and being so vitally necessary to the prosperity of the colony, should be maintained. How else could new colonists be induced to enter Texas from Louisiana? It was a vexing matter, as he indicated by questions he put to the authorities. What was he authorized to do if slaves ran away from their owners in the United States and came to Texas? "If the runaway remains here he is a nuisance to the Country—if his owner claims him and he is not given up it will destroy all harmony between the Citizens of that State and this—" And another tedious aspect of it all: what was he to do with "a free man who steals a Negro from that State and brings him here?" How was that crime to be punished?—for it was "certainly a very high Crime," and as punishment he could only propose whipping, a heavy fine and imprisonment. He busied himself with exhaustive drafts of how slavery could be maintained and regulated, and when he heard that the legislature of Coahuila-Texas was considering a measure to prohibit slavery "absolutely and forever in all its territory," he warned in wounded accents that the settlers could only regard its passage as "una acta de mala fé" on the part of the government, since they had come in with their slaves under the law. But he did not see his own strenuous effort to modify the law as an act of bad faith, and again and again he warned that the colony must face ruin if its slaves were freed. Now and then he gave ground, and to save slavery a while longer, asked that children of slaves be emancipated—though only at reaching the age of twenty-five.

So the struggle went on through the 1820s, and nowhere was heard a voice like that of Bartolomé de las Casas lifted on behalf, not of property, or the liberty of a restricted few, or of legalistic guarantees, but of the inherent humanity of men and women and children, who must not be owned like implements of work, and used as such. The arguments were all expedient, the reasons grubby, the eloquence geared to anxiety over material investments. Clumsy as it was, and even corruptible and at times bloodthirsty, the Mexican government, speaking with the voice of the Indian who had known the meaning of slavery under the early Spaniards, alone held any sort of moral posture in the long struggle whose stake was a measure of man's dignity.

Finally in 1827 Coahuila-Texas adopted a law freeing at birth children born to slaves, and permitting a period of only six months after the adoption and publication of the law during which additional slaves might be brought into the state. It was severe, but not so severe as the legislature's first draft of the bill, and it owed its final form to agitations led by Austin and his settlers. Austin wrote hastily to his brother-in-law to come to Texas at once, bringing his slaves, before the six months' period was over. But as with so many laws of the Republic, this one was not enforced in such an outlying land as Texas. Stephen Austin himself, in the face of the laws of 1822 and after, barring slave trade, bought his "decreped old woman" in 1828. New colonists poured into Texas from the East, and by 1830 the American population numbered thirty thousand—twice the number of the Texas Indians and Mexicans together. On the river in January, 1830, Captain Henry Austin told his cousin what he was hearing in Matamoros.

". . . The Mexicans appear to be very jealous of your increasing strength," he wrote, and he reflected another current topic: "I think the conviction that Texas cannot long remain theirs may determine them to sell to the U S now they have an opportunity." For though nothing had been accomplished officially, the United States minister to Mexico was known to have five million dollars available for the purchase of Texas, and perhaps a little over, if certain individuals in the capital could find ways to receive North American dollars quite privately—or so the minister hoped (though without the knowledge or approval of President Jackson). But his intrigues had little chance to develop. The government at Mexico City took alarm at the swelling immigration in Texas, and the growing establishment there of a society made in the likeness of the United States. Intelligence went from the Rio Grande to the capital, accompanied by various recommendations for the control of the North Americans and the reaffirmation of Mexican authority above the river; and in April, 1830, the government acted to repress the Anglo-American colonies in Texas. On the sixth, President Bustamante signed an Act of Congress that closed the frontier to Anglo-American settlers, though it held out inducements to Mexicans and immigrants from any foreign country other than the United States to take up claims in Texas. No travellers from the United States could enter even temporarily without a Mexican visa. Any settlement already in process of movement from the United States was cancelled. Existing colonies were not to be disturbed, but no slaves were to be brought into them henceforth. Texas coastal commerce was thrown open to foreigners for four years and at certain seaports the customs regulations were suspended to the advantage of Mexican and oversea colonists. These measures were to be enforced by military power, and at Matamoros, General Manuel Mier y Terán mobilized troops to march into Texas to do the job. The Texan settlers were to have their comeuppance.

After reflection, Stephen Austin wrote to the President and to General Mier y Terán, and drafted though did not send a letter to Lucas Alamán, the Mexican vice-president, who held jurisdiction over the colonies. He argued hotly against the exclusion measures of the new law, and especially its decree that cancelled settlements undertaken but not completed. Speaking for the colonists, and protesting their good faith, he asked, "Is it good policy to sour their minds and alienate their affections?" Already there were new settlers on the road from as far away as New York. They had sold their property at home, and had made all the complicated arrangements necessary for a new life in a new nation. From the moment of his acceptance of their applications, Austin considered them already members of the colony. He would not apply the new law to them. ". . . Immagine," he charged the government, "immagine for a moment the situation in which some hundreds of families had to be placed, by being stopped on the road to this colony after having sold all their property where they formerly lived and incurred heavy expences, they would be totally ruined, and"—let the government take note—"the odium would of necessity fall on the Govt that caused their ruin—public sympathy would be excited to a very high degree and public indignation would immediately follow. . . ." He asked flatly that orders be sent to "the Com^t Genl of this section not to stop the emigrants to my colony—". His protest was effective. In a few weeks he was assured by General Mier y Terán that his colony was not indicated under the article affecting settlements in progress.

But the rest of the Congressional act was to be prosecuted. It was plain to Austin that the article on slavery, confirming the state law already passed by Coahuila-Texas, could not be argued against; and he made no reference to it in his letters to the government—though in the one he wrote but did not send to Alamán, he took a mollifying line that reflected his sense of the expedient. "I have to say that I have always been opposed from principle to slavery and that I am well satisfied with the prohibitory laws on that subject." It was a statement hardly in accord with his earlier acts and protests. These he tried to explain away. "I have advocated the toleration of slavery in the infancy of the settlement because I at one time totally despaired of getting emigrants without allowing them to bring slaves." Having worked to implant slavery in the colonies it was difficult to know how he could ever hope to uproot it by a simple reversal of his own opinion. Still, he tried. "The country is now sufficiently advanced and as far as my influence extends I shall forever oppose slavery in Texas—I have made this declaratory to the settlers in public manner. . . ."

He even wrote to Henry Austin about his new mind. ". . . I am myself opposed to a union with the U.S. unless we first receive some *guarantees,* amongst them I should insist on the perpetual exclusion of slavery from this country. . . ." In 1830 union with the United States was already a real possibility to the Anglo-Texans.

But if he was now against slavery, suddenly in a scattering of letters written in June, 1830, he revealed why. It was the exposure of a morbid obsession. "The idea of seeing such a country as this overrun by a slave population almost makes me weep— It is in vain to tell a North American that the white population will be destroyed some fifty or eighty years hence by the negroes, and that his daughters will be violated and Butched by them." He shuddered to think of it, and he agonized over the answers he got when he gave warnings. The settlers dismissed him saying that "it is too far off to think of—" and "they can do as I have, take care of themselves—" and "something will turn up to keep off the evil, etc, etc,". Such, he said, "such are the silly answers of the slave holder." For the first time Stephen Austin gave a word to the ethical aspects of slavery. "To say anything to them as to the justice of slavery, or its demoralizing effects on society, is only to draw ridicule upon the person who attempts it—"

Luxuriating in the horrors of orgiastic explosions in the future, he rode ahead with his theme. "To those who do not reflect, I would say, 'take your pen—put down the number of slaves now in the slave states—calculate their increase for eighty years at the known rate of augmentation—Calculate the extent of country to which they are, and must be confided, and its capacity to support human beings—Then calculate the number of white population and their increase—deduct from said increase, the emigration of whites to other countries; (no such deduction can be made from the increase of blacks, for they cannot emigrate,) compare the two sums, and then suppose that you will be alive at the period above mentioned, that you have a long-cherished and beloved wife, a number of daughters, grand daughters, and great grand daughters . . . would no fears for their fate, a horrible fate; intrude themselves upon your pillow, and overcloud the evening of your life'? . . . If Texas is wisely and prudently managed, it will be saved from the overwhelming ruin which mathematical demonstration declares must overtake the slave states. . . ." What would the solution be, in wisdom and prudence? He seemed to see only one. "A few years more and Mexico will be the only resting place left for the whites South of Illinois, unless"—not that he advocated it, but there it was—"unless the blacks are exterminated by a general massacre by the Whites; and afterwards excluded from being brought into the country—In a century more either the whites, or the blacks must cease to exist in the southern States, or they must intermarry and all be placed on an equality."

8.
Bad Blood

But in 1830 there were other problems, too, for Captain Henry Austin reported from the Rio Grande that General Mier y Terán desired a meeting with Stephen, whom he did not deceive for a moment. It was Mier y Terán, and no one else, who had designed the government's measures against Texas, and Stephen Austin had "always known it." They were on the best of terms, of course, and observed all amenities, but just the same Stephen wished Henry would write him when "the long-expected army of Texas is to be on, and its number, etc.—" This referred to the movement of troops over the Rio Grande to enforce new revenue laws at customs houses to be established at various points in Texas, and to see that other provisions of the Act of April sixth were carried out. Enjoining calm at home, Stephen Austin reported that "The most perfect peace and harmony reigns over all Texas and will no doubt so continue—"

Henry saw otherwise on the Rio Grande. Mier y Terán on taking his army into Texas was planning, according to what Henry heard, to remove Stephen from the colony, because his influence with the colonists was "dangerous to the security of the province." It was a shocking rumor, and Henry dismissed it, "supposing it to be impossible for the Gen¹ to meditate so rash a measure." But soon he was not so certain. He wrote to Stephen that Mier y Terán was overheard saying that "he viewed the foreigners in this part of the country as the Most dangerous enemies of it particularly the North Americans whose sole object was to wrest from the Mexicans their property and so much of their territory as they could get— . . . You know," continued Henry, "You know the duplicity of the Mexican character—their general want of faith in all transactions and the necessity of being guarded against their villainy. . . . It may therefore be wise to keep yourself under cover of your own rifles, which Gen¹ Teran has not the nerve nor the power to encounter. . . ." and Captain Henry Austin added "you must take good care not to let it transpire that I communicate with you on this subject as it would probably consign me to the Calabose. . . ."

In Matamoros there were troubles for North Americans engaged in shipping in and out of the Rio Grande. A new state law required all foreign merchants except the English, the German and the Dutch to pay a tax on their capital in trade and on all importation during the previous year. The specific exceptions left only United States shipping subject to the tax. The regulations permitted the Texas colonies to ship goods to Matamoros, Veracruz and Tampico; but they had to pay the revenue. It may have been a measure in retaliation for abuses of the customs laws by the Texans, who for years had taken advantage of exemption from duty on goods to be used for building the colony to introduce all sorts of other goods in great quantity which they illegally used in commerce. Bad blood stirred at provocation from both government and settlers. "The Govts and people of Mexico appear to become more hostile daily to the citizens of the US.," as Henry Austin saw affairs on the river, "and I am of opinion will ultimately drive them from Mexico or reduce the U S to the necessity of compelling them to respect the rights of her Citizens—"

Matamoros was an armed camp. Mier y Terán's soldiers were on guard at every point. The customhouse was a fort, and collection of duties was accelerated, and its revenue was poured into the Commandant General's hands. It was the only source of funds with which to pay his troops. There were three hundred soldiers in town, and sixteen hundred more were expected to arrive soon, to be drilled and trained for the Texas entry. The army was raised through levies made on the Mexican people. The law stated that "vagabonds and disorderly persons shall be taken in preference for military service, recruits may be obtained by entrapment and decoy." Henry Austin did not expect the army to move north. He believed that affairs in central Mexican politics concerned Mier y Terán far more than the problems of Texas, and in fact, the General was changing his tune, protesting that he favored the Texans in all things. Perhaps there was a new reason for this, and Henry wrote, "I think he has more apprehension of a Grito for Centralism in the South and a separation of those northern states which are federal, than of the US or Texas. . . . I also suspect he counts upon much support from Texas in such an event. . . ."

But in that summer the vagabond army did move across the Rio Grande. Mier y Terán established a dozen or so military posts in Texas whose presence was an affront to the colonists, and returned to his headquarters at Matamoros. It was a hot summer, parched with drought. Henry Austin looked at the river to see it go drier and lower. Was he trapped with the *Ariel?* The searing winds came, and lifted sand into the air. It was choking, even while the air was sticky and humid. The land was flat and the lower sky presaged the sea and freedom and rescue, but the *Ariel* had to be readied, and there were officials to see, and six or eight thousand dollars to retrieve. Where was the image of the future that he had brought to the river—prosperity, and an estate with green lawns to the bank, and a heritage for a family? "Poor fellow," noted his brother Archibald in the East when it was plain that the Rio Grande steamboat venture was doomed, "he has traversed the world, beat the Bush, in every Hemisphere, contended with almost unexampled perseverance, with the freaks of fortune, had a fortune at various times as it were in his grasp, and have frustrated, Blocade, Wars and peace have so intervened as destroy his well-founded hopes of success, the all powerful ingine Steam does not appear to enable him to stem the current that has set against him. . . ."

But at last, in late August, he took the *Ariel* down the river and up the coast to the Brazos. He met Stephen Austin in due course, and discussed taking up a league of land. The prospect was not filling. He said it would "be folly for me to devote the remainder of my life to the occupation of a league of land." His past stirred in his memory, his scale of imagination would not let him be, and he shared with Stephen as with a kindred spirit the vague creative longings that made them both active, unhappy and relentless. "I must do something on an extensive scale with prospects of ultimate advantage of magnitude," he declared, "or do nothing. . . . You and I may indulge our imaginations with the pleasing prospect of passing the remainder of life in the tranquillity which a snug stock farm appears to offer, but neither you nor I could exist in such a state. . . ."

It was true; and Henry planned to move on to New Orleans and the States. He had a last word of advice for Stephen. There was political rumor that Mexico's federation was about to break apart into independent provinces. General Mier y Terán in such a case had his eye on his choice of land. "I strongly suspect Teran looks to Texas for his share. Flatter him in that point and make him believe the people of Texas look up to him as their political Savior and you may do anything with him. . . ." After this word, he was ready to go; but once again the *Ariel* was delayed by bad luck, for the beef rations packed for the homeward voyage spoiled overnight, and four crewmen deserted in the dark. He set about repairing his supplies and crew at the mouth of the Brazos, while "Farewell," wrote Stephen from San Felipe upstream, "I hope you may have a calm run to the U.S.—it is more than I expect to have for the next two years, and God knows whether I shall ever see much quiet—" And then the *Ariel* was ready, with her woodpiles replenished, and she set out to cross the bar into the Gulf. But she had taken on too much wood, and to lighten her for the crossing, the Captain set ashore to leave behind him his two brass cannon and other weighty cargo. The *Ariel* tried the bar again. This time she ran aground. In getting off, she was damaged. She ventured on, but her troubles had been too much for her; she sank and was abandoned in Galveston Bay. It would be sixteen years before steam came back to the lower Rio Grande. Captain Henry Austin, though still plagued by "prospects of ultimate advantage of magnitude," settled in his cousin's colony in Texas after all.

The head of the colony was also head of the militia, with the rank of colonel. The law required him to have the uniform of colonel in the Mexican army, of navy blue, with gold epaulettes, a scarlet waistcoat with gold round cord on the edges, a gold-mounted sword and belt, and a yellow sash; a set of holsters, a pair of boots and yellow spurs; pantaloons trimmed with black silk braid; a military surtout with a standing collar, that was to be "handsomely though plainely trimmed with black silk cord"; and a yellow-bitted bridle. Colonel Stephen F. Austin ordered all this out of New York in the summer of 1830. It was months in coming, for the embroidery of gold bullion on the coat took time, and cost forty-one dollars. It finally left for Texas by ship on December twentieth; but it would arrive too late to be taken to Saltillo by Colonel Austin, who was obliged to attend the next session of the legislature of the Twin Sisters, that would open in January, 1831. He travelled by way of Béxar, and struck out from there for the Rio Grande, which he crossed at France Way, as it was still called. He passed through the Presidio, where the population continued to take down grand yellow-gray stones from the ruins of St. Bernard's to make their shops and houses and corrals, and proceeded with an armed escort to Monclova and Saltillo. There was much to debate in the session, much to prove; her own identity for Texas, without loss of loyalty to Mexico. Behind the immediate issues loomed and pressed more relentlessly every day the energy of the United States as it reached toward the Rio Grande's two extremes of terrain, at the Gulf and in the Rocky Mountain north.

9.

The Mexico Trade

"We are caraing on a smart Trade with St. tefee from the boons lick country," wrote a Missouri merchant as early as 1824. For three centuries the flow of colonial life had moved by the compass needle north and south, from Mexico to the river and back again—captains and friars and householders; convicts paroled as colonists; an occasional bishop in his large, upholstered wagon; merchant trains with their Indian drivers; military inspectors of the Spanish Crown visiting frontier garrisons of forty men and four hundred horses and twenty firearms; journeyman artisans and now and then a student travelling between wilderness and a Spanish university: all in their slow glisten and wonderful persistence travelled north and south.

And then, with the nineteenth century, in a swing of the needle, the compass began to show life flowing toward the river along a new axis, from east to west, in a new measure of knowledge, and at a quickened pace. New paths were imagined. One much speculated upon in 1825 was the Red River, in spite of the immense "Raft" of tangled timber that hung over its course like a low thick canopy for almost a hundred miles, so that the river ran unseen as if in a subterranean current. But its upper end pointed generally toward Santa Fe, though its source fell short of there by a hundred and fifty miles, and the talk was that if the Raft could be cleared away, as men were now planning to clear it, then "Steam boats will be able to assend within a day or two's Journey from Sᵗᵃ Fee," and "if this is done the whole current of the Intercourse with New Mexico will be by way of Red River and the whole valley of it will Soon be settled. and the time may come when more cotton may go out of Red River than now goes out of the mississippi. . . ." For many reasons the Red River undertaking never materialized. For one thing, the clearing of the Great Raft was too difficult to do. For another, the upper reaches of the Red River could not float steamboats except perhaps in storm water. And finally, the Mexico trade already in progress overland to Chihuahua by way of the prairies and Santa Fe grew so fast that the Santa Fe trail quickly became the established route.

It had been Spain's firm policy to exclude all trade from the United States except through the severely controlled port of Veracruz. There came North American goods by sea, and, if any reached the Rio Grande and Santa Fe, went northward by the old cottonwood carts from Mexico. By the time it arrived, merchandise cost the New Mexicans dearly. One common item—calico and even "bleached and brown domestic goods"—sold for two or three dollars a yard.

But with the independence of Mexico in 1821, the restrictions were, if somewhat capriciously, relaxed. The trappers of the mountains showed the way to the Rio Grande overland. Both Anglo-Americans and Mexicans wondered whether trails might turn into roads; and in 1824, a group of citizens from Mexican Santa Fe crossed the plains to invite trade from the Mississippi valley. Stephen Austin's brother wrote to him about it: "A Deputation from Santa Fe arrived a few weeks ago at the council Bluffs—the object of their visit was to ascertain the most eligable Situation for a road to be cut from Santa Fe—to that place—and also to enter into some arrangement to Secure traders (to and from the

Province of New Mexico) —from attacks of the indians—and to appoint agents for the purpose of facilitating an intercourse and commerce to the United States—".

By then the Mexico trade was a reality. In 1821 William Becknell had taken out to the plains "a company of men destined to the westward for the purpose of trading for Horses and Mules, and catching wild animals of every description," as his announcement stated in the *Missouri Intelligencer*. His intention was to trade with Indians; but on the prairies he met a wandering group of Santa Feans who persuaded the Missourians "to accompany them to the new emporium [Santa Fe], where, notwithstanding the trifling amount of merchandise they were possessed of, they realized a very handsome profit. . . ." The expedition was equipped only with pack animals, and so were those few that went out again in the following year. In May of 1824 Becknell introduced an important innovation on the trail to Santa Fe, when taking out another merchandise train, he hauled his goods in wagons for the first time. The wagons were a success, for "no where else on the American continent," observed a trader, "can be found a route of 800 miles in extend more easily traversed by wagons than the one between Independence and Santa Fe."

The volume of traffic grew faster than the Mexicans had expected. Ready to measure by their own experience of the single, dawdling, annual train of the Rio Grande valley, and their own unhurried natures, they were hardly prepared to see so many caravans, and so many traders, and so much merchandise rolling past their vaguely defined boundaries. It was alarming. So much business could only mean so much power eventually in the hands of the Anglo-American visitors. Mexico went no further with deputations to the States to establish roads and propose commerce. But it was too late. The gates had been opened, and the flood had started, and would increase.

The first trade road led to Taos, where the trappers had gone. It was the port of entry for New Mexico, where papers were examined. The customs house was at Santa Fe, and there the serious business of taxation, and sometimes of confiscation, was done. As the trade grew, if Mexico could not exclude it, she could at least bear upon it every tedium and elaboration of government control that a Spanish heritage could suggest. Months before setting out, the trader had to have his entire bill of merchandise made out and translated into Spanish. This was copied in duplicate, and sent by traveller, or by mail if possible, to the point of destination, whether Santa Fe or Chihuahua, or any point between them. Once entered, the invoice could not be altered in any way, and any error in further copying it, even to a slip of the pen, was enough to subject the cargo to confiscation when it later arrived. The invoice was stamped, and a copy was returned to the trader with a "guia," or clearance. The guia was permitted to name three points of destination for the shipment, which thereafter could go nowhere else. There was a time limit on the validity of the guia. If its return to the trader were delayed by the officials, or by uncertainty of mails, the trader was sure to be late in his travel, for he could not start without the clearance in hand. And if he was late in arriving, then he was taxed double the duty levied on his goods.

But at last, if he had his papers, the trader could depart. The wagon train commander carried a document issued by the Superintendent of Indian Affairs at St. Louis, showing the names of all men in the trading party, and granting them permission "to pass into and through the Indian country, &c . . . to the province of Mexico." The trail to Santa Fe soon found an easier way than going by Taos, and down the black rocky canyon of the river west of the Sangre de Cristo mountains. It took a diagonal on entering New Mexico and came around the southern prow of the mountains and passing through San Miguel del Vado entered Santa Fe from the southeast. If the question was raised why the wagon trains, whose cargo was destined chiefly for Chihuahua, did not go directly there instead of so far out of the way as Santa Fe, a trader gave the answer. "I answer, that we dreaded a journey across the southern prairies on account of the reputed aridity of the country in that direction, and I had no great desire to venture directly into a southern port in the present state of uncertainty as to the conditions of entry." El Paso and Presidio del Norte were ports of entry on the Rio Grande below New Mexico, but received little traffic.

Every summer saw the traders come in sight through the blue-green hills southeast of Santa Fe. The long wagon trains gritted and creaked their way into the plaza, and the traders inhaled on the cool air the poignant scent of the piñon smoke that always hovered over the old royal city. An arrival was a great event. The Santa Feans came flocking to see the newcomers, who stared back at them, while both thought they had never seen such outlandish creatures. In the trading company there were many diverse men whom the taverns, gambling rooms and certain Mexican women prepared to entertain—city merchants, frontiersmen, wandering tinkers, farmers, hunters, wagoners. They often represented many nationalities, and in one train there were men of "seven distinct nations, each speaking his own native tongue," and a trader noted a voluble Frenchman who was given to "curious gesticulations," and "two phlegmatic wanderers from Germany," and two Polish exiles of a "calm eccentricity," and various Indians including a Creek and a Chickasaw, and "sundry loquacious Mexicans," and Americans who "were mostly backwoodsmen, who could handle the rifle better than the whip, but who nevertheless officiated as wagoners." Santa Fe had never seen the like.

They wore anything and everything. The merchant was the most elegant, in his dark, fustian long coat with its many pockets in which he could carry so much, his light trousers, and his round hat. The backwoodsman wore a shirt of linsey, that was made of mixed wool and flax, or a fringed leather jacket. The farmer's coat of twilled cotton cloth was already known as blue jean. The wagoner's vest had flannel sleeves. The party bristled with arms until they gave a "very brigand-like appearance." The hunter had his long rifle, and derided the "scatter-gun," as he called the double-barrelled fowling piece carried by Americans who back home went shooting for sport. But the scatter-gun had its serious uses, for on the prairies among enemy Indians "a charge of buckshot in night attacks (which are most common) will of course be more like to do execution than a single rifle-ball fired at random. . . ." Almost everyone carried pistols and knives. Now and then a large, rich train brought along artillery: "We had two swivels mounted upon one pair of wheels . . . one of these was a long brass piece made to order, with a calibre of but an inch and a quarter, yet of sufficient metal to throw a leaden ball . . . a mile with surprising accuracy. The other was iron, and a little larger."

The freight wagons of the train were long, heavy and narrow, with wheels higher at the rear than at the front, and double hoods of Osnabrück linen stretched over arched bows. From a little distance and seen from the end, such a wagon seemed to be wearing a great sunbonnet. The most popular wagons were made in Pennsylvania, first at Conestoga, later at Pittsburgh. Each could carry a load of about five thousand pounds. To pull it took three span of oxen, horses or mules. Each of these wore a collar of bells. The cargo was remarkably various, containing textiles of all sorts, from calico to velvet; clothes for men and women, including ribbons, handkerchiefs, hats, suspender buttons, rhinestones and kid gloves; building materials, cutlery, glassware, tools, baskets, furniture, paper, ink and paints; foods and spices of every kind and medicines and tobacco and almanacs and champagne and candles and colored lithographs and—a popular item—jew's-harps.

The wagons crowded into the plaza like fishing boats in a small harbor after long hazard at sea. The journey had taken ten weeks from Old Franklin in Howard County on the Missouri River. The eastern terminus moved westward for decades, to Independence, and then Westport, and then Westport Landing which became Kansas City. The road was an extension of the long westward walk of Daniel Boone, that had ended near Boone's Lick with his life. In the fourth year of the trade Congress authorized the President of the United States to "cause a road to be marked out from the western frontier of Missouri to the confines of New Mexico," and the government treated with Plains Indians for the right to cross to Santa Fe, paying the Osage and Kansa tribes eight hundred dollars each. Early encounters with Indians were peaceful; but it was not long until traders, regarding the Indians as inferior creatures, abused them; and Indians replied with all their ancient skill in savage warfare. Trading trains could not have protection by United States troops west of the Arkansas River because of treaty conditions. A trader of the 1830s thought that "such an extensive unhabitable waste as the great prairies are, ought certainly to be under maritime regulations," and considering the principal destinations of the trains, he recommended that "some internal arrangements should be made between the United States and Texas or Mexico, whereby the armies of either might indiscrimminately range upon this desert, as ships of war upon the ocean. . . ."

Traders often thought of the sea in their great prairie crossings. The vast open land looked like the sea, and the sky over it rimmed the world at the horizons without obstruction. "Seas of grass," they said, and "prairie schooner," and "prairie ocean." They found the journey, like a sea voyage, a giver of health, and many a frontier doctor sent a sickling on a prairie "enterprise" and saw him come alive of it. It was an affirmative experience. The voyagers believed in their work, which few others had performed; they had a sense of their worth and need; and they knew health of body and spirit. One said, "The insatiable appetite acquired by travellers is almost incredible, and the quantity of coffee drank is even more so. . . ." Each man did full justice to the rations he was required to bring—fifty pounds each of bacon and flour, twenty pounds of sugar, ten pounds of coffee, and salt, beans and crackers—and to the game he brought down with his rifle or scatter-gun on the way. His job was hard, and the bonneted wagons rarely made more than eleven to fifteen miles a day. He came through Indian alarms and terrifying storms and prairie fires. If he and the wind moved in the same direction a prairie fire ahead of him was no great trouble, for "fire burns so slowly back against the wind even through tall grass, wagons can be driven through it with safety." But if the wind came driving the fire from ahead, "it would often (particularly in tall grass) set both wagon and team in flames." Under a favoring wind a train once passed safely through a fire; but at night the wind changed, and the fire caught up with the wagons the next day.

At the end of the first lap of the journey, as night came down over Santa Fe, it was time to let go. The public rooms of Santa Fe were crowded early in the evening, and private ones later. Monte games—one trader of severe tastes called them "pandemoniums"—raged, and a fandango was called, and Taos whiskey and El Paso brandy flowed, and music, yells and ebullient salvos from firearms broke the mountain-clasped night. Tomorrow would come the ordeal of the customs house, with its rattle of papers, long official silences that chilled the hearts of the traders, and the glitter of greed in the eyes of the motley Mexican soldiers who watched the checking of the cargoes. The process might take several days; but once the papers were declared in order, and the duties paid, it would be time to tear the traders away from the rude joys of Santa Fe, and take the train down the river to El Paso, and beyond, to the city of Chihuahua.

They took the old road on the east bank all the way. After the empty plains the narrow valley with its many little villages of earth, its separate estate farms, seemed like civilization; and so it was, though odd to Yankee eyes. Yet the valley in the second quarter of the nineteenth century was so much terrorized by Apaches and even occasional Comanches that the traders could not hope to strike out on their own, however plain the road and frequent the settlements. If they staged few battles against riding Indians, it was because the trains made a great show of force and circumstance that discouraged attack.

The wagons wracked their way down the escarpment of La Bajada off Santa Fe plain, and along the valley road, soon passing in and out of cottonwood shade, a river grace. The bridge at San Felipe had long since been washed away by storm water, and all the way on the river until near to the mouth fifteen hundred miles away there was not a single ferry. This troubled few who wanted to cross, for during three quarters of the year, the river could be forded wherever there was an easy bank. Troubles mostly came otherwise, and took official form; for in any town where there was a squad of soldiery and an alcalde who saw his duty as a confusion of his personality, the long toiling train was apt to be halted by authority of the Mexican nation, and the whole customs inspection repeated, while the train commanders held their breaths, and wagoners bathed in the sweet-scented muddy river, and animals grazed, and summertime slipped away. It was no use to look for back roads that bypassed the little garrisons; for any train discovered off the main highway was, however orderly its papers, subject to immediate and entire confiscation.

But at last they moved on again, and saw how one little river town after another, only a few miles apart—Peralta, Valencia, Tomé, Adelino—seemed isolated from one another, with local differences in building style, costume and church furnishings. None of the river towns below Santa Fe had an inn or public house. Stopping for the night, the traders parked their train on the outskirts of a village, near water, and under trees, and built their fires and put down their blankets on the ground. The townspeople came to look at them as they pastured their animals and cooked their supper, and heard them talk, and sing, and recite to amuse one another, and watched them dance to fiddles and clapped hands under upward firelight on green leaves, and perhaps saw them take a man and bare his back and tie him to a tree to give him lashes with a bullwhip; and if they asked why this was done, they were told that the man was a bad debtor who was being made to pay off what he owed at a dollar a lash. In the morning with bellow and bray and holler, the rankle of harness bells, and the grind of axles and the complaint of wagon wood, the train moved on into the deserts above Socorro and below. There were no towns in that stretch but many camping sites that had been used for generations by riverside travellers—Pascual, El Contadero, Alemán, Robledo, San Diego, Fray Cristóbal—before entering the Dead Man's March. Such places had no permanent habitation or structure; but filled and emptied as travel went by.

The Mexican postrider carried the mail between Chihuahua and Santa Fe over this route, though since the raiding Indians had become active, he could not keep his schedule of two trips a month. Most writers sent their letters by private hands, to avoid loss, and also to keep them from being opened, and their business aired, in the post offices of Albuquerque and Santa Fe—the only ones in New Mexico. The postrider carried the leather post bag. It was locked. But because there was a shortage of keys on deposit at the post offices, he also carried the only key. His life was dangerous, and making a living was hard, and it came to him that a little extra silver would be his if he gave to inquisitive persons the privilege of ransacking the mail in his charge. One day in the Dead Man's March a Missouri trader saw a New Mexican ride up to the postrider who was passing by on his service. They conversed briefly, coming to an agreement; and then the postman unlocked his pouch and dumped its contents on the ground. His client searched the mail, and for the privilege handed him "the moderate price of one dollar."

Pressing on through the Dead Man's March as fast as they could, for water was still scarce, and their emergency casks were emptied all too soon, the traders returned to the riverside again and came upon one after another settlement that "had formerly been the seat of opulence and prosperity" but which had "long since been abandoned in consequence of the marauding incursions of the Apaches." Nearing El Paso, if the river was high at the ford six miles above town, they faced a hard job. Nowhere was there a sign of a bridge—the old one had gone in flood. The traders now had to unload the cargo and take the wagons apart, and using a thirty-foot dugout "canoe" that was at hand, float the wagon parts one by one across the river, and assemble them again on the opposite bank. The cargo followed. Sometimes they met quicksand at the ford, and then had to work fast to "drag mules out by the ears," and "to carry out the loading package by package," and "to haul out the wagon piece by piece—wheel by wheel."

Once across the river, the train rolled on, and in about three miles came to a dam of stone and brush that diverted the waters to the El Paso settlements for irrigation. Three miles farther loomed the tower of Guadalupe, at one corner of the plaza. Again the customs inspection delayed progress. The inspector was exacting and disagreeable. While he did his duty, the traders who could be spared from the ordeal wandered about the district, and ate local grapes "of the most exquisite flavor," and drank "Pass wine" and "Pass whiskey," and saw how the town hardly extended beyond the plaza, though as they resumed their march into Mexico, they realized that the settlements continued for ten or twelve miles down the river in a "series of plantations," with cornfields, orchards and vineyards under cultivation. At their end, the road left the river, and the train headed due south for the city of Chihuahua, and the southern terminus of the long journey from Missouri.

In an early year the Mexico trade did a business of about fifteen thousand dollars. Twenty years later, the total annual value of cargoes was nearly a million dollars, and a single enterprise brought back one hundred and fifty thousand dollars. Traders were paid by the Mexicans in gold and silver for their merchandise—gold dust from a placer mine near Santa Fe, silver bullion from the mines of Chihuahua. Silver was moulded into ingots weighing between fifty and eighty pounds each, and worth fifteen hundred dollars. Rich men in Chihuahua stacked silver bars in their cellars, where a Missourian saw such cords that looked like "a winter's supply of firewood." If the payment was made in specie, the traders poured their coins into newly made sacks of green rawhide, which as it dried stiff and hard compressed the money in a tight bale.

If all went well for a train, the traders could dispose of their wares in Chihuahua and return to Santa Fe in time to leave for Missouri in the autumn. But if beset by accidents, too many official delays, slow markets, or a wet summer that kept the rivers at flood, they might have to spend nearly a year on the round trip, staying the winter in Santa Fe; for once winter was on the mountains and on the plains, the men could not venture homeward. Pasturage was poor as autumn advanced, and the open road that was so passable in summertime was in winter a terrible passage exposed to the drive of blizzards. The traders hurried their business and their return to Santa Fe up the river. In addition to their bales and bars and buckskin sacks of silver and gold, they brought Mexican cargoes to sell at home—buffalo rugs, furs, wool, coarse blankets of Mexican and Indian make; and they drove herds of Mexican mules and asses. The wagonloads were kept light, with no more than two thousand pounds of goods in each, to ease the pull on animals who would feed poorly on the autumnal forage, and to make fast marches possible as the days became short and cold and promised trouble in a prairie winter. The westward drive to Santa Fe in early summer had taken seventy days. The return trip, with light wagons and increased knowledge, took forty. With every summer the number of trains increased, and with every trip, the traders, fixed upon their own concerns, and aware of no larger purpose, advanced the process that would in time make foreigners of the Mexicans in their own long valley of the Rio Grande.

IO.

Tormented Loyalties

In June, 1832, returning home by way of Matamoros from another
of his annual trips to the legislature at Saltillo, Stephen Austin declared
that he had had "a very hard and hot trip." The whole country was
"all parched up," and at many places in northern Mexico no rain had
fallen for eight months. It was fatiguing to travel so far from the Brazos
to Coahuila in vain efforts to bring order and government for Texas
out of the near-anarchy that prevailed in the northern provinces. All
of Mexico was in political turmoil, and the outlying districts wavered
between national and local problems, troubled by both and unable to
compose either. Texas was viewed with fixed suspicion. Her people had
resisted bitterly the repressive policies that followed the enactment of
the laws of April 6, 1830, and her delegate to Saltillo was obliged again
and again to protest loyalty, even while he argued in measured tones for
justice. It was therefore gratifying to Stephen Austin to find that in his
crossings of the Rio Grande he was treated "with more attention and
respect" than he had "any reason to expect." True, he still had enemies
who roved the river frontier trying to discredit him and blacken the
character of Texas. His reply to this was firm. "My character belongs
to the colony and any unjust attack upon me situated as I now am, is
in fact an attack upon all," he declared, and continued to examine frontier problems. It was a disgrace that the river towns were still without protection by the central government against Comanche attacks.
The mails were uncertain, and a connection must be made between
the United States and Mexican postal systems. There was a serious
threat to Matamoros, the Rio Grande's largest commercial port, in a
petition before the Mexican Congress, to favor Veracruz by closing
the mouth of the Rio Grande to shipping. Matamoros was spiritedly
defended by a colonist. "The natural advantages, which this place
possesses, in point of health, over the Southern port; the superior facili-

ties in the transportation of merchandise into the interior; its contiguity
to the frontier; and its importance as a military port, claim the consideration and protection of the general Government. . . ." It was a
touching view of a town that was beaten either by dust or downpour
the year round, along a river that was either an exhausted meander of
last waters among sand bars or a wide sailing flood.

Such extremes brought to mind the condition of the colony amidst
its opposing hopes and frustrations. To lead the way forward through
them called for nerve. "It has," said Austin, "it has been my policy to
slide along without any noise." It was galling that in his task he met with
difficulties not only from the Mexicans, but from among his own people,
and he was ready with another bitter opinion. "I fear (judging by my
own experience) that the predominant traits in the North American
character are ingratitude, selfishness, and avarice. The people of this
Colony have caused (what I formerly said was impossible) a shade of
misanthropy to pass over me. . . ." Of himself he had few doubts. "I
can with truth and clear conscience say that none of the sordid and
selfish motives which influence the mass of adventures had any weight
in determining me to attack the wilderness. I commenced on the solid
basis of sound and philanthropic intentions and of undeviating integrity." But when the Government pressed him to follow one course, and
his people another, he suffered. Did people not know how he toiled for
them? Lonely and isolated by his severe temperament and his flatness
of spirit—the wages of rationalism—it seemed that he must at times
reach for popularity by sudden changes of belief. Swayed by opinions
contrary to his, and that he despised, he must contradict himself in
crisis after crisis on the major issues of his world—slavery, statehood,
independence itself.

"Our situation is extremely delicate and interesting," he told
his sister in 1831, in an odd mixture of passion and objectivity. "To
remain as we are, is impossible. We have not the right kind of material
for an Independent Government and an union with the United States
would bring Negro Slavery—that curse of curses, and worst of reproaches,
on civilized man; that unanswered, and unanswerable, inconsistency
of *free* and liberal republicans"—and yet he had brought slavery with
him. "I think the Government will yield, and give us what we ought
to have. If not, we shall go for *Independence*"—the very idea of which
he denied indignantly when addressing suspicious Mexican officials—
"and put our trust in our selves, our riffles, and—our God. Adios."

It was true that the confusions all about him were greater, more violent, than his own. At Matamoros in the dry, hot June of 1832 he heard the latest news from both sides of the Rio Grande. For six months Santa Anna had been leading a revolution against President Bustamante. It had started in Veracruz and was now inflaming all of Mexico, and though Austin had hoped to keep Texas above the battle—"what is needed there is a *dead calm*"—in that very June, and in his absence, the colonists had met and passed resolutions supporting Santa Anna. Hastily Austin wrote home from Matamoros counselling "prudence and harmony and legal proceedings—no violence."

But violence was already bursting upon Texas. In rebellion against exorbitant duty charges and other abuses, three unarmed schooners in Texas colonial trade were sailed out of the Brazos River without clearing the Mexican port authority or paying tonnage fees. Presently one of the schooners, the *Sabine,* returned, bringing two brass cannon. They were the *Ariel's* old cannon that had been put ashore to lighten her for her last attempt to cross the bar of Galveston Bay. The Texans now possessed artillery. Ill feeling grew, and in the late spring the Mexican authority arrested seven colonists and took them into the fort at Anáhuac on Galveston Bay. Their neighbors took up arms and attacked the fort, to obtain the release of the prisoners. Negotiations ended in charges of bad faith on both sides, and the settlers sent for the *Ariel's* cannon. These could not come by land, and so were mounted on the schooner *Brazoria* behind bulwarks of baled cotton. To reach Anáhuac, she must sail past Fort Velasco, at Galveston. The garrison there refused her passage, and a land-sea battle followed that ended with the surrender of the fort, the disablement of the *Brazoria,* the release of the prisoners of Anáhuac, the abandonment of that post, and the withdrawal by summer's end of all Mexican troops from Texas. Most of them pronounced their support of Santa Anna and went to join him. It was the first victory of Texan arms against Mexico. Quiet was restored for the moment, and Stephen Austin once again from the Rio Grande proclaimed adherence to Mexico and the Mexican confederation.

At Matamoros in late June he saw the local effect of the Santa Anna campaign. "We have had a revolution here, or rather a change of garrisons and of officers. The Govt. troops very quietly marched off at one end of the town, and Col. Mexía with 300 marched *in* at the other end—he is of the Santana party. . . ." Mexía brought his troops from Tampico by water, accompanied by the Governor of Tamaulipas. They landed at the mouth of the river, marched overland without

incident except the firing of three cannon balls at a small party of
government cavalry that quickly dispersed itself, and many of the ten
thousand people of Matamoros and near-by settlements escorted the
invaders into town. "I have never seen anything conducted with so
much good order," Austin said. " . . . the ordinary business of the
merchants was not interrupted one hour—not one cent of private
property has been touched—not one act of confusion or even of disorder
has occurred since Mexía arrived. . . . he is . . . I think quite a liberal
and good man. I am much pleased with him." There was some concern
over reports that General Mier y Terán, who adhered to the government,
was in the neighborhood with an army; but this was dissipated presently
by news that Santa Anna had engaged him in battle and defeated him.
Austin presently heard what had followed on July third. "Teran killed
himself at Padilla on the 3—he ran his sword through his heart on the
very spot where Iturbide was shot." Santa Anna continued to drive his
way to the capital and the presidential palace.

Austin addressed him from the Rio Grande. " . . . I have
expressed my opinion," he said with vehemence that mounted with his
latest thought, "to the government of the Nation and to General Santa
Anna from Matamoros, with a particular notice of the slanderous, unjust
and Machiavellian lie, of that imaginary ghost raised by the aristocratic and designing enemies of the immigration of republican
settlers—that the inhabitants of Texas wish to secede from Mexico." In
a few days he took ship with General Mexía for the Brazos, and once
home, put himself on record in support of the current revolution. "The
colony and all Texas have but one course left which is to unite in the
cause of the Santana party, and if necessary fight it out. . . ."

For it was clear that the party in power under President Bustamante would grant little that Texas wanted. Bustamante's laws of
April 6, 1830, reduced Texas to a mere source of revenue that was to
be wrung from her by soldiery. New immigration was illegal under
Article II of the law. The appeals of Texas for loyal autonomy were
ignored. Bustamante actually threatened to make Texas into one vast
penal colony for the ejecta of Mexican society. No wonder the Texans
turned hopefully to Santa Anna, whose drive now looked certain of
success. He could not possibly do worse for Texas than Bustamante; he
could only do better. In the main, Texas wanted two things. One was
relief from the laws that cut off further North American settlers from
entering. The other was separation from Coahuila into statehood for
herself under the Mexican federation.

Many of the Texan complaints were like those laid before the Spanish córtes by the colonial delegates of Coahuila and New Mexico seventeen years before. Again the colony was too far from the view of the government for colonists to receive the most ordinary official services. Stephen Austin in 1832 stated that in all of Texas there was not one civil court, or even a lawyer, while the "supreme tribunal of Justice is at Saltillo, a distance of 300 leagues. The legislature understands neither the situation nor the wants of Texas, nor can it understand them. The military powers under the anti-republican anti-liberal administration of Guerrero's assassins . . . have treated the government and constitution of the State of Coahuila and Texas with a complete contempt. If the authorities of the State have borne such insults, there is no reason why the people should do so. . . ."

There were other conditions that tended to make a natural separation between Coahuila and Texas. Texas with her great Gulf Coast had access to foreign commerce, while Coahuila, all inland, lived on a straggle of internal commerce. Inhabited Texas with her meadowlands and rains from the Gulf was mainly farming country, while arid Coahuila was mostly given over to cattle ranges and mining. When Coahuila dealt with commerce and industry she provided for her own conditions, not those in Texas. "In short," said Austin, "you may say that Texas needs a *government,* and that the best she can have, is to be created a State in the Mexican Federation." And to justify, support and administer her own state government, Texas needed to grow: " . . . We want more population, and to obtain it the Article 11th of the law of April 6th, 1830 must be abrogated," concluded Austin.

As though to prove intentions of complete loyalty to Mexico, the Texans would ask that San Antonio de Béxar become the state capital. It was the oldest settlement, the seat of Mexican authority, in Texas. Its town council should be the nucleus of a Texas legislature. Let the council, urged Austin, "represent against the laws preventing imigration from other countries . . . let it complain against the maritime tariff, a barbarous contrivance ruinous to agriculture; let it expose clearly the abuses of the military power, and above all, let it be the first to urge a seperation from Coahuila and the formation of a seperate State." The San Antonians, if they would do these things, need not fear a lack of support. "The character of the people of Texas is interprizing and decided, they scorn dangers and laugh at obstacles; therefore if Béxar wishes to be at the head of these people, it must be decided in its course, it must be *Mexico-Texan.*"

There was little time left to make such decisions. The Texan colonists were in no mood to wait much longer for recognition and accommodation of their needs by the mother government. "Things have now come to such a pass," said Austin, "that lukewarm measures are ruinous, it is necessary to adopt a party, and to declare it publicly, otherwise I apprehend that it would be difficult to avoid difficulties, divisions, and local ill feeling throughout Texas." But the summer of 1832 passed, and no sign of official interest in the Texas question came either from Mexico City, or Saltillo or even San Antonio, and in September, the colonists acted. Boldly breaking the law of 1824 that prohibited citizens of Mexico from holding assemblies, the Texan aldermen of San Felipe de Austin on the Brazos called a convention to meet on October first to discuss ways and means to achieve separate statehood, and to take up other public questions.

The convention sat from Monday to Saturday in the first week of October. It was attended by only fifty-six delegates, for not enough time had been allowed for many more men to be present. But they aired their great principle in free debate. Among the delegates were native Mexicans who lived in Texas, and other foreigners than the Anglo-Americans. When they rose at the end of the week they had a sense of having done a momentous act. But "our consciences are clear," declared Austin. "Should the future drive us into an attitude of hostility in defense of what we have so dearly earned, the public opinion of good men, I think, will acquit us of wrong—we shall *then* expect that the sympathies which cheered the struggling Greeks and Poles—that sanctioned the independence of Spanish America—that applaud the liberals of France, and the reformists of Great Britain, will also cheer the humble watch fires of our undisciplined militia, and if necessary soon swell their ranks to a respectable army. . . ." But he hastened to make clear that separation from Coahuila was all that was wanted, not separation from Mexico. And yet—and yet when the first convention had risen and its members gone home, he could not help revealing in that autumn of 1832 a dreamlike possibility. Separation from Mexico, he said, was not to the interest of Texas "if such a thing can be avoided, unless"—and he underlined what came next—*"unless indeed we should float into the Northern Republic with the consent of all parties, ourselves included."*

It was like the completion of a design for another man and his purpose when Stephen Austin received a letter written from Nashville, Tennessee, September 10, 1832, by one of Austin's colonists, who was travelling. It came by hand, and on its cover bore the inscription,

"Politeness of Genl. Houston," and it introduced the bearer: "Genl. A. [sic] Houston of this town is going to depart for Texas in a day or two, he is going by the way *Arkansas Territory,* it will take him until in the month of Decr. sometime to reach you, I have given him a letter of introduction to you which he will hand you on his arrival there, I am not informed of his views in Visiting that country, I think he would be a great addition to Our country as a Citizen, he is a very intimate friend of the Presidents . . . I think it would be well worth your trouble to try and Make him a Citizen of your Colony. . . ."

The second statehood convention assembled on April 1, 1833. On the same day in Mexico General Santa Anna was inaugurated as President of Mexico. The Texans had guessed right in the recent revolution, and now prepared their address to the new president. Their labors were mainly given to two great matters. One was the drafting of a state constitution, and the committee to do this was headed by General Sam Houston, who had come to stay. The other was the framing of a petition to the national government appealing for statehood under the law of 1824 that said, "So soon as Texas is in a situation to figure as a State she shall inform Congress thereof for its resolution." For a fortnight the delegates worked on their papers; and ended by appointing three commissioners to proceed to Mexico with the Texan case. Of these, only one, Stephen Austin, went. He was confident of the outcome.

"I go with considerable—I may say—strong hopes of success," he declared. The petition was well argued from a legal point of view, its tone was respectful and dignified, and surely the government could neither take offense at it nor refuse what was asked. Every constitutional approach to the affair would be followed so long as there was hope of official agreement in the end. Stephen Austin hoped for a harmonious solution, for this mission was the last he intended to perform for the colony. He had worked tirelessly, and had launched a great enterprise, and now he hoped to retire with one more success behind him. "If however I fail,"—and he now reflected what was already in the minds of his people—"and war is the result, I will take a hand in that, and enter the ranks as a soldier of Texas." Who knew? In any case, on the eve of departure, he was not sorry for all the large impulses that had brought him through trouble and the ingratitude of small minds. "I had rather at least be capable of being moved by bright visions, never realized, than to pass through the world without being touched by the recollections of the past, the events of the present, or the anticipations of the future," he meditated, leaving for the Rio

Grande and the capital, and hoping to be home again in four months, if not sooner.

News of the convention had reached Matamoros in garbled form. It made much excitement. Along the Rio Grande it was believed that Texas had declared national independence and was raising an army to fight Mexico. Austin hastened to see the new Commandant General, Vicente Filisola, whom he reassured, with the result that Filisola ended by thinking well of statehood for Texas. The Commandant General was shocked by conditions as he found them on the Rio Grande, where smuggling was arrogantly carried on by officials, traders and clever lawyers. He discussed his problems with Austin, who was not well. Epidemics were sweeping the whole country in the summer of 1833, and Austin was a victim in May—"much debilitated by Dysentary or *Cholorina.*"

Waiting to take ship for Veracruz from the river's mouth, he was troubled by an old obsession that once again and in another sweeping veer of his convictions agitated itself into his correspondence. "I have been adverse to the principle of slavery in Texas. I have now, and for the last six months, changed my views of that matter; though my ideas are the same as to the abstract principle. Texas *must be* a slave country. Circumstances and unavoidable necessity compels it. It is the wish of the people there, and it is my duty to do all I can, prudently, in favor of it. I will do so." The dark dream of 1830 had passed off; and the climate of the society he had founded now prevailed over the justice and terror with which he had once viewed slavery, and over the morbid hatred he had then shown for the Negro. In the end he seemed like an individual torn asunder by the matter as a whole nation was later to be. He shook himself together for the trip to the capital—down to the river's mouth, up over the side of "a little schooner," and off for an expected voyage of six days to Veracruz, whence he would proceed overland to Mexico City, and the prompt dispatch of his business with Santa Anna and the government.

I I.

"God and Texas"

Nothing worked as so reasonably planned.

First, the week at sea—"I had a wretched trip. *One month* from Matamoros to Veracruz in a little schooner—ten days on short allowance of water—none but salt provisions—and sea sick all the time. But I am well now." He was in Mexico City by then, only to find that President Santa Anna was in the field with troops, putting down civil war. Vice President Gómez Farías was acting executive, and Austin called on him, and on appropriate cabinet ministers, on July 19th. He was cordially asked to return in four days to make a formal, oral presentation of his case, and when he did so, he was politely requested to submit his appeal in writing. In nine days he had it ready, and the hearings proceeded, while he felt by turns elated and hopeless. In his exhaustion, the cholorina returned to him, and he was "so weary that life is hardly worth having. . . ." But he was soon about and busy again, working on his great questions of statehood, and the repeal of the ban on immigration; and taking up other pendant matters opportunely, such as establishment of regular mails for the colonies and relief from import duties.

But however hard he worked, his little gains seemed to vanish in the toils of government—committees, interviews, debates in the Congress, all aggravated by the suspicion with which the Mexicans regarded the intentions of the United States. President Jackson's envoy in Mexico was once again pressing the purchase of Texas all the way to the Rio Grande, with a repeated offer of five million dollars. Beyond that, and in clumsy intrigue, the envoy was erecting a system of bribery that was an insult alike to Mexican pride and the dignity of the United States. Jackson in Washington, like Austin in Mexico, hoped to accomplish his different aims for Texas by legal means, with candor and good will. But all Mexico could see in either's approach was an insatiable appetite for her vast province of Texas; and in her alarm, which was entirely justified, she took refuge in the hesitations and elaborations of her bureaucracy; and Stephen Austin felt his patience run thin.

He heard from Texas. The news grieved him sadly. Cholera was spreading, his brother John was dead of it, and many close friends. He longed to go home, and one day in the fall while calling on the Vice President his taut nerves betrayed him, and he spoke sharply.

Either, he said, Texas must be made a state by the government, or she would make herself one.

Señor Gómez Farias was enraged. Was this a threat?

Austin replied that it was not a threat, only a statement of fact which he felt it his duty as a good Mexican to give to the authorities, that they might act wisely.

He thought the Vice President was mollified by his explanation, and he went to his lodgings. Once there, his own words echoed in his ear, and he sat down and wrote a furious letter to the Town Council of San Antonio de Béxar. It was dated October 2, 1833. In it he said that civil war conditions in Mexico made it impossible for anything to be accomplished. Nothing had been done for his mission, and nothing would be done. In such a state of affairs, he called for the settlements of Texas to combine without delay to form their own state government under the law of 7 May 1824. The central government was going to do nothing for Texas. "If the people of Texas," he wrote, "do not take their affairs into their own hands, that land is lost," and he was powerfully convinced that the course he urged was the only one that would save them all from total anarchy and ruin. Let them not lose an instant in uniting to form a local government independent of Coahuila even if the general government refuses its approval. "Dios y Texas," he concluded, and dispatched the paper which would travel for almost a month before being delivered in San Antonio, while he lingered in the capital.

The civil war suddenly took a new turn, resistance collapsed, and in early November the President returned to town and resumed his office. Austin soon gained access to him, and once again his volatile hopes rose. Santa Anna in gold lace and decorations was small, compact and stocky, with a large head and a gravely sensitive expression in his fine eyes, and a delicate smile that seemed to comment upon his own blood-won eminence with some detachment. If Austin was ready to face him with impatience, the President disarmed him. He seemed "very friendly about Texas," and quite as though he had never written his fiery letter of October second, Austin wrote home after his interviews with the

President—he saw him twice—"I am of opinion that if you all keep quiet and obey the state laws that the *substance* of all Texas wants will be granted. The appearance of things is much better than it was a month or even two weeks ago. . . ."

And in fact the government now moved swiftly to compose the Texas question. The ban on immigration was formally lifted. While statehood was not granted out of hand, and in any case would have to be voted on by all the other states of the federation, the government pledged itself to bring Texas as rapidly as possible to it, or to the status of a territory, and Austin sent word that "all will go right." Lesser questions of tariffs, mails, and establishment of local courts were, in government's timeless gestures, referred to appropriate offices for study. Eager to be off, Austin told the colony that "Texas matters are all right. Nothing is wanted there but *quiet*. . . ." But yes, there was one more thing. "It is now very important to harmonise with Béxar. . . ." for at all costs his letter of October second must not be acted upon now. He left Mexico City on the tenth of December.

At Saltillo, on January 3, 1834, on his way home he called on the local commandant to discuss Texan affairs, and was immediately placed under arrest by order of Vice President Gómez Farias. For the Town Council of San Antonio de Béxar, horrified even to receive the revolutionary letter of October second, had sent copies of it everywhere, and one had reached Gómez Farias, together with a copy of their reply, which groaned with loyalty and begged to be read by the government. "It is certainly regrettable," stated the San Antonians to Austin, "that you should breathe sentiments so contrary and opposed to those of every good Mexican. . . . This corporation neither can nor ought, or even wishes, to follow your suggestion, and it begs that you cease writing to it in regard to this matter"—they shuddered—"because you know very well what these communications render one liable to. . . ." The evidence was damning, and the prisoner could but recognize the fact.

"In a moment of irritation and impatience I wrote an imprudent letter to the Aynta. of Texas in October last," he informed a colonist, "for which I have been arrested and ordered back to Mexico . . . as a prisoner. I do not blame the govt at all for this—my treatment has been very good since my arrest . . ." and he asked the Town Council of San Felipe de Austin "that there may be no excitement about it." Looking back, he could not help listing the "calamities" of the past year in Texas —"floods, pestilence and"—what had brought him to jail—"conventions." It was an odd view to take of the democratic process by which his colony reached for new life. For the rest, he declared that all he had done was work "arduously, faithfully . . . and pationately" for statehood. . . . "This is all, and this is no crime. . . ."

He was kept for ten months in various Mexico prisons. One of them was the dreaded Accordada that had been used by the Inquisition, and there he knew solitary confinement. His only friend was a mouse who regularly came to see him and learned to eat out of his hand. "I . . . laughed at his antic miniature comedies," remarked the prisoner with one of his rare smiles, "and talked to him for hours." After seven months of confinement Austin saw his great mission to Mexico with new, and sad, eyes: "I hope the State question is totally *dead* and will remain so." His friends at home took to heart his requests that they do nothing to agitate for his freedom. No word, no plea, no funds, came from Texas. Presently he was moved to another prison, and then to another. His bitterness overflowed when he heard from one of his guards that certain Texans were at work arranging for him to be in prison for years and years. What if he *had* asked them to stay out of the case? They should have overruled his impulse toward self-sacrifice to make a gesture in his behalf. "A frank, manly, but mild and respectful representation from the people of Texas in my favor would have set me at liberty long since and would do it now . . . my situation is desolate. . . . I expect to die in this prison. . . . When I am dead," he threatened luxuriously, "justice will be done me. . . . This is man and mankind—a picture of human life."

It took months, a year, but finally Texans pleaded for him, and, touched, he declared that he had never believed a word of the stories about colonists working against him. He was released on bail, his trial was scheduled through many changes of venue and postponements, and he occupied himself with memorials on matters of government. He found time—there was plenty of time—to sit for two portraits in miniature on ivory, one in rich formal dress, the other in buckskin hunting costume with rifle, dog, books and leafy savannah, and both fashionably Byronic in feeling. Actually, suspended between the law in Mexico and his responsibilities at home, he was at liberty to amuse himself for the first time in fourteen years. He went to the play; to the opera; to assemblies and balls. He frequented drawing rooms. He wished he could take a long pleasure trip after his scrape was disposed of. Texas seemed curiously far from his thoughts. There, at home, forces were still growing that had sent him to Mexico, and a powerful new personality was increasingly known through the settlements, as General Houston, established in a law practice in East Texas, made himself felt in public questions.

"The little Gentleman," he ironically called Stephen Austin; and after reading one or two of Austin's mournful and suspicious letters from prison, he felt "pity mingled with contempt," and added that Austin "showed the disposition of the viper without its fangs."

But after so many delays of the law, Austin's enforced holiday was suddenly at an end, and under a general amnesty applying to participants in the civil wars, he was at last after two years given his passport and allowed to go home in July, 1835. He sailed from Veracruz for New Orleans, where he would take another ship for Texas. He believed he was bringing one more chance for Texas, if she would be patient and if the President had made his compromises in good faith, to win the place she wanted in the Federation. It was true that Santa Anna had mentioned a plan to send a corps of four thousand infantry, cavalry and artillery to San Antonio de Béxar to control Texas; but Austin thought he had dissuaded him.

Yet Santa Anna's victories in the civil wars were not comprehensive; and as rebellion broke out in one state or another, he was forced to put it down again; and he ended by suspending the federation, dissolving legislatures, and appointing his own creatures to governorships. When such revolution flared in Coahuila, he sent his brother-in-law, General Martin Perfecto de Cos, to the northern provinces to restore order. An army moved into position on the Rio Grande at Matamoros, facing Texas. Was Cos with his troops along the river ready to execute Santa Anna's armed occupation after all?

Texans seemed willing to give him provocation to do so. A customs garrison of forty men and a captain had been re-established at Anáhuac. Early in the summer of 1835 they were taken prisoners by thirty Texans under William B. Travis, and ordered out of Texas. They went. Once again Mexican arms had been thrown back across the Rio Grande. General Cos made his report, and was ordered to capture the five ringleaders of the latest Anáhuac affair, together with Lorenzo de Zavala, who was a refugee from the personal and political enmity of Santa Anna. Cos accordingly directed his subordinate commander at Béxar to arrest Zavala by force if necessary, and requested the peaceful delivery of the Anáhuac filibusters. It was an act that touched off all the latent explosive power in the Texas colonies. Rumors flew across the settlements. Mexico was coming to invade Texas and take the demanded men by force. The colonies were to be deprived of slaves. The Mexican constitution of 1824, which was the last refuge of Texan hopes, the actual charter of their contract, was nullified. Settlers who had

arrived since April 6, 1830, were to be expelled. Texans who had resisted
Mexican soldiery were to be court-martialled. A military despotism was
about to descend. . . . The colonists encouraged one another with
promises of defiance, and war was in the air.

It hovered over the Gulf. The government maintained a revenue
ship called the *Correo de México* to patrol the shipping for Velasco,
with orders to capture contraband vessels. In August she took an American brig. American captains thereafter vowed vengeance. The chance
for it came on September first, when the schooner *San Felipe,* of United
States registry, sighted the *Correo de México* off the mouth of the Brazos.
The *San Felipe* closed in and fired on the Mexican. The fire was
returned. The engagement lasted three quarters of an hour, until the
Correo de México withdrew.

One of the passengers on the American ship was Stephen Austin,
returning from Mexico. It was his first view of battle, and it told him,
after his long absence, how bitter were the animosities to which he had
come home. He landed from the *San Felipe* and all night long he "walked
the beach, his mind oppressed with the gravity of the situation, fore-
casting the troubles ahead to Texas." How many more armed encounters,
however small, could there be without an actual state of war? He was
hailed on his return as the only leader who could unify Texas and show
her where to go. What was there left to hope for from a Mexico too
ravaged by civil war to order her own national, let alone a provincial,
government? Santa Anna in destroying the federation of the states had
established a centralist government with himself as absolute ruler.
Who could deny to Texans the liberty of deciding whether or not they
would rest content under such a government? Who could tell the Texans
not to defend their rights under the 1824 Constitution? Who could
tell them not to oppose with a militia under arms Cos and his troops
from the Rio Grande if they should come? Austin found that another
convention—was it to be another "calamity"?—had already been called to
decide on the issue. It was plain that if they decided against the dictatorship, war must follow. Many counselled keeping the peace, at least
until Texas might organize for war. Many others called for immediate
war.

Austin was asked to address his colonists at Brazoria on September eighth, when they wanted to hear his counsel in their trouble. If he
asked them to defer or withdraw the call to the convention, they would
know he was against war. If he approved it—they would follow him
under arms. He rose to speak; and in a very few minutes, all knew the

answer. Only a gathering of the people of Texas, he declared, could justly determine whether they would accept the abandonment of the republican for the centralized government. The convention was to be held. The decision was made. Under its implications, a call to arms sounded throughout Texas; and facing the Rio Grande, the North American colonists made ready.

12.

From Mexico's Point of View

What had to be done was familiar enough to be thoroughly understood by General Cos and the citizens of the Rio Grande. It had been done often enough in the states below the river. When pronouncements were made against the government, and arms were brandished in revolution, there must follow long marches in prickly dust; passages and encampments in gritty mountains where a column of government troops was lost like any lizard; sightings of distant towns like images in mirrors of heat, approaches in wide circlings, and then contact, firing, a cavalry charge, confusions of personal valor; and whether after one day, or many, an end in some plaza with the reading of an official paper, a dropping sword, a volley, men crumbling dead and leaking crimson, while from arched shadows framed in white plaster the nonmilitary residents of Mexico regarded with fixed and fated eyes what an army was for.

Above the river, Texas—up to now the least troublesome of all Mexican political districts—invited suppression. The action that followed, seen from the Mexican point of view, was that of a sovereign national government doing its duty. It was a point of view to be maintained, in the way of nations, by force of arms, as long as possible.

In September General Cos again demanded the delivery of Zavala and the perpetrators of the Anáhuac outrage; and when they were not surrendered, he hurried his preparations to go and take them. He mustered five hundred soldiers at Matamoros. Some of these were trained and uniformed. Most were recently arrived criminals herded north for frontier service. He did what he could with them—issued arms, conducted drills, assigned them to units. They were of predominantly Mexican Indian strains, like all the soldiery of the nation. In their own village units lost in rock or jungle or desert with primitive weapons they were willing warriors and remorseless familiars of death. Now in squads, under heavy rifles, and subject to other authority than that of magic ancestors, they wondered at being soldiers. General Cos embarked them on small ships at the mouth of the Rio Grande on September 17, 1835, to sail up the coast on the Laguna Madre inside Padre Island for Copano on Matagorda Bay. He intended to go ashore, march inland to San Antonio de Béxar to join the Mexican garrison there, and by a show of power, to reduce the Texans, take his prisoners, and restore order above the Rio Grande. It was not known how long the general commanding the northeast provinces would be absent from his Matamoros headquarters; but information would be sent back from time to time, and as soon as the Texans had been brought to their senses, certain long-range plans would take effect. President Santa Anna was absent from the capital, preparing regiments that would in due course immensely reinforce the garrisons of Texas, and in any case, he had informed the Texans that he proposed personally to visit them in the following March—"as a friend." Meanwhile, the acting President had issued a circular from the capital which came to the Rio Grande forces to show them their duty, the reasons for it, and the promise of their own triumph. It was read with interest from Matamoros to Fort Rio Grande:

"The colonists established in Texas have recently given the most unequivocal evidence of the extremity to which perfidy, ingratitude and the restless spirit that animates them can go, since—forgetting what they owe to the supreme government of the nation which so generously admitted them to its bosom, gave them fertile lands to cultivate, and allowed them all the means to live in comfort and abundance—they have risen against that same government, taking up arms against it under the pretense of sustaining a system which an immense majority of Mexicans have asked to have changed, thus concealing their criminal purpose of dismembering the territory of the Republic.

"His Excellency the President *ad interim*, justly irritated by a conduct so perfidious, has fixed his entire attention upon this subject, and in order to suppress and punish that band of ungrateful foreigners, has directed that the most active measures be taken, measures required by the very nature of what is in reality a crime against the whole nation. The troops destined to sustain the honor of the country and the government will perform their duty and will cover themselves with glory."

The government made a strong case for the people and the army, and showed every confidence, even though it was a long march into Texas and the seat of the trouble. What if there were over twenty thousand settlers there now? They were not organized, their communities were scattered, and the two largest ones—in East Texas and along the Brazos—had few dealings together, and no political connection. Matamoros and its environs alone totalled around ten thousand people; and below Matamoros were the other states of Mexico where even in times of trial (the national treasury was empty and troops lived off the lands they crossed or the cities they invested) the sheer weight of numbers would certainly overwhelm the Texans, if they persisted in forgetting who owned Texas, after all. . . . News from General Cos was awaited with confidence and interest.

It was incredible when finally, by courier, and traveller, and scribbled field dispatch, it began to filter through the brush country into the sovereign Mexican establishments of the Rio Grande; and when, on Christmas Day, 1835, General Cos himself with an exhausted brigade appeared out of Texas at Laredo upriver, crossed, and settled his followers to lick their wounds. His campaign of four months could now be seen in its entirety from the Mexican point of view.

Entering Texas from the shore in September, General Cos heard how the Texans were organizing everywhere under committees of public safety; yet no one opposed him as he marched inland toward San Antonio, going by way of La Bahía, now called Goliad. He arrived there on the second of October and at once learned of a clumsy performance that had developed a few days before at Gonzales, a settlement east of San Antonio. The settlers there possessed a brass six-pounder that had been given them by the army four years before as a protection against Indians. Now in the unrest that prevailed so widely, Colonel Ugartechea, the commander at San Antonio, remembered the cannon, and even though it was known to be unmounted, he sent a small detachment to take it away. The settlers refused to give it up, captured the detachment, sent word to their neighbors that the government was about to attack them, and a force of Texans gathered fast preparing for battle. They removed their women and children to safety. They commandeered all the small boats on the Guadalupe River where Gonzales stood. They were ready when eighty soldiers under a lieutenant appeared from the garrison at San Antonio to free their comrades, take the brass cannon and arrest those responsible for outright revolt. The lieutenant held discretionary orders. If the Texans outnumbered him so far as to make it seem likely that he would be repulsed, and the national dignity impaired, he was to retire. Upon examining the situation he concluded that he must do so, and withdrew his position to "a slight eminence" six miles west of the Guadalupe River.

But that night—it was about eleven o'clock on October first—the Texans crossed over the river and then waited until dawn, which came over heavy fog. And then coming within a range of about three hundred and fifty yards, an advance party of Texans fired upon the army and were at once pursued by soldiers. The six-pounder was brought forward and set off with a load of grapeshot. As the fog lifted the army saw a piece of insolence. Over the cannon the Texans had placed a sign reading "Come and Take it!". The lieutenant from San Antonio gave an order to his trumpeter, who sounded a parley, which was held. No agreement resulted. The army would not surrender, and the rebels would not give up the old brass piece that was the cause of all the trouble. Instead, after the truce was over, the Texans fired it again, and then charged. There were over a hundred and fifty of them, fifty mounted. A loyalist soldier was killed. The army became disorganized, turned, and hurried off to San Antonio.

It was hardly a battle; yet the Texans had deliberately prepared for it as if it were to be one, and with effrontery had actually taken the initiative in attack. It was clear that the colonists had determined on war, were now enemies, and had fought their first engagement as such, with results unfortunate for the national dignity. General Cos had not arrived a moment too soon.

He inspected the supplies stored in the ruined mission of La Bahía at Goliad, which would serve him as an important base between San Antonio and the sea, and would also command a strategic road to Matamoros and the Rio Grande. In the old mission were stored for the large punitive operations planned by General Cos a number of pieces of artillery, three hundred rifles, ten thousand dollars in strongboxes, and plentiful supplies. After estimating the situation, General Cos stationed thirty soldiers and a colonel to guard the base, led his forces through the heavy autumn air over rolling hills and past green meadowlands threaded by bright little creeks to San Antonio, where he would hold consultations with Colonel Ugartechea. He hardly reached there before an exasperating report reached after him.

On the night of October ninth the Texans had descended upon Goliad, killed a sentry, chopped their way through a door with axes, and had captured the colonel commanding, all his men, and everything stored in the mission of La Bahía. It was bad, but what made it worse was that the outrage had been committed by only forty Texans, one of whom was a known troublemaker named Milam, who had in fact escaped from prison at Monterrey. With Goliad lost to him, General Cos had no base for either the lower Rio Grande or the seaports of Texas. The campaign was opening inauspiciously for the government. It was time to do something to reverse the trend.

General Cos established his men at San Antonio, and for two weeks examined the situation in staff discussions with Colonel Ugartechea; and then—was the initiative always to be in the hands of the enemy?—an army of many hundred Texans was reported to be approaching San Antonio. On September twenty-seventh a large advance party took up a position in the river hollows by the empty mission of the Immaculate Conception—one of the five clustered along the San Antonio river. The Texans were about a mile and a half across an open plain from garrison headquarters. Their very position was a challenge—almost it seemed like a threat of siege to the garrison. General Cos met it with decision.

When the Texans woke up on the morning of the twenty-eighth they found themselves surrounded by four hundred government troops. There was no escape for them, and no sensible course but surrender. Instead, under the heavy morning fog they formed two elements down in the river hollows, which afforded them natural breastworks, and there when the fog rose the army advanced upon them with blazing volleys, that seemed, however, to take little effect. It was the enemy fire that was effective—dreadfully so. It was amazing how the Texans handled firearms, they aimed like hawks, they fired with extreme deliberation, and all too often they hit their mark. They had a sort of drilled system. One man loaded while another fired, by pairs, so, along the lines, so that there never was a gap of silence and vulnerability while all loaded at once. The government force charged three times, supported by a brass six-pounder that hurled grapeshot into the shallow ravine; but the rifle fire from the river was so terrible that a hundred soldiers were killed or wounded, and it was not long until the rest were retreating to San Antonio, leaving behind them the cannon which became a prize for

the enemy. There could be no doubt that this, the Battle of La Concepción, was another defeat for the properly constituted authority of
Mexico.

An hour later the remainder of the Texan army appeared from
down the river course, where they had marched and camped by the other
missions—Saint Francis of Espada, Saint John of Capistrano, Saint
Joseph—and joined their victorious men who had been captained by
Texans named Bowie and Fannin. The fifth mission was within the town,
it was the one commonly spoken of as the Álamo, and though partially
ruined, served as a useful storehouse, shop building and fortress for the
garrison. There was every possibility in the encampment across the
plain to the south that the Texans would not be content until they took
the Álamo also. There were now about a thousand men gathered beyond
the Concepción mission with its arched cloister and its beautiful dome,
and their commander was discovered to be Colonel Esteban Austin, the
chief of the Brazos colony. General Cos still held the road that led back
to Laredo on the Rio Grande. Acting decisively, he dispatched Colonel
Ugartechea and a hundred garrison soldiers to Laredo to return by
forced marches with reinforcements of as many as five hundred con-
scripted convicts who were stationed there. Left with eight hundred men
in the town, General Cos directed operations, erecting barricades, plac-
ing batteries and strengthening all defenses.

In the following days the Texans were everywhere. Twice they
moved their position closer. They patrolled the approaches and kept
supplies from coming into San Antonio. They sent a demand for surrender which despite his shrinking stock of food and other supplies
General Cos disdained, just as he disdained breaking forth to give battle.
For nearly a month the garrison waited for the return of Ugartechea and
the conscripts, and the Texans in little sallies rode around the town
trying to force combat. It was plain that they had no heavy guns with
which to reduce the garrison from afar. They seemed restless and confused, and reports came in from their bivouacs that many of them were
leaving their camp in disgust because there was no fight. But they
received reinforcements now and then—three companies of volunteers
from the United States, one from East Texas—and their intention seemed
to be to hang on.

What they were determined to fight for was meanwhile being
declared in a civil assembly held in San Felipe de Austin early in the
same month. Those settlers who were not serving in the field with the
armed party met to create a state government, swearing loyalty to

Mexico under the constitution of 1824, and electing a governor, a commander-in-chief, and other officials. They had the idea that they were not pronouncing against Mexico, or sending men to fight against her, but only against the present government of Don Antonio López de Santa Anna and his system. They were supposed to believe that their policy would have the sympathy and support of many thousands of Mexicans below the Rio Grande who also preferred to cling to the abandoned constitution. But the President had more than once disposed of such Mexicans, and in any case, the Texan affair was rebellion against him, and the army, and the powers that were, and would be handled accordingly, as General Cos was handling them.

At San Antonio, General Cos faced increasing difficulties over supplies. Even fodder was scarce, and one day he sent a column of one hundred muleteers and soldiers out on the old Rio Grande road to cut grass for the hungry horses of the garrison. They gathered a pack-train load of grass in safety and were coming back to the town when a hundred mounted Texans attacked them, evidently thinking they were attacking Colonel Ugartechea with his reinforcements, and his saddlebags loaded with silver with which to pay troops and conduct the war. More Texans rushed to join the fight when they saw it developing, and the foraging party was obliged to break and run for the town, leaving behind all the mules, and fifty soldiers dead and a number wounded.

It became known later that a day or so before the grass fight Colonel Austin resigned the command of his forces to journey to the United States as a commissioner to raise money and support for the Texan revolt. Colonel Edward Burleson was elected, as North Americans always elected their officers, to succeed him in command. Shortly afterward events began to move more rapidly.

First, General Cos was betrayed by the escape of three Texan prisoners of the Anáhuac affair, and the desertion of a Mexican lieutenant. These men conveyed to the enemy camp news of how things were inside the besieged headquarters. The Texans evidently took much encouragement from what they learned of the state of the troops, supplies and defenses of San Antonio and the fortified Álamo mission. On the night of December fourth, the enemy moved to a new position by the old mill northeast of town, and just before sunrise on the fifth they attacked in three columns. One entered the town by way of Acequia Street, another through Soledad Street, both coming swiftly to the northern entrances of the main plaza. At the same time, the third attacked the Álamo east of the river, and a battle of four days began.

Every street and rooftop was fought for. Every house was the scene
of a delaying action. The Texans used their small arms with fearful
accuracy, and raked the narrow streets with their handful of small
cannon. It rained on December eighth and the day was cold. When the
Texans gained entry to the first room of a row of adobe houses, they
used battering rams to break through into the next, and the next, until
they held the whole row, and then a whole street. Even the arrival of
Colonel Ugartechea with men from the Rio Grande on the night of the
eighth could not hold San Antonio against the wildly fighting invaders.
General Cos withdrew from the plaza to the Álamo, which his men still
defended, and prepared to rally for a great effort that would make the
best use of Ugartechea's troops and save the town and the flag. But it was
a night of further betrayals. Three officers led their companies out and
left for the Rio Grande, and when the desertions were known, the remaining soldiers began to cry "Treason! Treason!", and the civilians joined
them in creating a panic. General Cos went among them calling out
counsels of courage and calm; but he was unrecognized or ignored, and
suffered brutal maltreatment in the darkness and the confusion of his
own people. He came to his final decision that night, and at sunrise, he
sent his Adjutant-Inspector forth from the Álamo with his surrender.

A treaty was signed on the eleventh, and on the fourteenth
General Cos began his return to the Rio Grande, having agreed for himself and his officers upon his honor not to oppose further the re-establishment of the Constitution of 1824. The conscript criminals were to be
removed from Texas beyond the Rio Grande, while the remainder of
the government troops were at liberty to remain in Texas or follow
their commanding general as they chose. All were allowed to keep their
arms and equipment. The wounded and sick were allowed to remain in
Texas until they should recover. No prisoners were kept by the Texans,
or shot. The campaign had taken a little less than four months, and
had cost Mexico hundreds of casualties in killed or wounded, the Texans
two killed and twenty-six wounded. The Texan army, its disloyal task
finished, scattered its units to their home neighborhoods. General Cos
on December fourteenth with eleven hundred and five men began the
march that ended on Christmas Day, 1835, at Laredo on the Rio Grande.

No proper adherent of the Mexican party in power could see
the Texans' revolt as anything but a personal affront to the President.
But if they were in revolt against his system, he was already arranging
to deal with them. It was known on the Mexican frontier that he was
raising ten thousand soldiers to take to Texas, and the news filtered over

the river to the rebels themselves, who hurriedly and with great confusion between military elements and political began in December to dispose their defenses. They secured the port of Copano, and bases at Goliad, Refugio, Matagorda and Velasco. Travellers still came and went between Texas and Coahuila, and there were also couriers and spies who brought news to the river. By such means it was learned that the Texans, after much dissension in their own councils, were preparing to mount an expedition against Matamoros. To do so they made a decision that could only be satisfying to the President and his generals; for to obtain troops for the invasion of Mexico at Matamoros, they withdrew all but sixty men from the garrison at the Álamo in San Antonio, and in two divided parties, started for the Rio Grande metropolis in winter weather of freezing mists and cold rains over the long stretch of barren country parallel to the coast. They moved slowly, which gave time for the Mexican northeast command to send heavy reinforcements to Matamoros throughout January, 1836.

Both the uprisen colonists and the generals of the republic considered making their opposing movements by sea; but neither had enough ships in which to transport their troops. The Texans had four precarious, if armed, schooners that gave them command of the Mexico Bay. The President, therefore, proceeded with plans for a land campaign. General Fernández was already at Matamoros with his reinforcements. General Urrea was ordered to join him there and cross the Rio Grande immediately, to seek out and destroy the Texan expedition. General Santa Anna with the main body of five brigades numbering just over six thousand men marched for Laredo by way of Fort Saint John Baptist and arrived on February twelfth. On the same day General Ramírez y Sesma crossed the river by the ford of France Way and headed for San Antonio de Béxar. After attending a ball at Laredo, the President took his troops across the Rio Grande on rafts and in his turn left for San Antonio on February sixteenth. On the next day General Urrea crossed the Rio Grande at Matamoros. The multiple invasion was launched. Mexico again watched her sovereign duty being done, this time by the President and his forces.

The main body was stretched out for miles, with distances between its brigades that would take days to close. It was a miserable march. The forces on leaving the Rio Grande had to cross hard brush wastelands until they came to the Nueces; and then began the difficulties created by the succession of rivers that looked on the map of Texas like veins in the half of a great leaf, all running more or less parallel, and equally separated, to the edge, which was the coast. Away from the rivers there was little water to be had for so great an army. Supply was complicated and the soldiers were forced to accept half rations. The country was too poor to feed them as they went. It rained and snowed; wagons and caissons were repeatedly mired. Or on other days the sun poured down its heat, and men and animals suffered from thirst. Soldiers fell ill and many had to be carried on the wheeled vehicles, adding to the burdens of the already punished draft animals. It was not long before wagoners recognized signs of dangerous disease in the horses and mules of the army. Many animals were stricken with the mal de lengua that was a swelling of the tongue from thirst and dry fodder; many others with the telele, a fever taken from drinking polluted water activated by the hot sun. Many soldiers died and were left in the wastes. There were few settlements where relief could be found, and what population he did encounter the President found to be apathetic in the face of the grand issue that was about to be settled by force of arms.

But he pressed forward, expecting to fall upon the rebels in San Antonio just before dawn on February twenty-second in a stunning surprise. His plan was ruined by a matter beyond his control. The heavens opened, a cloudburst fell, and his advance was mired down. It was not until the twenty-fourth that forward elements of the army entered the town. They met no opposition, and he joined them there two days later. A reconnaissance revealed that the only enemy position in the vicinity had been taken up in the structures of the Álamo, where artillery defenses on earthworks and behind the walls as established by General Cos in December were still in place. Barricaded behind them, and presumably with rations gathered to withstand a siege, was a body of Texans. Their cooking fires sent smoke above the walls, and their blinded gates and windows gave notice of their intention to remain. Above them stood their own version of the flag of Mexico—the red, white and green, with two stars, that represented Coahuila and Texas. In the face of General Santa Anna it flaunted the Constitution of 1824, under which the Twin Sister state had been founded.

The mission of San Antonio de Valero was of the usual pattern. It stood east of the river from which meandering acequias flowed past its enclosures. Built in the early eighteenth century it had stood empty since 1793, except for occasional use as a military depot. It had a great walled plaza, fifty-four by one hundred and fifty-four yards; a convent with a large patio; thick stone rooms used as a jail; a corral; and a church, whose roof had fallen in, filling the interior with hillocks of rubble. It took its popular name from the fact that a company of soldiers from El Álamo, a garrison post in Coahuila, had once been stationed there. The outer limits of the whole establishment, whether plaza, patio or church wall, enclosed about two and a half acres, and measured over a quarter of a mile. It did not seem possible that the party of Texans within the walls was large enough to man them effectively. General Santa Anna was in no hurry to open a full-scale attack, pending the arrival of other troops behind him on the long straggled march from the Rio Grande. He placed his batteries pointing across the river toward the Álamo, and established encampments with earthworks about the settlements of San Antonio at ranges measuring from three hundred to a thousand yards from the mission. His guns were light fieldpieces that could not be expected to break down walls; but he ordered cannonading, and for several days shells were lobbed into the mission enclosures, and cavalry detachments rode the perimeter to prevent escape of the occupants.

Yet a certain amount of passing in and out went on. Messengers got away, presumably asking for reinforcement by other Texas militia. One night a group of these managed to come in and join the defenders of the mission. During another night a small party dashed out to collect firewood and set some houses on fire near one of the army's batteries. By day they all worked at strengthening their works. From the walls, sharpshooters picked off soldiers who exposed themselves. It was an intermittent duel between six-pounders and small arms.

Intelligence reports indicated that a large force—two hundred men or more, under the Texan Fannin—were gathered in the neighborhood of Gonzales, and might advance upon San Antonio. General Ramírez y Sesma was ordered out with a cavalry regiment and an infantry battalion to find and dispose of them. What he was to do with them was plainly indicated in General Santa Anna's orders to him: *"En esta guerra sabe vd. que no hay prisoneros. . . ."* But if in that war there were to be no prisoners, Ramírez y Sesma found not even an enemy on the old road to Gonzales. He advanced eight miles, as far as the Espada mission, and returned on the following day to San Antonio. It was later learned that Fannin's column had started to the support of the Álamo but had turned back.

While General Santa Anna was waiting for his reinforcements, and the bombardment continued, and the defenders of the mission tried to build their safety out of the rubble within, the Texans took a fateful and defiant step on March second at the village of Washington on the

Brazos. Fifty-eight delegates, of whom three were Mexicans, signed a declaration of national independence from Mexico. They elected a full slate of national officers, including a commander-in-chief of the armed forces, and drew up a constitution, and set down their pretexts for their actions in a long bill of complaints against the mother country. For something over three months they had claimed to be a self-constituted state under the Mexican republic; now they claimed to be an independent and sovereign nation among the nations of the world. Far from the siege of San Antonio, the new government solemnly sent forth their resounding declarations against the power and authority of Mexico. If before the Texans had been guilty of serious civil disturbances, they were now guilty of outright treason, with its terrible terms of justice.

At last on Friday, March fourth, reinforcements arrived from the third brigade on the Rio Grande road, and the President called a council of war and heard his generals. Cos—who did not feel bound by the parole given to the Texans in the December treaty—was present, and urged that a full-scale attack on the Álamo should be delayed until the arrival, expected by Monday, of two twelve-pounders. Others disagreed. The President kept his own counsel until the next day, when he gave out a plan of assault to be staged before daylight on Sunday, March sixth. Of his five thousand troops, he assigned twenty-five hundred to the attack, divided into four columns, and equipped with axes, iron bars and scaling ladders in addition to the usual arms, to swarm against the walls simultaneously from the points of the compass. The President would direct operations from the headquarters of the reserve—with the river between himself and the Álamo.

Late Saturday night a silence fell when the cannonading, the sniping, were ordered to be stopped. Only meadow sounds, the low rattle of frogs in the river, and the random stirrings of bivouacs where many men and animals were awake in darkness were heard where for days and nights past the artillery had continuously thumped and the rifles had rung. At four o'clock the assault columns began to move into place in a silence severely preserved until some soldiers in one of them raised a shout—the kind of noise that soldiers made to stiffen one another and terrify the enemy. In this case it warned the enemy; and when at dawn on that Sunday the bugle split the heavy calm of the meadows about San Antonio, and the massive attack began, the army in all its four approaches was met with tremendous fire from the artillery and the rifles on the walls. The columns fell back and attacked again, and again, while the massed bands of the brigades across the river played the

"Degüello" to inspire their troops, for it was a word, and a tune, that meant the "throat-cutting," and when played in battle it signified that there was to be no quarter given to the enemy.

The Texan marksmanship, the speed, continuity and fury of their fire, were frightful. Soldiers fell by the score. But the number of their comrades was great, and gaps were closed, and presently there was a great swarm so near the bases of the walls, that the artillery above could not be traversed downward to bear on them. Suddenly a breach was made on the north side, and another on the south, and soldiers poured in to capture the Álamo plaza. The defenders fell back to the convent and its patio, and to the roofless church. The army turned their own cannon on them, and squad after squad advanced to take room after room in the convent cells, killing all whom they trapped in each. The Mexican bayonets whistled and darted in the early sunlight that rayed into the convent patio. The ground was strewn with dead attackers and defenders. But still the army strove and, when all was silent in the outer courts and rooms, threw its remaining power against the church, which was the last stronghold of the Texans. The main doors were forced, and everywhere—in the nave, the baptistry, the transepts, the sacristy, with their heaps of long-fallen stone and weedy mounds of earth, under the light morning sky within the open walls—the victory was won man by man until after an hour not one defender was seen alive anywhere in the profaned and mouldered mission.

But five who had hidden themselves were found and hauled out half an hour later, just as President Santa Anna, summoned from across the river by news of his triumph, arrived before the mission, where his troops were formed into line to receive him. General Castrillon showed him the prisoners, suggesting clemency. The President was shocked. Prisoners? How incredible. What had he already published in orders? "In this war, you understand, there are no prisoners." In a fury he turned his back upon Castrillon, and seeing his attitude, the formation broke ranks, took the unarmed prisoners, and killed them. The President's secretary, who was there, felt with certain others that this was a horror "que reprueba la humanidad"; but by an order that followed the President's policy was once more made clear.

The corpses of the Texans, numbering one hundred and eighty-two, were dragged from where they had fallen within walls and on floors that were pungent with burnt gunpowder and hardening blood to the open ground before the mission. There they were stacked in layers alternating with dry brush and branches and the whole was heaped with wood and set on fire, and left to burn and fall to the fingerings of the wind. The mission graveyard was reserved for the fallen among the Mexican troops. But so many had died in the battle that there was not room for them all in the consecrated ground, and the officer charged with their disposal ended by having the remainder thrown into the San Antonio River. He estimated that the army had lost sixteen hundred men in the hour's engagement. If this was exaggerated, the figures compiled by the President's secretary were studied. He spoke of three hundred dead after the battle, and another hundred among the wounded who died later. The President disagreed with all such tallies, and dictated to his secretary that while over six hundred Texans had perished, the army lost only seventy killed and three hundred wounded, out of an attacking force of only fourteen hundred. But however far such figures were open to question, the day had brought a victory, and Santa Anna moved energetically to exploit it against other Texan operations farther and south.

One had already come to its end—the expedition against Matamoros. General Urrea advanced from the lower Rio Grande in search of the invasion force, and learned that a large part of it was in barracks at San Patricio. Marching even at night through the freezing winds of a norther off the plains, he came before the village at three o'clock on the morning of February twenty-seventh and within half an hour attacked the garrison. All but four of the Texan enemy were taken. A few days later another portion of the invasion force was discovered returning from the Rio Grande where the Texans had gone to capture horses for their expedition. There was a running fight over the prairies twenty miles from San Patricio in which General Urrea held the field command in person. With lance, lasso and rifle his troops destroyed the enemy resistance and took many prisoners. The descent upon Matamoros was completely turned, and troops from her strengthened garrison were free to join General Urrea in Texas.

The President at San Antonio received news of Urrea's victories in the field, and felt much satisfaction in knowing that in all probability the Texan revolt was crushed. He disposed troops among the seacoast settlements and inland towns. Some he sent to Goliad, where they reinforced Urrea, who had been told of Texan forces there and at Refugio about twenty-five miles away. Urrea attacked Refugio first—again there was an assault upon a fortified mission, and again the Texans were defeated, though a great number of them escaped toward Victoria. But there they found the town in Mexican hands and, after a fight, were forced to surrender. They were marched to Goliad, which Urrea had captured. By the twentieth of March all enemy forces operating on the Guadalupe and San Antonio rivers were taken, and a force of prisoners numbering over three hundred, including the Texan commander Fannin, was under guard at Goliad. Word of the triumph was dispatched to the President.

Gratified, he was at the same time astounded that prisoners had actually been taken. When, when would his subordinates understand his orders? There was even a law, passed in 1835, requiring that all foreigners appearing in Mexico under arms should be considered as pirates, and treated as such. With some impatience he sent peremptory orders to Goliad that the prisoners were without exception to be put to death immediately. This command caused certain misgivings in General Urrea and other officers, for the surrender of the Texans had been accepted with an agreement that they would be paroled. But it had to be obeyed, and arrangements were made on the evening of March twenty-sixth to do so. The prisoners suspected nothing, and a number of them entertained themselves and their companions with music on several flutes, playing a nostalgic air popular with them entitled "Home, Sweet Home." At daybreak—the next day was Palm Sunday— the prisoners were turned out and formed in three groups under guard of the entire garrison. They were puzzled. What was the formation for? To preserve order it was thought wise to reassure them. One group was told that they were to be marched to the coast to take ship for their home settlements; another, that they were a work party to help with the slaughter of beeves; the last, that their barracks were needed to accommodate General Santa Anna and his escort who were expected in Goliad. They were marched out of town in three different directions for half a mile, in columns of twos, with guards flanking each column on both sides. The same action followed for each column. At the halt, the file of guards on one side moved through the column to the other, so that all guards were on the same side. And then before the prisoners knew what to expect, the guards fired, and the executions began. The first volley brought down almost all of the Texans; but a few ran away and there followed little localized pursuits for the next hour or so. In the end, only twenty-seven got away, so that, on the whole, the President's order was carried out successfully. Over three hundred were executed. Their bodies were jerked out of their clothes, flung naked into piles and with winter brush as fuel were set to burning. Days later there were still hands and feet to be seen among the ashes. With clemency that amounted to daring insubordination, the commandant of Goliad, troubled by his orders to effect the punishment, had spared the lives of four Texan doctors of medicine and a handful of others. Word of his mercy did not reach the President for some time, when other events absorbed his attention, and the survivors were safe.

Moving from success to success—the Álamo, the Matamoros movement, Refugio, Victoria, Goliad and its mass executions—General Santa Anna now laid plans to return to Mexico with news of his brilliant reduction of Texas—the Texas that called itself a nation. He meant to travel by sea, sending back to the Rio Grande by road the artillery and supply trains for which he might again have use in Mexico. But his generals persuaded him to remain until troop dispositions had been securely made through the humbled province, where now confusion and panic among the Texans created uncertainty for army and enemy alike. A great flight eastward began in all the Texas colonies, evidently in hopes that the power of the United States on the Louisiana border would protect the colonists. Their arms were scattered, their forces were in disagreement about how to organize further defense against punishment, and at best they could have had miserably inadequate numbers to hold the immense territory they claimed as their own. Their national government was ineffectual, and even their first and best-known leader, Stephen Austin, was absent from Texas, soliciting aid in the North American states. Another figure became known as the dominant leader of Texas; and as the nature of the crisis was military, so was he a military man. He was, as the President referred to him, "the so-called General Houston," who had been appointed commander-in-chief of the Texas national armed forces at the convention of independence.

It was he who led the remaining Texan forces eastward in a scattering retreat after the crucial news of the Álamo, Refugio and Goliad. When the settlers heard of his flight they fled also, crossing rivers that had risen in spring floods. In spite of the labors of travelling overland in heavy rains, the President determined now upon a vigorous pursuit of Houston and, so soon as he should bring him to bay, the destruction of the Texan armed forces once and for all. Accordingly he left San Antonio de Béxar on March thirty-first. His confidence was great. He assigned various brigades to occupation and policing duties apart from the main purpose of overtaking Houston, and with the remainder of the troops, he hurried eastward. In his advance he enjoyed one satisfaction after another. He came to the Brazos, and the town of San Felipe de Austin, on April seventh, to find this seat of trouble empty and in ashes. He caught a glimpse of enemy troops on the oppo-site shore of the Brazos, but he could not reach them, for the river was in flood, and the Texans had all the boats. Somewhere beyond them was Houston with his main body. The President marched down the Brazos, and crossed on the eleventh, at Thompson's Ferry. There he heard inter-esting information. At the town of Harrisburg, thirty miles northeast, the Texans who called themselves president and vice president of their nation, together with other prominent civilian leaders of the rebellion, were said to be; and General Santa Anna resolved at once to push ahead to take them as important prizes of the campaign. But they had fled when during the night of the fifteenth he arrived at Harrisburg. All he found were three printers, who said the Texan officials had left for New Washington. Wherever they were, there was the capital of Texas; and General Santa Anna learned later that they had made their way to Galveston Island, where in their persons they constituted the government.

The printers had other information. It seemed that Houston with eight hundred troops was falling back northeastward, attempting to put the Trinity River between him and the relentless chase that had moved so swiftly, in the face of such difficulties, over two thirds of the way across Texas. The President ordered Harrisburg put to the torch, and marched for New Washington, a wretched community of half a dozen houses on a spit of land jutting from the west into an estuary of Galves-ton Bay. Lynch's Ferry over the San Jacinto Creek was slightly to the north. In all probability Lynch's Ferry would be the escape route of Houston and his forces fleeing toward the Trinity farther east. The President ordered reconnaissance operations. If Houston was coming from the northwest down to Lynch's Ferry, he would have to cross Buffalo Bayou, a large inlet of Galveston Bay into which the San Jacinto Creek emptied. It would be a difficult crossing. The President resolved to reach Lynch's Ferry first, and when Houston's people came out of the swamp toward the crossing, to destroy them and end the war.

He prepared to set out, then, on the morning of the twentieth, first seeing that New Washington was burned. He then turned to the trail that led through a thick woods from the village to open prairie beyond, and was about to pass the word for the advance when a scout galloped into camp to report that Houston and his troops were fast approaching upon the rear guard of the army, and had already taken prisoners.

There were times when responsibility and power cost dearly in the lives of those who bore them.

Such a moment now came for the President, lonely in his awful position, and bending every skill and strength to the successful completion of his design. On hearing that Houston was about to trap him at the very exit of the flaming village of New Washington, General Santa Anna lost command of himself and by his actions cast the entire army into disorder and fear. He threw himself upon his horse, shrieking that the enemy was at hand and disaster imminent, and spurred his way wildly down the column of troops and animals waiting to depart. He scattered his own men right and left, trampling some in his fury to pass through the woods and out to the prairie. Others maintained order, brought the men through the copse, and formed them in battle order in the open land. But Houston was nowhere to be seen. The report had been false. Once again in control of himself, the President conducted a proper advance upon Lynch's Ferry, and at two in the afternoon of the nineteenth made the first contact with the "so-called General Houston," whose pickets were sighted near the junction of the bayou and the creek. Fire was exchanged. There was a sense of two major forces feeling each other out, wheeling for advantage, and wary of precipitating any action prematurely.

General Santa Anna took up his position on a low eminence crowned with a woods. There opposite to him at a distance of about a thousand yards was a screen of brush along Buffalo Bayou, with open ground between. The General described his position as an excellent one, "with water in the rear, a thick wood on the right down to the banks of the San Jacinto, a broad plain on the left, and open ground in front." With additional defenses worked up during the night of the twentieth, General Santa Anna felt confident in the face of any attack from the Texans, who were somewhere to the north and west. One thing was certain. The President and his troops lay squarely across the approaches to Lynch's Ferry. The whole place was a pleasant piece of country. The little creek, the deep bayou, were like scenes in a park. Wonderful trees lined their banks, magnolias eighty feet high, and evergreens, rhododendrons, arbutus, laurel, bay and firs. In the dense air against the varying dark greens of the background, drifts of musket smoke, and volumes from cannon, showed blue before vanishing in the afternoon and evening of the twentieth.

The President had sent Gaona, Cos and Urrea off to coastal missions with their brigades, but lately, about to close with his quarry, he had ordered Cos to rejoin him, and expected him momentarily. Early on April twenty-first the President directed the building of a further defense on the left of his line, facing the distant wood screen behind which the Texans at a distance of thirteen hundred yards were known to be concentrated. This breastwork was most ingeniously devised out of heaps of baggage, packsaddles, bags of hard bread and loose brush, to the height of five feet. A gap was left in its centre for a fieldpiece to speak through. While these preparations went forward, General Cos appeared with four hundred troops, having marched all night. In their exhaustion, they were considerately ordered to stack arms, dispose their luggage, and take their rest.

In fact, the whole army was fatigued. The entire campaign had been one of hardship; and it was a mercy that the day—it was April 21, 1836—was calm and without sustained disturbance. The President's encampment, with all the advantages that reassured him—including that of a retreat route across Vince's Creek to his rear, where for his convenience should he need it stood the only bridge over any watercourse between him and the Brazos—was quiet. It seemed the first day in months to allow soldiers to go about little chores for themselves. Some built lean-to shelters of brush. Others took unsaddled horses down to water. Many—most of the army, in fact—slept with the first ease in weeks. A few cooked themselves what they liked, and talked, and ate. The usual pickets were stationed about in the afternoon silence. General Santa Anna himself was in his tent, asleep, after the arduous duties of so many days. It was an open April day with light dancing on the varnished leaves of the magnolias and rhododendrons.

Suddenly, at half-past four, alert pickets observed movement opposite to the left of their line, and made report. A front of Texan cavalry was seen emerging into the clear, and feinting forward. The alarm given, troops on duty opened fire on the cavalry. Scarcely had they done so when from the timbered screen across the open area there broke forward a disciplined advance of Texan infantry.

They came fast and in silence. When they were three hundred yards from the President's breastwork of twigs, leather and stale bread, the Mexicans who manned it let go with a fearful broadside of musket fire.

The Texans did not pause or kneel to return the fire. They did not fire at all, but kept coming. Their faces and hands were white with tension.

The barricade fired again, and still the Texans did not reply but only came on, breaking into double-quick time. The Texan artillery advanced and poured in grape and canister over the breastwork. And then—it seemed to have been managed in an instant—the Texans were at point-blank range of the soldiers before the President's camp, and there they cried out in shaking unison, "Remember the Álamo! Remember Goliad!" and with their rifles all but in the faces of the soldiers, they fired then for the first time and swarmed through the crumbling breastwork in wild power.

When the federal soldiers, unable to reload and fire at such close quarters, swung their bayonets into play, the Texans, having none, grasped their own rifles as war clubs and broke them over bayonet blades, and heads, and bodies, with sharp crackings. The line at the barricade fell apart though General Castrillon came forward to rally it. He was soon killed. The barricade was lost. Panic seized the entire encampment. Within twenty minutes the men of the commander-in-chief's army were fighting each other to escape to the rear, before the white rage of the Texans, who fought like creatures possessed of demons, so that the federal troops had to face not only surprise, skillful use of arms, and superior knowledge of the country, but also some quality more terrible by far—a vengeful fury for which there was no match.

And now the President's advantaged position was seen to be disastrous; for the soldiers running away had nowhere to go but down the rear slope toward water of the bayou; and there they were shot, clubbed, and trampled, until whole companies of them were drowned in mud and dandled by the water's drift. Those who managed a safe crossing streaked for the bridge at Vince's Creek. But when they reached it, they found it burned away. Texan scouts had destroyed it before the attack; and once again there was slaughter on the banks and in the stream. The President's secretary was there and made a note of what he saw: "There were an infinite number of dead piled one upon the other, till they might have served as a bridge." The Texans pressed their victory full into evening. The war was ended with those few hours. Out of the President's battle force of thirteen hundred men, only forty managed to avoid being killed, wounded or captured. The Texans lost two men killed, and twenty-three wounded, out of seven hundred and eighty-three in the engagement.

If his soldiers asked that night where the President of Mexico might be, the story was soon told. Harshly awakened from his rest, he had taken a powerful horse and had ridden furiously for the bridge at Vince's Creek. Miraculously he escaped death. Eluding the fire of pursuers, he came to the crossing; and when he saw that the bridge was gone, he urged his mount down the steep bank into the water. There his horse was hopelessly mired down, and he left it, and disappeared in the gathering twilight. Night covered the confusions of the day and ended the fighting.

In the morning, Texan scouts ranged the surrounding country to make sure that no further resistance was possible. They came upon fugitives here and there, and took them prisoner. About ten miles west of the creek a scouting party came upon a Mexican hiding in tall grass. They ordered him to stand, but he lay prone. A scout said:

"Boys, I'll make him move," and aimed his rifle at him.

"Don't shoot," said another, and dismounting, gave him a kick, adding, "Get up, damn you!"

The fugitive slowly arose. His clothes were muddy. He was dressed in a leather cap, a laborer's blue cotton jacket over an expensive shirt, cheap linen trousers and red worsted slippers. Speaking in Spanish he addressed his captors, one of whom could translate what he said. The man said he was not an officer, but a plain cavalry soldier. A Texan hauled him up on the croup of his horse and the party returned to camp. As they neared General Houston's headquarters they passed by other prisoners who regarded them. Suddenly the mounted prisoner was recognized by his compatriots.

"The President!" they cried, and some saluted him. "Santa Anna!"

It was he. He was rapidly taken before General Houston, who had been wounded in the battle. The President's position was most serious. He had heard the terrible cries of "Álamo" and "Goliad" on the day before, and he knew he was held personally responsible for what they recalled. His agitation now was so great that before he could speak with General Houston he was obliged to ask for opium. This was given to him, and presently he was able to conduct affairs as President and commander-in-chief of Mexico.

First, with reference to the episodes at the Álamo and Goliad, he wished to make plain that he personally should not be blamed for the severe measures taken there, as he had only been the instrument of carrying out the clear provisions of Mexican law.

Second, upon being granted his freedom, he would, speaking for Mexico, arrange for the recognition of the national independence of Texas.

General Houston, replying only to the second point, stated that as military commander he could not discuss a matter that must be concluded by the civil authorities of Texas; and in any case, before further negotiations, he required General Santa Anna to order his remaining troops to retire from Texas soil, which meant withdrawal beyond the

Rio Grande. Accordingly, the President dictated a dispatch to General Filisola, who was at the Brazos, which said: "Your Excellency, The small division under my immediate command having had an unfortunate encounter yesterday afternoon, I find myself a prisoner of war in the hands of the enemy, who have extended to me all possible consideration." After this restrained remark, he went on to direct that all divisions of the army still at large immediately fall back, some to Béxar, some to Victoria, there to await further orders. He ended by saying, "I have agreed with General Houston upon armistice pending certain negotiations which may put an end to the war forever."

This was not true; the war was already over; and Filisola, Urrea and Gaona had not waited for orders to retreat, but immediately on hearing the news of San Jacinto, had begun their withdrawals toward the Rio Grande. Again the rivers of Texas were hard obstacles to armies with heavy equipment; for the spring rains stormed daily during the weeks of the marches, and the retreat was harder than the entry had been. But finally, on May twenty-eighth, the first units crossed the Rio Grande to Matamoros under Urrea; and there, on June eighteenth, the last, under Andrade, completed the evacuation. No national Mexican troops were left in Texas, other than prisoners of war.

Of these, General Santa Anna was in the gravest danger of harm. Citizens and soldiers of Texas demanded his life in return for the slaughters he had wrought among their comrades. Texan officials protected him with difficulty, and proceeded with treaty negotiations. Under these —there was one public and one secret set of agreements—he promised that he should never again "during the present war of independence" wage war, or encourage others to wage war, against Texas; that all fighting would stop; that Mexico's armed forces should leave Texas; that prisoners should be exchanged; that all property, "including horses, cattle, negro slaves or indentured individuals" captured by the Mexicans, should be returned to the Texan owners; that Texan independence should be recognized; that President Santa Anna should be returned safely to Veracruz; and that, as the boundary between Mexico and Texas, the Rio Grande should be accepted.

When news, first of the disaster in Texas, and second, of the terms of the President's treaties, came to the government in Mexico City, dismay gathered around a hard core of refusal ever to agree to the independence of Texas or the establishment of the Rio Grande as the boundary. But as Texas in her disputatious energy, and Mexico in her poverty and political instability, took steps to recover from the campaign of the President—he had gone free—it was plain to see which of the two nations remained the stronger. Texas, with twenty thousand people against the nine millions of Mexico, held her independence; and when her nationhood was recognized first by the United States, and then by England, France and other powers, her mother country, if she would not recognize, yet was obliged to accept a great portion of the Rio Grande as the actual boundary between the two nations that had for so long been one.

Within Texas, the Mexican point of view ceased to be significant.

13.

Fortunes of New Mexico

i. peoples and towns

Only along the Rio Grande above El Paso was the determining point of view still altogether Mexican, and it seemed more natural there than in Texas. Spanish life, the influence of Mexico, had been alive in New Mexico for three centuries as they had never been in Texas. The farthest forts and missions in Texas had been repeatedly abandoned by the Spanish power, while on the upper river, however poorly, they had lived even to overcome the terrible Indian revolt of 1680. The very land of New Mexico was more familiar to the Mexican memory than the land of Texas. New Mexico recreated the images of Spain and Mexico with bare mountain, tawny plain and narrow river grove; while for Mexicans in Texas few determining memories sprang to life out of the Texas landscape, with its wide coastal greenery, its prairies vaster than all Spain, and its belts of rolling green hills. In the 1830s, under Mexico, as for three centuries under Spain, organized life clung to the valley of the Rio Grande from Taos to El Paso, leaving the rest of the huge territory virtually without population except for the travelling Indians who had made their trails across it for so long, leaving hardly any other mark of life.

Along the New Mexican river lived about forty thousand Mexicans and ten thousand Pueblo Indians. Though the census was irregular, and records were ill-kept, the impression was that the Mexican population was growing, while the Indian was diminishing. An observant citizen was convinced that the loss of numbers among Indians must be blamed on only one thing. It was, he declared, "an abuse which is deeply rooted among Indian women; they refuse to bear more than four children; they succeed in this matter by drinking certain beverages which they prepare for that purpose." He called for the proper authorities—governmental or ecclesiastical—"to drive this practice out by any available means as soon as possible."

No new pueblos and only a few Mexican towns were founded after the turn of the nineteenth century. Above Taos, Arroyo Hondo, in 1823, and Questa, in 1829, were added to the Mexican communities. At El Paso, through the early 1820s, all settlement clung to the south bank of the river. James Pattie, the trapper, saw the old community as it lay spread out among its vineyards and wheat fields. He thought the town had a breadth of about three miles, but he did not know whether to call "the Passo del Norte a settlement or a town. It is," he said, "in fact a kind of continued village, extending eight miles on the river. Fronting this large group of houses, is a nursery of the fruit trees, of almost all countries and climes. . . ." In 1827 the settlement put out its growth in another direction—it crossed the river. A householder named José María Ponce de León made himself a new home on the north bank. Before long he had neighbors who followed his example. The result was a nucleus for the later, the American, El Paso.

But as new towns came to be, old ones endured through the years without much change of character, though with differences in detail. In 1832 "the wall of Santa Fe" was spoken of as crumbling . . . "an obstacle to the beauty of the city because it is becoming more dilapidated every day, and within a short time only its ruins will remain." It adjoined the old palace, which was itself "in partial ruins and in a general state of neglect." All towns were of earthen construction, with wooden beams, and were built around a central plaza from whose four corners the principal streets wandered off toward the open country. On these were situated shops and places of entertainment, and of supply, such as wood-yards. Behind the plaza, dwellings were disposed between the arms of the streets and followed no town plan, but found their places rather by the natural course of an irrigation ditch than by any severe grid laid out. Each house with its truck garden, its trees and its animal yard, was like a little plot of country life that showed the seasons. In spring pink and white blossoms of fruit trees sparkled in bright air beside pale tan adobe walls. In summer, when shade trees were leafed out, there were grand, slow-moving washes of shadow over the house whose rooms for their deep walls and thick earth roof stayed cool all day. In autumn when trees went bare, and sunlight thin, blue pencilled shadows of branch and twig played on the packed swept yard, and smoke from fires of piñon wood seemed to stand bluer and longer in the golden air. And when winter came, and snow fell, seen from the height of a valley slope the town, with all its boxlike shapes at odd angles about the formal oblong of the plaza with its continuous roof, looked like a scattering of great ingots of snow in sharp relief against their own shadows that lay like stripes on white ground.

The winter was long, for the river ran in high land, and towns were backed by hills, and hills by mountains. In some years the river froze almost to the bottom, and men working or travelling were able to cross without bridges or fords, for the ice was solid, and bore the weight of loaded oxcarts, pack trains and men on horseback from bank to bank. Even when the snow stopped falling and days were clear, the air was so cold that men could hardly work in the open, and women at their milking in the cowshed saw the warm milk freeze as it sprayed upon the cold pail.

But as the house stayed cool in summer, so it stayed warm in winter. The windows were small, the clay fireplaces deep and elevated so that they threw great heat, and the house was thick. People were comfortable if they stayed indoors; and if they went out, they were wrapped in furs that came in abundance from the creatures of the surrounding mountains. Barring disasters, men and women lived long— often to the age of ninety, or a hundred, or over. Age was honored. Old people when their days of physical usefulness were past yet had other uses, and gave of them to their own satisfaction and the continued creation of family law—the oracular wisdom of long experience, the power of tradition, the lessons that lay in conscious respect for the earthly source of life. These were values that knew little change throughout Christian Mexico. In the Rio Grande towns they abided late.

ii. politics

But if the family as a unit of human life seemed secure in its inherited ways, and was able to fulfill its precepts, the towns as the smallest subdivisions of political life had greater difficulties to meet in their need of order. A Rio Grande town was governed in the pattern of Mexico life—but in skeletal form. Mexican customs prevailed—but without a flow of refreshment through full contact with their source. Mexican ideas moved the people—but weakened by distance from their point of origin. For hundreds of years the northern river province had begged the central authority in Mexico, first under the Spanish viceroy, and now under the president and congress of the republic, for more troops, more money, more administrators, more clergy, more courts of law, more educational facilities; and had never received much more than an occasional visit by an inspector general, a bishop or a customs collector. The province had to be content with maintaining certain governmental forms, without the means to give them substance.

The New Mexican river province under the republic was ruled by a political chief appointed for an undefined term by the central government. Once he was in residence, he was answerable to no one else; but if his post was coveted by a man of influence, he might suddenly lose it, no matter how well he served. If his successor served ill, there was little recourse for the people under a ruler who alone had the ear of the government. His work was not easy—the budget of his office did not even provide for him a permanent secretary. His time was mainly taken up with the review of legal decisions made in the largest towns by their mayors, who served also as justices of the peace—though his duties were not supposed to include such a function. But in their inherent trust in and need for authority, the people could turn to no one else to appeal their cases. Thoughtful citizens saw the dangers in such arrangements— injustice, corruption, the impossibility of finding able men to accept public office under capricious tenure.

There were only sixteen towns considerable enough to have their own local government. These were grouped into three departments. Each department had a capital town from which lesser towns drew their authority. The capitals were Santa Cruz, Santa Fe and Albuquerque, and these alone had town councils and mayors. The lesser towns were commanded by a military officer who held no judicial powers. If an affair at law came up in his town, he referred it to the powers of his capital town for decision; and if they could not settle it to satisfaction, it must go to the political chief of the province at Santa Fe. If there it was not adjudicated to an end, there was one more recourse; but few citizens were able to spend what was required in time and money to make the last appeal, for the nearest practicing civil and criminal court sat at Guadalajara, distant almost two thousand miles through months of travel from the upper Rio Grande. There was no one in the long valley of New Mexico who was sufficiently trained in the processes of law to "conduct an examining trial, to prepare a defense, or to prosecute a case." Crime went unpunished and injustice had no orderly redress. When a man was arrested and put in jail, he entered an ordinary adobe room where with his cellmates he spent his time "in noisy revelry and conversation." He enjoyed free meals, and was not detained if during the day he thought of errands that must take him abroad, or if at night hearing the music of a fandango he resolved to join the dance. At his own pleasure he returned to his filthy cell and the congenial company of his fellow prisoners, all of whom took "their imprisonment with the greatest nonchalance."

iii. defense

If the province was unable to maintain internal order, it was even less equipped to face armed threats from beyond the frontier. A presidial company of a hundred men was stationed at Santa Fe to protect the northernmost boundaries of the republic, and to deal with civil disturbances throughout a province of over a hundred thousand square miles. What—intelligent citizens often thought of it—what would happen if an armed invasion, say three or four thousand strong, should appear from the United States? Even if the whole population of forty thousand sprang to defend New Mexico, how effective could they be without training, discipline, or adequate arms? The presidial company would be overwhelmed. The nearest important military headquarters was at Chihuahua, five hundred miles from Santa Fe, with stark deserts between. How could intelligent command be exercised over New Mexico from so remote a commandery general? Before a courier could reach there to report an invasion or a major Indian uprising the province of New Mexico could be lost.

Citizens saw what was needed and made urgent recommendations. New Mexico should be granted its own commandery general separate from Chihuahua's. Troop strength should be greatly increased to control the never-ending assaults by riding Indians who came from east and west of the river. The main garrison should not be stationed in Santa Fe, which was too far from the usual scene of Indian depredations, but should be located at Valverde, on the Rio Grande, just above the northern entrance to the Dead Man's March. There, where a ruined hacienda stood, a fort should be established, from which, as a midway point, troops could range forth upriver, downriver, or inland on either side, to meet internal disorder promptly. If this were done, the whole road to the south would be so well policed that in a few years along "the delightful banks" of the Rio Grande there would be "an uninterrupted cordillera of flourishing settlements!" The prospect was stunning. "Farewell, Dead Man's March! Farewell, gloomy and fearful desert, you would vanish forever . . . !" The citizen who urged this course even proposed a way to pay for it. Since the wall of Santa Fe was falling apart more every day, let the government sell its earthen bricks to people who wanted to build houses, and use the funds to erect the new presidio at Valverde. Thus there would be no drain upon the treasury of New Mexico—which in any case was empty.

With more troops, more officers would be needed. Where might they come from? A military academy was proposed, to be established at Santa Fe, for the training of cadets under a full curriculum embracing "military tactics, regulations . . . economy of administration, methods of conducting a trial, manner of directing a defense . . . procedure in a council of war . . . arithmetic . . . the elements of geometry, geography, and fortifications." The superintendent should be a gifted officer who would be paid a salary of one thousand pesos, which would be raised from tuitions and company funds.

And finally, the organization and training of a civil militia was strongly urged by those who took thought for New Mexico. "What a powerful defense would be presented by eight or nine thousand New Mexicans, expert in the use of weapons, equipped and ready for war!" Of all Mexico, the northern river frontier most needed such defenses. Those who lived in New Mexico knew that "the army is more useful and necessary on the frontier, as our unfortunate history proves"—for they were mindful of what had lately happened in Texas. They knew that the United States concentrated most of her standing army on her western frontiers. Could not the Mexican government read the significance of that fact? New Mexicans could read it even as long ago as 1810: "Once this territory is lost, it will be impossible to recover it. . . ." Such representations were made in vain. The Mexican government, though smarting under Santa Anna's loss of Texas, did nothing to reinforce the remaining province of the Rio Grande.

iv. church and school

Other defenses were crumbling, too, in a society that profoundly believed in the need of them. These were the ministrations, public and corporate, private and personal, of the Church. For seventy years there had been no visit by a bishop in the province. When Don Pedro Bautista Pino went from New Mexico to the Spanish córtes in 1810 he was already an old man; but he never knew "how bishops dressed" until he reached Spain. At last, in 1833, Don Antonio Zubiria, Bishop of Durango, came to tour the parishes of New Mexico. His progress was a triumph. Bridges over arroyos on his road were repaired and decked with wild flowers. He entered towns under ceremonial arches. For his passing, houses were dressed with whatever finery their owners could hang out the window— rugs, brocades, curtains. People knelt under his blessing in newly swept streets as his coach lumbered by. The only ones who were sorry to see him come were the few Franciscans who remained in the province, for the secularization of the missions, begun at the end of the eighteenth century, was nearly completed, and the Bishop was a symbol of the process, for now New Mexico came under the jurisdiction of his see of Durango, whose seat was four hundred leagues south of El Paso. Bishop Zubiría spent many weeks inspecting his northern parishes; and a year after his return to Durango the Franciscan system was gone from New Mexico; the secularization was fully accomplished.

With the Franciscans gone, secular priests were supposed to come from Durango to replace them in all the missions of the pueblos and the parishes of the towns. But they did not come in proper numbers, and the handful that came seemed to preside over a rapid dissolution of the church. In the pueblos, mission premises reverted to their Indian owners, and like the missions of Texas when secularized in the eighteenth century began to fall into ruin through neglect. Only five pueblos had resident priests. The town parishes were not much better off; for the secular clergy had no funds behind them such as the Franciscan Order had made available to its friars to supplement local support. Parish priests now lived, and church properties were maintained, wholly on what their parishioners could contribute. This was in most places miserably little. Few parishes had resident pastors. Most were vacant, to be visited two or three times a year by a travelling priest. Church buildings went to ruin without annual replastering with adobe. Pastors lived in misery and faced the old age and death of paupers. Some yielded to human failings and coveted a better living. Others valiantly pursued their duties through every hardship and deprivation. Still one or two others, far from ecclesiastical authority and the source of discipline, betrayed their vows and while still professing priesthood adopted ways of life they were supposed to correct in others. Such clergymen shocked foreign travellers who saw them at their genial indulgence. Devout New Mexicans also shook their heads, and bitterly regretted that in their province there was no administrative head of church affairs, a bishop, a vicar general, who would govern the clergy, preserve discipline, and let flower the faith that was so deeply rooted in the people.

It was to them a "truly doleful" matter "to see an infinite number of the sick die without confession or extreme unction." Regular Sunday Mass was said in only a few churches. Baptisms were arranged only with infinite difficulty. When death came, and a funeral Mass was needed, the corpse often remained unburied for days, until a priest could be found and brought to officiate. The penalties, and contrasts, of distance from the capital were severe: In 1838 the remains of Agustín de Iturbide were removed from Padilla to Mexico City, where they were reinterred in the cathedral with the highest pomp—the street outlining the grand plaza of the capital was entirely shaded by scalloped canopies, the populace made a lane through which the cortège passed, there was a black-plumed hearse drawn by six horses with outriders and followed by troops in a column of company fronts, while in the center of the Zócalo artillery fired a paced salute. But in New Mexico, where each parish and mission worked to pay its meagre tithe out of the year's labor with field and flock to support a religious, people more often than not died and were buried without his solace. As for the tithes—local corruption had its ways, and they went "only to enrich three or four private persons, without any spiritual benefit to New Mexico or temporal profit to the republic."

Another trouble to the view of a good citizen was the state of education in the province. There were primary schools in only six towns in the early 1830s, and the total annual expenditure for teacher salaries was only 1,850 pesos—and even so, it was reported that "relatively speaking, there is no better pay in the territory than that received by schoolteachers." But many of the teachers were indifferent and ignorant, the authorities paid no attention to the schools, and it could only be concluded that "no noticeable results are achieved by primary instruction." There were scarcely any books anywhere. Here and there the vocation of the teacher found expression when a priest took a class of young men to teach them a scrap of philosophy, or a young layman gathered others about him to study Latin and Spanish grammar. In 1834 the public schools were closed for lack of funds to maintain them. In the same year there was a glimmer of hope for public enlightenment. On the first printing press to reach New Mexico, a weekly newspaper entitled *El Crepúsculo*—The Dawn—appeared in a foolscap sheet for the benefit of fifty subscribers. But after one month, publication was suspended, and the only newspapers seen in the province were months-old copies from Mexico or the United States.

v. foreigners

For the traders, with their news, came all through the '30s in increasing numbers, and saw the poverty of the towns, the unworked capacities of the country, and the primitive methods of a nontechnical and incurious people. Food was raised only in the narrow straggle of farms along the immediate valley of the Rio Grande. Each family grew only what was needed to support its own members during the year. If hard times came, with drought or unseasonable freezes, or if the family had miscalculated its needs, there were months late in the year when hunger came as a familiar of life in New Mexico. The only commercial crops were cotton and tobacco, raised for trading within the province and for shipping down the river road to Mexican markets. Beyond the mountains on each side of the cultivated valley lay immense empires of unworked soil. There fortunes could be made, agriculture on a vast scale undertaken—but for two factors. One was the never-ending menace of the roving Indian; the other was that strain in the colonial character that had never recovered from the dream of Quivira, with its promise of free wealth, and its waking rejection of hard work as the price of its fulfillment.

And yet there were no paupers, for if a man did not have his own patch of land from which to gain a bean or an ear of corn for his family, he had recourse to an owner of large herds of sheep, proposing himself as a shepherd. Given a thousand ewes and ten rams to tend, he received as his pay a percentage of the lambs, with the remainder going to the owner. In time, after his own little flock had grown by the almost daily birth of lambs the year round—for the rams and the ewes were never separated—he was able to leave his employer and take on shepherds of his own whose work would yield him the owner's percentage in his turn. Sheep provided milk, meat and wool to the family; and lambs that were sold for the drive to Mexico. An American trader estimated that about a quarter of a million sheep and goats grazed on the valley slopes, and up to half a million sheep were walked to Mexico every year. In spite of such a great figure, sales brought little, for the price of sheep was very low, and the individual sheep was not heavy. As for cattle, the same trader believed that only about five thousand were maintained.

The Rio Grande Mexican was a rude craftsman. Where his work held primitive beauty of feeling or design, he was unaware of it; and when the United States traders kept coming, he turned to them for the products of their country, glad to buy instead of to make. Soon the province was served by foreigners who were expert craftsmen and adroit bargainers—carpenters, blacksmiths, tinsmiths, gunsmiths, tailors, hatters, shoemakers. The Americans set up water-powered mills. One spent a winter in Santa Fe building a public clock—the first one in an ancient city that previously took the time of day from a stone sundial at the old Palace. Others established a distillery up the Rio Grande at Arroyo Hondo, using water power in its machines. In a very few years all fabrication industry and commerce in the province were led by the foreigners. These men became a familiar sight in the towns and along the roads of the province. They had for sale services and objects that the natives wanted, they obeyed such laws as they could, and when the laws were unreasonable or administered with caprice, they circumvented them as cleverly and as quietly as possible. Gazing at them, the natives had a sense of what was inevitably coming; and seeing the Americans as agents of change and usurpation, they could not forbear expressing their bitterness. There were occasional brawls, attacks, robberies and murders. The American traders and tinkers kept a sharp eye out, especially when they travelled the well-worn roads on which New Mexicans were safe from banditry.

Yet even there the traditions of New Mexican hospitality showed themselves when the strangers stopped for a meal or a lodging for the night; and New Mexican women were gentle with the tall, energetic, and often blond men from the East, some of whom fell in love with the country, and resolved to stay, marry, and make their fortunes along the valley. A farm here, a flour mill there, a lumberyard, a brickkiln, a tannery—such establishments brought the techniques of the United States frontier far from home, and using the bountiful raw materials of New Mexico made so much visible change in the commercial life of the province that an upper Rio Grande Mexican cried out, "How long shall we continue to be foreigners on our own soil?"

14.

Revolt Up River

On this background of the New Mexican Rio Grande, with its natural beauties and its social poverties, there flared in 1837 a surge of violence whose causes bore some resemblance to those behind the uprising of the Texans in the previous year. New Mexico, too, was far from the seat of central government, and yet was denied full local government. With Santa Anna's revocation of the federal constitution of 1824, New Mexico lost the position of statehood and was demoted to the status of territorial department. New Mexico, too, was subject to an always-increasing population of busy citizens from the United States, who brought new notions of individual liberty and state autonomy. For the first time since Mexican independence, the political ruler of New Mexico, appointed by Santa Anna, was not a native New Mexican, but an officer of the Mexican Army. He was Colonel Albino Pérez, and he came to rule with Santa Anna's centralist principles. And finally, as

Texas had been seen by the capital chiefly as a source of revenue and as a vast compound for the criminal discards of Mexican society, so New Mexico in her wretched subsistence economy was suddenly in 1837 subjected to new taxes that would feed directly to the bankrupt national treasury.

Colonel Pérez laid about him with his taxations. Some of his levies affected the foreign traders, who had no recourse but to submit—though, it was said, not without seditious whispers that may have fanned the fires that were already taking light amongst the people. Others struck directly at the native occupations and pleasures. A woodcutter was subjected to a new license costing five dollars a month. A drover or a shepherd taking his animals through Santa Fe to market had to pay a tax of about twenty-five cents a head. A showman was taxed two dollars for each performance he gave, and to give a dance cost the proprietor fifty cents. All who lived without regular lawful occupations were to be arrested. It was not long until rumors, spread by the enemies of Colonel Pérez, enraged humorless citizens with stories of how a tax was to be laid upon every barnyard fowl, and how a husband was to be taxed for each performance of his marital duty. A new law re-established the public schools, but with elaborate requirements of parents that in many respects amounted to invasion of privacy and imposition of police rule. Popular resentment grew rapidly, and only awaited an incident to touch it off violently.

Among the enemies of the political chief was a certain Don Manuel Armijo, a man of substance who lived at Albuquerque. For a few months he had held an appointment from Colonel Pérez as a minor official of the territory, substituting for another who had been tried for peculation in office. When the peculator was restored to office, Armijo was turned out, and in discontent began to intrigue against the government. He found powerful allies who resented the new regime; and an underground movement was organized in the river communities, especially among the pueblos. In Taos, an upriver citizen, Jose Gonzáles, was a leader of the Armijo movement. The terrible days of Otermín and Vargas seemed to be looming once more, when the pueblos would rise again. But this time, the Indians were in league with Mexican leaders, and both were turned against the national authority.

Colonel Pérez was encountering troubles in maintaining his government. Having no public monies with which to buy supplies for his presidial troops, he turned to the American traders who were in town for the summer. They granted him large credits, and purchases were made; but they were filtered through graft, and the Governor was obliged to dismiss various grafters. When he disciplined native New Mexicans, his popularity sank again. There was a case in the north. A local official of Taos was put in jail at Santa Cruz by the Governor's prefect of the northern district. At once there was an outcry against tyranny. Organized rebellion sprang into the open. "Taxes! Taxes!" cried the rebels, gathering at Santa Cruz in great numbers from the northern pueblos. They marched on the jail and released the prisoner early in August, and on the third held a convention out of which they published a "pronouncement," a "plan," a "shout," in the familiar tradition of Mexicans in revolt. After several clauses that protested piety and valor, the plan of Santa Cruz became specific, and resolved not to accept for New Mexico any status of department or territory instead of statehood; not to submit to taxation, and not to obey those who would impose it. The milling throng grew. It was led by Juan José Esquivel, the mayor of Santa Cruz. Santa Fe was only twenty-five miles away to the south. Loyal agents hurried there to Colonel Pérez, with a warning of the numbers, the temper and the armament of the rebels.

The Governor decided from this information that what existed in the north was merely a state "of exaggerated unrest." He was a regular officer. Mobs were not armies. Still, he called for town officials to mobilize the militia at once, and made plans to march up the river to scatter the rioters. Response was apathetic; only a hundred and fifty men were mustered, most of whom were warriors from Santo Domingo. With these, and a wheeled cannon, and such presidial troops as were adequately equipped, Colonel Pérez marched from Santa Fe on August seventh. He camped that night eighteen miles from town, amongst the pale rosy fantasies of the eroded Rio Grande bottom; and proceeded on the following day toward Santa Cruz.

The enemy had come down the river to meet him and, breaking upon him from ambush near the black mesa of San Ildefonso, disorganized his force with surprise. He tried to parley, to listen to grievances; but the rebels fired and his troops deserted him. The Santo Domingo warriors joined their fellow Indians of the northern pueblos. Colonel Pérez and his few loyal men fell back about their cannon, which they fired. But numbers were too great for them, the rebels charged, killing six or seven men, and the Governor with twenty-three soldiers abandoned the fieldpiece and hurried south to Santa Fe, arriving at three in the afternoon.

He found the city in a state of general anxiety. The New Mexican residents expected a general sack if the rebels should be victorious. The American traders, having supplied the government troops, feared for their stock and their persons if the rampage reached the capital. They barricaded their wagons, and hid merchandise in the houses of friends, and carried arms. The Governor was powerless to protect his capital or to advise his people. He went through his desk, packed a few things, and with a handful of friends and defenders left Santa Fe at ten o'clock that night for the river road, and the south, and safety, like Otermín a hundred and fifty-seven years before him. Riding hard through the night he came to the hacienda of El Álamo near the river, and slept there.

But others were abroad in the night too—Indian couriers from the battlefield up the river who rode to advise other pueblo warriors along the road that the Governor with friends was trying to escape to Mexico, and that it was the command of the victorious rebels that he and his followers were to be caught and killed.

In the morning Colonel Pérez rode out again, and soon saw that the way ahead of him was guarded by Indians. He dispersed his party, letting each man save himself. Asking one to lead his saddle horse away, he dismounted and began to walk back to Santa Fe up the trail of La Bajada and over the wide Santa Fe plain where moving along on foot he might be inconspicuous. He walked all day, the ninth of August, toward the capital. From the opposite direction, the city was filling all day with the hordes of Santa Cruz, who came to take possession of property and government. Toward sundown Colonel Pérez came through fields to the farm of a friend where he sought refuge. But he had been followed all day by Indians from the river flats. They entered, seized him, beheaded him, and when he was dead, performed his symbolic unmanning by stripping him naked, and throwing him awry on the ground where they left him. Pushing on to the city they took his head along, and, meeting the victorious insurgents, with it entered upon a game of football.

Soon others who had sought to escape with the Governor were found in hiding among the farms on the outskirts of the capital. They were hauled forth, denuded, and run through with lances at leisure until they died. Another captive was taken to Santo Domingo and put into the stocks overnight. On the morrow while they execrated the crimes of the government, the Indians cut off his members one after the other and showed them to him in derision until they cut out his eyes and his tongue. After a long time dying, he was removed from the stocks and flung over the ground as carrion. In all a dozen supporters of the dead Governor were destroyed with protracted enjoyment.

On August tenth the rebels held a conclave for the election of a new, a native, governor. Don Manuel Armijo could not but hope that his efforts at rebellion, already so successful, must bring him the governorship. But the meeting elected Jose Gonzáles, the northern leader—"a good honest hunter, but a very ignorant man," as a trader said. Don Manuel Armijo, though repudiated, remained in Santa Fe to work with the new government. There was much to accomplish. All the property of the assassinated officials had to be divided among the new leaders. One of the rebels who had led the football game with Colonel Pérez's head on the day before found it hilarious to strut about in the Colonel's bloody coat. Lists of people to put in jail must be considered, and confiscations of property sketched out. Governor Gonzáles desired the convention to discuss the startling idea that help and alliance for New Mexico's new government should be sought in the Republic of Texas.

The citizens of Santa Fe and the visiting traders watched events with uneasiness, but a sack of the city did not develop, and the traders were not attacked. True, some of them faced great loss if not ruin, for they had given large credits to the defeated government, and could not hope that the rebels would honor the debts of their victims. A party of traders wrote to the United States minister in Mexico, asking him to obtain redress for them from the central government; but never received any. For in Mexico it was angrily believed that the insurrection had been fostered by the foreign Americans, even though they had supported the legitimate government of Colonel Pérez with goods and credit.

All in good time, Don Manuel Armijo came to his own plans. For several days he served the new government on committees, and attended a session of the new Governor's party in Santa Fe on August twenty-seventh, at which certain confiscations of property were made official. Many of the rebels out of the north were muttering about moving into the downriver estates and taking what they liked. Don Manuel Armijo's properties were downriver at Albuquerque. Suddenly the whole affair displeased him. He left Santa Fe, hurried to the Downriver, and began to gather about him a new party in opposition to Gonzáles. Most of the Santa Cruz army had been disbanded and its members had returned to their pueblos upriver. From Albuquerque, Armijo moved on south to the river village of Tomé, where on September eighth he issued a new pronouncement in defiance of the Gonzáles party. He had with him a parish priest, a mayor or two from downriver towns, and a number of

citizens who had discovered with him a burning devotion to the constitution and laws of Mexico. They drafted a paper. It noted with belated
horror the "iniquitous measures" being planned by the rebels of Santa
Cruz "to destroy the peace, harmony, and good order of the citizens,"
and it repudiated their authority, naming instead as the one surviving
legitimate officer of Mexican government in the river province the Prefect
of Albuquerque, who had escaped the massacres. The counterpronounce-
ment went on to declare that "no one shall be molested in their property
or privileges; if they have any," and that an armed force was to be
raised under the command of Don Manuel Armijo. Further, the pueblo
Indians were advised to "remain tranquil, and not mix in Mexican
affairs." To make certain of this, the pueblos were promised that they
might govern themselves until the re-establishment of legitimate authority in the province. Finally, the army headquarters at Chihuahua
would be asked for reinforcements, and the central government in
Mexico City would be apprised of all that was now being done—chiefly
by Don Manuel Armijo—in loyal efforts to recover the province from
the rebels who had forsworn allegiance to Mexico, and who had made
plans to ask Texas to protect them.

In Santa Fe, another loyalist movement was daring to show itself.
General José Caballero, the federal troop commander, who at the
moment had no troops, since the presidial company had been disbanded,
issued a call for resistance in the face of the Gonzáles government. The
new regime was a mockery. All was confusion in the capital, and "the
chieftains of the unsurrection, swollen with triumph, continued figuring
in the scene, and without any respect to the government which they
themselves erected, constantly concocted new machinations which they
have put into practice in an equally alarming manner. . . . Wretches!"
cried General Caballero. "Their savage ignorance precipitates them
from abyss into abyss in search of the punishment which divine justice
cannot forgive, but will prepare for them." It was clear that in this civil
strife, north was against south—Upriver against Downriver. General
Caballero called for the united effort of the downriver people, recognized
Don Manuel Armijo's title to command the volunteers, and proudly
announced that the old presidial company was re-enlisting without pay
to drive the rebels out of power.

All through September the forces gathered downriver; and toward
the end of the month Armijo led them north along the river road and
up the escarpment of Santa Fe plain. Governor Gonzáles fled before
them. The northern rebel authority cracked wide open, and Armijo

took possession of the capital without a battle, "the just cause of order and laws," he declared, "rapidly triumphing, in defense of which I grasped my sword, without the effusion of a drop of Mexican blood." He promised, pending the will of the federal government, to maintain law and order, and more: "if in order to attain these ends, it becomes necessary for me to make some examples of severity, I shall, without doubt, dictate them, although in sorrow. . . ."

Already in jail, incomunicados, were four leaders of the rebellion—though Governor Gonzáles was not one of them. He had escaped to the north where at Santa Cruz the rebellion was still in formal existence. Armijo assumed the office of political chief, and shuttled offices and duties about among his followers, and formed a government after the manner of Santa Anna, whom he resembled in such qualities as flexibility of conscience, political adroitness and an unusually strong instinct for self-preservation. The rebels were still to be dealt with in their northern country, but he was waiting for the Chihuahua reinforcements, and meanwhile, he composed an inflated report of his activities for the federal government, and sent it flying down the river road by courier, to earn him his confirmation as governor—which came from a grateful government in due course.

In the middle of October his private interests downriver called him, but before taking a few days' leave from his absorbing and agreeable duties he went into the matter of the prisoners in their filthy earth cells at the old Palace. On the whole, it seemed best to dispose of them without trial, and as examples. Accordingly, he left orders with General Caballero to have them shot, and rode out of the capital on the seventeenth for Albuquerque.

But something about the order gave General Caballero uneasiness, and he deferred carrying it out. Was the capital strongly enough garrisoned to withstand an assault when the rebels heard of the executions? Would it not be prudent to wait for more troops? Possibly he knew his man, though without expressing himself openly; but was it not conceivable that if in the future there should come a time of reprisals, it would be the actual executioner rather than the judge who might be paid off savagely? Governor Armijo would be out of town during the execution if it were performed as ordered. An order could be repudiated; not a volley from a firing squad. Whatever his reasons, General Caballero called a meeting of the chief officers of the government, and laid his problem before them on September twenty-first. They unanimously resolved that while the Governor's order must be carried out, the garrison must first be "strengthened by all the force necessary to repel any attempt that may be made. . . ." However, they provided that if news of an impending attack should come, then the prisoners were to be instantly decapitated in their cells.

The Governor returned as these policies were formulated. He accepted them, and advised the prisoners to put their affairs in order. This amounted to a reprieve of nearly three months; for the suitable strengthening of the garrison did not appear until early January, 1838, when two hundred dragoons from Zacatecas and two hundred regulars from Chihuahua at last arrived to join the Governor. They came opportunely, for another defiant proclamation of rebellion sounded forth from Santa Cruz, accompanied by threats to rescue the prisoners in the Palace. With the added troops from Mexico now under his command, the Governor felt strong enough to assume personal responsibility for the executions he had ordered months before. On January twenty-fourth, 1838, the four rebel chieftains were taken out of the Palace, and at the site of a sentry post three hundred yards from the plaza, were beheaded, while the Governor breathed in a state paper, "May God grant that this spectacle, so sad for peaceful New Mexico, be the last to present itself to its natural humaneness and good sense. . . ."

He was then ready, in the last week of January, to take his augmented forces into the field. As they marched out for the upper river, the capital was once more thrown into anxiety. The American traders made their wagons ready for immediate flight eastward, even through winter weather, if the rebels should win the impending battle; and the citizenry once again waited for the sacking of their town.

They were not long left in suspense. A courier came galloping in from Santa Cruz, where the rebels had met the army, and the capital breathed easy at his news—though the engagement had opened with a change of heart in the Governor. Seeing thirteen hundred Indians massed before him in their paint, pricked feathers, and bristled weapons, he wondered if perhaps after all he should not fall back with his five hundred and eighty-two soldiers. He had a familiar saying that his actions frequently illustrated—"*Vale mas estár tomado por valiente que serlo.*" But if it was better to be taken for a brave man than to be one, his reputation was saved for him by a certain Captain Muñoz of the Zacatecas dragoons, who seeing the Governor's faintness of heart, came to him and said:

"If your Excellency will allow me, I will oust that rabble in an instant with my little company alone."

The Governor superbly assented; the captain charged; the Indians fled, losing a dozen men, including José Gonzáles, the rebel governor, who was captured and brought before his old accomplice. Now Governor Armijo, with a great victory in his pocket, was once again a man of decision as he received Gonzáles, who extended his hand.

"How do you do, my colleague," said Gonzáles as between governors, if not accomplices.

"How do you do, my colleague," replied Don Manuel Armijo, and added, "Confess yourself, my colleague,"—for Chaplain of Dragoons Antonio José Martínez was present to hear the ex-Governor's confession. Don Manuel Armijo then turned to Don Pedro Muñoz and a squad of soldiers, and commanded, "Now, shoot my colleague."

The command was immediately obeyed, the rebels of the north were defeated for good, and the Governor returned to Santa Fe from the Upriver to reign for most of the next eight years in absolute power over what was left of the Mexican Rio Grande.

15.

The River Republic

Periodically, ever since her full retreat below the Rio Grande in 1836, Mexico threatened to return to Texas to punish the upstarts and regain the great province. But the shock of her defeat threw Mexico deeper into civil war, and the struggle between centralism with its dictatorship and federalism with its longing to re-establish the states under the Constitution of 1824 lasted for years and took all her official energies. Texas went unpunished, her independence was confirmed by leading powers of the world, and even in the midst of the agitating problems of creating her government, there were counterthreats on the part of Texas factions to invade Mexico. These were sporadic and largely matters of a familiar Texan temperament; and Texas too had her internal social

troubles which consumed all her armed power for some time, and spared
Mexico in her turn further chastisement.

For in the wake of victory, the Texans spread themselves increasingly over lands and privileges belonging for centuries to some of the
most predatory Indian tribes in North America. Clashes resulted. Indian
warfare with all its shock, speed and horror tried to arrest the widening
of pioneer settlement; and the new republic to save its life was obliged
to mobilize armed forces for relentless campaigns against Cherokees,
Comanches and other tribes. The job would take generations to complete, but by 1839 the worst of the formal Indian warfare was put down,
and many demobilized Texans who fought for the simple joy of fighting—the temperament—looked elsewhere for satisfaction.

They found it in the country of the Rio Grande, for there in
1839 swelled a movement of the Mexican civil struggle with a stunning
objective, in which the Texas government was earnestly invited to join.
Federal Mexican revolutionists proposed that an independent republic
be fought for and formed, to reach from ocean and ocean, and to consist
of Texas, Nuevo León, Tamaulipas, Coahuila, Durango, New Mexico
and the Californias, upper and lower. Though lively sentiment to join
in the venture arose in Texas, President Lamar and his government
declined, and even counselled Texans as individuals—an often precarious
undertaking—to hold their peace. Some hoped that the federal scheme
would soon burst into open warfare, for so long as Mexico's central government was occupied with revolt below the Rio Grande, it could not
hope to plan for invasion above. In any case, the North Mexican movement was a real one in 1839, and to fight its coming battles, it brought
together the strangest combinations of men.

For Mexicans were readying to fight against Mexicans; and, foot-
loose and spoiling since their release from Indian frontier campaigns,
Texans swarmed to help them. The Mexican revolutionary army was
commanded by a border lawyer. This was General Antonio Canales who
had been moving amongst the ranches of the wastelands raising a force
of volunteers who brought their own weapons and horses. For ten years,
off and on, he was to devote himself to the cause of an independent
border republic. Its outlines varied from time to time, but the general
idea possessed him, and he pursued it with everything but talent. Like
many Mexicans he was a man of double vocation, the more absorbing
part of which was to be a general. His lawyer's work could have detained
him but little. To have like-minded supporting commanders—Colonels
José María Gonzáles and Zapata; to lead horsemen who, like the

Mexicans, had little to lose, or like the Texans, simply went for the ride; to match wits with the weather, and one kind of brutality with another, and power with guile—that was the life. It was incredible how they moved about—how much ground they covered, and what ground! It lay vast, empty and gray under an empty sky. Its hard spiny growths lost their green under clinging dust. Dry earth ravines showed where storm water ran and would run again but all too briefly. An occasional trail, hardly a road, ran away into infinity to be lost southward in mountain passes of naked rock, hot by day and cold by night. The sun made vision into a narrow slit of distance where the land itself was an enemy and where clicking across the ancient dust like desert insects the enemy troops would move toward battle.

The one earth feature by which all places were oriented was the Rio Grande; and quite as though it were not the stated boundary between two established nations, General Canales took his way freely across it in either direction according to the urgencies of the moment. It was an eloquent comment on the condition of Texas that Texans did not stop him when he ranged north of the river as far as the Nueces. But he came not against Texas but to gird his forces and recruit Texans. In Texas territory at Lipantitlan on the Nueces where in the late summer of 1839 he maintained his headquarters, his little army was joined by a hundred and eighty Texans officered by Colonels Reuben Ross and S. W. Jordan. Each Texan was promised twenty-five dollars a month, a half league of land, and an equal share in the loot of war. Together they were ready to go, so soon as they should know whom they were to fight, and where.

Northeast Mexico was held by widely separated centralist garrisons. General Canalizo was at Matamoros with fifteen hundred troops, guarding the Rio Grande outlet to the sea. General Pavón with five hundred regulars and four cannon was at Revilla to control the immediate upriver towns. General Arista commanded Monterrey, the main inland approach to Saltillo and the capital. To fight these dispositions Canales had six hundred men—Texans, one hundred and eighty; two hundred and fifty mounted rancheros; one hundred and ten footmen; and sixty Indians with primitive arms. He organized them into two divisions, with Jordan and Zapata in command of one, and himself and Ross of the other. Of the three government garrisons, he picked Pavón's at Revilla to attack first; and on September twentieth he left the Nueces with all his men and marched for the Rio Grande. It took ten days to cross the wilderness between the two rivers. On the thirtieth the federal-

ists crossed the Rio Grande planning to fall upon Revilla in a surprise
attack. But federal informers saw Jordan's division at the river, where
he had trouble crossing his horses, and hurried to warn Pavón. Surprise
was gone; and when the centralists entered Revilla two days later, so
was Pavón, with most of his forces, who were retreating inland toward
Monterrey. Canales pressed after them, sending out scouts, while the
hankering to fight thickened in the Texans, so far denied what they
had come for.

At eleven o'clock in the morning of October third in the rolling,
rough country beyond Mier, near the Alcantro Creek, General Canales
found the centralists in battle formation. On sighting him in their turn,
they fired a ball from a nine-pounder, and Canales with his three
colonels agreed upon a plan of battle. It was never used. The Texan
elements under their command on seeing the enemy did not wait to
bother with orders. Leaving the Mexicans, the Indians and the high
command behind, they raced forward in wild zest until they were
within point-blank range of the enemy, took cover behind mesquite
bushes and in a little arroyo, and began to throw effective rifle fire at
the regulars. Colonels Jordan and Ross waited for General Canales to
support the Texans, but with his Mexicans he only watched the battle
from the rear, and did not move. The Texans were already committed;
and their two colonels went forward, commanded a charge, and after
twenty minutes of fierce, close fighting, forced the centralist lines to
break and run.

It was the moment to press a full-scale pursuit; but still Canales
hesitated, and Pavón was able to withdraw his cannons and wagons out
of range. Presently he sent a flag asking for a truce of twelve hours, to
which Canales agreed. When night came the centralist army pulled back
five miles to a lone ranch with stone corrals and established a strong
position. On the next morning, when the truce lapsed, Canales marched
again to overtake the enemy. The Texan troops were in advance, and
astonished Pavón when they appeared outside his walls. Major Joseph
Dolan demanded a surrender. General Pavón came forward. His men
were without water or provisions. He gave over his sword to Major
Dolan, who indicated that he would better surrender it to General
Canales.

"No, sir," replied the centralist commander, "I surrender to the
brave Texans. They are my conquerors!"

He had lost a hundred and fifty men in the battle of the day
before in killed, wounded or missing. The remaining three hundred and

fifty of his command were taken prisoners, and in the amenities of north Mexican warfare, these promptly joined General Canales to fight on the other side, with their own four pieces of artillery which now were his. The Texans lost fourteen killed and wounded at the battle of Alcantro.

It was a promising victory for the army of the proposed federation. News of it went down the river and inland to Monterrey, causing dismay. The population loved a victor. Sentiment would always swing to him, and bring him recruits, food, money and the atmosphere of success on which revolutions fed and grew. All wondered where Canales would strike next. Another such swift triumph, and another, and the new river republic might spring alive. But Canales, if not exhausted by the efforts of his Texan allies, was inclined to take his ease at Mier, where he established himself and his augmented forces for forty days, as October whiled away, and part of November, and the old brown stone town glistened and rang with the colors and music and chatter of the autumn fair with its carnival, and the government forces downriver and inland caught their breath and had time to prepare their defenses, and the Texans fumed at inactivity, and some went home.

Finally in the middle of November Canales proceeded downriver against Matamoros. It took twenty-eight days of hard marching to make the hundred and sixty-five miles from Mier. Canales now had one thousand and sixty men and his four recently captured fieldpieces. He intended to lay siege to Matamoros, where General Canalizo with eighteen cannon and fifteen hundred regular troops awaited him. On December twelfth the federalists reached Matamoros and laid down their siege.

There soon followed two gestures of extreme caution that had the air almost of an exchange of courtesies.

On December fifteenth Colonel Zapata took a platoon, half Mexican and half Texan, against a Matamoros outpost, killed thirteen of its defenders, and retreated. In consequence, Canalizo immediately withdrew all his other outposts into the city.

On the next day, Canales announced to a council of war that since the besieged government forces in Matamoros would not come out to meet him in battle, he did not think it proper for him to attack them in their city; and that therefore he intended to abandon the siege and withdraw. The Texans were thunderstruck at such reasoning, protested, offered to storm the city by themselves. General Canales refused their offer, and with that, Colonel Ross detached fifty Texans from the federalist army and in disgust led them across the Rio Grande and home to Texas.

Abandoning Matamoros on the same day, General Canales turned southwestward to Monterrey. He had heard that the town was garrisoned by only four hundred troops under Arista, and he counted on taking their ammunition stores to supply his own men. Somehow he still managed to give an air of success, for on the way his men were provisioned, and each received a contribution of five dollars, out of the resources of the population of Caderita. Near Monterrey the defenders, heavily reinforced, awaited the rebels in rough country. Arista did the handsome thing and came out to fight. Canales, freed of his recent qualms, judged it proper under the circumstances to reply; and artillery let go on both sides. The duel was continued bravely through the whole day. Swabbers and gunners labored to produce their roars and drifts of smoke. No shot from either side took effect, though the forces were only eight hundred yards apart. It was in many ways a satisfactory battle. It ended with nightfall.

On the following morning Canales found that Arista had fallen back a mile nearer the city to a strong position, and pressed forward in a double play. He sent three hundred cavalry on a feint to the line, while with the rest of his power he detoured Arista and came to the city itself. Monterrey was his if he but entered. But in another of his complicated decisions he settled in the large patio of a convent on the outskirts and fortified it, while his troops stared at each other in bewilderment. Late in the afternoon Arista returned to the city, placed artillery, and on the following day—it was Christmas Day—another artillery exchange began that lasted for two days and hurt nobody. On the twenty-seventh a cavalry skirmish took place during which Colonel Gonzáles turned and ran, leaving his colleague Zapata in the field. The gestures were all fierce—the spirit, if not frivolous, then preoccupied. The Texans again were scandalized.

It was their presence, in fact, that made Arista as reluctant as Canales to engage in real combat. He knew their powers. But he believed more than they in cleverness. On the night of the twenty-seventh he sent agents among the federalist bivouacs. There by campfire and over coffee and in shadows his winning scheme was carried out. Out of the twelve hundred and fifty men in the Canales command, Arista managed to bribe seven hundred Mexicans to desert to him. Canales now had a real pretext for a retreat and with energy he acted upon it. Arista's cavalry chased after him, a skirmish threatened but did not develop, and another hundred and sixty Mexicans abandoned Canales. The retreat continued to the Rio Grande with Arista's cavalry snapping at its heels like coyotes and turning to run if threatened with a fight. On the seventh of January, 1840, Canales brought his column across the river and on the next day forty-five more Texans said good-bye and went home.

And now, having ranged for five months over thousands of square miles of comfortless land, and with his forces at their lowest ebb in numbers and sense of motive, Canales chose the moment to proclaim to the world the purpose of his scattered campaign that had accomplished nothing. On the banks of the river in his character as lawyer he framed a proclamation calling for delegates to spring forth from the dusty wastes to organize the Republic of the Rio Grande. Horsemen took copies of the document up and down the flat valley and inland to ranches, villages and towns. On January eighteenth enough delegates were assembled to give form to deliberations and, at Canales's field headquarters on the Texan side of the river, were set to work. They drafted a constitution modelled on the long-lamented Mexican Constitution of 1824. A capital was selected—Laredo. A president was named—Jesús Cárdenas. A commander-in-chief and secretary of war was appointed—General Canales. A flag was devised. Various offices were filled. There was by its own statement a new nation on the Rio Grande. Its boundaries were yet to be determined by battle, its existence yet to be granted by the mother country and other nations. But those who created it felt, and behaved, like a government, and granted the armed forces of the Republic of the Rio Grande extra rations and an issue all around of mescal, with which to celebrate. On the twenty-eighth of January President Cárdenas was inaugurated at Revilla amidst whatever pomp and ceremony were afforded by the resources of a little river town made of earthen boxes and willow-edged acequias and jacals of brush and wattles.

The army stayed at Revilla for three weeks and then pushed upriver to capture old Fort Saint John Baptist from the regulars, who had retired before their approach. Canales now had only seventy-four Texans in his command, and Colonel Jordan proposed that the army retire to the Nueces to obtain many more Texan volunteers and to reorganize. Canales did not approve the suggestion; and for the third time lost a sizable body of his best fighters, for Jordan with sixty Texans quit the adventure and took the road home over France Way. The loss cost the army of the Republic very heavily. Twelve days later Canales, marching inland from the presidio, was found by Arista with a large force and whipped so badly that he was barely able to run for the Rio Grande and cross to safety.

After all, then, Canales, with his president, was obliged to retire to Texas to raise new strength to continue the struggle, for without Texans they could not seem to win battles. Cárdenas went to Victoria on the Guadalupe River, Canales to Austin, to spread their offers. Canales later established his headquarters and raised the flag of the Republic of the Rio Grande at San Patricio, using Texan soil as casually as Mexican for his purposes. Response came. Though warned by President Lamar that Texas refused to recognize the new republican movement, and in spite of previous experience with its conduct of campaigns, four hundred and ten Texans, with three colonels, including Jordan, who returned to the new flag, joined Canales at San Patricio. Three hundred Mexicans from both sides of the river also rallied to him. With seven hundred and ten men, he began the slow movement back to the Rio Grande.

Jordan, with a hundred and ten Texans, and Colonels López and Molano, with a hundred and fifty Mexicans, were ordered to carry the revolution down the river towns of the right bank in advance of Canales and his main body. In June, 1840, they made demonstrations and signs of victory at Laredo, Revilla, Mier and Camargo. Now López and Molano announced new orders to Jordan which, they said, had been given them by Canales. They were to leave the river and strike southward, to raise new companies, and collect arms, ammunition and money. Jordan acceded, and the march began. It soon took on the character of a triumph. In one town after another the new republic was hailed with cheers, bells, artillery salutes, and the fat of that lean land. Victoria, the capital of Tamaulipas, fell, and the new republic vanguard installed a new state government.

Now followed a series of curious movements directed by the two Mexican colonels, López and Molano. Though Colonel Jordan and the Texans could not see any real purpose in these orders, they obeyed, moving through the Sierra Madre by an unlikely route which the Mexicans said would lead to Saltillo. But soon suspicions of treachery on the part of López and Molano occurred to the Texans. These were confirmed when they realized that the column was being taken not to Saltillo but to San Luis Potosí. Jordan insisted that the march change its course and head for Saltillo where an enemy force was stationed. One day's march from Saltillo a courier brought Jordan a message from a loyal friend at Victoria de Tamaulipas that López and Molano were maneuvering the Texan force into a position where for a cash payment they would deliver the Texan volunteers to the enemy.

Jordan could not bring himself to believe this. He faced the Mexican colonels with the accusation. They were horrified. How could he even think such a thing of them? Bitterly they said that it was a personal enemy of theirs who desiring to ruin them had sent the wicked message. Jordan was moved. He reassured them of his faith in them, and preparations for an attack upon Saltillo began. The city, too, was busy in the golden October weather. Its flat roofs were prepared for spectators of the coming battle, and hillsides too were occupied by civilians. Everyone was an amateur of the arts of battle. Opposing forces moving in tight formations made grand patterns that were easy to follow. The spectacle would have amplitude, with land for a theatre, bullets for dialogue, and death for many climaxes much to the Mexican taste. Women shawled against the sun came out bringing children for a glimpse of their future. Merchants and clerks and old men came to let their blood stir at what they missed in their days. The Saltillo garrison had promised them a victory to watch.

Unknown to Jordan, Colonel Molano had been in town conferring with the local commander about the price of betraying the Texans. The theory behind the deal was true and simple—break the Texans, and you break the revolution and the Rio Grande republic. Colonel López was fully informed of the arrangements. The plan was ready. The regulars, a thousand strong, defended Saltillo in trenches on top of a hill three miles south of the town. The Rio Grande force faced them from another hill six hundred yards away. A ravine was between the positions. Late in the morning of October twenty-third the regulars moved forward. It was the signal, and Colonel López, commanding for Rio Grande, began to execute the plan of betrayal. He ordered the Texan elements to march from the line toward a gorge in the mountains. If they entered it, they would be in a box that could be closed behind them till they were all shot to death. As Colonel Jordan moved unsuspectingly to follow the order, one of his officers rode up to him and shouted,

"In the name of God, sir, where are we going? If you take us to that gorge over there, the enemy will not leave a man to tell what became of us!"

Jordan suddenly saw it all. He gave a command, the Texan march was reversed, the column rode down the ravine passing the garrison trenches only a hundred and fifty yards away, and threw his men quickly

into an abandoned hacienda in the direct line of fire from the enemy. It
was the only cover to be had. The regulars began to fire, and with that,
López, crying out, "Long live the Supreme Government!" broke for the
enemy lines. All the Rio Grande infantry also deserted at about the
same time. The Texans were left with the Rio Grande rancheros behind
the broken walls of the old hacienda.

    In short order they were surrounded on three sides. For a couple
of hours the centralists poured rifle fire and cannon fire upon them. The
Texans waited in silence. Their silence convinced the regular commander
that they were wholly reduced by his furious salvos, and at four o'clock
he ordered an advance. The hilltops quickened as the spectators saw the
great last act approaching. The centralists charged—and at thirty yards
were received with the usual Texas blast of terrible accuracy, and another,
and another. In a little while it was all over. When over four hundred
of the attacking regulars had been killed by the cold control of the
Texan fire, panic broke on the field. The regular soldiers turned and
fled to town. On the hills, the audience scrambled for home and safety
in dismay. The play had had an unexpected last act. The Texans lost
five men, won the battle, and embittered by treason gave up the war.
Organizing for retreat, they marched away home on the road to Monclova and France Way, holding off a force of regular cavalry that pursued them as far as the Rio Grande. The river republic lost another
defender when Colonel Antonio Zapata was captured near Morelos, and,
having refused to turn traitor to his cause, was executed and beheaded.
The Centralists brought his head in a barrel of brandy to Guerrero
on the river, his home; and there, on a pole set up opposite to his house,
his head was exhibited for three days for his wife and family to see.
Meanwhile, General Canales, far from marching in support of his various
divisions in the field, had moved aimlessly against San Marino in Tamaulipas, had retired hastily to Camargo on the San Juan, and there had surrendered to Arista.

    With that act the Republic of the Rio Grande with its spacious
notions—its constitution, its president, its commander-in-chief, its army,
its two-room adobe and stone capitol building on the high north bank
of the river at Laredo—was suppressed; though the separatist idea in
north Mexico was to be revived under varying forms and names for many
years. In imagining the success of his scheme, Canales had proposed the
eventual annexation of his Republic of the Rio Grande to the Republic
of Texas, with the Texan southern boundary extended to the Sierra
Madre—the rocky scales of the double continental spine that made Mex-

ico resemble on the map a great iguana curving southward through the
tropics. The Rio Grande remained as the actual, if disputed, boundary
of Texas on the south; and soon the Texas boundary question turned
westward to the long upper course of the river in New Mexico.

16.

The Santa Fe Pioneers

It fell to Governor Manuel Armijo to deal not only with all the
old internal hostilities—raiding Indians and civil complaints—but in the
autumn of 1841 with a new threat that loomed across New Mexico's
vague eastern border. The New Mexican rebels of 1837 and 1838 had
thought of turning to Texas for support and alliance; and while formal
appeals may not have been sent by Gonzáles, news of the strong dis-
affection of the northern Rio Grande communities reached the Texans
through traders and other travellers. Even after rebellion had been put
down, the Upriver remained resentful of defeat and the execution of its
leaders; and elsewhere in the province the airs and tyrannies of Governor
Armijo created an atmosphere of opposition to the government. The
discontent was not organized, its expressions were responses to long-
suffered hard times, and the Governor heard few threats to alarm him
unduly from within his domain. But if American traders in general felt
superior to the New Mexicans, and optimistic over future possession
of the river country, the Texans felt even more so, and moreover could
point to what they regarded as a legal support of their attitude toward
the New Mexican Rio Grande.

For in 1836, after the defeat of the Mexican armies, the Texan
Republic by an act of its congress laid claim to the entire Rio Grande,
from source to mouth, as the western boundary of Texas. Under such
act, all of New Mexico lying east of the river was held to be Texan territory. But a great wilderness six hundred miles wide separated inhabited

Texas from New Mexico, and the claim was not put to the test of action during the first five years of the Texan Republic, which had other, more immediate internal problems to meet.

But now in the summer of 1841 there came urgent warnings from Mexico City to Governor Armijo that an expedition was forming in Texas under the sponsorship of the Texan President Mirabeau Bonaparte Lamar with the object of crossing the high plains wilderness northwest to Santa Fe. It was to be a large party, and volunteers were openly solicited through the pages of the *Austin City Gazette*. The purpose of the enterprise was announced as mercantile, but its character was to be overwhelmingly military, in order safely to "escort the merchandise through the Comanche territory." Volunteers received assurances. "All who arm, mount, and equip themselves will receive the pay of mounted gunmen—will serve for six months, or until the return of the expedition, and will be supplied with subsistence, &c. The companies will consist of fifty-six, rank and file, and elect their own company officers. The Field and Staff Officers will be appointed by the President. Ten large road-wagons will be furnished by the government to the merchants who desire to send their goods to that market, and the troops will secure their transportation. As this expedition will not only furnish an ample field for adventure on the march, but conduce, by a successful result, to the benefit of our common country," the advertisement anticipated "on the part of the young men whose crops are already in the ground, a readiness to unite . . . and contribute by their discipline, as well as their courage, to sustain the interest and the glory of our young Republic." The announcement was signed by William G. Cooke, who with three others, was commissioned "to represent our government with the people of Santa Fe."

Represent? For what purpose? Why did a wagon train full of goods need commissioners? The Mexican authorities were exercised by the news. It seemed plain to them that Texas was about to test her claim to the country of the upper Rio Grande. Mexico City promised reinforcements to Governor Armijo. The expedition was to be guarded against at all costs.

Meanwhile in Texas all preparations went rapidly forward. Volunteers mobilized at several encampments. The parties called themselves the "Santa Fe Pioneers." Enthusiasm ran high. It was believed in Texas that the New Mexicans were eager for the enterprise to be launched. A letter was circulated that gave encouragement to the expeditioners. It was written from Santa Fe, and it stated that the Texans would be welcomed by two thirds of the Rio Grande Mexicans, and all the Pueblo Indians and American traders. The Governor, it asserted, knew all that was in the wind, and he was quoted as saying that if the Texans came he neither could nor would resist them. The pioneers gathered—six military companies totalling two hundred and seventy men with a cannon, under the command of Brigadier General Hugh McLeod; ten leading merchants from San Antonio de Béxar and their necessary employees; the commissioners; and a handful of guests and observers, including a young English lawyer named Thomas Falconer, and George Wilkins Kendall, a journalist from New Orleans. All men were mounted, there were fourteen wagons loaded with goods, two wagons that hauled the effects of the commanding general, another for the baggage of each of the six companies, and a doctor's wagon. These were each drawn by six to eight span of oxen, and the single cannon was pulled by mules.

President Lamar made careful preparations for the reception of his Texan commissioners. He chose three American residents of New Mexico then in Texas to serve as joint commissioners with his own men, and he addressed to the citizens of Santa Fe in Spanish and English a printed communication that revealed the real purpose of the whole undertaking. This was the annexation by Texas of the upper Rio Grande.

"We tender to you," declared President Lamar paternally, "a full participation in all our blessings. The great River of the North, which you inhabit, is the natural and convenient boundary of our territory, and we shall take great pleasure in hailing you as fellow-citizens, members of our young Republic, and co-aspirants with us for all the glory of establishing a new and happy and free nation. . . ." What greater gift could a Texan offer than to belong to Texas? The President continued, "This communication I trust will be received by you and by your public Authorities, in the same spirit of kindness and sincerity in which it is dictated," and if encouraged, he promised to send along later in the summer his commissioners who would "explain more minutely the condition of our Country, of the Seaboard and the co-relative interests which so emphatically recommend and ought perpetually to cement the perfect union and identity of Santa Fee and Texas. . . ." The copies of this proclamation were packed and confidently taken along by the Pioneers. If in the face of it there were any doubt about their purpose, a letter from the United States representative in Texas to Secretary of State Daniel Webster dispelled it on June 22, 1841: "An expedition . . . under the controul of three commissioners, left Austin, on the 6th instant, for Santa Fe. The object of the Republic is to open a trade with the people of that country, and induce them, if possible, to become an integral part of Texas."

All through the summer Governor Armijo received news of the Texan movements and made his own arrangements to deal with them. He had reason to suspect that many of his citizens might use the moment of the invasion to rise against him, and indeed, there was a plot in Taos to assassinate him when the Texans should appear. Many suspects were thrown into jail. The American traders and businessmen were watched narrowly by the Governor's people. Stories were put out that were calculated to terrify the New Mexicans into self-preservative loyalty. The Texans were coming to pillage, to murder, to usurp. Life and property would be in peril. If the Texans should succeed, they would profane and suppress the Holy Faith of New Mexico. Only the Governor could save all. His propaganda was poured forth, and as the Texans drew nearer toward the end of August, he had the satisfaction of observing that popular feeling in many quarters ran with him. It was not that he was loved—quite the contrary, for his oppressive and self-indulgent government was an offense to all who were not directly its beneficiaries in office. But a danger from without—this was enough to make his opposing measures seem like statesmanship, as his ragged men at arms were gathered to be drilled and provisioned and equipped out of the bottom of the barrel.

For his part, Governor Armijo, who was devoted to the good things of life, gave himself a certain state. He was always described as a fine-looking man, six feet tall, though inclined to stoutness that increased with the years until he was seen as "a mountain of fat." There was something Roman about his large head, with its dark, level-shadowed eyes, its long nose that emerged flush from the brow and sailed downward in a slight curve, its straight mouth with the thin upper lip that suggested timidity or worse, and the full lower lip that reached in appetite for the feasts of the flesh. His jaws were heavy and round. He was clean-shaven, and he wore his dark hair shorter than most men around him. His taste in uniforms ran to the lavish. In dress, he wore a cocked hat, braided heavily with gold lace, and crowned by a white ostrich plume that waved above his right eye. His blue tail coat had a high collar that rose against his jaws and revealed a white stock at his full throat. Epaulettes of thick gold discs with massive gold fringe weighed upon him as shimmering reminders of rank, and a silken sash bearing a grand medallion crossed his breast from his left shoulder. He

had a heavy, simple charm of manner. Strangers opened up to him with
pleasure at the pains he took to be agreeable. He disarmed them with
confessions of genial rascality on his part—what was it about the sheep?
Now well-to-do, he had founded his fortune by stealing sheep, and—
the listener was expected to laugh, and think of wicked but amusing
acts out of his own past—once upon a time he had sold a ewe to a man,
not once, but fourteen times, the same ewe, stolen back to sell again
to the same dupe. A sociable man, he loved to gamble, and did well at
monté in the rooms of *La Tules,* Doña Gertrudes Barceló, who queened
it over the society of Santa Fe. Moving about his functions in the long
house of earth whose dust fell a little more each day, Governor Armijo
was a focus of color and grandeur amidst poverty, a living and opinionated symbol of what government was like in the Mexico of 1842.

For in the capital itself, President Santa Anna was once more
returning to the absolute power he was to hold nine times over Mexico
before Mexico was done with him. While splendors were heaped on
him with his own approval, he bore his exalted condition with an air
faintly deprecating and surprised. When he dined in state, six colonels
"stood the whole time of dinner behind his Excellency's chair," as an
ambassadress observed, and when he was scheduled to appear at an
opera gala—they were giving Donizetti's *Belisarius* (it was thought to
be most appropriate)—the preparations were very grand. Two second-
tier boxes were thrown together and lined in red and gold to accommodate the President and his party. The stairway leading to them was
lined with solid rows of footmen in red and gold. On his arrival accompanied by a suite of generals uniformed like himself in red and gold,
the President was handed a libretto of *Belisarius* in a special red and
gold binding. The house was jammed, the "boxes were very brilliant—
all the diamonds taken out for the occasion," the ambassadress noted
further. The President took his chair, and the generals "sat like pea-
cocks" surrounding him. He looked "modest and retiring, and as if quite
unaccustomed to the public gaze"—an effect that took much experience
to attain. "Knowing nothing of his past history, one would have said
a philosopher . . . one who had tried the world, and found that all was
vanity—one who had suffered ingratitude. . . ." When he passed through
the capital, it was to travel "very much *en roi.*" There were outriders,
a great escort of cavalry, a string of coaches with his own drawn by four
white horses, and all proceeding at full gallop through dirt streets and
lanes of staring, dusty people.

His proconsul far to the north at Santa Fe proclaimed his own

state with what was to be had locally. Governor Armijo if he lacked
an opera house and a sumptuous household guard yet had a gang of
hard riders in ragged serapes, and a state coach—though this was really
nothing more than a long wagon—"a curious specimen of Mexican taste
and workmanship." The axles were widely separated, and to them were
heavily affixed two massive timbers on which, without springs, the body
of the coach rested. But to make up for its jolting unwieldiness the
coach carried on its front a brave display of gilt work. If it had none
of the lightness and elegance of the carriage brought to the Rio Grande
from England in 1813 by Don Pedro Bautista y Pino—the English
understood such affairs better—it told all who saw it that General Don
Manuel Armijo was coming. And if there was no corps of liveried footmen in the old Palace, and little red and gold, the Governor had his
own way of decorating his executive office. Tacked to its walls were
scalps and pairs of ears sliced from killed Indians or other enemies
of the state and brought to him as proof of duties done or bounties
claimed.

In August the Governor sent Captain Damasio Salazar, a trusted
officer, to the east to scout the approaching Texans. Almost at once he
made contact. On September fourth three prisoners arrived in Santa Fe
under guard. Captain Salazar had sent them. They were the commissioners Howland, Baker and Rosenbury who in all good nature and
confidence had come ahead of the Texan party, bringing copies of President Lamar's ardent invitation to treason. They were cast into jail, only
to escape a few days later, and to be pursued. After a skirmish in the
country during which Rosenbury was killed, Howland and Baker were
recaptured and imprisoned at San Miguel del Vado, on the eastern
frontier, to await the Governor's arrival.

For he was going in person to meet his enemies. First, however,
he wooed the loyalty of any New Mexicans who may have planned to
throw in with the Texans. Referring to the "ever accredited mildness
that in all epochs and circumstances has characterized the benignity of
the Mexican government, which as a guide, has ever been followed by
him who addresses you," he offered amnesty to any citizens who "seduced
with or deceived by coaxing words" had promised to aid the Texans,
provided such citizens from that day forward would "accredit their
patriotism, adhesion, loyalty and fidelity" to Mexico. He could not for
a moment believe that if they but gave thought to "the danger of losing
your religion, your country, and your property," they would come back
under the Mexican flag; and promising them a great victory over the

Texans, he concluded convivially, "with this, your fellow citizen and chief drinks to your health."

Next, he gave orders to guard against any sudden move of the North American merchants to join forces with the invaders. To the United States consul at Santa Fe, the Governor sent a stern command. "As Commanding General of this department, and, in the name of the Mexican nation I warn you, as Consul of the United States of the North, that neither yourself nor any one of the strangers staying or dwelling in this Capital leave it under any pretext or motive; that you all must remain in the city till my return. . . . Acknowledge to me at once the receipt of this precept. God and Liberty, Santa Fe, September 16th, 1841."

The North Americans had reason to be alarmed. A group of them met and composed a letter to Secretary Webster at Washington on the same day. "Sir:—In a moment of extreme excitement and danger we, a few isolated American citizens, together with a few other citizens of other nations, feel it to be our duty to inform the Government of the United States of the circumstances which surround and oppress us in these moments. It has been learned here that an invading expedition composed of 325 men from Texas is approaching this Territory; on that account, all the inhabitants and all the officials of the government have become so exasperated against all strangers in this place that we deem ourselves in danger of our lives and destruction of our property; there is danger imminent; and we fear that before this reaches Washington we shall have been robbed and murdered.

"The governor marched off today with his troops to repel the invaders. . . ." But the Governor's army had hardly gone when, with the effect of yielding to an afterthought of enraged self-righteousness, one of his officers suddenly returned to town with several soldiers, went to the house of the American consul, entered, and "grievously insulted him striking him on the face." Mexican citizens gathered for the fun, but a few "of better dispositions" intervened and stopped it. The officer and his men returned to the street, and there he announced for all to hear that once the Texans were disposed of, he "would return with his troops and would destroy all of us, the strangers. . . . We, therefore, hope that, with the presentation of these circumstances to our government, measures will be adopted that will avoid the recurrence of similar injuries to our citizens. . . ."

The Consul protested officially to the Governor, who sent back assurances from the field that provided they behaved themselves, the foreigners would be protected in their rights. The Governor, in his character as commander-in-chief, continued his march along the old Missouri trail that skirted the forested mountains southeast before it turned northeast at San Miguel. He was mounted on a huge mule that bore a magnificent saddle and a gorgeous caparison. With him were about a thousand men-at-arms—Mexicans with guns and cutlery, Indians with lances, bows and arrows. Just after sundown as he approached the ruined Pecos mission in the cold twilight that fell swiftly he came to a turn in the road to see Captain Salazar with a hundred soldiers and five Texan prisoners. The Governor's trumpeter sounded the flourishes that always announced him, and the Captain drew up his force in line by the roadside. The Governor rode forward to the prisoners showing all his hearty charm. Without dismounting he shook their hands—the prisoners were roped together—called them "friends," and remarking that he had been informed of their capture, asked who they might be.

One Texan—it was a Captain Lewis—nervously replied that they were merchants on the Santa Fe Trail from the United States.

Another—Van Ness—contradicted him by saying that all but one were Texans, and the last was Mr. Kendall, from New Orleans. But the Governor ignoring Van Ness leaned down to Lewis, took a handful of his collar and hauled him roughly up beside his mule and growled:

"What does this mean? I can read—Texas!" and he pointed to the word on the buttons of Captain Lewis's uniform that carried also a single star. Lewis trembled, and the Governor, outraged at being lied to, added, "You need not think to deceive *me:* no merchant from the United States ever travels with a Texan military jacket."

It was a bad start. The prisoners were in trouble. The Governor asked more questions. Where was the rest of the Texan column? How many were there in it? What were they after? He listened while they assured him that the Texans came on mercantile business with peaceful purposes. He considered the case of Mr. Kendall, who had a Mexican passport, and was merely travelling with the column to enjoy its protection. Mr. Kendall's papers were in order, but he would be left with the prisoners until his intentions were somewhat better understood. The Governor gazed at them, and reading in their faces what they had heard about him, he blurted out that he was a man of honor; he was no assassin; he would have them know moreover that he was a great soldier. They returned his look and held their tongues. He then asked who of the prisoners could speak Spanish, and Captain Lewis, who had lived in Mexico, came forward eagerly. The Governor ordered him untied from his fellows, mounted him on a mule, motioned him to a place in his

company, and turned to Captain Salazar, to whom he bawled an order
to march the prisoners that night to San Miguel where they had just
come from. The Captain was astonished, and dared to remonstrate with
the Governor.

"But they have already walked nearly thirty miles today, your
Excellency, and are hardly able to walk all the way back tonight," said
Captain Salazar, not entirely able to conceal his own distaste for the
return march that he must endure with the prisoners.

"They are able to walk thirty miles more," replied the Governor
with a mock-heroic gesture. He was of that order of men whose self-
satisfactions—and these must be large if they would satisfy—were all taken
at the expense of others: in money, honor, or, quite simply and commonly, in the blood and breath of life. "The Texans are active and
untiring people—I know them." And then, in the constricted voice of
a furious fat man, he added, "If one of them *pretends* to be sick or
tired on the road, *shoot him down and bring me his ears!* Go!"

And with a blast of bugles and a command to his troops he
rode by the prisoners on the darkening trail to San Miguel. The exhausted Texans took up their march in turn. At midnight they were
halted in a meadow when a cloudburst fell. They slept till dawn in the
rain and after two more hours on the trail reached the village of San
Miguel which was now teeming with the Governor's soldiery. The prisoners were confined in a house on the plaza, there to reflect on what
had befallen them since leaving home, and to wonder what was happening to the rest of their expedition, and to imagine the fate that was
taking shape for them in the capricious vapors of the Governor's mind.

In miserable truth, the Texans had to acknowledge that the
expedition was a failure even before it encountered the New Mexicans.
It had started too late in the season, for by the time the train was out
on the high plains, the best pasturage was gone—burned away by the
terrible summer sun. Nobody knew much about the route to follow
except two Mexican guides, who deserted one night. Indians harried the
pioneers—in one attack they killed five Texans, stripped them, and cut
the heart out of one. Supply was badly planned, and food ran out.
The travellers ate insects, reptiles, anything. A large part of the force
was detached and sent ahead under Colonel Cooke, the commissioner,
to find San Miguel and buy food to bring back to the starving main
body. Other groups—Harland, Baker and Rosenbury in one, and Kendall
with his four companions—were sent ahead at various times to scout the
New Mexicans and make cordial overtures; but with mournful results.

Colonel Cooke did not return, and neither did the others. Indians raided the main body one night and stampeded the animals, making off with eighty-three horses and all the cattle except the draft oxen and mules. As the train crawled slowly forward a great part of the company now had to walk. Many threw away their arms and ammunition, greatly reducing the company's power to defend itself. Many men fell ill for lack of salt to replace what they sweated away. Discipline crumbled, and the brisk intention of the expedition became a farce. Conquer a province, annex the upper Rio Grande? All they wanted now, the Santa Fe Pioneers, scattered in two large parties on the plains and one small party in cells at San Miguel, were rescue and something to eat.

On the morning of their arrival at San Miguel, Kendall and his three fellow prisoners looked out the window of their cell and saw a man led out blindfolded and pounded down to his knees against a plaza wall and shot in the back by a squad of soldiers at three paces. So close a fusillade did not kill him, and the corporal of the squad dispatched him by putting his pistol to the man's breast and shooting him in the heart. The flash set his shirt on fire. It burned until his blood seeped into the little flames putting them out. The victim was Baker, executed for running away from captivity at Santa Fe.

In a few minutes Kendall and his group were taken out to the plaza and lined up facing a window through which they could see the Governor wearing a blue uniform and a sword. Talking to someone out of sight in the room, he pointed to the prisoners outside, listened, spoke, nodded. The unseen individual within answered him about each prisoner. It gave them the feeling of being on trial. With Baker's body smouldering on the ground a few paces away they saw themselves grimly. And then the door opened, the Governor came out and weighing his own majesty with satisfaction on each step walked slowly to the prisoners and faced them. He was pleased to be gravely magnanimous. His charm was sobered, but it was there.

"Gentlemen," he said, "gentlemen, you told me the truth yesterday—Don Samuel has corroborated your statements—I save your lives."

Don Samuel? they thought, the unseen informant in the room? Who could he be? The Governor continued:

"I have ordered Don Samuel to be shot—he will be in five minutes. He ran away from Santa Fe, and, in attempting to reach Colonel Cooke's party, has been retaken."

They felt a shock of recognition. Don Samuel was Howland, the third of the advance commissioners.

"You now see the penalty of trying to escape," concluded the Governor, "his fate will be yours if you attempt it.—Sergeant of the guard, conduct these gentlemen back to prison."

But before they moved, Howland was brought forth to die. His hands were tightly tied behind him. He passed closely in front of the others. They blanched at what they saw. His left ear and left cheek were cut wholly away, his left arm was grossly hacked where the sword had finished its strokes. He turned to his friends, and their hearts beat when with the other side of his face he gave them a strong, sweet smile. They tried to go to him, were stopped by guards, and he said to them gently, "Good-bye, boys; I've got to suffer. You must—" but he was walked past them and that was all they heard. He was taken to see Baker's body, and then a blindfold was put over his ruined face, he was made to kneel and was shot dead by the squad, while the other prisoners watched sick with rage. They were then marched back to their cell.

The plaza was now gradually emptied of troops, and they wondered why, and were told that Governor Armijo with a thousand warriors was marching on Antón Chico, a village thirty miles away, where Colonel Cooke and his detachment of ninety-four men were encamped. All day couriers came and went—there were reports of a battle, and then of a surrender, unconditional surrender, which the prisoners could not believe. Surely Cooke and his men would put up a fight—but the report was true, and the plaza walls echoed with salvos, ringing of bells in the church tower, outlandish music on guitars, fiddles and trumpets, and cries of "Long live the Mexican Republic!" and "Long live the brave General Armijo!" and "Death to the Texans!" There was a procession, the tutelar saint of the village was carried from and to the church, a Te Deum was sung, and the celebration went on all night. Every ten minutes the prisoners heard the sentries dolefully cry out, "Centinela alerta-a-a-a!" in relay from post to post.

In the morning the Governor received the prisoners again. It pleased him to be candid. He said that of course he knew they were gentlemen—Howland had told him so, and indeed, they looked it; he had given orders that they must be treated accordingly. He waved them to seats. He then quizzed them about General McLeod and the main body of the Texans who were yet to be taken, and in fact he was about to go and take them, and if they put up a fight, he would kill them all. As his prowess reminded him of himself, and his department, his native talents rose within him, and he improvised a little epic, an aria, on the subject of his own valor, the splendor of his army, the glory, strength

and richness of New Mexico, while his captives could hardly believe
their ears. In time he dismissed them to new quarters, and in a few
minutes they heard trumpets, the clatter of a mounted column, and
watched him dash by on his great mule, leading his troops, in a superb
blue serape heavy with gold and silver bullion.

Three days later—it was September twentieth—Cooke's people
began to pass through San Miguel on their way to Mexico City under
guard, and roped together. The San Miguel prisoners, hungry for news,
were not permitted to talk to them; but could only speculate upon their
own destiny. But their spirits rose in the next few days, for they were
kindly waited upon by the women of the place, who brought them good
food, and amused them with attentions, and listened to their jokes, and
exclaimed at their general good nature. The young priest of the parish
was good to them, too. As the days passed the prisoners saw several
caravans go by on their way to Santa Fe. If only, they thought, if only
they might escape and make their way to the United States by the
Santa Fe Trail! But they were closely guarded. For three weeks they
waited for news of McLeod and the main body; and then, in driblets, a
few Texans were brought in at a time, and finally on October ninth
the bells rang again, and a procession was formed, and guns were fired,
and they knew that the Governor's victory was complete. Within the
next few days all the remaining Texans were driven into San Miguel.
They were in a frightful state. Most of their clothes had been taken
from them, they had only one blanket each to protect them from the
sharp mountain weather, they were starving. Their merchant wagons
followed, in the possession of the Mexicans, and once ranged in the
plaza, were emptied of their cargo which was promptly distributed among
the Governor's people, with great shares going to himself and to Captain Lewis.

For it now came clear what Lewis had been up to. Kendall and
his friends had been wondering where Captain Lewis had been during
their captivity which he had been spared; and now they heard how,
beginning as interpreter for the Governor, he had succumbed to a cruel
weakness of his own character, and had served as a traitor, inducing his
fellow Texans to put down their arms and submit to the Governor
under false promises of good will. The Texans, as soon as they gave up
their rifles, were tied together with lariats, and robbed of their personal
valuables, knives and baggage. It was a sad discovery.

October seventeenth came as a warm day. Little showers of rain
fell. The Texans were all turned out together into the plaza and counted

—nearly two hundred of them. For the first time in many weeks they were reunited—all but Cooke's party who had been taken through town without pausing a few days before—and they exchanged their news, while waiting to hear what was now to become of them. This they soon learned; for Captain Damasio Salazar was put in command of a guard of two hundred soldiers, for the purpose of marching the Texans on foot two thousand miles to Mexico City and the mercies of Santa Anna, while Governor Armijo flushed with achievement rode back to Santa Fe and the triumphal welcome of a hero.

Many of the marchers already knew Captain Salazar for what he was. Their hearts sank now. He drew his tradition from impulses deep in humanity at its most inhumane. His view of authority, and the value of life, and the meaning, and uses, of pain, was not unique. It had shown itself in his superiors—the President of Mexico, the Governor of New Mexico. If he was a man who could not read, so that subordinates had to make sense for him out of written orders and passports, yet in sustained effort he could bring his faculties to bear on other matters of quite respectable complexity—how to wound the human mind and body, how to torture them, how to kill them, how to dishonor them when killed, and all nicely devised to slake his own hearty appetites.

He now gave an order and marched the column out on the old Pecos road. By sundown he brought them to Pecos and without feeding them, turned the prisoners into the ruins of the mission to spend the night. After the warm day and its dancing rain showers the night was icy, for there was snow on the Sangre de Cristos and its breath came driving down on the wind. Having been robbed of most of their clothing, the prisoners had only one single blanket each. It was not enough. Nobody slept all night. In the morning, before the cold mists of the Pecos canyon began to thin, they looked hungrily to their custodian for food, and leaped with joy when he called them—all one hundred eighty-seven of them—to gather about him. When he was surrounded, Captain Salazar reached into a receptacle he had, and took from it a small cake. The men looked at it. He tossed it into the air above them, and they scrambled over each other to reach for it. He laughed to see the sight, and tossed another, and another, until he had thrown up fifty cakes—all he had for the whole party. He had the joy of making animals out of men who were comrades. The more they fought each other for the cakes the more his glee showed itself. When there was nothing left, and with more than two thirds of the men still sick with hunger, he fell them in and started the day's march. He was taking them to the Rio

Grande by way of Galisteo Creek. The ground was rough. Their feet bled, for many had no shoes. They passed the second night in an open corral after a pint of meal for their day's ration. The Captain would not resist what wells of rich humanity dwelt deep in him—he told the prisoners that his orders from the Governor were to keep them tied throughout every night; but as he knew they might be tired, he dared to disobey the order. Of course, if any man tried to escape, not only he, but every one of his companions would be shot to death.

On the third day he marched them into Santo Domingo on the Rio Grande, and a few hours later into San Felipe downstream. In both pueblos the Indian women were kind to them, bringing them food and sympathy. But Salazar pushed on as soon as possible, improvising tortures as he went. At Algodones, on the river, when the prisoners begged to be given house shelter against the cold, he thrust them all into two connecting rooms so small that they would hold scarcely twenty in ordinary comfort, and listened to their yells and thuddings with satisfaction, for they were slowly suffocating. In his own good time he released fifty to sleep on the ground. At Sandía pueblo he issued rations of one ear of uncooked corn per man. At Albuquerque he marched them through the streets. At Los Placeres ranch he gave out no rations, and when the men begged, he pointed to pastured horses and mules near-by and remarked that the "grazing was excellent." At Valencia on the old river road he issued a pint of flour around, but few men had energy enough to cook it into anything edible, and most sank to stupor while frost gathered on their blankets. In the morning the Captain found one of the Texans dead, and as an accounting for the Governor, cut off his ears, and threw the body into a ditch. Then calling the morning's roll, he was asked by another Texan for permission to ride in a cart for he had become too lame to walk; and granted it. A mile later the cart broke down, and the Captain ordered the Texan to walk, then, or be shot. "Then shoot, and the quicker the better!" said the Texan, and Captain Salazar did so, then cutting off the man's ears, taking his shirt and trousers, and leaving another body for dogs or coyotes.

The Captain could only relieve the tedium of his mission by rapid progress. At times he turned the command over to a subordinate and snatched a few hours of sleep in a wagon by day to supplement his night's rest. At Socorro he allowed a day's halt, and then pushed on toward the Dead Man's March. He was obliged to shoot another man who was falling behind, and take his ears. It did not suit him to permit any of the ailing prisoners to ride on any of the unburdened mules that were led by the escort. Reaching the Dead Man's March he announced that the crossing would be made without the usual overnight stops. They entered it after a heavy snowfall that came during the night and left five inches of snow on the sleeping prisoners. Once again a member of the stumbling and dragging detachment lagged in the rear, and the Captain ordered a soldier to make him keep up. The Texan was unable to do so, and the soldier knocked out his brains with a clubbed rifle, remembering to bring the ears to the Captain. During the crossing of the Dead Man's March the Captain met northbound troops from Durango—the reinforcements promised to the Governor to help him deal with the Texans. Already dealing with the Texans, Captain Salazar pushed them on to the end of the desert crossing and once more came to the Rio Grande, with the loss of only one more Texan, who died of pneumonia, complicated by a piece of drollery on the part of a Mexican soldier. The sick man, supported by friends, who heard the death rattle in his throat, came to a moment of lucidity and asked for water. Just then, the soldier, smiling for his joke, pointed a rifle in his face and pulled the trigger. The gun was not loaded, but the sick man was convulsed by the action, and threw out his arms in self-protection. The soldier could not resist repeating his success. He again took aim and snapped the trigger. It was too much for the patient. He shuddered once and died. His ears were cut off and taken to Captain Salazar, who now had a collection of five pairs.

Now that they were nearing El Paso, the Captain and his men found a new enjoyment—describing to the Texans what their fate must be once they entered the jurisdiction of Chihuahua. All that had passed before would be trifling compared to what awaited them farther south. It was a pleasure to torture the minds, as well as the flesh, of weakened men. The thought was left with them that upon the arrival of orders from President Santa Anna, they would all be executed. Pushing dutifully on, the Captain caused his charges to ford the Rio Grande, which at its deepest came to their chins. The water was bitter cold. Only a few miles ahead lay El Paso, where Captain Salazar was to turn the prisoners over to the commanding general of the Chihuahua department, Don José María Elias Gonzáles.

What followed was like a dream. The transfer was made, and within two hours the prisoners were billeted in small squads at different houses of the El Pasoans. After five months of never seeing a table or a chair, they were seated to partake of "well-cooked meats, eggs, the finest bread . . . even the wines of the place." General Elias was in a rage at the treatment they had endured. Salazar, coming to make his report to him, proudly stated that he had delivered every prisoner safely but five who had died on the way, and to prove the accuracy of his tally, threw down on the General's desk five pairs of ears strung on a thong. The General by now knew all, and held Salazar for the murder of three of the men, and for an accounting of what he had stolen from the prisoners.

El Paso could not do enough for the miserable Texans. The citizens fed them, let them bathe, gave them money, clothes and beds. The young parish priest, Father Ramón Ortiz, endeared himself to everyone with his handsome face, his sympathetic expression, and his openhearted help. General Elias ordered that they remain for three days of rest in El Paso. When it was time to resume the march, the whole city turned out to see them off, and many residents—the commanding general, the priest, several other leading citizens—rode part of the way with them and hoped that they would come safely to Mexico City and speedy liberation, and took an "affectionate farewell." So the Santa Fe Pioneers left "the lovely town or city of El Paso," in its "delightful situation in a quiet and secluded valley, its rippling artificial brooks, its shady streets, its teeming and luxurious vineyards, its dry, pure air and mild climate, and above all, its kind and hospitable inhabitants. . . . Surely," pleaded a prisoner, not one of the Texans could "ever think of El Paso, or the dwellers therein, without lively gratitude."

But El Paso was only an interlude of mercy. On arrival overland in the capital, they were distributed among several prisons—the dreadful Accordada and the Santiago convent in Mexico City, another in Puebla, the grimly isolated fortress of Perote. Those in the Santiago were objects of curiosity for fashionable residents of Mexico City. The Spanish Ambassadress—a former American—noted that "a good deal of interest has been excited here lately about the Texian prisoners taken in the Santa Fe expedition. . . ." She had heard that they were stripped of their hats, shoes, and coats. One day she went with a party to see them. The common soldiers were in the courtyard, the officers in the convent's large hall. She understood that President Santa Anna planned to "have them put in chains, and sent out to sweep the streets, with the miserable prisoners of the Accordada." But an officer with her pooh-poohed the idea. Actually, she found that there seemed to be "very little if any vindictive feeling against them"; and in June, 1842, the President to celebrate his birthday gave the bulk of the prisoners their freedom—though one singled out for severe treatment was isolated in the fortress of San Juan de Ullóa until January, 1845, when he made his escape and

returned to Texas. The Texan attempt on the upper Rio Grande—
General Andrew Jackson writing in retirement to General Sam Houston
called it "the wild-goose campaign against Santa Fe"—was done with.
The upper river faded into remoteness again; and the Texas Rio Grande
came into view through the smoke of little battles between Mexicans
and Texans over the boundary claims, and the sovereignties, that
divided them.

17.

Border Smoke

For vastly the greater part of its twelve hundred miles, the
border country of the Rio Grande was bare and ungrateful. Below the
El Paso settlements was the old village at the junta de los rios, called
Presidio del Norte, where amidst crumbling missions a garrison guarded
the river crossing and a port of entry. Then, reading downstream, came
the fantastic country of the Big Bend, where only Indian wanderers
penetrated. Old Fort Saint John Baptist and the half-dozen Escandón
towns and the Gulf settlements for river commerce were the only formal
communities below the Big Bend. Ranches and haciendas were scattered
along the valley, many of them established under Mexican grants after
1821—but the Texas rebellion, and Indian raids, and the scorching of
the land under demands of volunteer armies in civil conflict caused
many to be abandoned. Where once near the river sheep and goats were
raised, and farther inland, mules, horses and horned cattle; and where
after 1817 corn was grown and after 1830 cotton and sugar cane, the
lower valley was "turned into a desert." Commerce was reduced to a
trickle, and in the 1830s at Matamoros after the smoky withdrawal of
Captain Henry Austin with the *Ariel,* "wagons were almost as scarce
as steamboats." The great tract between the Rio Grande and the Nueces
was an empty wilderness buffer between populated Texas and the

boundary she claimed. Mexico had never recognized the independence of Texas, much less her Rio Grande border. Mexicans still freely used the north side of the river as far as the Nueces, and Texas was powerless to prevent them.

Under her first president, General Houston, Texas did not actually make a do-or-die issue out of the Rio Grande. After the victory of 1836 she asked the United States to annex her and grant her statehood, even going so far as to propose a new boundary, if it would expedite action. The boundary was to be the watershed between the Rio Grande and the Nueces, and the New Mexico Rio Grande was to be abandoned as the western limits. But the United States did not welcome the proposal to annex Texas, and the old boundary claim stood. It was emphasized in armed raids on Mexican establishments on the river—in 1837, when Texans attacked Laredo without results, and four years later in the Lamar project of the Santa Fe Pioneers. Again in 1837 Texas asked for annexation, and again the United States refused, finding the request "inexpedient, under existing circumstances." For Texas and Mexico were officially still in a state of war, while the United States was at peace with Mexico, and bound to her by a trade treaty to be observed scrupulously so long as it could be "reasonably hoped" that Mexico would "perform her duties and respect our rights under it." The Texas Republic was obliged to be content with recognition by the United States, which came on March 1, 1837, under a joint Congressional resolution.

Of all the factors that kept the annexation issue in a turmoil for twelve years the most emotional, and for a long time the most decisive, was in a sense a legacy from Stephen Austin. It was the institution of slavery, on which he had founded the working economy of his settlements. If, for a period, he had wavered in his view of the justice and the usefulness of slavery, the Texas Rebellion by its successful outcome confirmed his last view of the matter; for among the first laws drawn up by the Texan convention of independence in March, 1836, were those conserving and regulating the holding of slaves. What had Austin said? Texas "must be a slave country. Circumstances and unavoidable necessity compel it. . . ." By the time he died of pneumonia as secretary of state of the Republic in December, 1836, his slave policy was firmly embodied in Texan life.

As a fixed feature of that life, it became in the United States a hot issue between the northern abolitionists and the slaveholding masters of the south. Their respective views were expressed in Congress. If her system of slavery would come into the Union with the rest of

Texas, the abolitionists would fight against annexation, and the south would fight for it. The central struggle for power in the United States in terms of opposed views of living human property remained for almost a decade the dominant factor in all discussions of the annexation of Texas, and prevented any resolution of the matter.

After her early rejections by the United States, Texas, particularly under the presidency of Lamar, turned away from the idea of annexation toward a more vibrant nationalism. In 1839 she tried to bring about a state of peace with Mexico with an offer of five million dollars in exchange for national recognition and acceptance of the Rio Grande as the boundary between the two nations. The Mexican Congress was indignant at the proposal, and refused to consider even a truce that did not reaffirm Mexican sovereignty over Texas. But if a state of war continued, little indicated the fact. Private trading expeditions moved across the Rio Grande between northern Mexican towns and San Antonio, exchanging Mexican sugar, flour, beams, and leather goods for Texan tobacco and American calico and hardware—until early in the second presidency of General Houston.

In December, 1841, at Austin, General Houston was inaugurated as president for the second time, appearing "on the stage in a linsey-woolsey hunting shirt, and pantaloons, and an old wide-brimmed white fur hat. In this," thought an observer—it was Dr. Josiah Gregg, the Santa Fe trader, now roaming far afield in Texas with opinions tart as ever—"Gen. Houston demonstrated more vanity than if he had appeared in an ordinary cloth suit. He knew it would be much remarked, and thought it would be popular no doubt, with [the] body of the people." His vice-president, General Edward Burleson, "also appeared and was sworn in in his fancy Indian leathered hunting shirt—probably more for the purpose of being in unison with the president than for vanity. . . ." The president's speech was "rather dry and monotonous." Much of it was taken up with praising his own previous efforts on behalf of Texas, and much with severe criticisms of Lamar, his predecessor, who had sent the Pioneers against Santa Fe.

The issue was not dead; for in January, 1842, news reached Texas of the defeat, capture and treatment of the Texan Santa Fe expedition; and the public temper raged at the barbarisms of Governor Armijo and other Mexicans. Congress was in session under the new administration, and in a fury passed a resolution demanding that the boundary of Texas leap across the Rio Grande, and take in Sinaloa, Durango, Coahuila, Tamaulipas, Sonora, Chihuahua and the Californias

—in effect, the old huge design of the Republic of the Rio Grande that had been fought for and lost by Canales and his Texan volunteers two years before. Houston vetoed the resolution, and Congress passed it again over his veto. When word of such wild lust for Mexican territory came to Mexico, it was to inflame Santa Anna, supremely forgetful of the last scenes of 1836, with desires for a punitive war. In Texas there were two parties of sentiment. One was hot for an offensive war against Mexico. The other, represented by Houston, saw that defensive measures were the best Texas could manage at the moment. Both Mexico and Texas were without funds or credit. The scene of any possible warfare between them—the immense, starkly beautiful but barren lands of the Rio Grande —could hardly support a handful of towns and ranches, let alone mounted armies with their need of forage and their levies of money, food and animals of burden. The armed forces of Texas were not organized or trained. War seemed unlikely.

But suddenly, as a flourish against Texan designs on the eight vast states of north Mexico, on March 5, 1842, Mexican troops descended upon Refugio, Goliad and San Antonio. The Texan garrisons of all three places were too small to make any effective resistance, and all surrendered. For their part, the Mexican forces were too far from base, and too few, to do more than raise the Mexican colors over the three Texan towns; and after proclaiming the laws of Mexico to their enraged citizens, withdrew two days later and retired below the Rio Grande.

So after six years of preoccupied restraint, both Texas and Mexico again made the gestures of war toward one another. Houston alerted all military manpower in Texas. The Texan navy—five schooners and two brigs—was ordered to blockade Mexico's east coast ports and the mouth of the Rio Grande. Santa Anna promised to march across Texas and plant the Mexican flag on her eastern borders at the Sabine. Houston, in a letter addressed to Santa Anna and released to the world, told him his statement was a "silly gasconade," and in his turn pledged that Texans "will march across the Rio Grande, and—believe me, sir—ere the banner of Mexico shall triumphantly float on the banks of the Sabine, the Texan standard of the Single Star, borne by the Anglo-Saxon race, shall display its bright folds, in Liberty's triumph, on the isthmus of Darien."

Deeds fell short of such an exchange of rhetoric. Neither nation had funds to pay a full-scale army. Texas tried to borrow a million dollars in the United States and failed. The navy's expenses for overhauling could not be met and the blockade was never enforced. When the Texan congress voted an offensive war against Mexico, Houston felt obliged to veto the bill. All he could propose were defensive schemes along the border, and small forces were mobilized only to be infuriated by restraining orders.

In early June a Texan volunteer defense force of one hundred and ninety-two men under General Davis was attacked by five hundred Mexican cavalry with two hundred infantry and one cannon under General Canales, who was now in the national service against which he had plotted and danced about on horseback two years before. There was a ragged and enthusiastic cavalry charge, a feint or two, and a Texan bullet killed the Mexican officer commanding the cannon, whereupon General Canales flew back to the Rio Grande with his detachment, and the Texan volunteers disbanded.

Seen from far away in Washington, the state of affairs was a nuisance, and pressure was exerted by the annexationists in the United States to bring the war officially to an end. Once done, this would permit the United States to intervene in the Texas question without taking sides in a war—if an occasional brief scuffle between unsupported armed bands could be called a war. On June twenty-second, Secretary Webster asked the American minister to Mexico to lay before the Santa Anna government certain observations. After all, realities had better be faced: Texans and Mexicans were wholly different in their traditions, languages and ways; a vast distance separated their seats of government; they had now been disunited for many years; Texas was recognized as a nation by many other nations of the world, and maintained diplomatic and commercial relations with them. It did appear on the face of it that any future return of Texas to Mexican sovereignty "was among the things most to be doubted." The prevailing situation was harmful to commerce everywhere in the Gulf. To be sure, if the war must be continued by its parties, the United States could not interfere; but if she could help to compose a peace, she would be most willing to do so. Mexico must see that peace would bring the United States an opportunity to enter legitimately into the matter of Texan annexation. But Mexico rejected the offer, and in further repudiation set out to show by another armed thrust across the river that the war was far from over.

Like the others, the latest attack was little more than a brandishing of arms. It came on September 11, 1842, against San Antonio, where General Adrian Woll appeared with twelve hundred Mexicans. There was little local resistance; but the Texan militia was ordered to the counterattack, and volunteers marched from Gonzales to take back the old battle-pitted city. On the thirteenth there was an engagement on the Salado Creek six miles east of town between the Gonzales volunteers and Woll with eight hundred men. The Mexicans lost sixty killed and many wounded, the Texans ten wounded and none killed. "Huzza! Huzza for Texas!" cried the Texan commander in writing after the fight. But Texas suffered other losses that day when another volunteer band attempting to reach the Gonzales detachment was surrounded and destroyed with about forty-five killed and fifteen taken prisoners. Woll retired to the city and organized his train for retreat. By the eighteenth all his people were pulling back to the Rio Grande, taking along fifty-three prisoners, plunder, and a number of San Antonio citizens of Mexican blood who threw in their lot with Mexico. The Texans pursued the retreating troops for thirty or forty miles and then gave up to return homeward.

The Woll exploit was the signal for retaliation. The Republic's various bands of volunteers were ordered to meet in rendezvous at Medina, under the command of General Alexander Somervell. They were in high temper. Immediate invasion of Mexico was their hot hope. Seen from the ranks, any concern for the problems of supply, transport and military organization looked like merely irritating caution. Somervell had almost nothing with which to equip his men. There were intrigues and rivalries over the command positions, including the highest. The volunteers were not interested in making an army—they wanted to whip Mexico, at once, and many a man felt equal to the job alone, and became a corrosive malcontent at being restrained until some small show of order and discipline was achieved. But finally, after what a chafing officer called a "week of breeches-making," Somervell set out for the Rio Grande with seven hundred and fifty men. His orders from President Houston read: "When the forces shall have assembled, if their strength and condition will warrant a movement upon the enemy, it is desirable that it should be executed with promptness and efficiency." This left much to the discretion of the commanding general—a discretion that was the very opposite of the spirit of the volunteers.

On December seventh, at night, after seventeen days of difficult marching, the Southwestern Army of Texas reached the vicinity of Laredo on the north bank of the river. General Somervell kept the troops mounted, enjoined quiet, and "all was dead silence." The men noticed the "mysterious whisperings and grave concealments" of their commander that night, and concluded that plans were building for an attack at dawn. But with daylight, when they entered the town, all they encountered were "some women, children, and old men," for the Mexican garrison of one hundred troops had withdrawn across the river to the town's other part. The volunteers "felt they were badly humbugged," and sarcastically spoke of "the siege of Laredo."

Dissatisfaction with the campaign grew. Somervell first encamped his men a mile above Laredo, then three miles below it. He did not here cross the river into Mexico. His men were badly fed. In a day or two a large number of them broke restraints, entered Laredo and plundered it of "many articles of a useless character." Somervell collected the loot and restored it to the mayor. What sort of warfare was this against people who had murdered and robbed and burned their way in and out of Texas? But spirits rose with an order to march. All expected that now at last they would cross the river and sweep down the Mexican side taking town after town. Instead, Somervell led them down the Texan side, and presently edged away inland, through thickets of thorny brush that tore the men's breeches and legs. It was not long until they understood that he was leading them homeward. After protests, the General paraded his men and called for a vote. Of seven hundred and forty men present, two hundred voted to go home. They were released to do so under a colonel. The rest elected General Somervell to lead them into Mexico. A few days later, back at the river, he crossed them to Guerrero, and soon made contact with three hundred of General Canales' cavalry, who quickly retired. On the next day Somervell began to cross the Southwestern Army back to the Texan side of the Rio Grande on six large, flat-bottomed skiffs, and when the movement was complete, he ordered the boats to be sunk behind him. On December nineteenth his adjutant published an order: "The troops belonging to the Southwestern Army will march at ten o'clock this morning for the junction of the Rio Frío and the Nueces, thence to Gonzales, where they will be disbanded." Under his discretionary instructions, he had his reason for issuing it: ". . . Having been eleven days on the river, and knowing the various positions of the enemy's troops, I was satisfied that they were concentrating in such numbers as to render a longer stay an act of imprudence."

A large part of the army was astounded at the order, and, after hurried debates, refused to go with him. He departed inland with about two hundred officers and men, leaving three hundred and four, under five captains, to decide upon their own next moves.

18.

To Mier and Beyond

If they were not to invade and destroy Mexico, they would in any case use the Rio Grande settlements to obtain horses and provisions for themselves, before in their own good time they too should turn homeward. Their first move was to elect a commander. They chose Colonel William S. Fisher, who having served under Canales two years before knew something of the Rio Grande country. Among the other officers was Thomas J. Green, a spirited young veteran of the Texas. Rebellion.

The river was at high water. It was decided to take most of the force downstream by boat, while the rest marched parallel on the Texan bank. Despite Somervell's orders, his skiffs had been hidden instead of destroyed, and now were found and put to use. The men spoke humorously of them as their "navy." Tom Green was put in charge of them. His "flagboat" displayed a red banner with the Texan star. There were not enough men to fill all the boats, and the empty ones were left burning as the flotilla started downstream. They came to riverside ranches where they took provisions. The marching horses ate in cornfields. Scouts probed the Mexican bank for news of the enemy. The land and river-borne forces joined together each night. One night they found and disarmed a band of Karankawa Indians who had been on a raid into Texas. On the twenty-first of December the camp was made on the Texas bank opposite the way to Mier, which lay seven miles inland in Mexico. An officer was sent into the town for information, and returned to report that General Canales had just evacuated the place, but local residents told how General Ampudia and a large force was hourly expected to come to the city. It was, next to Matamoros, the largest town of the lower river, and would be able to supply the needs of the Texans.

On the next day, Tom Green accompanied Colonel Fisher to Mier and presented the mayor, whose name they understood to be Don

Juan, with a requisition for whatever government supplies might be stored there, "including cannon, small firearms, powder, lead, munitions of war of every kind, &c." In addition, the levy—giving an inflated estimate of the Texan strength to impress the Mexicans—demanded "5 days' rations for 1200 men, to wit: 40 sacks of flour of 6 arrobas each, 1200 lbs. sugar, 600 lbs. coffee, 200 pairs of strong coarse shoes, 100 pair of do. pantaloons, and 100 blankets." The mayor parted his hands. Though he would fill the requisition for the Texans as he had had to fill so many for Mexican armies, it could not be done instantly. The levy had to be apportioned among the citizens, who would patiently bring what they could afford.

All day the supplies piled up, and by nightfall were nearly complete, when it was found that teams and wagons to haul them had not yet been provided. Delivery to the Texan camp across the river must wait till tomorrow. The Texan commanders agreed, but inventing their own guarantee took Don Juan with them across the river. Tom Green assumed charge of him. He gave him a supper of mutton. It was a cold night. A "heartless norther" was blowing. Don Juan, said Green, was "a far more decent man than the majority of Mexican officials." To protect him against any temptation to escape, Green drolly thought of a milder restraint than chains. He took Don Juan under his blanket, and— mocking the episode later in the editorial first person plural—"gently placed one of his legs between ours, and though there was no community of language between us, yet we seemed to understand each other's motions, for when one turned over the other turned, we always maintaining his leg in the same affectionate position." When morning came Don Juan showed "a haggard countenance," and all day watched anxiously for the requisition train to appear. It did not appear, and at night "the norther continued to blow, and we again had the mutual honour of sleeping with each other in the same affectionate manner. . . . Don Juan, not knowing what the non-compliance of his order as to the provisions would bring about, grew still more restiff. His dreams were anything but pleasant, if we were to judge from his nervous excitability, and sleeping exclamations. . . ."

On Christmas Day the mayor's worries were given substance. A captured Mexican reported that the supply delivery had been halted by General Ampudia and General Canales, who had arrived at Mier with seven hundred troops and two fieldpieces. Five Texans who had been in the town were held prisoner. At their river camp the Texans held a council of war and all voted to attack the city. Green went to his

boats and found Don Juan asleep. He did not wake up until most of the
Texans had been ferried over the river a mile or two above the village
of Roma. He was astonished at the activity all about him, and asked
what it meant, and was told that his city was about to be invaded. In
the name of his wife and children he begged not to be carried into
battle. He was promised a position well in the rear. The crossing was
completed by four o'clock.

Shortly afterward gunfire was heard downstream. Scouts reported
that the Mexicans had taken up a position to prevent a lower river
crossing, had captured two Texans, and had retreated to the city. The
Texan main body pushed forward as twilight came. A mile from town
they met enemy pickets who fired and fled. By seven o'clock the winter
darkness brought a cold, drizzling rain that kept up all night. The
Texans moved to the crest of a meandering bluff that followed the left
bank of Alcantro Creek. Before them across the creek was the eastern
face of the town. The creek was about sixty feet wide, running rapidly
over stones with a watery roar that was all that could be heard, for the
town was quiet, and the Texans kept a hush. Scouts went out in the
rain to find a way down the bluff and over the creek. Above and below
the town there were easy fords. These were guarded by Mexicans, for
the scouts in the dark could hear the chime and creak of cavalry gear
when horses shook themselves. The crossing would have to be made
almost straight down the bluff and over the creek.

While their scouts threw a scattering of diversionary fire across
the regular fords, the bulk of the Texans keeping strict silence climbed
forty feet down the bluff, moved up the creek a little distance, and forded
it waist-high. During this movement Don Juan, the mayor, made his
escape. Coming up to the town they met a Mexican picket, opened fire,
and followed with a rush upon a steep street that led to the plaza. Mexican artillery was placed at the head of the street. The Texans fired upon
it, and took cover behind houses at a street intersection to reload. The
Mexicans replied with grapeshot, and pausing to reload in their turn,
were again fired upon by the Texans; and so the duel continued.

Mier was built of a river sandstone that weathered to a rich
brown. The houses, all one storey high, were contiguous in each block
of streets. At their street intersection the Texans forced entry to a corner
house, and once inside, found a crowbar with which they tore passage-
ways from room to room until they were only fifty yards from the plaza.
Breaking ports in the walls they bore their aim on the artillery and all
through the night kept up a harassing fire; and with dawn, when they

could see the artillerymen, they picked them off until the enemy field-pieces were silenced. Ampudia's soldiers then took to the housetops, threw themselves down on the flat roofs, and continued the battle against Texans who hugged walls and fired from behind windows and broke through roofs to level their "astonishing marksmanship."

Late in the morning the Texans looked across the creek and saw the eight men left in charge of the camp on the bluff receive a furious attack by first sixty, and then several hundred, Mexican cavalry. The camp guards fought well; but three were killed, including the son of Captain Henry Austin; three were taken prisoner, and the last two by supreme valor managed to run to join their comrades fighting in the town.

Many were wounded in the Texan main body, but Tom Green and others had the sense of moving close to victory, for the enemy fire slackened, and after one more furious charge, fell silent. In the charge Colonel Fisher was wounded in the right thumb. It seemed like a slight wound, but the shock to him was great, and he was seized with vomiting. Tom Green came to him and found him unable to exert his command. It was an awkward moment. Green was certain they were "in the midst of victory." He assumed command, and gave orders that would place the Texans for their final triumph. Just then a white flag was borne to them from the Mexican positions by one of the Texans captured shortly before on the Alcantro bluff—Dr. Sinnickson. The Texans were jubilant. Here was the white flag of surrender. Colonel Fisher received Dr. Sinnickson, who brought messages from General Ampudia.

But what he had to say was not at all what they expected to hear. Ampudia, far from surrendering, was offering the Texans a chance to surrender or be destroyed. If they should surrender, Ampudia promised that "they should be treated with all the honors and considerations of prisoners of war; that the Santa Fe prisoners should be treated so likewise"—there were several Santa Fe Pioneers present who had been released by Santa Anna the year before—"and that our men should not be sent to Mexico, but kept upon the frontier until an exchange or pacification were effected." Ampudia further assured them "that he had 1700 *regular* troops in the city, and 800 fresh troops near by from Monterrey, which would be up in a few minutes; that it was useless . . . to contend longer against such odds. . . ."

Most of the Texans were amazed to hear these terms repeated by Colonel Fisher. Some few officers and a number of men murmured that they should be accepted. Green stared at Fisher, who seemed seriously to consider making the surrender. Under cover of the truce the Mexicans infiltrated the Texan positions. Every moment was precious and Green pleaded for authority to renew the battle or at least to make a fighting retreat over the Rio Grande to safety. But Fisher, sickened by his wound, and shaken by thought of the losses that must come in fighting a way home, hesitated, spoke to the men, vouched for the honor of General Ampudia, and ended by taking Green with him to make the surrender. Green, miserable with rage, reflected upon the "effect of gunshot wounds upon the nerves, which, unlike those from the sword or knife, show a fall of countenance and a corresponding depression of spirits," and concluded bitterly that "in future the advice of a wounded commander should be received with great caution, if at all." In a short while, the Texan arms were laid down in the plaza, the men were herded into small stone rooms under guard, and General Jesús Cárdenas, the prefect of Tamaulipas, who had appeared in the city, wrote from Mier on December 26, 1842, to the mayor of Laredo—for the river towns were apprehensive—that "today at three o'clock in the afternoon the Texans surrendered after seventeen hours of continuous fighting . . . the only guarantee being that their lives would be spared."

For no sooner had the Texans given up than the Mexican commanders changed the terms of the capitulation. The guarantee that they would be treated as prisoners of war was left out of the written articles of surrender drawn up by General Ampudia. The Texans were apprehensive; and in the following days their bitterness had reason to grow. With only two hundred and sixty-one men in the battle, they had brought the enemy force of over two thousand to the moment of defeat—only to see it thrown away by their sick and frightened leader; for they heard from Texan prisoners who had been taken by Ampudia before the surrender that at the moment he sent out the truce flag, he and all his high command were ready to run away down the river road if the Texans refused his overture. The horses of the Mexican staff, saddled and ready, had been held waiting for flight at the south streets opening off the plaza. The Texans lost sixteen dead and about thirty badly wounded, while the Mexican losses were in excess of seven hundred. The victory had been wasted. Only the Texans left behind at the Rio Grande camp escaped: forty-two, warned by a good ruse of Tom Green's, marched for home.

The rest soon saw how the terms of capitulation were to be enacted. On the last day of December they were marched out on the Mexican river road toward Matamoros, with artillery leading and closing the column, and their files closed on the flanks by infantry with fixed bayonets and beyond these by cavalry. The weather was still bitter. The captives had lost their best blankets to the cavalry. One cold night they made little fires in camp, and when the flames died the men raked away the coals and laid themselves "in piles in the ashes" to keep warm. Their feet were raw. They were thirsty, having no canteens. The march was rapid, with few stops for water. As they entered the river towns— Camargo, Reynosa, Guadalupe—they were walked around the plazas to be exhibited like live trophies of a menagerie hunt, while bells rang, salvos were fired, fireworks were let off, and slogans of valor on strips of paper were pathetically shown by children—"Glory and gratitude to the brave Canales," "Eternal honor to the immortal Ampudia." In one town a company of naked painted Indians joined the jubilee, yelling, and firing blank charges into the faces of the prisoners. These were followed by a band of dancers—twenty little boys led by a tiny old man, "not larger than a boy of twelve," and all dressed in a profusion of colored scarves and ribbons, and wearing headdresses of small mirrors fastened to make obelisks. Shaking gourds filled with gravel, the dancers cut figures in time to music played by several marching violinists, "always keeping good time in step and motion," jigging first on one foot, then the other.

The Texans dismayed their masters with humorous commentary at times. One evening they were thrust into a cattle pen to spend the night in ankle-deep manure, and, treated like cattle, they "were determined to complete the character. They would get down upon their all-fours, bow their necks, paw up the dirt, and low like bulls." Another night corralled in a sheep pen, they "bleated more like sheep than any sheep in Mexico."

At Matamoros they were driven through streets under triumphal arches. It was, they observed, "the only American-built town" they saw in Mexico, with "many frame houses with shingled roofs . . . and built of combustible materials as most Southern towns in the United States." It was situated about half a mile from the Rio Grande, and thirty from its mouth, contained a population of about ten thousand, and was "the most defenceless city in Mexico." There they learned that despite General Ampudia's promise to the contrary, they were to be marched inland to Mexico City where—terrible thought—Santa Anna reigned. On January 14, 1843, in several detachments, the prisoners left the river for the interior, by way of Monterrey and Saltillo.

It was twenty months before those who survived saw Texas

again. Their story came across the river piecemeal. Much of it was
shocking, even beyond the conventional brutalities expected of certain
types of Mexican officers. Ordinary decent treatment was such a welcome
contrast that when it came Tom Green was invariably moved to compose a letter of courtly gratitude to the responsible official. He was just
as ready with stern letters of protest when—in repeated betrayal of the
prisoner-of-war agreement—the men were thrown into rooms so small
and airless that suffocation was a danger, or when they were badly fed
or not fed at all, or when at the caprice of a Mexican detachment commander they were all threatened with assassination. They went along
tied together by lariats, and plotted escape. A chance came at the
Hacienda Solado, a hundred miles beyond Saltillo. Led by Captain
Ewing Cameron, the Texans overpowered their guards one morning in
February, took their weapons and horses and dashed away for freedom,
leaving five dead and several wounded prisoners behind.

For two days they kept to the roads, heading for Monclova, France
Way and Texas; but afraid of being overtaken by soldiery, they turned
off the road into mountains to the west, hoping to find a secret way
across them to the open plains of Coahuila and finally the river. For
five days they struggled against rock and thirst and hunger. Always the
mountains opposed them. On the third day they were forced to kill their
horses for meat. Many of the men wept in the act. The party pushed
ahead on foot. Some fell behind dying of thirst and were left. The sun
was fierce by day, the thin mountain air bitter cold by night. Only a few
scraps of thorned plants grew amidst the unwatered rocks. Eating of
their puffy leaves, the men tasted fire, and drank worse, for in desperation
they drank their own urine and knew in consequence "a consuming
agony." Some scratched up cool earth from the shade of the bushes and
applied it to their bare bellies and throats for a second of relief. On the
fifth day they saw camp smoke and those who could went for it. It was
smoke from an army campfire. Excepting five who had died, four who
individually managed to escape homeward, and three who had vanished
never to be heard of again, all the prisoners were once again in the
hands of the Mexicans.

Driven back to the Hacienda Salado handcuffed in pairs, they
came under the touch of President Santa Anna, who had sent orders
that every tenth man was to be shot. One hundred and fifty-nine white
beans were placed in a small clay jug, and seventeen black beans were
added on top of those. The black beans meant death. The beans were not
stirred up. In a courtyard with high walls on which uniformed Mexican

dragoons in shakos and crossbelts stood guard, the prisoners were lined up to come two-by-two for their beans. Cameron, the leader of the escape, was told to draw first. "Well, boys," he said, "we have to draw, let's be at it." He drew. The first bean was white. He was spared. The prisoners shuffled up in turn. "Boys," said one, "this beats raffling all to pieces." Another remarked, "This is the tallest gambling scrape I ever was in." Drawing a black bean, another showed it to his fellows with a smile and declared, "Boys, I told you so; I never failed in my life to draw a prize." Another who drew black said lightly, "Well, they won't make much off me, anyhow, for I know I have killed twenty-five of the yellowbellies." He then asked for his dinner and smoked a cigar. A young man who drew a black bean said to the Mexican officer with the jug, "After the battle of San Jacinto, my family took in one of your prisoner youths, raised and educated him, and this is our requital." When the drawing was done, Captain Cameron, weeping bitterly, asked the Mexican officers to kill him and spare his fellows. The afternoon was failing. Those who drew death were roped together and taken to another courtyard beyond the high wall. Their comrades in the first courtyard could hear preparations, and then volleys, and dying groans, and then repeated shots—one prisoner had to be shot fifteen times before he died— and a scramble amidst the Mexican soldiery as one fainted at what he saw and as he fell was caught by the others. So evening came on March 25, 1843. In the morning the prisoners were once again placed briskly on the road to Mexico City. As they were marched out of the hacienda they saw the broken bodies of their friends scattered on the ground.

A month later they were near Mexico City when an order came from President Santa Anna to execute Captain Cameron, even though he had drawn a white bean. The execution was promptly carried out. In a sense, it was done as a courtesy to General Canales, who, having nursed a private grudge against Cameron since they had served together in the Rio Grande republican campaign of 1840, had requested it.

The Texans were assigned to various prisons—most of them to the formidable castle of Perote on the road to Veracruz. They heard that efforts were being made in behalf of their release by foreign governments—Britain and the United States. Their own government also made appeals for them; but they were embittered to hear that President Houston refused to accredit their invasion of Mexico as an official and authorized movement of the Texas army. ". . . They went without orders," he wrote, and "so far as that was concerned the government of Texas was not responsible, and the men were thereby placed out of the protection of the rules of war." Left at that, their situation would seem almost hopeless. But Houston went on to ask the British chargé d'affaires in Texas, who was negotiating as a neutral for the release of the prisoners, to plead a further point: ". . . The Mexican officers, by proposing terms of capitulation to the men, relieved them from the responsibility which they had incurred; and the moment the men surrendered in accordance with the proposals of capitulation, they became prisoners-of-war, and were entitled to all immunities as such. . . . Upon this view of the case, I base my hopes of their salvation, if it should be speedily presented, through the agency of her majesty's minister, to the Mexican government." The British and American ministers did what they could, an individual prisoner or two was released now and then, a daring escape from Perote was managed by Tom Green and some companions, but it was not until September 16, 1844, that all were finally set free by order of Santa Anna, who felt constrained to mercy while mourning his wife, recently dead.

Texas made only one more armed effort against Mexicans—another abortive one, commanded by Colonel Jacob Snively who led a company out on the north plains in the summer of 1843 to attack and rob a rich caravan out of Santa Fe which on its return trip from Saint Louis was accompanied by Governor Armijo in his amplitude. As a consequence of all the Texan incursions of the past three years, Santa Anna in August, 1843, closed the customs houses of the Rio Grande at Taos, El Paso and Presidio del Norte, ending the Santa Fe and Chihuahua trade from over the plains. But once again Mexico acting against the North Americans was too late; for events had moved into larger channels; diplomatic and political currents long agitated began to move fast and soon grew to flood, gathering to pour the great energies of the United States of North America across the plains toward the long Rio Grande shore of Mexico and Texas.

19.

Diplomacies

In 1843 political debate in the United States was sharpened over slavery, which promised to be a bitter issue in the coming presidential campaign of 1844. The abolitionists of the North made their strength felt throughout the nation; and the slaveholders of the South saw that only by the creation of new slaveholding states could their cherished feudal institution survive. Texas, with her system of slavery already established, would bring new strength to the Southern position; and proposals to annex Texas were again heard in Congress.

Now Texas became the object of rivalries between powerful European influences and the United States. England and France had already served Texas as mediators with Mexico. Fears and rumors in Washington gave color to incredible, and yet conceivable, possibilities—was Texas to become a British colony? would a French Bourbon prince govern a Texas pendant to France? President Houston seemed to favor annexation to the United States, if to any other power; but his republic had fared poorly in previous attempts to bring about American statehood; and in his second term he was willing to throw a scare into the Congress at Washington by accepting the good offices of Great Britain in diplomatic representations to Mexico. As a result of British services, an armistice between Mexico and Texas was at last after eight years of a state of war agreed to on June 15, 1843. Andrew Jackson wrote to Houston, "I see you are negotiating with Mexico, but be careful of the designing English." The press was full of alarms about the Texas-British intimacy, and Houston enjoyed it all, even assuring the British representative in Texas that in the midst of wild surmise in the newspapers, he was ". . . as cool as a shoemaker's lapstone in an open shop at Christmas. . . ."

His strategy of a European bias in diplomacy was successful in the United States, where annexation became a major battle cry in the gathering presidential campaign. Mexico was not deaf to the sound. Two days after the proclamation of the Texas armistice, Mexico issued a general statement of policy meant specifically for North Americans, reaffirming the old Mexican law that dealt with armed foreign intruders on Mexican soil. It did not matter whether any such foreigner "be accompanied in his enterprise by a few or by many adventurers . . . all such persons taken with arms in their hands shall be immediately put to death." This notice was reinforced by a note handed to the United States minister in Mexico saying that the Mexican government would consider any act of the American Congress to annex Texas a declaration of war against Mexico. Over the shoulder of Mexico gazed the British, and in the foreground, in newly found composure, reclined Texas, now for a brief interlude in a position to make her own choices among international partners.

These positions meant more than allegory. The political contenders in the United States suddenly saw that an issue more critical than slavery was now visible in the midst of all the turmoil over annexing Texas. The issue was whether Texas was to be allowed to come under the influence, and possibly even the dominion, of a foreign power—Great Britain. The Monroe Doctrine was seriously threatened by the possibility. The Southern slaveholders had an additional motive for fearing the encroachment of Britain, for if she gained control of Texas, avowedly she would put an end to slavery there. They redoubled their efforts to hasten annexation, while much of the hitherto immovable abolitionist strength that had resisted Texas-with-slavery came around to the view that the greater evil lay in permitting Europe to extend new colonial power to the Gulf of Mexico. As the campaign mounted in 1844, the fight was no less bitter over annexation and its terms, but the lines were more clearly drawn than before. The Democratic candidate, Mr. James K. Polk of Tennessee, was firmly in favor of annexation, and of denying the British claim to Oregon, which was also being agitated at the time.

As the campaign mounted in 1844 the Whigs held their national convention first. They nominated Henry Clay, and in their platform they failed to take notice of the leading issue before the people—annexation. A month later the Democratic party convened and concluded its platform with the statement that "the re-occupation of Oregon and the re-annexation of Texas are great American measures, which this Convention recommends to the cordial support of the Democracy of the Union." It was a realistic sounding of the public sentiment, which was expressed pungently in another way by General Andrew Jackson who in retirement had not lost his gift for reading the popular temper: ". . . You might as well, it appears to me, attempt to turn the current of the Mississippi, as to turn the democracy from the annexation of Texas." There was a clear choice before the American people, to be made by torchlight as the campaign summer went by, while Mexico was treated to the pleasure of watching the North Americans choose their president on the basis of annexing some two hundred and forty thousand square miles of what she still considered to be Mexican territory.

At one moment the matter seemed close to settlement even before the election. A treaty between Texas and the United States was signed on the executive level on April 12, 1844, granting Texas the status of a territory of the United States, with all the defense measures that might be necessary under that condition. But the Senate failed to ratify the treaty ten days later, the Texan Congress took no action on it, and the moment of decision passed. The vote in the presidential election would after all determine the outcome. General Jackson wrote to President Houston, "The rejection of the treaty filled me with regret; but the effect of this movement brings the subject directly to the attention of the people; and we shall, in the course of a few months, be enabled to understand what their verdict will be." President Houston replied, "It is now the duty of the United States to make an advance that can not be equivocal in its character; and when she opens the door, and removes all impediments, it might be well for Texas to accept the invitation."

For Texas needed help. The Mexican armistice had run its course without the achievement of peace. True, a peace conference had been held at Salinas on the Rio Grande near Laredo by commissioners of Mexico and Texas; but when its conclusions were presented to President Houston he refused to sign the treaty because in it Texas was described as "a department of Mexico." The nominal courtesies of the armistice were cancelled, and in June the central Mexican government instructed General Woll in north Mexico to resume any necessary acts of war against Texas. The Rio Grande was made a boundary in an odd new way, a line across which Texans were dared to step. If one did so, to the distance of a league south of the river, he was to be found guilty at a summary court-martial and shot. He was not to try to run away, either, for if he were "rash enough to fly at the sight of any force belonging to the Supreme Government," he was to be chased until he fell dead or was captured to be killed. A few days later General Woll dispatched to President Houston a formal declaration of war, and news came out of Mexico all summer of how armies were being trained for a new invasion of Texas. This was plainly to be Santa Anna's reply to the open agitation in the United States for annexation. With so much strength behind it, the movement seemed too powerful for Britain and France to oppose with further colonial plans for Texas. Though still cordial, they offered no strength to Texas in her decisive year.

Meanwhile in the United States sentiment ran high. It was made more acute by the publication of George Wilkins Kendall's *Narrative of the Texan Santa Fe Expedition,* which told a large public for the first time what Mexicans had done to North Americans in that scrape. As election neared, with internal struggles in the major parties, the issues were compounded—slavery and abolition, free trade and protection, the "Know-Nothing" movement, Oregon, and again the Bank of the United States—but dominating these was the issue of statehood for Texas on which the Democrats campaigned. As the campaign proceeded, Henry Clay also spoke up for annexation if Texas could be acquired "without dishonor, without war, with the common consent of the Union, and upon just and fair terms." But when he said further that slavery was not an issue in the annexation debate he lost the votes of the Liberty Party in New York State, and in consequence Polk was elected in November. The voters knew that "the election of Mr. Polk means that Texas will be annexed to the United States," as a Whig politician and editor put it.

Texans understood the same thing, and General Houston, now succeeded in the presidency by his secretary of state Anson Jones, saw that his hopes of many years must be fulfilled with the union of his second country to his first. In the early weeks of 1845 the press and public made annexation its own passionate topic while Congress debated. The Free-Soilers spent their last efforts to prevent so vast a new slave territory as Texas from entering the union and securing the Southern dominance in Congress—for one of the provisions of annexation was to be that Texas could divide itself into five states at her pleasure—and the annexationists rang every change possible on the theme of the Monroe Doctrine. But the Democrats had a Congressional majority safe in hand, and the matter moved toward the vote in Congress, while in Mexico Santa Anna was dethroned and banished into exile, and the new government under José Joaquín Herrera proposed to recognize the independence of Texas at last, in a desperate trial at winning Texas away from the United States. It was late. On February 25, 1845, the House of Representatives at Washington voted the resolution offering statehood to Texas, and on March first the Senate passed it. President John Tyler, about to leave office, signed it the same day, and the invitation to union was transmitted to Texas on March third. On the following day Polk was inaugurated, ready to face the implications of the major plank in his platform.

At the end of March, Mexico broke off diplomatic relations with the United States, and in May passed a law declaring peace with Texas, on a basis of Texan independence. A treaty was drawn up in discussion with the Texan Secretary of State that was to be offered to the people of independent Texas for their ratification. England and France again figured as the mediators. But Mexico was too late, and for the last time. Texas sentiment for annexation was so strong that when the Mexican treaty was submitted to the Texan Senate in June, a scandal resulted. The Texan Secretary of State was twice burned in effigy and, under a rain of abuse for having treated with Mexico in opposition to the spirit of annexation, fled the republic for Europe. On July fourth, a convention called by President Jones met at Washington on the Brazos to discuss the invitation from the United States and the Mexican treaty. The treaty was ignored, and with only one delegate dissenting, the convention recommended to the citizens of Texas that the invitation to statehood should be accepted.

On the same day certain cautionary army and navy orders went out from Washington on the Potomac. If, as she had promised to do in the event of annexation, Mexico should declare war against the United States and try to hold Texas, then Texas must be defended, like any other United States possession. General Zachary Taylor was at Fort Jesup, Louisiana, with United States troops. He was ordered to take his force to Corpus Christi on the Gulf Coast and establish a base from which the land defense of Texas might be managed. Commodore David Conner was ordered to patrol the Gulf ports of Mexico with the United States Home Squadron. By the end of the month Taylor was landing his soldiers over the difficult bar before Corpus Christi.

His mission was nonaggressive. His men had plenty of time to satisfy their curiosity about the new land. A soldier rode a mustang for the first time—"the animal was lively and frisky enough, but a mere rat compared with our northern horses." Many men traded for mustangs to use on pleasure rides over the flat coastal country. An odd thing happened to the mustangs during a horse trade. "The best look as if they had lost all the fire they possessed in a state of nature. Their look is one of regret. . . ." There was curiosity, too, about the putative enemy. Late in the summer a Mexican spying for the American service returned from Matamoros, a hundred and fifty miles distant on the Rio Grande, with a report that gave relief, and yet too a tinge of disappointment. "He

reports no warlike preparations, and that the two thousand men at
Matamoros have again dwindled to five hundred. He says the people in
that vicinity are opposed to the war."

On October thirteenth, in a general election, the people of Texas
voted all but unanimously to ratify the annexation resolution, and
adopted their new state constitution. Among the provisions for annexation made by Congress was this one: "Questions of boundaries with
other nations are to be adjusted by the United States." Texas was
relieved of making good her claim, now, to the Rio Grande. Having
brought the claim with her into the Union, she laid it at the feet of the
United States.

President Polk had made earnest diplomatic proposals to Mexico
that any dispute over Texas be composed through peaceful negotiation,
and on October fifteenth came a change in the sentiment of the Mexican
government. President Herrera agreed to receive a United States diplomatic representative on condition that Commodore Conner withdraw
his forces from the waters off Veracruz. Conner withdrew immediately,
and on November tenth, John Slidell was appointed as the United States
envoy extraordinary. He arrived at Veracruz on the last day of the
month. He was instructed to offer Mexico these terms: for a boundary
following the Rio Grande from its mouth to El Paso, and from there
due west, taking in the present areas of California, New Mexico, Arizona,
Nevada and Utah, the United States would pay twenty-five million dollars
(though President Polk declared himself "ready to pay forty millions for
it"); and in addition, if Mexico would recognize the Texas boundary
claim of the whole Rio Grande from mouth to source, the United States
would assume the debt of paying all claims of her citizens against Mexico,
to be calculated at a minimum of two million dollars.

Slidell set out for the capital only to encounter the afterthoughts
of President Herrera, who had discovered that his agreement to negotiate
with the United States was violently opposed by a new revolutionary
party in Mexico. Herrera fought a delaying action of excuses—Slidell was
not properly accredited; Slidell was coming as a "minister," which
implied that annexation was already recognized by Mexico, and Mexico
could receive him only as a "commissioner"; it was not proper for
Mexico to hear any Texas matters from anyone but the Texan government; and under these conditions, Slidell could not be received by the
President of Mexico. The American minister sent word of his rebuff
to Washington and lingered in Mexico hoping to persuade the government to receive his credentials. By the end of December he had a new

Mexican president to deal with—General Mariano Paredes y Arillaga, for Herrera had been overthrown because of his conciliatory attitude toward the Americans. Paredes took office on January 4, 1846, as leader of the war party. He declared an aggressive policy—Santa Anna's old claim to Texas all the way to the Sabine at Louisiana; and he promised to defend it. On January twelfth when Polk received Slidell's message of an impasse, he saw that despite repeated efforts to negotiate, war had come closer. On the next day he sent orders through Secretary of War Marcy to General Taylor at Corpus Christi to march for the Rio Grande.

It was a wet winter on the Gulf Coast. The American troops were delighted when a new indoor diversion was ready for them—an army theatre built in Corpus Christi, "a capital building," according to a soldier, "capable of seating some eight hundred persons. The scenes were painted by officers of the army. A very clever company was engaged, and many an otherwise dreary evening was spent by many of us with infinite pleasure within its walls." Taylor received Polk's new orders on February third; but he could not immediately execute them, for the whole coastal plain was a mire, and before he could move wagons, ordnance and columns of troops, he must know more about marching conditions. On February ninth he sent out an experimental wagon train to make a test of travel in wet weather. By the sixteenth he had his report, and could plan the movement. In the state capital of Texas, on that day, the flag of the single star was hauled down and in its place rose the colors of the United States, to complete the official annexation.

While Taylor's officers and men went about preparing for the southward march along the coast, there were opposing views among them about the task they were sent to do. Though they knew that the General was to "avoid any acts of aggression" against Mexican forces across the river "unless an actual state of war should exist," many believed that the United States had stung Mexico into defense of her rightful possessions. They saw that between the Nueces and the Rio Grande there was nothing but unsettled wilderness and that, as a soldier said, "so far as actual occupation was concerned, the Texan claim was tenuous indeed." Lieutenant U. S. Grant thought the armed march to Mexico was "unholy." He "had a horror of the Mexican War," but lacked "moral courage enough to resign." One of Taylor's regimental commanders recorded similar views. "As to the right of this movement, I have said from the first that the United States are the aggressors. We have outraged the Mexican government by an arrogance and presumption that deserve to be punished. For ten years we have been encroaching on Mexico and insulting her. . . ." A Pennsylvania lieutenant wrote, "How unjust! The march to the banks of the Rio Grande was, of itself, an act of hostility," and the United States behind a posture of solemn virtue goaded Mexico to assume "the odium of beginning the war." Such views were not mollified even by Taylor's orders, echoing instructions from Polk, that required all personnel "to observe with the most serious respect the rights of all the inhabitants who may be found in peaceful prosecution of their respective occupations. Under no pretext nor in any way will any interference be allowed with the civil rights or religious principles of the inhabitants. . . . Whatever may be needed for the use of the army will be bought . . . at the highest prices."

Not all, or even most, of the army had doubts about their duty. What they had heard of Mexico's actions—the inhumanities of Santa Anna, Armijo, and their imitators heaped upon Anglo-Texan and American prisoners—and what they began to learn of Mexican life as they neared the border gave them strong motives, beyond their sworn duty, for the job ahead. Rumors reached the army that nothern Mexico was again in a revolutionary temper. "No lover of freedom can refrain from shedding tears to witness the deplorable, degraded state into which the poor Mexican is cast. It is in the natural course of things that, sooner or later, the northern states will declare themselves independent." It was the old vision of the Republic of the Rio Grande, or of the Sierra Madre, that loomed again. A north Mexican emissary even rode into Taylor's camp to persuade him to hold back his advance and give the northern federalists one more chance to declare their independence, elect a governor— General Arista was mentioned—and spare the new republic the hazards of being a battleground between Mexico and the United States. "Not many years hence," added an American officer, "there may be another state still further west [than Texas] begging to be annexed. . . ." As for the immediate justification of the American occupation, "In annexing Texas to the union," he concluded, "we were bound to take her as she was . . . Texas with her prescribed limits. She claimed to the Rio Grande."

Finally, another, and coolheaded, American who had known the whole story through his own experience as a Missouri trader in two decades, disposed of his own qualms in a majestic period: ". . . Though when the subject was first agitated, I had my misgivings as to the consequences and policy, and I also thought the rights of Mexico should be to some degree respected, the discussion of the matter has dissipated the first difficulty, and the deportment of Mexico the second."

20.

The United States to the River

"We are off for the Rio Grande!" wrote an American diarist on March 8, 1846.

The diplomacy was done with, the high policy was released into action, the national energy was beginning to pour out, and the reality of the experience came into the scale of men who embodied it individually. If the stakes were continental, the terms, in the long columns that struggled through the bare country, were personal. The soldiers saw, felt, gave, endured and suffered. Much was new and strange; much—at times—beautiful; and they were moved to know in their personal experience what the nations more abstractedly opposed to one another.

The sober tenacity of Stephen Austin, the tormented loyalties of the early Anglo-Texans, the wild self-regard of the trapper, the organized and systematic ways of the Missouri trader, the physical power that served Texans ready to die for freedom or adventure—all these prophetic American qualities taken together seemed stronger than their sum; suggested destiny; and now approached their larger fulfillment as the Army of the United States every day drew nearer to the disputed border.

After the heavy rains the land was already dry. Water holes were sometimes a day's march apart. Prairie grass, recently burned off, left a quilt of black ashes through which the army marched, and the ashes rose and lodged on the soldiers' faces and made them "resemble Africans." But they were equal to all annoyances. They endured all, as Lieutenant Grant saw, "without a murmur," and another officer remarked that "there is a 'physique' and 'morale' about our 'little army' of which they never dreamed; well clad, well fed, and well armed; moving forward with an enthusiasm and 'sangfroid' which carries victory in their face. I feel more and more convinced that we can successfully contend with an immensely superior force."

There were things to stare at on the way—one day "a mustang taking it into his head to be a little restive, relieved himself of his load, a demure-looking campwoman." And there were sights to delight the eye. After the heavy rains of winter and early spring, the Gulf lands were bright with an illimitable reach of wildflowers. ". . . The flowers during today's march were gloriously rich; conspicuous above all were the Texan plume, a beautiful scarlet flower, the Mexican poppy, and the indigo. . . ." The very air in the Texas spring was wonderful. "I do not think I have ever felt a sweeter or fresher morning," wrote a soldier on March twenty-fourth. "The morning star and moon were about setting; the former, even as day broke, looked like a diamond set in the clear, blue sky. . . . We marched through a wilderness of mesquite and acacia thickets, fragrant with the blossom of the latter; the grass was rich; the peavine, with bits of delicate blossom, abundant. . . . The air from the sea was delightful, and everything in nature appeared so happy that it was perfectly exhilarating." The thickets were alive with singing birds. One day a mirage in the distance made the prairie look on fire; and once past the belt of mesquite thickets, they saw open prairie, with no trees, reaching all the way to the hazy Gulf. The nearer they came to the river the faster flew rumors that a battle awaited them; but still there were pleasures of the country to record. The country "was really beautiful; such grazing was never seen before. The ground appeared alive with quail, and every waterhole turned out its flock of ducks. As you approach the river chaparral increased in density. The soil is very rich. . . . The country is perfectly level, and the roads are in capital order. . . ." They had not seen a single habitation since leaving Corpus Christi.

As the army marched along the coast, a fleet of supply ships steamed down the Gulf toward Point Isabel, a little port nine miles up the coast from the Rio Grande, in a harbor formed by reaches of low land divided by a narrow entrance from the sea, called Los Brazos de Santiago—the Arms of Saint James. Here General Taylor intended to establish his base of supplies. Point Isabel, though in Texas territory, was used by Mexicans as a port of entry. Sea traffic put in there to unload cargo that was taken overland to the Rio Grande, in preference to anchoring off the mouth of the river and taking cargo inland over the far-reaching shallows by lighter. As General Taylor approached Mexico, two hundred and fifty Mexican troops of artillery and infantry, commanded by General García, defended Point Isabel, and its customs house, and the private trade in bribes that comfortably sustained the captain of the port, a certain Señor Rodríguez, who ruled over fifty or sixty residents in their shacks of twined reeds, timber from wrecked ships, and grass thatching. The customs house, though the largest, was "a miserable hovel."

On March twenty-fifth Captain Rodríguez saw stands of smoke far out above the Gulf approaches to the Arms of Saint James. In a rage, he concluded that these announced the vessels of the United States. A handful of his residents went inland to meet the army. Point Isabel was bracketed from sea and land. Saying good-bye to his little monopoly, Captain Rodríguez set fire to the customs house and as many other huts as possible, and with General García and the Mexican troops, ran away down the beach to Boca Chica, at the mouth of the Rio Grande.

Looked at again, the American ships were standing in closer; and almost on the heels of the port captain, General Taylor arrived with his cavalry and his wagons. Soldiers went to work putting out what fires they could, saving a few of the sea-grass houses. The General saw that his base was well-chosen, for in that low, level sea land, Point Isabel stood up, a bluff about twenty feet high, and made a prow out into the bay, commanding all approaches, and giving a clear view southward toward the Rio Grande. Sail now showed under the sea-borne smoke, and three hours after the General's arrival, the fleet entered the Arms, escorted by two brigs-of-war and a cutter—though with trouble. A high wind was blowing, the passage was unfamiliar, the *Monmouth* went aground and the *Neva*, fighting strong currents of air and sea with extra steam pressure, blew a hole in her boiler. But supplies came off at once, including four eighteen-pounders. The life line for the army was established, and two days later General Taylor, leaving a garrison, resumed the march with full wagons to join the bulk of the army that was camped waiting for him in a wide meadow edged by ridges of chaparral and mesquite that in flat land showed high, and gave its name, Palo Alto, to the place. It lay about halfway between Point Isabel and Matamoros, eighteen miles apart by road. With the return of the General and his detachment, the army was reunited in bulk, and pushed ahead immediately to the south. A few miles farther on they passed through an old dry lagoon edged with palms where the river had once run. It was called the Resaca de la Palma. They were stirred by rumors that four thousand Mexicans would cross the Rio Grande on the morrow and give battle.

And at last, late in the morning of March 28, 1846, the Americans came to the river. They saw its shallow brown waters forever taking the wide bend around the town of Matamoros, and there across the stream were two hundred people to return the stares of the American army, and in the town a Mexican army band marched and played, as sentries were disposed on both banks. After noon, and with first bivouac duties done, a number of young American officers eased their way down the north bank of the river and throwing off their uniforms went into the water to bathe. Across the river they were seen by a group of Mexican girls. In a few minutes with light laughter the girls came down to the water on the opposite bank and entered into it in their turn. The young men and women called to each other; and in answer both moved forward. Shining with water and sunlight the hard white and the soft earthen bodies approached to meet in midstream. Suddenly the rifles of the Mexican sentries took aim at the young men. The American soldiers kissed their hands at the Mexican girls and returned to their proper riverside. The allegory of life seeking itself through love before battle was broken and scattered; and other furies long gathering awaited release on the Rio Grande.

BOOK FOUR

The United States Rio Grande

I.

"*Way, You Rio*"

"GOOD-BYE. COME BACK A MAN," said an Indiana father to his son, a volunteer for the Rio Grande in 1846. The young man "gave him a shower of tears" and left for the war. It was the nation asking for fulfillment of the first significant task of its early maturity. The national policy on the river was at the start in the hands of the regular army—Taylor's three brigades, that represented only a small segment of the American people, and even included representatives of foreign populations. But it would not be long until, through expansion of the army by volunteers, the whole people would feel the war that was fought in their name. On town hall and courthouse the recruiting notices would soon be tacked up, and soon gaunt little coaches connected by swaying chains behind stovelike locomotives would haul volunteer companies to concentration points, and regiments would go down the wide tributaries on scroll-sawed steamboats to the Mississippi that led to the Gulf. Out of the eastern harbors already sailed other transports and supply ships under raked masts and tall funnels, to the tune of a capstan song:

> Oh, say, were you ever in the Rio Grande?
> Way, you Rio.
> It's there that the river runs down golden sand.
> For we're bound to the Rio Grande.

>   And away, you Rio!
>   Way, you Rio!
>   Sing fare you well,
>   My pretty young girls,
>   For we're bound to the Rio Grande!

The electric telegraph did not yet touch across Texas. News by fastest Army courier took two weeks to come from the river to Washington, and mails by steamer were even slower, and most newspapers came out only once a week. The families at home could only repose their confidence in what lay behind the whole people who had already turned to the west in so many other enterprises. The move to Mexico was full of anxiety; met with unpopularity in various quarters of the nation; and, from a certain political view, violated international morality. But its general direction seemed natural, for on an official and national scale it was but one more step in the westward march hitherto taken by individuals, and families, and business associates, and private communities. There was no surprise in its sudden call upon the country to go to the West and Southwest with the largest home army assembled since General Washington's. What had William Becknell printed in a Missouri newspaper so long ago as 1821? Calling for men to join him in a plains trading expedition after horses and mules, he had without intending eloquence or a heroic tone simply announced men "destined to the westward." Whether he meant immediate destination or large destiny, the effect was the same, and his countrymen after him showed no more uncertainty than he.

> Oh, New York town is no place for me—
> Way, you Rio!
> I'll pack up my bag and go to sea.
> For we're bound to the Rio Grande!
>
> And away, you Rio,
> Way, you Rio! . . .

Even if almost nothing was known about far Texas, and Mexico, and the problems waiting in distance, climate and the Mexican nature, the United States was confident as the war opened that it would be a short one.

> We'll sell our salt cod for molasses and rum—
> Way, you Rio!
> And get home again 'fore Thanksgiving has come.
> For we're bound to the Rio Grande!
>
> And away, you Rio! . . .

General Taylor's army on the north bank of the Rio Grande in March, 1846, represented the third of the three great peoples who came to the river. The American soldiers, taken together, were prophets of a time to come. The collective prophecy they carried was not plain to all its carriers, but it stirred in them like their own seed, and sow it they must. Its nature could be read from fragments out of the ancestries of idea, issue, motive and way of life that had created them in a society new to the world—a society formed around a central passion: the freedom and equality of democratic man. A taste of this—the American theme—had already come near to the river with the Texan settlers in the south, and the trappers and traders in the north; but now once again change, coming with a final sovereignty, was about to make its way along the whole river with an energy and a complexity unknown in the earlier societies of the Indian, the Spaniard and the Mexican.

2.

Collective Prophecy

i. new man and new principles

Until 1846 it was the frontier people from the United States who had made new life in the Far West. In that year the whole nation began to take part, through the national army, in the life of the West, which was tied to all the United States by longing, and letters, and hope. But what had made the frontiersmen had also made their successors; and out of the past of the seventy-year-old nation, and of the impulses—some of them as old as the great ages of Mediterranean life—that had created it, marched the Americans, who with all their differences showed common traits and beliefs that seemed to the rest of the world like the marks of a new order of associated men. In America, ideally, a man was an individual not merely to himself, but to all his fellows, under restraints and aids agreed upon by all, in the interest of each.

The settlement of eastern North America was not an expression of the parent state, like the colonial acts of Spain in Mexico first done eighty-eight years before the founding of Virginia. It came as a movement of various individuals and minorities out of England, the Netherlands, the German States and France who even under crown charters and with various motives—religious, commercial and adventurous—soon revealed if they did not first proclaim that their essential desire was for self-government, under a system of social equality. When this desire came plain in the various scattered colonies of the eastern seaboard, even with their differing localisms it seemed to draw them together to reinforce one another in their essential drive for realized individualism for their people. For whatever reason, they had all come to feel in the old world that they had reached the limits of their hopes for growth, freedom and self-expression. To attain these they proved themselves willing to take great risks and undertake great labors. They were plants turning toward the light and space of a new Eden. Cotton Mather said "the whole earth is the Lord's garden—why should men not tend its empty places?" The idea of liberty separated the early settlers from other people in European societies. Were there two kinds of men—those who feared liberty, and those who held it above earthly authority?

They who left "all the pleasant accommodations of their native country" to pass over "a terrible *ocean,* into a more terrible *desart*" in search of freedom under God brought an energy that was more powerful than any already established in the New World. The Indian society had always been arrested in an anonymous communal arrangement by the absence of the idea of the individual. The Spanish society was built on an inertia which allowed the high cultivation of the individual yet denied it any expression that was not in harmony with the prevailing official position of the state. Now imagining new experience until it occurred, the American settlers brought a frame of life in which the individual was not only permitted but obliged to create himself socially. The forces that obliged him so were the unexampled frontier environment, the swift emergence of a self-made culture, the extension of democratic doctrine, and the joyful sanction of anyone who grew to his own individualism, comely or rude. A poetry of action was inherent in all such obligational forces; and it both contained and exposed a mighty volume of spiritual strength.

That strength was great enough to bring the colonies together to make a new nation, and to survive the terrible hazards of the struggle to design a government for all citizens that would not destroy the essential freedom of each. That this was achieved, and swiftly, as the lives of nations were reckoned, was a matter of fame. European observers came among the Americans, to live their life, and record what they examined, and return with a book manuscript to Europe.

"The happy and the powerful," remarked one thinking about the occasion of the colonies, "do not go into exile, and there are no surer guarantees of equality among men than poverty and misfortune." And another seeing in his mind's eye the migration over the ocean, reflected of the Americans that "everything has tended to regenerate them: new laws, a new mode of living, a new social system. Here they are become men. In Europe they were so many useless plants, wanting vegetative mold and refreshing showers. They withered; and were mowed down by want, hunger, and war. . . . The American is a new man, who acts upon new principles. . . ."

When before had a new land and a new idea of man been brought together in their newness? Even the vast soil of America in its primeval bounty and beauty and untouchedness seemed ordained—"in this state it is offered to man," observed Tocqueville; man who was "not barbarous, ignorant and isolated, as he was in the early ages, but already in possession of the most important secrets of nature, united to his fellow men, and instructed by the experience of fifty centuries. . . ." He saw that in older migrations—say, at the fall of Rome—peoples scattering for new places carried with them destruction and death; while in America, each settler brought "the elements of prosperity and life." They knew full well the nature, and the might, of their achievement. They paid reverence to one of its humblest symbols, and moved Tocqueville as they did so. It was Plymouth Rock. "Here," he said, "is a stone which the feet of a few poor fugitives pressed for an instant, and this stone becomes famous; it is treasured by a great nation, a fragment is prized as a relic. But what," he asked, remembering Europe and its symbols, "what has become of the doorsteps of a thousand palaces? Who troubles himself about them?"

It was not to build palaces or make vast conquests that the Americans went to work on their new lands. Tocqueville saw that all they then wanted to do was to add a few yards of land to a farm, put out an orchard, build a room or two—and always to make life easier. He marvelled at how hard they worked to gain such ends—what "feverish ardor" and "avidity" they spent to improve their material circumstances. Indeed, there was a danger in their zeal, their "vague dread . . . lest they should not have chosen the shortest path" that might lead to their own welfare: for such a pursuit might "at last shut out the rest of the world," and even come between "itself and heaven." This was a meditation for a philosopher; it did not deter later emigrants from Europe.

For in swelling numbers they came to the American coast, and established themselves for hire, so freeing countless American-born citizens for their plunge into the interior of the continent. This "double migration was incessant," wrote Tocqueville. "It begins in the middle of Europe, it crosses the Atlantic Ocean, and it advances over the solitudes of the New World. Millions of men are marching at once toward the same horizon; their language, religion, manners, differ; their object is the same. Fortune has been promised to them somewhere in the West, and to the West they go to find it. . . ."

For in the early nineteenth century the American West was already the world's marvel. With the Louisiana Purchase Jefferson had committed the nation to a continental reach. But more, in his whole concept of democracy he had opened political frontiers in the thoughts of men that only the West, in its sheer space, could contain. "In early youth," said a pioneer toward the end of his days, "we removed to and settled in a country universally known over the continent as the 'Great West'. . . . Towns, steamboats, post offices and children were named 'Far West' in honor of that wonderful country. . . ." It was there for the taking. After 1820 land was to be bought from the government for $1.25 an acre. In most American families, as well as in the newer arrivals from oversea, the memory was still keen of how the old-world society was based on great landlords and their holdings. Space was narrow in Europe. Hierarchies and classes constricted men in fixed places into which they had been born. Who could simply go forth anywhere in Europe and take land to make a new life for himself out of it? And even if land were so available, how little of it was there at best, compared to what lay between the Alleghenies and the Rockies, and beyond. . . .

In their constant search for better, easier ways of life, the Americans as they moved on westward repudiated one past after another—that of Europe, that of the Atlantic coast, that of their first inland settlements. A Frenchman at the end of the eighteenth century saw this as "complete proof of the American indifference to love and friendship and of failure to form attachments to anything. . . ." The American abandoned, "without reluctance, the place where he first drew breath, the church in which he first perceived the idea of a supreme being, the tombs of his ancestors, the friends of his infancy, the companions of his youth, and all the pleasures of his society"—all for land, new land. If this was a desire deep in the individual, it must reappear as an element in the national character; and it was seen by some as a driving force behind the march of General Taylor's army to the river. Abraham Lincoln, who opposed the Mexican War, supported his point with a joke about an Illinois farmer who said, "I ain't greedy about land. I only want what jines mine." That farmer's self-pardoning greed suggested the temperament of some of the earliest settlers to cross the Alleghenies, who struck Tocqueville as "only an agglomeration of adventurers and speculators . . . we are amazed at the persons [there] invested with authority," and he asked how from such settlers could a proper life be made to grow.

But such pioneers were not for long alone on the frontier. Others—all kinds—kept coming; and among the adventurers who pushed out beyond the settlements were various Europeans of high degree who appeared to view the West as a great park where they might hunt, and explore, and record marvels new to the inquiring and cultivated intelligence. There were German princes with grand suites and striped canvas pavilions and personal physicians; British sportsmen elaborately armed and staffed with frontier scouts; and hired artists who sketched and painted for their noble patrons the Indians, the game, and the landscapes of the prairies and the Rocky Mountains. They took away with them after their grand tours a body of information to be published or exhibited abroad; while the settlers remained to enact the freedom they had designed for themselves.

As each succeeding frontier was settled, it was resolved into the form of a state government; and its most significant act was to give form to the convictions of liberty for which it had been populated. The new states spread their energy and influence not only westward, but eastward; for their new constitutions popularly adopted universal manhood suffrage, and under their example the old Atlantic states were required by their people to set aside religious and property qualifications for the vote and in their turn to adopt universal manhood suffrage also. The same impulse that thrust individual Americans westward returned a fuller democracy to the states they had left behind them.

But if liberty was not a new idea in mankind, then it was new to equate it with comparative solitude. The Americans brought distance with them as a virtue, dragging it along to separate them from their fellows, in an endless appetite for freedom. In Louisiana Audubon came upon the wilderness cabin of a Connecticut family. When he asked why they had moved to such a "wild and solitary spot," the husband replied, "The people are growing too numerous now to thrive in New England." The very nation was founded on the concept of the integrity and self-sufficiency of the individual. The frontier attitude was perhaps a caricature of this—its lines all too black, its features too coarse, its sentiments rising in balloons of comment too fiercely rude, and its shading too rough in its crosshatching; but, like many a wood-engraved political cartoon of the period, it was true in its essential quality. Freedom meant not only independence of spirit and belief; it meant also a chance to dominate the material environment. This was new in North America, where before the environment had dominated the Indian and the Spaniard.

Passing over the eastern mountains, taking the rivers if they flowed west or southwest, and coming to the forest frontier, the settlers took down trees if necessary to let their road go on. Almost at once organized communication followed them. The mail travelled by small cart, in a green darkness by day, and by night through firelight cast all about by torches of pine cut and held by the driver. Every so often the cart reached a hut in the woods. This was the post office. There, a bundle of letters was thrown off, the cart galloped on and, when they could, the forest settlers came from their hidden cabins to leaf through the folded, sealed papers for their mail. The cart now and then carried a passenger. One of them marvelled at signs of how fast and how soon settlers had deserted their recent clearings and cabins as they moved westward to look once more for a better life. And soon, too, the woods took back what they had lost to the clearings. The post traveller would come upon a little opening of light through the green density and there see a chimney in the woods, standing alone above its blackened hearth; or the remains of a cabin whose logs were sprouting anew, while vines and flowers hung like veils from the corner uprights, making a bower. The only sounds to be heard in the high green aisles were dove song and woodpecker drillings. The traveller asked himself if ruins, then, were already there; and like many who came after him, he tried to recreate in his mind the character of the men to whom the woods had allowed passage, only to spring up behind them as they went.

The Americans were

> "Those that look carelessly in the faces
> of Presidents and governors, as to say,
> *Who are you?,*

> Those of earth-born passion, simple,
> never constrain'd, never obedient,
>
> Those of inland America,"

sang Walt Whitman. The people, he said, were "ungrammatical, untidy, and their sins gaunt and ill-bred," and yet they had "measureless wealth of latent power and capacity, their vast, artistic contrasts of lights and shades, with . . . entire reliability in emergencies, and a certain breadth of historic grandeur, of peace or war . . . the peaceablest and most good-natured race in the world, and the most personally independent and intelligent. . . . Grand, common stock! to me the accomplish'd and convincing growth, prophetic of the future; proof undeniable to sharpest sense, of perfect beauty, tenderness and pluck. . . ."

From the first, the frontiersman saw himself as a new breed of cat, and behaved accordingly, in cutting himself off from the past. Whenever he saw that he was regarded as rude and coarse, he at once acted more coarsely and rudely. He jeered at any of his fellows who echoed the manners and tastes of the East, or of England. His patriotism was deep and true, but he pounded Eastern or foreign visitors into exhaustion with his defiant assertions of it. Yankee Doodle was a figure in a piercing little song, but he was more. He was a reality who made actual appearances among frontier crowds, when some fellow felt like dressing up in striped trousers, a blue tail coat and a tall beaver hat, to remind himself and all others of what an American looked like. He was regarded without surprise or question. Any man had a sanction for oddity. Audubon saw a man in New Orleans on the levee wearing a flop-brimmed hat, a bright green coat, wide yellow nankeen pants, a pink vest, and a frilled shirt. In his shirt was a bunch of magnolias from which the head of a live baby alligator swung to and fro. He carried a loud silk umbrella with one hand, and with the other a cage of brightly feathered birds. Stalking grandly, he was singing "My love is but a lassie yet" in a Scottish dialect; but when he talked, his speech was native American. He was a one-man drama, and his right to create a spectacle was granted. He was exaggerating his individualism, and his observers let him be in his dreamlike commitment, that was haunted by his passion—arising from buried discontents dimly understood by all—to be distinguished among his kind, in any way he desired.

In certain ways, the American not only created a new kind of society; he also began to look like a new kind of man. His inner likeness gave him a new and characteristic outer bearing, and his physical experience in overcoming a virgin land brought to him and his sons rugged health and taller, broader, harder bodies. Drawing contributors from many old-world nationalities, the American race in a few generations through common experience, spirit and belief, shaped them into a general type that even with its myriad variations yet stood forth as a recognizable ideal figure for Western democratic man. This American was tall and rangy, and he walked with a long stride, pressing his legs against the unknown distance and future in a steady gait that gave a breathing swing to his upper body. Beyond physical dimensions and details, it was his quality of movement that gave him his most characteristic appearance; for movement expressed nature and will. His nature was to be free, strong and original; his will was to succeed in these aims, against obstacles of tradition and wilderness country; and all that he had in mind and met in nature helped to make his aspect new among mankind.

Going West, he clothed himself in few garments, all designed for work. As such, they not only covered but revealed his body, ignoring style and ornament for the simpler value of leaving him free in the gestures of labor. If he worked in open prairies or on wide rivers his hat was wide-brimmed to shade him from the sun. If he worked in mountains or woods he had a fur cap for warmth, and for kinship with the animals he hunted and loved in their defeat. Now and then he wore a felt hat wetted and dried in the shape of the tricorne of the Revolution. His shirt was loose, cut to hang over his shoulders front and back, with sleeves seamed to the rest between shoulder and elbow, and tightened around the wrist with a lace or a button. His trousers were tight from waist to knee, and made either to hang over or fit inside his boots with their thick soles and squared toes. For jacket he often wore a cloth or hide vest, and for coat on occasions of leisure a long-skirted affair with pockets inside the tails. The materials were mostly homespun, and were often left undyed. When colored, they showed the colors of berries or spices—frosty blue, dark cranberry red, sassafras yellow, cinnamon or nut brown, leaf green. The trapper or scout in buckskin was deer-colored and from a little distance in a wood if he held still was hardly to be mistaken for anything but another deer. The farther he went from settled life the more he tended to resemble a creature of the wilds, until an occasional one could only be spoken of in animal terms, like the man who was observed "mounted on a mountain mustang, his face, what little of it could be seen besides hair, looking very much like a small piece of buffalo meat, and with hair standing out like porcupine quills. . . ."

Embracing the farthest wilderness, the first settlers struck an occasional cultivated observer as men who reverted to savagery. Crèvecoeur said they had "an instinctive fondness for the reckless savage life, alternately indolent and laborious, full and fasting, occupied in hunting, fishing, feasting, intriguing, amours, interdicted by no laws, or difficult morals, or any restraints, but the invisible ones of Indian habit and opinion." Again, "these men appear to be no better than carnivorous animals, of a superior rank, living on the flesh of wild animals when they can catch them, and when they are not able, subsisting on grain." And again, "remote from the power of example and the check of shame, many families exhibit the most hideous part of our society. They are a kind of forlorn hope, preceding by ten or twelve years, the most respectable" who "come after them. In that space, prosperity will polish some, vice and law will drive off the rest, who, uniting with others like themselves, will recede still farther, making room for more industrious people, who will finish their improvements. . . ."

What showed in a later light was the prophetic persistence of image of a new life which led the forerunners to enact their own folklore as they thought of it amidst surroundings for which there was no previous pattern. The real binder of the new society was a willingness on the part of all to endure poverty for the sake of independence— "Poverty & Independence," as Audubon wrote in his journal for 1820, ". . . the only friends that will travel together through the world." The nation had begun as "a people of cultivators, scattered over an immense territory," as Crèvecoeur saw. But among the Western settlers every level of social position was represented, and every degree of development in cultural aspect and expression, from the wildcat primitive to the classical scholar, the tinker to the craftsman, the lawless scout to the maker of communities of calm and organic order, the man who governed his fellows by a spirit of fire to the one who led them by rational science. Together they might seem to glisten and seethe inseparable as sands in light, but in their ways and manners, they could be remembered as separate grains each shining sharply for itself.

ii. frontier attitudes

As the individual felt equal to the vast wilderness, so he was able to get on with the job of turning a continent into a neighborhood. Despite the fifty centuries of social cultivation behind him, the instant he had to be ready to practice wilderness craft he was ready. An ancient atavism of man against animal sprang close in time and memory; and a fabled breed of hunters was the result across the Appalachians. As marksmanship was their craft, it became their art and their entertainment, even their inducement to waste what sustained them. General William Henry Harrison, writing to the Secretary of War and Marine from Fort Saint Vincent, Indiana, in 1801, said, "One white hunter will destroy more game than five of the common Indians, the latter generally contenting himself with a sufficiency for present subsistence, while the other, eager for game, hunts for the skin of the animal alone." The hunters, tenacious, wasteful, wilful, were men who would kill one bounty of nature to obtain another, and in taking the wilderness with violence would not be stayed by moderation or thought of the future's needs. Merely to take a treed raccoon, they would chop down the tree, at night, by a woods pool or bayou, with torches guttering and dogs dancing.

Compared to others, they were a nation of sharpshooters. Their skill was what won Texas, and plains battles against riding Indians. To prove their skill men held contests to show their wonderful handling of the long rifle. Audubon saw them at it. The rifleman first cleaned his barrel. He then took a ball from his leather pouch, cupped it in the palm of his hand, and from his slung horn poured just enough powder to cover the ball. He poured the powder into the tube, set the ball in after it, and wadded it with a patch of six-hundred-thread linen, and rammed it all home with a hickory rod. He then faced the target. Sometimes this was a nail, driven two thirds into a board forty paces away. In one of three shots, he was able to finish driving the nail. He could trim the wick of a lighted candle at fifty paces without putting it out. At a hundred yards he could cut off a turkey's head. At comparable distances, he could hit the eye of an enemy. He could bark a squirrel, as Audubon saw Daniel Boone do it. The hunter aimed at a branch just where a squirrel sat, and hit the bark. The concussion killed the squirrel and sent him spinning in the air, to fall to the ground with his fur and flesh undamaged. The report of the long rifle made a crack like a whip. Men who could shoot like that, and who otherwise knew how to use themselves against the wilds, made a close community.

They gave later comers a hard time until able to prove themselves in the same terms. This habit sometimes showed itself in a comic hostility that masked a process of shrewd appraisal and suspended judgment until the newcomer could earn acceptance in the occupations and diversions of the initiated. Such hazing sometimes went to the limits of test and danger. Dimly it wanted to prove that a stranger could take care of himself or if need be do his part for the common safety in situations of peril. But further, the attitude was so exaggerated, so preposterously more than itself, that it suggested some obscure but grinding necessity to enlarge and insist upon all the masculine attributes that were taken for granted by most men in most other environments. It seemed as though a predominantly male society like that of the frontier was obliged to accentuate its maleness to make an outsize virtue of it, and so preserve in eternal boyhood the secrets and discoveries of essential virility that in the boy's first awareness of them assumed such proud, obsessive and exciting value. In many of its social expressions the early frontier West resembled a vast boys' club whose members dealt with puzzling perils and uncertainties by shouting them down with incantations of prowess.

Wildcats? Such a man could lick his weight in wildcats, and so stated with truculence and often. He would cry that he was a blacksnake, the longest, slickest, wisest of all. He was a weasel, clever enough to steal whatever he wanted. He was a raccoon, a tornado, an earthscreamer, a river at flood, a gamecock; he used a pine tree for a toothpick and he drank a lake if he was thirsty; he was cocked on a hair trigger and it was sure death merely to look at him in a certain way. He would as soon fight as eat; and—he sighed like a gale and belched like a geyser —he just loved to eat. He would take anybody on with a gun, or a knife, or bare hands with thumbs to gouge out eyes, and all for the pleasure of it, both received and given. If anyone thought he was just fooling, let him take up the ultimate challenge, and consent to fight him naked, straddling a bench or a log and strapped to it within a few inches of each other, and armed with a knife each; and see who finally fell over cut and bleeding, and who still sat there able to spit when the onlookers came forward to untie the both of them, one live and one dead. It was a challenge that was actually given and taken when doubt or boredom reached desperation.

Aggressive humility was another frontier attitude, perhaps less to be trusted than open truculence. It suggested envy, and private schemes to take what was wanted. Many frontiersmen could manage their faces with an actor's control. This was a technique of shrewdness, to wipe off any expression from which another could read intention or attitude. It was the poker face, and it could conceal either a teeming mind or one absolutely empty and at a loss. If a man felt ignorant he did well to conceal his feeling; and in any case, who knew everything? If men believed in equality, then what one man didn't know was just as good as what another didn't know. Out of tact, knowledge was often as carefully concealed as ignorance. It appeared that the ideas of the democratic citizen either dealt exactly with small matters, or vaguely with large ones, with no thoughts in between.

But if there were few learned men in the new society, there were few ignorant. The American cared "more to know a great deal quickly than anything well," Tocqueville said, and further noted that "the habit of inattention must be considered the greatest defect of the democratic character." The citizen's mind was always busy with his own concerns— chiefly those of business, his own situation, the assertion in thought of his own plans. These were his diversion as well as his livelihood; and they left little room for the charms of useless but delightful ideas. Like all generations, those of the early republic went in for rages and fads of belief that seemed to enlighten the people even while giving them a thin authority in obscure affairs, which they could display with elegance. Among the most gratifying of these were phrenology and its offshoots, which seemed to provide a penetrating key to human capacities. It was a period accomplishment to know with finality the secrets of personality by a glance and a touch upon the skull; and it was a popular pleasure to say, as if it meant something, that Fauvel-Gouraud's system of Phreno-Mnemotechny operated "through the intellectual and not the mechanical action of the mind."

Gravely accepted at the time, such imported fantasy seemed to give tone to the society. But there were more local notions of fantasy that really caught something of its likeness. David Crockett passed from life into legend before his death, and was quoted in a body of literature written down long after its invention. One time, out hunting, when the sun rose he lighted his pipe from it, shouldered his bear, walked home, "introducin' people to the fresh daylight with a piece of sunrise in my pocket." The expression held something of the blitheness, the sweet fresh primality, the sense of outset as at dawn, of the early nation.

Confidence dwelled in such a large view, and reflected the trust with which Americans moved alone through solitudes. When they met one another, they fell into easy, immediate fellowship, a habit they would never lose. Despite natural dangers, Audubon said ". . . So little risk do travellers run in the United States that no one ever dreams of any to be encountered on the road."

—Though one night putting up at a forest cabin where he was allowed to enter and scrape a cake out of the ashes to eat for his supper, and make a bed of skins from a heap in the corner, he was seen to possess a handsome gold watch. Later in the night he heard his hostess, "an infernal hag," plotting with her drunken sons to murder him and steal the watch. He was saved by the arrival of other travellers and had the satisfaction of seeing the murderous family executed, their goods given to a wounded young Indian who also had taken refuge under the same roof, and their cabin burned. Justice so swift proved how rare was such a crime against a traveller's faith; and how trustworthy was the ordinary forest home.

iii. woman and home

It was woman who gave it grace and amenity, with whatever materials were at hand. Her courage was as great and her work as hard as her husband's. Her satisfactions were all tacit. Unlike the European who flattered women but did not treat them as his equal, the American almost never complimented his wife, but showed her in other ways how fully he valued and counted upon her partnership in a wilderness venture. If as a figure she was idealized in countless impersonal episodes of frontier lore, she was, like the men, also projected in the grotesque vein. Mike Fink, the river boatman who was translated into myth, had an incredible daughter. She was so huge she tamed a full-grown bear; and all at once she could chew with one side of her mouth, whistle with the other, and scream with the middle. Grandeurs and amenities abandoned with the East merged with the talents and symbols of the West in a description of another frontier maiden, whose bonnet was a hornet's nest. Her gown was a whole bear's hide, with the tail for a train. She could drink from a creek without a cup, shoot a wild goose flying, wade the Mississippi without getting wet, outscream a catamount, and jump over her own shadow. She had good, strong horse sense, knew a woodchuck from a skunk, and could dance down any fellow. . . . Such monstrous views of woman were in a perverse way a proof of her equality with men whose experience she wholly shared in the job of making the new life. After the troubles of migration, it was she who gave heart to the cabin home.

"A pleasing uniformity of decent competence," said Crèvecoeur, "appears throughout our habitations. The meanest of our log houses is a dry and comfortable habitation." It was put together of trees felled by axe to make a clearing. The stumps were burned away in a long chore that boys could do. Seedlings showed in the rubble, and were cut down or allowed to grow, depending on where they sprang. Larger trees with heavy foliage were circled through the bark to kill their shade and let light through upon patches of corn sowed between them.

The house was about thirty feet long, fifteen feet wide, and fifteen feet high. It was all one room, and it had a single window hung with a muslin curtain. At one end rose the chimney made of stones hauled from a creek near-by or dug out of the ground. The hearth was of packed clay. The fireplace was wide and high, to hold an immense fire, that not only heated but lighted the whole room. Over the hearth hung a long rifle on iron hooks, and above it, for decoration, perhaps a deer- or bearskin, and a clutch of eagle or hawk feathers. On the wall to the right of the chimney was tacked an engraved map of the United States on Pennsylvania laid paper. From its eastern parts where it showed dense hatching of towns, roads, waterways and mountains in lines of black ink, the map faded toward the Mississippi until beyond the river westward it showed little but the names of Indian tribes bitten into spaces of white paper, with a straggle of the Rocky Mountains like a spine of tiny pine cones, and a tentative broken curve for the empty Pacific coast. Near the map hung a single plank shelf on which rested the family's books—a Bible, the first six books of Milton, a volume of Shakespeare, an almanac. Along the wall instead of closets stood wooden chests. In the center of the room was a long table built in the clearing. Its legs still held bark. On the table was a teapot of English china, a handful of silver spoons by Revere or Hurd of Boston, some teacups, and a little pile of old newspapers. Such a dwelling as Tocqueville saw it was "a little world, an ark of civilization amid an ocean of foliage. . . ."

Here was enclosed all the life of the family, for parents, children and dogs; here ate and slept the traveller in the common firelight under the protecting rooftree made by the father; and here presided the mother. She was in many cases a woman of gentle cultivation who had left the home of prosperous parents to risk with her husband the trials of the Great West, bringing with her as best she could all the graces she had learned. Her life was hard. She bore children frequently and in countless cases without any aid but that of her husband. Her day began with sunup and until her daughters were old enough she did its womanly tasks alone. She aged fast. Her appearance was inclined to be "at once sad but resolute." If she seemed exhausted, yet it was with pride, that her life should be so insatiably used by her man, her children, and her place on earth; and when travellers came, she and her husband gave what they had of shelter, food and floor. This was done as a duty, impassively, with no pretense that uninvited guests were in every case occasions of joy.

Like an Indian woman, the mother cooked out of doors except on the coldest winter days, when she set her kettles and skillets in the great indoor fireplace. She lighted her fire with flint and steel, or punk and tinder, until about 1829, when something else came along that was described with amazement. A tall red-haired young man—he turned out to be Alexander William Doniphan who would appear on the New Mexico Rio Grande in 1846—"took from his pocket the like of which I had never before seen . . . rubbed it on the sole of his boot and lo! there was combustion fire." The phosphorus-tipped friction match quickly sprang into wide use. On a spit the mother cooked all sorts of game brought in by her husband and her sons. When they went on a bee hunt they came home with plenty of wild honey. In deep kettles she made a variety of stews, seasoned with herbs for which the woods were combed. Out of corn and wheat flour ground at home she baked bread and cakes. From wild berries and fruits she made sweets. In time she would be able to gather produce from her own orchards, after her little trees began to bear. Out of the woods she took her medicines, from which she mixed a general remedy called bitters. To a draught of whiskey she added sarsaparilla roots, dock roots, black snakeroot, the bark of dogwood and of wild cherry, and a few beads of black pine gum. This was fed to grownups and children alike when indicated.

When she wasn't cooking she was working toward cloth at her spinning wheel or loom; or making new garments; or mending old ones. It was said on the frontier that the first thing a young man did was to get him a wife so's to have her make him some clothes. When she wasn't sewing she was teaching the children their ABC's, and how to read, and how to cipher, and who the Lord Jesus was, and where their grandparents were, and what America was, and how a living was made. She had very little money and needed no more, for her husband obtained goods by trade; and what money they had was enough to pay the government, "as there were no unreasonable taxes." The mother told her young ones of what was dangerous in the surrounding country —wolves, snakes, big cats, bears. She made it plain that not all Indians were to be feared, for many went by on camping and hunting trips, and though queer and with outlandish notions, and a shock to see with all the cranky nakedness they showed, many of them were almost friends. She spoke of other kinds, of whom all had heard, who came with brand and scream and arrow and stolen rifle, to kill all who lived in a cabin like hers. Thinking of it, she raised her head, and put her hand under her children's chins and made them raise theirs, and said that fear was no excuse not to stay where you wanted to stay, if you did no harm there, and bore your share of work. There were days when she even found time to surprise the children with a cornhusk doll, dressed and painted, or a rag doll that she had made for the girls; for the boys, perhaps a little horse made of twigs and a spool, or a toy bear stuffed with pine needles, or a beanbag, or a buckskin ball worked and worked until its seams met just right to create the sphere.

She kept her girls by her till late; her boys she lost early. The boys had hardly a cubhood. They went from boy to man; for as soon as their bodies were lengthening and filling to meet physical toil, they were ready to do a man's work; and were granted leave to do it. None could read the prickling thoughts of a youth or guess where they would turn him. The father watched his sons come to independence; and he saw this with pride, as an extension of the national ideal of equality and democratic opportunity. If the son wanted to stay at home to work, he was welcome; he was equally at liberty to do what many did at fourteen or fifteen—make a bundle of what he owned, take a rifle from the family's armory, and with a sweet bloom of ignorance on his confident face, go out on his own to a still farther West than the one he grew up in. He went with trading trains, or trapping parties, or with exploring expeditions of the Army, or joined a wild and dissolute crew of rivermen; and what he learned he measured by the gaunt, strong image of life to which he was born in the forest clearing, where in little he saw the community of work that in the large held America together. Everyone worked, and no job for man or woman was high or low, but all were respectable if honest. No one was embarrassed to work for pay. The President himself was paid.

iv. community expression

As neighborhoods took form, and the habits of a family were united with those of others, a sense of community governed all; and after the time when every day required ceaseless work, the neighbors at last were able to keep the Sabbath. They came together for worship in a clearing, or presently built a meetinghouse where they could be enclosed with the spirit of holiness that, they felt, arose more powerfully from all than from each. Going to church they carried in hand their shoes and stockings to keep them clean and only when near the meetinghouse did they sit down on a log and put them on to enter into worship presentably. Democracy spoke through a frontier hymn of 1800:

> Come hungry, come thirsty, come ragged, come bare,
> Come filthy, come lousy, come just as you are. . . .

And when they were gathered, it was one of their number who emerged to speak for them. There was always one who could "preach a pretty fair backwoods hardshell sermon." His expression was geared not to vaults and ambulatories and transepts but to groves and clearings and roughhewn rafters. Emotion—raw, contagious—was what they came to release, in the name of God. When the spirit was on them, they worshipped somewhat in the vein of the frontier fantasy that gave them identity with wildcat, tornado, ring-tailed roarer, and earth-screamer.

For daily close to violent peril and the large acts of birth, life, and death with no specialized skills to meet them, when they gathered to deal with human destiny under God their prayer took violent forms in the forest revival meetings of 1800 and after. The wildcat was licked over and over in testimonials given in meeting against Satan. The earth-screamer rose and jabbered sounds that if they were words belonged to an unknown tongue; but their message of guilt and release was understood by all. Shouting people fell to the ground in convulsions of humility and brief lost-mindedness. They writhed, jerked, crawled and trembled, while their tears streamed into the dust, and those who watched and heard felt strange longings begin to shake within themselves, and soon they too were lost to the hard world and were thrown down by a power greater than each—the power of all together. Crying of David's dance before the Ark of the Covenant one would suddenly leap into the air, crack his heels as for a hoedown, and start to jig like a man on a river boat. Born of the intention to worship, there took form among them the essential acts of theatre, dance, and concert—every satisfaction, however rude, of the desire to find through formal emotion a delivery from the limitations of the flesh, in its connotations of hardship, suffering and sin. So led by one of their number they gave themselves up to each other in the name of the Lamb; and purged by spectacular emotion in which all took part, returned to their ordinary selves with sighs of renewed innocence and strength.

It was a mood, then, proper to other Sabbath pastimes, against the misted blue distances beyond woods, and river hills, and creekside meadows; the lyric, gold-washed afternoons of the frontier landscapes. A man would bring a horse to the meeting; and for hours the horse was judged by a ring of critics who squinted at his general conformation, felt his withers, counted his teeth, stroked his coat. Another, prosperous, donated a beef or a turkey as a prize for the best marksman; and the long rifles cracked like whips in a shooting contest. Others—men and women alike—fished at the edge of a stream with thoughts upside down in clear water. Others sat and "visited," feeling the past week in bone and flesh, and letting their weight rest till tomorrow. Someone sang— "The Soldier's Tear," "Long, Long Ago"—

> Now that you've come, all my griefs are removed,
> Let me forget that so long you have roved,
> Let me believe that you love as you loved
> Long, long ago,
> Long ago.

From the long-ago, drifts of the national heritage glowed and faded in memory, hearsay, and gossip—how General Washington used to hold a levee at Philadelphia in his black velvet court dress wearing a beautiful little sword and an expression of calm elevation, while Lady Washington watched him to see whom to speak to; how a man who when lightning struck a tree was reminded that as a boy-sailor on the U.S.S. *Constellation* he saw the foremast of the French frigate *Insurgente* crack and fall; how another who had sailed with Decatur never forgot the burning of the *Philadelphia* before Tripoli; how a woman watched Madam Madison carry a picture and a parrot out of the White House when the British came to burn the capital; how Daniel Boone tried out his coffin—there was a picture of him doing it—before he died; how you could ride from Lockport to Albany on the Erie Canal so smoothly; how the remarkable new hotels of New York, five stories tall, had parlors for ladies, and music in the dining rooms; how the word "Slavery" had best not be mentioned till you knew which side you were talking to; how the public still took passage on river steamboats even though so many burst their boilers and sank on fire; and the railroads—how you not only got cinders in your eyes from riding on them, but just from standing in your own field and watching them go by; how printing presses, if you could believe what you heard, would all be run by steam in the end; and why didn't Daniel Webster go the whole hog and go to England to live, where the whiskey was better, and he would feel at home if he loved them so; and if Santy Anno did what they said he did in Texas why did they let him go; and if so many men had seen the famous white mustang wild on the prairies how come nobody ever took and caught him; and how the women in Santa Fee, every one of them, young or old, pretty or plain, smoked what they called seegaritos and blew the smoke in the faces of men at dances; and—sooner or later the talk all got around to it —who ought to be thrown out of office, and why, and who was going to be elected. . . .

For, as to politics, every American was an expert. He knew this was true, for he *was* the government. To make him so his forebears had fought and died; and to keep him so, he would fight and die himself. He saw himself as the people at large, and the people as embodied in himself. He, the voter, projected into the people, was the source and object of everything. The people, observed Tocqueville, reigned in the world of the United States politics as the Deity did in the universe. If, as Crèvecoeur thought, the American was a new man who acted upon new principles, "he must therefore entertain new ideas and form new opinions." Politics was the supreme topic for American conversation; and its object was liberty. "In this country," wryly declared the French Bourbon royalist Montlezun, "where the word liberty is never omitted in conversation, there is the greatest tyranny of opinion; that is, of political opinion, for that is the only kind that seems important." What this royalist authoritarian failed to note was the immensely important fact that the opinion was not that of a single controlling individual, but of a majority of individuals who controlled. An art of collective living was at birth; and as it would govern the destinies of all, so it took the energies of all, at the expense of other values that in older societies were exquisitely developed as ornaments of life—the fine arts, the abstract pleasures of philosophy, all the tones of aristocratic systems that had for so long hidden matter under manner.

For man himself was the proper heart of the matter of life; and when the Americans rediscovered the fact, and the world heard them talk about it, they were listened to with a sense of recognition. Tocqueville observed that "the political debates of a democratic people, however small it may be, have a degree of breadth that often renders them attractive to mankind. All men are interested by them because they treat of *man*, who is everywhere the same." America seemed to stand not only for equality of opportunity; but to be also the land of mankind's second chance. To the degree that the Americans were interested in each other, the world was interested in them.

And indeed, Americans took a lively, sometimes a prying interest in one another's affairs. It seemed to one student of the new democracy that "if an American were condemned to confine his activity to his own affairs, he would be robbed of one half of his existence; he would feel an immense void in . . . life, and his wretchedness would be unbearable." What saved all was again the general consent to the will of the majority; and the majority on occasion not only made the laws, but even reserved the right to break them. For once law was established, if it appeared to bear too closely upon the rights of the individual, he was free to enlist others with him in an effort to change it to resist the power of central authority, and to remake, over and over again, the image of the nation in the likeness of his view of life. The citizen's training began early—schoolchildren made up rules for their own games and clamored for their observance among themselves. In any contingency developing in public—a traffic upset, a quarrel, a complaint against a merchant or innkeeper—the onlookers formed themselves into a deliberative body, and resolved upon what to do. Committees met to decide upon all manner of things—even to the drinking of alcoholic beverages. In the early nineteenth century temperance societies with over two hundred and seventy thousand members carried a stern influence. Their cheerless sway in Pennsylvania alone in one year reduced the consumption of alcohol by five hundred thousand gallons.

v. language

Such effect could arise only from an inexhaustible outpouring of speech. The Americans were talkative. With opinions sharply ready, they spoke their pieces freely. To rise and be heard was not only essential to their system of life; it was almost the only social joy they knew. In the absence of well-established theatrical life, and opera companies, and museums, the debating societies of the Americans had to serve as substitutes. They were popular. In their meeting rooms citizens rehearsed the postures and appeals that must serve them if they ever went to Congress; and the habits of debate became so satisfying that even in intimate conversation the member was likely to forget that he was talking to an individual and to fall into the larger airs of one who swayed a meeting, and if his style rose with his opinion, so that he became heated, he swept the air with his arm, and, carried away by his own sound, he addressed his lone listener as "Gentlemen. . . ." For oratory could always sweep him away, his own most of all. Newly the possessor of the parliamentary arts, he sometimes lost himself in them to the point of forensic nonsense. But more important to the habit of democracy than the nonsense of manner was the right of all citizens to be heard.

"Eloquence is, in fact, after gold, their highest ideal," said Father Grassi, an Italian Jesuit who gazed at the Americans during his five years as president of Georgetown College from 1810 to 1815. He went on to say that New World orators paid less mind to the inner values of a speech—originality and beauty of thought, weight of ideas, force of argument and logical development—than they did to its manner. They knew their success with a public waiting to be edified rested upon other details—florid metaphor, elegant words, grand periods. The American speaker confessed that he was impatient of "a vulgar and sterile state of facts." What the people wanted must be offered. "A people who have fresh and lively feelings will always relish oratory." The oratory of the West was "free, lofty, agitating, grand, impassioned. . . ." It was a people's art; and like a people's art, it had a curious double spirit. It both derided and imitated the richness of more aristocratic or better-educated models. It was aware of the idiom of a donnish class, an élite in whom all elevated expression was reposed by older societies; and rejected it in the name of a whole population who shared equally the joys and powers of making utterances that could sound splendiferous, whatever on earth they might mean. Much frontier oratory in its inflation took to kidding on the level. The inflation was perfectly conscious and was often meant to be comic—and yet at the same time, it hoped to intoxicate with its reminders of large acts, projected fantasies of patriotism, and a new historical spirit. For metaphor it drew freely on the

marvels of the unfolding continent—the might of Niagara, the sweep of
the prairies, the noble rise of the Rockies, the blaze of Western starlight,
the arc of heaven that embraced America from coast to coast, and endlessly the scowling American eagle who dwelt on pinnacles and crags,
and soared in freedom above the restraints of earth. Like all the arts of
the people, their oratory expressed desire and character. Its inflations and
exaggerations were brandished in reply to the vastness of the West, the
bulk of mountains, where man was so little. If there was vulgarity in its
expression, there was also pathos; for what showed plain was the violent
dancing of a spirit that must assert or be lost.

As the country—its land, political purpose and united energy—was
new, so must its most common means of expression—language itself—be
new. For the old forms of English the people laid down new rules and
made up new words. Inventing his character, and adopting wilderness
ways with which he had to achieve physical victory, the American needed
new means with which to express himself. By 1815 he had a new dialect
that was a distinct tangent of the mother tongue. Much of its vocabulary was consciously fantastic; and any man was privileged to coin vivid,
homely, and extravagant locutions, and might even become a virtuoso
of the process. The frontier talked the raw materials of a new literature.
Politics, work, and daily character in shrewd masquerade stimulated the
most vigorous flow of new speech expressions. Those that had a real
spark of aptness, a truth in their color, passed into current use. Stump
speakers flung them back at their creators; they were picked up by newspapers; and in time passed into general acceptance as correct. It was a
language that sought understanding at the level of least education. It
reflected a general suspiciousness of studied correctness, and in the beginning it even disdained formal recognition of different social levels. "Our
dictionary," noted Crèvecoeur before the nineteenth century, "is short
in words of dignity and names of honor." But it was not long until the
frontier granted titles to anyone whose calling or whose knack of im-
personation seemed to demand them—Judge, General, Colonel, Doctor,
Reverend. . . .

Tocqueville found American speech full of abstract terms which
enlarged and obscured the thoughts they were intended to convey, and
he concluded that democratic nations preferred obscurity to labor—the
labor of speaking and writing correctly and clearly. His observation again
caught something of the essential character of people working out a
great experiment in equality. Make it *sound* grand, they seemed to say,
and you *are* grand. Keep it loose, and you are not committed. Generalize,

and you are delivered from the concrete which in terms of your own life may be hard and graceless. Roar, and inconvenient truth or painful accuracy may be stilled. To the untutored ear, the accents of education sounded fancy. So, without education, adopt the fanciness, and you will sound educated. Upon such a trait much comic character was based—the itinerant preacher, the courtly Negro, the windy swindler.

American humor rested less on inherent wit or sharp observation of human failings than on rough drolleries full of exaggeration and strange usage for its own sake. The speech became noisy and profuse. It imitated sounds of sucking and smacking and cracking and slicing and chopping and sawing and thumping and poking and digging and clapping and exclaiming and hushing. It stuck in extra syllables for elegance and comic surprise. It liked to repeat in the same word the sound of dental consonants that gave a jerky, droll effect. It made comedy out of mouth-widening vowel sounds and speech-yodels whose effect depended upon a swallowed *l*—the gobble of the North American turkey. It was at times almost abstract sound. Its character, stripped of known words and their meaning, and left only with sound, might still suggest the meaning intended, along with the hard, simple, and at times lyrically beautiful life from which it came.

To throw fits into someone was to cornuck him. To mean huge was to say monstropolous. A total abstainer from alcohol abstained teetotaciously. An angelical character was angeliferous. Someone who wanted to flee skedaddled, which meant that he absquatulated. Something complete was bodaciously so. To defeat or overcome was to ramsquaddle and to obliterate was to obflisticate. A strong man was a screamer, and an important one a ripstaver. If a fellow took off his clothes he shucked himself; and a woman suffering from a certain nervous disorder had the peedoodles. If there was a kettle of meat and vegetable stew for supper, it was known as burgoo. To cheat someone, or to deceive with false love, was to honeyfogle. . . . It took only a few such words salted through an otherwise conventional passage of speech or writing to change its character into something entirely new in effect. The effect was that of imaginative enlargement of experience. Even place names reflected the tendency. Audubon on the Mississippi recorded in 1820 that "many places on this River are rendered More terrible in Idea by their Extraordinary Names than real difficulties—". And if the native speech could evoke pictures of rough, hilarious or absurd experience, it could also summon forward much of the accidental beauty that pervaded the memories of the westering people. Again it was Audubon who noted a lovely usage that made a picture of countless frontier encampments: firelight, he said, "is named in some parts of the country, *forest light.* . . ."

In both the grotesque and the lyric lay predictions of the national literature that was to come.

vi. arts and utility

With the open secret of the whopping lie the frontier made its own first conscious literature. Competitions of tall tales were held in which the people tried to create their own myths. Boasts of prowess, marvels of animal origin or reincarnation, farces of anthropomorphism, fabulous reversals of the natural order, minglings of Indian, Gaelic and huntsman's lore—these were typical raw materials for the made-up stories with which improvisers in camp hoped to entertain and stun one another. As they dealt highhandedly with the mysteries of nature, they were in great contrast to the mythologies of all Indians, who stood in awe before the elements; and as they celebrated the rebellious triumphs or howling humiliations of a man alone in the fantastic world, they were opposed in spirit to the decorousness of the Spanish character. So long as there were new sights to behold, new endurances to encounter, the frontier's own literature held the character of a mythology. But it was not long—a matter of a generation—before experience seen in those terms from the inside became the subject of a commercial literature that saw the West from the outside, and found for it a huge national audience. In the end, the commercial literature came back to the frontier, and there the living subjects of its formularistic romances read with credulity and love what it told about the West, very little of which was real or true.

The novels of Fenimore Cooper grafted the frontier forest upon the conventions of European romanticism, and soon a flood of imitations of Cooper's popular creations poured forth from the steam printing presses of the East, and were known as "steam literature." If these were full of wild inaccuracy, they met the desire of whole populations at home and abroad to participate in the early nineteenth century's only new physical adventure.

But truer meanings of the American adventure were gathering to be heard, and would proclaim through Emerson the American mind, that must convert the world, and through Whitman the American body, that must father upon it a new breed. The Yankee philosopher spoke for the freedom of the individual intellect and its responsibility in a democracy. The crowd-roaming poet, revealing the true polarities of the feminine and the masculine in himself, passionately celebrated the body of the recumbent land and the body of the democratic man who possessed it. In the central ideas of these two interpreters of the new nation lay seeds that would grow throughout all significant American literature after them; for they were mystically sensitive to the essential quality in the early national experience, and like prophets, spoke it forth to the future, over the heads of the people, as it were, to their common heirs.

Meanwhile, the people, close to what they had known on the frontier, gratified in countless ways the memorial impulse, creating the "old-timer." At a settlers' meeting in Missouri someone read a metrical catalog of early families, written in a tradition if not in a meter that recalled Michael Drayton and the Battle of Agincourt, with the names of common heroes standing forth to kindle the minds of those who had helped to win a wilderness, a century, a nation:

> Sam Lucas, Boggs and Swearingen,
> The Nolands and the Fristoes, then,
> The Greggs, with Owens two;
> The Davises and the Flournoys,
> The Kings and Staytons and McCoys,
> And Dailey with his twenty boys—
> All these and more we knew. . . .

In such a purpose, however humbly, literature came to the service of the people.

It was a service required of all the arts in early America. "Nothing," declared Dr. Franklin, "nothing is good or beautiful but in the measure that it is useful: yet all things have a utility under particular circumstances. Thus poetry, painting, music (and the stage of their embodiment) are all necessary and proper gratifications of a refined state of society but"—and here was suggested an admonitory glance from aside his small curlicue spectacles—"but objectionable at an earlier period, since their cultivation would make a taste for their enjoyment precede its means." But Franklin was looking east, not west, and thinking of opera houses, theatres and museums in the cities of Europe. He saw that utility must be a determining value for the arts of a forming democracy; but having little of the creative temperament he forgot that the arts would never wait for ideal conditions or a refinement of society

to bring them forth. Even as the frontier took its westward course they
came forth because it was in their nature never to be denied; and as they
appeared in the context of democracy they spoke both to the people
and for them.

vii. light in the clearing

By river and by road troupes of theatre players followed the settlers. Floating along waterways actors rehearsed in costume on deck, to
the astonishment of people working in riverside fields or travelling along
towpaths. In their costume hampers were stuffed the wrinkled habili-
ments of their repertoire—the blacks of Hamlet, the stripes of Yankee
Doodle, the crowns and swords and ermine and velvet for Richard III,
plumes for Pizarro. When they came to towns, they played in halls, meet-
inghouses, later in theatres; and the actors eddied in and out of the
public life offstage in grand strangeness, ample of manner, of swelling
speech, and garbed in bright colors that would not bear close inspection
after hard travel and measly pay. Every frontier American was a hot
critic, for he knew something himself about making a character and the
art of dissembling. The roving theatre brought with it the magic of a
heightened life, and in its freedom of movement and fancy, probed into
the longings of its audiences, revealing to them the hidden discontents
and shortfallings of the selves that glowed in their desires and that were
never so disturbing as when they watched the enactment of a heroic
play, however ragged its character, or poor its scenes. Many a playgoer,
facile with the emotions of revival and tall tale, fell into confusion watching the actors, and forgetting what was imaginary and what was real,
had to be restrained by neighbors from intervening in the acted drama.
In the face of such familiar transports the actors were patient; for it was,
every time, the greatest tribute they could receive; and for what it signified they stoutly and willingly fought like other pioneers the dangers
of frontier travel—Indian attacks upon their little troupe, an occasional
robber, uneasy threats by backwoodsmen who resented the appearance
of actors with their silky airs, their humbling literacy, their swagger and
color, their way with women. . . .

But towns were far between, and the theatre company was ready
to play wherever anyone would attend. A cluster of cabins on a river-

side, a clearing in a forest—anywhere. In such places the play was given out of doors, with no curtain, and for scenery, only what the woods provided. A space between thickets served as stage, with real trees for "wings" from behind which the actors could enter. Scene and location and date were affirmed, in Elizabethan style, in the spoken text. Tallow candles held in potatoes made footlights, unless the settlement was too poor to spare these, when the lights were made out of old linen rag wicks burning in pans of fat. If not even these were to be had, then the play was given in the dark, and imaginary life rode forth on the voices of actors unseen but speaking with doubled intensity to piece their listeners who sat on benches facing them, or on the ground. But perhaps the moon was out, and then silvered in common magic the forest, the animated figures striving with one another, the spectators, were united in a creation of spirit as powerful as it was mysterious, and as poignant as it was fugitive; a little point of light shining one night in the deep continental darkness.

The wandering players had their specialties, turns of song, recitation or dance which they gave between the acts of a play, or put together in a whole program as a minstrel show. Their plays were expedient versions of those popular in established Eastern theatres, and sometimes included a vehicle for a famous star, like Junius Brutus Booth, who found on the frontier a certain fulfillment of his mystical and libertarian nature. Some of the plays were of American origin, and many of these were written around a central stock character. They were Yankee plays—*Jonathan Postfree*, or, *The Honest Yankee* (1807); *The Saw-Mill*, or, *A Yankee Trick* (1829); *Solon Shingle, The People's Lawyer* (1839). A recurring figure in plays improvised within a strict convention was the rube who for four acts served as the dupe of clever, rich, educated and cruel men, such as lawyers, bankers, and land speculators; and who in act five turned upon them with blinking innocence that got the best of them every time. The hick in the city presented variations of this democratic passion in which the central figure—in his carrot-red wig, his blacked-out teeth, his baggy pants into which he kept looking with a squirm to see if what he lost was to be found in there, only to be embarrassed to discover the audience watching him in the act—raised the people by impersonating someone laughably lower than their lowest specimen. There were plays on episodes of early American history—*The Arab Chief and the Pirate of the East* (1834), which recalled naval adventures in the Barbary wars; dramas in which Washington appeared; and adaptations of Cooper's novels.

But the most popular native theme was the Indian. In the theatres of the East, and in the very clearings and at woods-edges where the people had killed and known killings by Indians, Indian plays were acted in such profusion that in time it was said that they had become "perfect *nuisances.*" They presented the tragedy of the Indian, and recalled promises made by white men and broken. In their explorations, and perhaps expiations, of the betrayals of human relations and rights, they accepted the Indian as a human being, with none of the legalistic debate as to his nature that had for so long occupied the colonial Spaniard. The Indian of the early American theatre was an ideal figure of natural man, echoing Rousseau's concept of the savage. In *Metamora, or, The Last of the Wampanoags,* written by John Augustus Stone in 1829, and played for decades by Edwin Forrest, the Indian hero ended the play with an apostrophe to the white soldiers who have killed him: "My curses on you, white men! May the Great Spirit curse you when he speaks in his war voice from the clouds! Murderers! . . . May your graves and the graves of your children be in the path the red man shall trace! And may the wolf and the panther howl over your fleshless bones, fit banquet for the destroyers! Spirits of the grave, I come! But the curse of Metamora stays with the white man! I die. . . . [Falls and dies]." With this play, and in nearly forty others on Indian themes, the audiences who made them so popular seemed to make gestures of poetic redress, and to bring into the light a sense of guilt toward the Indian who had suffered the destruction of his liberty and the loss of his land. Audubon's view of the Indian in 1820 found its echoes in the theatre of the people for many decades: "Whenever I meet *Indians* I feel the greatness of our Creator in all its Splendor, for there I see the Man Naked from his Hand and yet free from Acquired Sorrow. . . ." By what they responded to and thus made profitable the people shaped their own democratic image in the creative arts of America. The theatre seemed to make one further gesture in self-portraiture, for even as they continued to take the continent from the Indians, the people used the theatre as a medium of confession.

viii. sons of harmony

In their music, too, they found community, whether in joining together for religious, political, social, or working occasions. American music was essentially an art of performance rather than of invention. The Puritans brought their hymns with them; and as North American life became more polite than pious, grand musical societies with serious purpose were founded in the cities to produce works of Haydn, Bach, Pleyel, Mozart, Handel, Purcell, Dr. Thomas Arne and Sir Henry Bishop. The Revolution, with its achievement of freedom through martial valor, was followed by a new popularity of music. Francis Hopkinson of Philadelphia came forward as the first sophisticated native composer, composing songs that echoed the manner of Dr. Arne, and reflected the simple sweetness of morning light. His works for harpsichord were given in proper concerts, and a company came to present French opera in New York and Philadelphia, and soon there were attempts to shape dialogue-and-ballad operas on native subjects.

In a more popular vein the fife became the rage. Its shrillness and panic legerity suggested the state of the national feeling. With little stinging scales it challenged the conservatism of the past, forcing an animated vision of a future as brisk and insistent as its own voice. The fife presided at the head of parades and at rallies. If the fifer went travelling, his instrument provided a walking skirl to keep him company and announce him when he arrived at inns, fairs or parties, where being asked he would play solo airs and tweedling songs.

William Billings in the late eighteenth century brought a new formal excitement into the prevailing church music of Puritan psalms sung in unison. In primitive imitation of the high contrapuntal style he arranged them in harmonies for part singing. His tunes made an immediate appeal and on being published in engraved sheets sold widely. They were, he declared, "twenty times as powerful as the old slow tunes," and calling them "fuges," he described their new character in terms of contest between the parts, "each part striving for mastery and victory, the audience entertained and delighted, their minds surpassingly agitated and extremely fluctuated, sometimes declaring for one part, and sometimes for another,"—for all the world like partisans in democratic politics. "Now the solemn bass demands their attention, now the manly tenor;

now the lofty counter, now the volatile treble. Now here, now there; now here again—O ecstatic!" he cried to his creations, quite carried away by the sense of movement in his art, "Rush on, you sons of harmony!"

As music went west with the frontier settlers it lost the opportunity for formal performance offered by the cities. In the mountains and forests, it took the form of traditional songs from the British highlands and, through the Negro, from the west coast of Africa. The frontier made up few new songs, for the settlers were already past the phase of civilization in which primitive people originated a folk music. Appalachian and savannah and prairie song were all modifications of old expressions long before developed over the Atlantic in the British Isles and Africa, and were often corruptions of these. But they were augmented by accidental beauties of tonal expression that Western life produced in its work. On the crystal rivers when a flatboat or keelboat came to a bend, a boatman sounded a warning on a horn, playing a vagrant tune that drifted on the water and was lost in the trees—

> O, Boatman! wind that horn again
> For never did the listening air
> Upon its lambent bosom bear
> So wild, so soft, so sweet a strain!

In the golden mists of river perspective it made a signal of wonder, nostalgia and the stir of going over America, much as the sound of the railroad whistles would do in later times. Steamboats put the boatman's horn to rest, for with them came steam screams, a new sound in the nation's work that must in time find expression in its music. And so too, the ringing of anvils, the chinking of harness, the locust song of the power saw. . . .

If music in America drew all its substance from the Old World, and made little if any gift to the creation of new music, then the rhythms of work and simple social occasion led to a style of instrumentation and accompaniment that made do with materials caught up out of common life. Rough, witty, percussive, the style, listened to fastidiously, might have seemed almost antimusical; yet in the primitive sense it performed an essentially musical task—to make rhythm and beat with many percussive means, and assign melody to a single line for violin, flageolet, voice or group of voices. Western music devoted itself to a lively function—the levitation of the body. To hear it was to see physical gesture—cakewalk, dance figure, the waggles of convivial drollery. There was little contemplative or serious role for music. But in its simple repetitive drive there lay translations of work beats, the blows of mauls and axes and hammers which in a group of working men always fell into accidental syncopation that even more than Negro rhythms may have prefigured the jazz idiom of a century after. Of all percussion instruments, hands were the easiest to use. The gesture again prefigured the form, and evoked the scene with the rhythm of handclaps, either on the beat or off, with single clap or double to the beat—people in a ring, or in line, or in a square, dappled by sunlight through shade out of doors, or shown by the bloom of lanterns indoors, when intense conviviality erased distance and void and wilderness, with choral shrillings and the threeked echo of handclaps in the eaves; in high musical terms a performance rude and graceless, but worthy of respect as a means to let the people stand forth in their hunger for exchange and delivery of spirit. For popular music (like all other popular arts) held little abstract artistic value, but was wonderfully eloquent in describing its makers and users.

Percussion effects to express the simple rhythms that dominated frontier music came from anywhere and everywhere. George Caleb Bingham drew a young riverman sitting on a sawhorse and holding a skillet in one hand while he stroked and struck it with the knuckles of the other, to accompany the sound of a fiddle played by another man sitting on a keg. Negro musicians brought their drum-headed banjos into the people's music, and also taught countless boys how to hold polished pork rib bones between their knuckles, and shake, rattle and roll them with brilliant effect. The jew's-harp though capable of giving an illusion of different pitches made a humming monotone whose only variations were percussive. Drumsticks like knuckles performed on any surface. Flute, flageolet and violin sang melody—if they survived egocentric drives encountered on the frontier: Audubon hearing "a great uproar" one night in his guest room went to find Rafinesque, the naturalist, "running about the room naked, holding the handle of my favorite violin, the body of which he had battered to pieces against the walls in attempting to kill the bats"—of a rare species—"which had entered by the open window." The violin, a Cremona, was demolished. But Audubon still had his flageolet, and when he travelled, staying overnight with strangers, he repaid their hospitality with "a few airs" before taking his leave in the morning.

Popular songs heard in theatres brought together verse and music in strong declamation that swept the audience into joining the refrain, as in a piece that kindled every patriot with its narrative of Jackson's victory over the British in Louisiana:

But Jackson he was wide awake, and wasn't scar'd at trifles,
For well he knew what aim we take with our Kentucky rifles;
So he led us down to Cypress Swamp, the ground was low and mucky;
There stood John Bull in martial pomp: *but here was old Kentucky.* . . .

The actor, dressed in buckskins, threw down his fur cap, and took aim
with his property rifle, and the audience, with handclaps, foot-stamps
and roaring voices, crashed out the chorus between stanzas:

> Oh, Kentucky!
> The hunters of Kentucky!
> Oh, Kentucky!
> The hunters of Kentucky!

Such a song, in both its subject and its clean, hard style, would have the
power to evoke its singers and stompers long afterward.

Group song was a popular pleasure, and the singers developed
their own kind of literacy through a simplified system of musical notation. It was a system that employed notes of distinctive shape repeated
for the several intervals of the scale—some square, others triangular,
others oval, so that they looked like little scatterings of buckwheat
heads on the staff lines. From this resemblance the system, which originated in Lancashire, was called "Buckwheat Notation," at first in derision, later in simple acceptance, as its use spread fast among singers who
found conventional musical notation difficult for sight reading. With the
turn of the eighteenth century, when religious revival meetings swept
the West, shape-note singing became a general accomplishment that was
never to be lost among untrained but fervent folk singers of America.
Songbooks sold widely, and westering travellers took along copies of such
as *The Western Lyre,* issued at Cincinnati in 1831, and *The Missouri
Harmony,* at St. Louis in 1837. Even blank music books went with the
emigrants, who when they heard new songs wrote down text and tune
in buckwheat notation to share them with new friends when their journey allowed. In the hoot and glee of their mingled voices the early
travellers celebrated the community of their hopes, the power of their
faith, and an eternal trial at rising above sin. If what they sang was not
transcendent as music, it served a purpose in harmony with what they
were, taking the voice of each, and for a little while making them all
one, in still another image of the equality and democracy they strove
to create together with their lives.

ix. knacks and crafts

A frontiersman "boasted that with only hickory withes and a jack-knife he could make a very good wagon."

In such a statement lay the seed of all the arts and crafts—the "practical arts" as they were called—in early America. Dr. Franklin's concern for the marriage of beauty and utility was unconsciously answered by the men and women who in successive settlements were obliged by scarcity of rich materials to equip and ornament their daily tasks with objects of their own making. It was natural that the practical arts in a democracy were first of all functional. If the conditions of their lives denied to the settlers access to the fine arts, there was also in the crotchety plainness of the people a hint that the fine arts were suspect. Puritan bleakness was partly responsible for such a view. But another and overriding sense had effect too. This was a democratic suspicion that the fine arts had always been identified with aristocratic patronage. Palaces crammed with splendors, artists appointed to court, prestige and expense attached to the work of master-artists—such airs of luxury seemed highfalutin, and to partake of them called for a whole world of experience, education and allusion in which the democrat could only feel at a disadvantage. In their gnarled self-respect the people must earn their own evolvement of the arts. If at first they must be content with making a beautifully finished rake handle that felt good to the grasp, or a plain little chair that looked polite as it sat empty and felt good as it was occupied, or a wooden decoy duck carved and painted to fool a game bird in early daylight and otherwise to ornament a shelf with its sleek green, brown, gray, black and white reminders of sport and sustenance, then what they fashioned so honestly had the authority of answering honest needs.

In the pattern of ordinary social development the settlers would have climbed through primitive generations or centuries toward a flowering of refined art based on their utilitarian creations. But there were two reasons why such a sequence was not necessary. First, the settlers were not socially primitive people, but civilized people taking new land with a new social idea; and second, to their new idea of man and to new land in which to realize it there was soon added a third newness that swept the first two along at an amazing rate of historical develop-

ment. This was the discovery and spreading use of technological methods
—many new means of making corporate life closer, and individual life
easier, so that united to his fellows the individual was to be relatively
free from toil. The frontiering and completion of the American continent took place during the first years of a world revolution in technology.
The effect of this coincidence upon the people's expression in the arts
was to drive home more deeply than ever the love of usefulness over
beauty—if it came to a choice. The handicraft of the settler would soon
exert itself in designing for machine crafts. Machine crafts would make
possible through duplication of copies a widespread use of what before
had been limited to an original and its user, who was so often its maker.
The spirit of the copy said, My value is in serving as many people as
possible, to help in their lives. Has this work not its own beauty? The
spirit of the original said, I am unique, and my beauty lies in my
rarity, for the touch of my creator is on me everywhere. What matter
that I serve only one?

But there the matter came to a point. For the democratic impulse
sought to bring the goods and beauties of life to as many people as
possible, in contrast to the aristocratic impulse that granted patronage
to art forms for an élite. If traditional fine-art forms were the highest
expression of creative spirit in civilization, then the Americans seemed
to have forgotten the fact; and to have busied themselves with an expression of creative spirit for which the raw material was mankind itself,
in a powerful belief that the arts of living together must come first.
Their masterpiece of creative spirit was the forging of human liberty
and equality in a coherent society. In the process they illustrated the
difference between the practical arts and the fine or inutile arts, considered as historical records.

Through articles made for use, the practical arts left an uncritical
likeness of the society that produced them. On the other hand, the fine,
or inutile, arts always made a conscious criticism or interpretation of the
life from which they grew. This was one of their chief intentions. The
record they left was formal, and while it suggested the taste of the times,
it suggested even more sharply the personality of the designer. The position and character of the arts in America seemed to equate utility with
the anonymous people, and formal beauty with the individual creator
in the fine arts. And as it was the body of the people together who made
the conditions of life, it was their popular expression in the arts and
crafts that achieved originality, style and freshness; while to the scattered few "fine" artists was left the task of treating American subject

matter in techniques and visions imitative of European models. The universal American tinker became a maker of machines for work, the whittler became a sculptor of workaday signs, artisan and artist were one; and their genius for the practical became a national characteristic that would lead to a standard of material life new to the world.

In their conviction of purpose there could also be delight in how they worked; and in countless objects made for use they celebrated their own gaunt graces, and left a record of how, in their spirits, fancy and patience and good sense could meet.

Where color was used, they used it exuberantly, on wood, metal or in fabrics. On the other hand, form was frugal, as the gestures of labor were frugal, with the inference of meeting a purpose with not too little, or too much, but just enough energy. The Conestoga wagon illustrated both idioms of color and form. Shaped like a great open coffer, and slung on wheels to go away, it was just a plain receptacle; but with its bright blue sides, vermilion wheels and dazzling creamy hood of Osnabrück linen, it recalled the painting palette of the Pennsylvania Germans, who made flowers in such frank colors, and stars, fruit, doves, parrots, on their boxes, furniture and certificates of occasion.

Wood was the commonest American material. The continent had a seemingly inexhaustible supply. The frontier American craftsman used it for most houses he built; and for most of the objects that went into a house or served business. He made all manner of chests, none exactly alike, but all sharing a common plainness. If he made a tall clock case, it was severely plain. His benches, beautifully surfaced, remained as close as possible to their original parts of plank and branch. Such severity suggested not only that the maker was a plain man, for religious or other reasons unsympathetic toward rich ornament; but also that he was in a hurry, with many another task awaiting him. But when he came to make machines of wood, his pace of work must have been measured and easy; for what resulted sometimes were such masterpieces of functional design that their beauty would satisfy long later any interest in abstract art. Such machines were a Shaker spinning wheel, with its large delicate wheel suspended above a base remarkably light on slender legs; and a fork for pitching barley and straw that extended four wooden tines in repeated tapering curves in a gesture of work that combined exquisite efficiency with elegance. Something of the same beauty brought thoughtlessly to life out of a grave concern for a good feel and a perfect usefulness could be seen in the wooden stocks made to support the cast metal parts of American rifles. Their tactile appeal, combined out of finish and shape, was so great that no man could see a good one without wanting to run his hand over it, even if he wasn't thinking directly about how a white morning came over whitening water where game must rise with the day.

Wooden crafts and painting came together in various needs for painted sculpture, and for outdoor commercial signs. Ships built in the Eastern yards were given carved figureheads that were portraits of real men or women, great figures out of the young national history, or idealized allegorical creations. In their proud realism, these were often heroic in scale, and carved with wonderful, wavelike freedom of scrolling design. They were brightly painted and heightened with gold leaf, and when installed under the bowsprit leaning over the bosom of the waters, they made visible the personality with which men have always endowed ships. At the stern, there was often opportunity to create carving and gilding, where the ship's name and home port were shown. In such long horizontal panels a peculiarly American style of decoration, using letters and ornaments, treated space with the balance and grace of the printer's art.

Other figures of popular sculpture were life-sized wooden Indians or Turks or Negroes to stand before tobacco stores in bright paint and arresting stare. It took twelve days to make such a figure—six for the carving at a foot a day, and six for the finishing. To produce hanging signs for inns, shops, barbers, the craftsman again allied woodworking to painting, and often called again on the serene severities of typography to govern the spacing of his symbols and letters. Many such signs were beautifully contrived and when they called to the customer, did so calmly, offering, at inns, the one word, "Entertainment," and displaying, for shops, carved likenesses of wares in bas-relief.

Painting was allied to metal crafts in the production of such articles as tin utensils, canisters, pots, trays and boxes; andirons and bootjacks and hitching posts that represented human or animal figures; and various toys. The metal craftsman made weather vanes in every kind of symbol. The conventional cock was joined by new designs, with certain ones recurring to reflect the interests of the public—a fish, a whale, a grasshopper, a trotting horse, a horse in extended racing stride, a frigate in full sail, a locomotive and tender. These were painted or treated entirely with gold leaf or left in the black silhouette of wrought iron. Lanterns and candlesticks and trivets; locks, hinges and latches; firemarks in iron with designs that again recalled typography—all had simple grace and the occasional appealing falter whereby the hand of the originator could be detected. It was in duplicated objects of cast metal that the impersonality of the coming steam power era was suggested—rifle barrels, spread eagles for flagpole and cornice finials, plain iron kettles with their three little legs cast on the pouchlike belly.

In weaving, embroidering, rugmaking, quilting, women contributed to the idiom of American crafts. The richly colored floral and vinelike designs of crewel embroidery derived from Jacobean England were succeeded by plainer patterns in hard homespun cloth. Weaving tablecloths and bedspreads and coverlets, the housewife developed simple geometries that repeated variations based on squares and triangles, frequently in colors of blue and white. Her most personal style appeared in quilting. Here was an exercise in thrift, for she used patches of cloth saved from every which source; and in ingenuity, for her hope was to achieve symmetrical patterns out of scraps that came along with no rhyme or reason; and in patience, for a quilt was big, to fit on a man-and-wife bed, and to make only one six-inch-square patch of the ten dozen or so needed would call for thousands of stitches. But she persisted, and produced an original work whose simplicity and modesty told much about her life and the joys of her labors throughout many hours made up of a few minutes here, a few there, when in repose she was not idle.

x. first interpreters

Little—almost none—of the formal art of painting told as much about American life as such workaday crafts. Before the 1840s only two painters—Edward Hicks and James John Audubon—brought together matter and manner in styles that yielded out of imagination and experience true images of the new America. Hicks was a native artist whose painting arose from two other prepossessions—religion and his trade as a coach builder. He was a Quaker preacher, and the austere tenets of his church gave simplicity to his vision, and educated him in terms of Biblical literalism. His working trade called for decorative painting on the panels of carriages, and for it he learned to grind his own color, and to make his own brushes. Moving from Pennsylvania to New York, and on to Maryland, and Ohio, he worked as house painter, sign painter, and carriagemaker, rising in Quaker meeting wherever he might be. Something in his spirit told him that painting pictures was ungodly, yet something else told him more strongly that it was a delight and in the end a necessity. He tried to compose his warring spirits by devoting his paints to religious themes. His pictures took well with the public, and in time even the Quakers encouraged him in his art, provided he pursued it "within the bounds of innocence." Self-trained, his talent developed until in his most famous subject matter he gave forth in composed enchantment his vision of life. It described the human and animal worlds as he would see them, and it identified the act of colonization in North America with the ultimate equality of creatures promised by the prophet Isaiah:

> The wolf also shall dwell with the lamb, and the leopard shall lie down with the kid; and the calf and the young lion and the fatling together; and a little child shall lead them. And the cow and the bear shall feed; their young ones shall lie down together; and the lion shall eat straw like the ox. And the sucking child shall play on the hole of the asp, and the weaned child shall put his hand on the cockatrice' den. They shall not hurt nor destroy in all my holy mountain; for the earth shall be full of the knowledge of the Lord, as the waters cover the sea.

The Reverend Mr. Hicks painted a picture of that vision. If he had painted it only once, it would perhaps not have furnished sufficient evidence for his general emotion. But he painted it over thirty times, and its idyllic democracy stood for what he felt in his nation, believed of his God, and desired of his fellow creatures. His treatment of Isaiah's vision was perfectly literal. There were the animals, clustered together in peace—he called his subject "The Peaceable Kingdom"—and yes, there a little child led them, and other little children set their hands over the serpents' pits; and upon the animal faces lingered bewitched expressions that seemed to veil yet reveal human thoughts. In the middle distance was an allegorical group representing William Penn making his treaty with the Indians, and on a lovely bay beyond lay a ship with pearly sails. Come, said the painting, let all manner of men, as well as all manner of animals, dwell together in peace. Let this occur, it implied further, in our great land of North America, with its waters, mountains, and endless depths of forest. With one huge oak set against dense shadowy foliage Hicks suggested inexhaustible America; and in the prim, sweet compliance of his animals and Indians and colonists with the spirit of peace and equality he captured the desire that had con-

ceived America. Everything in the work was "within the bounds of innocence"—the concept, the drawing, the design, the color scheme; nothing
in it owed a debt to European conventions of art.

The reverend carriagemaker illustrated in his career how in
America's early arts they best saw and captured America who sought her
humbly, through crafts and other acts of work.

A number of beautifully gifted artists before Hicks painted
American portraits and historical subjects, but by the spirit of their
training and technique, they remained colonials. Copley was the American Reynolds, Stuart the American Romney, Sully the American Lawrence, and so on. However rich and copious their productions, they
could not suggest the new America so well as the work of another artist
who when he went to work had no conscious plan to catch a likeness
of America. But that was what he caught, in the general passion of his
first purpose, which was scientific. That he was not a native American
made no difference to his capture of the American essence in his work.
Beginning with Asiatic migrations after the ice age, America was always
peopled by foreigners. What mattered was how he saw a new land in
its new lights:

"Imagine," wrote a French critic who saw a first showing of his
work in 1827 at Edinburgh, "imagine a landscape wholly American,
trees, flowers, grass, even the tints of the sky and the waters, quickened
with a life that is real, peculiar, trans-Atlantic. On twigs, branches, bits
of shore, copied by the brush with the strictest fidelity, sport the feathered races of the New World, in the size of life, each in its particular
attitude, its individuality and peculiarities. Their plumages," and it
was of course Audubon's birds of which he wrote, "sparkle with nature's
own tints; you see them in motion or at rest . . . singing, running,
asleep, just awakened, beating the air, skimming the waves, or rending
one another in their battles. It is a real and palpable vision of the New
World, with its atmosphere, its imposing vegetation, and its tribes
which know not the yoke of man. The sun shines athwart the clearing
in the woods; the swan floats suspended between a cloudless sky and a
glittering wave; strange and majestic figures keep pace with the sun;
. . . and this realization of an entire hemisphere, this picture of a
nature so lusty and strong, is due to the brush of a single man; such
an unheard-of triumph of patience and genius! . . ."

If the French critic did not know America, it was likely that he
knew Europe; and the important thing in his impression of Audubon's
world was that it was strange and new, in its golden stands of light,

its vast river prospects, its blue perspectives stepping away into woods and mountains; all incidental to the bird or animal so studiously arrested in the foreground—incidental, but again, as though early America had to be seen obliquely lest she vanish, standing forth in the truth. Over his shoulder, so to speak, and beyond his scientific purpose, Audubon saw the land and fixed it forever in its spacious morning sense.

There were other painters who combined scientific interests with the arts, like little Leonardos. The Peales of Philadelphia operated a museum of curiosities that included scientific specimens. Samuel F. B. Morse along with his telegraph and Robert Fulton with his improved steamboat were literate painters in conventional styles. The American forerunner in any craft of life seemed required to possess various knacks, if he would be self-sufficient, and also serve his countrymen with all the talents needed to throw together a new culture.

xi. the american art

"It is not," wrote John Adams to his wife Abigail from Paris in 1780, "it is not indeed the fine arts which our country requires; the useful, the mechanic arts are those which we have occasion for in a young country." Wandering about Paris, he could have filled volumes with descriptions of temples and palaces, paintings, sculptures, tapestry, porcelain, and so on, if he only had the time. But this, he said, he could not do without neglecting his duty. And what was his duty? "The science of government is my duty to study, more than all other sciences." And as for the arts—"the arts of legislation and administration and negotiation ought to take the place of, indeed, to exclude, in a manner, all other arts. I must study politics and war, that my sons may have liberty to study mathematics and philosophy. My sons ought to study mathematics and philosophy, geography, natural history and naval architecture, navigation, commerce, and agriculture, in order to give their children a right to study painting, poetry, music, architecture, statuary, tapestry and porcelain. Adieu."

In 1817 he still had qualms about the general subject. "Is it possible to enlist the 'fine arts,' " he asked, "on the side of truth, of virtue, of piety, or even of honor? From the dawn of history they have been prostituted to the service of superstition and despotism." He even graded the arts in the order of their perfidy, "History and epic poetry are worse than architecture, sculpture, and painting, because they are more lasting deceptions." But though he felt that the sciences and arts, for all their failings, had "vastly and immensely ameliorated the condition of man, and even improved his morals," there seemed actually little to be done about disciplining them. "It is in vain to think of restraining the fine arts," he concluded. "Luxury will follow riches and the fine arts will come with luxury in spite of all that wisdom can do. . . ."

John Adams did not see how widely characteristic of the American people was Dr. Franklin's notion that beauty depended wholly upon utility. If what the people made for usefulness had beauty, it lay in abstract qualities that recalled the gestures of human purpose and use. Every act of building and equipping of America for work was admittedly a worthwhile social achievement. But was it any the less an aesthetic achievement to create the very subject of America at work than to comment upon the subject afterward in the formal processes of art? This was the question that America asked of the traditional arts, and would continue to ask in creating all forms of technological design. To make the society itself flower and sprout color and fulfill purpose—this was the American art, and its medium was the liberty of the individual citizen.

In the immense neighborhoods of the frontier the settlers came together from their scatterings in field and forest to help each other at tasks too great for a single family. And when they gathered, they made entertainment out of their work, at husking bees, flax-scutching bees, house-raising bees. Whiskey flowed, and great meals were cooked out of doors in pits of embers, and not only many hands, but shared ideas of how to do it, made light work. Holding strong desires for freedom from all bondages, including that of primitive labor, the Americans became virtuosos of convenience in living. What they discovered about the conquest of manual labor they were able to share by the same means that would in the end make them neighbors in common knowledge over the whole continent—instruments of communication such as those that came into being and use at the very time of the westward movements of the first half of the nineteenth century—the steamboat, the electric telegraph, developments in printing methods, the steam locomotive. An American song gave a sense of exhilaration that came with the railroads:

> Singing through the forest,
> Rattling over the ridges,
> Shooting under arches,
> Running over bridges. . . .

There was a national genius for "make-do." The boundaries of material development seemed to be pushed back in a new dimension of ingenuity; and the nation felt the brisk joy of working all technical limitations to their utmost limit. Common sense was put to work with uncommon energy; and Dr. Franklin's imported rationalism, the seed of technology, appeared to become an American trait. In its spirit of inquiry, it faced the Americans not only to the west, but also to the morrow. If the Indians in their dateless time had been bound by the present, and the Spaniards by the past in their collective memory, then the Americans had a passion for the future. The future was the American theme. To make a better life today, yes, they strove; but there would be tomorrow a still better one, right there on earth; and to achieve this, as surely it would be achieved, every citizen believed he had his chance, in his own way. Because enough people believed so, they created a nation of the many, governed by all, for the benefit of each in his own terms of life, liberty and the pursuit of happiness so long as these did not undo the voted will of the majority.

3.

Bivouac

This creation was the inheritance of the troops gathering on the Texas river in the mildness of March, 1846; and in all their separate persons and various fashions they bore living evidence of the national character. If it was a complex character, yet through all the common expressions of its owners—their vision of human life, their energy and materialism, their politics and oratory and language, their dominant

religion and mythology, their theatre and music and crafts, their dedication to the affairs of work and business—shone a single faith. It was
faith in democracy, whose power in national terms was about to meet
another test facing Mexico.

> Oh, say were you ever in Rio Grande?
> Way, you Rio!
> Oh, were you ever on that strand?
> For we're bound to the Rio Grande!

The song was heard on the supply ships standing in for General
Taylor's depot at Point Isabel; and in a plowed field on the north bank
of the river opposite Matamoros on March twenty-eighth where the
Army was camped in a square with its wagons in the middle which
seemed to a young officer "a very bad position for defense." In the afternoon a flag staff was planted on which the Stars and Stripes were run
up "in a prompt and spirited manner while a band of music struck
up our National air," creating "a momentary stir among the spectators
on the opposite bank." Presently General Taylor sent Brigadier General
William J. Worth across the river to make representations to a Mexican
general officer who "viewed with great indignation our flag planted on
Mexican soil." A United States lieutenant read a paper, prepared in
French, stating for General Taylor that his troops were present under
orders of President Polk to take peaceable possession of the country as
far as the left bank of the Rio Grande and that General Taylor hoped
the Mexican commander would see nothing in the act to produce hostility between the two countries. The Mexican general—it was R. D. de la
Vega, who represented General Mejía, the commander of Matamoros—
listened while a subordinate translated the message into Spanish, and
then asked,

"It is the intention of General Taylor to remain with his army
on the left bank of the Rio Grande?"

"Most assuredly," replied General Worth, "and there to remain
until directed otherwise by his government."

General Worth now asked to see the American consul at Matamoros. The request was refused. Worth frowned. Was the consul a
prisoner? he asked. No, Vega said, not at all, he was "in full exercise
of his functions." Moreover, no American in the city was in arrest.
Worth drew himself up.

"I have now to state," he said, "that a refusal of my demand to
see the American consul is regarded as a belligerent act; and in conclu-

sion, I have to add, the commanding general of the American forces on the left bank of the river will regard the passage of any armed party of Mexicans in hostile array across the Rio Grande as an act of war, and pursue it accordingly."

The interview was over. Worth and his officers were ferried back across the river by Mexican boatmen. Evening came in like sea mist from Mexico Bay. Soon there was formations of firelight outlining the American bivouac. In the darkness no lights showed in Matamoros. Through rain that fell all night long the American soldiers heard men digging and piling earth across the river; and when morning came saw that there were new earthworks facing them with a Mexican twelve-pounder siege gun in position.

4.

The Army of the Rio Grande

Matamoros seen from the opposite bank in morning light appeared to be embedded in a great garden, with the unfinished plaster towers of the church rising out of greenery. Beyond the town lay gardens and cotton fields. The settlement reached up and down the river for a mile. It was still the river of palms, though no longer so named. Tall ranks of palm trees stood along the banks, and inland, along the ridges of old resacas, that were former beds of the river. The river's course in 1846 made deep meanders about Matamoros. The town lay half a mile back from two wide sandy lobes of ground into which fitted a single lobe of the opposite bank. In the center of the Texas lobe that bulged into Mexico American soldiers on the morning of March twenty-ninth began to build a defensive position for the first battery to be placed. They named it Fort Texas. Its guns stared straight at the headquarters of General Mejía across the way. Earth was hauled and piled by a different regiment each day, as the design of a fortress was laid out with six bastion fronts. In plan, the fort looked like a great snowflake. It was large enough to hold four or five regiments. The flagpole rose from within its massive sloping walls that went higher every day.

The Mexicans were busy too. Following the river bend opposite Fort Texas they too raised earthen banks to protect newly placed batteries of mortars and bombs. Upstream they threw together another defense, a hollow square of piled earth, that they named Fort Paredes. Over the town flew four Mexican flags; and the flags of England, France and Spain, to locate their national consulates, and in the event of bombardment to proclaim immunity. It was easy to see both ways across the river; even to hear. The two armies watched each other over the shoulder, as it were, while each continued preparations for what to do to the other. Mexicans were confident of winning if war broke out. Mexican troops greatly outnumbered American forces, and even to European observers the United States seemed to be risking defeat in Mexico's great northern deserts.

United States troops wandered about off duty on their side of the river and saw their first scraps of Mexican life. About twenty houses stood in the fields near the bivouac. Most of their families had fled across the river after the arrival of the army. Every family had a goat in the house, and a gamecock tied under every bed. Up and down river were gardens where grew lemons, oranges, figs, peaches; and lines of palms bearing plantain and cocoanut. From the little farms came those few Mexicans who had stayed home, and who now brought chickens, vegetables and milk to sell to the troops. After a day or two, vendors from Matamoros came and went freely among the Americans, selling food and oddments. Among them, the Army was certain, there were many spies who saw and heard all they needed, while "we are doing nothing," observed a young Kentuckian early in April, adding that "an enterprising general might have cut us to pieces any night since our arrival here." He sighed. He did not want to censure General Taylor who, he could only assume, had information denied to others.

Watching each other prepare for war, the armies kept up a social tone across the river. Work and drill were plainly visible both ways, and were observed with interest and often with admiration. The Mexicans made frequent rumpus with drums and trumpets during the day. Detachments were marched and countermarched, and American regulars lounged on their bank and applauded. The Mexican river front became a promenade where in open carriages the best society drove along to greet the Americans. Gallant conversations were held across the stream.

Compliments flew. Friendships were pledged. Many of the Mexican officers were handsome, beautifully uniformed and wonderfully graceful in their manners. Beside them, their soldiers were "half-starved-looking devils" who excited in the Americans "only feelings of contempt." Both armies loved band music, and gathered to listen to each other's at sundown. While the women of Matamoros dawdled by in their lacy rebozos on the opposite shore, the hungry men so far from home gave them music. "We played 'Yankee Doodle' because it made a loud noise, the 'Star Spangled Banner' because it waved over us, 'Hail Columbia' because it was inspiriting, and the sweetest airs from the operas for the beautiful señoritas." But when the Mexican music came, it was "exquisite . . . surpassing anything ever heard from a military band." And then the warm April night was on them in darkness, and the riverside amenities were done, and back in camp, at tattoo, the American soldiers heard how a large force of Mexican cavalry was thought to have crossed the river below them, and all were ordered to memorize the watchword— "Texas"—and to sleep on their arms without undressing. But morning came without incident, and work went on, and in the afternoon, perhaps, there was something curious to be seen at Fort Paredes, where the work was nearly done. There, if they would stroll to the river, the Americans could see the Mexican soldiers kneeling on the ramps and parapets of earth they had thrown up, while a priest in a white cope heavy with gold bullion blessed the fort, scattering holy water everywhere on it, that it might with divine assistance stand with them against wound, death and defeat in their cause. In the mystery of the blessing there lay somewhere embedded the mystery of the common soldier's thought of war—how little he might gain for himself, how much of himself he might lose.

Some thought about it until it made them change their minds. One afternoon early in April both armies heard rapid volleys of rifle fire downstream from Fort Texas, below the central ferry crossing. On hearing the fire, the Mexican pickets at the ferry ran away "like scared dogs" to Matamoros. Soldiers from Fort Texas swarmed to the bank and saw that their own sentries were firing at a deserter who was trying to swim the river to escape to Mexico. He was hit. He sank and drowned. It was a scene to be repeated many times. Upward of thirty men deserted the American flag in the first few weeks on the river.

While work went forward at Fort Texas the depot at Point Isabel was daily growing. Dispatch riders and wagons moved back and forth between the two posts. Troops built quarters and warehouses and dock facilities at Point Isabel. The installation was called Fort Polk. New shipping came in almost daily. The bar at the entrance of the Arms of Saint James was only eight feet under water, and the broad side-wheeler steamers took it gingerly. There was a story that in ancient times one of the largest and richest of Mexican cities stood at the entrance only to be swept away by the sea in a storm; and another that a later Mexican village with a fort and a garrison of sixty Mexican soldiers was wiped away in a single night by a hurricane, leaving only the low, bare sand islands that paralleled the coast. The only other settlement on the nearby beaches was a village called Bagdad that stood on a sandspit on the last Mexican bank of the Rio Grande at its mouth. There came Mexicans from as far away as Monterrey to enjoy bathing in the sea. It was subject not only to Gulf storms, but to high water when the river overflowed its low dunes in flood, and the waters shifted back and forth in dispute over ocean floor and beach. The bar at the river's mouth had even less water than the Brazos entrance, and the Army had not yet received vessels shallow enough in draft to enter the river, where no steamboat had entered since the departure of Captain Austin's *Ariel* in 1830. All supplies in the first weeks of April, 1846, came over the road from Point Isabel to Fort Texas. On the fifth, the Army's heavy guns, eighteen-pounders, arrived from Point Isabel to be emplaced in the fort.

General Taylor regarded in patience the preparations made at his command. Certain of his officers wished he might move a little faster. It had taken over a year since annexation was approved by Congress to bring an army to the Rio Grande. And now that it was there, could not something more be done, if not to give battle, then at least to smarten up the camp, guard against spies, drill the troops . . . ?

But the General was calm. He rode his horse, old Whitey, among the tents, the working parties, the soldiers lounging off duty, and gave homely reassurance just by his looks. His face was wrinkled and dark yellow, and he took less trouble about a uniform than any of his private soldiers. Now he wore an old oilcloth cap, and again a farmer's broad-brimmed straw hat, or even a big Mexican sombrero. His coat was either of blue-checked gingham, or a faded green homespun, or a linen roundabout duster, or a brown fustian. Sometimes he wore linen trousers, or attapakas pantaloons, or "a common soldier's light-blue overalls," or blue Army pants without braid. Someone said he looked rather like Fenimore Cooper. The men knew his goodness of heart, for like them he felt as "honest and as good as anybody." He lived in a

plain unguarded tent under a cottonwood tree a little way from a pond
that had an island in it. From it he could watch Fort Texas and the
granular glisten of camp life under the Mexican sun.

Some of his officers chafed under his limitations of mind and
education. "Slow of speech," with "a stammering voice," he could make
his wishes known, but before they could become official, someone had
to put them into readable English. If he took a dislike to a man, he was
passionate and implacable forever after against him. For most men in
the American government he had a suspicious contempt, like any voter
jealous of power held over him even by his consent. Theoretical refinements of strategy and tactics were foreign to his mind; but "a certain
bull-headed obstinacy" in his character gave him the force—the slow,
undeviating force—he could throw into a fight; and the common Army
received it through his presence in his wanderings among them; and
through what they heard of him in his headquarters. Missing nothing,
giving a minimum of orders, he waited for the American position on
the north bank of the river to develop; while he sat in his camp chair
and told and listened to stories that would make him laugh till the tears
ran down his face—preferably the same stories, over and over, by the
hour—in the comforting drone of a simple man who had no love and
no brilliance for anything but his uncomplicated vision of duty.

The troops of General Taylor's command were regulars. Volunteers would join him later. For the present he had not more than twenty-
three hundred men, while his staff estimated that the Mexicans could
certainly oppose them with three or four times as many. More than
one American officer thought it "a mistake to come with so small a
force . . . no one seems to think a disaster to our Army a thing possible,
and most of the Army are disappointed and impatient that General
Taylor does not create a pretext for taking the town." True, it did not
seem plausible that the Mexicans had any discipline; but the Americans
also labored under a disadvantage—some of the senior officers were incapable of drilling them. "We ought to have the best-instructed troops
in the world," sighed a brilliant lieutenant colonel commanding the
Third Infantry, "but are far from it." General Taylor knew nothing of
army movements, and only one brigade commander out of three could
"give the simplest command . . . 'break to the right or march to the left,'
for instance—" without the prompting of an adjutant. The common drill
of the battalion was impossible to execute, much less the movements of
a brigade or an army. It was a comfort that the Third Infantry, at least,
was well-trained, "for every officer and every man knows his place and

duty." Lieutenant U. S. Grant did not agree entirely with such an estimate of the army as a whole, for he believed that "the officers of the regular Army, from highest to lowest, were educated in their profession." A more efficient army for its number and "armament" never "fought a battle than the one commanded by General Taylor on Mexican—or Texan—soil." But then Lieutenant Grant was not yet of the line; he was a quartermaster, to whom an infantryman would deny an opinion on the fitness of troops.

The enlisted soldiers were men who had gone into the Army in peacetime to serve for seven dollars a month. At that rate few officers expected to find a very superior breed of individual in the ranks. The opportunities of American civil life drew men of ambition with their expanding rewards; and only when volunteers later came to the Army, to fight for patriotic reasons, was the quality of the enlisted soldiers improved. Among the regulars were many soldiers of foreign birth—English, Irish, French, German, Polish. Many of these were veterans of the Napoleonic wars. To them Mexico offered free land—three hundred and twenty acres to a private soldier, more to holders of higher grades—and immunity if they would desert. Enough did so to form what was called the San Patricio Battalion of the Mexican forces.

Except for a few companies that carried recently developed percussion-cap muskets, the infantry under General Taylor was armed with flintlock muskets that were charged with paper cartridges packed with powder, buckshot and ball. Their range was only a few hundred yards. Everyone wore blue—the men, jackets, trousers and fatigue caps of light blue; the officers, dark blue frock coats and light blue trousers with braid. In the artillery was vested most of the dash and prestige of United States arms. Taylor had four twelve-pounder howitzers that threw shell, and four deep-voiced eighteen-pounders for siege. Beyond these, he commanded the latest glory of the Army, which was the mobile, light, horse-drawn cannonry trained to maneuver fast in the field, and which was known as the "Flying Artillery." Its weapons were brass six-pounders that fired solid shot. Its officers—Ringgold, Duncan, Bragg, Ridgely—were young men all trained at West Point. They had the spirit of those who knew they belonged to a corps d'élite: and who swore that their new weapon—the Flying Artillery—was the key to victory in all future warfare. Even their vocabulary reflected their high style: in 1846 a shot from a cannon was called a "blizzard."

As April wore on, preparations continued on the river. Soldiers soon found it dangerous to explore the countryside. One, Colonel Cross, the chief quartermaster, rode out alone on the tenth of April and did not come back. All the American power was concentrated in Fort Texas, with its heavy guns. Outside its bastions loomed a battery containing two howitzers. The Mexicans completed six batteries, strung along the river, and—it was somewhat dismaying—planted in deep pits protected by high embankments in front, until it seemed that "they could not be knocked out, or only with luck or difficulty, by the American fire." From such hidden positions the Mexican fire, if it came, would rise in high lobs to sail heavily across the river and fall from almost directly above into Fort Texas, and upon the tenting grounds gathered about it. The weather was odd—warm nights and cold, alternately; and one afternoon a sheeting rain came in on a sudden gale and swamped the camp. Tents were blown down in the company streets, and everything in them was soaked. If General Taylor went on waiting, so did the commander in Mexico.

5.
The Cannonade

What General Mejía was waiting for became clear on April eleventh, when the Americans heard the bells of Matamoros suddenly clamoring in jubilee and a salute of twenty guns going off. They piled toward the river to observe a grand affair. With two hundred new troops, General Pedro de Ampudia, the old North Mexican campaigner, was arriving in Matamoros to relieve General Mejía of command. The Mexican garrison paraded in honor of their new commanding general, while the Mexican bands of music "excelled all former efforts." Late in the afternoon Ampudia came down to the riverside to inspect the fortifications. On his left breast he wore a decoration awarded to him for his triumph over the Texans at Mier. Stories about him came across the river by pedlar, and flew through the American camp: he was a great general, he was a brave man, he was a bloodthirsty fiend who in marching to the river just now had refused to be encumbered by sick and straggling soldiers and had ordered such wretches to be shot.

The next day at three o'clock two Mexican officers came down to the ferry on their bank with a trumpeter and sounded a parley. Matters were beginning to move. Ampudia's representatives were brought across. They were taken to General Taylor's tent under its cottonwood. There they handed a document to the commander of the Army of the Rio Grande. General Ampudia, it stated, would not insult the good sense of General Taylor by explaining "the many grounds for just grievances felt by the Mexican nation," but required him "in all form, and at latest in the peremptory term of twenty-four hours" to break up his camp and retire to the north bank of the Nueces river, so allowing the two governments to regulate "the pending question of Texas." If General Taylor insisted "in remaining upon the soil of the department of Tamaulipas," war must follow.

General Taylor accepted the message, and said that he would answer it at ten o'clock the following morning. The Mexican officers were escorted back to the ferry, and the staff went to work that same afternoon to elevate General Taylor's wishes into a proper dispatch. He wanted it said that as an Army commander he could have no truck with another government in diplomatic affairs. He would remind Señor General Don Pedro de Ampudia, though, that the United States government had done its best to settle the Rio Grande dispute by peaceful means, but without any success. Meantime, he was ordered to occupy and hold the country up to the left bank of the river until the whole shebang was definitely settled, and in obeying his orders, he had made no hostile moves. To wind up the argument, he could not, under his orders, back up from where he was—or, as the educated adjutant put it, "to retrograde from the position which I now occupy." The General wanted it added in there somewhere that he was sorry for the other choice left to him by General Ampudia, with "the individual suffering that may result"; but he wanted it understood that he would "by no means avoid such alternative, leaving the responsibility with those who rashly commence hostilities." He had the honor to be—and here the adjutant nodded—"very respectively, your obedient servant."

Promptly at ten o'clock in the next morning the answer was delivered across the river; and at two o'clock an American dragoon patrol rode up to headquarters to report that Mexican troops were crossing the river into Texas some miles below camp. Nothing further was heard of this Mexican movement. But if the enemy was receiving supplies by ship at the river's mouth where there were no American troops yet posted, access to the sea was denied Ampudia by General Taylor's next move, when he requested Commodore Connor to blockade the entrance with units of the United States Home Squadron.

The General had a Mexican man of affairs on his staff, a certain Chapita, who had connections in Matamoros. On April fifteenth Chapita flourished a piece of information—Ampudia, so lately installed as commander of the north, was soon to be displaced by another veteran of Texas and north Mexican campaigns, General Mariano Arista, a tall, redheaded soldier who having lived in Cincinnati, Ohio, presumably knew how to treat with Americans. The opinion went around the American officers' messes that his appointment indicated peace for a while—"the war is put off till June. This ends the chapter. There will not be a hostile gun fired, but we shall have to drag through a hot and tedious summer here without our families, infinitely worse than all the horrors of war. It is nonsense," declared an American major, "for our government to temporize any longer with Mexico." Were there not provocations enough?

Colonel Cross, for example—what had become of him? Were Mexicans responsible for his disappearance? On the seventeenth of April a detachment was ordered to the field under the command of Lieutenant Theodoric Porter (son of Commodore David Porter) to find out. Two days later men from Porter's detail came straggling into the camp to hack out a sobering story. In a hard rainstorm at night they had been attacked by Mexicans, members of a guerilla band led by a border bandit called Roman Falcón. In the downpour, the Americans found most of their powder wet. Lieutenant Porter was killed, with several of his soldiers. The survivors came home sure that just so had Colonel Cross been killed, though his body had not been found. But in another two days it was discovered by another scouting party. There was nothing left but his skeleton and a few scraps of equipment. Coyotes and buzzards had picked the bones clean. Was nothing to be done about such an outrage? But a state of war did not yet exist.

And then, on April twenty-third, President Paredes appeared before the Congress of Mexico to declare that "from this day defensive way begins," and was received with enthusiasm.

His statement was timed to give strategic—and legal—support to the command at Matamoros; for on the following day Mariano Arista arrived to relieve Pedro de Ampudia, with orders to go into action immediately. One day later a large force of cavalry under General Anastasio Torrejón crossed the Rio Grande above Fort Texas. The movement was met at Carricitos Ranch by a scouting party of sixty-three men under Captain Seth Thorton. Eleven Americans were killed, several wounded, and the rest captured to be taken to Matamoros. It was the first engagement of the war, and word of it was sent by express courier to the President and the Cabinet at Washington, who still hoped to make their point by peaceful means.

Close on such a first success, the Mexican forces now crossed the river, above and below Fort Texas, by-passing the American main body, and manoeuvring to close behind it to cut it off from the supply base at Point Isabel. Communications with the base were already precarious. So many Mexican troops were massing on the coast that reports came into camp telling how Point Isabel had already been attacked. Not Chapita, but his nephew, had the best story—how two regiments of Mexican infantry and one of cavalry had been "cut to pieces" by American artillery. The whole story was false. Point Isabel was still safe, and Commodore Connor had sailed for the Arms of Saint James to land five hundred marines and sailors, having left another large detachment on land at the river's mouth. On April twenty-eight for an hour before nightfall there was a continuous fire of musketry in Matamoros. American officers wondered if a revolt had broken out across the way. But the matter was never explained. General Taylor informed his staff that evening that he would march in six days—on May third—with the bulk of the Army to protect Point Isabel and throw back the enemy, "wherever he found him." To defend Fort Texas, he would leave the Seventh Infantry behind, and the "sick, lame and lazy, with Land's and Bragg's artillery." Major Jacob Brown was assigned the command of Fort Texas. His orders from General Taylor were clear: he must maintain his post, he must on no account risk his position by making a sally, and if he were surrounded and besieged he must inform the General by firing the eighteen-pounders of Fort Texas at regular intervals, which would be heard at Point Isabel through the heavy sea air. At last a young officer was able to exclaim to his diary, "Glorious times these!"

He left for glory three days sooner than the Commanding General had planned, for on the morning of May first a large Mexican force crossed the river below Matamoros, moving up the coast toward Point Isabel. General Taylor alerted the army and at two o'clock began to pull away from the Rio Grande on the narrow road that was bordered by old river beds edged with palms. "I go to meet the enemy," recorded

the young officer, "with my feelings all schooled to do my duty regardless
of personal consequences." They marched for eighteen hours and
encamped at midnight without having seen the enemy. At daybreak the
long column of infantry, flying artillery, dragoons and wagons moved out
again. By noon they were arriving at Point Isabel where across the
low dunes tufted with sharp grass they could see the etched black
spars and idle smoke of the fleet in the harbor. The troops were hungry.
They'd had no coffee and little else to eat or drink since leaving Fort
Texas. Soon they found oranges and lemons to suck for thirst, but there
was only one water well—a new one dug by the army—to meet the wants
of nearly two thousand men. They slept on the ground that night
without fires or blankets, and only the officers had tents. Pickets strained
for sign of the enemy in the dark.

    None came.

    A little while after day broke over the sea, and before reveille, the
sleeping camp was awakened by heavy sound from far away. Men lifted
their heads to listen. They heard cannonading from the Rio Grande, and
knew Fort Texas and its little garrison were under bombardment. The
stifled thumps of the distant cannon "were listened to with feelings
so intense that our soldiers fairly ceased for a moment to breathe."
In a few minutes the "camp was wild with excitement," for as Lieutenant
Grant said, "The war had begun." Worried by what they could hear,
they yet dreaded to have it cease, for continued cannonading was the
"best proof that the Fort" had "not fallen. . . ." It kept up all day;
and at night, riding hard with four voluntary companions, Captain
Samuel H. Walker, of the Texas Rangers, on orders of General Taylor,
returned to Fort Texas for news.

6.

Fort Texas

He approached the fort early the next morning and made his way carefully into the dry moat that surrounded it. There he signalled and was recognized by Major Brown, who had him brought up by a ladder. They exchanged their news. The bombardment beginning at five that morning, said Major Brown, must have thrown over fifteen hundred shots and shells at Fort Texas throughout the day. Remarkably little damage was done to the fort, though one soldier was killed. Even the tents of the Seventh Infantry, set up within the walls, and the horses of the dragoon company, tied to picket lines there, were not hit. The garrison's gunners knocked out two of the heaviest Mexican cannon, and most of the bombardment from across the river thereafter was laid by mortars. The fort seemed secure. Captain Walker was glad to be able to take such good news back to Point Isabel. In his turn he described to Major Brown how coming overland he had found the country "literally filled" with Mexicans. To communicate between Point Isabel and Fort Texas was "desperate service." Walker snatched some rest and spent the day—May fourth—with the garrison.

As the day wore on, the Mexican artillery resumed its fire. The ramparts of the fort were manned by riflemen, but it presently seemed safe to assume that the Mexicans were not going to storm the position with troops. Major Brown ordered his men off the parapets, but kept them immediately below their positions on the alert. Because his magazine held very little ammunition, he decided to conserve what he had "to use against assault"—should it come—"rather than spend it against enemy batteries." Work continued on bombproof shelters near the rifle posts. These were made by setting out barrels close together to form small rooms, with timber laid across their tops and packed with earth to a thickness of several feet.

The artillery observers in the fort could plainly see each Mexican battery over the river before Matamoros. One was a little way upstream in a grove of trees. One tree towered above the rest. In it was a Mexican observer with a spyglass. The next one downstream held mortars in a pit; the next was protected by sandbags; the next, by a line of piled earth; and the last was enclosed in a large earthen square. From these positions came sailing either shells of bronze or iron balls. They came slowly enough to be seen in their heavy rise and fall. The shells were round, like bombs, with protruding fuses, and they hissed and whirled in their trajectories. On landing they exploded, and reflected by the ground their force was spent upward in the air, throwing metal, and showers of sand that settled back slowly. When a battery fired over the way, the observers in Fort Texas called out which one it was—"Sand-bag battery," or "Lower fort mortar battery," or "Tree mortar battery," and if it sent over a bomb, easily identified, that too was called out, and the men fell face down on the ground to take open shelter under the narrow point of the cone-shaped explosion at impact. In his high tree the Mexican soldier with his spyglass saw the Americans falling every time a shell went off, and reported, "so it looked to him," that those who fell were killed. His reports were repeated in Matamoros and soon it was believed that the Americans were "dying by scores." Encouraged, General Arista considered plans for taking the fort by assault. Late in the afternoon of May fourth Captain Walker left Fort Texas to find his way through the enemy movements inland and report to General Taylor that the river garrison was holding well.

Soon after Walker left, Major Brown's attention was suddenly turned from the river to the country in the rear of the fort when musket fire was heard from there. Mexican troops were established about four hundred yards away, firing toward the fort. Though at that distance their fire fell short, Major Brown concluded that they were making the frank gesture of an assault. He ordered the parapets and all bastions manned to repel attack. Evening fell, and no storm came, but the defenses were ready all night. In the dark there were sounds of activity inland— the gear of moving horsemen, murmur of men massing, the grunt and scrape of shovels. There would be something to see at dawn.

With daybreak on the fifth the garrison saw that an "immense force of thousands," both horse and foot, was aligned behind Fort Texas with its left end anchored on a point of the river below the fort and its right on a point above, for a distance of a mile. In the country behind the line was a new battery emplacement—the "Country Battery," as the Americans immediately called it. The fort was now encircled by the enemy. The garrison went to work training eighteen-pound and six-pound batteries on the new line from their positions in the two south-easterly bastions of the fort.

At five o'clock in the afternoon all Mexican guns on both sides of the river opened on the fort with "a galling crossfire of shot and shell." It was returned by all batteries of the fort, until after an hour the enemy barrage ceased on both sides as if by prearrangement. Presently a Mexican informer, named Valdez, made his way to the gate of Fort Texas and asked to be admitted, for he had news. Glittering with a native talent for intrigue he was taken to Major Brown.

What was his news?

He replied that in Matamoros they were telling how a party of United States dragoons on a foray out of Point Isabel had been driven back to the base.

Was that all?

No, there was more: General Arista's troops were "becoming dissatisfied, and were deserting in great numbers."

Anything else?

Yes, it was said that a revolution had broken out in Mexico.

While there may have been general encouragement in some of this, Major Brown faced harder information at hand. In the last evening light a party of Mexican cavalry made a reconnaissance within eight hundred yards of the fort. One of Brown's junior officers came to ask permission to take dragoons and sally out to "return the reconnaissance at closer view." Major Brown approved; and in a few moments the lieutenant and his men rode out of the gate of Fort Texas. They were gone for an hour, and returned with all safe to report that they had ridden close to the Country Battery forcing Mexicans to retire behind it. There were thousands of enemy soldiers deployed about the open plain behind the fort. General Taylor's headquarters under the tree near the pond was occupied by the enemy, who had posted guards along the ditches thrown up by the General's detail. The garrison's situation was now unstable. It was time for Major Brown to think about signalling over the dunes with paced salvos of the eighteen-pounders to General Taylor, twelve miles away as sound travelled.

The sun was hardly up on Wednesday the sixth when the eighteen-pounders began their heavy intervals. Their pace was so measured that the enemy as if understanding their message began to reply with salvos from the Lower Fort Mortar Battery and the Country Battery. Mexican guns found the range that day. Their shot and shell tore down tents within the fort, and wounded many horses on the dragoon picket lines. If there were too few men in Fort Texas to offer a strong defense, they were lucky in one way; for in the great area of the fort they were also too few to offer compact targets. All they could do was watch for the sailing cannonballs and shells, and avoid them if they could. They had so little ammunition that Major Brown held the fire of his batteries, hoarding what he had against a mass attack. His men made a game of the bombardment. They laughed and jeered and hopped aside when the balls landed. An old mess cook making coffee for his fellows saw a ball roll into the ashes of his cooking fire. It spilled his pot. He walked up and kicked the spent ball, saying in disgust, "There! Those [profane] Mexicans have knocked over my coffee."

After nearly four hours of shelling the fort was showing damage. Major Brown, with his adjutant, went on a round of inspection. He came to a bomb shelter on which soldiers were making repairs. He stopped to direct them. Amidst the general shelling a bomb struck on the parapet just above the work party. It threw up a curtain of sand. The soldiers fell waiting for the explosion; but none came. The shell buried itself as a dud. The men rose again—all but one. They turned to see Major Brown who lay among them with his right leg blown off by a direct hit from another ball. They saw the end of his thigh bone bluish white amid raw muscle. He was conscious. As they took him up to carry him to the hospital tent he said,

"Men, go to your duties. Stand by your posts. I am but one among you."

While surgeons operated, amputating his leg above the knee, his command was taken over by Captain E. S. Hawkins. After the operation the Major remarked that it was fortunate for the United States that the wound had come to him instead of to a younger man. He was put to bed in a bomb shelter. The shelling continued.

At about four o'clock it ceased, and at half-past, two Mexican officers advanced with a white flag. They halted before the fort. To meet them, Captain Hawkins sent two officers, who brought back a proposal made by the Mexicans "on humanity's grounds" that Fort Texas surrender, and spare further bloodshed and destruction. Captain Hawkins examined the proposal. It would have been useful to know, just then, where General Taylor was, and whether he had heard and understood the signal salvos of the heavy guns, and what conditions were governing his own decisions across the seaside plain. Fort Texas was in trouble. It could be only a matter of time until—but Captain Hawkins disposed of the surrender demand without solving his own uncertainties. At five o'clock he sent his spokesmen out to reject the Mexican advice. The garrison made ready with what they could. The Mexican shelling was resumed immediately, but Fort Texas could not reply. As darkness came the assault was expected. It did not develop, but the bombardment continued for the first time into the night. It made a picture, as a soldier saw. "As the shells rose into the air, the burning fuses gave them the appearance of fiery comets, and at times so rapidly did they fly, that streams of seemingly continuous, hissing light, formed magnificent arches from the Mexican batteries to our fort, where they found a common centre. The continued reverberations of the heavy discharges, the constant explosion of shells, the sheeted flame from the mortars and howitzers, that in the darkness of night seemed bursting volcanoes, formed a picture of war at once sublime and terrible. . . ." Quiet did not come till late.

It came only to be broken at dawn of Thursday, May seventh. The garrison was feeling the strain of fatigue and uncertainty. There was no word from the General. Who knew how long they would have to keep on dodging shells? They noticed that the Mexican shells this morning were not of the usual bronze, but were now of iron. It was something for the soldiers to talk about. Firing continued intermittently all morning. A number of horses were killed. In the afternoon the firing grew steady and went on till sundown. One shell smashed through a tent and blew up in a chest that held all the instruments of the Seventh Regiment band. Bits of brasses and woodwinds flew into the air.

That afternoon in Matamoros a formation was held to commit and encourage Mexican infantry to lead the long-expected assault on Fort Texas. It was to take place at midnight. General Arista's assurances were conveyed to the small brown soldiers who stood in ragged garments, listening immovably. The time was excellent, said their officers, for the attack. It was well known that vast numbers of the North American soldiers in the fort had been killed: resistance would be weak. Moreover, those wretches who somehow had survived the tremendous artillery demonstrations of the Mexican army were by now so exhausted and worn down that they could never make a proper defense. The assault troops had the honor of leading the arms of Mexico to victory. An inspiring name for the detachment was therewith bestowed upon them—they were to be called the "Forlorn Hope," in the spirit of those who dare the powers of fate by voluntarily recognizing hazard so great that only the greatest of soldiers could overcome it. The ranks of the Forlorn Hope sent up no cheers, while their leaders continued "to nerve them for the work," and "every passion was appealed to, and prejudice consulted. . . ." When midnight came, and the hour of attack, the Fort Texas garrison heard sudden discharges of muskets, and then bugles in the darkness sounding the charge, and all braced to meet what must come—but it did not come. The Forlorn Hope remained impassive in the dark. Was it true, then, that General Arista was having trouble with his troops? Now instead of a swarming assault from all sides against the fort, artillery fire was resumed and lasted till day broke, and the garrison did not sleep, and looked at one another, and wondered where the General was.

The firing went on all morning, Friday, May eighth, in hot, sticky weather. The garrison was tired. They had not even the satisfaction of returning the bombardment of the enemy. The soldier's greatest privation—not to know what was going to happen to him—troubled the men. Their apprehension fed on idleness. They were not yet starving or thirsting—but who knew when they might be, especially if General Taylor had not heard the eighteen-pounders, or having heard them, could not for various reasons come back to the river? And still the Mexican batteries threw in shot and shell, until it was impossible to think, day or night. It sometimes seemed that not another explosion could be endured—and then, sometimes, suddenly there was quiet, like an answer to a mortal need, and the firing stopped.

It stopped at two o'clock that Friday, and in the deep relief of silence, the garrison heard nothing, for a few moments. And then, from far away, a great meaning trundled through the hot, dense air. The soldiers of Fort Texas jumped to their feet and listened, staring at each other. What they heard was "a severe cannonading towards Point Isabel," whose sounds "continued to roll on the plain," and they knew what they were hearing, and they pounded and hugged one another for joy, and sent up together a "simultaneous shout . . . that must have sounded in Matamoros more terribly than our severest cannonade." The General, somewhere, out there on the sandy plain, was coming back to the river, and in his march had met the enemy, and was giving battle.

At the shout that went up from Fort Texas, the Mexican batteries on both sides of the river opened again with a harder barrage than they had ever thrown before. Every time there was a momentary silence on the river, the sounds of the battle on the inland plain came through, and the garrison cheered. They cheered that afternoon when they saw great numbers of Mexican infantry and cavalry crossing the Rio Grande above and below the fort to head rapidly inland toward the battle. The

movement could only mean that Mexicans were badly needed to reinforce their comrades who were trying to stop General Taylor's army from
coming back to Fort Texas.

Shortly before sunset the bombardments ceased, both near and far;
and a little while later an accommodating Mexican, carrying a white
flag, approached Fort Texas and was admitted. He had news. It was
true—the United States forces had engaged the Mexicans at a place
called Palo Alto, and had pushed them back toward the Rio Grande.
Nightfall had ended the battle, which perhaps would be resumed in
the morning. Who could say?

It was quiet all night that night on the river. At two o'clock
in the morning, when Major Jacob Brown died in the bombshelter, the
quiet seemed stiller. The night sounds of the river pressed closer.
Crickets asked and asked in the rushes. Now and then a catfish came up
for air and strenuously slapped its way underwater again. A goat bell
sounded faintly on the other side. Voices were talking somewhere. Someone waded the river—thighs, coming slowly, and creating two new
skeins of current. Jacob Brown was enfolded in an army blanket. His
garrison slept and would soon awaken.

7.

The Listeners

The ninth of May, Saturday, was a day of wilting heat, worse than
any other so far. The distance everywhere was lost in a pale milky haze.
Blurred ranks of palm trees seemed to float upright without touching
earth; their thick stems were cut by the shimmer of heat at the sandy
ground. There was fine dust over greenery until all looked pale olive in
color, under a sky more white than blue. Fort Texas was still surrounded,
though only an occasional shot was lobbed into it. Many of the siege
troops from behind the fort were gone to reinforce the Mexican lines

farther inland to the north. The garrison listened for sounds of renewed battle. None came all morning, and they wondered again where General Taylor had gone, and what General Arista was doing. They watched upriver and down, and the road leading from the main ferry across the open country toward Point Isabel. From the elevated banquettes of the fort they could see the whole countryside and all the river approaches—the sandy flats, and the easy slopes to the river, and the river itself with its sand bars, and its deep and shallow channels, marked by difference in the current, and the banks about a hundred yards apart. No carriages rolled along the Mexican bank now, and no gallant banter flew across. Matamoros was oddly quiet, as though a carnival of war and jubilation had been interrupted by an announcement not yet quite understood. Here and there someone crossed the river, a handful of soldiers, a vendor in his white shirt and his wide white pantaloons wrapped almost twice about his frank brown belly. If a horseman went off at a gallop up the road to the north, in the odd stillness of the simmering day he seemed momentous: but only because the soldiers who watched him from the fort strained so hard to see, and to hear, where there was nothing to see or hear, that their thoughts ran away with them after such a simple event as a rider vanishing up a dusty road.

Noon passed, and there was no news, and the hours of early afternoon, until at last, somewhat after three o'clock the garrison once more heard the opening claps of battle from over the plain. There were statements from the artillery—but today few and far between when compared with yesterday. Now it was the flat sputter of musket fire that seemed incessant. The listening soldiers said to each other that the fight today was closer in—they could not be sure, but under such sustained rifle fire and with so little cannonading, there must be rushes of small units of men, maybe even fighting hand to hand. There was not much wind on a day of such wet heat, but now and then it shifted, with the effect of a great, distant door opening or shutting on far decisions, and the listeners remembered marching from that quarter, and some estimated that the battle was happening about five miles away from Fort Texas, at the place where the Point Isabel road passed through the old dry lagoon where once the river had run edged with palms—the Resaca de la Palma. Anyone who remembered it and how the road ran there saw that it made a natural situation for ambush. The Mexicans outnumbered the General's troops by nearly four to one; and furthermore, knew the country well. The garrison's fate depended on which soldiers would return to the river from the plain.

At about five o'clock they saw what looked like the first sweepings of a coming storm. Dust rose in a long line to the north and east; the whole line seemed to come toward the river before an impelling wind. Presently they heard sounds—little scraps of audible indignity, and then saw the mortal humility of men running for their lives, who had thrown away anything that would hinder their flight, the Mexican army of the north in rout and terror breaking as fast as they could for the Rio Grande. The garrison roared with joy. They could not see the whole force in retreat, but the portion they saw, in its panic and volume, was enough to assure that upstream and down, out of sight, more thousands were in a wild scramble for individual survival. The river front was jammed with men who fought to slide down the softly caving bank into the water and across to Mexico. Their voices cried for safety. They climbed across one another to swim. Many were drowned, including wounded who were carried in sacks on muleback. It was like a mindless swarm of brown-skinned animals that ran breathless before a prairie fire.

It was not long until what they ran before could be heard and seen—the United States Dragoons, Artillery and Infantry "in one mass at full run, yelling at every step," and firing whenever they could as they came. In the midst of their cheers that "reached high heaven" as they swept toward the river, they faltered only once, when three shots from an eighteen-pounder broke toward them, and narrowly missed them. They stared toward Fort Texas, thinking their own men had mistakenly opened fire on them; but the eighteen-pounder was across the river, and as it did not speak again, perhaps its crew had run away with the soaking-wet fugitives who went by it. The Americans rushed on, "yelling like mad." General Taylor's Army of the Rio Grande was once again at the river. The siege of Fort Texas was lifted.

Before nightfall the army was formed into improvised marching order and withdrawn to make camp near their supply wagons that were established on the day's battleground. So complete was the rout of the enemy that few security measures were needed along the north bank of the river that night. "Thus," recorded an officer, "thus ended the day in the most brilliant victory of the age."

By late afternoon of the next day, the army was making its encampment once again around Fort Texas by the river; and the Seventh Infantry and the other garrison troops, free among their countrymen again, listened to the stories of the two famous battles which they had heard but had not seen

8.

Palo Alto

First, the Battle of Palo Alto.

They heard how General Taylor with two thousand men left Point Isabel for Fort Texas, on the evening of May seventh, bringing a train of two hundred and fifty wagons loaded with stores. He knew from the signal guns that he was needed, and soon. The army made seven miles that night and pushed on early the next day, the eighth of May, crossing a great open prairie where on their right and left were ponds of fresh water. Ahead of them three miles rose the ridge of tall ancient mesquite trees—the place called Palo Alto where General Worth and the rest had camped on the first march to the river. Everybody remembered it. Now, right before that background of gnarled greenery, the army saw the Mexicans, drawn up in line a mile wide, with their cavalry on the right, artillery in the center, and infantry on the left. The enemy arms sparkled, for it was light and hot in the early sky. Between the two forces there was nothing but long, dry grass.

The General ordered a halt between the ponds, and the men after stacking arms were sent to fill their canteens and water the horses, half a regiment at a time. The water was sweet, after the brackish water of Isabel. The soldiers drank and washed. They stirred up dust from the long grass and in their bellies were knots of wonder before battle. In half an hour the regiments were reassembled. The wagons were ordered to remain in the rear at the ponds when the army was formed in a solid square and ordered to advance.

Breaking from solid square into line, the army moved forward in an order of battle that put the Fifth Infantry on the right, and then reading to the left, Major Ringgold's Flying Artillery, the Third Infantry, the Sixth Infantry, two eighteen-pounders, the Dragoons, Duncan's battery, and the Eighth Infantry. The grass was so thick that marching tread and roll of caisson were muffled. In some places the prairie grass reached as high as a man's shoulder, and was stiff, each blade "pointed at the top, and hard and almost as sharp as a darning-needle!" It was dry and brittle.

The Mexican ranks made a long blur of color reaching from wing to wing of the woods of Palo Alto. It was useful to know their number, and, to count it, Lieutenant J. E. Blake of the Topographical Engineers rode out ahead of the Fifth Infantry and, coming opposite the Mexican left end, turned parallel to the Mexican line and rode alone, in full view and at brilliant speed, down its whole length. An embodiment of the spirit rising in the Army of the Rio Grande as it sparkled and creaked and tinkled its way on the grassy plain, Lieutenant Blake returned, safe and admired, to report to the General.

Captain May's Dragoons left the line to gallop forward and mark the spot at which the Flying Artillery would establish their batteries. Shortly afterward the Mexican cannon let go with ball and grapeshot. The range was about seven hundred yards, and the salvos fell far short of the advancing troops. Clouds of dust came up, and sulphurous smoke. The army pressed on, and coming into the Mexican range, soon learned, with jokes and laughter, to watch the enemy cannon balls come rolling on the ground and dividing the thick grass, and to break ranks to let them rumble harmlessly by. The Flying Artillery leaped forward to their planned positions. The line was halted behind them. They fired, and in a few minutes the General's two eighteen-pounders opened up, and the battle was on. It was two o'clock. For over an hour the cannon duel kept up, with twenty or thirty pieces of artillery raging. That was the fury whose sound travelled to Fort Texas.

Soldiers were always accompanied by dogs. At the first exchange of cannon fire, two army dogs turned and with tails tight went yelping for Point Isabel. Another, belonging to a battery officer, watched his cannon fire, and started to chase the ball every time, but always lost it to the airy distance in bewilderment. The infantrymen were too far removed to use rifles, and so stood at order arms as spectators, "watching the effect of our shots upon the enemy, and watching his shots so as to step out of their way." Though some suffered wounds from the enemy fire, the rest stood their ground "with a coolness and steadiness almost incredible, cracking jokes the whole time and sending up, whenever one of our guns made a big gap in the Mexican lines, a shout that must have struck terror to their hearts. . . ." The battle began, and continued, as an artillery duel, with rushes by the dragoons to head off enemy cavalry thrusts. The infantrymen were ready with General Taylor's order of the day before in mind: "The General . . . wishes to enjoin upon the battalions of Infantry that their main dependence must be in the bayonet."

While the artillery exchange raged in the center, the Mexicans sent out two flank attacks. On the left, lancers under General Torrejón made a wide circle at full gallop to attack the supply wagons in the rear of the ponds. It was thrown back by Ridgely's Flying Artillery who raced around the line to take up a new position. There they let go with blizzards of shot. On the right, enemy artillery and cavalry tried to circle behind the line, but were met by the Fifth Infantry, supported by the Third, to be scattered by muskets fired from square formations. Major Ringgold's light batteries pressed this advantage and took a new position to rake the enemy lines from the left. To meet the threat, the Mexican front was forced to shift into a new angle, and General Taylor ordered a corresponding oblique march in his line to face it. While this formal evolution took place, both lines ceased fire.

In the sudden silence a new sound was heard over the plain—the hiss of flames. For a wad from an American battery had set the grass on fire, and now, banking upward from a fast-moving front of flame, heavy clouds of black smoke rolled between the forces and hid them from each other. Lieutenant Duncan drove his battery under the smoke to establish a new position only three hundred yards from the Mexican right. From behind the wavering protection of the smoke cloud, he "opened so unexpected and destructive a fire" upon the enemy that "their ranks were broken and hundreds of them moved down and the whole right wing of their army was thrown into utmost confusion."

The sun was beginning to set, and the coolness of the coming night was forcing the smoke down on the plain. Major Ringgold rode to the rear to order up more ammunition for his battery. An enemy six-pound ball struck him, cutting off his right leg at the thigh. He was laid upon the ground. Quietly he gave over his watch and his purse to be delivered to his sister. He then "appeared to have closed his connection with the world, and calmly to await death." Another officer was grievously wounded: the whole of his lower jaw was shot away. A veteran of Napoleon's armies was killed when both his legs were blown off. The army rolled forward against the haze, and the Mexicans were lessening their fire. They made one more infantry advance, in full pomp, under the deepening sky, with a band playing—such music as had sounded a week before out of Matamoros, in the idle evenings. The band was struck by a salvo of shells that silenced it. The musicians fell. Their brave instruments were torn like paper. It was the day's last fight. Dim beyond the smoke the whole Mexican force that survived fell back into the Palo Alto along the low ridge that bounded the plain to the south, and night came, and ended pursuit, and brought silence.

General Taylor encamped his men that night on the enemy's original battle line. His staff came together to reconstruct a coherent pattern of the battle. The enemy had fought with six thousand, the Americans with two thousand troops. Three hundred and twenty Mexicans had been killed, over four hundred wounded. General Taylor lost nine men killed, and forty-seven wounded. The enemy's greatest mistake was his first—opening fire at a range of seven hundred yards, at which he could not hope to be effective, so allowing the Army of the Rio Grande to gauge his strength and take up positions of advantage at will. It was clear that "the manoeuvres of our corps were made with great coolness and precision," and that the "management of our batteries" was "skillful and prompt." While the staff conferred by torchlight, surgeons moved among the wounded of both nations on the field, and burial squads dug graves for the dead, and all night long, the United States Dragoons were on guard, riding in a circle about the army that slept victorious.

9.

Resaca de la Palma

Morning came hot again. The dead were still being buried. Soldiers, as they had a chance, wandered over the rubble of battle left on the field—scraps of uniform, abandoned weapons. The wounded were still being brought in. One party of Americans came upon a startling sight. They saw a handsome young Mexican officer in a beautiful uniform lying down with his head resting against his reclining horse, with its splendid saddle. They were like sleepers who had forgotten to leave the scene of battle. Were they asleep? The soldiers leaned closer, and swore they were asleep; but when they touched to awaken the serene young officer, they saw that the back of his head had been shot away, but without disfiguring his face; and that the horse must have been killed at the same instant by another shot; so that both fell together. The soldiers wondered.

The enemy forces were seen moving amidst the Palo Alto to the south early in the day, but they soon vanished beyond it. General Taylor called a staff council. What went on in it leaked out afterward, and the troops knew that seven out of ten commanders had voted to desist from battle, preferring to entrench where they were and await reinforcements by volunteers who surely would soon land at the Arms from New Orleans. The General listened, and turned to the three who voted to pursue the enemy at once. He agreed with them. He dismissed the council with orders to establish the supply train there in camp, and to assign the two eighteen-pounders and a twelve-pound battery with artillerymen as its guard. He then sent out a reconnaissance in force to locate the enemy, and after that assembled the main body in one massive column and started forward at the pace of the foot soldier.

The army was soon past the ridge of Palo Alto on the road that led to Matamoros. After marching for three miles, the General received information from his advance party. The Mexican Army of the North was in battle position at the old lagoons that flanked the road. It was an ideal position, for they commanded the only road to the Rio Grande in that vicinity. The lagoons were long and shallow, three of them, lying end to end, and linked by natural little causeways over the nearest of which passed the highway. The road ran beside the first lagoon, and then turned to cross before the second. The third lagoon lay broadside to the road within musket range. All three together made a natural fortification as if designed to control any passage on the road. The lagoons were edged on both near and far sides with thickets of chaparral and stands of palms that gave cover to entrenched troops. In the lagoon beds here and there stood stagnant ponds where once long ago the Rio Grande flowed. The old river bed—the Resaca de la Palma—was now bristling with Mexican troops. Ranks of them stood below the breast-high, near rim of the beds, and other ranks of them crouched on the far rim as a second line of defense, and past them must go the United States troops if they wanted to take the Rio Grande road.

General Taylor moved forward a detachment to draw the enemy's artillery fire and so reveal his battery positions. In half an hour the contact was made. The Flying Artillery was sent ahead on the road and ordered to engage the Mexican batteries. Two infantry regiments were deployed on each side of the road to move forward in support of the artillery. The artillery flew, and working hard under the beating sun the cannoneers pulled off their clothes to their breeches and let go with terribly sustained fire. The infantry regiments swept forward in line on each side of the road, and met the Mexican rifle fire as it ripped out across the near parapets of the resaca. The defensive fire was heavy, but it did not stop the oncoming infantry, who in a little while were pouring down over the rim of the resaca into the lagoon bed, to force the Mexicans in close combat to run for cover behind the second rim.

Meanwhile the American artillery was having less effect. The enemy batteries protected by dense thickets continued to rake the main approach of the road. One Mexican battery in particular was placed squarely on the road where it led through the far side of the resaca. Try as he might, Ridgely (who had succeeded to Ringgold's command) could not silence it. General Taylor jogged up the road on Old Whitey to examine the situation. All about him "the balls were falling like hailstones," and when he was cautioned that he was too close to the enemy, he answered, "Let us ride a little nearer, the balls will fall behind us." He sent for Captain May of the Dragoons, and ordered him to attack the troublesome battery, saying "Charge, Captain, *nolens volens!*" May took his mounted squadron down the road. He wore a gold tassel on his blue cap, above long hair and beard. His men, like the cannoneers, had stripped to their bellies. They rode up to the position of Ridgely's batteries, that blocked the road. May indicated that he must go by, and Ridgely answered,

"Wait, Charley, wait until I draw their fire!"

The Dragoons remained at the halt while the Flying Artillery threw in blizzards. The Mexican guns replied. And then, working by hand, Ridgely and his fellows pulled their guns off the road, and at full gallop May led the Dragoons out on the causeway with their sabres whistling and their bare sweated skin flashing. They came down, up and over the lagoon bed and drove the enemy gunners from their guns. As the Dragoons swept down the other side of the resaca, the gunners returned to their posts, and General Taylor, from his place on the road, sitting with one knee cocked over his pommel, shouted,

"Take those guns, and by God keep them!"

By the time May and his riders had turned and formed to charge the battery from the rear, elements of the United States Eighth and

Fifth Infantry regiments were already charging it, and soon took it for good. The resaca was crossed at the most important place.

Elsewhere in the other lagoons the fighting took the form of rifle volleys followed by rushes of infantry in small units that threw the Mexicans back from the near ridges down through stagnant pools, and across the beds, and up the far ridges into tangled chaparral. Suddenly, first in one quarter, then another, the battle seemed to go against the enemy. The Mexican batteries, in turn, ceased to fire. Nerve seemed to ebb away from the Mexicans. No longer hearing their cannon, and pressed by the United States infantry, they went wild. There were courageous thrusts by isolated groups of Mexicans, but a moment came when both forces, in the midst of absorbing individual combat, realized that the way to Fort Texas at the river was breached. "A deafening shout of triumph went up from the whole of our men," noted an American officer, "which struck such terror into the Mexican ranks that they fled in all directions."

The combat surged beyond the resaca into flat country studded with chaparral groves. Daylight was changing as the sun came lower. The Mexican cavalry and artillery horses broke and ran away. Mexican officers ran like their men. The pursuit became a race. Behind the Mexican lines was General Arista's field camp. The Americans found it abandoned, but full of signs of surprise. There was a sumptuous canvas marquee displaying every comfort and crowded with chests and chests of administrative equipment and trunks of personal possessions. About it lay piles of supplies—thousands of musket ball-cartridges in boxes, and about five hundred packsaddles, and many stands of small arms. Near the headquarters tent simmered great vats of stew in pepper sauce, and mounds of half-butchered animals, all suggesting preparations for a grand victory celebration. General Arista was gone—barely in time. In his tent he had left his personal portfolio of papers, "containing the most important information." It was taken by an American staff officer, along with a stack of the General's personal stationery, on which letters afterward went home to families in the United States. The order was given to pursue the enemy, "and on we went," said a man who was there that day, "yelling and firing with the Mexicans in full run before us until we reached the river and found their General, officers and cavalry had outrun us. . . ."

The engagements of the two days were really episodes of the same battle. In the second, the Americans lost thirty-three killed, eighty-nine wounded. The Mexican losses were, in proportion, frightful—almost two thousand men killed or wounded, eight cannon captured and one dismounted, more than a thousand stands of small arms and all ammunition in about twenty wagonloads, all pack mules of which there were nearly seven hundred, all provisions and the personal baggage of officers, all drums and a great many colors. Among the prisoners was General de la Vega, who would be sent by ship to New Orleans.

Prisoners gave a piece of curious information. The Mexican army went into the Battle of Resaca de la Palma depressed by "rumors of treachery in the high command." General Arista knew nothing of them, for they had been circulated by his political enemies, including, some said, General Pedro de Ampudia, whom he had superseded. General Arista, further, knew little of what his army would face that day, for when word came to him that General Taylor was moving upon him, he dismissed the report, "insisting that the advance was a mere skirmish." Throughout the battle of May ninth, he sat in his marquee absorbed and happy, hard at work on piles of official papers, undisturbed by the "skirmish" that cost him sole possession of the Rio Grande —though not, some years later, the presidency of Mexico.

IO.

The River Dead

The American commanders had much comment to make on the two-day battle. At ten o'clock at night General Taylor worked on his report, the heart of which lay in the statement, "The enemy has recrossed the river, and I am sure will not again molest us on this bank." His officers all agreed about one thing: "It is a glorious fact for the army," as one put it, "that there were no volunteers with us." The greatest victories since New Orleans belonged entirely to the regulars. They were justly proud, for the officers, especially the subalterns in the Army of the Rio Grande, were mostly out of West Point, which at the very time was threatened with abolishment by a Congress that had listened to charges that the military academy was a school for aristocratical popinjays who cost their country much and could give it nothing. The first Rio Grande battles would change the tune, for it was soon known everywhere that "on their first encounter, the subordinate officers, chiefly from West Point, executed their orders with the precision of a field day exercise, showing beyond all question the utility of military education and discipline, and putting to rest at once the attacks on the Military Academy which had become so formidable that few believed it possible to sustain the institution a year longer. . . ."

The officers discussed the qualities of the enemy. How odd that all through the dripping heat of the day, while American soldiers threw off every stitch possible, the little Mexicans wore their heavy quilted overcoats buttoned tight or tied about their shoulders. What a difference, noted the military critics, there was between the Mexican officers and men! The officers were elegant, elaborately uniformed, full of style and address—and almost to a man incompetent. They did not really lead their troops, or see to their welfare, or use their endurance wisely. The common foot soldiers were marched thirty miles a day, sometimes fifty, while the American infantryman averaged perhaps fifteen. The dark little Mexican Indian was courageous, and "with an able general would make a good fight," as Lieutenant Grant said. But what could he do if even his weapons were faulty? Why, even at close range, was his marksmanship so poor? American officers examined the Mexican ammunition, and found the answer: the Mexican cartridge held twice as much powder as was necessary, and because of that, a fired rifle kicked bruisingly, and because of the excessive kick the Mexican aim was poor and the cost, to Mexico, terrible.

The United States had its own failures at the high administrative level. If anyone asked the officers why, when the Mexican forces were driven yelling across the river a few hours ago, the American army did not cross, pursue and wholly destroy them, the answer came with the bitterness and scorn which the field always felt for the War Department: there were no boats, no materials to make a bridge, to take the pursuing troops across. Why had nobody foreseen the need? But someone had. A year ago, General Taylor had written to ask the War Department to equip him with "a ponton train" for river crossings. The request was never acted upon in Washington; and he now wrote that if he had had what he asked for, it "would have enabled the army to cross on the evening of the battle, to take Matamoros, with all the artillery and stores

of the enemy, and a great number of prisoners; in short, to destroy
entirely the Mexican army."

Still, there was enough glory to go around, and even Lieutenant
Grant, of the Quartermasters, got his share, for during the battle at the
resaca he was given temporary command of an infantry company, ". . . an
honor and responsibility I thought very great," as he said. He smiled
later over the flourishes he executed in the fight. He led his company
at a charge, captured a Mexican colonel, and then learned that the
ground he fought over had already been taken by the Americans. He
could only conclude "that the battle of Resaca de la Palma would have
been won just as it was if I had not been there. . . ."

Matamoros had been decorated with cloths and garlands to celebrate a Mexican victory. On the night of the retreat the women of the
city tore down the festive array and ripped their ball gowns. Violent
disorder broke out in the streets. Crime and confusion gratified distracted
appetite in every way.

For the next two days, squads were at work burying the dead of
both armies. On the battlefields lay bodies mouldering open to all
nature, as it worked to purify corruption—the sun, the sky, the buzzards,
the burrowing insects, the coyotes. "Already," wrote a soldier, "the
vultures were at their widespread feast, the wolves howling and fighting
over their dreadful meal. . . ." The scent of decay was dense over the
land and along the river; it was what many young soldiers would most
remember for a long time after the battles. For several days the river
fell, and as it went lower it revealed many bodies of Mexican soldiers
drowned while trying to escape on the ninth. Some of the bodies were
lodged in low tree branches lately submerged but now high and dry;
and hung there in the air until they dropped "piece meal into the river
below." The river itself, for a while, became offensive; and the awed
soldiers watched how the mutilated corpses drifting downstream would
be attacked by catfish, "causing them to twitch and roll about, as if still
in the agonies of death. . . ."

General Taylor rode over to Fort Polk at Point Isabel on the
eleventh of May, "on public business." A steamer stood out for New
Orleans. On board were General de la Vega, with other prisoners of
high rank. Courier officers sailed with General Taylor's news of the
great victories. From New Orleans it would be relayed by express
messenger until within reach of the telegraph; and then by wire, to
Washington and New York.

II.

The Nation's War

The cabinet met with President Polk in Washington on May ninth—the day of the second battle—and, as he noted in his diary, "All agreed that if the Mexican forces at Matamoros committed any act of hostility on General Taylor's forces I should immediately send a message to Congress recommending an immediate declaration of war. . . ." The President adjourned the meeting without having had any word of encounters on the Rio Grande.

But about six o'clock in the afternoon of the same day theAdjutant General of the Army appeared at the White House with dispatches for the President that had just arrived by the southern mail. They were from General Taylor, and they told of the attack made on April twenty-sixth by General Torrejón's lancers, in which Captain Thornton and his men had all been captured or killed on Texas soil. The cause for war was established. The President immediately prepared his war message, which was passed by the House two days later, and by the Senate on the day following. Polk signed it on May thirteenth, as Congress voted a war appropriation of ten million dollars and authorized the President to call for fifty thousand volunteers.

And now the national position toward Mexico was immensely shifted from a localized stance on the lower Rio Grande in protection of a border claim, to an all-embracing purpose of defeating Mexico wherever she could be touched. The President already had his grand strategy in mind. His first move toward its execution was to order an expedition to be organized out of Fort Leavenworth, to march against Santa Fe and the north Mexican provinces all the way to the Pacific. Colonel Stephen Watts Kearny was to have the command.

On May sixteenth the President presented his plan to the cabinet. A huge pincers movement was to embrace Mexico simultaneously with many claws. In addition to Taylor on the lower river and Kearny on the

Rocky Mountain Rio Grande of the north, an army was to march from San Antonio to Chihuahua crossing the Rio Grande at old Fort Saint John Baptist—a move that was later to inspire Doniphan to meet it by marching down the New Mexican Rio Grande to El Paso and from there to Chihuahua City. Naval forces in the Pacific were to capture the coast of California, as General Kearny went west from New Mexico to take California from inland; and other naval forces in the Atlantic would blockade Mexican east coast ports from Tampico to Yucatán. Finally— though it was a later addition to the plan—an invasion would be mounted with landings at Veracruz and an overland sweep to Mexico City. Four of those movements would take in the Rio Grande at widely separated places along its great length. The plan in its spacious strategy comprehended a vast portion of the continent. It was at once approved by the Cabinet, and before the day was over, also by Senator Thomas Hart Benton, the Senate leader, for whom the President sent in order to make certain its support by Congress.

The raising of volunteers next came up for discussion. The President saw that a truly national effort would be required by the war, and he knew how to call it forth. He had already sketched a "distribution among the States of the 50,000 volunteers authorized to be raised," and he now submitted it to the Cabinet, who approved his scheme. "A portion of this force was assigned to each State and Territory in the Union," he explained, "so as to make each feel an interest in the war. . . ." By this decision Polk made the Rio Grande a household word, a family concern, in the nation. As the whole nation had debated—taken sides— passionately on the Texas issue, so the war for the Rio Grande was in everyone's awareness, and the river was a national feature. But not until their men went to it in great numbers from every quarter of the land would the Rio Grande become personal—the property, the sorrow, the pride and the romance of the whole American people. Its name acquired an evocative power it was never to lose, even though people might forget in later generations how this came to be.

With the publication of the news of Torrejón's raid, the war spirit began to rise at home. Recruiting began at once, and in many states the quotas were filled immediately, with immense overflows—in Tennessee thirty thousand volunteered for the three thousand who were called; in Indiana, where four regiments were authorized, fourteen could be formed. With his volunteer program launched, the President considered other problems of winning against Mexico. He sent for Bishop John Hughes of New York, the Roman Catholic primate, to enlist his advice and support on how to assure the Mexicans that their religion was safe under the Constitution of the United States. "The false idea had been industriously circulated by interested partisans in Mexico," explained the President, "that our object was to overthrow their religion and rob their churches, and that if they believed this, they would make a desperate resistance to our army in the present war." Could not Spanish-speaking priests accompany the American troops as chaplains, and even "visit Mexico in advance of the army," to reassure the Mexican clergy, who would thus be less inclined to encourage resistance by their Mexican parishioners? The Bishop thought this an excellent idea, and offered to do all he could to help solve the problem—even to paying a visit himself to the Archbishop of Mexico, whom he knew personally. "I found Bishop Hughes," noted the President, "a highly intelligent and agreeable man, and my interview with him was of the most satisfactory character. . . ." In spite of Whig opposition in Congress, the President's war program was finding popular support everywhere.

It received tremendous response when the next news came from the river. On May twenty-third, "the southern mail this evening brought intelligence of two decided victories obtained by General Taylor's army over the Mexicans on the Del Norte," recorded the President, adding that "no official account of these battles was received." But Taylor's reports arrived a day or so later, and meanwhile the papers had the stories. Bells rang out in the Eastern cities, and men and women danced in the streets, and by torchlight gifted citizens delivered orations as was their right and need, and bonfires flared in downtown squares. If so many rose with enthusiasm to the national commitment, no one was obliged to, and some didn't. A New York lawyer told his diary, "Great news from the frontier; two great victories; the Mexicans smitten hip and thigh and General Somebody"—it was Vega—"taken prisoner. 'Nothing equal to it,' said my extra, 'in all Napoleon's campaigns.' Hurrah, hurrah, crow and cackle . . . and no end to the glorification. I do believe we're the windiest people extant. . . ." But he was a Whig, and a skeptic, and his wry view was a lonely one.

For in every salable medium the war and its leading personalities were kept before the public. Fashion, with its reflection of what the people thought about, took up war subjects for lithography, glassware, china, fabrics, pottery. Print publishers rushed to press with scenes from the war lithographed in color. Sarony and Major presented the death of Major Ringgold at Palo Alto, who was shown reclining against two comrades, while his fallen horse turned its head to heaven with a look of intense sorrow in its welling eyes. Nathaniel Currier offered the Battle of Palo Alto, with General Taylor in the foreground, while United States Infantry advanced in solid ranks upon Mexican artillery shown eighteen feet away. Kellogg and Thayer printed the capture of General de la Vega, and both Currier and Weber issued gallant scenes of Captain May's charge at Resaca, with his gold tassel and hair tossed by his speed. In their emotional style, the prints told more about the people at home than about the events illustrated.

Some of the print subjects were issued on fabrics—silk kerchiefs and curtain materials. One chintz showed Zachary Taylor, in brown, green and ochres, wearing a stovepipe hat, sitting sidewise on "Old Whitey," with the American flag floating over battling troops in the distance, the whole wreathed in roses and leaves, and repeated mechanically. General Taylor was also fixed in likeness on jugs, cups, plates, snuffboxes, and on twenty-six different flasks made by the glassware craftsmen of Baltimore, Philadelphia, New Jersey and the Monongahela-Pittsburgh district. Presently from England came sets of Staffordshire china, known as "The Texian Campaigne," showing scenes of the Army on the Rio Grande. It was the theme of the day toward which all interest turned: ". . . me toward the Mexican sea . . ." said Walt Whitman for himself, and, poet as prophet, for everyone. The popular imagination could not have enough given to it about the war. Long later Ulysses Grant read "of deeds of heroism attributed to officers and soldiers, none of which we ever saw. . . . I do not suppose any war was ever fought with reference to which so many romances were invented."

But never before had the nation set out to extend its reach over so vast a theatre of war; or to use so many of its men in armed service. Its scale of operations was commensurate with its new sense of the continent; and so was its imagination.

I2.

Invasion Summer

Once more after Resaca the army was massing on the Rio Grande's
north bank, and the days were spent in re-establishing supply lines from
Fort Polk, resting the troops, and consolidating a grip on the river's
defenses. On the fifteenth American troops seized the village of Barita,
their first conquest on the Mexican side of the river. The village lay a
few miles upstream from the mouth, and consisted of a customs station
and many huts. A breastwork was at once thrown up to command the
river and all its approaches. For want of boats or bridging elements, no
crossing had been yet possible upstream where the main bulk of the
army was gathered. Fort Texas was now called Fort Brown, in memory
of its dead commander, and would soon be the town of Brownsville.
There were still Mexican troops in Matamoros, but Fort Brown commanded the river front now, and hostilities were all but suspended.
General Taylor had every intention of crossing the river once he had the
means. Again on May fifteenth a small element of his army moved
against the Mexican shore. Lieutenant Richard Graham commanded a
detail of soldiers who were given the job of swimming the river to the
south bank where Mexican boats were moored. Covered by American
guns, they crossed, cut free a number of boats and brought them back
safely. The next two days were spent in examining the river for a suitable crossing place. Upstream three or four miles there was a Mexican
ferry that was operated by pulling barges along a rope stretched over the
river. It was noted by American scouting parties.

At noon on the seventeenth of May Mexican trumpeters sounded
a parley on the opposite bank. It was clear that the enemy had recognized
General Taylor's intentions to enter Matamoros, and now a Mexican
general asked for an interview with him. He was brought over with his
aide to make a proposition for General Arista.

Would General Taylor agree to an armistice while a courier could go and return from Mexico City "with a view . . . of settling our controversy by negotiation?"

No: General Taylor "peremptorily refused, saying that he had once offered that course to Arista, who, supposing that we were weak and an easy prey, refused it."

The Mexican General reviewed his instructions, and then "proposed to surrender the public property including arms and ammunition if General Taylor would promise not to cross the river."

On the contrary: General Taylor would take Matamoros and all the public property found there for the United States, and would establish his headquarters in that city. His mind was made up. He had been reinforced by "a large accession of troops from the United States"—volunteers were on the way—and he had ample armaments to batter the city down. He had already distributed orders to move up the river to the ferry, and his troops were alerted to start over at half-past one. However, he would make one concession: he would hold off crossing until three o'clock, to await General Arista's surrender.

The Mexican officers went to their boat and returned to their commander; and at half past one the Army moved out on the north bank to the ferry upstream, and halted there for General Taylor's next order. At sunset he appeared in the new riverside camp and declared that he had heard nothing from Arista. His officers at the ferry were able to give him news. All afternoon, Mexicans had been crossing to return to their homes on the north side of the river, and had told how the Mexican army had retreated from Matamoros, taking along all their artillery. The General was hacked. How could he ramsquaddle somebody who had skedaddled? He supposed the report was true enough. There was nothing to do but settle down for the night and cross in the morning.

The crossing began early on May eighteenth. It was slow, for the ferry could take only about fifty men at a time. A junior officer trying to swim his horse across was drowned, and so was a soldier of his company. At eight o'clock the ferry on a return trip to the north bank brought a deputation of Matamoros city officials to see General Taylor. He received them, spent two hours with them, and sent them back to town with assurances that he would treat all their people as he would American citizens. Meanwhile the Dragoons, Ridgely's Flying Artillery battery, the eighteen-pounders and a battalion of infantry were getting over the river. The General ordered them to march down the Mexican bank, while he set out downstream on the north side to the ferry opposite Fort Paredes, where he would take the main body across. There was no

battle in prospect, for the Mexican army had all gone. Taylor's men
were excited and jubilant to be entering Mexico as masters of an important town. The elements on opposite banks moved downriver, and just
as the General's forces arrived opposite Fort Paredes, the American flag
broke out from the flagstaff of the fort where on the evening before the
Mexican flag had hung. As it went up, the lead regiment on the north
bank "gave three deafening cheers which were taken up successively by
those in the rear until the air was fairly rent by the glorious shout. . . ."
The patriotism of soldiers was spontaneous, robust and loving.

At the Fort Paredes ferry there were three boats manned by
Mexicans. The Army would have "the felicity of being *ferried across by
the enemy*." A ferryman worked at each end of the flatboat, which was
hauled across by pulling at a rope tied to each bank. On one barge, a
ferryman was naked, the other wore a scrap of shirt and something on
his feet. The crossing went rapidly, the first troops went up the south
bank, and over a sandy plain north of the city, and entered Matamoros
to the tune of "Yankee Doodle." Only a few troops occupied the town;
the remainder made camp on the plain precisely opposite Fort Brown
where they had first encamped on the river. "Much has been accomplished today for the United States," wrote an infantry officer.

In the next few days the army went to see the sights. Matamoros
was laid out in squares. The houses were mostly of brick, and few
windows had glass in them, but were protected by iron grilles. It was a
flat-roofed town. The Americans found it odd that there was so little
damage from the bombardment by Fort Texas. The wounded, though,
were everywhere. Public buildings and private houses held long rows
of suffering Mexican soldiers lying on cowhides. Visitors could "tell at a
glance the wounded of Palo Alto or Resaca de la Palma." The first
showed many amputations, for Palo Alto was an artillery battle; the
second, wounds from bullets, for Resaca was mostly a small-arms battle.
An American officer saw a dying Mexican soldier who held "in his hand
the grapeshot that had passed through his breast. He showed it to us
with a sad countenance." The town was orderly, though one night a
Kentuckian disarmed several Mexicans who were "cavorting about the
streets with drawn swords."

If the conquerors had entered Matamoros expecting to find an
exotic atmosphere and a colorful society they were disappointed. The
town was dusty, hot and still. The best society had fled with the Army.
The air and ground, especially at night, were alive with stinging insects.
There was little stir of commerce amongst the population of eight thou-

sand. "It is not," wrote Lieutenant Grant, "a place of as much business importance as our little towns of 1,000." The odor of sickness and suffering drifted everywhere from the improvised hospital wards. There was little to fulfill the "glowing pictures of Spanish beauty and grandeur" that had filled the heads of the invaders before they crossed the river. They accepted what they found quietly. "The behavior of our army after victory," an officer found, "is as highly honorable as the victories themselves." The Americans invaded neither the civil nor religious rights of the residents. Mexican judges still sat in their courts, law and order prevailed, and if an American soldier disturbed the peace he was punished. "The army, instead of entering the city as conquerors, encamp quietly in the suburbs. . . ." Their tents stretched "out before you for miles, until they grow into seeming white spots, looking like snowballs resting on the bluish sward."

Such conditions reflected the temperament and the mild power of the commanding general over his regulars. His new headquarters were set up in four tents under a clump of stunted and ill-shaped trees overlooking a bend in the river. No sentinels were posted near him. While the camp trained to make ready for his next movement of the Army, he sat and worked and told stories in his tent. Whatever was to be done with General Arista's captured marquee with its magnificent appointments, he didn't want it. For a table he used two rough blue wooden chests set together. It was covered with papers in which he could burrow after an idea he needed. When he had visitors he yelled for Ben, his servant, who brought refreshments—a pitcher of Rio Grande water and tumblers on a tin tray put down on a stool. To visitors seated in canvas camp chairs, the General waved an invitation to drink, saying "Help yourselves." They saw him as "a very thickset, farmer-looking old gentleman, in a linen roundabout, and remarkable for short legs and long body." His eyes shone brightly in his seamed face. Behind them, they soon saw, his mind missed nothing.

It was not long before visitors came, in profusion and great circumstance. General Taylor was the national hero. The Congress and various state legislatures voted him medals and swords of honor, and delegations arrived to make presentations with appropriate remarks, hampers of champagne and delicacies. An ode was offered to him in Latin, which he could not read. Two French artists went at him with odd squintings and crayons held forward to take measurements in the air, and reporters from the Eastern papers besought him for interviews. To such, he said, "Help yourselves," and retained a sandy composure,

for he knew honeyfogling when he saw it, and what it was worth; while
at home, the Albany *Journal* predicted that he would be the next
President of the United States.

He was more at home in the immediate problems of command. On
crossing the river he had sent a mounted force to pursue Arista and the
escaped Mexican Army. After a thrust of sixty miles south of Matamoros,
the pursuit was abandoned because there were so little water and forage
to be had in the harsh country. When he was ready to take up his campaign again, he would have to devise other measures than marching
inland from Matamoros. On May twenty-fourth appeared the first sign
of a solution to the problem. It was the high-pressure steamboat *Neva*
which arrived from the estuary to tie up at Matamoros. The troops went
down to see her. She was of light draft. With enough like her, high
enough in the water to get over the bar at the river's mouth, the Army
could in large part be carried up the river to invade Mexico from such
a point as Camargo, a hundred and thirty miles upstream, and to move
against the important cities of Monterrey, Saltillo, Victoria. With the
arrival of the volunteers, General Taylor would have ten thousand men,
four thousand animals, and all commensurate supplies to transport upriver. He ordered the quartermaster to send to the United States to
procure light-draft river steamers in use there. The mission left within
four days, to go up the Mississippi, and up the Ohio as far as Pittsburgh,
and along the Alabama, the Chattahoochee, the Apalachicola, to find
steamboats. Within a few weeks the first of them were already churning
their way down to the Gulf, and across to the mouth of the Rio Grande—
the *Big Hatchee,* the *Hatchee Eagle,* the *Troy,* the *Corvette.* Captain
Austin's *Ariel* was remembered. General Taylor was assured that steam
navigation, under certain conditions, was practicable on the river.

Until the ships came, and the volunteers in greater number, there
were other matters for him to ruminate in headquarters—even one or
two about which to feel a shaking anger beneath a calm, blinking
exterior. On May twenty-seventh the mail expected from the States was
"lost by the express who got drunk on the way up from Point Isabel."
The matter was not merely awkward, it might also give a dangerous
advantage to the enemy, for the mail contained instructions from Washington for the next moves against Mexico—possibly even the President's
whole continental design for the war. A few days later headquarters
believed what it heard next—that General Winfield Scott, the commander
of the whole United States Army, would presently arrive on the Rio
Grande, with all his spacious ways, and his bludgeoning opinions ex-

pressed in rhetoric as majestic as his uniforms. General Taylor hated to think of it. He could not abide him. Perhaps—if the boats came, and the volunteers—he might be able to take the Army up the river before the terrific General-in-Chief could arrive.

13.

Recurrent Frontier

Meanwhile, he mildly presided over what was happening to Matamoros, imposing restraints only when public order required them. Through the first weeks of occupation, the city had kept its formal Mexican character. Officers dined with friendly local families, and learned to drink wine at table. Some studied Spanish for "several hours in the forenoon, and then fell asleep"—after the local custom. Attendance at Mass was a novel diversion for non-Catholics who at home had never risked it. In the town the General had found a huge storage of seegars—eleven or twelve wagonloads. He caused them to be distributed to everyone in the Army who smoked. The troops drilled, held target practice, and late in the hot afternoons found their steps taking them out of increasing habit up the river a little way to Fort Paredes, where they would sit down on the bank to watch with swollen thoughts as the girls of Mexico, unembarrassed by an audience that exuded longing, bathed in the warm stream, and called, and played. In the evenings the soldiers dawdled in the streets, now and then catching a glimpse of a private garden through a patio gate, to see flowering vines and orange and lemon trees heavy with ripe fruit. Sometimes at the grilled windows women lounged smoking their seegaritos, willing to talk to lonesome men. In the plaza regimental bands played after evening mess, and on Sunday mornings Ridgely's Flying Artillery Battery gave exhibition drills. Now and then a trooper whiled away time training a donkey. The Army of the Rio Grande was nearly bored out of its wits.

But then, in a few weeks, the commerce of appetites arrived to assuage the Army; and in a very short while Matamoros was a bear pit. A powerful strain of the United States energy came into play, with high animal spirits, rowdyism, bright lights and noise and waste and extravagance and arrogance that pardoned itself with a marvelling smile that grown men could be so boyish. The Army society soon presented another picture of an American frontier in its first, most awkward age; but here superimposed on an existing civilization. Wherever they went in great numbers, the Americans re-enacted the frontier experience. Out of the violent humor of boredom, and with the new resources of American commerce, they made of Matamoros a raw American town in the summers of 1846 and 1847.

Gamblers and saloonkeepers from the States swarmed up from Point Isabel and opened their shops to a rush of custom. Dance halls, equipped with musicians and girls and upstairs rooms, found a large trade. All the classic trash of a displaced society looking for pleasure was soon visible. Discipline suffered. Local jails and military compounds were crowded with arrested officers and men. The volunteers were arriving now in numbers, and a regular officer declared that they were "playing the devil and disgracing the country in Matamoros." Sutlers came with stores of goods, to be sold at sky-high prices. "A long step toward civilization" was taken when shipments of ice arrived, and whiskey juleps could be had at the bars. An American vaudeville company, true to the tradition of the pioneer theatre, appeared and occupied the old Spanish opera house, playing to a "most motley audience," according to one of the actors—young Mr. Joseph Jefferson. A playbill announced, for Sunday evening, August ninth, *The Dumb Girl of Genoa* in a world première, and *The Desert Rose,* and "a great variety of dancing; the whole to conclude with a dance in wooden shoes, that will be a caution to corns and cockroaches." After a few profitable weeks the company was disbanded when its manager ran away with all its cash. Mr. Jefferson next found employment selling seegars and tobacco at Mr. William Foyle's "Grand Spanish Saloon," whose most prominent rival was a saloon called The Resaca House. Drinking was so general and troublesome that General Taylor in midsummer issued an order forbidding the sale of spirits after August fifteenth. In honor of the order, Mr. Foyle convened a "sarcastic meeting" of the "Friends of Temperance" in his drinking parlor. Another businessman had already done well with a soda fountain, where he sold "soda water with syrups" to another great appetite of the troops. And presently arrived four thousand Bibles, shipped out by the American

Bible Society, and soon the moan and stammer of the voluntary revivalist were heard amidst the carousing. Two Catholic priests, appointed chaplains to the Army in line with the President's discussion with the Bishop of New York, arrived early in July. There was plenty of work for all, as the volunteers continued to join the camps.

Over the river camped the Texas Ranger companies that had volunteered as separate units. They made their own shelters out of reed and brush, for the Quartermaster issued them no tents, or any other equipment. Some of the Rangers were veterans of the Mier fiasco; and having marched over much of north Mexico, were valuable guides to General Taylor on conditions of the country and surprises of the Mexican character. Wondering yet if it were possible to march against Monterrey from Matamoros without first going upriver to turn inland, General Taylor was advised by the Rangers that it was not: the country, dry, was too barren—the country, wet, was impassable. He proceeded with the Camargo plan. The Rangers were, in their tradition, "not only the eyes and ears of General Taylor's army, but its right and left arms as well." Their view of Mexicans was deplored by the General, however; and after a number of cool outrages committed by Rangers against their hereditary enemies, he trusted them less with missions in north Mexico.

It seemed for a time important to work for the good will of the northern provinces, where sentiment was still active for secession from the central government, and for revival of the independent Republic of the Rio Grande. "By judicious management," thought an American officer, "nothing would be easier than to separate all the Northern provinces from Mexico." Coming while the American forces were preparing deep invasion of Mexico, such a political loss might be a fatal blow to the enemy government.

One day very soon after the Army was settled on the Mexican side, a man arrived to present to the staff a plan that would, he felt sure, help to divide Mexico against herself. He was General Hugh McCleod, the late commander of the Santa Fe Pioneers and released prisoner of the Mexicans. He proposed to publish a newspaper in Matamoros, in both Spanish and English, called *The Republic of the Rio Grande And The People's Friend,* whose job it would be to persuade "the people of the states of Tamaulipas, Nuevo León, Coahuila and Chihuahua to an appreciation of the merits of a separate Northern Mexican federation." The Army approved the idea as an instrument of propaganda and psychological warfare, and the first issue of the paper appeared on June second. It was "very well received by the Matamorians," and would surely open the eyes of the northern Mexicans "to the degradation of their condition under the existing and former Governments and the contrast presented to them of what they might be under a Government of equal and just laws and free institutions." A week later the second issue was out, and "the Mexicans read it with much avidity." After another issue, however, the paper passed into new hands, and the new owners while promising to continue publication—"single copy, one bit"— stated editorially that they did not "feel themselves altogether qualified to work out a republic on the Rio Grande." The paper's name was changed to *The American Flag,* and publication continued for two years, all in English, with straight news. The great secession above the Sierra Madre once again faded away.

It was a summer of tremendous storms over the Gulf and the Rio Grande littoral. Time and again the huge American encampment was beaten down by wind, rain, thunder and lightning. The issue tents were unequal to the tempests—even if they stood, the tents "afforded but little shelter from the rain," wrote a field soldier. "The Army is treated shamefully with regard to tents. There is unpardonable neglect somewhere." Not only comfort was at stake—the very armament was in danger. "Inspected my company and found the muskets in bad order. Can't be helped, the frequent rains and no tents to protect the muskets must rust them. . . ." And still the furies blew, screaming through the swayed palm trees, and bringing up the river in sudden flood, and darkening the whole sky to the color of smoke over half of Tamaulipas and Gulf Texas.

If the regulars, with their old soldier ways, were baffled by the weather, the volunteers found it even more discouraging. Untrained and hardly disciplined, the volunteers soon found that their patriotic fervor faded out as they encountered the daily realities of their service on the river. Everything was strange—strange, but without interest. What had been undertaken as adventure soon became miserable duty. If there were occasional beauties to see, not every man could see them, though one soldier would never forget his last night on shipboard nearing the river's mouth under a summer moon. "The moonlight . . . was of a whiteness to shut out the stars. . . . A strange object within pistol-shot was moving swiftly in a direction the opposite of ours. It seemed infinitely large and high. The silence of its going deepened the mystery. It acted as if self-controlled. Then I realized that it was permitted me to see a spectacle fast disappearing, and the most imposing and majestic of the

apparitions of the sea—a three-masted merchantman full-rigged, every
sail set, and laden so deep that the light waves gave it no lateral motion.
On it went, glacial white, mountain high, deathly still, a spectral, glid-
ing glory of moonlit space. . . . It passed, vanished, and made no sign. . . ,
My standards of the sublime are few—it is one of them." The soldier was
Lieutenant Lew Wallace, of the first Indiana Volunteers, who over thirty
years later at Santa Fe would be governor of the New Mexico Rio Grande.

But with the daylight landings, the volunteers saw the muddy
stream of the river pouring angrily into the Gulf, and nothing but
dunes north of the river, and the village of Bagdad south of it, where
smugglers trafficked, and along the shore only wreckage silvered and
rotted by the furious sun and the sandy wind and the salty tides. All
through the summer the volunteer camps were built upon both sides
of the river from the mouth to Matamoros until over twenty thousand
soldiers were in the Rio Grande theatre of operation. Sick from the
crowded, tedious voyage the volunteers landed to find confusion. As one
regiment arrived another pulled out for upriver, vacating an unsanitary
camp. The volunteers elected their own officers, few of whom had military experience. Command was infirm, and obedience, even co-operation,
whimsical. The regiments gave themselves great airs, with brave titles—
the Killers, the Gunmen, the Guards—and fanciful uniforms recreating
the styles of the Revolutionary War and the War of 1812 and the Napoleonic adventures. Some wore thigh-boots tricked out in red morocco,
and tunics of brilliant color faced in bright contrasts, and tricorne hats,
or shakos with pompons, or plumed sugar-loaf caps. In the moist heat—it
was often over 120 degrees—sweat poured down under such headgear,
and after seeing General Taylor ambling about on Old Whitey, or a big
gray mule, "like an old man a-going to mill," wearing his straw sombrero,
many threw away their elaborate caps and bought Mexican hats for
themselves; and if their officers ventured to object, the volunteers, "as
honest and good as anybody," made hard faces and cited the General.

All their equipment and provisions were unsuitable for men in
that climate. Rations, issued three times a week, were beans, coffee, sugar,
pickled pork, and flour or hard biscuits. There were no vegetables, "not
even onions." The biscuits were "alive with brown bugs . . . the men
frequently substituted pieces of them for gunflints." Now and then
against orders men went to shoot beef cattle and sneak them back to
mess. When this was not possible, they dragged the river for shrimps
to supply fresh meat. The only drinking water to be had came from the
river, "a tepid mixture about thirty per cent sand and the rest half

yellow mud." A full draught of it was a sure purgative. Now and then a
ship put in from Boston with ice which could be bought for a dollar a
pound—while it lasted. Firewood was scarce on the dunes. Most cooking
was done on coal brought from Pennsylvania or Ohio. For the thousands of men sifted along the banks it was life in unrelieved wilderness.
By night, they tried to sleep in spite of blowing sand, stinging flies, burrowing chiggers and "night fowls," as they called mosquitoes. By day,
fellows had little to do but walk along the beach, chasing the huge white
crabs that jumped like great spiders, or swim in the surf, or pick up
shells, open them, pull apart the sea creatures within, and throw them
to gulls and curlews. When the fun wore out, "there was nothing left to
do except speculate upon what was to become of them."

Comrades sickened of each other. Some actually died of home-
sickness. And soon there were epidemics of physical illness—smallpox,
mumps, measles, and worst of all, violent intestinal infections. If drinking the river water led to dysentery—the familiar Rio Grande "cholerina"
—unsanitary conditions in camp, and unrefrigerated food, and improper
diet brought enteric fevers to a fearfully increasing number of men.
Over and over Lieutenant Wallace saw it happen. "The soldier may
have been in perfect health the day we went into camp . . . ; at rollcall,
three weeks having passed, I notice the change in his appearance. His
cheeks have the tinge of old gunny sacks; under the jaw the skin is
ween and flabby; his eyes are filmy and sinking; he moves listlessly; the
voice answering the sergeant is flat; instead of supporting the gun at
order arms, the gun is supporting him. . . . The surgeon gives him an
opium pill"—or calomel and jalap—and "another week and his place in
ranks is vacant. A messmate answers for him. . . . There is no hospital
of any kind. It will go hard with him, one of six in a close tent, nine
feet by nine, for the night will not bring him enough of blessed coolness
to soothe the fever made burning through the day. His comrades not
themselves sick are his nurses. They do their best, but their best is wanting. . . . A delicacy of any sort would be a relief; he prays for it pitifully,
and they bring him the very food which laid him on his back in the first
instance—bean soup, unleavened flapjacks, and bacon. Another week
and he is giving his remnant of strength to decency. At last he has no
vigor left; mind and will are down together; the final stage is come. . . ."

One regiment lost five hundred men in six months. There were
too many to bury in daytime, so funerals were held at night. Lumber for
coffins was soon exhausted, and the burial squads used gunboxes and
the staves of cracker barrels; and when these gave out, army blankets,

and then nothing. "And then, the poor men," wrote Lieutenant Wallace, "the poor men were not always allowed their natural rest in the sands of the dunes where we laid them, for the winds, blowing fitfully, now a 'norther,' now from the Gulf, thought nothing, it seemed, of uncovering a corpse and exposing it naked." In their tents the living could not shut out the sound at night of the dead march played by fife and muffled drum "heard first faintly and scarcely distinguishable from the distant monotone of breakers." It sounded incessantly, and even when the burials were briefly interrupted the soldiers were not free of its tune, for hearing it all night long in the pouring moonlight, the mockingbirds of the Gulf whistled snatches of it in the hot daytime. The nation heard with growing anger of the number who died in the river camps all summer.

In desperation many volunteers gave in to mischief, license, and finally crime. The Mexican residents came to hate and fear them. They foraged recklessly for Mexican corn, cattle and women; they stole Mexican fence posts to burn in campfires; if a Mexican displeased them, he was in great danger of being killed. Murders were common. The soldiers in river camps drank even more liquor than those stationed at Matamoros. It was their need to do violence. Volunteers camped opposite Matamoros amused themselves by coming down to the north bank with their muskets and firing at random across the way at the American camps opposite until a staff officer at headquarters said a day in his tent was like a day in battle. The Texas Rangers accepted recruits many of whom were "desperados and ruffians and renegades from the States" as wild and dissipated as "Russian Cossacks." Such men, it was noted, were not Texans. Spoiling for action against the enemy, which was denied to thousands in the summer encampments, volunteers fought one another. One day a soldier of the Baltimore Battalion and a soldier of the Ohio regiment, fishing at the river, both claimed the same catfish. The quarrel nearly became a pitched battle with loaded rifles between the two organizations, and was ended only when the colonel of the Ohio used the flat of his sword on the Baltimore fisherman. Stories of all such disorders went to home newspapers, and Whig editorials in opposition to the war called the volunteers a national disgrace.

In vain General Taylor issued orders commanding proper conduct—soldiers were to pay for what they took from Mexicans, firearms were not to be discharged off duty, the men were not to fight one another, and so on. But still the outrages persisted, and the Army took little disciplinary action. The volunteer officers held command only by a sort

of hair-triggered compliance on the part of their men, who had elected
them, and who could undo them as well. Now and then an officer—most
probably a regular serving with volunteers—tried strong measures to
subdue in an individual example the general insubordination. A French
priest assigned as chaplain saw with pity and shame how "the most
barbarous chastisements are inflicted for offences which in France would
be fully expiated by a few hours' imprisonment. I have seen soldiers
suspended by the arms from branches of trees for drunkenness. Sometimes, too, they tie their arms and legs, and fling them repeatedly into
the river, and then drag them to the bank with a cord. A soldier, stricken
with a severe malady, lay on his bed of suffering in chains. He died in his
chains; and, perhaps, in consequence of being kept chained." He was
happy to add that "such cases of cruelty . . . are rare. They are individual acts for which, ordinarily speaking, the American officers, who in
general are men distinguished alike for their high intelligence and
accomplishments, are in nowise responsible."

Of all the river camps, the one—never given a name—at the mouth
was the most wretched. The First Indiana were supposed to guard the
important entrance, but there wasn't a Mexican to be seen except an
occasional smuggler scratching himself, and the beach, at Bagdad. Twenty
men could have held the strategic location, according to Lieutenant
Wallace. New regiments would arrive overland from landings at Point
Isabel, and if the First Indiana thought relief was at hand, they were
wrong. The sight of the new troops bound upriver "marching by, flags
flying, drums beating, and hurrying aboard boats as if they smelled the
contagion in our camp or feared an order for them to stop and take our
place, was maddening. . . ." They heard little from upriver, and what
they did hear was mostly distorted. "A steam-boat man would stray in
among us with the news. . . . Occasionally, too, an inspector came down
and took a snap-look at our tents from the guard of his steamer. . . .
There was not a soul among us so simple as not to see that we were
practically in limbo. . . ."

14.

Upstream and Inland

On his level, too, the Commanding General had special problems. Late in June General Taylor received an infuriating letter. It was from Major General Winfield Scott, at Washington, and if it held any welcome note it lay in the implication that Scott might not after all appear on the Rio Grande, but remain in Washington, content to issue plans for the defeat of Mexico. But what plans! Working with maps, and making grand assumptions about the geography of Mexico, he issued a stupefying command to Taylor on June twelfth, 1846:

"Take up the line of march beyond the Rio Grande, and press your operations toward the heart of the enemy's country. . . . The high road to the capital of Mexico will, of course, be one of those lines."

How easy he made it sound! A brisk walk, the cutting of an arterial highway, and Mexico City must fall. But where was any knowledge of the scale of Mexican distance, or understanding of the north Mexican desert, or recollection of what it took to feed, water and shelter an army?

General Taylor replied at once to the Adjutant General at Washington, determined, "nolens volens," to describe certain realities. He was already planning to move upriver to Camargo. But "from Camargo to the city of Mexico is little if any short of 1,000 miles in length. The resources of the country are, to say the best, not superabundant, and over long spaces of the route are known to be deficient. . . . I consider it impracticable to keep open so long a line of communication. It is, therefore, my opinion that our operations from this frontier should not look to the city of Mexico, but should be confined to cutting off the northern provinces—an undertaking of comparative facility and assurance of success." His strategy meant to capture Monterrey, Saltillo, and other key cities of the northeast, just as he had been planning all along.

He received another letter from Washington by the middle of

July which gave some comfort. It came from Secretary of War Marcy, and, written before the Secretary had seen Taylor's reply to Scott, it indicated that there were some in the War Department who could look at a map and see more than the Army's General-in-Chief: ". . . If it should appear that the difficulties and obstacles to conducting a campaign from the Rio Grande . . . for any considerable distance into the interior of Mexico will be very great, the Department will consider whether the main invasion should not ultimately take place from some other point on the coast—say Tampico . . . or Vera Cruz. . . . The distance from Vera Cruz to the city of Mexico is not more than one-third of that from the Rio Grande. . . ."

General Taylor replied, somewhat stiffly making reference to General Scott's design, that he could not determine whether he could win the war alone in his northern frontier campaign. Practice alone would show whether his army could subsist beyond Monterrey. As for Tampico, he felt it was impossible, and about Veracruz he had no views. He was not disposed further to extend his advice. He knew what he could do with his present resources, and he intended to proceed. Did Washington aim to catch him in a trap? Get him to give advice, then take it, and if it went wrong, blame him? He knew what was behind their attitude—Scott, and Polk, and who else: they were trying to kill the sentiment that was building up all over the country—Taylor for President. They were scared by the Whig mass meetings that had been held at which in spontaneous demonstrations he had been acclaimed as the necessary nominee for '48. That was part of it—the other part was the enraging ignorance of politicians in walnut-panelled offices on the Potomac of what actualities governed the Army of the Rio Grande, two thousand miles away. It was, in the face of these, almost an impertinence for the War Department to have an opinion, way back there, on the staff level, when the reality was here, on this muddy ditch, in this heat, with soldiers dying of their bowels. General Taylor told his fellow field-soldiers, speaking of those safe in Washington, "They have an intention . . . to break me down." His army was to be thrown away, and the venture wasted, "for all of which I shall be made the scapegoat."

But the high pressure steamboats were already on the river, and on July twenty-sixth the first detachment had gone upstream on the *I. E. Roberts*. The rains had continued, the river was running almost at flood level, and on August fourth General Taylor boarded the *Hatchee Eagle* with his staff for Camargo. He arrived on the eighth and at once reviewed the troops that had preceded him. The rest of the

invasion forces were coming up both by river and by land for the jump-
off into Mexico. Like ten thousand others back home, the wife of a
young major felt her heart turn westward. "My thoughts," she wrote in
a diary kept for her husband's return, "my thoughts have wandered to
the Rio Grande."

After the fall of Matamoros, upriver towns were occupied by
small infantry forces without opposition and as the heavy movement by
road began and continued in late July and early August, the troops
found their flag already flying over Reynosa and Mier on their way to
Camargo. The march was an ordeal that lasted eight days, through rain
and mud, or blasting sunlight and dust. The old Escandón towns
offered little shelter—they looked deserted but the men soon saw that
"there is scarcely an old wall standing that some family does not live
behind." In many places the river road was flooded, and the columns
had to make detours to the south. Water holes at evening were brackish
and some were contaminated by cattle who to escape the extraordinary
heat of that summer stood in them for weeks. There were few reliefs
for the troops, though now and then they passed little ranches where
young girls gladdened them with waves and laughter. After passing a
little beyond Mier, they saw their first mountains—faint blue crowns
on the southwest horizon. They started up coveys of plover and sent
bands of wild horses glaring and plunging away. One regiment met a
Mexican driving his cart full of fresh melons to Matamoros, and in a few
minutes, to his delight, bought his whole load at high prices. The heat
was presently so frightful that the troops were halted to rest after
midday. Reveille sounded at midnight, and the march was taken up
again by moonlight, while fifers and drummers, "with a perfect *vim*,"
did their best to inspirit their fellows with the tune of "The Girl I
Left Behind Me." It was necessary, though dangerous, to rely on Mexican guides: an infantry regiment was taken astray on the road to
Linares, which was a Mexican army station, and was saved only when
the treachery of their guide was discovered. Finally, after a march of
one hundred and thirty miles—the air-line distance was eighty—the
columns came up the rise of land that enclosed the San Juan River
and saw Camargo lying below on the near bank, a little way above the
confluence with the Rio Grande.

As the army made its way down into the valley, one of its officers
was moved by the sight of it. The Rio Grande, "seen in stretches, had
the appearance of so many lakes embedded in green foliage. The smoke
from several ranchos curled gently and lazily upward . . . and a steam-

boat—a *high-pressure steamboat*—true emblem of an American, lay moored at the bank. . . . lazily working off steam. Add to this the long line of covered wagons—the troops, upon whose bayonets the sunbeams glistened, marching on their winding way, and you have a picture unsurpassed. . . ." Entering Camargo they heard that General Canales had just evacuated it, "after inflicting numerous pains and penalties upon the good people," who "hailed with great joy" the new occupation troops.

The steamboat voyage up to Camargo took from four to seven days. By the middle of August there were twenty vessels in service. They were officered by American masters, mates and engineers from the inland rivers, and manned by hired Mexicans. None of the steamboats drew more than five feet of water, some as little as three and a half loaded, and eighteen inches light. They burned wood, gathered every evening at the banks. The green mesquite was a slow fuel, and many a boat had to pull into the bank during the day to get up steam before resuming her voyage. If the river was free of snags, it presented a channel that shifted among soft sand bars, so that a master had to feel his way on each trip. Even so ships went aground all too often. One—the *Neva* —sank one night while tied up to the bank, and everyone believed she had been scuttled. The voyage was slow, and men were crowded together amidst bales of supplies, but progress was sure, and it was better than the overland march. The Rio Grande was "a noble river at the present stage of water," and the country along its banks "decidedly pleasing," where mesquite thickets alternated with open cornfields and little ranches or villages whose people came down to watch the little steamers puffing amazingly along. When the soldiers took off their hats and kissed their hands to the girls, they would all "shout and laugh and make themselves most merry." In general the upriver inhabitants were friendlier than those at Matamoros, and at Reynosa especially, said an officer, because of two facts: "first, the Texas Rangers have not been let loose on them, and [second], only Canales has . . . committed outrages upon them, which have rather turned the current of their feeling in our favor." The river voyages of that summer had interludes of high spirits and antic pleasure for soldiers who crowded the little steamers. One night a boat tied up near a solitary hut as darkness fell. An old Mexican came out of the hut to see the arrival. A fiddler, he was soon playing for the soldiers. They begged permission of their commander to go ashore so they could hold "a stag dance." This was granted. The men swarmed to the bank, where some built a fire and began to roast a goat. It was almost like a symbolic sacrifice to the pagan deity who soon inspired them all. An American fifer joined the Mexican fiddler in making music. A soldier who heard them play said they "imagined themselves possessed by the spirits of Pan and Paganini." Scratching and squealing away, they seized the troops with their tunes, and soon all the men were dancing. They danced "by couples, but without much regard to time or order. . . . The dancing . . . became stronger in proportion as the wild strains grew louder" and the soldiers "vied with each other in the extent and singularity of their saltations." Every so often something swept over the whole detachment, and to the light of the goat-roasting fire and the banked furnaces of the moored steamer, they all "indulged in a promenade or rather *gallopade* of two or three *heats* around the hut." In a scene of color, smoke, glow and animation like a lithograph of the period brought to life, the men feasted and danced and galloped on the riverbank—and then suddenly "a heavy rain terminated the sport on a seasonable hour, and the men returned to the boat much amused and refreshed by their exercise. . ."

The high water lasted all summer between Camargo and the sea. Regular navigation was more difficult farther upstream, though later in the year the *Major Brown* arrived at Laredo with supplies for a new army station there; but before she could cast off to go downstream, the river fell, and she was unable to sail for two years.

And now at Camargo the army repeated the spectacle of Matamoros. On a little stone and clay town with its squared streets and central church and plaza and peach-laden trees descended some fifteen thousand soldiers, with all the animal trains and heavy equipment and greedy hangers-on that accompanied them on the river. Before they could make camp the soldiers had to clear dense mesquite off the ground. The summer floods had swelled over town and field, and receding, had left heavy silt that dried as fine dust. When the wind blew, dust sifted everywhere.

And as always, after flooding, the Rio Grande bred disease. The new base of operations in a matter of days was pest-ridden. Thousands of men went down with the cholerina and hundreds died. The epidemic had come upriver with the transport of troops, and conditions at Carmargo spread it. Men bathed and animals drank in the San Juan River that was the camp water supply. Sanitation was poorly regulated, and hospital facilities were limited and little was known or understood of germs, or antisepsis, and though in Camargo there was a druggist's shop—it was the only shop in town—it sold only soda water. Once again deaths were so numerous that military funerals became a mere shuffling of wasted bodies into sandy troughs, while the dead march was sounded by fifers and mockingbirds. Camargo was known as the "Yawning Graveyard." Tremendous heat by day and noisome fogs by night and insects persistent in their millions made matters worse; and the Army, through appropriate officers, attributed the epidemic to "noxious gases and deadly miasmas."

But still the slow work of supply build-up went on, and until it was done, General Taylor would not budge, though he had sent advance elements toward Monterrey on reconnaissance. He was in an odd mood, as one of his officers recorded. "The general was advancing in a strangely divided frame of mind—had supreme confidence in his men, but he had little confidence in the movement on which he was embarked." Were those people in Washington trying to cornuck him? If he thought so, it might take the starch out of him, until the time came to move into action, and then a man would get back to where he felt like himself again. . . .

The rains went on, and soldiers were so wet all day that whiskey was issued to them. Tent canvas was rotted till it resembled a sieve. Sometimes after a storm the air was cool for hours—a delicious change, and one night there was a brilliant display of meteors over the immense Mexican plain. The camp heard that Comanches were on the loose near Mier—three hundred were said to have killed the mayor, even though an American infantry company was stationed there. Letters came from home. One from his wife so moved an officer that his heart leaped "at the reflection that she does not outdo me in devotion. Never for one moment has my fidelity been tempted to give way." In an atmosphere of pathetic license, he had his own resources: "Have been all afternoon on my bed reading 'King Henry the Fifth,' one of Shakespeare's best plays"—best, even though it trembled with the soldier's lust:

> And the flesh'd soldier, rough and hard of heart,
> In liberty of bloody hand, shall range
> With conscience wide as hell, mowing like grass
> Your fresh fair virgins. . . .
> What is't to me, when you yourselves are cause,
> If your pure maidens fall into the hand
> Of hot and forcing violation?
> . . . Why, in a moment look to see
> The blind and bloody soldier with foul hand
> Defile the locks of your shrill-shrieking daughters. . . .

Many volunteer units had enlisted for stated, short terms of service. Now at Camargo when all the energy of the army was needed for the coming campaign in the interior, hundreds of men said good-bye and returned downriver on the steamboats that were headed for the Gulf to bring up more troops and supplies. Of those going home, "the great majority" were "pretty well disgusted with their service," which for them had meant only heat, and illness, and inaction on the outlandish river. But enough were left with the General to make a great display, and on August seventeenth he reviewed them, all drawn up in order of battle. Their line was over three quarters of a mile long —"one of the most magnificent military displays we have had since the last war." With General Taylor four other general officers inspected seven regiments of infantry and two battalions of horse artillery. All were in dress blues, the officers with gold stripes, except the General, who rode the line "in plain undress." He was himself again. He "never looked in better health or spirits," for action was soon to be resumed.

On the following day the first division moved into Mexico, by way of Mier, to be followed by one division a week until all but small holding forces were gone from the Rio Grande. The transport problem over the deserts had been solved—nineteen hundred pack mules with Mexican drivers took the place of most of the horse-drawn wagons. General Scott should have witnessed the difficulties of loading tent poles and canvas and mess chests and sheet-iron kettles and a hundred other articles on the little beasts, which took several hours at the outset of each day's march, so that the first-packed grew tired of standing, and broke and ran, sometimes bucking or rolling till they managed to scatter their burdens. Still, there was no better way to cross the wastes with an army's duffel.

As the movement got under way, the staff at Camargo heard that Mexico was in a state of revolution. President Paredes, who had marched toward the frontier as far as San Luis Potosí with eight thousand troops, was thrown out of office, and a provisional president had sent for the one man who despite his record could unite all Mexicans under his familiar name—Santa Anna. Under a safe-conduct honored by the United States, Santa Anna on his way home from exile in Cuba had landed at Veracruz an August sixteenth, and was proceeding to the capital to take charge. General Taylor now had his principal adversary.

Monterrey lay a hundred and fifty miles southwest of Camargo. The last of the Rio Grande divisions moved out on September first

and camped that night under a young moon. The General with his
staff accompanied the Fourth Infantry on September fifth. He was now
in such high spirits that his people wondered if perhaps he were over-
confident. Mexicans whom they met assured them that there would be
"Mucho fandango á Monterrey," and wondering what this meant, the
Americans—correctly—translated it to mean that there would be something of a fracas at Monterrey. The country they passed over was dead
level, with unending clumps of mesquite. Those who kept up their
journals every night had to write by the light of the new moon—there
was too much wind to let them light a candle. So under a wide movement of air over the great empty plain the combat forces of the Army
of the Rio Grande slowly faded out of sight into Mexico.

15.

The Army of the West

Meanwhile, at Santa Fe, Don Manuel Armijo was once again
established in the Palace. After six years as governor, he had been succeeded in turn by two Mexican generals sent from the interior—Mariano
Martínez de Lejanza and Francisco García Conde, during whose terms
the civil and military conditions of the province fell off miserably. For
a time progressive New Mexicans held hopes that prosperity was at last
come to sustain commerce and feed the government. The fur companies
of Taos alone spent up to sixty thousand dollars a year for supplies,
and taxes were paid on a hundred thousand dollars' worth of skins
shipped out of Abiquiu. But envy led certain businessmen to seek a
larger share of such profits, and a new law was proclaimed to require
that trapping parties would be licensed only if composed of equal
numbers of native New Mexicans and visiting Americans. It was not
long until the Americans by-passed the government to deal directly with
Indians.

The results were wretched—doubly so, for not only was revenue lost, but also relative peace with Navajo Indians, to whom the American trappers traded firearms, giving them the awful power now to attack the Mexicans with superiority of weapons. Depredations increased sharply, and the Mexicans were in general powerless to resist, for their laws prohibited the introduction of firearms among the population. But for a handful, ranchers, farmers, and town dwellers were armed only with bows and arrows. It was clear that the government feared to give them weapons for self-defense that could as well be turned against corrupt officials. And when outlying communities pleaded with Santa Fe for troops to be send to protect them, the answer was always no, as what few soldiers there were had to be kept in Santa Fe to defend the governor and his crowd. If the militia—with bows and arrows—were called out to avenge an Indian raid, it was noted by observant New Mexicans that it was not "by any means usual that the rich go out to follow the savages when they commit depredations."

And if at last the governor did happen to take steps against raiding Indians, he was more likely than not to create trouble instead of quiet it. The administrators sent from Mexico did not understand the problems that they had to deal with, especially those of the Indian nature. To General Martínez de Lejanza all Indians looked alike, and when he went to chastise a band of murdering Navajos, he seized with them a party of innocent Utes, with whose nation the New Mexicans had never known any organized trouble. Bringing his prisoners to Santa Fe, he punished Utes along with the others. Ute chieftains came to ask for the release of their people. The Governor received them in the Palace, and mistaking their vehement protests of injustice for personal threats, he called for his guards to defend him. Their defense was extreme: they assassinated the chiefs in the audience chamber; and it was not long until Utes swept down the Chama from the Rio Grande headwaters country to kill and burn. Enraged New Mexicans demanded troop patrols on the northern frontiers to give them security against the Utes, but the Governor proposed instead to march out and "chastise them severely in the spring, carrying the war to their country." There spoke the Mexican administrator who had no knowledge of the land he governed. "All his great imaginary movements had to be made, if done at all," said a disgusted New Mexican, "in the Ute country, rugged and mountainous, where there are no trails except those made by the mountain sheep and rabbits." Meanwhile, to those who asked for troops where the raids came, the governor "was so weak at all times as to try to

persuade them that the point of peril was Santa Fe . . ." where he
lived.

If the New Mexicans hoped for relief when at last General
Martínez de Lejanza was "removed to the sweets of private life," his
successor, though he reigned briefly, was a disappointment. General
García Conde openly misappropriated public funds to his personal uses;
and upon his departure, the return of Don Manuel Armijo positively
seemed like a blessing. At least Armijo was a native who as such knew
what he had to deal with, and if his failures resounded, he was like
Santa Anna another phoenix of disaster—a personage with a gift for
the spectacular, for which the Latin soul could forgive much. He returned
to preside over a bankrupt citizenry who had been permitted no means
and no experience of self-defense, and who found themselves in the
early summer of 1846 at war with the United States. Already he had
acted in response to news of how the North Americans were advancing
to the lower Rio Grande. To Albert Speyer, a Prussian resident of Santa
Fe who operated wagons in the Missouri trade, the governor gave an
order to bring back on his spring trip two wagonloads of arms and
ammunition.

Speyer made his purchases at St. Louis and prepared to turn
West again. Trailers for Oregon were gathered there too—among them
young Francis Parkman with his notebook, and many others who looked
past the Mississippi with the hungry American eye. One was a young
midshipman bound for the Columbia River with dispatches, who in
spite of his immediate destination had "a wild plan of raising a body
of men, and *taking Santa Fe.*" The travellers left for all points west
from St. Louis by river, floating down to Independence, where the trails
began—northwest, southwest. "Speyer," noted Parkman, "had an immense number of goods on board," tended by "piratical-looking Mexicans" who wore "broad, peaked hats." There were others bound for
Santa Fe—"a vulgar New Yorker, with the moustache and the air of
a Frenchman," and a young man who had "one brother on the Atlantic,
another on the Pacific, and a third on the Mississippi, while he is going
to Santa Fe. So much for American wandering." There was also a young
fellow from St. Louis who when the steamer tied up near Independence
"harnessed his mule into his waggons, and drove off for Santa Fe, bent
on seeing. He seemed about eighteen years old, open, enterprising, and
thoughtless. He will come back a full-grown man." Speyer pulled out
on the Santa Fe trail in early May for his ten-week crossing of the
prairies. Three weeks later, at Fort Leavenworth, Colonel Stephen Watts

Kearny, after he had his orders to march against New Mexico, heard of Speyer's consignment of arms and ammunition for the enemy, and ordered out two troops of dragoons to overtake the train and seize its military supplies. But slow as it was, the train had enough of a start, and went safely on to Santa Fe.

There, by the end of June, the citizens knew of General Taylor's victories at the seacoast; but even if those were Mexicans troops whom he had whipped, the whole thing had happened far away, and a travelling scientist wrote that "The people at Santa Fe appeared indifferent to the defeat at Palo Alto; only Governor Armijo felt alarmed, because he had been informed that troops would be sent over the plains to occupy New Mexico." News came to the Governor "by extraordinary express" that Mexicans out on the plains had seen United States military forces at the Vermejo River headed for New Mexico. They were described as six hundred men, "the advance guard of the Army destined to invade this Department." The main body was said to be at the Arkansas River. The Governor immediately issued a call for the militia to arm. Two companies were to report to Santa Fe, one to remain on guard at Taos, with their pikes, spears, bows and arrows, and a few antiquated muskets. A light scouting party was sent to Vermejo to bring further details of the advance invasion force.

The detachment was back in a few days with an easing report. They had found traces of an encampment on the Vermejo, but these reflected only a small party, and could have indicated either hunters or soldiers. The Governor was relieved. On July eighth he disbanded the militia, but with a cautionary order to "hold themselves in readiness at the first notice." But two days later—it was exasperating—he received more serious news. It came in a letter to him from four Santa Fe traders who were not Mexicans. Writing from Independence, they told him that a "considerable body of the North American army was on the march" for New Mexico with "the purpose of occupying the same, by order of the United States." The American commander had assured the merchants that "their mercantile interests would be in no danger," and that they might even send this letter with his permission, announcing his advance; and that all he required of them was that they not precede the army, but travel in its rear. There could be no doubt about the truth of the letter; and Governor Armijo was forced to heave his thoughts from position to position in search of what to do.

He chose to ask for a solution of the difficulty by someone else. He called a meeting at Santa Fe of leading citizens, officials, and two solicitors from Chihuahua who happened to be in New Mexico. First he read them the merchants' letter; and then he astounded them with what he said next. He asked the opinion of the meeting "whether he ought to defend the Department or not." One of the lawyers rose to say that "a question of that nature should not be propounded." The Governor held the inherent power and obligation to defend New Mexico. All that should be asked was how "the defense should be made." The other lawyer and the rest agreed vigorously. In danger of being misunderstood, the Governor scrambled to protest, not once, but twice, that he was "ready to sacrifice his life and property . . . on the altar of his country," and he thanked all for their "most sincere patriotic sentiments," asked them to "be in readiness at a moment's notice," and adjourned the meeting.

His position was impossible and no one seemed to understand it and feel for him. It was easy enough to cry for valor—but where were money, arms and troops? Reports kept coming into town of the advancing army—how powerful, how steady their approach, how familiar the land they so strangely moved across. If citizens asked why the Governor did nothing, he could reply that they were wrong—he had told all to hold themselves in readiness, and moreover he was preparing a proclamation.

On August eighth he issued the latest of his state papers. "Fellow Patriots," he trumpeted, "the moment has, at last, come when the country requires from her sons, the unlimited decision, the reserveless sacrifices, which circumstances, extreme under any point of view, claim for its salvation." He went on to refer to the eagle of Iguala, the value of unity—"a house divided against itself cannot stand," he declared—the illustrious President of Mexico, and the god of armies. But if the citizens looked for a plan, an order as to what to do in the face of the threat that every day drew nearer, they found none. True, he did hope for victory, but his hope was qualified: victory "if it be possible," he said, and added, with an eye to his future, "for no one is obliged to do what is impossible. . . ." Thereupon, he heavily shrugged off his burden of leadership onto those who only waited to be told what to do: "Your governor is dependent upon your pecuniary resources, upon your decision, and upon your convictions." In conclusion, he assured the New Mexicans that "he who actually governs you is ready to sacrifice his life and interests in defense of his beloved country." It was an excellent proclamation in every respect but one: it said nothing.

Two days later the Governor asked the New Mexico Assembly,

then in session, to vote one thousand dollars for the support of the regular troops. The Assembly could not vote him the actual money. There was none in the public treasury. But they authorized him to float a loan for the sum, to be guaranteed by future revenues of the government, and then adjourned, never to meet again at Santa Fe. If the Governor tried to raise the loan among the local men of business, he did not record any use of the monies. Meanwhile, into Santa Fe thronged volunteer militiamen "to be ready." And as they came, leaving their ranches unprotected, the Navajos struck at the outlying frontiers, and killed or captured people of at least twenty families. The capital was in an uproar. The question was asked: Why had the Governor not assembled his men through the weeks of July, and moved out to meet the enemy on the plains long before now? There now remained only one natural position of defense between Santa Fe and the relentless progress of the American force. This was Apache Canyon, where the road passed through a rocky defile. Fifteen miles distant, it was the eastern gateway to Santa Fe. If it were breached, all would be lost.

16.

The Secret Agent

But if there was reason to think that the Governor believed all was lost already, his views were not shared by his second in command, Colonel Diego Archuleta, who for himself—and many others—favored a furious defense. First reported as four thousand strong, the Americans were now known to consist of only twelve hundred regular and volunteer troops. Properly inspired and energetically led, over four thousand New Mexicans could be raised to save the province even now, even with bows and arrows, even in the face of the impossible. But it was late—how late was made clear on August twelfth when under safe-conduct an officer and a civilian, with a guard of twelve dragoons, appeared in Santa Fe as emissaries from Colonel Kearny, and presented themselves at the Palace.

They were Captain Philip St. George Cooke and Mr. James Magoffin. Captain Cooke brought a letter from Kearny to the Governor, which he was to present at a suitable moment. Magoffin, as a Santa Fe trader and resident of Chihuahua, knew Spanish, and was an old acquaintance of the Governor. But to protect what he must do later he resolved not to go with Cooke for an official interview, and left with him an interpreter to manage introductions. While Magoffin went to see friends among the traders, Cooke entered the Palace and was soon conducted into "a large and lofty apartment, with a carpeted earth floor." He saw Governor Armijo "seated at a table, with six or eight military and civic officials standing. There was no mistaking the governor, a large fine-looking man . . . he wore a blue frock coat, with a rolling collar and a general's shoulder straps, blue striped trousers with gold lace, and a red sash." He received the Captain agreeably.

In the meantime Magoffin sought out Henry Connelly, a prominent trader who also lived in Mexico, whom he had known well. The two could talk frankly.

What did Connelly think the Governor intended to do about resisting the invasion?

The Governor, Connelly replied, "was not determined to resist," as things stood.

That was gratifying. What about others? Was there strong sentiment elsewhere to give battle?

Connelly, "being intimately acquainted with Colonel Diego Archuleta & and having opportunity of conversing with him on the subject of impeding the entrance of the U.S. forces into that city," was able to answer for him: "the Col. was decided in making a defense. . . ."

Magoffin was glad to have the information. He now knew how he must proceed. Leaving Connelly, he presently paid his respects to the Governor without having shown himself publicly as a member of Kearny's mission. Official affairs were over for the moment, and when the Governor invited his old friend Magoffin, and the American captain to dine with him, they accepted. It was such an occasion as the Governor always enjoyed. Turning on all his old, florid good-fellowship he beamed upon his guests. Captain Cooke was an able officer, well-educated, and a credit to any man's table. James Magoffin was a handsome Kentucky Irishman with a robust wit and a stock of hilarious stories. The candlelight was bright, the wine flowed, the food was rich and hotly spiced,

Indian servants moved silently in and out of the shadows, and presiding as the first gentleman of New Mexico, the Governor was in his element, among men, with his general's tunic unbuttoned, his duties forgotten along with tomorrow, and other morrows.

But a little before ten o'clock, when dinner was over, the Governor rose and accompanied his guests to Cooke's quarters, and there, in private, they got down to business. Magoffin was fluent in Spanish. He knew the country and its ways and its chief. He carried now a private authority that came from intimate councils with the great; for a few months ago, in Washington, Senator Benton had taken him to see President Polk and Secretary Marcy, who appointed him to accompany Colonel Kearny as a secret agent, with the mission—proposed by the Senator—of persuading the powers of New Mexico, by whatever means, to submit to conquest without resisting. His work was to be unofficial, done in shadow, but nonetheless binding in its results. For the official gesture of the occasion, Magoffin now nodded to Captain Cooke, who produced Colonel Kearny's letter. To the Governor's heavy face with its eye for the main chance, Magoffin translated it.

Fully written in official style, it contained really only two ideas.

The first announced that by the annexation of Texas the boundary between the United States and Mexico was now the Rio Grande from its source to its mouth. The United States Army of the West was now marching to take possession of New Mexico as far as the east bank of the river.

The second advised the Governor "to submit to fate," and surrender peaceably. If he should do so, all would go well with him and his people. If he should not, he and his government would be treated as enemies. They would be overcome and would receive the curses of their countrymen.

There followed a long conversation. Magoffin was able to use powerful arguments. He was pleased to say that the President of the United States himself had sent him to bring assurances to the distinguished Governor of New Mexico and his good people. The United States hoped "only to give peace and prosperity to the inhabitants." Why not take a realistic view of the situation? Kearny was coming with enough troops to defeat any resistance, and even stronger reinforcements were to follow. It was possible to use the tone of one reasonable man talking to another, for Magoffin already knew from Connelly that the Governor was not disposed to fight. Possibly, even probably, there was offhand mention of financial embarrassments that so often visited a

gifted public servant who retired from office having suffered heavy
personal losses in consequence of living up to his position; and there
was evidence in time that a large sum may have changed hands in the
sealing of Magoffin's argument; for he later asked the United States
government for fifty thousand dollars to reimburse him for "secret
services rendered during the war." It was known that the Governor
suffered from a fatalistic venality. Already convinced that there was
nothing he could do to save his state, he would show a business sense
compatible with his nature if he consented to be paid for what must
inevitably come.

As everyone knew, the only strong defense of Santa Fe lay at
Apache Canyon.

The Governor now "promised not to make a stand at the defile,
after which the invaders would have no difficulty." It was an entirely
satisfactory interview. The Governor's only remaining problem was
how to keep up a plausible show of resistance to satisfy public sentiment
while avoiding a real fight. There were gestures that he would have to
make—mobilization, levies of supply, a sortie to the canyon—but somehow, when the time came, he would manage to go through with his deal.
Captain Cooke was strongly impressed with James Magoffin's skill in
using his old influence over the Governor. The meeting broke up with
cordial exchanges.

It was now Colonel Archuleta's turn. Magoffin conversed with
him separately—probably on the following day. Magoffin immediately
saw that "fight was in him." He was a young man, a veteran of service
as captain of the New Mexican rurales. He would have to be "drawn
off," or his influence might control the Governor, and a smooth design
might turn into nuisance and bloodshed. Magoffin had a suggestion for
him, and the fiery colonel listened. He listened with increasing attention as Magoffin touched home to the heart of personal ambition. What
had Kearny proclaimed? Only that he was coming to occupy New Mexico
as far as the Rio Grande's east bank. Nothing was said about what lay
beyond—the immense empire west of the river. Why should not Colonel
Diego Archuleta give up the costly and in the end useless defense of the
eastern part of the province, retire to the west bank of the river, and
there pronounce himself chief of state over a great province in which
the United States had no interest whatsoever? Surely he would succeed
in holding such a position. Speaking as a presidential agent, Magoffin
added that the western half of New Mexico would be "too far off to be
protected by the central government" at Washington. The opportunity

was stunning. Colonel Archuleta was shaken. Magoffin pressed his advantage, and went on to suggest that in addition, or perhaps even as a substitute arrangement, Archuleta might well be given a post of responsibility under the United States government in its own area of New Mexico. He could rest assured that Magoffin would recommend him to Kearny for such appointment, if he liked. A quick light of a great future in the Colonel's eye, a moment's pause for the sake of dignity, and it was all over. The Colonel submitted. "The Colonel would have fought," Magoffin could say. "I quieted him."

Magoffin then, with these successes behind him, dropped in on a number of the other leading citizens of Santa Fe, "many of the rich" with whom he "had ample intercourse." He repeated his courteous threats and appealing arguments—"the only object of our government was . . . to give peace and quietude to the good people of the country"— and was glad to see that he "gave them entire satisfaction." If the promises he had received were sincere, the battle of Santa Fe was already won. He took pains to hide his arrangements, and even assured his friend Connelly that a "strong stand would be made a few miles from the city." Out of caution, Connelly and a number of other American businessmen left Santa Fe under permits issued by the Governor. Magoffin— they could not imagine why—stayed in town; and Captain Cooke returned to join Kearny, who was almost at Las Vegas, to bring him the favorable news.

And now the Governor entered upon a bustling program of public measures for defense. He commandeered horses and mules. He dispatched a large force toward Apache Canyon to make camp and await his arrival. He ordered every male citizen between the ages of thirteen and fifty-nine to spring to arms and march to the front. In the end, four thousand New Mexicans would be posed at the defile. The father of a boy not yet thirteen asked that the child be excused from service and the Governor answered, "No, sir, he is a cadet, and is, therefore, subject to the ordinances, and he is a military officer, and, therefore, must go to the front." The little boy reported long later that "Armijo placed at my disposal a piece of light artillery with its equipage and artillerymen under my orders; we marched to Apache Canyon. . . ."

Others were more fortunate in their requests to be excused: those who paid the Governor any sum between twenty and one hundred dollars were let off. At the same time he opened a subscription for a public war chest. Patriots gave what they could. He turned his eye to the church, and ordered the pastor of Santa Fe to give over all the money, plate and livestock in his possession. Ignoring the right of succession of the lieutenant governor he secretly signed over control of official as well as private affairs to a business friend, who could protect his interests if the time came for him to absent himself. His old henchman, Damasio Salazar, risen to the title of general since the happier days of the Texan Santa Fe Expedition, now demanded—as though he suspected the Governor's intentions—the command of the defense forces.

But he was denied the glory, for on the sixteenth of August Governor Armijo rode off to join the encampment in Apache Canyon. Las Vegas had fallen. In another day or two the Americans would be upon him. He brought with him a guard of dragoons, the last of the militia, and—to their astonishment—the members of the legislative Assembly of New Mexico. He found the armed citizenry barricaded behind evergreen branches, and he heard how among them there had almost been mutiny. Once with them, he gave an energetic display of leadership. First he planted his artillery out in the open one hundred yards away from the mouth of the canyon, "by which he evidently intended that the gorge should be passed before his fire was opened," as an American officer later observed. It was a gesture of defense that would yet prove convenient for the invaders who had bought him off. Then in a great sweat to shift responsibility from his own shoulders to those who later could be vilified as traitors, he had recourse to a familiar habit. There in the canyon he called a series of meetings to demand indignantly what his people would have him do. The answers were not what he hoped for.

He first convened the legislative Assembly on the red hillside with its cedar clumps, and asked them "to say whether he should defend the Department or treat with the enemy." An assemblyman answered for his colleagues that the question was improper: they were there not as legislators but as soldiers, "and their duty was to act as such, and obey orders." The Governor dismissed them. He could not pin the blame for a retreat upon his Assembly.

He next sent for the officers of the militia and volunteers, and repeated his question. A citizen replied—and his reply was allowed to stand by his fellows—that they "had assembled in camp to fight, and that was what they should do and it was their wish to do so." Again the Governor was denied the pretext he longed for. But someone, either then or a little later, brought up the proclamation issued by Kearny from Las Vegas, in which New Mexicans were promised every consideration in their way of life and religion if they would submit peacefully, and the Governor was able to seize the opportunity to insult his citizen soldiery.

"Cowards!" he shrieked, and went on to declare that he "would not compromise himself by going into battle with people who had no Military Discipline." Forthwith he commanded them to disband and go to their homes—with the enemy five leagues away and advancing steadily. The regulars, he stormed, with the regulars he would meet any situation that approached. He tried desperately to seem like a victim of fate. But he was acting. In turn he kept showing all the tricks of his repertory—the man of decision, the fearless patriot, the reasonable democrat, the statesman in command of a high rhetorical style if not of an army; and all the while he was obliged by his profitable secret commitments to keep his gestures hollow. Giving every appearance now of being "very much exasperated" at what he chose to regard as his betrayal by the bewildered volunteers, he saw them begin their immediate retreat from the canyon. All was confusion. Each man took any horse he wanted, and galloped away home.

Lastly the Governor and Commanding General assembled the regular officers and once again asked his famous question. They replied that "they should march at once, meet the enemy and give them battle." He hastily dispersed them, but a few minutes later, hearing cheers from the troops who had been told what their officers had said, he was obliged to announce that he would attack. But not yet, not quite yet, for he had a letter to write. Dating it "Camp in the Canyon, August 16, 1846," he addressed Colonel Kearny with sentiments that were plainly intended to be seen afterward, to the writer's credit, by the central Mexican government. Step by step, he described the measures he had taken to save his province. He recorded how ardently he desired to defend it; he made plain that defense was impossible because reinforcements could not come in time from central Mexico, so far away; and he announced that he was withdrawing to the left bank of the Rio Grande, there to await decisions made by the two warring governments. He then launched into the flourishes that came so naturally to him: "I protest to Your Excellency before God and man that I do not recognize the Department of New Mexico as the land of the Republic of the North"—but what did that matter, since he had sold it out privately? "My heart is grieved with pain, on seeing that from my hands the country in which I first saw light passing to another nation"—which was another way of assuring Kearny that the deal held. "I do not deliver to Your Excellency the Department, and I only make my military retreat, until I shall receive orders from my government"—but he closed by tacitly recognizing the new authority that was coming along the old Pecos road: "I recommend to your Excellency the inhabitants of this beautiful country. They are most worthy, as your Excellency will see, of the kind consideration of the government."

He gave the letter to Colonel Archuleta to deliver, and in spite of his announced intention to fight, or to retire to the west side of the river to keep vigil, he ordered the regulars to accompany him at once to Santa Fe, where he gathered up all the money, plate and supplies he could load on pack animals, herded the requisitioned horses and mules of the defense forces into a private band for himself, and with hardly a pause, fled down the river taking all the regular dragoons along as his personal bodyguard. Over a doorway of the Palace was an inscription, *Vita fugit sicut umbra.* If life fled like a shadow, so did the Governor. News of his desertion flew through the city, and many of the propertied residents in panic ran away also. One who remained stated bitterly, remembering Francis I, "It can be said that Mr. Armijo did absolutely nothing, nothing, and can say 'All is lost, including honor' . . ." His accomplice Archuleta also ran away, taking refuge on his downriver ranch, probably without delivering the Governor's letter. He had not proclaimed himself political chief of the west bank of the Rio Grande. Perhaps the time for it was not yet ripe. Perhaps he should wait and see what office would be offered to him, under assurances of the presidential agent, by the new masters of Santa Fe.

17.

Bloodless Possession

For the moment, Lieutenant Governor Juan Bautista Vigil y Alarid assumed office as provisional governor in the midst of the popular terror caused "by the flight of General Manuel Armijo, the desertion of

his soldiers . . . and the fear brought . . . by the approach of the military
forces of the United States. . . ." His first act was to post everywhere
copies of Kearny's letter to Armijo promising kindness to the New Mexicans. His second was to send his acting secretary of state, "quite a youth,
and dressed in the fashion of the Americans," to meet Kearny with a
letter announcing the governor's abandonment of his post, and extending a welcome to Santa Fe. Various Americans in the city also went out
to meet the Army.

August eighteenth was a rainy day and the road was muddy. In
midafternoon the first troops of the advancing column were seen from
the edge of town moving along the base of cedar-covered hills. Most of
the Santa Feans who were left went indoors. A few Mexicans lingered to
peer around adobe corners as the army arrived among the houses. Not
yet certain that there would be no resistance, the soldiers came with
"drawn sabres and daggers in every look." The column was in close
formation. At five o'clock General Kearny—he had just received his promotion—rode to the plaza. The artillery rolled on by him to take up a
position on a hill that commanded the town from the north. The officers
of Vigil's provisional government were waiting at the Palace. As the
General arrived before them and dismounted, the sun broke through
the heavy sky in a waft of splendor, Vigil greeted the General and
turned over to him the office of governor, the United States flag was run
up above the Palace, and from the north hill sounded a "glorious
national salute" of thirteen guns. Soldiers still marching through the
earth-walled lanes of the town heard a "wail of grief" from the men and
women within their houses. A lieutenant noted that "there was not the
least show . . . of resistance in any way." Magoffin, Cooke, Armijo and
Archuleta had done their work well.

While the troops wound up to camp on the artillery hill, the
General and his staff entered the Palace where they were given El Paso
wine. They were hungry and thirsty. They had marched twenty-nine
miles with nothing to eat since five in the morning. The staff went to
dine at the house of a Mexican officer, "very much after the manner
of a French dinner, one dish succeeding another in endless variety."
Later, "in fine spirits," General Kearny showed his officers through the
Palace. They saw a long ballroom with a dirt floor, and doors panelled
in buffalo hide painted to resemble wood, and offices, bedrooms, guard-
room, kitchens and prison cells and the patio garden, all "suitable to
the dignity of a governor in New Mexico," though many parts of the

building were "in a state of decay. . . ." Up on the hill the soldiers found little wood to burn, and in the sharp night kept their fires flaring with the tops of green cedars.

As soon as they could on the following days soldiers ranged through the town and some wrote notes on what they saw. Santa Fe was shabby, with no signs of either taste or wealth. There were no gardens— but the visitors had not yet looked within patio walls. Cornfields were laid out in the very center of town. Everything was a queer jumble of the clever and the primitive. Public walks enclosing the plaza were covered by a continuous roof, which was capital in case of rain; but there were no "public lights" anywhere in the streets at night. Delicious fruits were to be had at the market—peaches, grapes, melons, apples. The residents were poor and beggarly, and if the women were not handsome, they were "rather more intelligent than the men" and all loved parties, for there were "phandangoes almost every night." The army erected a hundred-foot-high flagpole in the plaza for the American colors. Odd little discoveries were made now and then. One brought to light Governor Manuel Armijo's state coach, with its now shabby gilt. A young officer examined it, and concluded, "as to going out in it, no one in his senses would risk his neck in such a clumsy and crazy affair." If there was one general impression shared by all, it was about the bells. There were five in the main church, and the other two had one or more each, and they all rang, it seemed, all the time, night and day. Dawdling about the famous old city, a soldier decided that in what he saw there was "nothing to pay us for our long march. . . ."

The General saw it all with a different set of values. It was no small matter to have taken the capital of the upper Rio Grande province at so little cost and in such good order. He could be well satisfied with the completion of the first phase of his mission. Stephen Kearny was fifty-two years old, a small man with a plain, thoughtful face that with its large, pale eyes and seamed cheeks suggested the looks of Andrew Jackson. His hair was gray, brushed forward on his brow and temples in the style of his youth—the period of the War of 1812, in which he had first seen service. The wings of a narrow white collar were folded across a high black stock under his jaws. His long blue coat piped in gold and bearing gold bullion epaulettes and twelve gold buttons fitted his trim figure closely. He was "very agreeable in conversation and manners," he conducted himself "with ease," and with gallant charm he could both "receive and return compliments." Candid and plain-speaking, he was an immediate success with new friends in Santa Fe, and with much to occupy him, he found time for both official and social affairs.

On the day after his entry he delighted the public with a speech he made before the Palace, in which again he pledged his government to honor the civil and religious rights of all. He called for peace and harmony, and announced that "being in possession of Santa Fe, I am therefore virtually in possession of all New Mexico. Armijo," he said, "is no longer your governor. His power is departed; but he will return and be as one of you. When he shall return you are not to molest him. . . . I am your governor—henceforth look to me for protection."

Vigil y Alarid replied to the address. With dignity he gave New Mexico's allegiance to the new flag, and added, "To us the power of the Mexican republic is dead. No matter what her condition, she was our mother. What child will not shed abundant tears at the tomb of his parents? I might indicate some of the causes for her misfortunes, but domestic troubles should not be made public. It is sufficient to say that civil war is the cursed source of that deadly poison which has spread over one of the grandest and greatest countries that has ever been created. . . ."

The conquest was completed on the following day when chiefs came from the river pueblos to declare their allegiance. The General had a "long and interesting" interview with them, "a fine, hardy, robust-looking set, with bows and arrows and Indian dress." They fascinated the staff with a recital of their tradition that had long promised how "the white man would come from the far east and release them from the bonds and shackles which the Spaniards had imposed" upon them. "Three hundred years of injustice and oppression" had "failed to extinguish in this race the recollection that they were once the peaceable and inoffensive masters of the country." A deputation of the clergy also appeared and joined in the new allegiance. In the evening a message arrived from Don Manuel Armijo, hinting that he might return, and "asking on what terms he would be received." But this turned out to be only a dodge to give him time to make good his escape to the south, in case pursuit and capture were planned. As he went he ravened upon his countrymen, driving off their cattle and horses with those he had previously stolen. A dedicated, and scared, materialist, his philosophy knew no limits. Scrambling toward Chihuahua he did not know that five hundred Mexican troops under a regular colonel were marching north to help him to defend New Mexico. With them, and supported by the rich resources of the Downriver district, he might have—but it was idle to imagine an act of duty and fidelity by which he might have defended the river kingdom; for its easy loss was long since determined by the facts of his character.

On August twenty-second General Kearny issued another proclamation to the New Mexicans. In it he repeated all his previous assurances protecting their rights. And then he went one step farther in defining the limits of New Mexico now under his command. He announced his intention "to hold the department, with its original boundaries (on both sides of the Del Norte), as a part of the United States, and under the name of 'the Territory of New Mexico.'" There went, at one stroke of the pen, the old fiction about the Texas boundary at the east bank of the upper Rio Grande; and with it went Colonel Diego Archuleta's chance for a personal empire. Kearny was acting in accordance with confidential orders issued to him on June third by the Secretary of War, which stated that in case he conquered Santa Fe, with it would be "included the Department or State of New Mexico." The news was quietly taken, though it remained to be seen what Colonel Archuleta's reaction would be.

The citizens saw with pleasure through the following days that the General meant quite simply what he had proclaimed. Their habits, religion, civil rights and unofficial customs were left undisturbed. He was able to give brisk attention to details. He abolished the use of "stamp paper" which the Mexican government had sold for eight dollars a sheet, on which, to be legal, all business and official transactions had to be drawn up. He went to Mass as a gesture of courtesy. He called on the American traders, and he dined with Mexican families. He worked on plans for a march to California, in which he would be followed by a battalion of Mormons who had volunteered on condition of receiving their discharges once they reached the Pacific coast. With him in Santa Fe, in addition to his regulars, was a volunteer Missouri regiment under Colonel Alexander Doniphan, which, in the grand strategy of the war, would march down the Rio Grande and on to Chihuahua in an attempt to meet American forces under General Wool.

All through the last two weeks of August Santa Fe was alive with rumors that Governor Armijo had not, after all, gone very far south, and that indeed he was busy raising five or six thousand men in the Downriver, and would soon return to his capital, force it to surrender, and resume his station in the Palace. The citizens watched the General to see if he would send soldiers out against Don Manuel. But even though he did nothing, the rumors were believed by many of Armijo's former followers, who fled the city, "lest on his return they should be considered as traitors and treated accordingly."

James Magoffin was still busy at the center of things, still dissembling his true purposes behind his character as Chihuahua trader—a disguise that had the virtue of truth. His brother Samuel was in Santa Fe, headed south with his caravan, and had brought along his new wife, Susan, who was much in love and interested in everything—conditions that she revealed in her diary. "Brother James" came to supper frequently, and the military came to call, including the General, who made a flutter at the end of August by announcing that he was about to take a strong force and march to the Downriver for a look around. It would be as well to examine the rumors of Armijo's activities there, and meet the population, and know the country better. James Magoffin was to precede him by one day, and once again prepare the way; after which— though this was still a secret design—he would go on to Chihuahua, where before the arrival of General Wool with his American troops he would undertake to "quiet" the Mexican authorities just as he had done at Santa Fe.

James Magoffin still had Colonel Archuleta on his mind, and sometime before the departure of the downriver reconnaissance, he made a point of seeing General Kearny about him. He reminded the General of the private agreement with Archuleta, and recommended him for an official post under the new Territorial government—some job "which would compromise him," and bind him to the United States cause. Yes, the General remembered. Yes, of course, he intended to take care of the matter. Magoffin left it with him, and spent his last two evenings with Samuel and Susan, and "cracked jokes and spun yarns, laughed, drank &c." There was a supper of "oysters & champaign," and at night on September first he left for Downriver.

On September second the General led seven hundred soldiers out for the country below. "We passed through S.Fé with our banners flying to the breeze," said a volunteer, and "the Ladies looked intently from the housetops as we passed—" Three days later an army grazing detachment out on the plain to the south heard cannon fire from the direction of Albuquerque. It was a salute to the General on his arrival there. He sent word back to Santa Fe that "all was quiet and no armed force of any kind in the field." By the eleventh he was in the capital again, well-satisfied with what he had seen. As soon as he had time he called on the Samuel Magoffins and amused Susan with his description of life down the river. At Santo Domingo the Indians, mounted, costumed and painted, gave a stunning exhibition of a sham battle; and later the resident pastor gave a collation to the staff, while behind his back the young soldiers and the Indian servant girls flirted in a "little exchange of the artillery of the eyes." On down the valley people turned out to offer melons and other fresh fruit. The soldiers bought quantities, using their uniform buttons for money. A button passed for twenty-five cents. Hundreds of Mexicans and Indians trailed along after the Army, and seemed "well pleased with the change of government." At Albuquerque the General called on Mrs. Manuel Armijo, who seemed to be "a good-looking woman and rather cheerful." Another traveller saw her a little while afterward as "a comely dame of forty, with the remains of considerable beauty, but quite passée." Her husband, said the natives, had "gone to the Devil," and a volunteer entered a mysterious rumor in his diary: "Don Manuel emasculated."

The troops went as far as Tomé. They saw large flocks of ducks, geese and swans on the Rio Grande, and plenty of fish. The weather was pleasant until the last few days, when sandstorms came up. At Tomé there was a fiesta in honor of the Blessed Virgin Mary, with processions, bonfires and fireworks. The volunteers gave trouble and seventy or eighty of them had to be given extra duty to discipline them. The staff took part in the fiesta, walking in the procession, and the General carried a lighted candle, "making," as he said to amuse Susan Magoffin, "a fool of myself." The whole tour was reassuring, in its pledges of loyalty, its "most flattering treatment," with some of the towns exhibiting fireworks and theatrical entertainments, and giving balls. If Armijo had been busy raising a force, there was no sign of it, or of him. New Mexico seemed secure, and as soon as final plans were ready, the General could leave for the West.

He ordered Colonel Doniphan to remain at Santa Fe until relieved by another volunteer force that was coming from Missouri under the command of Colonel Sterling Price for occupation duty. In his reports to Washington the General, after noting the satisfactory state of the population, went on to describe the Rio Grande. It was a stream, he said, that needed engineering controls; and he recommended that the War Department plan them. He attended to the final details of his movement across Arizona toward California, and fixed his departure for September twenty-fifth. The night before leaving, he was the guest of honor at a ball given in the Palace by the merchants of Santa Fe. Many of those invited did not attend, said Mrs. Magoffin, "owing to the death of an old gentleman a few days before, who was related to half the city." But the company was sprightly, and wearing her scarlet Canton crepe shawl, Susan was "soon surrounded by the Gen. and his officers." The local ladies were turned out in the Mexican style, "large sleeves, short waists, ruffled skirts, and no bustles." They all smoked seegaritos, and one who made a flashing appearance was "the old woman with false hair and teeth"—Doña Tules, who ran the leading monte game of Santa Fe. The dancing was lively. They danced the *cuna*—"the cradle." Susan Magoffin thought it beautiful. It was somewhat like the waltz. A couple stood face to face, encircling each other's waist with their arms, to make the sides of a cradle. As they swung around, both leaned back, to close the bottom of the cradle. The music of a violin and a guitar scraped and thumped, clouds of cigarette smoke hung under the ceiling, and in a corner a local matron of position sat with her foot on a human footstool—her servant, who crouched before her.

The Army marched out at noon the next day. The General was busy with last-minute details, one of which "for some reason" he had neglected until it was now too late. He had not made any arrangements for the future of Colonel Diego Archuleta. It would prove to be a costly oversight. The command of New Mexico was turned over to Colonel Doniphan.

Eleven days later, opposite Valverde Mesa on the Rio Grande General Kearny was preparing to leave the river and turn westward when he met "Mr. Kit Carson with a party of sixteen men on his way to Washington City with mail and papers—an express from Commodore Stockton and Lieutenant-Colonel Fremont, reporting that the Californias were already in possession of the Americans . . . ; that the American flag was already flying from every important position in the territory, and that the country was free from Mexican control, the war ended, and peace and harmony established among the people." Two large phases of President Polk's grand strategy were accomplished with the taking of New Mexico and California. General Kearny, offering to detail a substitute courier, persuaded Kit Carson to turn right around and guide him to California. Keeping with him only his battery of two howitzers and a hundred dragoons, the General sent the rest of his force back to Santa Fe, and pushed on for the Pacific. James Magoffin took leave of him and rode for El Paso on his way to Chihuahua, where, if all went well, he would do for General Wool what he had done for General

Kearny. It was for him a satisfaction to be able to say, in simple truth, "Bloodless possession of New Mexico was what President Polk wished; it was obtained through my means. . . ."

18.

The Army of Chihuahua

Another thrust in the American grand strategy of the war came to the river on October eighth, 1846, at France Way. The old ford of St. Denis, and the Spanish founders of Texas, now saw Brigadier General John E. Wool's Army of Chihuahua coming to Mexico at a point about five hundred river miles inland from the Gulf. Wool came on the old trade route from San Antonio that skirted at great distance the highlands rising from the deep coastal plain. As they neared the river his soldiers saw passages of purple and yellow limestone, occasional canyons, and far-reaching surfaces of pale gray dust broken by thorny brush; and to men marching in war so far from home, at the end of day after day, over so great a waste, night came like a vast sinking of the heart.

They had taken eleven days to march about one hundred and seventy-five miles from San Antonio. As they neared the river their order in column read first, four companies of dragoons; and then, six infantry companies, both regulars and volunteers from Illinois; General Wool and his staff; the Arkansas volunteer artillery regiment; the wagon trains, and a rear guard. Each soldier was issued twenty cartridges, and all guns and cannon were heavily loaded. Across the river, old Fort Saint John Baptist was now called the Presidio del Rio Grande. It was known to be garrisoned by Mexican troops. Wool's men expected a fight. There would be no long interval of posed yet suspended hostilities on both sides of the river such as had delayed General Taylor's operations downstream for so long; for General Wool, before undertaking his march, had made certain to equip the division with a "flying-bridge," the parts of which were hauled in wagons—framed timbers, and spans of various lengths, and pontoons—under the charge of two engineer officers, Captain William D. Fraser and Captain Robert E. Lee.

It was like General Wool to insist upon extraordinary preparations for a campaign. He had been for twenty-five years Inspector-General of the Army, and had formed a habit of furious interest in details and a dear love of uniformity. He required all personnel to shave daily, even beardless volunteer boys, no matter where the Army of Chihuahuas might find itself. Units that took his smallest order less than awesomely he disciplined with hardness, and when the Arkansas Volunteers insisted on behaving like frontier democrats in military matters he conducted a running feud with their colonel, Archibald Yell, former governor of their state. He brawled primly with other senior officers, too, and with Dr. Josiah Gregg, whom he had engaged at San Antonio as an expert on Mexico to accompany the Army in the post of interpreter. If Gregg saw him at first as "an amiable gentlemanly man," it was not long before he was calling him a man "of a very unpleasant, whimsical temperament— decidedly old-womanish"; and the volunteers referred to him as "the old Woolly Devil," and "Old Granny Wool." But he continued to demand strict order on the march, proper sanitation in camp, and sustained training; and in the end his troops remained more healthy than those in other invasion units, and when they were tested in battle proved to be well-prepared.

They were on the alert now as they came to the Rio Grande on October eighth and looked across at Mexico, expecting to see the Presidio garrison drawn up to fight. But, as a young volunteer German immigrant noted, "with the exception of two Mexicans who held up a white flag, and waved their hats, there was no one else to see." The Presidio garrison had abandoned the town and retired to the interior. The mayor of Presidio del Rio Grande crossed and gave his old stone town into "the protection of the United States." The men dismissed from ranks broke for the river, whose water "was muddy, but good to drink." The current was "very rapid," and the stream "about as wide as the Ohio at Cincinnati." The troops found refreshment by bathing at once.

The engineers went to work on their flying bridge, and also assembled ferry barges, while the troops waiting to cross hardened their spirits with grim little jobs. "There has been," wrote Captain Lee to his wife, "a great whetting of knives, grinding of swords, and sharpening of bayonets, ever since we reached the river." Within three days the flying bridge and the ferries were ready, and under a hard rain the Army of Chihuahua crossed to Mexico and marched over brushy bottomland to Presidio five miles inland. "We were lucky," scribbled the German youth, "to find cornbread instead of bullets awaiting us. . . ." The residents were friendly, but charged "exorbitant prices for everything." The Mexican officials sought out General Wool with a great piece of news. A hundred miles southeast beyond mountain and desert General Taylor with the Army of the Rio Grande had captured Monterrey in engagements lasting from September twentieth to twenty-fourth. It was not so much to rejoice the Americans with this news that it was given them by the Mexican town authorities, as to report further that General Taylor after his victory had agreed to an armistice of eight weeks. The Presidians gave General Wool a copy of the articles of capitulation of Monterrey, in which the cease-fire was clearly provided for. Surely he would honor it?

The General found nothing in the articles to keep him from continuing his march, and he agreed to abide by the armistice after arriving at Monclova, another hundred and seventy-five miles away. Meanwhile he took a few days to rest his men, replenish supplies, and consider possible routes for his descent upon Chihuahua, should the war continue. In another day Brigadier General James Shields arrived from Camargo to command the Infantry brigade and confirmed the news of Taylor's third big victory. General Shields—who later quarrelled with Wool—earned a line or two in Dr. Gregg's notebook: ". . . a military monomaniac—crazy—his head addled by his elevation . . . one of the veriest *military* simpletons." The Army of Chihuahua had its notables. Another was the wife of Major David Hunter, Paymaster USA. Amidst the small but varied crowd of women on the campaign, most of them attached to enlisted men, Mrs. Paymaster Hunter loomed as "a very amiable, meritorious and remarkable lady who is truly the heroine of Gen. Wool's campaign, having been the only respectable female in the army," as Gregg saw her. She had marched from San Antonio, and she would proceed into Mexico, to suffer "innumerable sacrifices, privations and dangers—and all for affection to her husband." If Dr. Gregg heard some "contend that she has been out of place," he thought this was possibly true in one sense. "Nevertheless," he insisted, "I must consider that there is at least no *demerit* in her course: in fact"—his head swam with generosity—"in fact, I think it merits more than a mere negative. . . ."

Few of the soldiers saw Presidio, for their camp was four miles west of town, and they were marched to it without pause, much as they would have liked to gaze about. But "I always forget," sighed a volunteer, "that I have no will of my own but that I am a part of a machine." Still, in glimpses, the Army could see that Presidio, with its stone town gate, was colorful. Its earthen houses carried architectural ornaments frescoed in pale earth colors. Weeds worked on the ruin of Saint Bernard's. Private gardens of sugar cane, cotton and fig trees attracted the invaders. Two thousand people belonged in Presidio, but now in the war only about half were still in town. It was not a healthful spot, for swamps and bogs stood on all sides, caused by overflow from irrigation canals. In their brief stay, the Army picked up "considerable chills and fevers."

One day two starving men lurched their way into camp to be taken care of. They were Texas Rangers who had been captured a few weeks earlier in a previous American touch at the river. It was an episode unauthorized by the Army, and it ended in recall of the troops, and reprimand for its commander—Colonel William S. Harney, who had been unable to contain himself at San Antonio until General Wool's arrival during the summer. He had taken Presidio in August with only a few companies of rangers and regulars. When he was ordered to withdraw his impulsive invasion, the Mexicans returned, and fired at his rear guard over the river, and took a few prisoners. One man, a civilian sutler, had a strange story to tell, and he came in his turn among Wool's men to tell it.

With seven companions he had been ferrying supplies for Colonel Harney when the Mexicans fired upon him in the river. He jumped overboard. He couldn't swim, but crawled underwater to the Mexican bank where he hid till dark, when he pushed a log out in the current to bear him across to the American bank. But he could not make it, and ended by floating thirty miles downstream before he could manage to land. He walked up to the campsite opposite Presidio only to find that the Americans had left. Mexicans then captured him, and the night before he was to be marched to the interior with other prisoners, he escaped, and again entered the river, found another log, and floated down again, this time for eighty miles, to Laredo. Hoping to meet Wool's Army at France Way, he walked up from Laredo, found the encampment, introduced himself—he was a Mr. Riddle—and told his story.

In camp, volunteers greased the wagons, and regulars let them do it "—the volunteers have to do all the extra work," one of them observed—and got on with their washing and everybody prepared for inspection which meant, under General Wool, buying new clothes if old ones were worn or unpresentable. A regimental sutler asked "10 dollars for a pair of coarse boots, and 6 dollars for linen trousers." On the private soldier's pay of seven dollars a month, it was hard to meet the General's standards. Sardonically the private soldiers referred to themselves as "seven-dollar targets."

And yet there was pride in the Army, and a sense of affirmative purpose, for at Presidio a young private recorded quite simply, "I had the honor of doing guard duty soon after our arrival in Mexico. The guard parade of 300 men make a grand appearance. They parade daily under command of the staff officers, Captains, etc." He did not see the ceremony as merely a formal flourish of arms that took up his time and set him to trudging at somebody else's pleasure. He noted further that "Our lieutenants have the least to do, and can take it easy." And when it was time to go to work, the Division could respond swiftly. On October fifteenth, "this morning at 9 o'clock the alarm was sounded, and then a call to arms. In ten minutes we were in readiness to meet the enemy. In the distance . . . shots were heard. The Dragoons went out to investigate, but soon returned to report that the Mexicans at Presidio were celebrating a feast day, and were shooting volleys in honor of the day." But the Army was leaving the next day for the interior, and General Wool must review them all before starting, and so "We had a big review in the afternoon. . . . Later," about to leave for the unknown, and obscurely aware of how poignant might be the idlest words if they were the last from a soldier who might never return, "later in the day I wrote two letters to the home folks. . . ."

At four in the morning on October sixteenth the advance elements of the Army of Chihuahua moved away from the river, on the Monclova road, over a land perfectly level, and without water in a day's march. Some of the soldiers had picked up at Presidio a "kind of scurvy" that made "lips, teeth, gums and tongue sore," so that it was agony to eat. There seemed nothing in prospect for days but the repeated chores of marching overland, for no enemy forces appeared, and Dr. Gregg, on his mule, with his red parasol, riding beside the marching men who were heavy-belted and pendulous with scabbarded blades, remarked, "Verily our war-seeking soldiers are becoming desperate for want of an enemy upon whom to display their valor."

Once at Monclova, General Wool waited four weeks under the terms of Taylor's armistice. While he waited, he studied obstacles and solutions to his proposed move upon Chihuahua City. To his west lay the great and all but impassable Bolsón de Mapimí, an elevated desert

shaped like a huge pouch and rimmed by mountains. Dust-gray, waterless, silent, it rose between five and ten thousand feet in altitude, and
covered nearly ten thousand square miles. He could not cross it with
an army, but would have to detour around it to capture Chihuahua
City and paralyze north central Mexico—if the armistice were lifted and
hostilities resumed. It was lifted, suddenly, for the Washington government ordered General Taylor to rescind it; and Taylor notified Santa
Anna, who was now in the field as Mexican supreme commander, that
the war would be renewed on November thirteenth. Three days later
Taylor's Army of the Rio Grande occupied Saltillo, basing Worth's
division there.

And now, studying his most suitable route to the west, Wool saw
that he must march south from Monclova to Parrás in order to skirt the
Bolsón de Mapimí before turning west and north toward Chihuahua.
He saw further that Parrás was only ninety miles from Saltillo, and the
United States forces there. It seemed to him that, coming so close to the
main body of invasion, his division would be more useful as a part of it
than as a lone expedition crawling through weeks of wilderness travel
on a mission whose success was by no means certain. Accordingly, he
sent an express to General Taylor at Monterrey suggesting that orders
be issued to change his objective, attaching him instead to the Monterrey-
Saltillo-Parrás line. Taylor promptly approved; and the Army of Chihuahua marched on November twenty-fourth for Parrás, to go no
farther west.

But Colonel Doniphan at Santa Fe knew nothing of the change
in plan, and proceeded with his part of the design against Chihuahua
City, which he had persuaded General Kearny to approve.

19.

The Free Missourians

Colonel Sterling Price and his Missouri regiment had been in Santa Fe since October third, preparing to take over from Doniphan. The Mormon battalion was also there, outfitting under Captain Philip St. George Cooke to march for California. Their condition appalled their new commander. They were hardly a military force. They were "too much enlisted by families," as he saw. "Some were too old, some feeble, some young; much embarrassed"—in the Mormon style—"by too many women." They were "undisciplined; much worn by travelling on foot . . . from Nauvoo, Ill.; . . . clothing scant, no money to pay them . . . or clothing to issue." Another officer observed that "A more ragamuffin looking set than the Mormons it would be hard to find. . . . From the officers down I could see nothing like a genteel-looking man. . . ." There was a general eagerness to leave Santa Fe and be on the move. Out of various motives—freedom for the Mormons, adventure for the soldiers, business for the traders—everyone wanted to be up and going. The troops were all "anxious to get away, each one wishing to be the first." A lieutenant said, "Some prefer an expedition to California, some south, and all are fearful they will not get to go where they wish."

On October seventh many of the traders at Santa Fe started downriver, including the Samuel Magoffins, with their wagons for Chihuahua. Their march was planned to take advantage of protection by the Doniphan column, and they would make rendezvous with the troops at Valverde before driving on for Mexico and—who knew?—perhaps battle. On the same day Colonel Doniphan received a dispatch from General Kearny ordering him to take a crack detachment and enter the Navajo country to wring pledges of peace out of the Indians who had taken advantage of the unsettled conditions of a change of government in New Mexico to ravage the countryside.

Preparations were stepped up. On October fifteenth and sixteenth the Mormons moved out. Soldiers knowing they were about to depart suddenly felt nostalgic about what they would leave. One made a note of the "artillery band at tattoo, who play several tunes every evening between the calls. To hear the martial notes of a bugle on a clear calm lovely evening is always soul-stirring, but to have three or four good musicians in a land destitute of taste or rational amusements nightly play some old and favorite air, when one's mind is running upon home, friends, and the many luxuries and enjoyments we have deprived ourselves of, is certainly a pleasure . . . one of the few enjoyments I have in Santa Fe is the music. . . ." And then came darkness, and the lively nighttime, until the army's curfew at ten, when "the gun fires." Then the citizens "can be seen running in all directions, the monte tables are deserted, and the merry fandango is no longer heard . . . and the stillness only interrupted by the tread of the sentinels, the rattling of their arms, or the reliefs going on post. Occasionally a sentinel is heard calling the corporal of the guard, having taken a prisoner, some unlucky individual who is caught straying from home or returning from a gambling house. . . ."

Colonel Doniphan with three hundred mounted troopers left Santa Fe on October twenty-sixth. The rest of his force—some five hundred men—would follow on the river road to await him at Valverde while below Albuquerque he turned west for the Navajo plains. On the day of his departure the Navajos, as though to confirm the need of his discipline, raided the old river villages south of Albuquerque—Tomé, Valencia and the rest—killing many people and driving off five thousand sheep from the valley farms. The Mexican ranchers, now territorial citizens of the United States, sent their remaining herds and flocks to the eastern mountains for safekeeping, and organized bands of "voluntarios" to chase after the Navajos in their western wilderness, where Doniphan would soon force a great roundup of chiefs for a council of peace.

The rest of the First Missouri Volunteers toiled down the river in their own free style. Their column stretched out for miles—at one time for as far as a hundred. Parties of traders were intermittently scattered along their line, until at times soldiers could not be told from civilians. Their uniforms were incomplete, and such as they had were of summer weight. There was already snow on the mountains above Santa Fe, and winter followed the marchers down the valley. Many suffered, for they had thrown away their tents to make light their loads. The nights were hard. One morning the troops awoke to find themselves under four inches of snow. In the valley they saw great passages of geese flying south, and shot a few, but the weather was "too cold for sport." Large blocks of ice floated down the river. Fording was difficult. The river road was sandy in spots, and gave trouble to teams and teamsters. Soldiers "had to spend half of their time at the wheels." Oxen died on the trail and men took ill and were sent back to Santa Fe. Soldiers foraged in mountains twenty-five miles away from the road to bring firewood to the column. The human climate was not pleasant, either; for as they marched south the troops felt that "the people generally have hostile feelings and would be able to render efficient aid to any force sent against us from below. . . ." The spirit had changed from the first enthusiasm for the new regime. There were powers at work in the dark to change it. But so far, in early December, the Americans, only sorry that as conquerors they were not better loved, suspected nothing.

Presently, at Lemitar, and below, at Socorro, the column came into what seemed like a new climate. The weather moderated. Soldiers found diversions in Socorro, if at high prices. An English traveller, George Frederick Ruxton, was also there in December, 1846, and made notes on what he saw of the old river town. Its appearance was "that of a delapidated brick kiln, or a prairie dog town, indeed from this animal the New Mexicans appear to have derived their style of architecture." The people seemed to him dirty, mean, lazy, beggarly. ". . . In his rabbit burrow," with his tortillas, his chile, and his corn shuck cigarette, "the New Mexican is content; and with an occasional traveller to pilfer, or the excitement of a stray Texan to massacre now and then, is tolerably happy—his only care being that the river rise enough to fill his acequia . . . that sufficient maize may grow to furnish him tortillas for the winter, and shucks for his half-starved horse or mules, which the Navajos have left, out of charity, after killing half his sons and daughters and bearing into captivity the wife of his bosom. . . ."

Ruxton had come up the Chihuahua Trail, and now in December he was among the traders and Missouri volunteers. He marvelled at the loose formation of the column, and its disorders, and its lack of uniformity in all things. Even the ammunition and provision wagons, he noted, were travelling through enemy country without an escort. At Valverde, where the camps of the soldiers and traders were made while awaiting Colonel Doniphan, Ruxton, an officer in a British regiment, could hardly believe what he saw. "From appearances no one would have imagined this to be a military encampment. The tents were in line, but there all uniformity ceased. There were no regulations in force with regard to cleanliness. The camp was strewed with the bones and offal of the cattle slaughtered for its supply, and not the slightest attention was paid to keeping it clear from other accumulations of filth. The men, unwashed and unshaven, were ragged and dirty, without uniforms, and dressed as, and how, they pleased. They wandered about, listless and sickly looking, or were sitting in groups playing at cards, and swearing and cursing, even at the officers if they interfered to stop it (as I witnessed). The greatest irregularities constantly took place. Sentries, or a guard, although in an enemy's country, were voted unnecessary; and one fine day, during the time I was there, three Navajo Indians ran off with a flock of 800 sheep belonging to the camp, killing the two volunteers in charge of them, and reaching the mountains in safety with their booty. Their mules and horses were straying over the country; in fact, the most total want of discipline was apparent in everything." It was all true, and shocking to a cultivated observer with professional military standards. What a foreigner could not see was that the volunteers were frontier individualists, enacting a primitive stage of democracy, even if it often proclaimed the self to the disadvantage of its fellows. But in the end, what did it matter, mused Ruxton: "These very men, however, were as full of fight as game cocks," and when a fight was coming, that was what was wanted.

For Mexican troops were massing in northern Chihuahua. Ruxton had seen them. There was every sign that they would defend El Paso, the gateway. He brought news, too, of others he had seen—Ex-Governor Manuel Armijo, travelling southward with Albert Speyer, the Santa Fe trader, and all their wagons. Speyer's large consignment of arms and ammunition, so laboriously hauled from St. Louis, was seized by the Mexican army, in spite of a hired escort of "thirty strapping young Missourians, each with a long rifle across his saddle."

Armijo had other worries. Ruxton told his listeners at Valverde about him. "A mountain of fat," the fugitive governor "rolled out of his American Dearborn," and asked,

"What is the price of cotton goods at Durango?" He had seven wagonloads with him to sell. Next he asked,

"What are they saying in Mexico of the doings at Santa Fe—" its capture by the Americans without any resistance?

"There is but one opinion," replied Ruxton, "expressed over all the country—that General Armijo and the New Mexicans are a pack of arrant cowards."

"Oh, my God!" shrieked Armijo. "They don't know that I had but seventy-five men to fight three thousand. What could I do?"

Other news came to Valverde. Traffic through El Paso was closed. Traders camped farther down the valley sent word that a large force was coming up from Chihuahua to capture all travellers and goods. Drivers made corrals of their wagons, sinking their wheels to the hubs "for a breast-work in case of attack." Worse, a party that had managed to get through to El Paso had been captured and jailed, and one—it was James Magoffin—had been led away to Chihuahua City where he was tried for his life as a spy. His secret work at Santa Fe had been discovered. He was in great danger. Samuel and Susan Magoffin heard this with distress at Valverde.

Colonel Doniphan returned to the river from the Navajo country on December twelfth at Socorro, bringing with him a treaty signed by the chiefs with X's, promising "permanent peace, mutual trust and friendship." He hurried down to Valverde to join his main body of troops, and set to work preparing "our train," as he said, "to obey the order of General Kearny, requiring me to report to General Wool." He animated the command, took them down to Fray Cristóbal, and without incident led them through the Dead Man's March. They emerged from it at the river on December twenty-second and found the last traders camped downstream. There was no communication with El Paso. Mexicans living at the new settlement of Doña Ana would say nothing. There was battle in the air. The Colonel shook together his units for regular inspections. Ammunition was passed out, and without recourse to voting, pickets were stationed at night. The fighting strength of the long, scattered column totalled eight hundred and fifty-six men—all riflemen. There were no cannon at hand for, as Wool's forces were well-equipped with a regiment of artillery, the Missourian batteries had been left behind at Santa Fe.

20.

Brazito and the Pass

It seemed odd not to have news of General Wool. Presumably, by now, he should have drawn near to the city of Chihuahua, if he had not actually entered it. News of so striking an event would surely have come north, despite all the Mexican army might do to censor it. And yet there was not even a rumor of his invasion. But in any case, Colonel Doniphan's orders read to report to General Wool at Chihuahua City, and there he must go to find him. The column straggled on past Doña Ana—the last settlement above El Paso forty-five miles away. The weather was pleasant as the march began on December twenty-fifth. It was to be a short march, perhaps out of respect for the great feast of Christmas. Coming near to a fine camping site with leafy river bottoms and an easy approach for leading horses to water, the Colonel ordered a halt and a camp made around one o'clock. He sent out scouts to survey the neighborhood, and south of the campsite they suddenly saw and chased a small party of Mexican observers who as they ran away left behind a fine horse. The horse was captured and taken back to camp.

The Americans were being watched, then, and Colonel Doniphan had his first direct warning, and his first captive—the horse. While the wagons were being unloaded, and the teams and cavalry mounts were led to the river to drink and forage, the Colonel called for a deck of cards, and sat down to play the scouts for the ownership of the Mexican mount. It was a gesture in the democratic volunteer style. The game was not yet finished when to the south on the flat valley a cloud of dust was seen to appear and grow. The Colonel estimated its size and behavior; and gave the order to sound "boots and saddles." In another moment he cancelled it, for the cavalry mounts were all at the river. There was not time to bring them back and saddle them. He commanded everyone to form in infantry line, and established the teamsters as a guard around their wagon park.

In less than half an hour the dust was near enough to reveal its source—a Mexican army of eleven hundred men—lancers, cavalry and infantry—with a howitzer. They advanced steadily, coming along a high level parallel to the river and to mountains that rose a few miles away as the eastern limit of the valley. Once opposite the camp, whose site was called Brazito, they wheeled into front and halted on the elevation half a mile away from the Missourians, who were drawn up in line with the Rio Grande in their rear. The Mexican front reached north and south for two miles. The regulars among them were uniformed in red "& made quite a cavalier appearance," as a volunteer saw. The American Army of the West had not yet fired a shot in battle. Now with the moment of decision upon them, they drew together out of their rambunctious disorder as volunteers, and presented a hard, clear, disciplined force, waiting for the command to fight. The scene on the riverside plain had a third group of observers: a large party of Apache Indians who from the mountains in the rear of the Mexican line proposed to watch the encounter.

The day was sunny, and the valley's winter colors shone in the clear air—pale russet reeds, silver grass, and gold straw; gray-violet mountains above the speckled bench where the Mexican arms glimmered; and in the river groves, copper, gold and bronze leaves clinging to the cottonwoods like trophies of beaten metal waiting for conquerors. From the Mexican lines emerged a rider who cantered to within a hundred steps of the Missourians. There he halted and displayed a flag. It was black, with two white skulls above crossbones on one side, and on the other, white lettering that read *"Libertad ó muerte!"* Doniphan's adjutant with an interpreter rode out to meet him.

"Let your commander come to our line and speak to our General," said the Mexican.

"If your General wants to see our commander," replied the Missourians, "let him come here."

"We shall break your ranks, then, and take him there!"

"Come and take him!"

"Damn it all, we will neither give nor ask quarter," said the Mexican waving his flag, "prepare for a charge!" and galloped back to his line.

Colonel Doniphan passed an order down the ranks: "Prepare to squat!" The men laughed, but knew he was in earnest, for he followed it up by ordering them to hold their fire, and let the Mexicans shoot over their heads until their advance was so close that the volunteer marksmanship could take terrible effect. The Mexicans moved. Their infantry was on the American right, their howitzer in the center, and their cavalry on the left. As they came they fired and paused, fired and paused, five times, without any return fire from the ranks before the river. They turned to ask one another what kind of people were these who stood up to be shot at without shooting back. They shrugged. It was clear that the Americans meant to surrender.

But the long rifles were cocked, and the officers were watching the Colonel, and the files were already told off, one and two, one kneeling to reload while the other stood to fire, and when the Mexicans had come within a hundred and fifty yards, the word came, and "number one fired, and then number two . . . and it was well done and had a fine effect, their cavalry reeling under it, and their whole line giving," recorded a Missouri lieutenant. The Mexican cavalry charged around the end to get at the parked wagons, and there too the teamsters held fire until it could be given with maximum damage. When it came, the Mexicans veered away in confusion.

At the same time, the Missourian right charged the enemy howitzer and captured it. It was at once put to work by volunteers who formed a battery of artillerymen about it. The whole Missouri line now surged forward at the command to charge, and the Mexican front rolled back at some distance before it, as though blown over the ground by a shock wave. By the time the Americans reached the high level of the first Mexican stand, the Mexicans were nowhere to be seen. At a full run they had retreated out of sight. Some who fled to the mountains were stopped and killed by the Apaches there. Others headed south to flee through El Paso. One was a woman who had followed the Mexican soldiers into battle. At the defeat, she jumped on a mule and whipped it into a frantic trot southward. Another woman was killed at the capture of the howitzer, and her body carried away. There were Mexican dead over the field, and much abandoned property.

The soldiers were allowed to pick up what they could find; and soon retreated to the Brazito camp, loaded with wine, and trinkets, and garments, and little crosses, and scraps of equipment, and dropped weapons. All were in roaring spirits. They had come ably and safely through their first battle. They had proved that frontier democrats were capable of discipline when the necessity for it was presented in terms of life and death. "Our men behaved like veterans," declared an officer, "and exhibited a coolness and obedience to orders worthy of any troops." Once again in camp, they knocked open the Mexican wine jugs and

took the day as a "Christmas frolic." Colonel Doniphan was amused at
the Mexican aim with the howitzer. It was always high, and he said that
"about a bushel of copper ore" from the howitzer must have passed
over his head "by at least ten feet." He settled down to resume his interrupted card game, finished it, and agreed that the Mexican horse was
won by one of the scouts. The losers had the last laugh when it turned
out that the horse had been allowed to escape during the battle. "It
was late at night before all was quiet in camp," noted a lieutenant,
"being greatly exhilarated by our victory without the loss of a man. . . ."

Leaving camp early the next morning they wore their trophies
of victory. "One had on a Mexican dragoon cap, another a serape, some,
beads and crosses, almost everyone something. . . ." The volunteers
were themselves again. They marched south, passed the Mexican base
camp of the day before, found "some of the fires still burning," and
came upon a handful of Mexican dead left behind. "We thought only
of reaching El Paso," wrote a soldier, "and solving the problem whether
we shall have another fight or not."

It was solved the next day when in sight of the earth city on the
south bank they were met by a deputation come "from El Paso to surrender the place, and to inform us that the Mexicans were totally
defeated and never stopped but continued on to Chihuahua in squads,
dispersing in all directions." The conquerors crossed the river by a ford
between two vineyards, marched through the town accepting "grapes,
apples, wine, pears, peaches, etc., in great abundance" from the residents,
and camped in a vineyard at the far side, with open country beyond.
The wind was blowing, and the fine alluvial soil of the valley's old river-
beds came up in long hauls on the air against the exposed camp. At the
end of December at El Paso the river was a meagre stream winding by
the dusty violet mountains of the pass, and between groves of valley
cottonwoods with their hammered dark-gold leaves. Above the banks
rose freckled sandhills, and bare trees in the distance looked like arrested
gray smoke. The earth, and the houses that came up from it, were of a
pale, skin-brown color. Washed sunlight bore down through thin white
cloud, and flocks of huge crows made commotions in the fields. The
country was dusty and flat; and in its open winter airs all things, even
the low, extensive town, were absorbed, from a little distance, by golden
space.

The regiment found El Paso very different from Santa Fe. The
old northern capital seemed in retrospect to be rude and graceless by
comparison with the charms of the wide irrigation canals of El Paso,

and its beautifully set vineyards, orchards and fields, and the patios with so much greenery, the fine workmanship of the houses, and their superior furnishings and—presently—their hospitality. For at first the populace had run away, but soon began to return when it was plain that the Americans, while they might be infidels and heretics, as Governor Trias had proclaimed in Chihuahua, were not barbarians, as he had also called them. But neither were they notably virtuous. As the people returned, and enterprise saw opportunity, victor and vanquished combined in the commerce of appetites; for the regiment was in town to stay until Colonel Doniphan's plans and equipment were complete.

Now in the northernmost city of Chihuahua, he was positively assured by surrendered Mexican soldiers that General Wool had made no move at all against the state. Here was a dilemma. Should he advance to Chihuahua hoping that in time Wool would appear? Should he undertake such a march deep into enemy country without artillery? Or should he ignore his orders from Kearny and not proceed? In a sense the decision was not his alone, for the men under his command were all volunteers with decided views. He explained the problem to them and put the decision to a vote. All but two or three voted to continue the march. One, "a blacksmith in Company F, was shoeing a horse when told of the result of the vote," reported a Missouri cavalryman. "It frightened him. He was opposed to going on. He dropped the shoe of the horse upon which he was at work, and began to talk of the foolishness and danger of the march. He talked of nothing else and talked incessantly. It preyed on his mind and deranged his reason. In two weeks he had talked himself to death, and was buried at El Paso. . . ."

Now with his answer firmly provided, Colonel Doniphan "determined to order a battery and a hundred artillerists from New Mexico." Until they should arrive from Santa Fe, there was nothing for it but to wait at El Paso; for lacking the certainty of meeting Wool and coming under the protection of his cannon in the event of a fight deep in the interior, it would be foolhardy, in the Colonel's judgment, to march without heavy guns. He sent an express to Colonel Price at Santa Fe with his requisition, and the volunteers unbuttoned themselves for a high time during the pause.

"The army," saw a lieutenant, "was composed of men of a restless and roving disposition, and the little discipline which prevailed was totally insufficient to prevent rioting and dissipation, which endangered the health of the troops as well as their efficiency. . . ." While some officers and men did the jobs of setting up supply, taking possession of the primitive gristmills of the town, and sequestering captured arms and ammunition in warehouses, others thronged the old plaza where amidst the market stalls were the stands of "perpetual gambling—monte-dealing, chuck-luck, &c," at which Mexicans and soldiers blocked the street. Fandangos were given for the officers. Three soldiers were arrested to be court-martialled for ravishing a Mexican woman. Horse and mule racing for high stakes drew enormous crowds. The native wines and brandies poured forth. By the middle of January Colonel Doniphan, like Taylor at Matamoros, was obliged to issue orders curbing the opportunities for excesses. Gambling, fandangos and racing were officially suppressed, but without practical success. Drills and inspections were held, and men were trained in the mounted charge with sabres.

Rumors came into town of Mexican forces mustering in the south, at Carizal, and of movements downriver near the old presidio at the Junta de los Rios. The Colonel sent scouts in both directions. At the end of the first week of January the Carizal scouting party returned with three prisoners one of whom was the parish priest of El Paso, Father Ortíz, who had been so kind to the captured Texans five years earlier. He was questioned by Doniphan who gave him a furious lecture, for if he had not been acting as a spy, he had at any rate been taken in the company of spies reporting to Carizal on American affairs at El Paso.

But if the pastor was a patriot, he was still a figure of charity and even elegance in the hospitality he bestowed on foreigners. The Samuel Magoffins were taken into his rectory to stay, and were served by his two sisters who kept house for their popular and charming brother. "We have chocolate every morning on rising," Susan told her diary, "breakfast about 10 o'k, dinner at two, chocolate again at dark, and supper at 9 o'clock, all are attentive, indeed we are so free and easy, 'tis almost a hotel, meals are served in our own room, one of the ladies always being in attendance. . . ." The weather was so mild that trees were coming into leaf. In patios hidden from the streets visitors took their ease surrounded by flowering plants in pots, and rose bushes and beds of lilies, and tropical birds in wicker cages, and nibbling pigeons, and cats eyeing them. Business was bustling, and the residents were "well pleased by the conduct of the American Army." The troops had received no army pay since their enlistment. Their clothes were in tatters, but with what funds they had brought along, or had made in gambling or in other improvised ways, they bought what they needed from local merchants at high prices. The wind blew on some days, and on others a fine crystal sunshine warmed everyone with a sense of common well-being. At night, in the January cold, sentries were bothered by "a great many wolves, which come down from the neighboring mountains into the suburbs of El Paso" to kill sheep and feast on "the offal about the shambles and slaughter-pens." The wolves, keeping up "a dolorous serenade during the nights," frequently attacked the sentry posts, where the soldiers shot at them. Hearing musket fire from the outskirts, the town woke up to fears of battle; but then quiet could come again, and morning, and Colonel Doniphan would wonder why the artillery from Santa Fe had not yet arrived. There was a reason—a highly disturbing one; but he did not know it yet. All he could do was wait in the early weeks of January, 1847.

21.

Counterdance

On December twenty-eighth—the day following Doniphan's entry into El Paso—a majestic arrival occurred twelve hundred miles away at the Arms of Saint James on the Gulf, when a steamer put in to deliver, with his staff, a major general six feet four inches tall, of glaring eye, heavy build, and a manner of solemn amplitude, all sumptuously uniformed in blue and gold. It was Winfield Scott, at sixty years of age the General-in-Chief of the United States Army.

His journey had been crammed with inconveniences most unsuitable to the progress of a major general. It was impossible to imagine how so many "cruel uncertainties" could seek to impede him who so loved the splendid comfort of high rank, even with its unending duties of manner, rhetoric and ceremony. He had left from New York, where he caught a heavy cold. Sailing for New Orleans, he had been delayed almost a week at sea by vexatious head winds. In New Orleans for four days, he held official conversations, and dined with Senator Henry Clay, and—it was astounding and supremely impertinent—the purpose of his journey which was the highest strategic secret of the war appeared in print in a Spanish language newspaper of the city, and was at once copied by other papers, and sent off to the Eastern press as vital news. In a trice a public that grew by hours knew that General Scott was on his way to the Rio Grande to confer with General Taylor, and to lay down the final arrangements for a landing of American troops at Veracruz to invade Mexico from the east coast. It was hard to know which would be worse—the embarrassments or the dangers that might result from the leak.

Where it had come from, nobody could imagine. He had been particularly careful in writing to General Taylor from New York on November twenty-fifth, announcing his coming, but not to identify Veracruz as his objective. To do so would not have been "prudent at this distance." All he had said was that he was "not coming to supersede you in the immediate command on the line of operations rendered illustrious by you and your gallant army. My proposed theatre is different. You may imagine it. . . ." It was awkward that some Mexican had also imagined it, and had printed a story absurd in detail but correct in general. The letter went on to state that the writer would proceed to Camargo in order to be "within easy corresponding distance from you." It said further, "But, my dear general, I shall be obliged to take from you most of the gallant officers and men (regulars and volunteers) whom you have so long and so nobly commanded. I am afraid that I shall, by imperious necessity—the approach of yellow fever on the gulf coast—reduce you, for a time, to stand on the defensive. This will be infinitely painful to you, and for that reason distressing to me. But I rely on your patriotism to submit to the temporary sacrifice with cheerfulness." If the letter had been intercepted—though nobody knew —the yellow fever at the Gulf and the diversion of troops from one to another theatre may also have told too much. Perhaps the leak occurred at Washington, where the plan had been laid down. What would President Polk think?

He had been most cordial to General Scott of late. Certainly the President had no confidence in General Taylor, and spoke out freely against him. "I am now satisfied that anybody would do better than Taylor," he stated even after the victories of Palo Alto, Resaca and Monterrey. "Taylor is no doubt brave and will fight, but is not fit for a higher command than that of a regiment. I have no prejudice against him, but think he has acted with great weakness and folly. . . ."

General Scott could but concur—though earlier his opinion of General Taylor had been favorable. But now it seemed discreet to agree with the President, with whom he had "many long personal interviews on military matters," and to accept the command of the great expedition to come. In only four days of staff discussions throughout "the great bureaux" of the War Department, the grand campaign had been mapped, and before leaving for the Rio Grande, the General-in-Chief magnificently wrote a circular to the leading Whigs in Congress commending the President and the Secretary of War for their handsome treatment of him in his hour of added responsibility. He left Washington "highly flattered with the confidence and kindness the President has just shown me." At New Orleans on December twentieth he wrote again to General Taylor, enlarging upon the campaign plans, and now calling him to a meeting at Camargo. He marked his dispatch "most confidential . . . outside and in," and sent it by officer express to General Taylor at Monterrey, and prepared to sail from New Orleans for the Rio Grande on December twenty-fourth.

There was one last exasperation at New Orleans before sailing. General Scott was informed that on the heels of his departure from Washington, the President had sent to Congress a bill creating the office of lieutenant general of the Army, and proposing its bestowal upon Senator Thomas Hart Benton, who would thus supersede all other general officers. The President had remarked to a legislator that he had been "compelled to send Gen'l Scott to take command of the Army as a choice of evils, he being the only man in the army who by his rank could command Taylor." The news was incredible. General Scott dismissed it with grandeur.

"If the rank were asked for," he stated, "it could only—remembering Mr. Polk's assurance of support and reward—be intended for me on the report of my first success," and left for Point Isabel.

When he arrived, he found no word from Taylor, and resolved to go upriver without delay. He was in a genial mood as he renewed old acquaintances among the officers, even, in a general amnesty, restoring to favor such as had once felt his ire. One, Lieutenant Colonel Ethan Allan Hitchcock, who had served under him in Washington, hardly expected to meet him now, remembering that General Scott had once "found a place for a flare-up and did flare up in the highest sort of style" against him. But now the General sent for him at Point Isabel, rose, offered him his hand, and made him "a very complimentary speech," ending up with an appointment to his staff.

"Are you ready to move forward?" asked the General.

"Perfectly," replied Colonel Hitchcock.

"Got a horse?"

"Two, General."

"Glad! Glad! You will join me tomorrow?"

"With great pleasure."

"Clever! Very clever! Right! Right! We start early."

"I will be ready, General."

They boarded the *Big Hatchee* the next morning and steamed along the wide loops of the Rio Grande through dunes and marshes, coming to Matamoros by nightfall. There was still no word from General Taylor. Nobody knew what was happening at Monterrey. Matamoros was "wild with rumors," one of which spread the word that Taylor's communications had been cut by the enemy. Transferring to the steamer *Corvette,* the staff continued its progress the next day, with observations upon the natives who seemed the next thing to "Indians in mud huts," who came to sell wood for $2.50 a cord to the captain; and a pause for an exchange of intelligence with a down-bound steamer, whose news was that Mexican troops were massing below Saltillo under the command of Santa Anna; and hours on deck, when the little ship moved slowly between the banks, while General Scott was "particularly civil," lolling immensely and rumbling on in the satisfactions of high-level reminiscence, amidst subordinates who could not take away the topic, but who remained content under the tall funnel to breathe of smoke and sparks and greatness.

General Scott explained at length the orders which brought him there. He outlined in detail the "ultimate objects of his movement." He re-enacted with relish his many interviews with the President—"what Mr. P. said, what he said," back and forth, back and forth. If there were brief, ever so brief, moments of silence in which the General undertook to "look so wise as the Sphinx," it did seem that he accomplished only "a puzzled, dubious gaze into vacancy." And then, perhaps in "bad French," he would resume his satisfied soliloquy, or sober his hearers with a "flat joke," or treat them to "agonizing pedantries of connoisserhip in wine and cookery." Since his temper was uncertain, all he said was taken with deference, even, in some cases, with fondness, for those who worked closely with him knew his qualities of bravery, skill and warmheartedness.

The anticipated conference with General Taylor was odd to contemplate. There could be no two men more antithetical. General Scott

exploited every massive grace of high position; General Taylor in rumpled overalls shambled about on a yellow mule. Where one condescended,
the other fraternized. If one delighted in exercising his mind and displaying its florid contents, the other—but it was General Scott himself
who said of General Taylor that "few men ever had a more comfortable,
labor-saving contempt for learning of every kind. . . ." Their opposed
qualities were never more sharply stated than by the soldiers themselves,
who with their timeless knack for truth in caricature, spoke of Scott as
Old Fuss and Feathers, and of Taylor as Old Rough and Ready—nick-
names joyfully taken up by press and public.

Given such differences, the conference at Camargo, with its delicate issues of command prerogative, the distribution of troops and the
opportunity for victory, seemed likely to be difficult. And there was even
one further bone of contention buried under more official matters: each
man, with much popular reason to do so, saw himself as the next President of the United States.

But on January 3, 1847, when the *Corvette* arrived at Camargo,
General Taylor was not there, and there was still no word from him
directly. It was the staff at Camargo who gave General Scott the information that General Taylor, far from coming to meet him at the Rio
Grande as ordered, had instead pursued a project of his own—an extended
march eastward into Tamaulipas. He was out of reach for the time being.
It seemed to the General-in-Chief that—really—he had done all he could
to invite General Taylor's participation in the next immediate decisions;
and he now acted with firmness. He wrote orders to General Butler,
who was in command of the Monterrey-Saltillo line in the absence of
Taylor, to abandon Saltillo, hold Monterrey for defense only, and detach
and send at once to the Brazos under General Worth's command a whole
division of General Taylor's army. Certain others of Taylor's troops were
ordered to Tampico. The dispatch included further details of the Veracruz campaign plan, and closed with General Scott's reflection that
though Providence might defeat him, he thought the Mexicans could
not. Marked *Private and Confidential*, the papers went not only to General Butler, but in duplicate to General Taylor, for his perusal when
he could receive them. There was little more to do at Camargo. General
Scott and his people looked over the town and camp the rest of the day,
and one of the staff remarked it as "one of the most miserable places
I ever saw, dirty and dilapidated and but little better than a Seminole
village." They returned to the *Corvette* with relief and the next day
started downriver. Five days later they were again at the Arms of Saint

James, where General Scott pushed preparations for the armada he would lead to the Mexican coast.

All his communications to General Taylor so far ran into trouble. The first, from New York, which was delivered, Taylor dismissed saying, "a more contemptible and insidious communication was never written." The second, from New Orleans, was never delivered, because of what Scott later called "gross neglect of the officer who bore it." The third, from Camargo, reached Taylor on January fourteenth upon his return from the Tamaulipas reconnaissance. On reading it, he was outraged in every personal and professional consideration. General Butler had already acted on the orders it contained. But there was also a dreadful probability that the Mexicans were reacting in their turn, for the copy sent by Scott to Taylor had been intercepted, its officer courier killed, and its contents hurried on to Santa Anna. The copy that eventually reached Taylor was sent to him by Butler.

General Taylor at once saw the implications of the orders, and their effect upon the enemy. If all the best troops of the Army of the Rio Grande were to be pulled out and sent to Scott, then what an opportunity was left for Santa Anna, with his forces massing below Saltillo! It could lead to a disastrous defeat for General Taylor. He saw it all as a wicked affront, with overtones of persecution. Scott's demands for his troops were leaving him with only eight hundred regulars and less than seven thousand volunteers without battle experience. Six general officers were also removed from his army, leaving him only two or three none of whom had had command experience in combat. Once again the bland decisions of the War Department, and the incomprehensible and therefore hateful personality of General Scott intruded upon the bleak realities of the front lines of the desert war, with all its labors, its experience and its human stakes. Washington! What could they know there, where everything was reduced to papers in a conference room, "with its long, official, green-covered table and chairs ranged in official order around it," as another public servant saw, "and official stationery in front of each chair. One could not sit there a moment without official sensations of dignity and red-tapery. . . ." General Taylor's responses were lively.

He wrote to Scott declining to report for a discussion, as he would be busy with matters at Victoria and later at Monterrey. He declared that if Scott had relieved him of his whole command, he would have registered "no complaint." But to reduce his forces so radically, and then to leave him to face over twenty thousand men under Santa

Anna, this was hard to understand—or perhaps it could be understood only too well. "I feel," he wrote bitterly, "I feel that I have lost the confidence of the government, or it would not have suffered me to remain, up to this time, ignorant of its intentions. . . ." Nevertheless, "however much I may feel personally mortified and outraged . . . I will carry out in good faith . . . the views of the government, though"—his darkest suspicions welled over—"though I may be sacrificed in the effort." To his son-in-law he raged, "It seems to me the great object so far as I am concerned . . . is to keep me as much in the dark . . . as it was possible to do; particularly as far as the authorities at Washington are concerned." And as for Scott's orders to pull back from Saltillo and cool his heels at Monterrey, General Taylor flatly informed the Secretary of War, "I shall do no such thing without orders to that effect from proper authority." So much for his recognition of the powers of the General-in-Chief.

General Scott continued to be "the most urbane of conquerors." Replying to Taylor, he said, "There are some expressions in your letters which, as I wish to forget them, I shall not specify or recall. . . . If I had been within easy reach of you . . . I should . . . have consulted you fully on all points. . . . As it was, I had to act promptly, and, to a considerable extent, in the dark. . . ." Elsewhere, and later, he commented that his orders for the reassignment to him of Taylor's troops "began to sour [Taylor's] mind in proportion as he became more and more prominent as a candidate for the Presidency," and he spoke of "the senseless and ungrateful clamor of Taylor, which, like his other prejudices, abided with him to the end. . . ." But General Scott was not to escape his own sense of betrayal, and to speak of "the perfidy of Mr. Polk," for it turned out to be true that the President had made every effort to appoint Senator Benton to the supreme command and had only been thwarted by Congress; and furthermore, the President had suspected General Scott himself, "from his inordinate vanity or from some other cause," of having given out at New Orleans the story of his coming invasion of Mexico. In the President's view, "the truth is neither Taylor nor Scott are fit for the command of an army in the great operations in progress and which are contemplated."

General Taylor, in another statement to his son-in-law, set the tone on which the formal counterdance of vanities ended. "One of the expectations of those who perpetrated the outrage against me was, that I would at once leave the country . . . in disgust & return to the U States which if I had done so, would have been used by them to my disad-

vantage. . . . But in this"—his countryman's ire crackled—"in this I
shall disappoint them, as I have determined to remain & do my duty
no matter under what circumstances until I am withdrawn. . . . I recd
an answer from Genl Scott to a communication I wrote him from Victoria, in which I did not disguise my feelings; he is somewhat tart in
his reply. . . . He & myself now understand each other perfectly, & there
can for the future be none other than official intercourse between us."

The whole scene of the Rio Grande appalled General Scott. He
could not forbear writing to the Secretary of War his impressions in
which lay a strong if implied rebuke of General Taylor's management
of volunteers. He was "agonized" by what he had heard from reliable
witnesses. "If a tenth of what is said be true" the volunteers "have
committed atrocities—horrors—in Mexico, sufficient to make Heaven
weep, & every American of Christian morals *blush* for his country.
Murder, robbery & rape on mothers & daughters in the presence of the
tied up males of the families, have been common all along the Rio
Grande. . . . The respectable volunteers—7 in 10—have been as much
horrified & disgusted as the regulars, with such barbarian conduct. As
far as I can learn"—where was Taylor?—"not one of the felons has been
punished, & very few rebuked—the officers, generally, being as much
afraid of their men as the poor suffering Mexicans themselves are afraid
of the miscreants. Most atrocities are always committed in the absence
of regulars, but sometimes in the presence of acquiescing, trembling
volunteer officers."

But at Point Isabel, General Scott's problems were more immediate. At the War Department he had ordered all the complicated gear
for his amphibious invasion—troops, ships, supplies and equipment, including one hundred and forty-one surfboats for the landings, and casks
of drinking water from the Mississippi, and enough firewood to last sixty
days. But all these were slow to arrive. There would hardly be time for
training in the tactics of putting an army ashore for battle. The weather
was foreboding—northers and high seas. But at last on January 22, 1847
the build-up began. Worth arrived downriver with his division. His
men were jubilant, thinking they were homeward bound until, at the
mouth, they discovered that they were assigned to the invasion. Inland
at Saltillo, they were replaced by Wool's brigade. On the same day the
first detachment of new volunteers arrived at Point Isabel from the East.
Presently, out of New Orleans, the transports began to appear. Their
character was disappointing—they were brigs and schooners of light tonnage that rode the stormy Gulf with difficulty. On February fourth a

steamer brought the surfboats—not all that had been requisitioned, but only sixty-five. Five days later General Scott suffered a more severe blow yet—he heard that the Mexicans had captured his third letter to General Taylor, and were in possession of his plans for the assault. It was imperative now to move fast, and he redoubled the efforts of the Army. Even without sufficient ships or all his supplies, he must move. But one more woe beset him. A furious norther blew in on February twelfth. Sand flew, the shipping strained at anchor, the Army shivered amidst the dunes, until finally on February fifteenth General Scott was able to embark with the advance detachments for rendezvous, first at Lobos Island, then at Tampico on the Pánuco, and the massed descent upon Veracruz. In a few days the site of the invasion jump-off at the Rio Grande beaches was once again occupied by only the garrison at the Fort Polk supply depot, and the forgotten regiment on the tide-washed wastes at the river mouth.

All through the weeks of preparations on the coast, Santa Anna, far inland, was moving up with twenty-five thousand troops, from San Luis Potosí to Encarnación, and finally to a mountain-sided plain below Saltillo. General Taylor, having been pressed, had agreed to run for President if nominated in 1848, had taken and abandoned Victoria, and had retired to await Santa Anna at Buena Vista. There on February twenty-second and twenty-third the desert armies met; and in a great if costly victory Taylor with his weakened forces won northern Mexico— and the Presidency. Ten days later General Scott's men began their landings near Veracruz. On March twenty-seventh the city surrendered, and on April eighth the coastal army began its march inland over the route of Cortés to the heart of Mexico.

22.

The Avengers

Meanwhile Doniphan's Missourians waited at El Paso for the artillery to come from Santa Fe. Suddenly on January tenth there was news from the north. "A New Mexican taken up" by a patrol near El Paso, jotted a volunteer, "states that a revolution is on foot in Santa Fe." For over a week Colonel Doniphan heard nothing further; and then on the nineteenth two lieutenants rode into El Paso with more information. There had been rumors of revolt ever since Kearny's departure. The sentiment of the people toward the Americans seemed to have changed. Even the Pueblo Indians, at first glad to see their Mexican masters overcome by new powers out of the legendary east, soon told each other that they had been "outraged—their lives at stake— their possessions in danger." New Mexicans complained of the "bullying and overbearing demeanor" of the conquerors. There was tension in the air. Colonel Price, in command at Santa Fe, and Governor Charles Bent, who had been appointed to rule the territory by General Kearny, felt it. It looked to his troops as though "indecision" ruled Colonel Price. He was not given anything to act upon until one day just before Christmas 1846 he learned of a visit paid to Lieutenant Governor Vigil by the figure who presided over much of the vice of Santa Fe. It was Doña Gertrudes Barceló, La Tules, with her wig and false teeth, who whispered that a large group of conspirators—men who had voted against the surrender of New Mexico under Armijo—had been meeting secretly to plan a revolt for Christmas Eve. All over the territory, as well as in the capital, native patriots were to rise and capture or murder every North American in New Mexico. The preparations had been going on for months—whispering campaigns, encouragement of malcontents, and organizing of armed bands. Even El Paso was included in the pattern of rebellion, and Father Ortíz was its agent there. The whole scheme was led by an angry man to whom promises had been made—and broken: Colonel Don Diego Archuleta, who had been left with neither an empire west of the Rio Grande nor an official post under the new government. His vengeance had deep roots and but for La Tules it would have burst forth on Christmas Eve, in the style of the terrible revolt of 1680.

The territorial government moved swiftly. Fifteen of the ringleaders were arrested, though Colonel Archuleta made his escape, along with one or two others. All the artillery of the Army was parked at all entrances to the plaza, and sentries were everywhere. After a nervous day vigilance was relaxed, for with the leaders in arrest the rebel organization seemed to melt away. Colonel Price again spoke of sending the artillery downriver to Doniphan. An officer observed, "The artillery are making ready to march . . . ; the clanking of the anvil is incessant; caissons and gun carriages are strewn around the forges." He had an afterthought: "At this juncture it is almost doubtful whether the safety of our citizens does not require that the artillery should remain. . . ." But Doniphan had waited long enough, and Price ordered the ordnance and its men to be ready to depart January eighth. The report of success in the Battle of Brazito later encouraged him in his decision. Any threat from Chihuahua by Mexican forces now seemed remote.

Governor Bent said as much, among other things, in a proclamation to the New Mexicans in early January. "You are now governed by new statutory laws and you also have the free government promised to you. Do not abuse the great liberty which is vouchsafed to you by it, so you may gather the abundant fruits which await you in the future. Those who are blindly opposed . . . also those persons who dream that mankind should bow to their whims, have become satisfied that they cannot find employment in the offices which are usually given to men of probity and honesty, exasperated have come forth as leaders of a revolution against the present government. . . . Their treason was discovered in time and smothered at its birth. Now they are wandering about and hiding from people, but their doctrines are scattered broadcast among the people, thereby causing uneasiness, and they still hold to their ruinous plans. . . . There is still another pretext with which they want to alarm you and that is the falsehood that troops are coming from the interior"—Chihuahua—"in order to reconquer the country." But what, asked the Governor, what help could a Chihuahua torn by internal weakness and opposing factions bring to the far north? He advised the New Mexicans to remain quiet and attend to their work, while he prepared to leave for Taos to visit his home there. Warned that his life was still endangered by the extremist followers of the absent Archuleta, he shrugged off all concern and went home.

Days passed, until at El Paso on February seventh two artillery officers riding in advance of the batteries and their troops hurried to Colonel Doniphan and reported that "Gov. Bent & all the Americans at Taos were assassinated," and that soldiers from Santa Fe were ordered to march up the Rio Grande to Taos to destroy a rebel force composed largely of Indians of the pueblo there.

It was heavy news for the Missourians; but when by the following day the remainder of the artillery column had arrived, there was nothing for Doniphan to do but give the command for the departure southward into the Chihuahua desert, where—who knew?—he might find safety with General Wool in all his power, or alone might face destruction by a Mexican army before Chihuahua City. With his eight hundred opinionated volunteers he left the Rio Grande at El Paso on February 8, 1847.

Far to the north, nearly the whole length of the river away in New Mexico, the after-convulsions of the Taos Massacre were still being felt.

23.

Massacre at Taos

For on January nineteenth—the very day when Doniphan at El Paso heard that the revolt of Christmas Eve had been smothered—Archuleta's latest plans had erupted at Taos with pitiable results. He was not personally on hand to witness or to pay for the horror wrought by his infuriated vanity, which was enfolded in the rags of his patriotism. His local accomplices had aroused the Indians of the pueblo and the Mexicans of the village of San Fernando not only against all Americans but also any natives who had joined the new government. Even the local pastor, Father Antonio José Martínez, was said to encourage the rebels. All day on the eighteenth the rebellious Indians crowded into San Fernando; and throughout hours of drinking the fiery whiskey of Taos their vague sense of injury became a clear and inspired vision. The uproar grew until Governor Bent was advised to leave town for his own safety. He declined. The rebels made drunken speeches to one another far into night; and before dawn of the nineteenth were ready to enact their evil dream.

The family of Governor Bent were all awakened in the dark by the noise of a mob crowding into the plaza where his house stood in a row of connected buildings. Under his roof with him were his wife, his children, and two friends, Mrs. Christopher Carson and Mrs. Thomas Boggs, whose famous husbands were absent from Taos—Carson still with Kearny in California, Boggs on his way home bringing United States mail over a newly established route. The Governor rose from his bed and went to the *portal* to face the shouting faces under torchlight.

What did they want?

They told him that "they did not intend to leave an American alive in New Mexico; and as he was governor, they would kill him first." They surged toward him.

He tried to calm them, appealing to their "honor and manhood."

They laughed. They drew their bows, lightly so as not to kill but only hurt him, and let fly their arrows, aiming at his eyes, his cheeks, his breast. He fell back into his house. They followed. They took him, threw him down, and tore away his scalp with knives. In the next room the women were digging a hole with a poker and an iron spoon through the earthen wall into the adjoining house. When they could they thrust the children through and followed. The Governor crawled to join them, "holding his hand on top of his bleeding head." Indians came after him through the hole. Others swarmed down over the flat roof into the yard and broke into the house next door. Throwing aside his wife who would protect him they killed him with guns. Someone brought a board and brass nails. Spreading his scalp they tacked it to the board and glaring with joy went through the village to show their trophy. The women and children of the Governor's household were left behind with his body. It was secretly buried at three o'clock in the morning of the following day by Mexican friends who risked much to bring such a mercy, and food and clothing, to the family.

From the Governor's murder the rebels moved on to others. Sheriff Stephen Lee was killed on his own rooftop. Young Narcisse

Beaubien, home from study at Cape Girardeau College on the Mississippi, was tortured, scalped and killed. J. W. Leal, the United States District Attorney who had accompanied the Governor to Taos, was awakened, denuded, marched through the village before the rebels who sang as they pricked him with lances and arrows, and scalped alive. Praying them to kill him, he instead received arrows that drove delicately into his eyes, mouth and nose. He was thrown broken and alive to freeze in a ditch for several hours. At last the rebels in their terrible sense of virtue returned from other work and killed him with a few final arrows. His body was given to hogs who feasted upon it until in the afternoon Mrs. Beaubien, who had lost her son, dared to see that it was buried. Upriver at the same time seven Americans were killed and their property burned at Arroyo Hondo, and two at the Red River. In all, twelve were massacred in the uprising of the nineteenth, and at once similar outbreaks followed in other northern towns. Their successes encouraged the conspirators to hold meetings, organize a government, collect an army to march against Santa Fe, and send dispatches to the Downriver urging more revolts. An Indian loyal to the American authorities hurried down the river canyons and over the plateau of Santa Fe to notify Colonel Price of the catastrophe. There in the capital Donaciano Vigil assumed office as acting governor, and worked with Price to organize strong counterblows to the revolution.

While the rebels were gathering forces from the countrysides, Colonel Price called into Santa Fe various units that were scattered as grazing parties and as town garrisons. By January twenty-third he was able to move upriver with three hundred and fifty troops and four brass twelve-pound mountain howitzers. The rebels had come downriver from Taos as far as Santa Cruz. There during the next afternoon all about the once-important town surrounded by broken hills Price's regiment fought two thousand rebels, and drove them to retreat into the Rio Grande canyon through which at the river's edge wound the road to Taos. Before giving pursuit the American soldiers, wrote one of their officers, "destroyed the grain, wood and residence" of Don Diego Archuleta, who was "one of the richest and most influential of the leaders. . . ." The Taos road was primitive and the snows obliterated it entirely in many places. Encumbered with heavy equipment the American troops struggled northward breaking trails as they went, while the insurgents swarmed as individuals among the carved hills and faces of the canyon keeping out of range until they could assemble again to make a stand on the east side of the river, behind a little mountain shaped like a funnel without its stem from which the place took its name—Embudo. On the twenty-ninth in bitter cold amidst the tumbled black walls of volcanic rock brushed with snow and spotted with the dark olive green of piñon trees, Price found the enemy massed against him and attacked. Once again he drove them upriver, and followed at his slower pace until on February third he brought his power up from the river on to the windy sweep of Taos Plain.

No obstacle remained now, and later the same day coming through groves of silvery trees he arrived before the ancient twin pueblos of Taos that faced each other across a wide plaza where Taos Creek ran under broken ice. The howitzers were run forward to bombard, but night fell before a battle could be fully mounted. The main body camped for the night at the village of San Fernando de Taos a few miles southward. In the cold, sunny morning, all companies moved on the pueblos to surround them. Taos Mountain, streaked with snow, rose in the north as a background for the fury that followed. Many of the seven hundred warriors of Taos were collected in the pueblo church that stood at the northwest corner of the plaza. It was manned as a fort, with holes on the parapet and in the walls through which the defenders could shoot. The great terraced steps of the two pueblos were silent and empty, their ladders drawn up, their occupants waiting within like creatures in burrows listening for a favorable change of weather. In the fields on all sides the troops were drawn up, facing the clay wall that surrounded the town area. The howitzers were planted to effect a cross fire at a range of four hundred yards. Cannonading opened the battle, with flashes of fire, drifts of brown smoke, and black explosions over the snow. Dismounted soldiers charged in waves, the artillery moved up between salvos, and all converged toward the church. Its earthen walls were stout. "An attempt was made to cut through the walls of the church . . . with axes," reported a young artillery officer who commanded a six-pound howitzer in the battle, "but they were so thick and the fire so deadly that it was found to be impracticable." Still, the axes had thinned the three-foot thickness of the walls, and the young officer brought his howitzer up within sixty yards of the church and fired at the hacked part of the wall and "soon made a breech large enough for five or six men to enter abreast. The roof of the church was then fired, and I ran the 6 Pdr. up within 30 feet of the breech, and poured grape shot into the church. Lighted shells were also thrown in, which bursted handsomely." The attackers could see the interior. It was teeming with Indians, great numbers of whom fell dead and wounded. Rafters caught fire from the explosions.

The noise was fearsome, chorded together with the cannonades, the rattle of muskets, the shouts of the attackers, the cries of those hurt inside the church, and the roar and crack and tumble of burning timber. "The order to storm the church was then given . . . and the storming party rushed it, so as we entered we found the smoke and dust so dense, that it was impossible to exist in it unless near the openings, and that the enemy had all retired except from the gallery, as we entered they fled, and were shot down by our troops from the neighboring walls." Soon the roof fell in, and blackened beams hung down, and the cold sunlight poured in from the bright blue sky. The church was a ruin and a charnel house. "In 20 minutes we had possession of the church and the houses in that part of the town, and the white flags were flying from the two Pueblos . . ." Before sundown the north pueblo was abandoned, and the soldiers took to it for the night.

It was still dark the next morning when in the acrid air of smoking timber and spilled blood the elders of the pueblo, bringing their women and children and sacred objects, came before Colonel Price to plead for peace. He granted it on condition that they surrender the leaders of the insurrection, who were given to him. In his three battles he had lost ten men killed and fifty-two wounded, some of whom later died. The rebellious Indians and Mexicans lost a hundred and fifty killed and more than that number wounded. The engagements of the Taos Rebellion were the last to be fought near the Rio Grande in the War with Mexico.

24.

Chihuahua

While the rebel leaders were marched to San Fernando de Taos for imprisonment and trial, Colonel Doniphan and the Missouri Volunteers were finding their way deep into Chihuahua. The traders waiting at

El Paso to hear of the outcome of his march, upon which would depend their future business on the Chihuahua Trail, heard throughout the month nothing but rumors. Most came from Mexican sources, and told of heavy reverses put upon the Americans by Mexican arms—Santa Anna had defeated the Army of the Rio Grande at San Luis Potosí, and General Taylor was a prisoner of war; General Wool was surrounded at Monterrey; a great force was marching from Durango to destroy Doniphan and recapture New Mexico; Santa Anna was about to invade Texas—not one of which was true. But such reports had power, and the Samuel Magoffins, waiting at the Pass, were troubled by them, especially the latest which promised that the residents of El Paso were about to rise up and murder all Americans in the place. They were sure the end had come when early in March a Mexican friend came to them "with his hair somewhat in ends and features ghastly. At once our minds were filled with apprehensions," wrote Susan, "lest the dread sentence had been passed. Without seating himself . . . he took Mr. Magoffin by the hand and led him out of the room in haste, and with tears in his eyes told him that 'he was a Mexican, and it pained him to the heart to know that the American army had gained the battle and taken possession of Chi.' "

For on February twenty-eighth, without Wool, who never came to the western interior, and with traders pressed into service to help him, Colonel Doniphan and his thousand citizens had met four thousand one hundred and twenty Mexicans in the valley of the Sacramento Creek north of Chihuahua City at noon, and after a fight lasting three and a half hours, had defeated them. On the next day he took formal possession of the city of Chihuahua and freed all American prisoners including James Magoffin. Among his spoils was "the black flag which cut such a conspicuous figure at Brazito." When news of his triumph reached the United States, William Cullen Bryant compared him to Xenophon for his great self-sustaining march through so many thousand miles; and the President, in his diary, was proud of what the soldiers under both Price and Doniphan had accomplished: "The number of troops engaged was comparatively small, but I consider this victory one of the most signal which has been gained during the war. . . . The truth is our troops, regulars and volunteers, will obtain victories wherever they meet the enemy. This they would do," he added like any proper Western democrat, and out of his scorn for such as Scott and Taylor, "if they were without officers to command them higher in rank than lieutenants. It is injustice, therefore, to award the generals all the credit."

25.

Trial at Taos

In Taos the war on the river entered upon its last scenes when the rebel leaders were brought to trial before Judge Beaubien, whose son had been one of their victims. The hearings were opened at nine in the morning on April 5, 1847, in a "small, oblong apartment" with adobe walls and two narrow windows. The judge's bench was at one end, and near it were chairs for witnesses and jury, all divided from the rest of the room by a thin railing. The room was jammed with spectators who stood. The prisoners faced the judge. On a plank bench at one side sat the three main witnesses, Mrs. Bent, Mrs. Boggs and Mrs. Carson. All three were Mexican women. A young American onlooker from Cincinnati stared at them. "Señora Bent was quite handsome . . . good figure for her age; luxuriant raven hair; unexceptional teeth, and brilliant, dark eyes, the effect of which was heightened by a clear, brunette complexion. The other lady"—Mrs. Boggs—"though not so agreeable in appearance, was much younger." He looked longest at "the wife of the renowned mountaineer, Kit Carson," and a century later what he felt still moved with life. "Her style of beauty was of the haughty, heart-breaking kind— such as would lead a man with a glance of the eye, to risk his life for one smile. I could not but desire her acquaintance. The dress and manners of the three ladies, bespoke a greater degree of refinement, than usual. . . ."

The jury included Mexicans, French Canadians, and Americans. Six prisoners were on trial. The prosecuting attorneys were an American twenty-two years old and another from Missouri who in the blowsy longing of frontier eloquence had "fought, bled and died" for his country in the war. The counsel for defense was a volunteer private on furlough to serve the court. The trial lasted two days, and seemed to the young man from Cincinnati "a strange mixture of violence and justice," for "it certainly did appear to be a great assumption on the part of the

Americans to conquer a country, and then arraign the revolting inhabitants for treason." (President Polk was later to agree with him, in principle.) The three main witnesses told their stories of the sorrowful
night. "When Mrs. Bent gave in her testimony . . . pointing out the
Indian who killed the Governor, not a muscle of the chief's face twitched,
or betrayed agitation, though he was aware her evidence unmistakably
sealed his death warrant—he sat with lips gently closed, eyes earnestly
centered on her, without a show of malice or hatred—an almost sublime
spectacle of Indian fortitude, and of the severe mastery to which the
emotions can be subjected. . . ."

When the jury retired, a Canadian juror could hardly wait to
cast his verdict, and needed only to know what it should be. Dancing
with excitement, he asked the foreman,

"Monsieur Chadwick! Vot sall I say?"

"Keep still man," said the foreman with a sense of propriety, "until
we talk awhile to the rest about it. Don't be in such a hurry."

"Oui! Oui! c'est bon; très bien! Mais, monsieur vot sall ve do
avec sacrés prisonniers—sacrés enfants—"

The foreman was not troubled too far by niceties of procedure.
He replied,

". . . Why, hang them, of course; what did you come in here for?
Wait till I'm done with these Mexicans"—part of the jury—"and I will
tell you what to do."

The jury returned to the courtroom in less than fifteen minutes
with verdicts of guilty "in the first degree—five for murder, one for treason." Judge Beaubien, recalling that the jail was "overstocked with
others awaiting trial," fixed the following day for executing the sentence
of death, saying solemnly, "Muerte, muerte, muerte." There was a
moment of terrible silence, and then the guards came forward, the
prisoners "drew their serapes more closely around them," and impassively returned to jail.

The next day was Friday, the death day, the day of Golgotha. A
few clouds drifted in a brilliant sky. Convivial interest in San Fernando
de Taos brought a crowd of morning drinkers to Estes's Tavern where
Metcalfe the sheriff—a son-in-law of the saloonkeeper—was glad to see
them. Needing ropes for his day's work, he had none, and must borrow
them. From traders and a teamster he obtained what he needed and
went to a room next to the bar to tie the hangman's noose on one end
of each rope or lariat. One or two mountaineers helped him. One
found the lariat too stiff to work. Metcalfe brought a royal's worth

of Mexican soap with which to soften all the ropes. He did not forget
to note in his bill of expenses,

To soft soap for greasing nooses . . . 12½.

After they had washed the sticky soap from their fingers the helpers
were given a drink of Taos whiskey by Mr. Estes.

Then lighting cigarettes and carrying their nooses, they all
accompanied Sheriff Metcalfe to the jail. Seeing the nooses, onlookers
exclaimed. The jail was at the edge of San Fernando. There were no
houses between it and the fields to the north. A hundred and fifty yards
away in a field a scaffold of two uprights and a crossbeam now stood.
Not far from it was a large tree. The mountaineers with their lariats
went into the jail. Across the patio they saw a brass howitzer with its
muzzle four feet from the room in which the prisoners were held—a
long, cold room, badly ventilated by one small window and the open
door where the sun came in on the earthen floor. In its patch of light
two prisoners were lying on a *serape,* wearing brightly colored shirts,
open on their brown skin showing "a wilderness of straight black hair."
They were filthy. They were silent to greetings. They were to die in two
hours. Leaning about the room were the other prisoners—eighty in all—
ragged, lousy, miserable.

At nine o'clock there was a stir. The soldiery were being mustered.
Priests came to administer the last rites. A crowd collected outside. Soon
the word passed that the condemned were coming. Eighteen armed men
made a square at the gate to receive them. They were marched to the
scaffold in the field with their hands tied behind them. On the backs of
their heads were white cotton caps that would be pulled over their faces
when the moment came. At the nearest houses the roofs were crowded
with spectators. On the jail roof was a mountain howitzer—the same one
used in destroying the church. It was loaded and trained on the gallows.
A soldier stood by it with a lighted match in his hand. Two hundred
and twelve soldiers were formed in the field. Under the gallows waited
a government wagon with two mules in harness.

The condemned were marched to it. The escort of soldiery made
an evolution, forming a hollow square about the scaffold, from which
the soaped lariats now depended. Strongly shadowed by the clear sun
the condemned men were placed in the wagon. The scaffold was so
narrow that they touched one another as they stood on the wagon bed—
men waiting for other men to do mortal things to them, while hundreds

watched in bated quiet. Now the nooses were set loosely about their throats. They were asked if they would speak. *"Mi padre, mi madre—"* the little words were scarcely heard. Their white caps were pulled forward from rakish angles until their heads, all covered, were six white stumps. Harness was twitched and slapped, the mules started forward, the wagon was drawn out from under what weighted it. The rawhide ropes creaked and straightened and swung in narrow compass. Convulsed, the bodies swayed and turned and bumped one another, and two gripped hands, and held so, till dead.

Forty minutes later the soldiers were marched away, the howitzer came down from its roof, and the population broke forward toward the gallows. The ropes were slacked off. Some of the knots, despite the sheriff's soap, were hard. A hunter was cutting one such knot when the owner of the rope, a teamster, came forward and said,

"Hello, there, don't cut that rope. I won't have anything to tie my mules with. . . . I'm in government service, an' if them picket halters was gone, slap down would go a dollar apiece."

The hunter desisted, worked the knot loose, and gave him his halter whole. Relatives claimed the bodies. Indian widows went to their dead men and each took hers up, tied him to her back, and set out walking in grief to the pueblo three miles away, to bury him at home, with ghostly Indian honors. The Americans who had helped with the whole affair took up a collection of five dollars and sent it ahead to Mr. Estes's bar to have eggnog prepared. When dismissed they took their rifles and walked to the tavern where in the back room by one o'clock they were drunk on eggnog, made with real American brandy. One of them danced an Indian dance till he fell down unconscious, while the rest roared with laughter. At the end of April when five more Indians and four Mexicans were hanged at Taos, the war on the Rio Grande was over.

26.

All on the Plains of Mexico

All summer long in 1847 troops were homeward bound along the Rio Grande. They were volunteers whose terms of enlistment were completed. It was safe to let them go without replacement, for the war was all but won with General Scott's inland battles to the South—Cerro Gordo, Puebla, Contreras, Molino el Rey—though in the atmosphere prevailing at home not everyone was confident, and some were critical. A New York diarist, George Templeton Strong, expected in March to hear "that Taylor and his force are prisoners of war and that we're driven across the Rio Grande (and I can't see what's to hinder)"; and in May he recorded "Rumor of a defeat in Mexico: 'Col. Doniphan' licked somewhere near Chihuahua. . . . Hope it's true, for the only way of bringing the war to a close is to prosecute it totissimus viribus, and a little defeat or two will open up the administration"; and in August, "Nothing further from Mexico; everybody waiting with mouth wide open for the first reliable statement of what Scott's doing; there are about three new lies every day. . . ."

As the American movements of the whole Mexican War, but for the California naval campaign, had been based on the Rio Grande, so now in the summertime many of the forces came back by the river. The Missouri thousand, who had entered upon the Rio Grande in the New Mexican north, now completed their great loop from Chihuahua to Coahuila, Nuevo León and Tamaulipas, and approached it again through Mier, Camargo and Reynosa. Doniphan's men kept their character to the end. A homeward-bound soldier of Wool's division saw them: "They look wild and have a peculiar manner, and don't seem to have any discipline." Their commander, at the end of his campaign, was satisfied with them. "High spirits and a bold front," said Colonel Doniphan, "is perhaps the safest policy. My men are rough, ragged, and ready, having one more of the R's than General Taylor himself . . . all have done their duty, and done it nobly. . . ." The volunteers were not to be judged by the occasional individual whose exuberance took a wrong turn—like Ben Leaton of whom Dr. Josiah Gregg spoke as "a desperado." Leaton with three other men deserted from Doniphan's force to live as bandits on the Rio Grande near Presidio del Norte. They established themselves in one of the large ruins of the early eighteenth century missions at La Junta de los Rios, called their stronghold Fort Leaton, and preyed on the Indians and Mexicans of the region until Leaton's death in 1852.

Coming out of Mexico to the river, soldiers urged their officers to hurry the march, for steamboats were scarce, and the first units to arrive at the little river towns would have first chance to go on board for the long journey home. One regiment marched all night to beat another to Reynosa; and when they reached there, secured the only two boats on hand. Three other ships were mud-bound below the town. The river was alternately high and low that summer. When a steamer went aground the troops had to wade ashore to lighten it. If it did not come off the mud, the troops had to wait for wagons from upstream to carry their supply, and the trip was resumed by land. And then it might rain, and for hours, for two days, even, the men without tents "stood like cattle in the mud both day and night" until steamers floated down to pick them up. A change in weather brought a change in travel, with shifts from muddy roads to ships, or stranded ships to dusty roads. Roads and steamers were rarely used at the same time.

The boats were so crowded that on the lower decks men could not lie or sit, but had to stand; while those on the upper decks spat their tobacco juice upon those below. Only officers were allowed in the cabins. Guards were posted to keep the rank and file out. As well as they could, the men played cards, drank whiskey and talked all night. The weather was hot. Many had fevers, and all felt "depressed and ill." They longed to be clean of the vermin of Mexico. A river captain said to a soldier, "I took up some New-Yorkers not long since; they scratched themselves in a leisurely sort of way. But you fellows scratch with great earnestness—scratch yourselves all over—scratch rapidly—violently —scratch all the time. What's the matter with you? Got fleas?"

The veteran replied in the vein of frontier grandeur,

"Fleas! Do you think we are dogs, to go about infested with fleas?" He snorted. "These are lice! We work harder than the New-Yorkers because we have more to do. Our lice are big handsome fellows, and we have plenty of them—got them in Mexico!"

But there were satisfactions, too. It was heartening to clean guns for the last time and turn them in to the ordnance companies; and to be paid off for the first time in months; and to burn "saddles, and other horse rigging"; and on a road-march to come upon a company of tight-rope walkers at an isolated ranch—the men were "especially interested to see Preciosa, the prima donna, perform," who with her troupe "displayed fine talent. . . ." Soldiers went to bathe in the river during a halt, and now and then were shot at from bushes along the bank. But the river was generally at peace ever since March, when "depredations of the guerrillas, and the large force under General Urrea, in the Valley of the San Juan, caused much uneasiness and alarm throughout the Valley of the Rio Grande." When they could go ashore for a little while at a river town, the soldiers tried to buy a meal. All they found was "bread and ginger pop." They hoped for better at Matamoros, the the river metropolis, where they must surely find "newspapers, bread, cheese and cigars." But if rain did not keep all on board, the steamboats would pause only an hour or two, and the soldiers would get up their hopes for the next stop, at the river's mouth. Matamoros had begun to "assume quite an American appearance—brick and framed houses, with shingled roofs." The population of the Mexican period —ten thousand—was reduced to between three and five thousand. The steamboats took the bends among the dunes, and came to the mouth, where on the left bank was a roaring American army depot which the soldiers called Sodom, and on the right down the beach a quarter of a mile was Bagdad, where in an eating house they ordered up breakfast and "ate potatoes for the first time in a year." There was only one stage left before leaving for home—a walk up the nine-mile beach to Point Isabel where the Gulf steamers docked.

Waiting, the men filled the days with bathing and running on the beach, picking up shells, and eating oysters, and the nights with gambling, drinking, and fighting to pay off old scores of enmity accumulated during the year of serving together at close quarters in arduous and boring duty. Some units were discharged from the service of the United States before embarking at Point Isabel, others after arriving at New Orleans. In either case, they were treated to a ceremony, when an orator—an officer of their regiment or a civilian master of the high style—rang in their ears the martial sounds of their story. "Bearded and bronzed as were the soldiers" who listened hungrily to what they had done, "they cried till the tears left glistening paths down their cheeks." Lieutenant Lew Wallace declared after hearing the oration on the occasion of his discharge, "I alighted from my perch sore and cramped; but from that day to this I have never regretted the year left behind me as a soldier in Mexico. . . ."

And all through the long hot summer while the armies of the northern campaigns were turning homeward, the troops under General Scott were toiling across central Mexico toward the capital. "We had to throw away the scabbard and to advance with the naked blade," stated the General-in-Chief in the style of Clarendon. As his army swept inland he ordered distribution among the Mexicans of a broadsheet that adroitly summarized the issues of the war and the purpose of the United States. It reminded the natives that in 1824 Mexico established a government after the model of the United States, in which each state elected its own governor, and that in 1834 Santa Anna destroyed the federal constitution, proclaiming a central government and taking to himself the appointment of governors. Zacatecas and Texas resisted such usurpation of local power. Texas declared her independence and fought for her rights. In the Texan war, Santa Anna's subordinates, under his order, massacred five hundred Texans at Goliad after they had surrendered. The Texans defeated Santa Anna at San Jacinto and took him prisoner. Texas, independent, applied for admission to the United States, which denied and postponed annexation for ten years. The war between Mexico and Texas abolished all boundaries. The United States sent a minister to Mexico to negotiate a boundary. He was repelled. The United States then having accepted Texas as a state ordered an Army of Occupation to the Rio Grande. Mexican troops crossed the river and attacked the American army, were beaten, and had been beaten ever since, though Santa Anna boasted of victories. The United States had only good will toward Mexicans. The broadsheet concluded, "We are here for no earthly purpose except the hope of obtaining peace." The battles of the summer having brought Scott to the Valley of Mexico, peace seemed as desirable to the Mexicans as to him; and on August twenty-fourth he granted an armistice during which peace negotiations were undertaken.

Nicholas P. Trist, chief clerk of the State Department, arrived from Washington under commission by President Polk to deal directly with Santa Anna, president and military chief. The move gave General Scott another opportunity to "flare up in the highest sort of style" but in time he forgave Trist his intrusion, sent him a gift of some guava jelly, and thenceforward co-operated with him in efforts for peace. The armistice was abruptly ended by Scott on September sixth when it was clear that the Mexicans were using its period of grace to reinforce their troops, newly fortify Chapultepec Castle, and arouse public sentiment to support renewed fighting; and further when the Mexican peace commission proffered terms that were patently unacceptable. There were dealings backstage in which Santa Anna accepted ten thousand dollars as a down payment on a bribe for surrender that, it was whispered, might go as high as a million. Hostilities were at once resumed, the battle of Molino el Rey and the storming of Chapultepec followed, and on September fourteenth Scott and his generals led the army into Mexico City. Mexicans continued to resist elsewhere—Puebla, Huamantla, Atlixco. Santa Anna's government fell, and he was superseded in command of the army. It was not long until all major military resistance ceased, and once again, but now more realistically, peace talks were undertaken by the Mexicans. For it was plain who must prevail: Mexico had only 8,109 men under arms, and of these less than three thousand were on guard at Querétaro, the temporary capital; while the American forces numbered 43,059, of whom thirty-two thousand were under Scott's immediate command in support of his position at Mexico City.

All through the fall of 1847 and into the winter of 1848 the peace talks continued, with discussions of boundaries and lands as the spoils of war. New Mexico was suddenly taken out of consideration for outright cession when in December at the order of Colonel Price delegates of her citizens gathered at Santa Fe to organize a territorial government under the United States. The act amounted to a voluntary annexation which Mexico would be powerless to undo.

The rest of Mexican territory was in jeopardy from other forces; for with the suspension of the fighting, sentiment in the United States spoke out from every quarter with violent and even virtuous appetites for Mexico's land. The President told Congress in December that the United States "might have to take the full measure of indemnity into its hands"—which all understood to mean the annexation of the whole of Mexico. The possibility had wide support in the press and among the more radical members of the President's party. There were cries of "Destiny"—"God ordained that Mexico should be an integral part of the Union." A mission of terrible sternness lay upon the conquerors— "The Mexicans are aboriginal Indians and must share the destiny of their race—extinction!" Without a qualm feelings of racial superiority were brought to support greed: "Look at the gold and silver glittering there in masses that await the pick of the Saxon." The issue was seen through many bigotries—religious, political and educational. Mexico's religion was attacked as the enemy of republicanism, and Mexico must be rescued from it. The clamor was heard in Mexico, where General Scott while reserving his personal views stated that "two-fifths of the Mexican population, including more than half of the Congress," would favor annexation of their whole country to the United States. Polk's opponents were outspoken in their turn: "It is folly to absorb such a country into our own, to exhaust such a nation into the healthy veins of a republic like this," and Daniel Webster declared that California and New Mexico were "not worth a dollar."

But what Trist was asking for, upon instructions from Washington, were terms that fixed the United States boundary at the Rio Grande from the mouth to the thirty-second parallel, and thence west to the Pacific; and through weeks of meetings he gained substantially what he asked for, with only a small concession to modify the boundary between the Californias a little north of the thirty-second parallel. For all of New Mexico (which then included Arizona) and upper California, he agreed to pay fifteen million dollars, and he further pledged the United States to pay the claims of its citizens against the Mexican government. His task was accomplished under extraordinary conditions, for after the collapse of the armistice in September he had been recalled by Washington, but had refused to obey, certain that he would be able to resolve the meetings into an acceptable treaty. General Scott appeared to agree with him, and with reason. On February second a treaty was signed at Guadalupe Hidalgo, a suburb of Mexico City, and the commissioner hurried to the States to submit it to the government.

News went through Mexico that peace was made, though official notification of the outpost garrisons could not be managed with dispatch. In the same week, Colonel Sterling Price, at El Paso, heard that a Mexican army in Chihuahua was preparing to march north to reconquer the central Rio Grande. At once he began to lay plans for an expedition of his own to follow Doniphan's path and once again subdue Chihuahua.

In Washington, though the public exulted at a settlement, the Treaty of Guadalupe Hidalgo met a mixed reception. The President accepted it with reservations: "If the treaty was now to be made," he wrote on February twenty-first, "I should demand more territory, perhaps to make the Sierra Madre the line." But with minor adjustments in articles dealing with land titles in Texas and other ceded areas, he sent it to the Senate, where it encountered stormy fortunes, mostly equated with party sentiment. Daniel Webster and Sam Houston opposed it outright. Jefferson Davis called for the acquisition of most of Tamaulipas and Nuevo León, all of Coahuila, and much of Chihuahua. Secretary of State Buchanan hoped for the Sierra Madre partition, and the extremist Democrats demanded all of Northern Mexico. But as the Preisdent had noted, it was doubtful whether additional territory "could ever be obtained by the consent of Mexico," without which renewed war would be necessary to gain more land. The nation was done with war for the time, and even though a soldier in Mexico wrote home that "Some one said that we ought to continue the war and whip them"— the Mexicans—"until they consented to take back all Texas," Trist's Treaty was ratified on March 10, 1848, by the United States.

The last military gestures of the war were made by Colonel Price's force, which moved south from El Paso on March first. At Doniphan's battlefield of Sacramento they were met under a flag of truce by Governor Trias, who announced that a treaty had been signed. Colonel Price did not accept his statement. Trias retired, Price entered Chihuahua City without opposition and drove on to pursue Trias to Santa Cruz de Rosales sixty miles to the south. Once again Trias tried to convince him that a state of peace existed. In reply, Price mounted a blockade of the town to await reinforcements of cavalry and artillery. When these appeared, he attacked without choosing to verify the protestations of the Mexican commander. The battle for Santa Cruz ended in victory for Colonel Price just after sundown with the loss of four Americans killed and nineteen wounded, and an uncounted but much greater number of Mexican casualties—all suffered forty-two days after the signing of the treaty. At Querétaro on May twenty-fifth the treaty was ratified by the Mexican government—now again rid of Santa Anna, and for the second last time—and ratifications were exchanged by spokesmen for the two nations. In the same month, just as an impoverished Mexico was about to deliver over her lands in North America by ratifying the treaty, gold was discovered at Sutter's Fort in the California she was signing away.

And now there was settlement at last of the old disputes over the southeasterly Rio Grande as an accepted boundary. The Emperor Charles V had first posed the river—the Rio de las Palmas—as the western boundary in 1525 of the great, the imagined, province of Florida. In 1682 La Salle had claimed for France all lands east of it, and in 1716 St. Denis urged his government to designate the Rio Grande as a French boundary. In 1802 the French declared it the farthest limit of Louisiana, and Jefferson had repeated the claim in 1803 after his purchase of

Louisiana from Napoleon. Monroe in 1811 had terrified Gutierrez de Lara with the same notion, which persisted untried until in the Florida Treaty of 1819 the United States renounced it "forever." Henry Clay in 1821 attacked the Florida Treaty and again claimed all of Texas to the Rio Grande for the United States, though inconclusively. In 1824 the river was debated as the dividing line between the Mexican provinces of Coahuila and Texas, in the event of their political separation. Many Americans in 1825, with the accession to office of President John Quincy Adams, expected that Texas would be acquired peaceably all the way to the Rio Grande. Henry Clay as Secretary of State in 1827 attempted to buy it so from Mexico for a million dollars. In 1832 and 1833 the Texas Statehood Conventions under Mexico saw the Rio Grande as the new state's southwestern border. President Andrew Jackson, like Clay, tried to buy Texas to the river, though for a higher figure—five millions—in 1833. An independent Texas fought for the river line and won it in 1836, though without the agreement of any Mexican official except Santa Anna's, and his—once his skin was safe—he repudiated. In the early summer of 1848, what so long a sequence of claims had labored over and over to effect was now confirmed by overwhelming power: that the southeasterly Rio Grande had always seemed a natural boundary between different sovereignties, kinds of country and types of society. Under the sense of destiny of the American people, and their weight of arms, the issue—passed from trappers to traders, traders to soldiers, soldiers to citizens—was at rest. The Rio Grande in Colorado and New Mexico, and its left bank in Texas, belonged to the United States. It was won by the whole nation. Walt Whitman in New Orleans in 1848 remarked that "Probably the influence most deeply pervading everything at that time through the United States, both in physical fact and sentiment, was the Mexican War. . . ." It was won by the tradition, the skill, of the frontier rifleman. And it was won by a spirit drawn from deep in the national character. As a volunteer in the war concluded, "There was a *national* feeling in the army. . . . Every soldier felt he was a *freeman;* that he was a citizen of the MODEL REPUBLIC; and that he ought to look upon the disgrace of the AMERICAN ARMS AS INDIVIDUAL DISHONOR. . . ."

While Winfield Scott remained at Mexico City throughout the peace talks (later with many fulminations against the President and the administration he would make his way to the United States and two unsuccessful stands as presidential candidate), Zachary Taylor returned to the river in November, 1847, for the long journey home. At Mier he was honored by the officers of the Third Dragoons with "a light collation." Going downstream on the steamboat *Major Brown* he was received with artillery salutes at Camargo, where he reviewed the Tenth Infantry. Continuing his voyage on the *Colonel Cross* he came to Matamoros where he found that leave of absence had been granted to him, and boarding the *McKee,* he wound down to the Gulf and up the beach to Point Isabel, where on Friday, November twenty-sixth, he entered the *Monmouth* and sailed for New Orleans, a hero's reception, and—a year later—the Presidency, which would give him an opportunity to pasture his horse on the front lawn of the White House. "The only respectable female in the army"—Mrs. Paymaster Hunter—thought of travelling to the United States in his company; but at the last minute she was unable to leave her husband, and at Matamoros "she resolved to remain—being now, as she remarked, within 'striking distance' so that she can go home when she may wish. . . ."

In vessels drawing away from the river, the Gulf, with homeward-bound troops, the sailors sang a new song:

> When Zacharias Taylor gained the day,
> Heave away, Santy Anno;
> He made poor Santy run away,
> All on the plains of Mexico.

> So heave her up and away we'll go,
> Heave away, Santy Anno;
> Heave her up and away we'll go,
> All on the plains of Mexico.

After the marches, the battles and the camps, the ingenuities, the lawlessness, the energies of the army and the steamboats, the river gradually went back to quiet. The little river towns of earth and rock, baked at some seasons, icy-winded at others, had been suddenly awakened by the arrival of the army to know a year or two of prosperity, violence, change—the world passing through; and now they fell back into their sempiternal dust to serve only as hubs for the life of rancherias in the countryside, where only the elements made motion amidst the daily cycle of color in the skies, above the slow-circling birds, the obscure snakes, and the silence broken only by the slide and roll of the heavy river water.

> General Scott and Taylor, too,
> Heave away, Santy Anno;
> Have made poor Santy meet his Waterloo,
> All on the plains of Mexico.

> So heave her up and away we'll go,
> Heave away, Santy Anno. . . .

Captain Robert E. Lee of General Wool's brigade bought his little son a mustang pony in Mexico, and had it shipped to Baltimore. The pony's name was Santa Anna. At the abandoned wastes of the river's mouth rooted in sand and the white dust of shells lay the blackened wreckage of "the numberless vessels" grounded during the war. The beach was now an empty prison, where once troops had been sent to be punished—yet not quite empty so long as there was someone to remember what lay there. For a young officer waiting for the ship that would take him home from the Rio Grande made a note of what he saw. ". . . I strolled out to the dunes so thickly peopled with our dead. The revelations were shocking." Wind and wash had hauled away the covering of the graves, exposing their contents. His colonel ordered him to "take a working party and rebury all remains." As he did so, the lieutenant wondered if the government would ever take home the bodies of the fallen. It was not done in his lifetime, or after. "The poor fellows are abandoned," he thought, remembering his comrades. "Only the Great Gulf lifts a voice for them—an inarticulate, everlasting moan." Soon his ship was ready in its turn, and with the living he sailed away from the Rio Grande.

> Santy Anno was a good old man,
> Heave away, Santy Anno;
> Till he got into war with your Uncle Sam,
> All on the plains of Mexico.

27.

El Dorado

Of the war's consequences, some were small, of concern to perhaps only one or two. At noon one day in February, 1848, President Polk had a caller—the ex-Empress Ana María Iturbide who came from Philadelphia with her friend, a Miss White, to interpret for her, to ask about her pension from the Mexican government which owing to the war she was not receiving. In her anxious isolation of language, Doña Ana gathered from Miss White that the President would do what he could. He would ask for a grant from Congress, and did so. There the matter was lost in committee, until thirteen years later the exiled and so briefly imperial matron died in Philadelphia.

Other consequences were national. When the terrific news of the discovery of gold came from California, Mexico knew what she had lost with the war, the Americans what they had gained—the Golden Land, El Dorado, at last—and, as an American magazine put it, "then began the rising and the rush." It rose in such appetite and fury that Henry David Thoreau was moved to groan, "Going to California . . . it is only three thousand miles nearer Hell. . . . What a comment, what a satire on our institutions! The conclusion will be that mankind will hang itself upon a tree. And who would interfere to cut it down?" In a sense, the rush was never to end for the rest of the nation. With varying objectives in the popular imagination, there would always be something lying in wait to be taken on the golden strand. Once again the Western frontier called, and the United States replied with movement.

Some travellers went by clipper ship from the Eastern ports, sailing to Panama for a jungle passage to the other ocean and a precarious coastwise shipping to the north; or continuing around Cape Horn and up the west coast of the Americas. Some landed at the Arms of Saint James in the Gulf, sailed up the Rio Grande in rusty steamboats left over from the war, and went overland across northern Mexico from

Camargo or Mier. Other overland routes spanned the continent at the waist, or again touched out from San Antonio toward Eagle Pass, a march across Mexico to Mazatlan, and a northbound vessel. Another reached from San Antonio to El Paso, to follow the river up to a ford north of the new town of Las Cruces, and turn west. And still another came from over the prairies to find the river below Santa Fe, follow it southward to Socorro or Doña Ana, and take the westward turn there. The stakes looked enormous, but in the end, they seemed only a pretext, for relatively few of the tens of thousands of emigrants made great fortunes out of gold. But all found new land, new opportunities in life according to their tastes and abilities; and to satisfy what compelled them within, all endured troubles and even perils, in the classic frontier style.

The journey by the Gulf and the river took in the new town of Brownsville, that had grown up around Fort Brown. In 1849, along with all the lower river towns but Mier, and with only one doctor of medicine in the valley, Brownsville was swept by an epidemic of cholera. Upriver California travellers lost many of their companions, who died in Rio Grande City, Roma, Camargo, and on river steamboats. Some of those who escaped the disease fled home to the Eastern States. Others who went on westward saw services of intercession at Mier, where the cholera had not come—a Te Deum and Mass in the old brown stone church, with the organ shaking the air through the open doors, and bells ringing, and a procession of the Host to the plaza which was decked with bright cloths, and children waving little flags made of kerchiefs tied to sticks, and rockets rising into the sunshine.

One emigrant coming up from Brownsville to Roma to strike inland across Mexico travelled the river by "the splendid, fast-sailing, high-pressure steamboat 'Tom McKinney,' propelled by an engine of four crab power, the steam being furnished from two enormous boilers formerly used on a first-class Mississippi boat . . . she was of very light draught. . . . ." He had advice for "all parties coming by this route. Do not form parties to exceed fifteen in number, as it will be difficult to procure subsistence en route for larger ones. . . . Do not encumber your-selves with unnecessary baggage. No man's ought . . . to exceed 150 lbs; and it is folly to bring any amount of provisions. A few cooking utensils are necessary, and also saddles and bridles. . . ."

A party of gold seekers crossing Mexico for Mazatlan was attacked by Indians, their stock and horses were stolen. The animals were recov-ered by soldiers from Fort Duncan on the river. The travellers rested near the fort. Their place was called California Camp. Used by later emigrants, it became the town of Eagle Pass, named for the great bird who for several years lived on the river, and was seen to make his way slowly from one bank to another always by the same airy course.

Overland parties from San Antonio for El Paso helped to incise the road that later stage lines would use. American society awheel, carrying all its amenity and structure with it, found it reassuring amidst daily strangeness to hold meetings, elect caravan officials, and to celebrate patriotic anniversaries with oratory, recitations and "readings." When it was necessary to pause to "let the oxen blow," the train made camp and voted a social evening. Coming to the river at the site of Fort Quitman the emigrants found shade—their first in hundreds of miles—with cotton-woods and willows. The road was sandy, and if a horse sprained an ankle, its owner dismounted to join "what the boys call the walking commit-tee." The river in June, 1849, was often in flood, and one morning "rose from fifty feet wide to five hundred," at the rate of "nearly a foot a minute." To ford it a man had to tie his clothes and firearms with his belt to his horse's neck, and swim hanging on to his horse's tail.

At El Paso the travellers camped near the town but on an island— La Isla—made by a division of the river's flow round a sandspit "from 2 to 4 miles wide & about 20 miles long." On it were the three ancient mission towns of Isleta del Sur, Socorro del Sur, and San Elizario. By another change of the river's course the island later became part of the American bank. The emigrants traded with the Mexicans for fruit and vegetables—"250 large onions for an old sword which cost about ten shillings in New York new"—and shot ducks and quail, and cleaned river water with a filter made of prickly pears. Six pecks of wheat cost five dollars, and of flour, seven. The Americans rendered their own tallow— "invaluable"—and were watched with interest by Mexican men dressed in white muslin shirts hanging open and pants "tight around the thighs" but wider down the leg and wide-leafed straw hats, and Mexican women in scarves and separated blouses and skirts, and smaller children "nearly naked."

The El Paso valley was more than ever a crossroads. By late August, 1849, four hundred wagons had passed through on the way to the gold fields, and even though "accounts from the gold region is good," many travellers had become discouraged and had lingered there at loose ends. Another emigrant said they "look blue," listening to rumors of the hard passage ahead. So many talked of wintering at El Paso that he declared "The Pass, no doubt, will be a great place this winter, as

gambling, drinking, &c, are all the rage," and "The Pass this winter will
be the theatre in which many a horrible scene will be played. . . ." Already, displaced emigrants had abused the Mexicans, demanding house-
room, and turning into horse thieves, gamblers and even murderers. One
set up a business killing Apache Indians and selling scalps to the Mexican
government for two hundred dollars each, and collecting two hundred
and fifty for each prisoner. If Indians were scarce, he even killed Mexicans to profit from their scalps.

But those who went on followed the river up from El Paso. A few
miles north of town they met a man and a boy who sold "wiskey & gin"
for fifty cents per third of a pint—"extravagantly low." They passed a
ranch house fenced with "timbers from the wagons brought from
Missouri by Col. Doniphan in 1846," and came to Las Cruces with its
few houses, and a few miles later saw the American flag for the first time
in "many a day" flying above Doña Ana. Turning there toward San
Diego, California, they forded the river—there were no longer any bridges
on the whole course of the Rio Grande—and continued their passage
westward.

The overlanders who came across the central prairies to the Rio
Grande below Santa Fe had much to do every evening when camp was
made. One left a record. "Now comes the busy scene of pitching tents,
collecting wood, preparing food, etc. The sound of the axe, the metallic
ring of the blacksmith's hammer, the merry voice of children, the bray-
ing of mules, is heard. Some children are playing near the water . . .
ladies are attending to their domestic concerns, the preparing of a good
meal for their families." Music rose, and the "sweet sound of the flute . . .
will come floating on the ear, or the well accorded voices of a band of
vocalists, or the merry notes of a violin accompanied with the tripping
sound of feet. . . ." Another left practical warning. "The march down
the Rio Grande was most arduous and difficult; the road is very bad after
reaching the river. . . ." The only good thing was that for a large part
of the way "before leaving the river, green corn, onions, grapes, fresh
meat, and fish" could be "procured in abundance," and there was "no
scarcity of wood, water and grass." One party in the summer of 1849
paused near Socorro to celebrate the Fourth of July. "Our messes all
joined together and purchased 20 lambs at a rancho nearby our camp,
which made us a good dinner. We had the Declaration of Independence
read, and an oration, after which we drank the health of our friends at
home and the prosperity of our country. . . . One mess brought out some
of the best Hollands [gin], another cognac, while your humble servant

and a few others were lucky enough to find at the bottom of a trunk some sparkling champagne, reserved for this occasion. At sunset we fired a grand salute, and in the evening we had a fandango at which, by special invitation, there were present a crowd of the fair señoritas. They waltz 'devinly' and their dancing is 'dem foine'. . . ."

Not far from Socorro, at Lemitar, a year later, ex-Governor Manuel Armíjo, established on one of his properties, was hoping for political preferment under the American government of New Mexico. His eyes were on election to the post of delegate to the Territorial Assembly. He supposed it was necessary to swear loyalty to the United States in order to occupy any position. He had not done it, but he could not believe that that would "militate against [him] in receiving votes as delegate." Others "whose names it would be a shame to mention" had received votes. Why not he? "I would to God," he cried, "they would vote for me for President of the United States." But if nothing came of his unbounded ambitions, he could sigh, "I am here as a saint whose day has passed—but well content, because I know how to philosophize." Though rumored to have buried much treasure, he was out of funds, and was forced to offer his silver table service to an American lieutenant for three hundred dollars.

28.

Contraband

Brownsville began as a scattering of huts and jacales that were soon brought into a grid of streets at right angles by order of the local sheriff, who destroyed any dwellings that were not in line by a certain date. The first population was made up of French and American merchants and Mexican families. Four years later there were five or six thousand residents, "chiefly Mexicans." New houses were built of brick, and the streets were edged with rows of Chinese lilac, willow and acacia.

On windy days both Brownsville and Matamoros, opposite, were obscured by a flying haze of the river's fine pale sand, and on rainy the streets were runnels where little rivers ran down to the town quay, which was shaped like an amphitheatre, where bales of goods came and went with the steamboats. It was a busy town, alive with horsemen, and ranch carts, and aguaderos in loose white cotton who sold water brought from the river in little casks with axles fixed to their ends so that casks were drawn like rollers.

Once again the society enacted the extreme individualism of the frontier. Bankrupts, escaped criminals, deserters from the armies of the recent war, gamblers and swindlers set the tone. The barrooms were fighting pits. Pistol duels added style to murder. Murderers and other offenders were lynched at the town shambles by hanging from the timbers on which beeves were butchered. The place was "without roof or shade, roasted by the sun, and the resort of dogs which fought for the bones of the animals." The sheriff—a huge man of great strength and a brutal force—usually killed the men he set out to arrest. Bloodhounds guarded the gate of his jail. One prisoner who served time under him and was discharged alive was a drummer boy who had deserted in the war, had been sentenced to be shot, but because of his extreme youth had instead been drummed out of the army. He lived at Brownsville as a boy-drunkard, terrorizing the streets with his threats and oaths. One day he appeared naked on horseback, riding in and out of stores and saloons, defying arrest. The sheriff shot him in the arm and lodged him behind the bloodhounds. On being released, he found a rifle, shot the sheriff with a ramrod still in the barrel, and fled to Eagle Pass, where he continued to enact his doom as a public nuisance until a quartermaster's carpenter of Fort Duncan shot and killed him, to the general applause of the upriver authorities and citizens.

Local elections at Brownsville were held with violent partisanship. Opposing parties staged parades with the colors of their candidates worn by supporters, horses and even dogs. On election day voters were offered free whiskey from tables set up in the streets. By comparison, Matamoros across the way was calm. On the last three days of Holy Week, no vehicles ran there, and all year the Mexican customs guard, with its well-uniformed officers who had "a very distingué air," had so little to do that its soldiers slept "nearly the entire day in a grove of the *Palma Christi* planted near the shed."

They slept not because the cross-river traffic in goods was small. It was large—but almost all unofficial, for everywhere on the lower river the smuggling of contraband goods was highly organized. Matamoros might be the official port of entry for Mexico on the lower Rio Grande, but upstream, whole towns were established as stations for the illegal passage of merchandise by enterprising Americans. Davis Landing, where wartime steamboats refueled, was soon transformed into Rio Grande City, which was seen as "a vast assemblage of American stores and Mexican huts, where smuggling progresses on an extensive scale." Several companies of the United States Army were stationed a little south of town at Fort Ringgold (later Ringgold Barracks). There was no customs office on the Mexican side, for Mexico had no funds to pay for adding to her border ports. The smugglers operated on so great a scale that their calling was accepted as respectable business. They prospered so long as they were willing to suffer inconveniences, one of which was the climate. "Trees and verdure are rarely seen," noted a visitor to Rio Grande City, "so that the heat reflected from the river sand, and from the rocks and gravel of the hills, makes the place a veritable furnace. One should possess the incombustible nature of the Salamander to live there. . . ." Roma, farther north, suddenly grew after the war with "fine houses and warehouses" for the American exporters. An American boundary surveyor was puzzled to explain how so remote a little town could support such prosperity. One night while he was out in the open away from Roma taking observations he found the answer. In spite of the calmness of the night, the mercury of the artificial horizon in his instrument was "very tremulous." Calculations were useless in such odd conditions. He packed up his case and started to town through the dark only to meet a "long train of mules, heavily laden, going toward the Mexican side. The motion of the animals caused the disturbance of the mercury, and their rich burden of contraband goods, intended for the Mexican market, explained the prosperity of the town. . . ."

American and Mexican businessmen collaborated in breaking the customs regulations. At Roma in a certain period of two months over a hundred thousand dollars' worth of goods went across the river illegally and efficiently. Cotton cloth was the main article of sale, and there lay the reason for the whole contraband trade. For the Mexican government maintained a monopoly of cotton manufacture. The industry was large. At its peak it employed over two hundred thousand workers, and produced over a million bolts of cloth a year. To protect this business, the government placed an exorbitant tariff on imported stuffs, and along the border, this amounted to an invitation to cheat the garrisons at Matamoros, Mier and Camargo.

But officials there were not above the battle. Winking at the official duty rates, the customs houses of the three towns bid against one another for the American trade; and—in a typical instance—if Mier offered a lower rate than Camargo, Mier prepared to receive the custom, pass the American goods, and keep the fees for her officers. But watching what went on, Camargo's soldiers were waiting for the American merchants as they crossed near Mier. In a flourish, the soldiers captured the pack train and its men. Camargo took that trick from Mier. But the game was not over, for a party of Texas Rangers and mustang hunters were paid two thousand dollars by the American exporters to spring across the river and rescue the goods. This they did, returning with the cargo, together with the clothes and firearms of the Camargo troops.

Such conduct of business held much to recommend it to the border spirit. It was illegal, it was adventurous, it was a game. But it was also expensive and complicated, and much could go awry in the process. How much better, thought the merchants of Brownsville and Matamoros—the largest business towns on the river—if the Mexican government, or better yet, a new government established by revolution, were to abolish the intolerable monopoly, and establish a system of competitive trade with a reasonable duty fee! There would thus be legitimate markets and fair profits for both American exporters and Mexican merchants. A committee of businessmen from Brownsville and Matamoros was organized to arrange for a revolution, calling upon an instrument already at hand.

For ever since the war the mirage of the separatist republic had intermittently appeared over the Rio Grande states of north Mexico, and its champion now was a certain General Carvajal, who had fought under Canales in the earlier campaigns to establish it. Carvajal had the nucleus of an army whose ranks included veterans from the American forces of the Mexican War who were not yet done—might never be done—with the binding miseries and the sandy little glories of warfare on the thorny deserts below the river. "Of middle size, symmetrically formed," General Carvajal "had regular features: his lively eye spoke at once address and energy—" and now before it clearly loomed once again his vision of the Republic of the Sierra Madre. If he received financial support from the merchants who came asking him to lead the revolution and end once and for all the tiresome contraband laws with his new republic, he could not fail. He agreed to make war on the Mexican government along the river, whose troops were commanded by General Ávalos at Matamoros. Carvajal's first target was Camargo. He captured it readily and paused to recruit his ranks, and to wait for hard cash and supplies from his backers down the river.

But the days passed, and no funds arrived, and presently it was known that the merchants were no longer with him. They were instead dealing with Ávalos, whom they invited "to a grand entertainment, at which they discussed the measures to be taken against Carvajal." The merchants had won their point in a deal with Ávalos by which—over the protests of the Mexican customs chief—American cotton could enter Mexico at a low duty, with a suitable extra fee for the general himself. It seemed that the merchants could not wait for the successful issue of a revolution, for huge shipments of goods had accumulated on the American shore, and must be moved. Now under their new arrangements they pacified Carvajal with promises for the future, if he would but hold his fire. He camped at Reynosa waiting for his promised support once again; and while he waited, for eight days cotton shipments worth half a million pesos went over the Rio Grande. It was a great stake of business for the big operators, and it was done quietly—and at the expense of the smaller frontier brokers who now had no prospect of selling their goods to a flooded market. The little operators told Carvajal what had been done to them, and he saw his own betrayal too. He attacked some of the pack trains bearing the goods to the interior, burned what he could, and then marched to besiege Matamoros.

The siege lasted twelve days during which Carvajal twice occupied Fort Paredes and once penetrated into the city with sappers and skirmishers. But when news came that his old commander and fellow revolutionary, General Canales, was on the march to relieve the city, he retired upriver to Rio Grande City. Canales followed him, and after circular retreats executed with great spirit, both armies, by the inexorable laws of Mexican border revolutions, "found themselves face to face by their very efforts to escape each other." A battle resulted near Camargo with many casualties until Carvajal's ammunition was exhausted, and Canales seized the opportunity for retreating in "a strategical movement," taking with him a number of American prisoners who a few months later under pathetic circumstances were executed "rather as rebels and assassins than as prisoners of war." Smuggling was continued undisturbed. The Republic of the Sierra Madre was once again done for. Its Mexican veterans scattered to their ranches in the wilderness on both sides of the river.

29.

A Thread of Spirit

During many decades after the war, life on both sides of the river held the same flavor, without sharp differences resulting from the American ownership of the left bank. Settlers and vagrants from the United States attached themselves to the towns, to engage in trade and wagon-driving. Almost none took up ranching or agriculture. The back-country life of the rancherias continued in the Mexican tradition, apart from the world of commerce, news and ideas. There was only one thread that bound together the isolated families on their ranches lost in dusty space, and it was an invisible one—the thread of spirit that tied them to their religion, and that was traced for them whenever he could do it by the parish priest from Brownsville, who every year or so rode out on his horse, alone, to find them so far apart, and yet so close to him, in the bitter brush deserts.

Such a man in the 1850s was a missioner from France, cultivated, patient, courageous and inexhaustibly curious about the outlandish country where he found himself. He was happy to receive a warm wel-come from "Catholics, Protestants, Jews all alike" who "offered their best services," wherever he went. First he went to work on his church. He planted a garden beside it, and trained a wild boar to serve as a watchdog to keep people from picking flowers during the sermons which they moved out of doors to escape. He ordered an organ from Mexico. The church was ugly, and he "contrived, after a time, to cover . . . the walls with certain paintings on cotton." He took his place as a vigorous citizen of Brownsville. On his errands he was often chased by the sheriff's bloodhounds. He warned the sheriff to keep them chained, but to no avail. One day he was obliged to shoot the dogs. He regretted having to do so, for he liked animals, and even for his own pleasure and the instruction of others developed a small zoo.

When he had time he wandered over to Matamoros and was

charmed with what he saw—the plaza with its lilac hedges, the patio gardens with their orange, pomegranate, peach, palm, and fig trees, the quiet hot days, and then the lively evening when as the Angelus rang out before sunset the shuttered doors and windows opened, the streets filled, ladies in bright muslins came to their iron balconies, and promenaders drifted among the lilacs, to chat, laugh and smoke till midnight. All was animation. Chocolate and coffee were served everywhere. "Conversations," he recalled, "turn mostly on poetry, on religion, on love, horses, music and dancing. Scandal and politics engage but little this sequestered people, favoured with a sky the most beautiful, a climate the mildest in the world."

Again, he ventured down the river to the mouth, where he remarked that "the Spaniards of the 16th century well designated this coast by calling it *Costa Deserta*." When he saw Bagdad he was not reminded of "the abode of Harûn-al-Rashid." A dozen Mexican families lived there in reed huts plastered with mud and oyster shells, with no trace of near-by cultivation to provide food for them. On the other shore of the mouth in half-ruined wooden sheds left over from the war abided a group of American beachcombers who fished and hunted by day, and by evening, met "to smoke, to read the papers aloud, and to discuss politics." The busy pastor concluded that "eccentricity and feelings of independence must be pushed far enough to make people live thus in deserts, without name or shade, and spend in solitude and inaction a life without aim." Now and then a sloop arrived at Bagdad from Tampico, bringing bananas, ananas, cocoanuts and lemons, which were sold upriver in the towns.

It was not long until the father missioner found that church relations in his vast parish of the lower Rio Grande were decayed where not simply abandoned. In the last Spanish years visiting priests had made their rounds amongst the ranches every year or two. But after the achievement of Mexican independence such visits almost ceased; and—as happened in New Mexico during the same period—"all pertaining to doctrine and morality fell into the shade," and only "what struck the senses was more tenacious in its hold. The substance was lost in the form, and external practices, as is natural to the Mexicans, became the chief objects of attention. This religious decadence was a sad sight. . . ."

A month after his arrival from France he went up the river to start setting matters right. He packed a set of light silk vestments from Lyons, a chalice, a pyx, a catechism, a chrismatory containing holy oils, certificates of baptism, first communion and marriage, and a few personal necessities, and sailed upstream on the steamboat *Comanche* until she stuck fast on a sand bar. Thenceforth he proceeded on horseback.

The land was empty, silent and wavering in glassy heat. The only living thing he encountered in the early stages of his journey filled him with pleasure because it lived. It was—must he say it?—a rattlesnake, and were its bite not mortal, he reflected, he could have dismounted "to embrace the creature." In the little towns he found the Mexicans were poor and few in number, and "most anxious to have a priest to instruct them in their duties, to support them in their misery, and to close their eyes at the supreme moment of death." His riverside road was intersected by straggling trails made by cattle going to water. In the waters of Alamo Creek he saw "people of every age and each sex" bathing. He visited Mier, and found it a beautiful town, "with its church spire, palm and aloe trees, cut in profile against the azure firmament." The local pastor gave him information, and he called to see various families in town, with whom he smoked a cigarette, ate a sweet cake and drank a mug of chocolate. It was a pleasure to see how "strikingly handsome" were the men and women of Mier, and to hear what good Spanish they spoke, "less corrupted with Indian words and phrases."

One time when he left Mier it was late at night. Lost in the dark, he kept wondering where to turn to reach the Rio Grande across the markless plateau. Suddenly out of the night appeared "the shadow of a man," quite naked, making his way home to Mier after working in the fields all day. The missioner asked him the way to the river. Without a word the peon took the bridle of the missioner's horse and led him for ten minutes across the plateau, and then said, "Let the horses take their own course," and "vanished like an apparition." At Camargo the traveller encountered simplicity of another kind no less deeply Indian. He assisted at high Mass in the parish church. Sacred music "was played on a large drum, a trombone, two clarionets, and several violins. . . . A great surprise awaited me. During the elevation they commenced playing the *Marseillaise*." True, he recalled, "throughout all America the *Marseillaise* is quite the rage. . . ."

If he wanted to progress from one ranch to the next on the Texan side of the river, he found that the only roads were the old Spanish trails in Mexico. "Often the shortest and even the only route between two Texian *ranchos* is to cross the Rio Grande and travel the Mexican territory, and to recross the Rio Grande again near one's destination." But whichever side he was on, the back-country life was the same, for the ranchers were all Mexicans. They seemed "just as indolent as their countrymen in town," with "all the characteristics and all the defects of an infant people." He studied them with a professional eye, and came to a conclusion. "Voluptuousness is surely their damning vice." But he added that this came not so much from depraved morals as from ignorance and enervation. He could not imagine how a ranchero made a living, overpowered as he was by the mere notion of effort—"save in pleasures." The Mexican rancher could sleep anywhere, better under a tree than a roof. Poor ranchers lived on coffee, chocolate, tortillas and sun-dried beef; the rich on rice, spices, lamb cooked with raisins, tamales. Neither walked, even to go half a mile, but always rode. He might live in "a wretched hut," but on his horse the Mexican lavished every splendor, with gold and silver studdings on saddle and bridle. His horse was his inseparable companion. Riding out, the rancher wore his best— a broad-brimmed hat trimmed with gold lace or a gold chain, and lined with green; an embroidered shirt; velvet trousers with broad facings of black braid slashed at the calf to show his long white cotton drawers; a bright scarf of China crepe at the waist; and silver spurs.

The missioner saw many a company of such horsemen on high occasions. Going to a feast celebrating a baptism, a marriage, or a fandango, they rode "like a horde of madmen let loose, or of Indians. . . ." Their women rode with them. At full gallop, they went shouting, singing, in a cloud of dust, and pulled up at a cluster of ranch buildings made of stakes and reeds laid out in a miniature plaza, with a long street intersecting it. If the ranch was decked for a wedding, tables with food were set out under brush arbors. The missioner was pressed to partake of the feast. He nearly choked on the "horrid sauce of beef-suet, pepper and spices," which tasted like melted tallow. There was nothing to drink but whiskey, which he refused, though the hot sauce made him think he could "quaff the Rio Grande at a draught." After the feast and a siesta in the shade there were horse races down the long dusty street between the jacales; and after the races the riders linked arms and strolled around in groups, singing to the music of a guitar or an accordion. Though none had musical training, everyone played and sang "with no less taste than talent." Now and then a young fellow took a woman en croupe and in a flourish of violent gallantry galloped her to the end of the street and back, then seizing others in turn, repeated his strenuous compliment.

When evening came, the horses were tethered, lanterns were lighted in the trees, and benches were set out to make a square. The women laid aside their mantillas and formed a line while the men came to make a row behind them. When two violins, two clarinets and a bass drum began to play, the fandango was on. The missioner watched for a while, and then withdrew to seclusion behind a hut, wrapped his blanket about him and lay down to sleep. It was useless. "During the whole night, the bum-bum of the big drum, the shrill discordant notes of the clarionet, the roars of merriment, and the thundering acclamation of the dancers" kept him "from closing an eye." And if the dancers rested for a moment, others sang. It was true that their voices were sweet and their songs "racy with the poetry of nature." Still others sat under the trees smoking and "relating fantastic stories as history." An "itinerant troubadour" might be present in his wanderings from ranch to ranch, and in return for a meal and a corner in which to spread his serape for the night, told stories—making a hit with tales of witches who lived in the river country—and sang ballads to the sound of his guitar. At one such wedding feast the bride was admitted to be the "living descendant of Montezuma." She was an orphan, and of all her immense family wealth nothing was left to her but vast lands in Texas, whose title since the war it was impossible to hold. Offered six thousand dollars in settlement, "she accepted this miserable sum, and married the man she loved,"going with him "to continue in obscurity, her existence unknown, indeed, to the world, but withal peaceful and happy. . . ."

Resuming his rounds, the missioner came to his remote families after long, hard rides, to bring them the blessing of God upon their stages of life, temporal and eternal. He baptized new children. He sat with the older children and gave them their lessons in catechism. He instructed them for their first communions. Through him they learned the true meaning of the stories of the Holy Family and the saints told them by their parents in fragments half remembered and half invented. If young people waited to be married he performed the sacrament of matrimony for them. If old people were ready to die he brought them the grace of a happy death, while the ranch women wept and shrieked, striking their breasts and tearing their hair in propriety. He was an honored guest and he became a friend. He was the world, with its news, its powers, and its sense of form. Through him the lost clusters of humanity scattered about the blinding prickly wilderness were brought into the great design of life, and given dignity, and their rightful share of an all-enfolding love, and salvation through it. When he had renewed their understanding of these things through an explanation of the Mass which they could attend so seldom, he prepared to celebrate it for them.

Taking two meal tubs, he set them at the foot of a large sycamore tree under its embracing shade. Over the tubs he laid a door from a hut. This was his altar. He dressed it with two bottles covered with moss to serve as candlesticks, and he took the crucifix he wore and hung it on the stem of the tree. With muslin mantillas and shawls fixed to branches he made a drapery about the altar. Then—it was still early in the hot day—he went to the bank of the Rio Grande to read his breviary. After that it was time to call everyone to Mass. He walked through the settlement of the ranch ringing a little bell, and they came. They knelt on a patch of green grass in the sycamore shade, all silent, and attended the repetition of the Holy Sacrifice first done and now done again in their behalf; and vastly away the plain was gilded by the sun, and overhead in the branches birds sang.

The missioner, so far away from the cultivated graces of life in his beloved France, learned to know different graces in the people he came so far to serve. One night he had a companionable visit from the old Mexican soldier who was his man of all work—"cook, butler, sacristan." It was a lovely night, and the missioner was taking his ease in the garden of his rectory where he had contrived a gallery of board from which depended a hammock. There he liked to doze, or consult his thoughts, or gaze at his flower beds in the summer starlight, or watch the lights of Fort Brown as they went out one after another when the bugle ended the day. The sacristan sat down on the ground near the hammock and for a while neither he nor the misioner spoke, but simply dwelled together in the night. Then puffing at a cigarette, the old campaigner launched in a loud voice a monologue "on the beauties of the heavens and the earth."

"See," he said, "what a charming night it is! what sweet mellow temperature! what pure and balmy air! what silence in all nature! How this silence of night ravishes my soul!" And yet all was not silence. "Do you hear the cry of the widow"—the great-tailed grackle that made hilarious clatter in the treetops everywhere on the lower river—"as she flies and flutters in the distance? Why does she not sleep beneath the broad shade of the ebony tree? Mystery of God," he said, and fell silent under it. And then he was moved to continue. "Do you see those myriads of stars whose twinkling splendor lights the plains like the timid doubtful twilight? And those majestic palm-trees, whose graceful branches gently poise themselves against the clear sky, seeming as if at night-time they bear fruit of fire, suspended from every branch? And those stars that fall and fade away, leaving behind them a light narrow cascade of diamonds? Oh!" he cried, "how wonderful are the works of God!"

However much the misioner may have elaborated the translation of what he heard that night, he could still say, "I was wrapt in amazement and delight at the poetic rapture of my old soldier. . . ."

30.

Boundaries

Words put forth in campaigns—military or political—sometimes had to be overcome. Though General Kearney on approaching New Mexico had said that he proposed to take only the lands lying east of the Rio Grande, soon afterward he swept his claim across the river all the way to California. With the signing of the peace, Mexico succumbed to the terms of the United States; but not Texas. Texas in 1836 claimed all New Mexico's area east of the river, amounting to some ninety-eight thousand square miles. In 1848 she reaffirmed the claim by another act of her legislature, and sent a Texan judge to hold court in New Mexico. This was Spruce M. Baird, who travelled along the New Mexican valley agitating the Texan cause. Near Socorro he made an ally of a returned refugee. "Genl. Armijo," he reported to Governor George T. Wood of Texas, "Genl. Armijo espouses our cause with some zeal and is decidedly the first man in that region." Baird soon measured him. "I bought him out lock stock and barrel." Armijo was living on past glories, and could not refrain from showing the Texan certain spoils left over from the victory over General McLeod's Santa Fe Pioneers of 1841. "He showed me General McCloud's regimentals and says no other Mexican general can exhibit such trophies."

But New Mexico was now a ward of the United States, and her citizens—though without prior approval by the national government—moved to achieve territorial status. Ignoring the claim of Texas and the presence of her jurist, they held an election to choose a New Mexican delegate to Congress, with voters eligible in the vast disputed area. The

Governor of Texas drew his sword. Texas, he declared, would seize New Mexico to the east bank by force. But he was not dealing now with an Armijo whom earlier Texans had even so not been able to overthrow; he was dealing with the United States, and the government at Washington assured him promptly that if he sent Texan troops to New Mexico they would be received and disposed of as aggressors.

The local quarrel suddenly flared into larger significance when other Southern states threw in with Texas in her sense of injury, and against the government made bitter charges of an overreach of federal power. The Northern states as automatically sided with the national government; and a premonition of tragic things to come could be read in the argument. For embedded in the question of states' rights against federal authority was the issue of slavery. Texas had long since been committed to slavery by the policies of Stephen Austin. Texas held a further promise of value to the Southern faction, for at the time of her acceptance into the Union she had been guaranteed the right to divide herself by vote of her citizens into as many as five states, all of which would presumably declare for slavery. The possession of immense new tracts taken from New Mexico would make such a sub-division not only politically powerful in national questions, but also locally rich in material resources. Again in 1850 Texas by joint resolution of her legislative chambers asserted her New Mexican claim and promised that "the State of Texas will maintain the integrity of her territory."

The question was taken up by Congress in the summer, and an omnibus bill—the Compromise of 1850—was passed with provisions that settled the local status of new lands won by the Mexican War, and postponed the ultimate challenge to the union inherent in sectional animosities. California became a state without slavery. New Mexico was separated into two federal territories, one of which embraced the later statehood areas of New Mexico and Arizona, the other comprising those of Utah and Nevada. Both were to decide for freedom or slavery upon becoming states. Fugitive slave laws were tightened, and in the District of Columbia, while slavery was continued, the slave trade was outlawed. And the disputed lands between Texas and the upper Rio Grande were given to New Mexico, with a payment of ten million dollars awarded to Texas. President Millard Fillmore promptly signed the bill and sent it to Texas.

It created a furor in Austin. The Governor convened the legislature in a special session to take action. The bill had many features to infuriate the Texan houses. It required their acceptance of its provisions.

by a deadline—December 1, 1850. It assumed that Texas interests could be disposed by the federal government. And its proposal to pay the ten millions was hedged with conditions that seemed to reflect upon Texan honor, for only half the great sum was to be paid outright, the other half to be held until Texas herself had paid off claims against the United States that accompanied Texas into the Union. Were Texans to conclude that Texas could not be trusted to meet her obligations if she obtained the ten millions all at once? Focussing the furies of his legislature, the Governor proposed the immediate occupation of Santa Fe by force of arms, and then made another suggestion—that the disputed lands be sold to the United States, but with the reservation that Texas retain jurisdiction over them. The halls at Austin echoed much high feeling in debate; but in the end, opposition collapsed, and on November 25, 1850, safely before the deadline, the terms of the United States were accepted and affirmed by act of law in the Texas legislature. The New Mexican Rio Grande was not to be an interstate boundary after all, except for a little jog of a few miles above El Paso on the modern map.

But in addition to marking Mexico off from Texas, a portion of the river as it turned north from El Paso was indicated as the boundary between New and old Mexico. A precise survey of the international boundary was still to be made under the articles of the Treaty of Guadalupe Hidalgo. These provided that the line "shall commence in the Gulf of Mexico, three leagues from land, opposite the mouth of the Rio Grande, otherwise called the Rio Bravo del Norte, or opposite the mouth of its deepest branch, if it should have more than one branch emptying directly into the sea; from thence up the middle of that river, following the deepest channel, where it has more than one, to the point where it strikes the southern boundary of New Mexico; thence, westwardly, along the whole southern boundary of New Mexico (which runs north of the town called *Paso* to its western termination; thence, northward, along the western line of New Mexico, until it intersects the first branch of the river Gila; (or if it should not intersect any branch of that river, then to the point on the said line nearest to such branch, and thence in a direct line to the same; thence down the middle of said branch and of the said river, until it empties into the Rio Colorado; thence across the Rio Colorado, following the division between Upper and Lower California, to the Pacific Ocean." In these provisions the river's habit of changing its course was taken into account. For centuries the channel had wandered, creating the old resacas of the littoral; and, more recently, the isla at El Paso; and, a hundred years later, leaving as farmland—marked "No Dumping"—the site of the steamboat dock at Davis's Landing half a mile from the new bank. Far into the twentieth century the vagaries of the river's course would keep an international commission at work adjusting problems of ownership and sovereignty raised by sudden storm changes in the channel.

In 1849 President Polk offered Lieutenant Colonel W. H. Emory the post of boundary commissioner if he would resign from the Army to conduct the survey, which he "respectfully declined" to do. Colonel John B. Weller was then appointed, and Emory became his chief astronomer and commander of the escort troops that would accompany the survey expedition. They embarked from the east coast for the Isthmus of Panama with the news of California gold ringing in their ears—news that made trouble for the survey when later in California many members of the party quit to seek their fortunes in the gold fields. The boundary commission in 1849 and 1850 was able to accomplish little. The commission was repeatedly bankrupt because the government failed to send the monies appropriated, promised and needed for the field work. John Russell Bartlett was appointed to replace Weller, and once again the expedition was organized. The new commissioner had a lively interest in the country he went to study, and was proud to see gathered by eminent scientists under his leadership much striking new scientific information, and quoted his experts to the effect that, "It will be perfectly safe to say, that one hundred undescribed species of North American vertebrate animals have been added to our fauna. The entire annals of zoological history scarcely present a parallel to this case."

He took delight in the social amenities of the Pass, at Magoffinsville on the north side of the Rio Grande—one of three American settlements there. It represented "the American El Paso," and consisted of "a large square, around which" were "substantial adobe buildings of a better description than usual, embracing some six or eight large stores and warehouses, well filled with merchandise." The commissioner found the town "admirably situated," and belonging "wholly to James W. Magoffin, Esq., an American, long resident in Mexico, whose energy and public spirit will undoubtedly make it the principal place on the frontier. . . ."

Magoffin had lost none of his savoir faire since the war. With "delicacies prepared in New York and Paris for the foreign markets" he could serve "a cold collation . . . that would have done credit to the caterer of a metropolitan hotel." Bartlett stayed in quarters on the Mexican side three or four miles away, and when James Magoffin gave an evening party, the guests forded the river in carriages, sometimes getting stuck fast in midstream until Mexicans came to carry them ashore. The company remained at the party till the next morning, returning home by daylight. When the commissioner in his turn desired to give a party, Magoffin invited him to use a large hall at Magoffinsville. It was a success, even to four great "new-fashioned chandeliers improvised for the occasion" out of sardine tins fixed to a hoop off a pork barrel, wrapped with Apache calicoes and supplied with a "dozen burners each," that "shed such a ray of light upon the festal hall, as rendered the charms of the fair señoritas doubly captivating. . . ."

But if the impromptu delights of El Paso broke the monotony of a hard job, Commisioner Bartlett still seemed unable to get it done. He was a man of many gifts—scholar, antiquarian, bibliographer—and his interests yielded much of value about the nature of the new country taken by conquest. But there were complaints that he spent too much time away in Mexico, and in February, 1853, he was relieved of office. Colonel John C. Frémont who was named to replace him never assumed active part in the direction of the survey. Colonel Emory was still a member of its staff. Presently he appeared in Washington to complain vigorously about the government's handling of the commission; and after all, he was appointed as commissioner, and undertook his command in 1854.

It was his mission to survey another and final southern boundary of the United States, for in 1853 the Gadsden Treaty had been concluded with Mexico which for a consideration of ten million dollars gave the United States new lands in southern New Mexico and Arizona. This was an important acquisition. It embraced a great east-west strip of high flat country ideal for the course of a railroad. If the United States had not bought it, her southernmost rail lines to the West would have had to pass through Mexican territory.

In his survey report Emory made a striking picture of the character of the land by imagining it as a passage by sea. He found that the "depression" of the continent from east to west was wide, stretching from the confluence of the Pecos with the Rio Grande to the Gulf of California. "If the sea," he said, "were to rise to 4,000 feet above its present level, the navigator could cross the continent near the 32nd parallel of latitude. He would be on soundings of uniform depth, from the Gulf of California to the Pecos River. He would see to the north and to the south prominent peaks and sierras, and at times his passage would be narrow and intricate. At El Paso he would be within gunshot of both shores"—the gap through which the Rio Grande ran. He had noticed "this remarkable depression in the continent, in an exploration made by me in 1846," while he was campaigning as a lieutenant in the Army of the West. He had pointed it out to James Buchanan as a basis for fixing the boundary under the Mexican peace terms, and the Secretary of State had instructed Trist "not to take a line north of the 32nd parallel." The instruction had been ignored, and only with the Gadsden Treaty was Emory's original recommendation carried out.

Emory's border mission took two years to complete. He was harassed not only by Indians but also by the raids of Rio Grande freebooters—Carvajal and others—who were still making dust along the river. It was his impression that conditions in the long, speckled valley had "steadily gone backwards since the days of the Spanish rule." With his small party and all their topographic gear he followed the river line between vast stretches of unknown land; and in some places even the river itself had to be taken on conjecture, notably in the Big Bend. He was an able and orderly soldier, "calm, dignified and firm," with all the versatility of so many officers in the mid-century army; and it was particularly exasperating that again and again the government let his men go without pay—once they mutinied in protest—and repudiated his scrupulous requisitions on monies appropriated for his work. He tried to resign but his resignation was refused, and, despite all, he was able to finish his duty. There were compensations. The longer he worked the more he seemed interested in the harsh country that slowly yielded itself up to his knowledge. James Magoffin—an old friend with whom he had campaigned in '46—gave him much help. Best of all, the Mexican officers on the boundary commission who worked with him were intelligent, co-operative and courteous. The interpreter who officiated at joint sessions of the survey was Don Felipe de Iturbide, "the younger son of the late Emperor." In the journals of the joint commission, the daily entries were signed alternately in first place by the Mexican and United States commissioners, to balance the precedence of the two nations in their common effort. The survey was harmoniously concluded, to the satisfaction of both governments.

The youngest river town to be affected by the final boundary was Mesilla, New Mexico. It was established in 1853 through Mexican land grants just across the first boundary between the nations. Las Cruces and Doña Ana lay a little way to its north in United States territory. Those two towns were suddenly crowded after the war by "Texans and other Americans who exercised Texas 'head rights' and took up grants of land" so thickly and forcibly that native Mexicans living there were obliged to move away. Mesilla was founded by those Mexicans who sought safety and peace in the near-by Mexican territory, protected by the line of the first treaty. The town was made entirely of adobe. Its roof lines on one-storey houses rose and fell gently like natural earth contours, on a valley background of willows, cottonwoods and cat-tails. Principal houses in the plaza were developed in a style that could be called Rio Grande Palladian. Wooden windows and door frames, topped with beautifully proportioned classic pediments in miniature, were let into the earthen walls. Square panelling on shutters or doors accompanied them. Such refinements could turn a long, uneven, hand-plastered mud wall into the façade of a palace. The line of inheritance was clear through centuries from Rome to Spain, to Mexico, and up to the Rio Grande. Spirit moved. It survived, as it always survived materials. It would ring, too, in the bells of Mesilla, when two decades later they were cast there of articles of bronze and silver brought by the parishioners to be melted down.

The Gadsden Treaty, carrying the boundary farther south to Magoffiinsville, included Mesilla in the United States—and also Lemitar, where General Manuel Armijo had died on December 12, 1853. He was buried in the northwest corner of the parish church at Socorro, and shortly afterward was memorialized as one of New Mexico's "greatest benefactors" by the Assembly at Santa Fe, which having forgotten certain details of his career then adjourned out of respect for the "memory and distinguished services" of the enterprising sheep-thief who had risen to govern and to betray the upper Rio Grande. He did not live to see his remaining property formally annexed with southern New Mexico.

Residents there were at first apprehensive at the change in sovereignty, but the new government protected the grants they had received from Mexico, and on July 4, 1855, Governor David Meriwether of New Mexico, escorted by General John Garland and United States troops from Santa Fe, arrived to take formal possession of the town and valley of Mesilla. After entering the little town with his parade the Governor made a speech which was translated into Spanish. The United States flag was raised in the plaza while the soldiers cheered three times. The Third Infantry Band played "Hail Columbia," "Yankee Doodle" and "The Star-Spangled Banner." Local Mexican officials came forward to swear allegiance to their new government. Any who did not want to live under it were "notified to leave and to take refuge in Mexican dominions," said a soldier from New York state, and he added, "This was the best 4th of July I have passed since I have been in the Army. . . ."

31.

Flag and Lamplight

But there was yet another reason why the Gadsden Purchase was necessary. In the great strip of land which it comprehended there had been since the war an unremitting terror laid down by Apache, Comanche and Lipan Indians, who preyed on Mexican residents and American settlers and travellers alike. Since many of the Indians raided from within American territory, Mexico filed huge claims for indemnity against the American government. But lacking sovereignty in the terrorized borderlands, the United States could not there make its power felt. The only answer was to acquire the strip—and continue to add links to the chain of army posts all the way up the Rio Grande from the Gulf to the headwaters country. From the eighteen-fifties to the eighties, when the Indians were finally pacified on government reservations, the immense river empire was policed by only a score of little garrisons. A flag by day, lamplight in a window by night, signalled from these posts often hundreds of miles apart a ready and thoughtless valor that stood against the alien faith of the Indian in his own cause that was now seized by the destructive convulsions of a dying mythology. To guard a fifteen-hundred-mile frontier containing fifty thousand Indians—of whom over twenty thousand were actively hostile—New Mexico in 1854 had a total of sixteen hundred and fifty-four officers and men, scattered among less than a dozen forts.

The forts of the Rio Grande system fell into two general groups —those in Texas and those in New Mexico. Many of the Texas river forts had been established during the war, and after 1849 were maintained "to protect the peaceable inhabitants," observed the Army's Inspector General in 1856, "and preserve our own neutrality in all revolutionary movements in Mexico for some years to come."

The military headquarters of the Department of Texas was at San Antonio. From there orders were relayed to the little regimental components stationed together for garrison duty at outland forts. A complete regiment was almost never held together at a single post. Its companies were assigned separately to different stations. Each fort on the border river had units of artillery, infantry and mounted infantry, a band, quartermaster's and ordnance departments, occasionally a chaplain; and invariably a component of laundresses—some of whom were soldiers' wives—living in a row of tents behind their respective companies.

Some of the lower river posts were adjacent to towns—Fort Brown at Brownsville, Ringgold Barracks at Rio Grande City, Fort McIntosh at Laredo, Fort Duncan at Eagle Pass—and were named for officers who had died in the river campaign. Others—often named for veterans of the war in the Mexican interior—were alone in the wilderness, like Fort Inge, Fort Clark, Camp Hudson, Camp Peña Colorada, Fort Quitman, Fort Davis and Fort Hancock, and, far back from the river, guarded its approaches.

They were all examined by the Inspector General in 1856. On the whole he found officers and men in good shape, in spite of comfortless living conditions. Desertions were few and discipline was good, even though there was much sickness—yellow fever and dysentery—in the river forts. The companies turned out everywhere to show him how "handsomely" they could execute the "broad-sword exercise," or bayonet drill, or battalion drill, or artillery practice, though on the target range at one post rifle fire was not what it should have been. Repeatedly he noted that barracks lacked "iron bedsteads," and that the men's bunks were "miserable," and the kitchens "worthless." It was shocking to find that the powder magazines at Ringgold Barracks had leaking roofs, and that the lightning rods "want pointing." If there was a useful small library in the quartermaster's house, there was no school for the handful of children on the post. Lumber was the most scarce of materials, with barely enough to make coffins. Water was hauled from the river into settling tanks.

No station on the Texas river was "ever considered desirable," wrote an officer's wife, "on account of its unfailing sand and heat." There were "no comfortable houses at Fort Duncan," the laundresses lived in "hackales," the hospital windows had cloth in them instead of glass, and the summers were so hot that the Inspector General recommended for the men, instead of their issue tunics of thickly lined broadcloth, a light summer jacket that could be washed. At McIntosh the entire garrison lived in tents, except for two officers who built and paid for a little house themselves. Everyone else suffered by heat in summer and cold in winter. Noting that a bastioned field fort had been built of stone and earth on the high river bluff of Fort McIntosh, the Inspector General wryly recommended that before any further effort and money were spent on fortifications and officers' comforts, the men should be given adequate barracks. There was no shade anywhere on the post.

"The Troops have been extremely exposed to the burning sun on the Rio Grande," he commented, "for instance at McIntosh and Duncan, where they have not been allowed by their own labour to cut posts & make shades & elevate their tents." The reason was that "the population on that river expect pay for all trees & stakes cut," and the department commander "prohibited any expenditure for the temporary accommodation of the troops." Even the "horses of the mounted men," he found, "have been much exposed without shades." He must have seen, if he did not record, how little wood there was to cut in that rocky passage of the river.

And another thing: the post sutler sold "ardent spirits," though there existed a regulation against the practice. It seemed that the post commander considered it preferable to condone the sale of spirits rather than face the inevitable cluster of bootleggers who would meet the needs of soldiers just outside the fort. The Inspector General observed that "the regulation should be either rescinded or enforced. . . ." He found that there were no Indians on the north side of the river, and that depredations were traceable to Lipans who crossed out of Mexico. It was gratifying that "A very good understanding exists with the people and authorities on the Mexican side of the river"—a circumstance that through the century became a tradition for the border cities that faced each other across the Rio Grande. A final cordiality complimented the Inspector General at McIntosh when the enlisted men's theatrical society gave a play "whose performance was very creditable to them." Hoping that the post gardens could manage to produce more vegetables and so hold down the scurvy, he was off to see other forts and the same problems.

Though he ran into occasional variations on the military theme and these made his tour more amusing. One was about the system of supplying the river forts by boat. The head of steam navigation in the 1850s (and in fact until the twentieth century when the last steamer ran in 1907) was Roma. Goods were transshipped upriver to the forts by pack and wagon from there. But the report of an early quartermaster of Fort Brown was extraordinary, even though his claims and recommendations came to nothing, as so often happened with Army reports. First of all, until steamboats were released from wartime troop duty, he supplied the river garrisons by keelboat. And then in 1850 he sent an expedition up the river with orders to navigate to the farthest possible place. He hoped to discover that shipping could utilize far more of the river's length than it had so far done. A keelboat and a skiff, manned by sixteen men, ascended the river by channel to a point a thousand miles above the head of steam travel, or about thirteen hundred miles above the mouth. It was an astonishing penetration for a river with so little water, and the expeditioneers came back, all safe, to report optimistically that if the channel were improved in certain passages, steam navigation would be entirely feasible all the way "up to Babbitt's Falls." These falls were described as "not perpendicular, but a rapid descent of some 200 feet in about half a mile." They were walled in by a perpendicular gorge hundreds of feet high—so high, with such rocky darkness below the slit of sky overhead, that "the stars could be seen at mid-day." It was a new piece of knowledge of the Rio Grande, and it may have described one of the canyons of the Big Bend. In his enthusiasm the leader of the expedition could see steam navigation having its terminus in the profitless canyon. But even though such pioneer quartermasters argued how practical it would be to fit the river for steam commerce, nothing was done to extend the steamboats' range; for by the international treaties of peace, both Mexico and the United States were bound to consult each other in any engineering works on the boundary river. Such combined action would have to wait for a new century, and then it would turn not to meandering travel by channel, but to irrigation and power projects, such as the international Falcón Dam, which would be dedicated by the American and Mexican presidents in 1953.

In another notion, the Army's quartermaster department hoped to transplant a form of transportation suitable for desert operations, and the Inspector General was in a position to report on its progress. In May, 1856, an American officer arrived at Indianola on the Gulf bringing with him from Smyrna "a drove of Camels of 34 in number,

as follows,—1 Tunis Camel a mule, Bactrian Camels mules, I male
Booghdee Camel a mule, 4 Arabian male Camels of burden, 14 Arabian
female Camels of burden, 1 Arabian male calf camel, 1 male Senaar
Dromedary, 1 female Muscat dromedary, 2 male Siout dromedaries,
4 female Siout dromedaries, 1 male Mt Sinai dromedary, and 1 female
and 1 male calfs." In addition to American personnel, his staff included
three Arabians and two Turks. "I inspected these animals," declared
the Inspector General. He had no doubt they were "designed by the
Creator for beasts of burthen." But he could not yet say, "before a fair
experiment," whether they would answer the needs of the Army for
durable pack animals in long hauls over waterless lands in the Southwest. He noted their obvious advantages—they were convenient to pack
as they crouched on the ground, and the humps on their backs made it
easy to keep in the saddle—and approved the first stage of the experiment, which was to keep them for breeding. In later stages, the desert
beasts were to be marched across the Southwest into Arizona. Their
military practicability in their new environment was never conclusively
established; and the drove gradually perished—though in the tourist
mythology of another century, reports of wild camels seen amidst the
illusory rocks of Arizona would recur with some regularity.

As the Army brought its organization with it, so the form of its
frontier forts reflecting this tended to be repetitious. But there were
local variations, and between the river posts of Texas and New Mexico
there seemed to be one general difference. Those in Texas were laid
out in an open order of buildings and tents, arranged for the living
convenience of a small community rather than for defense against attack
or siege. Those in New Mexico were typically fortresses, one-storey
castles of earth, which even when not actually surrounded by revetted
walls were guarded by the placement of the outermost square of buildings in a design for defense. Fort Bliss in its early sites and Fort Thorn
were enclosed by walls, Fort Craig had many interior squares enfolded
by an almost continuous quadrangle of buildings, Fort Marcy showed
in clay the classic flanks of a crenelated field fortification. But whatever
their variations, they were all, upriver and down, created in remarkably
short times by the men who would first garrison them. Their materials
were mostly those to be had on the ground. These were put to use without imagination in detail, but certainly in response to imagination in
the large, that projected the nation's task over the immense river empire,
and brought there the Army's likeness, in all its rigidities of order, duty
and hardship.

The Army's first style along the upper Rio Grande was Mexican—adobe construction, long rows of rooms opening out on a plaza, one-storey high. Later, as posts became permanent, and decades of duty seemed certain, the New Mexico Territorial manner succeeded. Milled lumber took the place of stripped logs, and fired bricks of sun-dried adobe, and even two storeys of one. Windows and doors came from lumberyards back East, and the buildings of an important post assumed the look of a segment out of a small city east of the Mississippi, with the frank, neighborly gesture of the wooden front porch, a grassed yard and a picket fence, and a central parade ground like a small park. The Army was the medium through which the airs and manners of life in the United States came to the river frontier to stay.

Early in their establishment the scattered garrisons, particularly in Texas, seemed to Commissioner Bartlett to be misdirecting their efforts. It was the policy of the Army to grow at each fort as much of its food as possible. Soldiers farmed while Indians ranged. In his boundary report the Commissioner urged that "a change should be made in the system pursued at the frontier posts. Soldiers should not go into quarters, and then quietly remain devoting themselves to agriculture. Better would it be for the government to pay double the price it now does for its wheat and corn than to employ the soldiers for cultivating it; for the consequence of the present system is, that by their attending to the fields, they become unfitted for and neglect their proper duty as soldiers." The Commissioner suggested that "with the opening of the spring, the soldiers should leave their quarters, and be kept moving from one point to another. Let them be a few days in a mountain pass, next at some oasis in the desert whither the savage must resort to satisfy his parching thirst, and again in some of those beautiful valleys covered with luxuriant grass, which are also his resort after his predatory excursions, that he may recruit his animals. This active life," he concluded, writing in comfort far from the scene of his proposals, "would be much more agreeable and healthy for the men than the inactivity of a garrison, and would tend more to overawe and subdue the Indian. . . ." In any case, it was not long until the Indian's own tactics called forth the frontier Army's constant movement in and out of the river forts for endlessly repeated parleys, battles and punishments.

Until 1851 most troops in New Mexico were garrisoned in Santa Fe, Albuquerque and other towns. But in that year the new department commander, Colonel E. V. Sumner, was appalled at what he found of soldier life in the towns, particularly Santa Fe, a "sink of vice," and for

both moral and administrative reasons, he ordered the department headquarters moved from Santa Fe to a new site near Las Vegas, where Fort
Union was immediately established and construction begun. For thirty
years Fort Union was to be the headquarters and supply depot of the
Army in New Mexico. All Missouri trails converged there. It was the
eastern gateway to New Mexico. The river posts were provisioned and
governed from it.

For two years after the war American troops were quartered in the
ruined church and presidio of San Elizario on the long sand island below
El Paso. In 1851 Fort Bliss was founded—though it was not so named
until a little later—at Smith's Ranch, the site of the village of Franklin
near Magoffinsville, and was to know two other adjacent locations before
its final one. Upriver near Mesilla, Fort Fillmore was erected on the east
bank in 1851, and three years later with the arrival of new troops it
received four officers' wives "who had the courage to accompany the
army on its toilsome march of three months across the plains." They
were "the only American ladies" seen by Commissioner Bartlett between
San Antonio and the Pacific, and he believed they were "the only ones
on this portion of the frontier" in 1854. Fort Thorn was established
on the west bank opposite Doña Ana in 1854, and guarded the San Diego
road as it turned away from the river for California. At the foot of
Valverde Mesa, Fort Conrad was built in 1851 but two years later was
abandoned and its garrison moved a few miles south to found Fort Craig
with a spread of twenty-two buildings—"the best and prettiest fort in
New Mexico," according to a soldier, who added, "It is situated on a
table land beside the Rio Grande. It is set in a grove of cottonwood
trees." Only small garrisons were left at Albuquerque and Santa Fe.
Cantonment Burgwin, eight miles south of Taos in a mountain canyon,
and Fort Massachusetts, in the San Luis Valley through which the river
wound after its passage out of the mountains of its source, were the
northernmost of the riverland posts at mid-century. In later decades
Fort Macrae (whose site would be covered by the waters of Elephant
Butte Dam in the twentieth century) and Fort Selden were added to
valley defenses.

On all sides, invisible until they acted, were the enemy people—
Navajos north and west of the river, Apaches in its mountain flanks,
Lipans along its southeast stretches, and Comanches who wintered in
the Bolsón de Mapimí and ranged from Mexico to the buffalo plains
north and east of Santa Fe. Movement according to the seasons and the
presence of prey or spoils was their medium of life. They used the deserts

as no soldier ever could; for their very identity lay in that land, and knowing its common secrets they could make its thinnest resources feed them, and hide them, and answer their beliefs of spirit, and give them power.

In that great open country where the Army's forts and wagon trains were so small, the Indians crowded upon them unrelentingly. No one could safely venture alone more than three miles from Fort Bliss in 1852. Every small party travelling the road from San Antonio to El Paso was attacked by Comanches, and the prairies along its course were burned by Indians to deprive the trains of grass for their animals, so that the Army had to haul extra feed in wagons. An Indian fighter said that in twenty years of raiding in New Mexico and Arizona the Apaches cost settlers over fifty million dollars in destruction and theft. New Mexicans, between 1846 and 1850, according to figures of United States Marshals, lost 453,293 sheep, 12,887 mules, 7,050 horses and 31,581 horned cattle. The Apaches perfected a method of making off with flocks of sheep. They shaped the flock into an oblong pattern never wider than thirty feet, and as long as required. Choosing the strongest sheep they lashed them together by the horns two by two, forming them into a living fence that enclosed the flock on each long side until the sheep within could not stray. Indian drivers strode along beside and behind the flock, and at its head a squad of young, hardy Indians set the pace. Running night and day, the desert thieves could take twenty thousand sheep from fifty to seventy miles in a day, sometimes making swift marches of up to fifteen hundred miles, far out of reach of organized pursuit.

In the face of such tactics the Army tried to establish order by treaty. It seemed that each new commander as he came to take over a Department tried to parley with the enemy. Indians were generally willing to accept an invitation to a conference at some bare place in the wilderness. There came the mounted Army column with its blue wagons under their white tops, each drawn by six mules and escorted by six cavalrymen. The soldiers made camp with tents, and strung picket lines for horses, and established the precise, frugal and unchanging order of their housekeeping in the field.

All about at a little distance camped the Indians in their own way, with tepees, arranged according to no order, hundreds of them, alive with warriors, their wives, children, old men and women, horses for the best fighters, and countless dogs. While the bulk of Indians sat in a great demilune facing the soldier camp, watching but pretending not to watch, and the troopers, lounged at hair-trigger ease with their weapons, the commanding officer and his staff deliberated with the chiefs. The commander made gifts to the chiefs which they appraised expertly and in silence unless they felt more was due to them, when with injured dignity they would say so. If one chief received more than another trouble flickered and if it broke out hasty adjustments had to be made. And then the discussion proceeded to the agenda.

The commander recited a list of things to be recovered—stolen horses, sheep, cattle, and even children. The Indian spokesman understood him through an interpreter, and in his turn replied, with little gestures of the chin that poked at places faraway and dim, and speaking in sounds that exploded in the throat, or drilled against his teeth, or yelped like the mindless voicings of a coyote, he said that he had no knowledge of stolen horses, sheep, cattle or children, but that if he discovered any such, he would—and here with his fingers bundled together he made a dabbing motion of delivery—he would give them to the commander. Strange things did happen, he conceded. He was an old man, and the other chiefs were old men in their wisdom. If what the commander said was true, then the blame must be put on the young men of the Indian nation, for who could control them in the years of their pounding blood, animal splendor and pricking desire to do great deeds? The commander sighed. So the excuses always went. All he could do was propose pledges of future peace, and make impressive to the meagre degree possible in the surroundings an act of scratching a large sheet of paper with an X whereby some part of the signer would seem forever to be held captive to ceremony and honor. The commander could only reflect that some day, such an act, such a document, would turn out to be the last one necessary; and only hope that this might be it.

The parley was adjourned.

The soldiers relaxed, and a few drifted among the Indians to see them closely, and discover if they carried gold bullets, and if so, as many did, to trade a dozen leaden balls for one gold. By dark the soldiers were back in their own camp, behind sentries; and in the night, looking out of the bivouac toward the Indian positions, what they saw was written down by a young sergeant: "At least 1000 little fires were to be seen about us. . . ."

In the morning, if they were camped near the river during a cold month, soldiers might see how Apaches hunted ducks. From a brushy shore several large gourds went bobbing on wavelets toward ducks who swam on the shallow water. Lightly, randomly the gourds moved among

the ducks who murmured and circled but did not fly. Suddenly a duck
here, another there, and another, vanished below the water, while
alarmed at last the remainder went to the air, and the hunters arose to
stand in the river. They wore the gourds over their heads with holes cut
for their eyes. For days they had practiced floating empty gourds among
the ducks until the ducks were no longer alarmed by them. Then the
hunters wearing their gourds entered the water unseen and perfectly
imitating the motion of the empty gourds bobbing on the river waded
in a crouch on the river floor until they could seize their game from
below, pull them underwater, and stuff them into the bags. The
soldiers knew too that Apaches wearing the horned heads and tied skins
of antelopes could go in perfect masquerade among those sensitive
animals and at close range kill their quarry. Such craft at hunting wild
creatures compelled admiration and wonder. But more—it measured too
the skill of desert Indians at their other work of surprising and destroying their human enemies. It was a skill never to be matched in kind by
the Army. It had to be overcome by other techniques and the compounded courage of fellows-at-arms who, outnumbered in the wilderness, yet put forward in a conviction of massed power the policy of the
United States when there came a time for battle.

For after parleys and treaties, when the soldiers returned to
their forts and the Indians to their light-stricken and distant country,
troubles began all over again, with raid, thieving, murder and fire. From
the fort nearest to the trouble a column of troops moved out in pursuit
of the enemy. Often they had with them an Indian scout in the service
of the Army. With his help they read the vacant land. They watched
the horizon for smoke of campfires. If they came upon the trail and
found campfire ashes they studied these to learn how long ago the fire
had been put out, how much stirred by winds, what kind of desert fuel
had been burned, how many people it had served by its size. If grass grew
at the site, was it trampled, and how widely? Were there animal droppings and evidence of animal urine? These by their condition might
tell passage of time. Were there signals for other Indians—little markers
of twig and stone? If there were even a single bush near-by, throwing
a lacy shadow, was there an enemy scout hiding there?—for soldiers
recorded how using the barest ground an Indian plainsman could wholly
conceal himself from unpracticed observation at a distance of only a
few feet.

And then, sooner or later, perhaps in a rocky canyon, or a shallow
in the plains, or the shadow of a mesa, the war party was found posed

for battle. Sometimes they had with them their rag-bundled women. The warriors were polygamous, and their striding women were fiercely contentious for the man who owned them. Aprowl like cats across the thorny land, they clawed their way after their thieving, murdering, lying lords. When the troopers formed for battle, they would see an occasional Indian rise up out of cover in jeering defiance. He turned his back and showed his naked posterior, clapping it obscenely as he shouted words of challenge and contempt. When the battle came, it might be brief. Both parties were accoutred for light, rapid movement. A siege was rare. Leaving their transport and supply guarded well behind them, the soldiers advanced using what cover they could find. Their rifles sounded. The Indian fire was returned with both arrow and bullet. Twenty minutes, an hour, more or less, and the skirmish was over, with dead and wounded on both sides. Sometimes the greater part of the Indians escaped while the rest fought off the attack. Again, the whole war party might be taken. And again, the troopers might have to retire or all be destroyed. However the issue went, what all knew beyond its decisive moments was that though the battle might be final for men who fought it, there were many more battles to come before the prairies and deserts would be at peace.

When the fight was over the soldiers buried their dead. They dug a common grave and lined it with pack tarpaulins. They wrapped the fallen in their bedding rolls and laid them in the grave. An officer read or repeated prayers for the dead, and earth was closed over the dead troopers. The bugler sounded taps. A squad fired a salute. Sometimes the commander's tent was pitched over the grave. Sometimes fires were built on the grave to blacken all marks of burial. But if the Army column moved on to pursue escaping Indians, and returning days later passed by that way again, they might find that the fire-scarred grave had told all too plainly what lay there, and that another Indian party had thrown it open to steal the burial blankets, tossing the bodies about to be picked by carrion birds and animals. Then the soldiers would gather the remains and reduce them to a stern safety. "We built a large pile of pine wood; put on bodies; burned the flesh; took the bones away," observed a young cavalryman. He helped to bring the bones of an officer back to a Rio Grande fort in 1855. The captain's wife was waiting there for him. She was one of the only four American ladies stationed between San Antonio and the Pacific. In her doorway she asked where her husband was when the troops returned. They evaded her questions. But she knew, and in some persistence of a desire both to deny what must come and to leave others their ease for yet a little while, she accepted their poor evasions, and spoke lightly, and went about her tasks in quarters, until an hour later at their duty and in their time the others came to tell her what she knew they would tell, and she wept. Later, a new post in the mountains was named for the captain—Fort Stanton.

Along the lower river some of the Texas forts had their counterparts in Mexican garrisons across the way, as at Matamoros, Laredo and Eagle Pass. Courtesies and entertainments were exchanged by officers and their families. At Piedras Negras, opposite Eagle Pass, American officers and ladies went to eat Mexican food, and see bullfights, and hear the music of the Mexican army band "—so sweet and thrilling—", and watch the "superb drilling of Mexican soldiers, who marched and countermarched for at least an hour without a single order being spoken, they responding merely to a tap of the drum as each new movement was initiated." American troops, thought an officer's wife, "could never be kept in such slavish subjection." Sometimes the Mexican band came across to play at Fort Duncan, serenading the ladies—perhaps a little dangerously—who "listened as in a dream to its rendering of various operas and Mexican national airs, played with such expression that all the sentiments they indicated were aroused.".

And once during the 1850s there was another sort of excitement to discuss, when an American border freebooter named Callahan crossed the Rio Grande with a band of followers to recover some Seminole Negro slaves who had escaped from him into Mexico. He was met by a force of seven hundred Mexican troops whom he defeated. They fled the city of Piedras Negras, which he occupied and looted. A citizen of Eagle Pass saw some of Callahan's men. "Every one that I saw had more or less of jewelry displayed about his neck and breast"—gold earrings, necklaces, finger rings, watches. The raiders stole food, and other supplies, and silver-mounted saddles. When the Mexicans showed signs of returning to fight, Callahan as an American citizen appealed for support to Major Burbank, commanding at Fort Duncan. The major replied that the raiders had no business in Piedras Negras, and should withdraw. All he would agree to do would be to cover their retreat with the guns of Fort Duncan. Callahan was pressed by the returning Mexican force. With a single round of grapeshot from a four-pound cannon, he discouraged the Mexican attack and returned to Eagle Pass where the whole town had watched his affair from the riverbank.

But most of the Rio Grande forts stood in isolation. Cantonment

Burgwin near Taos was so remote and dull that when an officer and his wife had a chance to visit Fort Union with its complement of a hundred residents, they exclaimed that "the post seemed very gay to us, with the band and so many people." Coming back to the river from the Indian country in 1856 an officer paused at Fort Bliss, which seemed to him a "most unmilitary" post, and went on to Fort Fillmore, where matters were far better conducted. On his way upriver to Fort Craig he and his command were overtaken by a blizzard, and made camp hurriedly. They built a great ring of fires within their circle of parked wagons, and there, in their own climate, the soldiers were almost as warm as in spring, while the commander spent the evening reading in his tent by the warmth of his small portable stove, and the norther clapped away outside. It was a joy to arrive at Craig in a day or two, and dine at the officers' mess, and play poker, and run into Army talk again—who was getting married, which way the last promotions had gone, was there any hope for a new pay bill in Congress, would an officer always have to pay his own travel expenses on leave and put up with half-pay to boot, was that a new daguerreotype over there of the General's youngest daughter—all the enfolding and reassuring trifles that held together an isolated society between its occasions of hard, and at times heroic, professional duty.

Enlisted men talked of other things. Once in dangerous Indian country the entire command of three hundred men were put on guard all night, while their five officers slept in tents pitched at the center of the camp. "Oh," said an enlisted man, "oh that our government only knew the courage of some of her officers! Nothing happened during the night." They talked about a colonel who with his sword cut a soldier who fell in the field from thirst and could not march further. "The man fell, bleeding profusely. We went on and left him . . . a poor victim of an inhuman tyrant." They talked about a captain who enraged by clumsiness shown at drill "ran his sabre into a man's back, injuring him for life. The captain says it was accidental. I don't know." They talked about troubles between enlisted men, too—the soldier at Fort Craig who refused to obey an order by his corporal, drew a knife, was shot through the heart by the corporal, and was buried "without the honors of war," while the corporal received no blame. . . .

Both officers and enlisted men and any women stationed at a fort did what they could to lighten the weight of wilderness. A melodeon was shipped in by cart, and someone played it for chapel. Someone else organized burro races and everyone took part either as jockeys or laughing spectators. On holidays and Saturday nights a committee cleared the floor of mess hall or armory, put up decorations of paper and lights, arranged a bay for an orchestra of band musicians, and all came to enjoy a "social hop," for "nothing now offers the soldier more joy," said a soldier's letter to a newspaper, "than when he is carried away by the excitement of the dance," in the polka, the schottische, the lancers, and— an intoxicating innovation—the "glide waltz." It was a convention that the enlisted men should form a dramatic society to present in one gala evening a number of specialty acts, an exhibition of gymnastics, and a play. One post theatre was always referred to as the "opera house." Its offerings were watched by all of the garrison not engaged in the performance, and earnestly overpraised at the last curtain. Any soldier gifted with a public accomplishment was in demand, like a young sergeant who wrote in his notebook at a Rio Grande post: "Stopped with Company I, 1st Dragoons, at Fort Thorn. By invitation recited Plato's 'Soliloquy on the Immortality of the Soul' at a kind of theatre established here." Out of the *Phaedo* he repeated for other men in the wilderness whose business it might be to die of their duty, ". . . if the soul is really immortal, what care should be taken of her, not only in respect of the portion of time which is called life, but of eternity! . . ." In such ways the tedium of garrison life was relieved. But soon the forts of the Rio Grande would have a mission larger than guard duty.

32.

The Rio Grande Divided

Just as the election of Polk in 1844 had signified that Texas would join the Union, so the re-election of Lincoln in 1860 made it inevitable that she would leave it. Following the lead of South Carolina and other states early to secede, Texas called a convention to give form to the views about human relations with which since the troubled times of Stephen Austin she had justified her slave-operated economy. On February 2, 1861, the convention "passed an ordinance dissolving all political connection with the government of the United States, and the people thereof," and called an election for February twenty-third at which Texans would ratify it.

How unnatural, cried Texas, that the Northern states should feel hostile toward the "Southern states and their beneficent and patriarchal system of African slavery!" How could the North proclaim "the debasing doctrine of the equality of men, irrespective of race or color—a doctrine at war with nature, in opposition to the experience of mankind, and in violation of the plainest revelations of the divine law"? Forgetting the passion for equality that had led to the founding of the nation, the statesmen of Texas labored to clothe their pretext for disunion in self-righteous and finally in pious terms: "We hold, as undeniable truths, that the governments of the various states, and of the confederacy itself, were established exclusively by the white race, for themselves and their posterity; that the African race had no agency in their establishment; that they were rightfully held and regarded as an inferior and dependent race, and in that condition only could their existence in this country be rendered beneficial or tolerable: That, in this free government"—only a few white Texans wondered how the word "free" could be used if it did not apply to all human beings—"ALL WHITE MEN ARE, AND OF RIGHT OUGHT TO BE, ENTITLED TO EQUAL CIVIL AND POLITICAL RIGHTS; that the servitude of the African race, as existing in these states, is mutually beneficial to both bond and free, and is abundantly authorized and justified by the experience of mankind, and"—though no scripture was cited—"by the revealed will of the Almighty Creator, as recognized by all Christian nations; while the destruction of the existing relations between the two races, as advanced by our sectional enemies, would bring inevitable calamities upon both, and"— here was exposed the material motive behind earlier, more elevated protest—"and desolation upon the fifteen slaveholding states. . . ."

Sentiment for secession was so clearly formed in Texas that even before the public voted on it, preparations for war went forward. General David Emmanuel Twiggs, commanding United States troops in the Department, repeatedly asked Washington for instructions to follow if Texas seceded. None came. At last, when a "committee for public safety" demanded that he surrender all Army posts and property in Texas to the state government, he agreed. For this "treachery to the flag of his country" he was dismissed from the service. A few months later he was solaced with a commission as major general in the Confederate Army. On February 23, 1861, Texans voted overwhelmingly to quit the Union, and when word came of the Confederate attack on the garrison of Fort Sumter at Charleston whose commander had refused to act like Twiggs, Governor Clark of Texas, like President Lincoln at Washington, called for volunteers and moved into war measures. Lieutenant Colonel John R. Baylor with Texas militia occupied the forts west of San Antonio, even as far up the Rio Grande as Fort Bliss, and, later, Mesilla. Loyal citizens fled before him. One, a native of Maine named Babbitt, with two other men, escaped from El Paso in two dugout canoes lashed together by which they floated on the Rio Grande all the way to Brownsville—some twelve hundred miles—in the first known continuous voyage of the boundary river.

New Mexico meanwhile remained loyal to the United States, and the Rio Grande was divided between its own north and south, like the nation at large. Many memories helped the old river kingdom to abide with the federal authority. Her population was largely Mexican. The decision of Texas to default her statehood aroused little sympathy among a people whose traditional relations with Texas had been marked by earlier Texan disloyalties and aggressions—the Texan revolt, the Texan border adventures, the Texan attempts to annex New Mexico first by arms and then by boundary claims. Further, when Mexico, displaying a degree of social and political maturity, outlawed slavery by the decrees of 1829, New Mexico as her province was governed by them. After New Mexico became United States territory it was with the provision under the Compromise of 1850 that on reaching statehood she would vote for or against slavery within her limits. But she was not to wait so long. Though in 1859 her legislature passed a law protecting slave property already introduced into the territory, at the next session, in 1862, she would repeal the law and thereafter support the antislavery philosophy of the national government in both form and spirit. That New Mexico even under her brief legal sanction did not encourage modern slavery was indicated by the small number of Negro slaves there at the outset of the war—some twenty-two in all.

As war came in the spring of 1861 Colonel William W. Loring, commander of United States forces in New Mexico, left his command and joined the Confederacy. He was succeeded by Colonel Edward R. S. Canby to whom fell the preparation of the river garrisons and other outposts for defense. Resources were few, and though militia men of Latin blood responded to his call, they were untrained and unready for battle.

In July he was obliged to remain inactive when Colonel Baylor, with several companies of artillery and mounted rifles, marched up the river from El Paso as far as Mesilla to give battle to the Union garrison at Fort Fillmore.

The fort commander was Major Isaac Lynde, a kindly, gray-bearded veteran of thirty-four years in the Infantry, who soon heard that the Texans were coming. In spite of what he knew, he ordered no extra precautions against surprise. "Great God, what brainless imbecility!" exclaimed his post surgeon, who clearly saw present danger and later raged at what followed. On the night of July twenty-fourth Baylor's troops camped six hundred yards from the fort intending an attack at daybreak. Two of his men deserted to enter the fort and give warning. Major Lynde ordered the long roll on the drums, the garrison awoke—but not to action. No scouts were sent out to measure the enemy, and the next morning, Baylor and his men were calmly permitted to ford the Rio Grande near the fort and occupy Mesilla, where they were received with "vivas and hurrahs" by the people. Soon afterward Major Lynde ordered almost his whole force of seven hundred men to form for an advance upon Mesilla. If its purpose was worthy, its execution was, as the post surgeon declared, "one of the most extraordinary, imbecile, and childish military movements ever perpetrated. . . ." Lynde demanded the surrender of the invaders. It was refused. He then ordered cavalry out on a frontal instead of a flanking movement, with the result that four men were killed and several wounded. On a near-by hill were clustered women, children and unarmed men of Mesilla who came to watch the fight. Lynde ordered his artillery to fire upon them, and luckily the fire fell short. Presently the Major rode up to the post surgeon at his field hospital wagon and ordered,

"Doctor, get your wounded ready to retreat."

"Where to, sir?" asked the doctor, thinking the battle was about to begin in earnest.

"To the fort," replied the commander.

"Great God!" thought the doctor, "is this the disgraceful finale . . . ?", but he must obey. The garrison withdrew to the fort two miles away to the amazement of most of its officers. The next morning the Major ordered another retreat, now to Fort Stanton in the mountains a hundred and fifty miles northeast of Mesilla, leaving Baylor, with only two hundred and fifty troops, in possession at the river.

The summer weather was merciless. The high plains east of the river were dry. There were the Organ Mountains to cross. The retreat was a misery—and in another day the Confederates came after the fleeing command. In a "sublimity of majestic indifference" Major Lynde was taking lunch at San Augustín Springs when his officers came to beg him to fight. He exercised his authority, refused their protests, and—"suicidal, cowardly, pusillanimous"—in a little while surrendered his force unconditionally to Colonel Baylor. A few days later on August first Baylor issued a proclamation announcing southern New Mexico and all of Arizona as a Territory of the Confederate States, with Mesilla as its capital and himself as its military governor. On the following day Fort Stanton was abandoned by Union forces that withdrew to Albuquerque. The garrison of Fort Thorn retired upriver to Fort Craig, which was now the only strong United States defense below Albuquerque. Major Lynde's surrender yielded all of southern New Mexico to the Confederacy, and along the Rio Grande opened the way to objectives of immense, perhaps decisive, importance to the whole Southern cause.

For the Rio Grande invasion was not merely a matter of subduing a handful of earthen towns along a drought-parched river, and of converting a primitive, scattered population of Indians and Mexicans to a belief in states rights, and ownership of certain human beings by certain others. It was a matter of gaining a pathway to vast lands and resources whose possession—so argued Southern strategists—might actually tip the scales in the struggle for power between the South and the North. These were the gold fields of Colorado and California, the mountain west running to the Pacific from Denver through Salt Lake City, the ports of California, all of Arizona and New Mexico, and even—either by conquest or purchase—Chihuahua, Sonora and Baja California. Such a huge acquisition would give the Confederacy a transcontinental scope with world outlets in two seas; and by taking in the gold fields, which Lincoln called "the life-blood of our financial credit," it would go far toward crippling the Union's power to sustain the cost of war. The first move in such a grand design was to secure New Mexico. The river was the land vein along which that mission must be pursued.

While Baylor with his little force was opening the southern gateway, another Confederate commander was preparing a larger army to execute the grand strategy. This was Henry H. Sibley, who as a United States officer had served with the Army in the Rio Grande Valley before the war. Because of his knowledge of the river country he was commissioned brigadier general by President Jefferson Davis at Richmond and given command of the Army of New Mexico, a brigade in strength, which he undertook to raise in Texas during the summer and fall of 1861, to the number of almost thirty-five hundred men.

Colonel Canby, working at his defenses, had one thousand New Mexico militia to start with in support of his components of regular troops. He now raised five regiments of volunteers to be commanded by prominent New Mexicans, including Kit Carson, and distributed them to strengthen the garrisons. He heavily provisioned Fort Craig. He improved the defenses of Albuquerque, Santa Fe and Fort Union. And as Sibley began to move across Texas toward Fort Bliss, Canby asked Governor Gilpin of Colorado for a re-enforcement of volunteers. Their first detachment arrived, two companies strong, and joined the force downriver at Fort Craig where Canby was massing four thousand men for a campaign southward to recapture Fort Bliss. But before he could move, Sibley's brigade began to march up the river on February 7, 1862, and by the eleventh was within twenty miles of Fort Craig. The first major battle of the Civil War on the Rio Grande was shaping up, with the Confederate invaders holding the initiative.

Isolated probing actions by scouts of both armies followed, but without clashes. Late in the day of February nineteenth the main body of the Texan brigade began to draw into view across the river from Fort Craig, and by nightfall a large force was marked out by its campfires, and soldiers watching from the fort could hear voices across the water when the wind came from the east. The Confederates were camped on an open plain on the river's east bank opposite the fort. It was the only clear ground between black lava beds and ravines to the south and the abrupt mesa of Valverde two miles to the north, which sent the river on a wide bend toward the west. Two miles farther north, the mesa ended at another open plain with easy banks at each side of the river, where russet reeds clustered at the water's edge, and golden winter cottonwoods stood in groves. On the west side were fields where Fort Craig soldiers grew feed for their horses, and the place—once the site of Fort Conrad—was now called the Hay Camp.

Canby at Craig expected an attack upon his strong position, perhaps a siege. But when on the twentieth he could see that the enemy supply train, a mile and a half away across the river, was moving north, he concluded that Sibley was about to by-pass him, taking his way around the mesa's eastern end. Canby ordered an attack. His troops forded the river and came up the opposite shore toward the Confederate camp in the face of rifle and cannon fire. Unable to advance or find compact cover on the mild slopes of the open plain, the Union troops scattered to cling to isolated positions. There they spent the night, and returned across the river to the fort at dawn of the following day. By then the Texans had moved in strength to the upriver side of the mesa. Canby provisioned his men and hurried them off to the Hay Camp. When they reached it, they saw the Texans on the open land north of the mesa, and fired on them. The battle of Valverde was opened at nine o'clock in the morning, to last all day.

It was a hot winter day, with a strong wind blowing that hauled long shifts of dust, and tore away smoke from the muzzles of cannon, rifles and shotguns—for the Texans carried many of these. The Union forces charged through the river in strength early in the fight, and met a terrible fire that killed many in midstream whose bodies floated away in the gentle current of winter's low water. Artillery duels continued across the river until the Union cannon were dragged to the east bank, where from a strong position beyond the range of Confederate small arms they drove the invaders back from the river toward sandy ridges that marked a former bed of the river. The Texans made flanking charges with cavalry, but were thrown off. Three times the Texans tried to charge from their sand hills, and each time were forced back.

After noon more Union troops were ordered across the river, including the Second Regiment of New Mexico Volunteers, five companies of which refused to obey out of fear of the furious capacities of Texans in battle. In the course of the day occurred shifts in the commands of both sides. Colonel Canby came to take personal charge of the Union troops, relieving Colonel Ben S. Roberts, and General Sibley, becoming indisposed—some said drunk—turned the Confederate command over to Colonel Tom Green, who though older by nearly twenty years since the Mier adventure, was still a spirited and original soldier.

The battle seemed a draw until late in the day, when the strongest Union battery of six guns established at the northern end of the battleground was charged first by cavalry, and then in a fury of daring ordered by Tom Green, by the whole Texan force that had been pinned down most of the day in the sand hills. The charge was tremendous, and the fighting for eight minutes "was terrific beyond description." But the Union battery was inadequately supported; and all its officers and men were killed at their guns. It was the turning point. Seeing their crack battery taken, the Union forces broke toward the river, "more like a herd of frightened mustangs than men." Many more were slaughtered in making the ford. The rest were hastily formed once they reached the west bank. The Confederates gathered a cavalry force to charge after them and complete the victory, but before it could ride through the river, a truce party came from Canby's command asking for a cease-fire to permit burial of the dead and care of the wounded. It was granted. Under its protection, then, Canby's army hurried south to Fort Craig in entire defeat, while on the field of their victory the invaders camped that night, eating luxuriously of captured "Yankee light bread and other most delicious eatables," and drinking the whiskey they found in many a Union canteen, and believing the story they heard—how the canteens of the Union battery that had fought so hard had been "tinctured with ether." The first phase of Sibley's mission to conquer the mountain West was accomplished, for with the main New Mexican forces disposed of at least for the time being, he could now turn his back on them, march north to the chief cities of the territory and prepare to take its last major garrison at Fort Union.

On the very night of his defeat, Canby sent orders by courier to the northern posts announcing Sibley's victory, and giving orders that all public property, "and particularly provisions," were to be destroyed if necessary to keep them from falling into the hands of the invaders. So it was that Sibley, coming into sight of Albuquerque a few days later, saw three great columns of smoke standing above the town, and knew that a rich depot of supplies had been burned in anticipation of his arrival—and his need. "If it could have been possible for us to have hindered this," said a Texan soldier, "the Confederate Army of New Mexico would never have experienced any inconvenience for the want of clothing or commissaries." The Union quartermaster officer who gave the order to burn all public property in Albuquerque at half-past six on the morning of March second said that all was destroyed but supplies of "molasses, vinegar, soap and candles, and a few saddles, carpenter's tools, and office furniture." Most of these were pilfered by New Mexican residents. The Union garrison fled to Santa Fe, and Sibley's men took Albuquerque unopposed.

From Santa Fe a Union inspector-general sent a gloomy report to General Halleck at St. Louis. ". . . It is needless to say that this country is in a critical condition. The militia have all run away and the New Mexican volunteers are deserting in large numbers. No dependence whatever can be placed on the natives; they are worse than worthless; they are really aids to the enemy, who catch them, take their arms and tell them to go home." It had not been possible in one generation to erase the effects of the long periods of Spanish and Mexican rule when poverty and corruption had denied the people any proper lessons in self-defense. But help was coming. Another "force of Colorado volunteers is already on the way to assist us," added the inspector, "and they may possibly arrive in time to save us from immediate danger." The Federal troops at Santa Fe were too few to defend the capital; once again Army property went up in smoke, and the garrison pulled out for Fort Union.

There on March tenth the First Colorado arrived in tearing spirits after a brilliant march through heavy winter. The Colorado volunteers were mostly recruits from the frontier mining towns. They had come West to make their fortunes, and now they had marched South to earn their fame. They drilled and trained for two weeks at Fort Union, where the territory's last defenses stood. Colonel Canby, still immobilized downriver at Fort Craig, had sent orders that a supreme effort must be made to hold Fort Union. If it went, the whole territory went, and Colorado would be next. Meanwhile, the seat of New Mexican government had been moved to Las Vegas, and between March sixteenth and twenty-fourth three Texan regiments moved into Santa Fe. Other Texan forces were based at Galisteo twenty miles to the south. "We felt like heroes," wrote a Texan soldier to his wife, telling how his army had swept past Fort Craig leaving it cut off from its supply source in northern New Mexico. "We marched up the country with the fixed determination to wrench this country from the United States government. . . ." Fort Union was the great prize to be taken next. The Texan was confident. Fort Union, he said, "was ours already; and then New Mexico would belong to the new government of the South, and it would then be so easy to cut off all communication with California. . . ." A Texan picket of six hundred men left Santa Fe on March twenty-second to stand guard at the entrance to Apache Canyon. Las Vegas lay beyond, and Fort Union. Soon the main body of Texans would join the camp at the mouth of the canyon, and the sweep to the northeast would continue.

But on March twenty-sixth in the afternoon the Confederate picket heard that a small force—"200 Mexicans and about 200 regulars" from Fort Union—was coming through the canyon on its way to attack Santa Fe. It sounded like folly, and it constituted a nuisance to be brushed off as lightly as possible. The Texan camp sprang to arms and taking two field guns marched up the canyon to meet and dispose of the foolhardy Union troops. Four miles up the canyon they saw the Federal column coming at the double time, and opened fire. The trotting column halted and the Texans went about forming into proper battle line. But before they could manage this, every expectation was upset, for the Federal infantry "were upon the hills on both sides of us," wrote the Texan to his wife, "shooting us down like sheep." In the rocky trough of the canyon the Texans retreated, and their attackers pressed along above them—"they could be seen on the mountains jumping from rock to rock like so many mountain sheep." Time and again the Texans retired to new positions and delivered fearful fire. Nothing could stop their enemies. How could this be, wondered the Texans; when had New Mexicans ever fought like this? But they soon discovered whom they were facing. "Instead of Mexicans and regulars, they were *regular demons,* upon whom iron and lead had no effect, in the shape of Pike's Peakers, from the Denver City gold mines. . . ." Falling back beyond a deep arroyo near the canyon's entrance, the Texans made a last stand. Surely there they would be safe—but a company of Union cavalry came flying down to the arroyo, jumped it, and with drawn sabres and revolvers and in incredible immunity won the battle. The Texan picket surrendered, losing seventy-one prisoners, while the rest fled toward the rear.

Two days later, on the twenty-eighth, the battle was renewed, now between the main bodies of the two armies. The Confederates moved up from Galisteo into the canyon, and met the Federal forces who were much augmented by reinforcements from Fort Union, between the slopes of Glorieta Pass. The fight in the Pass surged through the day without decided advantage to either side. From high ground amid red rocks the batteries exchanged their salvos, and dismounted soldiers fought among clumps of cedar and mountain oak on the gritty slopes. The contest looked like a draw—until the Texan commander received word late in the day of a disaster that had overtaken him in his rear, at the west end of the canyon. There a Federal force under Major John M. Chivington, a Colorado preacher, had come by a hidden march behind hills above the canyon to fall upon the Confederate supply train of eighty-five wagons and nearly six hundred horses and mules which had been left lightly guarded. Charging down on the supply camp, Chivington and three hundred men of the First Colorado captured the guards, burned the wagons with all their contents, and bayonetted all the animals. News of this calamity came to the Confederate commander in the canyon during an armistice he had requested in order to bury his dead and attend to his wounded. The battle was adjourned until noon of the following day. It was never resumed, for without his supply, the Texan colonel knew he could not sustain his forces for another engagement. He led them away to Santa Fe. Word of his defeat went to General

Sibley, who was still at Albuquerque. The losses in the two phases of the battle cost the Confederates about three hundred and fifty killed, wounded and captured; the Union forces, about one hundred and fifty.

The Coloradoans were eager to press on after the retreating Texans and wipe them out; but direct orders had come from Colonel Canby to retire to Fort Union and keep it "at all hazards, and to leave nothing to chance." He feared an attack on the fort from the East, if a Confederate force was still available to move out of the Rio Grande valley and up the eastern plains of New Mexico. Further, he was himself once again in the field, for he was able to leave Fort Craig on April first to overtake Sibley at Albuquerque. There were now assembled the remnants of the Texan brigade. Santa Fe was once again free. On April eighth Canby arrived before Albuquerque, exchanged artillery salvos with Sibley, and then retired to the Sandía Mountains to await reinforcements from Fort Union.

Sibley looked upon his own situation. His artillery ammunition was gone. He ordered his brass fieldpieces buried. His supply train was destroyed, and could be replaced only by capturing another from the Union forces. But they were now victorious, thanks to the First Colorado, and could hold on to their wagons and animals. The countryside was too poor to offer the invading army subsistence for a long campaign, such as had for its purpose the capture of the whole mountain and desert West. He was not the military governor of a conquered territory whose resources he could wring dry at will. He was the leader of a now hungry, tired and ragged army. On April twelfth he ordered a retreat to begin. His main body crossed the river at Albuquerque and went down the west bank to Los Lunas. During the next day the remainder straggled down the east bank and camped at Los Pinos, the ranch of Henry Connelly, then Governor of New Mexico. The ranch stood at Peralta, almost opposite to Los Lunas. On the same day Canby's reinforcements arrived, and on the next, he marched to pursue the retreating Texans, whom he overtook at Peralta on the fifteenth, and engaged in a skirmish before nightfall. "As we galloped across the bottom towards them they fluttered like birds in a snare," wrote a Colorado volunteer. During the night the Texans forded the river, and came up with their main body on the west side. They left behind them their sick and wounded "without attendance, without medicine, and almost without food."

For the next several days the retreat continued on the west bank, while the pursuit paralleled it on the east bank. Both armies were within cannon shot of each other, but no battles followed. Union troops wondered why Colonel Canby did not cross the river and destroy Sibley's Texans once and for all. Was it because Canby was Sibley's brother-in-law? Or was Canby content to save his own men, and let the earth do his work for him? For Sibley, without resources, was crossing some of the hardest country in the river kingdom, where back of the narrow valley benches there lay nothing but desert. To shake his pursuers Sibley turned, after a few days, into even harder lands. He left the river terraces and detoured westward into the San Mateo Mountains. Lost to sight, he continued southward then until he arrived at Fort Bliss, where before sending his broken forces home across the western wastes of Texas he composed his impressions.

Reporting to the Confederate government at Richmond, he was convinced "that, except for its geographical position, the Territory of New Mexico is not worth a quarter of the blood and treasure expended in its conquest"—forgetting how in that very geographical position rested the whole hope of the Confederate design for empire, now lost. Able to ignore the very purpose of his mission, he went on to cite further exasperations. In New Mexico, "the indispensable element, food, cannot be relied on. During the last year, and pending recent operations, hundreds of thousands of sheep have been driven off by the Navajo Indians. Indeed, such were the complaints of the people in this respect that I had determined, as good policy, to encourage private enterprises against that tribe and the Apaches, and"—he was a consistent Confederate—"and to legalize the enslaving of them." In the face of the record, he managed to sound like a conqueror. "We have beaten the enemy in every encounter and against large odds. . . ." In the act of retreating, he thought it wise to smother any hopes for a return to New Mexico. ". . . I cannot speak encouragingly for the future, my troops, having manifested a dogged, irreconcilable detestation of the country and the people. . . ."

On May fourteenth, at James Magoffin's, he assembled his troops and took leave of them. He told them what they had been through, he congratulated them upon "the successes which have crowned their arms . . . in the short but brilliant campaign." He listed their engagements. "The boasted valor of Texans has been fully vindicated, Valverde, Glorieta, Albuquerque, Peralta, and last, though not least, your successful and almost unprecedented evacuation, through mountain passes and over a trackless waste of a hundred miles through a famishing country, will be duly chronicled, and form one of the brightest pages in the history of the Second American Revolution. . . ." It was a commander's valedictory in the style of the Mexicans he so despised, for it referred to everything but his total defeat. In early summer of 1862 the Texans were gone, Colonel Baylor's Confederate Territory of Arizona was undone, the threat against the whole Federal Far West was lifted, and the Civil War, so far as it concerned the Rio Grande in New Mexico, was over.

33.

The Desolate

But not every problem that had come with it. "The whole country was a theater of desolation," wrote a newly arrived officer of what he saw in the summer of 1862. "What the Confederates failed to appropriate, the Apaches destroyed. The inhabitants were literally starving and utterly demoralized." He came to the river at Mesilla in August, 1862, with Brigadier General James H. Carleton's column of troops ordered from California to reinforce New Mexico against the Texans. When they arrived the Texans had departed, and New Mexico was struggling with her old internal enemies, the roving tribes—and extreme hardship complicated by a ten-year drought. As the California Column came to take the ford at Mesilla they found that the river was so empty that they "crossed the river-bed on foot, dry-shod."

Plenty of stories about the river's exhaustion were heard during the 1850s. At El Paso people dug holes nine feet deep in the dry bed in order to tap a little groundwater for domestic uses. Herds of goats and sheep were driven up from Presidio del Norte to El Paso in the river bed which when dry made a fine path. Once when the river was revived by a little runoff a few miles above the Pass, residents on the Mexican side diverted all the flow to their fields and orchards. The people of Franklin on the American side "raised the question as to their right." The matter was "compromised" through a division of the waters between the users in both nations. In the winter of 1855 the river "disappeared

about 25 miles above Las Cruces (about San Diego Crossing) sunk in
the sand and did not appear again until it reached the . . . fall about
3 miles above El Paso." Here was the same curious concept as that held
by the Spaniards in 1541, when one of Coronado's officers reported
that the lower New Mexico river "disappeared underground like the
Guadiana in Estremadura . . . while farther on it reappeared as a large
stream." But there was no flowing subterranean passage; only an exhaustion of surface flow, and a lowered level of groundwater unable to seep
above to make channel water. Here and there in such an interrupted
passage the people might find deep holes or pools where quantities of fish
gathered to survive; and they fished for these all they liked. But fish out
of a few pools could not sustain the population, and Carleton's troopers
found that "instead of being able to furnish us supplies, we were compelled to afford them occasional assistance." Luckily the Californians
had been well-provisioned by their commander with rations that included
pemmican, which they hated, and they were "consequently in a condition
to be independent until such protection could be granted as would
induce the resident population to re-commence farming operations."

For if there were no Confederates to fight, Carleton soon found
that his well-trained soldiers would have plenty to do to control Indian
raiders. He made a rapid reconnaissance of the Pass country, and then
hastened to Santa Fe to become commander of New Mexico, relieving
Canby who departed for the East and the star of a brigadier. Carleton,
with the support of Governor Connelly, soon resolved under martial
law to throw every resource of the Territory into controlling the Indians.
For the first time in New Mexico they were to be confined on a reservation. The site chosen by Carleton was on the Pecos River in southeastern
New Mexico, where a cottonwood grove sixteen miles long and half a
mile wide at its widest bordered the red, muddy stream. A fort was
constructed and named after General Edwin V. Sumner, and there first
the Mescalero Apaches and later the Navajos were gathered and guarded.
There were no Mexican or American settlements anywhere near the
Bosque Redondo, as the reservation was called after its grove that
curved along the Pecos. The Indians were encouraged to raise their food
now instead of steal it. They took glumly to such a life. To the Army
all Indians looked alike—but the Apaches and Navajos were hereditary
enemies, and combining them on a single reservation caused extra problems of supervision. They were dispirited. When the Apaches had finally
surrendered to Carleton their leader told him, ". . . We are worn-out; we
have no more heart; we have no provisions, no means to live; your troops

are everywhere. . . . Do with us as may seem good to you, but do not forget that we are men and braves." It was an affecting speech, but soldiers remembered how relentless and how clever the Apaches had been for generations in their thieving. "These Indians are a decided institution in New Mexico," noted a trooper, "they seldom kill their tenants the Mexicans. It would be bad policy. Dead men raise no stock. . . ." As for Navajos, soldiers concluded that in addition to their terrible warfare the Navajos could claim a curious distinction. "Persons who speak the Welsh language find no difficulty in understanding them and being under-stood by them. . . ." It seemed obvious to soldiers that Navajos were descended from Welsh families who long before had been cast away on the Texas Gulf Coast.

The Apaches in their hundreds and the Navajos in their thou-sands suffered from cold and hunger at the Bosque Redondo. General Carleton inspected Fort Sumner and found they were not raising enough food for themselves, and ordered full government rations to be made available to them. Further, he organized a cattle drive to bring stock animals to the reservation. The first movement of its kind under Amer-ican administration, it was the forerunner of the cattle trail industry of New Mexico. One member of the inspecting party with General Carleton was Juan B. Lamy, first bishop of Santa Fe. He reviewed the misfortunes of the Indians, and of these the one he felt able to relieve was the lack of education for their children, of whom there were nearly three thousand at the Bosque Redondo. The Bishop offered to find teachers for them. It was the best hope for the future, as he always felt. But though the Army authorities might agree with him in general, they made nothing of his offer.

The Fort Sumner experiment lasted for five years. It was aban-doned because of many difficulties. The two tribes could not learn to live in harmony at close quarters. Their hardships were discouraging. They were not pastoral people who took naturally to farming. Govern-ment policy in Washington knew little of the realities that had led to the captivity of the Indians, and saw only its effect upon them as inhumane. When first the Apaches and later the Navajos broke out of the reservation, they were allowed to return to their old lands. The Apaches were to make trouble for many more years; but the Navajos were for the most part pacified. Going west across the rivers, they were exiles coming home, and one old man among them said, "When we saw the top of the mountain from Albuquerque we wondered if it was our mountain, and we felt like talking to the ground, we loved it so. . . ."

The interlude had its value. Farming and ranching, the settling of towns, greater safety in travel, had opportunity to develop. Further, Carleton, a stern administrator of martial law, put down disturbing elements in the civil population. For during the years before the Civil War, and after its suppression in New Mexico and Arizona, the territories had been "cursed by the presence of two or three hundred of the most infamous scoundrels it is possible to conceive. Innocent and unoffending men," said one of Carleton's captains, "were shot down or bowie-knived merely for the pleasure of witnessing their death agonies. Men walked the streets and public squares with double-barrelled shotguns, and hunted each other as sportsmen hunt for game. . . . Since Carleton's occupation of those Territories with his California Column, a great change for the better has taken place, and this melioration promises to gain ground. . . ."

34.
Confederate Border

Private inspiration was also the cause of much public disorder and suffering on the Texas river in the years that bracketted the Civil War—but with a difference from the pattern of trouble in New Mexico. Along the Texas Rio Grande it was organized into bands of outlaw Mexicans (sometimes allied with Indians) that killed ranchers and travellers, destroyed property, and stole stock animals. Chased by United States and Mexican authorities, they were seldom inconvenienced by both governments at the same time, and to escape had only to cross the river in either direction, depending upon which nation pursued them at the moment. Sanctuary always lay over the river. When the law pursuing a criminal asked "Where is he?" the famous answer on the lower Rio Grande was always, "al otro lado—on the other side." The design of pursuit and escape, with repeated tales of boldness, quick wits and inventive cruelty, led to a confused tradition among the people. Through long experience as connoisseurs of border butchery, they came to glorify the more expert criminals who made victims of their kind. When out of the welter of torture, murder, burning and theft there emerged an occasional Mexican virtuoso of remorseless savagery, he was celebrated in folk songs, for mingled with the terror which greeted his sudden appearances was a sigh of admiration. His type, with few variations, was the reigning folk hero along the boundary river for a century.

One such who played his character about the river towns of Mier, Roma, Reynosa and Camargo in the early 1860s was Abram García. As it was his whim always to ride a white horse, he was known as the White Cavalier. He and his band of followers were as handsome as they were brave, and as vain as they were cruel. They rode superb horses, saddled in gear that flashed with silver and gold mountings. Their immense hats heavy with gold and silver threads threw capes of shadow over their upper bodies and in the shadow flashed brilliant eyes and dazzling teeth. Their short jackets and tight trousers were made of velvet or the thinnest buckskins, loaded with silver buttons and bullion lace. They bristled with weapons. It was their convention to affect an elaborate courtesy of manner while hot with lust they reduced their victims to an animal state, and in the process gave pain. The White Cavalier enjoyed causing men to dance or have their feet shot off. When they had danced enough, he saw that they were stripped and beaten until almost, or—what could it possibly matter?—or in fact, dead. Then taking their horses, money, merchandise, or other portable possessions he spurred his mount till it bled and with marvellous grace vanished in a cloud of dust.

An even more ambitious example of the type was Juan Nepomuceno Cortina who beginning as a private murderer, later, like Canales and Carvajal, sometimes took whole towns and even provinces for his game. His title in the folk convention of his time was "Red Robber of the Rio Grande." In 1859 he captured Brownsville after a battle and in the following year he was pursued by Lieutenant Colonel Robert E. Lee, who was then still an officer of the United States Army on duty in Texas. He eluded Colonel Lee, who was restricted in his efforts by international policy governing the penetration of United States troops into Mexico. After another year Cortina made a brilliant reappearance on the Rio Grande to burn the little river town of Roma. It was his specialty to posture as the defender of Mexicans in Texas, which gave a spurious dignity to his passion for destruction. His career was to know strange periods of official sanction, when after revolutionizing Tamaulipas he became its governor, and when under President Juárez, and the later republic, he was to serve as a general officer. For fifteen years or more he was intermittently the scourge of the lower river—and he became the subject of a ballad that would survive to commemorate him.

The two governments at the river, with whatever help from orderly American and Mexican citizens, could not overcome the outrages of Indian and bandit raiding parties. It was the Confederate state of Texas that controlled the troubles better than any earlier authority. In 1861 a regiment of cavalry was raised by Texas to patrol the border. Its troopers rode the main routes of travel to police Indian trails and keep constant watch on the towns. They kept outlaws from coming in organized bands over the river from Mexico; and they searched for travellers crossing south out of Texas who were escaping from the conscription of Texans for armed service, or who were deserting the Confederate Army, or who were Northern sympathizers seeking refuge. In the early period of the war there was a large traffic of such people for whom the river was a boundary beyond which lay freedom. Doing their duty, the troopers of the Texas cavalry captured many of them. A further duty of the regiment was to keep order on the Confederacy's only international border outlet to world trade; for cotton from Texas was marketed across the Rio Grande in immense quantities.

From 1861 to the end of the war, the Texas Gulf ports were blockaded by the United States Navy. The West Gulf Squadron—commanded from 1862 to 1864 by Admiral David Farragut—patrolled the ancient Spanish kingdom of Florida from Pensacola to the Rio Grande. Confederate blockade-running ships sailed between north Mexico ports, including Bagdad and Matamoros at the mouth of the Rio Grande, and Atlantic ports of transshipment in the West Indies. The blockade-runners were built for invisibility and speed. With long slender hulls they sat low in the water displacing about five hundred tons. They were powered by steam and propelled by side paddle wheels. Their raked funnels were built with telescopic joints so they could be lowered to escape sighting. Their boilers were stoked with hard coal to show as little smoke as possible. Over their foredecks was a turtle-back shield to throw off heavy seas, and they were painted sea-gray to escape notice by day. Running the blockade by night they showed no lights, and blew off steam through underwater exhausts. Eastbound they carried cotton for the Europe trade, and westbound they brought crucial war materials such as lead, mercury, sulphur, and woven goods. If they passed the Gulf

Squadron safely, they were free to use the Rio Grande ports of Bagdad and Matamoros quite openly; for as Mexico was neutral her ports, under a convention honored by the United States Supreme Court, could not be directly blockaded. Even vessels destined for Matamoros, if captured by the Union squadron, had to be released to proceed on their way—though in at least one such case the war contraband cargo was seized.

In 1862 the Confederates held Brownsville, which meant that cotton shipments could be most conveniently made across the river there. Shallow draft steamers of many foreign nations came direct to the docks of Matamoros. Larger ships anchored in the Gulf off Bagdad and their cargoes were landed by lighter to be carried up the riverbanks to the Matamoros customs house, and transshipped into Texas. The southernmost Rio Grande towns became the greatest cotton markets in the world. Cotton was sold at fifty cents a pound, or more, in gold. Once again Matamoros experienced sudden growth, now to a population of thirty-five thousand, until she became Mexico's most important doorway to North America. In 1863 there was suddenly a prospect that through Matamoros the Confederate States might receive new and substantial support for their cause.

For the French were in Mexico. Since 1861 French troops had been arriving in increasing strength—at first with the support of Spain and Great Britain who soon withdrew—for the purpose of establishing a Mexican government that would pay up Mexico's huge and defaulted foreign indebtedness. Struggling to maintain his revolutionary regime, Benito Juárez worked to settle national economic problems without foreign intervention, and resisted the French. It was soon apparent that the fortunes of France in Mexico were linked with those of the Confederate States of America. If the South were successful, and if in her success she should receive aid from French Mexico, then the Monroe Doctrine would be nullified by the natural alliance that would follow. Once again there would be European power in the western hemisphere. The United States while honoring the neutrality of Mexico, recognized the Juárez government and opposed the French invasion. But occupied by the Civil War, Washington could spare no resources for active intervention. Resistance to the French had to be made within the strategic limits of the war at home. These, extending everywhere in the states, included Texas and the border; and there, in November, 1863, a force of six thousand Union troops under General Banks arrived from the Gulf to capture Brownsville. Fort Brown and the river shore and the old sea meadows all the way to Point Isabel were once again occupied

by an army. Its first purpose was to take part in the large-scale Federal
invasion of Texas from her two borders, by way of the Red River and
the Rio Grande—a scheme that was never executed. Its next move was
to discourage by its presence any effort of the French—who now had
almost forty thousand troops in Mexico—to reinforce the Confederacy
through Matamoros. No French troops threatened Matamoros during
the Union occupation of Brownsville.

The occupation interrupted the cotton trade out of Brownsville.
Cotton was now hauled overland from San Antonio warehouses to Eagle
Pass far upriver, where remained the only Mexican port of entry above
Matamoros. Confederate troops, in garrison at Fort Duncan, preserved
the secessionist authority of the town, though out of eighty-three votes
cast there in the Texas election on secession, eighty went for the Union.
Those loyal to the United States fled to Piedras Negras across the river,
and were joined by others from elsewhere in Texas, and all knew every
trouble of exile. Few of them could speak Spanish. All found it hard to
get jobs. Many who tried to return over the river on their way to the
United States were captured, and some were hanged.

Immense cotton shipments were crossed from Eagle Pass to Piedras
Negras. A founding citizen of Eagle Pass saw in 1864 how at one time
"the whole river bottom from the bank of the river to the edge of town
was covered with cotton." It was a fine volume of business for the Mexican customs officers, who took an export duty from the Confederacy of
one bale for each bale passed through the port. From Piedras Negras
the cotton was transported by road down the Mexican side of the river
to Matamoros or Bagdad, where the ocean-going ships waited.

In the summer of 1864 the affairs of Mexico touched toward the
border river with increased energy. On June twelfth the Archduke
Maximilian of Austria arrived in Mexico to ascend the throne as emperor. The French troops that armed his régime—for he was the candidate of Napoleon III for the crown of Mexico—pressed closer to the
border and forced Juárez to transfer his roving government to the
extreme north, at El Paso on the Mexican bank. In July the Union forces
at Brownsville were withdrawn and only a small garrison was left to
hold Point Isabel and the Arms of St. James. The Juárez forces held
Matamoros, where Cortina, in one of his periods of official respectability,
was the commanding general under the republic. He was, extraordinarily,
now tacitly an ally of the United States, in opposition to the Confederate
garrison that moved into Fort Brown when the Federal forces left it.

Late in the summer a French army of five thousand men landed at Bagdad and marched inland to take Matamoros from the republic. General Cortina led three thousand men and sixteen cannon down the river to meet them, drove them back to the sea, and then turned to defeat a Confederate force from Brownsville that had supported the French by attacking his rear guard. On the ninth he captured Brownsville, ran up the United States flag, and offered the city to the Union commander at Point Isabel, who with his troops was unable to accept it. Presently General Cortina was off on other campaigns in northern Mexico, the Confederates were back in Fort Brown, the Emperor Maximilian's power was established at Matamoros under General Mejía, whom the river populace knew of old, and the spring of 1865 saw the Confederacy fall into ruin. As Lee surrendered on April ninth at Appomattox, the Confederate Trans-Mississippi Department consisting of Arkansas, Louisiana and Texas, continued to resist. It was not until May sixth that the three states were surrendered. But even after that, on May thirteenth, Confederate troops from Fort Brown and Union troops from Point Isabel met in battle near Taylor's plain of Palo Alto. The Confederates forced the Union detachment to retreat, but could not break their line, and when evening fell overland from the Gulf the engagement ended— and with it all Civil War hostilities on the Texas river.

35.

The Second Mexican Empire

There remained under the command of General Kirby Smith a large Confederate army in Texas to be surrendered or captured. On May seventeenth, at Washington, one Rio Grande veteran issued orders to another for the final pacification of Texas. Lieutenant General U. S. Grant, the quartermaster-officer with Taylor in 1846, wrote to Major General Philip H. Sheridan, who had served at Fort Duncan as a lieutenant in 1854, to "proceed without delay to the West to . . . restore

Texas, and that part of Louisiana held by the enemy, to the Union. . . ." Sheridan was to "place a strong force on the Rio Grande, holding it at least to a point opposite Camargo, and above that if"—the supreme commander well remembered the river country—"if supplies can be procured. . . . I think," he added, "the Rio Grande should be strongly held, whether the forces in Texas surrender or not, and that no time should be lost in getting troops there. If war is to be made, they will be in the right place; if Kirby Smith surrenders, they will be on the line which is to be strongly garrisoned. . . ."

Was it odd that even after all resistance in Texas was ended there should still be a need there for a great army? Grant mentioned the Fourth Corps, the Twenty-fifth Corps, and thirty-seven thousand other troops as available to occupy Texas and hold the Rio Grande. General Sheridan hastened to see him and soon heard him speak of what could not be written in orders. The United States still maintained official neutrality toward France and her invasion of Mexico, while actually holding every sympathy for Juárez and his republic. It was to show great potential strength in support of the Juárez army that the river line was to be held in force by United States troops. "As a matter of fact," wrote General Sheridan later, General Grant said that he "looked upon the invasion of Mexico by Maximilian as a part of the rebellion itself, and that our success in putting down secession would never be complete until the French and Austrian invaders were compelled to quit the territory of our sister republic." Grant cautioned Sheridan "to act with great circumspection, since the Secretary of State, Mr. Seward, was much opposed to the use of our troops along the border in any active way that would be likely to involve us in a war with European powers."

Sheridan left at once for Texas by way of New Orleans. Near the mouth of the Red River he heard from Edward R. S. Canby—now a major general—that General Kirby Smith had surrendered to him on May 26, 1865, under terms like those offered to Lee, by which the defeated officers might take home with them their animals, side arms and possessions, to apply them to the needs of peace. With that act, Sheridan's second, and unofficial, mission became his first. He hurried on to Brownsville, arriving June first, to animate his river command with every scheme short of battle to harass Imperial Mexico. The task was well within his grasp as an able professional. "That bold dragoon," he was called by a New Yorker who once entertained him at dinner. His host saw him as "a stumpy, quadrangular little man, with a forehead of no promise and hair so short that it looked like a coat of black paint. But his eye and his mouth shew force" and "his talk is pleasant. . . ." This diarist saw him as "a brilliant practitioner" in military affairs, and—a connoisseur in his mountainous antiquity—General Scott said of Sheridan's battles in 1864 against Early that they were "among the *most finished* affairs of this war. . . ."

Once at the river, Sheridan saw that if he was to supply a great army along its valley he must do better than haul supplies by wagon and mule over the Point Isabel flats. There was no railroad anywhere on the Rio Grande. He immediately began to build the first one—a narrow-gauge line running from Point Isabel to Brownsville, that used wood-burning locomotives with extravagant cowcatchers and commodious wooden cabs. He soon heard disagreeable news. General Kirby Smith's command, though surrendered, was making an effort to remain intact, with the object of fleeing to Mexico to serve under the Emperor. Sheridan sent troops in force up the river to "make demonstrations" that would discourage the Confederates from crossing. Already they had delivered to General Mejía in Matamoros a supply of munitions. Sheridan sternly demanded the return of these. He saw a perfect pretext for invasion if Mejía refused. He was not alone in his sense of a possible war against the Emperor. The Eastern papers were saying that Napoleon III was about to send heavy reinforcements to Mexico, and readers noted that the United States would have a hundred thousand troops on the Rio Grande to oppose him, and war seemed "clearly in the cards" to an observant civilian who had served in Lincoln's administration. He thought it not entirely undesirable. Like all intelligent and sympathetic citizens, he was grieved by what the war had done to the nation. Was there a cure waiting at the Rio Grande? "Six months," he mused, "six months of campaigning by Virginians and Mississippians and Texans, shoulder to shoulder with New Englanders and Westerners . . . might be wonderfully reconstructive in its effect and reunite our fractured young national bones faster than any other treatment could possibly do. . . ."

Still the Secretary of State refused to sanction direct intervention at the border, even though after General Sheridan's "demonstrations" the French everywhere in northern Mexico, demoralized and agitated, seemed about to withdraw to the south. But General Mejía delivered up the Confederate munitions, and "a golden opportunity was lost," as Sheridan said, "for we had ample excuse for crossing the boundary." Encouraged once again by Seward's policy, the Emperor, said General Sheridan, "gained in strength till finally all the accessible sections of

Mexico were in his possession, and the Republic under President Juárez almost succumbed."

The General admitted to "growing impatient at this," and decided to "try again what virtue there might be in a hostile demonstration." First he reviewed the Fourth Corps at San Antonio in September as though to prepare "with some ostentation for a campaign," and then "escorted by a regiment of horse" he dashed to Fort Duncan at Eagle Pass on the river. He hadn't been there since he was a lieutenant fighting Lipans, hunting for turkey, geese, deer and antelope, and observing the bird life of the valley. Now he made contact with agents of Juárez in Piedras Negras, "taking care not to do this in the dark," and in a day or two all north Mexico was convinced that the American general was only awaiting the arrival of a great force of troops to cross the river and fight for Juárez and the Republic. The results were most promising. The Emperor's army abandoned all of north Mexico as far south as Monterrey. The only imperial garrison was the handful left at Matamoros with Mejía, and they were confined there by "that unknown quantity" General Cortina, who harassed the town so that none dared venture out of it. Republican troops were collected at Camargo, Mier and other river towns.

The moment was ripe for a crushing blow at the Empire—but once again the State Department, after protests from the French Ambassador, ordered "a strict neutrality," and Sheridan was obliged to stay on his side of the river.

He could only spend his energies on lesser excitements than invasion. He put down a colonization scheme organized by ex-Confederate personages who had been promised titles of nobility, land grants and the comforts of a new system of peonage by the Emperor if they would migrate to join him. He worked to compose the rivalries of General Cortina and General Canales who while fighting for the Republic "were freebooters enough to take a shy at each other frequently," and to unite them in a single command he recruited General Carvajal to come from Washington. But Carvajal, "the old wretch," was quickly unseated by Canales, and efforts at harmony failed. Matamoros was again in the hands of the Republic. General Sheridan sent frequent shipments of munitions "by the most secret methods" to the Juárez forces—in one shipment there were thirty thousand muskets—and by midsummer of 1866 the republican armies held the entire Mexican Rio Grande, and "in fact," wrote General Sheridan, "nearly the whole of Mexico down to San Luis Potosí."

Such news changed policy at the Tuileries in the following winter. Napoleon III cabled to his commander in Mexico—Sheridan saw a copy of the cable—to withdraw French troops under Maximilian. The message was sent at the very time when at Saint-Cloud the despairing Empress of Mexico was beseeching the French Emperor to send more aid to her doomed husband. By February, 1867, all French soldiers in Mexico were gone, some having embarked from Matamoros for the voyage home. Through the spring Maximilian fought his last battles until at Querétaro in June he was taken prisoner and the Empire was lost.

When the news of his capture reached the river, a ball was given in the Customs House at Piedras Negras to which "all the foreigners in Eagle Pass were invited . . . together with all the best people in that part of the country." The next word that came was spread there by a Mexican colonel who coming to the river from the interior told how the Emperor had been condemned to death, and how after his sentence the people of Mexico felt great sympathy for him. In Mexico City—had they heard this at the river?—five hundred ladies dressed in mourning marched in procession to present a petition for clemency to the authorities. It was denied. On the morning of June nineteenth everybody went up the hill at Querétaro—the Colonel had been there and had seen it all—to watch the Emperor as he was brought out by platoons of soldiers. When the Emperor and the two generals who were to die with him—one was Mejía—were lined up facing the firing squad "Maximilian advanced and presented each of the firing party with a gold doubloon, with the request that they would take good aim until he gave them the signal to fire by removing his hand from his breast. After resuming his position he eulogized his generals and resigned to them the honor of dying first. After they fell he calmly confronted the death that awaited him and met it with a fearlessness that became him. . . ." The news shocked the world, and a New Yorker made the wry comment that Juárez's Liberal party ". . . could hardly be expected to depart from the settled practice of all Mexican administrations in their hour of victory. . . ."

If there were few battles, or even skirmishes, on the Texas Rio Grande in the Civil War, its final phase was its most important one. General Sheridan observed, "At the close of our war there was little hope for the Republic of Mexico. Indeed, till our troops were concentrated on the Rio Grande there was none. Our appearance in such force along the border permitted the Liberal leaders, refugees from their homes, to establish rendezvous whence they could promulgate their plans in safety, while the countenance thus given the cause, when hope was well-nigh gone, incited the Mexican people to renewed resistance. Beginning again with very scant means, for they had lost about all, the Liberals saw their cause, under the influence of such significant and powerful backing, progress and steadily grow so strong that within two years Imperialism had received its death-blow. I doubt," concluded the General with satisfaction, "I doubt very much whether such results could have been achieved without the presence of an American army on the Rio Grande, which, be it remembered, was sent there because, in General Grant's words, the French invasion of Mexico was so closely related to the rebellion as to be essentially a part of it."

In the Civil War campaign of the New Mexico Rio Grande the Rocky Mountain and Pacific West was saved for the Union; while the Federal occupation of the Texan Rio Grande helped to sustain the Monroe Doctrine and Mexican autonomy. Soon the United States troops were pulled away from the river in great numbers, with only small garrisons left in the river forts; and across the way in Mexico, those who had fought the Empire returned to their prewar occupations. Among them was General Cortina, who with refreshed vigor resumed his career of raider and destroyer in and out of Texas.

Of all Western problems remaining after the Civil War the greatest one was that of the unpacified Indians. It loomed in menace behind every growing expression of civilized life in the river empire, where it was estimated that the Comanches, the Apaches, the Navajos, and the Lipans with their allies totalled eighty thousand. But as early as 1866 there was promise of a solution—of sorts—for it appeared that "the government in Washington," as a New Mexican churchman noted, was "contemplating a plan, which if carried out with prudence and humanity" would lead to the conversion of the Indians, "particularly of their children. . . ." Under the power and need of the whole nation in its westward reach the freedom of the Indians was about to be lost. Its last expressions glared the more brightly and terribly for the twilight that gathered to close over the long Indian day.

36.

The Mexico Moon

To the old Spanish question, "What is an Indian?", the Americans found various answers, depending upon their nearness to frontier experience. The Washington government, farthest away, when appealed to time and again for help, either replied, like Madrid or Mexico City in their periods of sovereignty, that local troops must suppress the savages, or sent Congressional commissions to investigate rumors of Indian outrages. One such commission, sitting in Texas in 1873, summoned any who had complaints, and many responded. "Several of these men," stated the executive document of the hearing, "while appearing before the commission to record their losses by Indian raids, were called away by the news of fresh attacks upon their residences and property. . . ." So at the very instant when unwieldy government at last was listening, though not yet acting, the human reality and trial of the people was dramatically proved. It was important that this was so, for removed far from the scenes of depredation, the government at times seemed skeptical of the alarms and supplications it heard so often from the West. The whole problem was confusing, for not all Indians were murderous aggressors—the Pueblos of the Rio Grande abided in peace, and their governors each held an ebony cane headed with silver that had been bestowed as symbols of authority in 1863, bearing the engraved name of the bestower: "A. Lincoln Pres. U.S."

But the others, the nomads? What hope was there for peace with them? Commissioner Emory in the 'fifties said they had "but two settled principles of action—to kill the defenceless and avoid collision with a superior or equal force." Some reformers proposed a gentle approach, in Quaker courage and passivity, on the grounds that the Indian hardly knew right from wrong, and could not be held responsible, really, for what he did not consider criminal. An Indian fighter of long experience bitterly disposed of such a view, to his own satisfaction, anyway.

"It is all very well to argue that the Indian knows no better," he wrote of the Apache, "that he merely possesses the teachings of his race, that his cruelties are the results of untaught savage disposition, etc.; but . . . is it true policy that intelligent, christian people should be sacrificed, year after year, and their massacres excused on the ground that the murderers were only Indians? . . . Must we forever continue to accept the wild and impracticable theories of parlor readers on Indian character? Can we continue to pay millions annually for the short-sighted and pernicious policy which has heretofore"—he was writing in 1867—"regulated our Indian affairs?" As for the old question about the Indian nature, he had a grim and certain answer. "The American savage is no idiot. He knows right from wrong, and is quite as cognizant of the fact when he commits a wrong as the most instructed of our race. If the reader should feel a particle of doubt on this point, all he has to do is to commit a wrong upon an Apache, and he will very soon become convinced that the savage is quite as much aware of the fact as he can be. . . . The capacity to discriminate between right and wrong is not the exclusive property of christianized people. . . ." The Apache understood his own acts. What he misjudged was their effect on the white man. "When an Apache mutilates the dead body of his enemy, he knows that he is doing a wrong and cowardly act; but he persists in doing it, because he judges us from his stand-point, and imagines that sight of the muti-lated corpse will produce terror in the beholders"—a mistake. The Indian "has not arrived at that amount of information which would instruct him that disgust and anger, with a determination for redress at the earliest opportunity, are engendered instead of dread. Like the rest of mankind, he is apt to measure other people's corn by his own bushel."

Many observers conceded that the Indian had his provocations to resist the white man. The earliest settlers broke promises made to him, and later on a great scale so did the government. As the frontiersmen were individualists by necessity, they made their own first laws, and destruction of an Indian was hardly treated as a crime. If there had ever been a time to handle the Indian with Quaker gentleness—and after all this had a simple resemblance to the Franciscan touch upon the Indian—that time was at the very first contacts with the Indian plains-men. But it was now too late for a policy of trustful brotherhood. When one after another the governors of Texas were refused substantial in-creases of the Army garrisons along the river, Texas recruited three battalions of rangers and did what she could to patrol the river plains above Laredo where the Indians came and went on their terrible business against American settlers above the left bank and Mexican on both.

There was nothing new in the warfare now pursued by the Indian—except its scale. Where in the Spanish and Mexican periods Apaches, Comanches, Lipans, had all been famous for raids, these were occasional strikes against a few obvious settlements scattered in a great empire largely Indian in its ownership. But after the Civil War every continental gesture, every new reach for natural wealth of the United States drove the Indians a whole nation at a time from their accustomed haunts, and Indian nations in solid though not co-ordinated response swarmed out on the offensive as their world was contracted about them. Exploitation of gold discoveries in the Rocky Mountain territories drove them from some of their best hunting grounds. Buffalo drives on the prairies forced them southwest toward the river, and so did the thrust of railroads across the land, followed by new American towns. Cattle trails cut across the ancient Indian paths and interrupted their free travel. The essential nature of the Plains Indian life—movement—was in jeopardy. To a Comanche warrior who said, "I know every stream and every wood between the Rio Grande and the Arkansas," the American expansion plainly meant the death of his nation as he had known it. Everywhere in the whole immense region of the arid lands of North America, of which the central vein was the Rio Grande for nearly two thousand miles, the Indian atrocities rose to a new intensity.

Indians out of Mexico raged over the river into Texas, and Indians from the plains crossed in the other direction. From Arizona on the west and from Texas on the east Indians descended upon New Mexico. Ten thousand horses a year were stolen from the north Mexican frontier, and cattle stolen in Texas were driven to New Mexico to be traded along the pastoral river. Comanches and Apaches fought each other for their spoils. Mexican wagoners if captured might be tied upside-down to their own wagon wheels with their heads a foot off the ground, where small fires were built to boil their brains until they burst from their skulls. A red and yellow American coach lettered "Butterfield Overland Dispatch" above windows that gave a glimpse of an interior lined with pink brocade and biscuit-tufted leather seats might be over-taken in its journey, and its occupants turned out to die, and its animals stolen, and the coach itself burned. Children—especially boys—were stolen, and both boys and girls were beaten and otherwise abused, and if they cried were killed, and a surprising number survived to grow up as tribesmen. Women, American and Mexican, were taken away into concubinage and slavery. Adult white men were killed rather than captured. The dead were dishonored by mutilations that hideously mocked their reduction to final impotence. If destroying Indians rarely entered the center of a remote town, they were bold and brilliant about striking at its loose ends where streets faded into open country, and stealing, killing, burning and vanishing all in a moment. At Eagle Pass when an avenging party rode out in pursuit, its men gave "the Terrible Texas," which was "a concert of sounds before entering an Indian fight accompanied by volleys of pistol shots. . . ." A man, knowing there were Indians about, once whistled to keep up his spirits, and a friend hearing him remarked that "there was no tune to his music," and did not blame him. In the American river towns where Indians struck there was bitter feeling toward the Mexican authorities on the other side, who sometimes did less than their share to take and punish the raiders. Citizens riding out after escaping raiders might see nothing of them but a line of smokes standing across the plains at intervals as signals to show other Indians where rode success and safety.

It was the Comanches who in the beginning had brought captured wild horses from the Spanish lands to the plains, and they remained the leading nation in the swift, always shifting warfare against the growing power of the Americans. As constant enemies they became familiar to the settlers, who saw them not only with rage and fear but also with a sense of wonder at many details of their mysterious life.

Their visions were like the weather over mountain and plain, their laws came from the creature powers of the earth. Needing assurance or protection from life beyond himself, an Indian plainsman went alone into the open land to undertake an ordeal of thirst, hunger or other suffering, that would bring him a vision. When he was worthy, it came to him as another man who spoke to him, giving him a song for his own, or a sacred ritual. He was both prostrated and exalted when the vision on leaving took animal form so that he would know what creature had blessed him, and whose feathers or fur or bone he must ever after keep by him as sacred protection. When an Indian drew pictures of what he knew, he left out some things it would be dangerous to set down, for in itself a drawing could exert wicked power. To the white strangers, some of the daily realities of the Indians seemed poetic—the very name of the largest division of the Comanche nation, the one that ranged about the river, was "the Honey-Eaters."

From the horse they took their style. Dismounted they were awkward and sluggish, but the moment they were on a horse they showed every ease and grace, as if they took lordship from the animal who was lord of the prairies. Comanche children learned to ride early. The warrior would never ride a mare. Maleness was superior, and any expression of its attributes enhanced his own. War chiefs each owned great bands of horses, by the hundreds. Even apart from what they would bring in trade, these represented wealth and splendor—and yet more, they carried in them their master's essence; for when he broke a wild mustang, the Comanche roped and threw it, and then made it his in another way. He put his mouth to its nostrils and exhaled his breath into them and, with it, his controlling spirit.

In September every year the Honey-Eaters in great numbers went to the Rio Grande and deep into Mexico to take horses. Then the heat of full summer was waning, and the rains were over so that no marks of travel would be left in mud for pursuers to follow, and the nights were fragrant and clear, and the grass was still succulent before winter. Because of where they went, and when, they called the month of September the Mexico Moon.

The raid was carefully organized. It began with ceremony—dances and songs and tales in honor of war, around a great fire, at night. Of the men, only the warriors going on the raid took active part. Each had a woman to dance with him. Leaving the firelight some vanished into the trembling shadows to make love, while men too old to accompany the raid told of their great days and struck drums for emphasis. The raid leader was absolute in his command. He said where they would go, who would be the scouts, who would do the camp work, where they would camp. Gathering his lieutenants, he mapped for them on the bare ground the trails they would take, and designated natural features, and showed the distance and time to be passed between halts. He knew the spaces, the trees, the water, the canyons, the mesas they would pass; and where in Mexico were the best animals and women and children ripe for taking. Preparations were soon completed—often in a single night; and at dawn the party moved south. It included enough women to perform the usual menial services—pitching and striking the tepees, gathering fuel, dressing or undressing the horses with their riding blankets.

Comanche women were short-haired. Their dress was voluminous, exposing only face and hands. On their long tunics they embroidered designs of flowers or animals in colored porcupine quills. When travelling exposed to sun and wind they covered their faces with red ochre. It seemed their only vanity, for they spent little attention on clothes or ornaments. It was their men who took trouble over appearance. They made themselves magnificent in every possible way. Their hair was braided in two queues that hung to their thighs, and studded with silver discs graduated in size as the queue narrowed, or interwoven with bright cloth strips or scraps of fur. Earrings of silver, gold, shell or bone hung from their pierced lobes. Soft, wonderfully tanned buckskins provided their long shirts, and the tight leggings that reached from foot to waist, and the breechclout drawn through the belt front and back. A wide strip was left where the buckskins were seamed, and this was sometimes cut into long fringes and tipped with silver or bead ornaments. Well-cut moccasins, a buffalo robe or a blanket from New Mexico, a cap of swept-back feathers finished the dress. The Comanche man had many suits of such a costume—so many that he kept a particular bag to carry them in. For special occasions he painted himself—black for war, and otherwise bright reds, blues, yellows and white, in any designs that pleased him. The general effect was so grand and so careful that an American traveller said of the men in a Comanche encampment that he had "never seen as much foppery displayed in our cities," and concluded that the "adjustment of toilet must occupy several hours of each day." Some of the young lords even "carried umbrellas to protect them from the sun."

Superbly mounted, they used cured sheepskins or pieces of buffalo hides to ride on, and their bridles were made of rawhide. They were armed with bows made of bois d'arc, metal-tipped arrows, ash-wood lances, shields of stiffened buffalo hide edged with turkey feathers, a flint-stone battle-axe, and sometimes with rifles, bowie knives and machetes.

In camp their tepees rose and fell as if by magic—the women were expert at handling the long poles and skins with which the shelters were made. The tepee seemed like a great garment, as it were, drawn about the shoulders of a seated Indian giant. In the evening on the trail when the leader lighted his sacred pipe all his aides smoked it with him. They ate game taken during the day's travel, or if none was to be had, they killed a horse and cooked it. They drank from a water bag made of a buffalo paunch, or a whole antelope skin. To obtain a great delicacy they cut the udder of a cow or goat and sucked the mixed blood and milk. Their active life and diet of lean meat kept most of the warriors slender, though there was one Comanche chief so fat that he could not heave himself upon any of his fifteen hundred horses, and was obliged to travel sitting on a travois.

Scouts journeyed a day ahead of the main war party. They would select the site for a temporary base camp from which the actual raid would be sprung, and the attack would be timed to come at night during or just after the full moon. The upper Comanche Trail to Mexico was a famous thoroughfare. To a resident of the lands it crossed it seemed in the nineteenth century like "a great chalk line on the map of West Texas from the Llano Estacado to the Rio Grande." Nearing the river, it forked westward to cross about forty miles below the junta de los rios, where the Conchos entered the Rio Grande; and it forked again to cross the river about thirty miles farther east. There was a garrison at Presidio del Norte near the junta. Both forks were well to the southeast of it. Going into Mexico, the warriors took the western fork. Returning they took the eastern. Their objectives were ranches, farms, villages, mines in northern Mexico, even as far as Durango.

When September came, the Mexico Moon, the residents of the river lands took their annual precautions. Sentinels were sent out to stations on the highest peaks and crags of the western approaches to the Big Bend. There they set up piles of brush and faggot to light as signal fires when the time came. They stood guard night after night as the moon rose later and fuller, until in its fall of turquoise light the whole fantasy of the rocky night seemed visible in sharpest detail and distance. Mountains were clear on the horizon, and declivities of the earth far away were like shadows, and even the colors of rock—yellow, rose, purple —were discernible in the calm shower of moonlight.

And then one night, far across the land, a pinpoint of rosy light would show like a fallen star burning on the ground; and near it another, and another, in the order of campfires; and the farthest sentinels on their cold platforms would know that they saw what they were watching for—the advance elements of the Honey-Eaters. Striking life to their fire high in the sky they gave the signal that was awaited by watchers on the next height, who in turn lighted their wood; and soon the news was taken south all the way to the river by the chain of watch-fires, telling men and women on their scattered ranches to gather their children and their animals and go to the river villages for protection.

In another day and a night came the rustling and glittering front of the war party, standing forth in the pour of the moon. Progressing amidst pointed rocks they bristled with gleaming points of their own, and passing over dry ground crusty with mica they winked and flashed with their silver jewels. The land they crossed was banded with every color, and so were their painted faces and breasts, their arms and bellies. If mystery was suspended in the very landscape of the Big Bend, it also clung around their spirits; and as they contended with a land of the utmost hardness, hardness hung like conviction in their hearts. In oddly stirring ways they seemed like direct expressions of the fantastic lands where they roved.

They approached the river whose sandy slopes were made of powdered mountains. There they would camp; water the horses; smoke and rest and ignore the poor settlements upriver and down, at least on the southerly journey, for they were after greater spoils than those huddled about the darkened jacales and earthen huts near-by. At day-break they would cross over the Rio Grande and be on their way, together a living embodiment of the land they called their own.

It would not long be theirs.

In 1867, either by treaty, or by direct order of the President of the United States, the Plains Indian nations were limited to reserved lands. The borderland tribes were assigned to the Indian Territory, to share it with the Five Civilized Tribes who had been moved there in President Jackson's time. Land was to be held by the tribe rather than owned by the individual, until 1887 when an act of Congress opened the way for individual Indians to hold title to property.

The "Peace Policy" of the government, with its negotiation of treaties as between two sovereignties, was not wholly a success. Indian leaders were eloquent in opposing the idea of reservation lands. "The world was made for all to live in," said a Kickapoo chief to a govern-ment commission, and ". . . the white man has no right to encroach on the hunting grounds of the red man, and has no right to cut the land up into little squares. . . ." A Comanche statesman declared, "My people have never first drawn a bow or fired a gun against the whites. . . . It was you who sent out the first soldier and we who sent out the second." So much for the past. As for the future, he said to the American com-missioners, ". . . You wanted to put us upon a reservation, to build us houses and make us medicine lodges. I do not want them. I was born upon the prairie, where the wind blew free . . . and everything drew a free breath . . . we only wish to wander on the prairie until we die. . . ."

Government gave the Peace Policy a chance to work. But the Indians could not observe the terms of treaties voluntarily, and raids and strife continued when war parties broke away from their reserva-tions. In 1871 the Congress took the Indians into legal custody as wards of the nation. They were to be supported by the government, with their affairs administered by Indian agents. The system had its failures. "What," demanded an officer long experienced in Indian warfare, "what can a political camp-follower, who has done party service in our cities, and been appointed Indian Agent as reward for such service, possibly know of Indian character?" Again the Indian met bad faith on the part of his conquerors. If he was a great enemy the white man had made him so, thought many of those who had borne the battle against him in the realities of the frontier. And—national policy was sometimes incredible— if the Indian was corrupt and slow to throw off his dangerous ways, then again it seemed clear that he had been greatly tempted: when the government announced that a ransom of one hundred dollars would be paid for the return of each white captive held by Indians, the Indians, becoming used to the value of money, were only induced to arrange for more captives. It would take two decades for the forcible pacification of the Indians to be successful. In the same period, an intermittent war of depredations was laid down over the river lands from Laredo to the Gulf, not by Indians, but by white men, of Mexico and Texas.

37.

Bad Men and Good

The Indian terrors represented an effort by a whole society, in the full power of its sanctions, to carry out an essentially conservative mission. Indians in trying to save their empire and their ancient ways were not outlaws. On the contrary, they were obeying their own laws to the utmost. It was the American and Mexican bandits of the river lands who broke the laws, even of their own countries. Their mission was one of private lawless gain, and in the crazy desperation of the vicious acts of a leader and his band lay an expression of human character adrift from its natural foundations of society and nationality. After the period of relative calm during the Civil War on the border, river outlaws came back to dominate the country with more violence than ever. Some of them were lost to society as a result of the war—men who came to the river owning nothing, and reflecting the spiritual displacement from which great sectors of the nation had to recover. Some were Texans embittered by the hardships and indignities of reconstruction within their own state. Others were children of adventure who had to be nourished on excitement at no matter whose expense of property and life. All these came in such numbers that in 1877 the Texas government published a list of five thousand "men wanted in Texas" by the law.

From the Gulf to Laredo; in the passes of the Big Bend; over the river at El Paso; in the Mesilla Valley of New Mexico the outlaws worked. They were gamblers, smugglers, stealers of horses and cattle, and all too often murderers, some of whom in a suspension of moral values came to be admired as the ablest of their vocation. One of these was William Bonney, called Billy the Kid, with his succession of dazzling murders, brilliant escapes from jail, and languid insolence in the face of the law. Of many a domineering outcast it was often said on the border river, "He's killed several men and no telling how many Mexicans. . . ."—for his victims were often those who lived over the river.

These retaliated in kind, in a spirit illustrated by the remark of a Mexican at Matamoros: "Shoot the first gringo who comes over here and tries to look at a hide." Depositions by the hundreds made before government commissions testified to the volume and fury of raids by Mexican marauders on the Texas side of the river. "Throughout the valley of the Rio Grande," declared an Army report of 1875, "and for a hundred and forty miles back from it, crops and herds have been abandoned; people dared not travel except in armed parties; civil law outside of the towns was suspended, and sheriffs and judges reported . . . that it was unsafe to attempt to execute processes of law outside of the towns, unless the officers of the law were accompanied by soldiers to protect them. . . ." A United States customs official at Edinburgh, Texas, wrote to General E. O. C. Ord, commanding the Department of Texas, ". . . We, the Americans living in this county, live all the time in dread. It has become so common for the bandits to cross the river and murder Americans, that we think it is only a question of time as to ourselves."

Overland traders were attacked and robbed—one lost "over four thousand in gold" near Mier—and the horses, cattle and lives of ranchers were taken by thieves who struck and raced for the Mexican bank, where lay complete sanctuary. "In an area of fifteen thousand square miles," said a deponent, "from the Nueces to the Rio Grande, and from San Antonio to the Devil's River, they have stolen nearly all the stock at different times and taken it to Mexico, selling it there, with the knowledge and sufferance of the local authorities. . . ." A Mexican army captain who was seen on his side of the river driving a herd of four hundred stolen cattle remarked, like an Apache speaking of New Mexican farmers, "The gringos are raising cows for me." Mexican bandits sometimes went disguised as Indians. The mayors of Mexican river towns admitted that the trade in stolen cattle was immense, with the average price of five dollars a head paid by buyers in Mexico. The illicit trade found complete protection in a "Free Zone" officially established by Mexico along her entire northern border, from the Pacific to the Atlantic Gulf. The limits of the Zone were loosely defined. Its purpose was to grant relief from customs fees to northern Mexicans, but its freedom was taken to grant immunity to any fugitive from Texas, against whom the local Mexican authorities refused to move if he were in the *Zona Libre*.

Volunteer parties of American ranchers went to the river in pursuit of their lost animals, and some ransomed them for three dollars apiece. If such a bargain could not be struck, they might resort to battle at fords where cattle trails crossed the river. The Mexican federal government stationed two or three companies of troops on the river, ostensibly to control bandit parties. They were a poor lot, and a Texas militia captain told Congress, "The Mexican cavalry is very indifferently armed and mounted. The men are armed with all sorts of guns. I believe they all wear a uniform cap, but they wear hardly anything else; they are shamefully naked." Even under such an able officer as General Falcón, the miserable troopers were unable to succeed in their mission.

If raiders were deterred by the American military escorts that accompanied a commission from Washington on a tour of the river lands, it was only briefly, for no sooner had the commission closed its hearings and returned to Congress than "an increase in the number of raids occurred," with the cattle thieves more furious than ever "in bitterness and determination." General Ord found a parallel in history for the conditions that so incensed border Americans. "It seems to me that the circumstances of the plunder of the stock ranches on the Rio Grande are almost identical with the piracies committed on our commerce at one time by the Algerines, who fled in safety to their own ports with their prizes. There the offenses were committed on the open sea; here they are committed with the same ease on the open plain. In both cases the pirates found a ready sale for their captures in the ports where their expeditions were fitted out, namely, Algiers and Tripoli, &c, for the Moors; Matamoros, Reynosa, Camargo, Mier and Guerrero for the Mexicans. And in both cases the pirates were rewarded by promotions and honors." Sure of their power, the desert pirates hardly bothered to hide. An Army officer going upstream as a steamboat passenger in 1876 said that his vessel passed right through a herd of stolen cattle "that the Mexicans were driving across the river. Part of the cattle were on one side of the river and part on the other, and the Mexicans were stripped, and had the saddles off their horses, and were in the river driving the cattle across."

When Americans on the border hoped for war against Mexico to force an end to the outrages, they considered how the cure might be worse than the ill; for the Mexican side was far more populous than the Texan side, and, said a Texan witness before Congress, "We are not so foolish but that we know that a war with Mexico, unless premeditated and our Government fully prepared for it, would result in the immediate occupation by Mexicans, for a time at least, of all that country bordering on the river, and would, consequently, involve the loss of the larger part of our stock and the destruction of all our property." Certainly the Army was not "fully prepared" for war on the border in 1876, when out of his Departmental troops General Ord could assign only four hundred to the Rio Grande, of which only three hundred were cavalry. It was all he had to work with, though in the previous year he had asked for a regiment of cavalry "for service on the lower river, and, if practicable, a light-draught iron clad" to be sent to Point Isabel by the Navy "provided with a sufficient number of steam-launches to patrol the river Rio Grande." He was sure that the vessels would be even better than a regiment "to stop the marauding." Cruising launches "could show continually where parties had recently crossed into American territory, or might be crossing, and as the telegraph" was "being laid on the banks, cavalry stationed along the river (an exceedingly crooked one) could get notice to the point and take the trail. . . ." The river's own action made the task of patrolling hard and the pursuit difficult, for in flood or freshet the river chopped away banks, and destroyed roads and trails, and in the lower flats inundated great tracts with mud, so that troops were forced to keep to the high ground. Further, as the river changed its course after storm, it also changed the boundary, so that soldiers were not always certain where they might act on their own ground.

On both sides of the river the "bad man" ruled. If he was a Mexican, he was, at his most impressive, a "general," like Cortina or Canales, both of whom were busy at the congenial task of combining theft with revolutionary gestures, and with fighting each other. If he was an

American, he was typically an unreconstructed Civil War veteran, or a displaced outcast of Eastern American cities who displayed to exaggeration the frontier trait of extreme individualism that once had mastered a continental wilderness, and now remained to terrorize it. There was much in his nature—even as it was misdirected—that was typical of the pioneer settler in the river wilderness. "Well," said a rancher who joined a volunteer band to invade Mexico illegally in hazardous pursuit of cattle thieves, "we loved living more than we loved life." And, he noted, the American bad man "got no mail." In such a detail there was a glimpse of how the bad man was divided from society and personal ties.

Every activity was affected by violence in an atmosphere where it so often prevailed. Elections in American river towns were signals for riot, destruction and even "little wars," as a peace officer said, and—revealing something of the river frontier character—he added that they gave him, a "hot-blooded youngster . . . a thrill that was hard to beat."

Political violence had an international setting. The 1870s saw many revolutionary movements organized by Mexicans conspiring in American river towns—Las Cruces, El Paso, Ysleta, Laredo, Brownsville. In 1874 the frontier was occupied with the revival of the old Rio Grande revolution of the north, that sought once again to create the Republic of the Sierra Madre. Twelve north Mexico governors signed a declaration of independence, and for a year the desert republic again struggled to be born, while the central government sent a few troops, and Canales and Cortina fought them as well as one another, and an American Army observer noted that in his opinion Mexico City would "undoubtedly be glad to get rid of most of the territory, which yields nothing but pronunciamentos and revolutions," and would "promptly accede to what it will be plain it cannot prevent."

But again, after its repeated apparitions throughout thirty years, the desert glimmer of a new nation faded away, and a year later, at Brownsville and Piedras Negras another pattern of revolution took form under Porfirio Díaz, which opened with the capture of Matamoros and flared all across Mexico to success at the capital. A merchant upriver at El Paso said, "Everything is quiet here," though he was certain that the Díaz revolution in Mexico would "kill business there and probably make it bad here. Our business in Paso del Norte, Mexico, will be levied for taxes in advance," and he knew these would have to be paid again at the regular taxation period. "Politics," he sighed, "furnishes the excuse for the revolutions in Mexico, but the real purpose of the revolution is robbery and the enrichment of new elements. . . ."

Meanwhile, the larger affairs of Mexico left the frontier north to its own impulses. Early in 1877 Cortina threatened new raids over the river into lower Texas, and to discourage him, the United States gunboat *Rio Bravo* was moored to the riverbank opposite Matamoros. She could not patrol upriver waters because she took too deep a draft except in floodtime. The vessel knew a further disadvantage—her captain was a drunkard, and his removal was advised by General Ord. But if the Army could proceed against an indiscreet naval officer, it could do little against the Mexican raids that continued unchecked along the river. Lieutenant General Philip H. Sheridan, commanding the Military Division of the Missouri, that embraced the Southwest all the way to the border, knew why: American troops were without authority to cross the border and on Mexican territory overtake and punish the raiders. "As I have heretofore had occasions to observe," he wrote to the Adjutant General in May, 1877, "the Rio Grande is a very long and difficult frontier to protect." Under the circumstances, all he could recommend was that Washington "take some steps to require the Mexican government to aid in the protection of that frontier."

Three weeks later a vigorous solution was at last ordered by President Rutherford Hayes, at whose direction the Secretary of War told General William T. Sherman, commanding the Army, "You will . . . direct General Ord that in case the lawless incursions continue he will be at liberty . . . when in pursuit of the marauders and when his troops are either in sight of them or upon a fresh trail, to follow them across the Rio Grande, and to overtake and punish them, as well as retake stolen property taken from our citizens and found in their hands on the Mexican side of the line." The President, "while anxious to avoid giving offense to Mexico," was "nevertheless convinced that the invasion of our territory by armed and organized bodies of thieves and robbers to prey upon our citizens should not be longer endured."

The presidential order brought furious objection from Mexico. Her foreign office declared—with some justice—that raids came as often from Texas into Mexico as the other way round. About El Paso in the early summer months of 1877 still another revolution against Mexico had been organized by Lerdo de Tejada, whose troop commander, Colonel Macharro, gathered an army in the great natural fortress of the Hueco Tanks, where spring lakes were walled in by sheer castellated rocks. In his forces were many Texans. Again it was difficult to know who of the confused border population were the aggressors—Texans or Mexicans. United States troops were sent from New Mexico by Colonel

Edward Hatch "with the intention of breaking up" the revolutionists
who organized on American soil. But Macharro succeeded in taking the
Mexican El Paso, though he held it only briefly. "One of the 7 day
revolutions ended last night," wrote a young German storekeeper to his
family in Europe in early June, 1877. He resisted the revolutionists
throughout, even when they threatened to jail him for refusing to contribute a hundred dollars to their funds. His protection lay in the power
and prestige of the United States. "I fastened the U. S. consul's shield
above the door which was sufficient notice to them that they had to
respect the American flag. . . ." His gesture gained power from the sudden
tension that had developed between Mexico and the United States during
that summer. Rio Grande Mexicans were at last face to face with the
realities of their northern boundary. For nearly thirty years after the
Treaty of Guadalupe Hidalgo, and forty after the Texan revolution,
they continued to view the lands divided by the river as one grand unit—
from the Sierra Madre to the Nueces, and from the Conchos to the
Pecos—and to treat them as such. Old loyalties, old joys, old spirits of
strife and brio made the official boundary seem insignificant. Blood,
language, mores were stronger than law, nationality, and order.

But now there were strengthened powers at work to enforce the
implications of the boundary concept. One was the policy of the Hayes
administration. Another was the enlarged and resourceful operations of
the Texas Rangers. And another was the effort—Mexico's first real one—
by Porfirio Díaz to keep the peace on the border by armed force. It was
General Ramon Treviño, governor of Nuevo León under Díaz, who
"more than any other man below the Rio Grande," said a Texas rancher
of the period, "was responsible for quelling the *bandidos*." Still, through
the summer, American cavalry columns crossed into Mexico after raiders,
in the face of Mexican official protests.

In the border cities more was anticipated. "We have been expecting a declaration of war by the United States against Mexico all summer,"
said a citizen of El Paso in August. "If this came about it would be the
best thing that could happen and of great importance to us." In October,
he believed "war was at hand," and if it was, he had second thoughts
about it. He had been following the news of the Russian campaign in
the Caucasus against Turkish troops and their Circassian mountaineer
allies, and if war came in Mexico, he wondered how professional American soldiers would prosper. "It is not at all improbable that the
Americans will fare as the Russians are now doing. The more one de-
spises one's enemy," he remarked with an eye open on an occasional

American attitude toward Latin neighbors, "the greater the danger of being defeated. It is very difficult and dangerous to invade a country that has no railroads, no roads, no bridges and very little water. On the other hand it is ideal country for guerrilla warfare. The Mexican has lots of endurance. He can take long trips and hard marches with only corn and sugar for food. If the American soldier does not have his rations of bacon, coffee and sugar for a couple of days he easily becomes exhausted. . . ." But by mid-November the war sentiment was much abated, and he saw it for what it was. "The demand for war in many of the American newspapers and especially in Texas is caused by speculators who want to make fortunes furnishing war supplies. The freedom of the press is abused and many of the papers pay no attention as to whether they print the truth or not. . . ."

In the autumn of 1877 a disturbance arose in the El Paso region that set in motion all the opposed powers of border loyalties. Eastward of El Paso about a hundred and ten miles lay a group of saline lakes from which Mexicans of both sides of the river had taken salt since 1863. They took it free from what they saw as a resource of nature open to all, and they hauled it in cartloads to the Rio Grande about ninety miles away to sell it to the boundary settlements. The salt trade became the livelihood of several river villages. In 1866 and in 1873 attempts were made by Texans to file legal claim to the lakes, but their claims were not valid, and it was not until 1877 that other Texas interests acquired a legal right to the saline deposits. The new owners at once established a fixed fee to be paid by all who came to gather salt. The traders who had used the deposits as a free public commodity raised bitter complaint, and in the social climate of the time and place, the outcome inevitably was civil violence. The Mexicans—greatly in the majority—had energetic leaders, including their parish priests and an Italian settler with political gifts. Opposed to these, the Texan interests, with a stubborn and reckless representative on the spot, held grimly to their legal right to the lakes.

Every classical element of a borderland dispute was present in the situation. The affair was international. It grew up around an issue of profitable property and enterprise. It posed Texans against Mexicans, and since the Mexicans involved lived on both sides of the river, it created a "racial" issue of Anglo-Saxons against Latins. It pulled in politics and the Church, and when the dispute was laid before the courts of law, these had no immediate means to enforce the peace. On one side the Mexicans formed a mob and on the other the Americans were represented by a force of volunteer rangers. There were no Army troops in garrison at El Paso, and when a detachment came from another post, its members were under orders to maintain order—but without taking sides in a local conflict. Threats of assassination were exchanged by the factions, and presently one came true when the Texan claimant killed the Italian politician who championed the Mexicans. These, inflamed by the advices of their pastor—who was later removed by the Church for his unworthy behavior—organized their revenge in the villages downriver from El Paso, and ended by killing the Texan leader and two of his supporters, and taking most of the volunteer ranger force as prisoners.

The American El Paso feared an attack, for the Mexicans seemed to expand their discontent to include hatred of all Americans, and additional troops were called to the scene from New Mexico. When they came, under the command of Colonel Edward A. Hatch, they succeeded in preventing further organized violence—but not individual violence on the part of other Americans who came to help in putting down the troubles. Rape, robbery and murder went unpunished on the American side, and across the river Mexican lawbreakers seeking immunity found it when Mexican officials in El Paso del Norte refused to bring them to justice. A United States Army commission arrived to make an investigation for President Hayes. The re-establishment of Fort Bliss at El Paso on the American bank resulted. For the rest, after nearly six months of uproar, bloodshed and suffering, the troubled residents of the El Paso valley once again knew comparative quiet, and the very cause of the Salt War was accepted, under superior force, by the people whom it had inflamed. Now when they went with their cottonwood carts over their ninety-mile desert trail to procure salt, they paid for every load after all.

Some of the Americans who had hurried to El Paso during the height of the troubles to fight Mexicans looked elsewhere for a release of their compelling energies, and found it in New Mexico, where the Lincoln County War was developing between rival cattle interests. It continued with such disruption of civil peace that the territorial authorities seemed unable to enforce order. In Washington General Sherman, echoing the remarks of a veteran of '46 about Texas, said, "We should have another war with Mexico to make her take back New Mexico," and General Lew Wallace, the Rio Grande veteran of Taylor's campaign, was sent to Santa Fe as territorial governor to restore the influence of law, which he managed to do only after Washington gave reluctant approval to his request for permission to use United States troops against the outlaws. In 1881 Texas Rangers were in the Big Bend to deal with bandit raiders from New Mexico, and as part of their severe duty made partial surveys of the huge, secret canyons of the river there.

Slowly, then, but inevitably, all such extensions of society in its order came to prevail over the vicious tedium of fear and destruction laid over the river frontier by the lawless. If it seemed inescapable that the successive frontiers of the American West had first to endure periods of terrorism imposed by irresponsible outcasts, it was true that at the same time, all the elements needed for organized social life made their courageous first bids in the new lands. Among the most effective of these were pioneer merchants, who came to set up their stores in the river cities of New Mexico and Texas, and by importation of goods began to link them to the great complex world of manufacture and production. Many such men were German immigrants who brought with them not only an understanding of business, but also a background of good education. One of them was a youngster who came to the towns of the North Pass in 1876. His experience was typical, and in letters sent to his relatives in Germany he shared it.

He left home to escape the militarism of the Bismarck empire. Its antithesis was the American West with its freedom. There he had relatives—earlier immigrants—for whom he was going to work. Crossing the sea he encountered new wonders—porpoises, whales, gamblers and luxury. In America as he travelled westward he met family friends and connections at New York, Chicago, St. Louis, Las Cruces. He found his journey by stagecoach from Kansas interesting but strenuous. The coaches were light and strong, with gray canvas sides and leather straps instead of iron or steel springs, which would break on the rough roads. The coach stopped three times a day for twenty minutes to let the passengers feed, and at other times, for five minutes to change mules. Otherwise the coach never stopped, day or night, but was pulled at a steady gallop, up hill or down, over good road or rocky. The passengers got no sleep. When the coach by a freak of the road was upset, which happened often, the driver did not seem to mind. Once arrived in New Mexico over the Santa Fe Trail, the passengers found the road better. It followed the river, and at Las Cruces made a junction with the highway to California, which ran through Silver City, Tucson, Yuma to San Diego, where travellers took a steamer for San Francisco. A coach ran daily from Santa Fe to El Paso, and an optimistic petition was being circulated to ask for the building of a railroad—"they are not asking much," observed the young German, "only the little stretch from St. Louis via San Antonio, Texas, [and] El Paso to San Francisco, California."

The young apprentice merchant reached El Paso—now a community on the American bank—a few days before Christmas. Ten minutes after his arrival he sat down to eat the last scrap of a sausage given to him by his mother. It had fed him all the way from Hamburg, where he cut the first piece. On Christmas Eve he was forlorn. The German tradition of Christmas meant nothing here. Mexicans observed the feast only as a religious event. For himself, he wrote, "there does not seem to be much to do about it." Looking at the valley cottonwoods he noted that their dead golden leaves were still on the branches. He hoped for letters, and asked that they be addressed to El Paso, New Mexico, instead of El Paso, Texas, in order to pass them over a shorter route to earlier delivery.

Looking about him at first he concluded that he was not likely to "make a fortune in a short time." The country was poor, the river carried very little water, and what flow there was seemed hardly enough to irrigate the farms and supply the urban needs of the eight thousand people who depended on it. There was a dam of brush and stones two miles above the town, but it was too porous to divert much of the flow, and he heard that when floods came the dam was swept away every time. He thought a new and stronger one should be built upstream. Of his fellow citizens he saw that many were "fugitives from the States." He missed his beer. Few of the Americans and Germans drank it because it was too scarce and too expensive. Whiskey and tequila were the usual beverages.

It was not long until he made friends, for he was young, energetic and personable, and through his uncle who employed him as a clerk he had a respectable introduction to society. He enthusiastically attended dances given at private houses. Beginning at nine o'clock in the evening, the dance was held in the patio whose swept earth floor was covered first with carpets and then with large tarpaulins. He was proficient in quadrilles and other dances known at home, and he learned a new one—a native dance called "la chubana." Supper was laid after midnight. Mexican gentlemen served the ladies first, standing behind their chairs until they were done. Then the men sat down to eat. The party lasted until eight o'clock in the morning. On other evenings he went calling, and stayed to play lotto and sixty-six. He thought he was doing very well at learning English, and already spoke some Spanish.

His prospects in the general mercantile business soon looked better to him. "It will not be long before I have made a fine place for myself," he wrote, even though he was not to receive any salary during his first six or twelve months. "I will try and make $100,000," he told his family grandly, "and then things will boom." The store carried nearly every class of merchandise, and he handled "everything from a corn plaster to a wig"—including dry goods, shoes, hardware, grain, feedstuffs, medicines, textiles from San Ildefonso and Chihuahua. Most women wore dresses of calico, and even in January he saw men in pants and shirts of unbleached muslin. Business had its extraordinary aspects. The prevailing interest rate was from ten or eighteen per cent annually. One day he saw a wagon train crossing out of Mexico on its way to San Antonio that carried one hundred and ninety thousand dollars' worth of coin and silver bars, and three thousand pounds of copper, some in coin, the rest in bars, for export to England. On another day he put his hand in the mail chute at the United States post office and found a snake. Wagon freighters taking goods from El Paso to Santa Fe were sometimes attacked by Indians, in spite of patrols from the recently established Army post at Fort Selden up the river. Now and then a band of freebooters swarmed into town from Mexico. One such consisted of a hundred Mexican cavalrymen. The young clerk had "never seen so many cut-throats together at one time." Even their officers knew their kind, for they confined them in billets except when accompanied by a sergeant. One night some of them broke out and stole a brass clock from a house thinking the brass was gold. When they discovered their mistake they threw the clock in bits "on the roof of the church." What odd creatures they were! "The complexion of these soldiers who come from the states of Sinaloa, Zacatecas and Durango (as well as that of some of our local inhabitants) is that of dry wood-ashes, neither black, nor brown, but grayish." The troop stayed for two days, and after damages, levies and pilferings were reckoned, would end up costing the store two hundred dollars.

The apprentice knew his family wanted to hear how he lived, and he wrote, "I am going to enumerate the members of my household, *1st* my old woman Doña Andrea who attends to my food and drink, *2nd* my porter who keeps the flies off me while I eat and is good for many things, a boy who helps in the store, 1 horse, 2 dogs, 1 rooster, 2 hens, 9 chicks and also countless bugs. . . ." He was being newly shaped by such a new life. Did he look any different? They would want to know at home. When a photographer "drifted into El Paso" he intended to have his picture taken for them, though he did not do so. But no matter how he looked, he felt different. He was becoming an American. They sent him some newspapers from Germany, full of "Your Excellencies" and "Your Highnesses," and the like. He could not help saying, "As this sort of address and cringing are not known here the whole thing makes a funny and ludicrous impression. . . ." When he was given a commission as a vice-commercial agent of the United States consulate at Paso del Norte, his family back home preened themselves and bridled proudly at his success in the new world, which had brought him an official title. To their congratulations he replied drily, "To tell the truth I do not consider being vice-commercial agent of very great importance. I look upon this honor very much like the title of an obscure book, 'Sad But True. . . .' "

His tradition was general along the Rio Grande wherever a business community was evolving out of primitive beginnings of trade in Mexican earth towns. The immigrant took his place with the American merchants and he seeded their society with memories of European styles and ways that added a degree of grace to the pursuit of gain. Such memories could have visible embodiment. At Albuquerque a successful German merchant built a Schloss on the marshy sweeps of the river bottom. It was made of adobe, wood and stone, with a central tower, and several wings, all painted white, set amidst a park of trees with fountains, arbors and meandering acequias. It contained a ballroom at one end of which was an organ with gold pipes. The castle's high narrow windows brought in dim daylight upon dark wooden panelling. There was materialized a propriety that echoed sentiment out of Schiller, and the courts of provincial Highnesses, and the dreams of Wagner; and it was all paid for by the freighting of goods over the trail from Missouri and down the river. The castle's owner watered his park with river water in summer, and in winter took his children on a sled over the river when it froze solid. He wore skates. The sled had wooden runners, and a board bed with a small chair fixed to it. He used to freight goods over the ice to the small stores and trading posts in the villages on the opposite bank below Albuquerque. A romantic castle in a river grove became possible only as civil peace began to prevail on the Rio Grande frontier.

Already the work of civilization had reached far into the wilderness of Indian savages, Mexicans and Anglo-Americans through the one institution that was able to make its benign energy felt in hacienda, pueblo and city. This was the Church in New Mexico, and in its effect upon the civil good of the whole river empire there rested an image of a man. He was the first bishop and archbishop of Santa Fe, Juan Bautista Lamy. When he came to the river in 1850 as vicar apostolic he found a sorry state of affairs. The nearest bishop had always been at Durango, fifteen hundred miles away. The Franciscans had been removed altogether. The handful of secular priests sent from Durango—there were only nine in New Mexico in 1850—were all too often dispirited and indifferent at their duties. The population lacked not only for spiritual help but also for civilizing aids in other matters. There were no schools, no hospitals, no agency to provide a sense of the future to the young in terms of their rightful growth of spirit and mind. The churches were almost all in ruins. An immense task faced the young bishop. He attacked it with a sort of grave passion, and for the rest of his life he was to see grow under his touch a revived society that found its connection with the great world.

He began his teaching at the simplest point of contact with his diocese—any point, across desert and mountain, which he could reach by going on foot or mounted on a burro or a horse. He travelled tens of thousands of miles in order to find his people and know their country. Finding and knowing these, he loved them, whether in a remote pueblo, a forgotten river town, or a mining camp. He took his knowledge of their needs to Baltimore, where the Council of American Bishops sat, and to Rome, where the Pope gave him encouragement and support, and to France, his homeland, where he enlisted scores of young priests to join him in the toil that waited in America's oldest frontier. His thoughts and deeds were woven in and out of the life of the river frontier like fine threads among coarse. He stood as a man of mind and spirit in a society of physical, often brutal, preoccupations. He represented knowledge and charity where all too often prevailed ignorance and self-interest. In opening the window of New Mexico upon the world, Archbishop Lamy expressed his own belief in freedom through enlightenment, without which her people would continue to live as victims instead of as masters of their environment. A willingness to advance the condition of man through social change was first expressed through him of all those who ever governed in the river kingdom. Such advance had been excluded by the Indians through ignorance, by the Spaniards through policy, and by the Mexicans through poverty. The Archbishop by his works seemed to anticipate the precept of a later teacher of his faith who said, "All our raw material of sanctity is in the now, just as it is."

So with the raw materials that he found he created the image of a life that had its design in the all-encompassing terms of his Christianity. His love of enlightenment came to show in the form of schools. He founded conventual academies in several cities all the way from Santa Fe to El Paso. He established a college in Santa Fe and led the citizens' support for New Mexico's first system of public education. His love of charity created the first hospital and orphanage in the Southwest, to which he gave up his own house. Where he had come to find nine poor and indifferent priests, in a few years he had over forty who strove to match his exquisite example of probity and dedication. He built eighty-five new churches, repaired the old ones and ended with almost a hundred and fifty altogether, including the cathedral of Santa Fe which he raised in the likeness of the romanesque temples of his native Auvergne. His good, clear sense of the uses of the world led him to do all he could to bring the railroad to Santa Fe and to foster the establishment of industry. He encouraged the slowly learning population to answer the call of new opportunities of work under new forms of commerce and to be provident with their honest gains.

If he loved growth for itself he revealed this faculty most simply in his garden behind the cathedral of Santa Fe. There within meandering walls he grew wonderful fruit of many varieties and planted several species of imported trees, hoping by his example to lead his fellow citizens to find joy for themselves and others in bringing shade, flower and fruit to a land so sparing of its own offerings of these.

Not the least of his personal contributions to his people was his plain, tall presence among them. When he would walk about the plaza of Santa Fe, or ride into an earthen town on a burro, or step off an afternoon train at Albuquerque, or an early morning train at Las Cruces, he seemed to lift up every heart by his encompassing smile, that so wholly changed his gaunt face and deeply shadowed eyes. He was spare and weathered like any other plainsman, the worst of whose endurances and dangers he had learned for himself. There was no other way in which he could have come to grips with the great duty of his life, and the land that embraced it.

In 1875 when he was created archbishop the whole territory celebrated the honor with him—the plain citizenry, the government, the army, men of business and industry, the students in his colleges, and the Indians in their pueblos. Upon his death in 1888 he was mourned both as a humble missionary priest and as a creative citizen who by his double example gave to the severe land that he loved its first secure sense of the values that could not fail no matter how complex the world of the future might become.

38.

The Last Wagons

And now, during the 1870s, the nation showed recovery from the effects of the Civil War. In this recovery it expressed the national genius for technology, by which, even in the unfinished West, ways of living would soon be changed as though in response to new laws of faith. The troubles of reconstruction were largely modified. The roving Indians were in process of recession. Law and order, if not entirely effective, were at least organized in frontier communities. The nation was getting on with its work. It would not be long until the Rio Grande line would begin to feel the energy of the machine in life, which would bring to the river societies their last and most pervasive change. Meanwhile, even with the old resources of animal power, there was a quickening of communication over the Rio Grande empire.

For all peoples the problem of overland travel had always been the same—the making of roads that followed the shortest, easiest way to a destination. So, from the time of the first, lonely walkers, had Indian trails been made, and so the primitive Spanish and Mexican roads, and the trade routes of the United States, and the paths of cattle drives that crossed New Mexico and Texas. Stagecoach travel continued along the river in New Mexico, and another route came from San Antonio, Texas, to cross the Rio Grande at Eagle Pass, on its way to Monterrey. In dry weather the road was good, and the trip took six days. Muddy ground prolonged the passage to seven or eight days. Seventy-two good mules were kept at post stations along the way. Six mules pulled the coach in United States territory, and eight in Mexico, where the going was harder. Moving along through a landscape dazzled with light and emptiness, the equipage maintained a steady, rapid pace, in spite of its great weight. The coach weighed three thousand pounds, its carrying capacity was four thousand pounds, and the harness of the team weighed twelve hundred pounds. The vehicle was built by Abbot, Downing and Company, of Concord, New Hampshire, and cost its Texan proprietor $1,250. It was commodious—eighteen passengers of average size could be seated "very comfortably." There were three seats inside, each with room for three people. Three more seats of the same capacity were on the roof, one close behind the driver, one in the middle, both facing forward, and one at the rear, facing backward. The coach's flat top was covered with heavy waterproof duck, and guarded on all sides by an iron railing two feet high. The body was built of the choicest hickory, and was slung on leather braces. All metalwork was of the best steel—axles, door handles, hinges, angle irons, bracings. The seats were upholstered in fine brown calfskin over horsehair and steel coil springs. At the rear was a capacious boot in which trunks and other heavy luggage were carried.

Indians presented a constant danger in the Texas part of the trip, but once at Eagle Pass, the passengers were sure of comforts; and over the river in Mexico, at the stage's overnight stops, a dance was sometimes given in honor of the travellers. The most respected people from the country around were invited. Mexican ladies came dressed in their finery, carrying French fans in little brocaded scabbards, and when the fans were opened out, they sparkled with brilliants and gold threads. At daytime stage stops in Mexico, native musicians came to serenade the passengers, for a few cents, with flutes "made of burnt clay and cane. . . ."

In the 'seventies trade over the Missouri trail to Santa Fe served chiefly to supply the New Mexican Rio Grande, while shipments for the interior of Mexico were for the most part drawn from Europe. After the two great river wars of the 'forties and 'sixties Mexican commerce turned away from the United States, until European nations held virtual monopolies. Texan freighters rarely heard English spoken in Mexico. Foreign business agents were German, French, or British, all of whom worked in the language of the country. Many cargoes from Europe were landed on the Texas coast to be freighted across Texas under bond. The wagons crossed the Rio Grande at the old ford of France Way, where the town of Guerrero now stood; or at Eagle Pass, Presidio del Norte, or El Paso. Texas freighters used huge blue wagons with beds twenty-four feet long and four and a half feet wide, with sides almost six feet high. They weighed four thousand pounds and carried a full load of seven thousand. On irregular roads they rocked steadily from side to side, until the weight was carried by two wheels at a time, which lightened the drag on their teams of mules. To control the heavy momentum of a wagon going downgrade the teamster hauled on a stout hickory brake that reached from his seat to the rear wheels. Mexican freighters used carts of cottonwood balanced on two wheels seven feet high. Their axles were of pecan or live-oak wood, and worn by rough travel, often took to making an intolerable screech. To stop the noise by lubrication, the Mexican carters fed the fat, succulent leaves of the prickly pear one at a time into the wheel housing. Such a cart carried five thousand pounds in its bed, that was fifteen feet long and six wide, with a shade cover thatched out of straw. Its cargo was equally distributed so as to balance on the single axle, and the whole was pulled by five or six span of oxen lashed to their wooden yokes by rawhide straps.

At each end of the freighting trip, whether at Matamoros or in the interior, the Texan teamsters were always astonished at the skill and strength of the little Mexicans who loaded their cargo. The cargador, who rarely weighed over a hundred and sixty pounds, conquered his burdens with ingenious means. Across his brow he wore a loop of strap that passed over his shoulders and down his back. Just between his hips it held a muelle, or pad, six inches thick, ten wide and fourteen long. It was a cushion upon which his load would rest as he bent forward, and lodged against the top swell of his buttocks it moved up and down with them in time with his steps. In that movement lay the secret of his power. About to receive his load, he turned his back to it and began to step up and down in place, like a soldier marking time. The several men who were ready to put his load upon him also took up the rhythmic step in time with his and, at a signal, gave the load on to his pad. He held the load with a steel hook in each hand, and as soon as he felt it secure, and without stopping his light, rapid steps he trotted off with it. The cargador was able to carry a load of five hundred pounds or more, so long as he received it in motion and never halted until he was relieved of it. A Texan freighter who never ceased marvelling at the little brown figures in white cotton, pumping their legs up and down under their tremendous burdens, said he "never saw one of them use the least exertion."

Taking European goods from the Gulf to upriver crossings, Texan freighters sometimes found themselves halted on the American shore by north Mexican revolutions on the other side. Then there was nothing to do but wait until the little war was over. After such an experience, one wagon master entered Mexico, delivered his cargo, and returned with three hundred and fifty thousand dollars in Mexican silver and forty thousand pounds of copper, addressed to Europe. To protect his train he engaged a Mexican officer with thirty men for a thousand dollars to escort him to the border. For his round trip which took him back to the seaports of the Gulf, the freighter earned $17,500. Young, hardy and adventurous, he found the freight-trail life not only profitable but enjoyable, for in camp every night, the freighting company, whenever possible, held a dance after supper. They "laid several wagon sheets on the ground inside the corral made by the surrounding wagons." On the tall wagon wheels they stuck lighted candles. If they were near a town, Mexican musicians came with stringed instruments to play, and otherwise, teamsters made music with what they might have—a violin, a banjo, bones, and hands to clap. The wagon sheets "on the level, hard ground furnished a splendid surface for the dancers," who enjoyed themselves "to the utmost." They danced all night, until the train corporal drove in the herd to be hitched at daybreak. Whenever possible they invited guests from ranches in the open country, and "after breakfast in camp, 'the best people' returned through the wilderness to their homes. . . .", and the freight train rolled and pitched slowly off on its way on the great flat lands through which the river ran. As they went, they encountered other long movements of men and animals in the open territory—herds of cattle and bands of horsemen who represented the largest and most characteristic industry of the nineteenth century on the Texas Rio Grande, and the last of the forms of life peculiar to the West.

39.
The Last Frontiersman

Ever since the eighteenth century the raising and tending of large herds of beef cattle had been practiced on the Texas river's wide, flat borderlands. All descended from animals brought to Mexico in the sixteenth century by Spaniards, there were several types of cattle on the river plains, of which the most distinctive had tremendously long horns doubled up and backward for half their length; heavy thin heads; tall legs, and narrow, powerful flanks. They were haired in various colors, with white patches. By the hundred thousand, wild cattle roved at large over the uninhabited land on both sides of the border, and constituted its prevailing form of wealth. As such they were always prizes for Indians, Mexicans and Americans who in an unbroken tradition of border violence raided the herds—preferably those already gathered into ownership by other men—and drove away thousands of animals to sell on the hoof, or to kill for their hides which were bailed and sold to traders, while the carcasses were left to carrion, and the bones to workers who gathered them up and hauled them for sale as fertilizer to Texas farming towns.

Even in the face of such hazard a few cattle traders drove herds east to New Orleans, north to Missouri, and west even as far as California, before the Civil War. But the trade was unorganized, and the principal markets, New Orleans and Mobile, were supplied by cattle steamers that sailed out of the Texas Gulf ports. The longhorn cattle they carried were called "coasters" or "sea lions." The coastwise cattle trade was limited by a monopoly held on Gulf shipping by the Morgan Line. "To anyone outside of the ship company," wrote an early cattle trader, "an enormous rate of freight was exacted, practically debarring the ordinary shipper." And when the Civil War took levies of man power from the cattle business, the trade was further constricted. In consequence of such conditions, "for a quarter of a century or more," the trader remarked, "the herds of Texas continued to increase much faster than the mature surplus was marketed. In fact, no market accessible existed sufficiently to consume this surplus, and of course the stock [became] less valuable in proportion as it became plentiful." But shortly after the Civil War the cattle trade was revived, and by the 'seventies, the herds of Texas owners were the largest in the United States. Of these, some of the largest belonged to great companies operating where the nation's range cattle industry had its origin—along the Rio Grande between the Pecos and Mexico Bay.

It was the brasada, the brush country, stretching from the Nueces to the Rio Grande. It was profuse in growths—but almost all were thorned. It was either swept with gray dust borne on blistering winds or beaten by deluges that hissed as they first struck the hot ground or raked by blizzards that came whistling out of the north. In its interlocking thickets that enclosed small clearings where grew curly mesquite grass, cattle could graze by thousands and hardly be seen by horsemen who sought them. There cicadas sang of the heat, and sharp-haired peccaries rooted among the thorns, and blue quail ran amidst the wiry shadows, and rattlesnakes sought the cool and sometimes were drummed to death by wild turkey gobblers at whose destroying wings they struck and struck with no effect on nerveless quill and feather. It was a land of hard secrets, the best kept of which was the location of water. Its few rivers ran in abruptly cut trenches walled with pink or yellow or slate blue limestone, and could not be seen except from their very brinks. In every direction the wilderness looked the same. There were no distant mountains to be seen. The land swelled away toward the white sky in slow rolls and shimmered in the heat that blended the ashen color of the ground with the olive greens of the brush until across the distance there seemed to hang a veil of dusty lilac.

It was astonishing how much human activity there was in a land so hostile to man's needs. It was the scene of habitual Indian travels, and of the military campaigns of the Mexicans and Texans in their wars, and of the United States Army in its Rio Grande movements, and of travelling traders, missioners and criminals. In its thickets there was even an occasional small ranch, locked in isolation by sun, distance, and the poverty of its occupants, who possessed even few wishes. And it became the scene of organized work in the cattle business. Animals born and grown there were taken in herds to the milder prairies above the Nueces, and across the rest of Texas and Oklahoma to beef markets in the north. ". . . The cow boys, as the common laborers are termed," said a cattleman who saw the industry develop, "go in squads of four or five scouting over the entire range, camping wherever night overtakes them, catching with the lasso upon the prairies every young animal found whose mother bears their employer's brand." It was "legal and a universal practice to capture any unmarked and unbranded animal upon the range and mark and brand the same in their employer's brand, no matter to whom the animal may really belong, so be it is over one year old and unbranded. . . ."

The cow boy was the last of the clearly original types of Western American to draw his general tradition and character from the kind of land he worked in, and the kind of work he did. His forerunners were the trapper of the mountains and the trader of the plains. Of the three, he left the fullest legacy of romance and to see him as he first was, it would be necessary in a later century to clear a way back to him through a dense folk literature of the printed page, the moving picture film and the radio that in using all his symbols would almost never touch the reality that supported them.

His work was monotonous in hardship and loneliness, and occasionally it was shot through with excitement that rose from danger. The country where he worked was in its dimensions and character his enemy; and yet it was also in an intimate way almost a completion of his nature, that revelled in vast vacant privacies, and fixed its vision on the distance as though to avoid any social responsibility. He had for his most constant companion not a man or a woman, but an animal—his horse, on whom his work and his convenience and even at times his life depended. His duties took him endlessly riding over range country, where he sought for cattle to capture, calves or yearlings to brand, herds to drive to water, individual cows or bulls of a proper age or condition to cut out of a herd for segregation into another group. Such a group would then be driven to another location—a different pasture or a market.

In dealing with cows through the consent of his horse, the cow boy needed to know much of the nature of both animals. Through experience he learned to anticipate the behavior of cattle, and to judge the effect upon them of every stimulus. He saw that the laws that governed them were the laws of the crowd; and he developed extraordinary skill in handling great crowds of cattle at a time. His horse, broken to riding, and subject to his will, he had to know as an individual creature, and dominate relentlessly its nature by turns sensitive, stubborn and gentle. Living with these two animal natures, the cow boy seemed to acquire in his own certain of their traits, almost as though to be effective at living and working with them, he must open his own animal nature to theirs and through sympathy resemble them. If he could be as simple as a cow, he could also be as stubborn; as fearless as a wild mustang, and as suspicious of the unfamiliar; as incurious as an individual bull, and as wild to run with a crowd when attracted. Even in his physical type, the cow boy might tend to resemble his animal companions—a certain flare of nostril and whiteness of eyelash could recall the thoughtless face of a calf; a leanness of leg and arm was a reminder of a horse's fine-boned supports and further suggested the physique best adapted to, and developed for, the horseman's job—the hard, sinewy body, light of weight but powerful, tall for high vision over the animal herd, long-legged for gripping the mount around its breathing barrel. His state of body and nerve had to be ready to fight, for his job sometimes included battle, when Indians or organized cattle and horse thieves came down upon his herd. Then like any soldier he had to shoot to kill, under the sanction of his duty. For his labors, he was paid in the 1870s from fifteen to twenty dollars a month in gold or silver. He saw himself at his task, and his self-image survived in his anonymous folk literature:

> All day long on the prairie I ride,
> Not even a dog to trot by my side:
> My fire I kindle with chips gathered round,
> My coffee I boil without being ground.

In any group of nineteenth century cow boys, more were bearded than clean-shaven. Their costumes were much alike, though with individual variations. But all their garments were "coarse and substantial, few in number and often of the gaudy pattern." The cow boy wore a wide-brimmed hat with its crown dented into a pyramid or flattened. If the brim in front was sometimes turned up off his face, it could be turned down to protect him from the pressing light of the sky under which he spent all day. Around his neck he wore a bandana of tough silk. It served many purposes. Tied over his face it filtered dust before his breath. It served to blindfold a calf or tie its legs. It was a towel, a napkin, a bandage, a handkerchief, or simply an ornament. His shirt was of stout cotton flannel, in a bright color or loud design of checks or stripes or plaids. Over it he sometimes wore a cloth or leather vest but rarely a jacket. His trousers were either of heavy denim, dyed dark blue, sewn with coarse yellow thread, and reinforced at points of great wear with copper rivets; or were of odd colors and materials, mostly dark, that could stand tough use. They fitted tightly. The trouser legs were stuffed into boots that reached almost to the knee. At work, the cow boy often wore leggings of thick cowhide. They were made after the pattern of Indian leggings—two long tubes, with wide flaps at each side cut into fringes or studded with silver disks, that reached from ankle to groin, and were tied to a belt as though to the string of a breechclout. Their purpose was to shield him against thorns in the brush he rode through, and the violent rub of haired animal hides, and the burn of rope when he pulled it against his leg as he turned his horse to control a lasso'd creature. On his boots he wore large spurs, of silver or iron. He wore gloves to work in, and around his tight hips he wore a cartridge belt from which depended his pistol—most often a Colt's single-action, 45 caliber revolver called the Peacemaker. He had no change of clothing. He went unwashed and unbathed unless he camped by a stream or a pond. "I wash," he said in his multiple anonymity,

I wash in a pool and wipe on a sack;
I carry my wardrobe all on my back. . . .

Like the object of his work and its chief instrument—the cow and the horse—his Texas saddle, in its essential form, came from Spain. Its high pommel and cantle, heavy stirrups and great weight suggested the squarish, chairlike saddle of the jousting knight, though its design was modified by Mexican saddlers until all contours were rounded and smoothed, and the pommel, of silver or other metal, was developed to serve as a cleat about which to secure the lariat whose other end was noosed about a captive cow or horse. When not in use the lariat was coiled and tied to the saddle. There was little other baggage on the saddle, except now and then a leather scabbard containing a short rifle. If two cow boys travelled together they carried their camp equipment and bedrolls on a pack animal. Otherwise, when a large group worked daily out of a central camp, their equipment was carried in the camp wagon to which they returned during the day for meals and at night for fire, food and companionship.

The wagon, pulled by four horses and driven by the camp cook, was a roving headquarters for the grazing party. Its form was invented by Charles Goodnight in the 1850s, who adapted an Army vehicle to the needs of the cow camp. Rolling in movement, it had a compact look, with its sheets over bows, that concealed the contents, which consisted of bedrolls for the workers and at its free end a high, square chest standing upright. Parked, free of it horses, and with its tongue propped level to serve as a rack for harness, and with its sheets extended and supported by poles to make a generous pavilion of shade to one side, the wagon seemed to expand into several times its own size. It was amazing how much it carried, and how much immediate ground its unpacked equipment could cover. The chest at the rear was faced with a wooden lid which when opened downward became a worktable supported by a central leg. Then were revealed in the chest many fitted drawers and hatches in which the cook kept every necessity for cooking and every oddment, including medicines. Behind it in the wagon bed, along with the bedrolls, he carried his heavy pots and skillets and tin dishes. Beneath the wagon frame hung buckets and to its sides were lashed water barrels.

The cooking fire, which at night served also to give its only light to the camp gathering, was made a few feet from the wagon and its profuse scatter of equipment. There the cook prepared his meals, always the same. If brush or wood were scarce, he made his fire of dried animal droppings, like the Spanish soldiers who centuries before had found these the only useful product of fabled Quivira. If he had no matches he could start his fire by pouring gunpowder into his pistol, wadding it loosely, and firing it with its muzzle close to a scrap of cloth or other dry kindling. He prepared a great pot of coffee boiled from whole beans. A cow boy drank a quart or more every day. Of such coffee it was said that "you would hesitate, if judging from appearance, whether to call it coffee or ink." It was drunk without cream or sugar. There was a kettle full of stew in which using his pocketknife—his only table service—the cow boy probed for a lump of meat. With thick biscuit or cornbread he soaked up the gravy and like an Indian ate from his fingers. There were no green vegetables to be had. A pot of kidney beans finished the meal. The cow boys squatted near one another, or stood idling by the wagon, and ate in silence and with speed. A meal was not an occasion of social interest. It was an act of need, disposed of without grace or amenity. Inseparable from it were the taste and smell of dust and cow-hair and horse sweat and leather—sensory attributes of everything in the cow boy's working life.

> For want of an oven I cook bread in a pot,
> And sleep on the ground for want of a cot.

But before the bedrolls were opened up from their heavy canvas covers, and the work party went to sleep, there was a little while for talk and other diversion. Such a miniature society created its own theatre. There was always someone who would be moved to perform, while the rest gazed at the intimate, never-failing marvel of how one whom they knew—a man just like them—became before their very eyes somebody else. The campfire put rosy light over the near faces of the gathered men and their cluttered possessions, and threw their shadows like spokes out on the flat ground until the immense darkness absorbed all. At the very center of light a fellow rose. He had a joke to tell. He acted it out. It may have been well known to all, but they listened in fixity. It was likely to be an obscene jape. The cow boy, observed a cattleman of the 'seven-ties, "relishes . . . a corrupt tale, wherein abounds much vulgarity and animal propensity." His delight was a practical joke on one of his fellows. The joke was good if it made a fool of someone. It was better if it mocked the victim's personal peculiarity, and it was even better if it played upon "animal propensity"—for the sake of symbolic relief of the enforced continence under which the work party lived on the range.

There were other stories to hear—many dealt with experiences in the Civil War, to which the early cow boys were still close in time. There were wrestling and other trials of strength to perform. There were songs to sing, some of whose texts were lewd parodies of sentimental ballads. All knew the songs of the cattle trail, and could sing them together. If in one of his cubbyholes the cook carried a violin for its owner, there would be fiddle music of an astonishing legerity that yet managed to seem tuneless, while a cow boy danced a clog in firelighted dust, and the rest clapped hands. Often a mournful piety stirred in someone, and when he began to sing a hymn, others joined him, and like a sigh of innocence, their united voices rose over their lonely fire where they camped, a little knot of men with every potentiality, to one or another degree, for every human attribute. The bedrolls came out of the wagon and were spread. Nobody had a book to read, and in any case, the firelight was dying and would soon be down to coals.

> My ceiling's the sky, my floor is the grass,
> My music's the lowing of herds as they pass;
> My books are the brooks, my sermons the stones,
> My parson a wolf on his pulpit of bones. . . .

As his artless song implied, the cow boy belonged to the type of man who was not, actually, domesticated. He chose freedom in the wilds over responsibilities of hearth and home. He thought more about work than he did of a family. He made love on almost a seasonal schedule, as though in rut. He visited a prostitute, or took a sweetheart, only to leave her, with sighs about how he must go roaming, as though all would understand his natural state. He departed for work or went off to fight wherever he would find other men like himself. He preferred the society of men to that of women: for only with men could he live a daily life that was made up of danger, and hard exposure, and primitive manners. These did not seem like disadvantages to him, for he liked them for themselves, and, further, they brought into his life excitement, freedom and wilderness, all of which he sought.

If he saw himself as a simple creature, and if tradition so accepted him, both were wrong. His temperament and character were full of tempestuous contradictions and stresses. The life he chose resembled the Indian's more than any other, but it lacked the sustaining spiritual power of the Indian's nature-mythology, and so it could not really hold for him the unquestioned dignity of a system that tried to explain—in whatever error—the whole of human life. He was close to the frontiers-man many of whose ways he repeated, but he was neither innovator, builder nor explorer. His love of hardness and primitive conditions could be turned either to serve his comrades in unbreakable loyalty, or to lead him, as it did in individual cases, to a career as gunman or cattle thief. His longing for love was so great that he felt an exaggerated chivalry for womankind, but in his worship he made women unreal; and yet through his song literature he lamented, ". . . between me and love lies a gulf very wide." He sanctioned his state by romanticizing it in ballad and story; but he refuted it symbolically by his periodic violent outbreaks of gunplay, drunkenness and venery. And with all his hardness, he gave in to a soft core of sentiment whose objects were the animals he worked with, and the comrades who worked with him.

"I and they were but creatures of circumstance," said a cow boy of his fellows in his domesticated old age, "—the circumstances of an unfenced world." From their unfencedness came their main characteristics. Solitude was put upon them by their chosen environment, which thus modified their character. "Adhesiveness," in the jargon of the nineteenth-century parlor science, was a human trait. The nearest living being to whom the cow boy could turn with affection was his horse. It was his daylong companion and helper. It obeyed his orders and made him master of distance and took him in and out of danger. Responding to his signals, it seemed to him to possess more than animal intelligence. His horse, a masterpiece of anthropomorphism, joined him in a partnerhip, and was paid every honor due to such a position. "My horse," continued the retired cow boy, "my horse was something alive, something intelligent and friendly and true. He was sensitive, and for him I had a profound feeling. I sometimes think back on . . . remarkable horses I owned in much the same way that I think back on certain friends that have left me. . . . I went hungry sometimes, but if there was any possible way of getting food for my horse or if there was a place to stake him, even though I had to walk back a mile after putting him to graze"—and cow boys hated to walk—"I never let him go hungry. Many a time I have divided the water in a canteen with a horse." If it was expedient to take care of his horse in order to assure his own mobility and safety, and if it was ordinary human kindness to care for a dumb creature, there was yet more than such promptings in the cow boy's devotion to his mount, as many a song and story attested. The professional cow boy rarely had a cultivated mind; and in his incurious thought he was lowered and his horse was elevated until they drew together in common identity. It was a process typical of a juvenile stage of character, and it may have suggested why the cow boy and his legend should appeal forever after as a figure of play to little boys. In much the same sort of emotion the cow boy felt a mournful fondness for the animals he herded—the little "dogies" to whom he sang on the trail to keep them quiet, and to whom he attributed something of himself as they were objects of his vigilance and labor, day and night. In its innocence and pathos his system of projected sentimentality for his animals suggested that only by making of them more than they were could he have survived his lonely and arduous duty with them. One of his songs said of the cow boy that "his education is but to endure. . . ."

Another song celebrated the life of cow boys together in their wandering yet coherent community. "The boys were like brothers," they sang of themselves, "their friendship was great. . . ." Alike in their extreme individualism, their self-reliance, their choice of a life wild, free and rude, the companions of the cow camp gave to one another an extreme loyalty. It seemed like a tribute to the hard skills they had to master to do their jobs. A man who proved himself able at it deserved membership in a freemasonry unlike any other. Its physical tasks caused a high value to come upon the life of action, in which there was no place for the values of mind and spirit. These were relegated to the world of women; and in the towns and cities that later completed the settling of the last frontier West, for the better part of a century it would be the women's organizations that would try to rescue the fine arts, education, religion, and social amenity from being held as simply irrelevant to civilized life—an attitude even more withering to mankind's highest expressions than one of mere contempt. For its purpose in its time, the brotherhood of the cow camp was all that was needed to make an effective society. Diverse like all individuals, and sprung from various backgrounds and kinds of experience, the cow boys taken together seemed to merge into a type more readily than most workers in a common job. Their environment directly created the terms of their work, and their work in its uncomplicated terms created their attitudes and points of view. And if they were like one another in their principal traits, it was because so many of them chose their calling for the same general reason.

This—it was attested to again and again in the cow boy's anonymous ballad literature—this was flight from one kind of life to another. Many cow boys left home, "each," said a ballad,

"Each with a hidden secret well smothered in his breast,
Which brought us out to Mexico, way out here in the West."

In this lay a suggestion of doom, a rude Byronism that was echoed in other songs by allusions to unhappiness, guilt, escape. Some were driven to the new society of the cow range by a faithless girl at home, or a dissolute life, or a criminal past; others by inability to become reconciled to their home societies following the Civil War, or by bitterness in family life, or even by a cruel stepmother. Romantic conventions of behavior in the nineteenth century could move the cow boy, who punished those who had betrayed him. "I'll go," he threatened,

> ". . . to the Rio Grande,
> And get me a job with a cow boy band."

He did not mean a band of musicians, for not until the next century would the cow boy's public identity be chiefly that of an entertainer who in a commercial adaptation of the cow boy costume would spend more time with a microphone than with either horse or cow. No, with companions on the cattle range, the cow boy, deaf to dissuasion by loved ones who had proved faithless, promised to go

> ". . . where the bullets fly,
> And follow the cow trail till I die."

Unable for whatever reason to accept the bindings of conventional society, within the one he sought and helped to make on the last frontier, he was capable of sure dependability in any cause for the common good of his comrades, whom he did not judge, even if sometimes a propensity to go wrong should overtake them in the very land where they had thought to escape their doom. Who knew when a man might encounter the moral frailty of one of his friends of the brushlands?

> As I walked out in the streets of Laredo,
> As I walked out in Laredo one day,
> I spied a dear cow boy wrapped up in white linen,
> Wrapped up in white linen as cold as the clay.

It was a dirge for a young man who in his dying words revealed a longing for a gentler land than the dusty empire of his work, and confessed his errors. "Oh," he said,

> "Oh, beat the drum slowly and play the fife lowly,
> Play the dead march as you carry me along;
> Take me to the green valley, there lay the sod o'er me,
> For I'm a young cow boy and I know I've done wrong."

Unashamed of their grief that sprang from their close living, his bearers saw themselves in him, and if he had sinned, they could not condemn him.

We beat the drum slowly and played the fife lowly,
And bitterly wept as we bore him along;
For we all loved our comrade, so brave, young and handsome,
We all loved our comrade although he'd done wrong.

For here was a clan feeling, a solidarity, with a realistic view of character and its capacity for error. Idealizing one another in the all-male society of their work and play, the cow boys remained loyal above, or even because of, the weaknesses they shared and assuaged with violence. In conclusion, the dirge moved from the individual to the group.

Then beat your drum lowly and play your fife slowly,
Beat the Dead March as you carry me along;
We all love our cow boys so young and so handsome,
We all love our cow boys although they've done wrong.

In another valedictory the cow boy spirit, after reciting the perils of "some bad company" which could only lead to being "doomed for hell," ended in the presence of the hangman with an admonition to morality.

It's now I'm on the scaffold,
My moments are not long;
You may forget the singer
But don't forget the song.

In the cow boy's lonely character there were extremes of feeling and behavior. If in his work there seemed to be a discipline of dedicated steadfastness, a purity of vocation, then when he went to town, he threw himself into indulgence. Perhaps the town was a reminder of the coherent social life he had fled at home, and perhaps it was now a guilty joy to outrage it by his behavior. Certainly the town was the very opposite of the desolate open range from which even the cow boy needed periodic change.

His best chance for it came when men of the range party were told off to drive a herd of cattle to the marketing and shipping towns. The main trails along which he drove went north from the Texan Rio Grande to Kansas, and another—the Goodnight-Loving Trail—led westward to New Mexico and California. It passed the Pecos River at Horsehead Crossing about a hundred miles above the Rio Grande, and presently divided into two forks. One pointed north to Colorado. The other crossed the Rio Grande at Las Cruces and followed the old road to San Diego.

The cattle made trails that showed many narrow grooves side by side—marks of the strict formation in which the animals in their thousands were driven for upwards of a thousand miles. A cow boy said that trail life was "wonderfully pleasant"—this in spite of continuing hazards. There still might be trouble with Indians. All the cattle were wild, and were easily stampeded by attacks, or by thunderstorms, or by hail. If the weather was wet, rivers rose, and to take thousands of cattle across swollen waters was at best a tedious job, and often a perilous one. Against the drovers on the move there pressed at one period a whole organized enterprise of thievery. Outlaws captured drovers, tortured them, sometimes killed them, and stole their herds. When one drover was captured, he tried to talk his way out of his trouble, but the bandits were immovable and a reporter of the incident said bitterly that "it was like preaching morality to an alligator."

But in swelling volume the animal trains passed through to their destinations, and the cow boys were happy on the trail. They played tricks on one another, and shot game on the prairies, and after supper sang, told stories, danced to a fiddle, lay back to look at the stars and speculate about them, and listened for the sounds of the herd settling down for the night. "I do not know anything more wholesome and satisfying," mused a cow boy long after his trail days, "than seeing cattle come in on their bed ground at night so full and contented that they grunt when they lie down." It was like a communion of creature comforts in which man and animal could meet. Three shifts of night guards were posted over the herds. A sleepy cow boy rubbed tobacco juice in his eyes to keep awake. Morning must come, and another day to be spent at the pace of cattle walking with odd delicacy in their narrow grooved trails, and after enough such days, the shipping town would take form like a few scattered gray boxes on the severe horizon, and the cow boy would feel his various hungers begin to stir.

It was in town that he got into most of his trouble. Every facility was there to help him do it. As a cattle shipper observed, in frontier towns "there are always to be found a number of bad characters, both male and female; of the very worst class in the universe, such as have fallen below the level of the lowest type of brute creation." These pandered to the cow boy's howling appetite for dissipation.

Sometimes he rode into town and without cleaning himself or

changing his clothes but just as he had dismounted in hat, damp shirt, earth-caked trousers, and boots and spurs, he strode into a dance house, seized a "calico queen" or a "painted cat," as he called the dancing women, and with Indian yells and a wild eye went pounding about the dance floor under a grinding necessity to prove in public, most of all to himself, that he was at last having a good time. The music to which he danced was "wretched . . . ground out of dilapidated instruments, by beings fully as degraded as the most vile. Few more wild, reckless scenes of abandoned debauchery can be seen on the civilized earth," remarked the cattle shipper, "than a dance house in full blast in one of the many frontier towns. To say they dance wildly or in an abandoned manner is putting it mild. . . ."

And sometimes the cow boy, at large in town with his accumulated pay, went first to improve his looks. In a barbershop he had a bath, and then had his three to six months' growth of hair trimmed, and his full beard cut down, shaped and dyed black. In a clothing store he bought completely new clothes, from hat to boots, and then, strapping on his pistol, he was ready to impose himself like shock upon the town. Gambling rooms, saloons, a theatre, a row of prostitutes' quarters like cattle stalls, dance houses—from one to the next the cow boy could make his explosive way, to be catered to by "men who live a soulless, aimless life," and women who had "fallen low, alas! how low . . . miserable beings." Among the conventions of the cow boy's town manners was free use of his firearm, whether he might harm anyone or not. The pathos of folly long done and half forgotten would make his murderous antics seem unreal to later view. But they were real enough in the frontier towns of the 1870s. "It is idle," sighed the cattle shipper in that decade, "it is idle to deny the fact that the wild, reckless conduct of the cow boys while drunk . . . have brought the *personnel* of the Texan cattle trade into great disrepute, and filled many graves with victims, bad men and good men. . . . But by far the larger portion of those killed are of that class that can be spared without detriment to the good morals and respectability of humanity. . . ." And "after a few days of frolic and debauchery, the cow boy is ready, in company with his comrades, to start back to Texas, often not having one dollar left of his summer's wages." All he had was a memory that found its way into one of his songs, about "The way we drank and gambled and threw the girls around. . . ."

The cow boy triumphed at a lonely work in a beautiful and dangerous land. Those of his qualities that did the job were the good ones—courage, strength, devotion to duty. His worse traits, exercised for relief, were not judged in relation to his task. All aspects of his complex nature entered into his romance. He saw himself for his own achievement, and like the earliest individuals of the frontier, he consciously created his character and his tradition, and whether his emotion was honest or not, it was so energetic that by it he made his nation see him in his own terms. In him, the last American to live a life of wild freedom, his domesticated compatriots saw the end of their historical beginnings, and paid him nostalgic tribute in all their popular arts. Soon, like them, he would lose his nomadic, free and rough form of life before the westward sweep of machine technics by which Americans made their lives physically more easy—and socially less independent and self-reliant. In the very exercise of their genius for convenience in living, the Americans sacrificed to the social and commercial patterns of mass technics some part of the personal liberty in whose name the nation had been founded. The cow boy in his choice of solitude held on to his whole liberty as long as he could. But domestication of his West by machine technics began in the 1860s and, once started, went fast.

For in response to such technics, the cattle industry grew with suddenness, and then became stabilized. The first of these was the westward advance of the railroads with which the northbound cattle drives could make a junction. It was not easy to arrange for the earliest rail transport of western cattle. A young Illinois cattle shipper who was the first to establish a livestock market in Kansas was astonished to have his new idea rejected by two railroad presidents and the leading businessmen of several Kansas towns to whom he went in turn. Finally the Hannibal & St. Joe Railroad gave the young shipper a contract "at very satisfactory rates of freight from the Missouri River to Quincy, thence to Chicago." He selected Abilene, Kansas, as the site for his stockyards, and in 1867, the first cattle were driven there from Texas. During the next four years 1,460,000 head of cattle were brought to Abilene. Other trails and shipping centers were soon established, and it was estimated that during a period of twenty-eight years nearly ten million cattle worth almost a hundred million dollars were moved from the Texas ranges to market. In the process of developing so great a business, the whole practice of cattle raising became formalized through changes that sought greater efficiency.

One of these used a technical machine product that soon conquered the open range where wild cattle once drifted according to weather. It was barbed wire, first used in 1875 to fence pastures in which with fewer and less skillful cow boys the herds could be restricted and more easily managed. When land was enclosed, ranch dwellings were needed. Permanent headquarters buildings followed. Cattle no longer were driven to rivers but found their water in earth tanks supplied by dug wells, with still another machine product to keep it flowing—the metal windmill. The main trunk lines of the railroads ran east to west across the continent; but soon feeder lines were built—sometimes following the flat terrain of the old trails—and machine transportation reached nearer and nearer to the great ranches of the border where the whole cattle industry had had its beginnings. The Missouri, Kansas and Texas Railroad was the great Texas cattle line. It tapped the Rio Grande brush country ranges. The Atchison, Topeka and Santa Fe main line crossed New Mexico and a branch line ran from Belen on the Rio Grande all the way down the valley to El Paso. The Texas and Pacific reached eastward from San Diego to El Paso in 1877, and bridges now came back to the Rio Grande to stay. The whole river empire was soon tied to the rest of the nation by rails. When packing houses were established at Kansas City, Fort Worth and other Southwestern cities, the final pattern of the organized beef cattle industry was realized. In it there was little room for the figure, the temperament, of the original cow boy, with his individual lordship over great unimpeded distances and his need of freedom as he defined it. His cow camp literature recorded yet another stage—the last—of his history. "The cow boy has left the country," he could sing, "and the campfire has gone out. . . ."

On barbed wire fences, like symbols of the new order of affairs over the controlled range lands, dead, skinned coyotes were impaled in a frieze—twenty or thirty of them at a time. They were stretched in mid-air with a lean, racing look of unearthly nimbleness, running nowhere; and their skulled teeth had the smile of their own ghosts, wits of the plains. In the dried varnish of their own amber serum they glistened under the sun. The day of unrestrained predators was over.

40.

Treasure

Illusion was the very nourishment of treasure seekers. Watching westward in 1858 for their first sight of mountains a party of prospectors entering Colorado saw on the horizon what one of the company said looked "like a thunder cloud." What he saw were the Spanish Peaks in the Sangre de Cristo range. His party turned north and followed the base of the mountains to the camps of Pike's Peak and Cherry Creek, where first discoveries of gold were followed by disappointment. Early stories in guidebooks and newspapers, all too often written by men who had never been west, told how gold was lying "on the plains, in the mountains, and by the streams, only waiting to be gathered up." The realities were different. Mineral treasure was present, but it had to be found in its secret lodgments and taken out by hard work. Many immigrants turned away homeward in disgust, making a wish in a popular jingle to

> "Hang Byers and D. C. Oakes
> For starting this damned Pike's Peak hoax,"

and some drifted southward to New Mexico, where one couple, "with wagon and mess," settled at Taos when the wife was offered a position teaching school. But others persisted, and the Colorado gold fields soon flourished. For about its first decade Colorado mining was located in the great central ranges of the Rockies, far removed from the Rio Grande and the San Juan Mountains of its source.

For though the New York *Herald* declared in 1857 that in "the Sierra San Juan, where, if we recollect rightly, both Pike and Frémont lost their way, gold, silver, cinnabar and precious stones are found in immense quantities," there was no mining of any significance in the Rio Grande basin of Colorado until after the Civil War. Settlement was limited to a few farming communities in the grand San Luis Valley, whose mild slopes and level floor recalled its origin as a huge lake. Through it the river ran a gentle course along which a handful of Mexican families established themselves in 1853 distant from the most northerly New Mexican settlements by only a few days' march. Using the river to irrigate their little fields, and the wide grassy valley to graze their small herds, they recreated the scene of slow water, bounteous cottonwood tree and earthen house that was so familiar in the river's New Mexican passage. They looked no farther for treasures of the earth.

In 1860, as though re-enacting in miniature an earlier pattern of conquest, a small party of Americans passed through the Mexican settlements of the San Luis Valley and followed the Rio Grande out of sight into the mountains of the source. They were looking for gold in the San Juan. Their search took them through summer and autumn, until they were caught in the snows of winter. In the following spring they were joined by other prospectors and all spent the next summer in the San Juan Mountains, but without finding gold. Before another winter could trap them they returned eastward to Fort Garland, where they heard that the Civil War had broken out; and the leader of the prospectors hurried to Virginia to enlist.

At the end of the decade other attempts were made to find the riches of the San Juan, and scattered strikes led to the establishment of mines on the western slope of the continental divide. By 1870 there was enough traffic along the headwaters of the Rio Grande to call alive the town of Del Norte as a supply point, at the gateway of the river between the San Luis Valley and the mountains. In the same year gold was found at Wightman's Gulch and other sites in the Del Norte region, the most thriving of which was Summitville to the southwest. The population of the district grew to six hundred. Stamp mills were set up at the largest camps. During the short summers pack trains bringing ore came from over the divide by way of Stony Pass which was over twelve thousand feet above sea level. On the eastward road out of the mountains a new town was founded in 1878—Alamosa.

It came as the new western terminus of the Denver and Rio Grande Western Railroad. The town itself came by rail, for from the old terminus of Garland City houses, churches, stores and other buildings were hauled on flat cars to be set up at the new end of the line. With heavy transportation now available, a new commercial interest was developed in the San Luis Valley that soon overshadowed mining as the main business of the region. Large-scale irrigation projects were organ-

ized and supported by foreign capital—principally British. Between
Alamosa and Del Norte a huge grid of irrigation canals reached out
from the Rio Grande for thirty or forty miles north and south. A land
boom resulted. Speculation in land values and water rights went wild.
As in so many other Western localities toward the end of the nineteenth
century, company promoters preached a new paradise and trainloads
of colonists came in response to the dazzling promise. For a little while,
so long as competition was fresh and vigorous, the San Luis prospered
in the vision of a future nourished by inexhaustible resources. Monte
Vista, a third railroad town, was founded in 1887. But within a decade
the vision bagan to pale, for what ended so many other organized
Western dreams elsewhere presently took effect in southern Colorado—
there was not enough water. Sapped by the greatly overextended system
of canals, the river could not supply all. The euphoria of the pioneer
faded, many immigrants abandoned their hopes and went away, and
those who remained came to a regulated sharing of the waters whose
stabilized flow was made possible by the building of reservoirs at the
head of the valley. In the same period the mining ventures of the San
Luis Valley began to lose energy. The camptowns of the Summitville
region were left to the weather, and turned into silvered ghosts. Raw
pine boarding turned gray, and weeds climbed the rusting machinery,
and the character of the wide valley became wholly agricultural, supplied and drained by the railroad in a stabilized economy.

But farther up the river a major find of precious minerals was
made in 1889 that suddenly brought the Rio Grande source country
into the national news. For several years prospectors had been scratching
at the rocks beyond Wagon Wheel Gap—where Kit Carson had once
fought the Ute Indians—but without making significant discoveries. In
that country they saw diamond clear creeks that were shadowed all day
by narrowing mountains but for a little while at noon, when straight
fingers of sunlight reached down through forest. On slopes open to the
sun in summer, groves of quaking aspens showed here and there, creating little gardens of their own within immense wild parks. In winter
the only green was that of the evergreens, solemn and frowning amidst
the silver and brown of lichens—the colors of age—set off by heavy banks
of snow. Far above, at timberline, like fixed images of the winds on the
inhumane peaks, the last trees clutched the naked rock with gestures of
agonized survival. Emerging from between two flat-cliffed mountains of
flesh-colored stone streaked with olive lichens came a little stream which
the prospectors named Willow Creek. They saw that it was a tributary

of the Rio Grande, and that it had its own smaller tributary which they called West Willow Creek.

On a summer day in 1889 two experienced prospectors who had made successful discoveries elsewhere walked up Willow Creek through its formidable gateway. Presently one of them—Nicholas C. Creede—saw in the stream what surely seemed to be evidence of silver ore on the washed sandy bottom. He followed the creek and turned into its west branch, and when he reached the head of it, found rocks flecked with quartz and stippled with silver. Creede and his partner George L. Smith staked a location and went to work sinking a shaft at the spot. They were soon rewarded, for they struck a silver vein so rich that Creede on first making certain of it, exclaimed, "Holy Moses!" The mine was given that name. Winter would soon close in. Creede and Smith gathered specimens of their mine, and went to Denver where word of the discovery presently reached David H. Moffat, president of the Denver and Rio Grande Western Railroad. With other investors, Moffat bought shares in the Holy Moses after inspecting it when travel became possible the next spring. Creede was retained to continue prospecting for the new syndicate. In the summer of 1890 a rush began to Willow Gap, and by October there was a town of tents ready to survive the winter.

A year later the Denver and Rio Grande Western tracks reached Creede, as Willow Gap was now called, and by December trains ran regularly up the Rio Grande canyon past Wagon Wheel Gap and the confluence of Willow Creek, which entered the river along a peninsula of heavy gravel. Twenty months after it was founded, Creede displayed an energy that reached far beyond its own rock-bound limits. A gentleman journalist felt it in Denver on his way to examine the new camp. The word Creede "faced you everywhere from billboards, flaunted at you from canvas awnings stretched across the streets, and stared at you from daily papers in type an inch long." In Denver shops there were photographs of Creede, and "the only correct map of Creede," and ore specimens from the Holy Moses. Miners' outfittings were advertised everywhere. A druggist pleaded in the newspapers for an investment of five hundred dollars with which to start a drugstore in Creede. Wherever the visitor met other people—in hotel lobbies, or the Denver Club— "Creede" was in the air. On the train from Denver to Creede every passenger "showed the effect of the magnet that was drawing him—he was restless, impatient, excited." The daily train had fifteen or twenty cars, and even so there were not enough seats for all its two or three hundred passengers. Some of the men sat on the others, while women of a certain class "smoked with the men and passed their flasks down the length of the car." As the train pulled into Creede the journalist jumped from his car "into two or three feet of mud and snow," and saw that "the ticket and telegraph offices on one side of the track were situated in a freight car with windows and doors cut out of it." The next thing noticed by the incoming passenger was that Creede already had electricity. A single electric light burned high against the pink cliff of Willow Gap at whose base huddled the town, and incandescent carbon "glow-lamps" shone in white, red and blue brilliance along the street front.

As a familiar of the great clubs and smart restaurants and polite drawing rooms of the world's capitals, the journalist was entranced by the simple rudeness of all he found in the mining camp. The approaches and slopes of Willow Gap were "covered with hundreds of little pine boxes and log cabins." It was "a village of fresh pine." There was "not a brick, a painted front, nor an awning in the entire town," which looked "like a city of fresh cardboard." The street was all confusion and movement. He saw "oxteams, mules, men, and donkeys loaded with ore . . . sinking knee deep in the mud," and "furniture, and kegs of beer, bedding and canned provisions, clothing and half-open packing cases, and piles of raw lumber . . . heaped up in front of the new stores—stores of canvas only, stores with canvas tops and foundations of logs, and houses with the *Leadville front,* where the upper boards have been left square instead of following the sloping angle of the roof." At the base of the superb rock panels rising above the town, all such clutter looked to him "impudent and absurd"—more like a "gypsy camp in a canyon," really, than a town. And the nomenclature of the establishments!—The Holy Moses Saloon, The Théâtre Comique, The Keno, The Little Delmonico. . . .

And the accommodations!—there were dozens of hotels, most of which afforded the traveller only a cot in a common room teeming with other sleepers. Beds were so scarce that the railroad company often left a number of Pullman cars on a siding to provide a lodging for the night. The population by now was about ten thousand, and included every type of commercial frontier character. The journalist saw gamblers, prospectors, miners, engineers, bankers, bartenders, itinerant evangelists, actors, prostitutes, schoolteachers, family men and women, jobbers, merchants, and confidence men to whom in his observations he could condescend with easy bad manners, and adventurous younger sons of rich Eastern families, with whom he was more at home. Luckily, he was able to find a bed for the night with a group of these young men who, like him, had come just for the lark. To go West to see such a spectacle as Creede was a gallant and correct thing for them to do, and he was their prophet, for his career had been full of just such fashionable exploits.

The night life, even though at the moment Creede was "not at all a dangerous place," with a lawlessness that was "scattered and mild," was worth an amused glance. There were things to see—a prize fight at Billy Woods's, a pie-eating match at Kernan's, a Mexican circus in the bottom near Wagon Wheel Gap, a religious service in Watrous and Brannigan's saloon where two electric lights hung in the middle of the room and a stove stood below them. The prayer meeting over, the house resumed its own character, and took in three hundred dollars an hour, while the women of the establishment, wearing "sombrero hats and flannel shirts and belts" above their long skirts, "were neither dashing and bold, nor remorseful and repentant." Actually, people seemed to use the gambling houses as clubs where they might keep warm and talk business and find company and gossip. One night Nicholas Creede was offered $1,250,000 for his share in the Holy Moses Mine, and refused. The journalist winced. How could anybody choose this life over what that much money would buy back East? But if the visitor read the Creede *Candle*—the local newspaper—he saw self-critical and outspoken opinion. Some of the citizens, it said, "would take the sweepstake prize at a hog show," and from time to time, it documented examples of the usual murderous antics of official "bad men" who in Creede as elsewhere on the recurrent American frontier enacted the dreariest convention of character in United States history.

The journalist went by day into the canyon to observe mining operations. Now he saw the prosperous, well-developed shafts, and again, "a solitary prospector tapping at the great rock in front of him, and only stopping to dip his hot face and blistered hands into the snow about him, before he began to drive the steel bar again with the help which hope gave to him." Long lines of burros went down the gulch "carrying five bags of ore each, with but twenty dollars' worth of silver scattered through each load." The voice of the driver echoed on the upright stone walls and the tinkle of the little burro bells carried far in the enclosed air. Other loads, often of ten tons, were brought down in sleds drawn by horses. The trail was slippery with packed snow and once their momentum was released, the sleds came flying heavily down the twisting canyon course and into town, where all scattered out of their way, for they must not stop until they stopped by the railroad tracks, which they reached in a great circle on the flat land where their cargo would be removed to freight cars.

Within a year after the mines were opened in Creede and its near-by camps of Sunnyside, Bachelor and Spar City, six million dollars' worth of silver was shipped out. In its sudden rise to fame and prosperity, Creede was typical of any mining town of the period in the West—and so it was, too, in its early fall to decay. After 1893 the price of silver declined, many mines were abandoned, and others if they were kept running were greatly reduced in operation.

Socorro on the river in central New Mexico knew much the same history. Silver was found in the Socorro mountains in 1867, and for over a decade was hauled upriver by mule train. When in 1880 the Santa Fe line went down the river toward El Paso, the Socorro region drew a new population of exploiters until Socorro itself was the largest town in New Mexico—one estimate fixed the total at thirty thousand. Magdalena, twenty-seven miles west of the river, was established by silver miners in 1884, and a railroad spur soon reached it. But again, in the familiar cycle of such mining towns, decline followed until both Socorro and Magdalena were primarily focal towns for agriculture—here, the supply and shipping points for cattle and sheep raisers. Only an occasional die-hard among prospectors continued to go alone with his burro, his pick, his skillet and his coffeepot into the blue rocks of his visions, determined, if he had one, to be faithful to his secret until the end.

One such was found in after years near Socorro when a group of students on a Saturday exploration came upon a jug pit or cave whose open mouth, invisible from a very little distance across flat ground, was narrower than its interior. The students knew that the cave like others in the area must be a repository of an ochreous dust so dense and fine that to breathe it freely was dangerous. Equipped with a respirator and a flashlight, one of the students was lowered into the pit by the others. In a few moments he was hauled up to tell what he had seen. His find was awesome. When he landed in the pit he disturbed from its floor a swiftly billowing cloud of yellow dust. It roiled in the air shutting off the sight of anything about him. He peered with his lamp toward the pit walls and suddenly through the suspended motes he was shocked to see at his very side the figure of a man that seemed to be molded of the dust, leaning on a sloping wall of earth with its brow on its forearm. It was the body of an old prospector, wearing a short coat hanging open and trousers poked into high boots, and over all a softening layer of

dust. Half buried near his feet was his pick. It seemed probable that
he had gone alone into the pit with no protection against the dust that
instantly rose to choke the air about him. Leaning his head upon his
arm against the wall as he struggled to breathe he had died of suffocation. Through the years he had been mummified by the dry air and the
little desert whirlwinds that having created the pit must have continued
to spin in and out of it now and again. In his open grave he was a
classic rendering of dust to dust itself, and a symbol of solitary man,
killed by the country of his love, faith and work.

41.
The Last Earth Secrets

For almost four centuries after the Spaniards first began to record
the river's history a long passage—over one fifth—of its course went undescribed. This was the country of the Big Bend, where one after another
great canyons and rocky deserts turned away travellers and settlers—all
but the few Indians who had once lived in cliffside caves and others
who migrated ceaselessly north and south and who may have seen most
of the secret river land that lay between the entrance of the Rio Conchos
into the Rio Grande and the confluence of the Pecos nearly four hundred miles downstream. But such Indians left no records of the country.

The Spanish settlements nearest to the blind channel were those
temporarily made by missioners in 1683 and 1684, and those by government forces in 1747, at the Junta. From there, looking downstream, the
Spaniards could see the first of the mountain fantasies that would have
closed off the river to ordinary navigation even if there had been enough
water to carry it. The Army quartermaster party that ascended the river
in keelboats in 1850 left a report that told how they had gone upstream
from Fort Brown a distance of about thirteen hundred miles and how
finally they had been halted by falls in a great canyon. But if they

reached one of the Big Bend canyons their record was not explicit. In 1852 and 1853 Colonel Emory's boundary surveyors followed the river's course wherever possible, but in the Big Bend they were forced to view the canyon system from a distance, or from the tops of the gorges, where precise measurement and description of the channel could not be made. The three men who declared that they had escaped the Confederate Army at El Paso in 1861 by floating all the way to Brownsville in two dugout canoes lashed together left no narrative of the unknown Big Bend country through which their voyage would have taken them. In December, 1881, and January, 1882, a detachment of Texas Rangers set out from Lajitas, below Presidio, to navigate the Big Bend in three boats. They worked their way downstream to the mouth of Maravillas Canyon and there, after fifty-two days, their expedition ended, with a great stretch of the river—all the way to the Pecos—still unobserved by boat. Having kept no daily record of their observations, they made their report from memory. If it was a testimony to adventure and courage, it did not serve the purpose of a survey.

It was not until 1899 that the last secrets of the river's conformation were penetrated and recorded in systematic detail. In the autumn of that year Robert T. Hill, an officer of the United States Geological Survey, arrived at Presidio bringing five companions and three specially built boats for an expedition down the Rio Grande through its entire Big Bend career. As they made their preparations the travellers—one of whom was Hill's nineteen-year-old nephew—examined the local character of the river.

Above Presidio the river in some years vanished in the desert. Colonel Emory had told of how a herd of goats was driven all the way to El Paso in the dry stream bed. But relief and replenishment came to the Rio Grande just north of Presidio from the waters of the Conchos. With this tributary came new power for the Rio Grande in the struggle of water against rock, and another of those beautiful easings of desert into bounteous pastoral land that recurred along its course. This relief was here so striking that earlier travellers familiar with only the border country spoke of the Conchos as "the mother stream of the Rio Grande," and said that it brought "the first permanent water to the main river." Such a limited view was often taken of the Rio Grande throughout its history; for along its great length, and in different times, on different missions, travellers discovered the river in segments, named them differently, found contradictory characters in them, and for many generations did not form a comprehensive theory of the river's continuity, variety and use. After the bare and voracious desert in which it nearly died, the river at Presidio came among willows again and cottonwoods, lilac mountains with attendant clouds, emerald-green fields and pink sand, through a sweetness in the air made from all these together.

On October fifth Hill gave the order to start the voyage. Two men entered each of the three boats. Soon after leaving Presidio they heard a roaring noise and presently encountered rapids foaming over huge rounded boulders of volcanic rock. They had to get into the water to guide the boats. They all knew, with Hill, that "loss of balance or a fall meant almost certain death." They were in the rapids all day. Other dangers ran along the river course and against these they kept loaded rifles beside their oars. "Every bush and stone was closely scanned for men in ambush," for bandits and assassins abounded. The most famous and frightful was a Mexican named Alvarado, who was called "Old White Lip," as one side of his mustache was white, the other black.

In the hazy heat on the downriver horizon images of another country began to loom, almost like premonitions. Fantasies were made manifest. Unimaginably long ago, mountain nature had gone capricious in stunning terms. The land had opposed the river before this passage; but never on the scale of what lay ahead. The Rio Grande was heading for all the old conditions of its course—desert, mountain, canyon—but now raised to prodigious dimensions of height, depth, length and power in furies of sky action, and earth response. The scene could be understood only in the scale of what created it. Continental dimensions and eminences of the hemisphere itself must be invoked. North America at its waist was twenty-one hundred miles wide. Along its eastern shelf the mountain chain of the Appalachians ran almost continuously from north to south. Along its western shelf the Rocky Mountains ran almost continuously from north to south. Towards the ends of their courses these, the two major mountain systems of the continent, threw out spurs toward one another which, incredibly and immensely, intersected. A cataclysm so great using elements so huge could only leave fixed signs of colossal turbulence in rock and earth, fantasies of shape and color and atmospheric temper, including the dead but enduring evidence of volcanic action. The whole rind of the earth in the Big Bend country was dropped in a great tilted slab to a depth of two or three thousand feet on the north, and six thousand feet on the south, as though a cut were made in a watermelon, and the segment pushed in below the surrounding surface. Mesas, volcanic mountains, plains, interior basins, deserts, badlands, lava flows, beds of dried rivers and dead and vanished seas, all profuse in number and fantastic in shape and often violent in color made that country in its vast freaks of light seem like figment instead of fact.

Upstream the river had always been in touch with mountains; but they lay generally parallel to its course. In the Big Bend the river encountered mountains in a new and extraordinary way; for they lay, chain after chain of them, directly across its course as though to deny its passage to the sea. But the pull of the sea was stronger than rock. The Rio Grande with its shallow flow did not turn aside, or dam itself into a system of lakes, but for ages wore its way as an antecedent river through the escarpments as they rose, some to a height of almost a mile above its course.

Late in their second day's voyage Hill and his men entered the Bofecillos Mountains with their chocolate-colored cliffs—"the first of the series of canyons of the Rio Grande" in which they "were to be entombed for the succeeding weeks." It was called Murderer's Canyon, for in it had been found a supposed victim of "Old White Lip." A little farther down they came into Fresno Canyon which like the first one was made by vertical cuts six hundred feet deep through walls of red volcanic rock. The river flowed muddy yellow. On the tops of the canyons was desert, out of reach of the water below—a condition that moved Hill as "shocking and repulsive."

Suddenly they passed out of the canyon, leaving behind vertical walls which continued north and south of the river, and into a valley with every variety of form and color. The outermost hills were of dazzling chalky white capped with black tufa. Slopes were vermilion foothills of clay. Still lower were river terraces of yellow clay and gravel, all threaded by the narrow green ribbon of river vegetation.

Hill's party included Mexicans who promised to kill White Lip on sight, a distraction to which Hill was cold. "Only a most fortunate mistake prevented my men from carrying out their threat," he wrote. "Alvarado had a surname as well as a Christian name, and when they were told that the next ranch down the river was Ordoñez's, they did not understand that this was another name for Alvarado until after we had passed him with an infant in his arms, serenely watching us float down the stream. . . ."

Below the bandit's home came "great bluffs of a dirty yellow volcanic tuff, which weather into many fantastic, curvilinear forms. One of these, two hundred feet high, stands out conspicuously from its surroundings, an almost perfect reproduction of the Egyptian sphinx." In

late afternoon they came to another wall cut ahead of them by the river,
and entering camped with a sense of safety, "hemmed in on each side
by vertical walls and out of rifle range from above." In the morning they
emerged from this mile-long canyon and entered a sinuous course
through what they called Black Rock Canyon, cut a thousand feet below
the summit of a level plateau, and lined with buttes whose tabled tops
and lower slopes showed thick bands of white chalk, with between them
an immense bed of black lava. At evening they sailed into an open basin
and passed the mouth of San Carlos Creek, a meagre flowing stream, the
first tributary of the river below the Conchos.

   At this point they had come one hundred miles by water, though
in air line they were only fifty miles from Presidio. They camped on the
Mexican side, and regarded a mile downstream "a vast mountain wall,
the vertical escarpment of which ran directly north and south across the
path of the river, and through which the latter cuts its way."

   They were face to face with the first of the three mightiest
obstacles of the Big Bend. It was the Santa Elena Range, running fifty
miles from north to south. Ten miles of it lay in the United States;
forty miles of it, sawed off by the river, lay in Mexico. The range was
half a mile high and twelve miles wide. Its top was a plateau, tilted
slightly to the west. From the top the river's cut was so clean that—as
other observers noticed—it could not be seen until they came to stand
at its very edge. Even from the crest of the canyon wall the running
water a quarter of a mile below was not always visible, and when it could
be seen from overhanging ledges, the stream looked like "a mere thread."

   The next morning Hill's party came to the awesome gateway in
the face of the escarpment. The river made a sudden bend as it entered
the canyon, "and almost in the twinkling of an eye we passed out of the
desert glare into the dark and silent depths of its gigantic canyon walls,
which rise vertically from the water's edge to a narrow ribbon of sky
above." The channel was only twenty-five feet wide. They could almost
touch the walls with their oars. There was a deathlike stillness all about
them as they floated without using their oars on the slipping waters.
"Their flow is so silent as to be appalling," noted Hill, and "the solem-
nity and beauty of the spectacle were overwhelming."

   They had drifted in this mountain oubliette for a few miles when
they were halted by a disheartening discovery. Part of the huge southern
wall had fallen in a great rock slide to obstruct the path, not for the
water, which pounded its way beneath a pile of fifty-foot boulders, but
for the boats. The slide rose to a height of two hundred feet, and though

it was only a quarter of a mile in length, it cost Hill and his men three days to cross it—for there was no way to go but forward. They hauled their boats and equipment over the slide with the hardest effort, climbing to a height of one hundred and eighty feet and descending the other side. Even as they passed their freight hand over hand up the rugged slope they could still regard the magnificence of the scene with awe. Yellow and red marbles in the cliffs; gigantic columns five hundred feet high that had been undermined by the river to drop a few feet without tumbling and to lean against the walls; great caves below the skyline, and others at the waterline; fortress and castle and bastion of natural making; silence—all worked upon them.

And so did fears. What if the river should suddenly rise with storm water? What if they should wreck one or all of the boats on the rocky portage? They called the place Camp Misery. "While buried in this canyon at Camp Misery" they were "constantly impressed by the impossibility of escaping from it" if their fears came true. "For its entire length there is no place where this cliff can be climbed by man." Acutely conscious of their situation, they struggled on, hauling at the boats, each of which weighed three hundred pounds, with lariat and bare hands, over the immense limestone cubes "around and between which the water dashed with the force of a mill-race, and where a slip of the foot on the smooth rocks meant certain death." But they prevailed, and at last made ready to take to the water again early one morning. But "before the boats were loaded a tremendous roaring sound like distant thunder was heard up the canyon, and we saw that what we most dreaded was happening— the river was rising." They hurried their preparations and sprang aboard the skiffs. "It was either stay and starve or go and chance it. Fortunately, this particular rise proved to be a small one"—and in this they were lucky, for the river could rise thirty feet in half an hour in the Santa Elena canyon—"just sufficient to give impetus to our craft, and our course through the canyon was rapid."

The skyline was of always changing interest. There was no animal life at all in the canyon except for a small species of bat, and a family of quail which had ventured into the deep slot and found themselves unable to soar out again. As the enclosing walls rose to their greatest height—seventeen hundred and fifty feet—the boats sailed suddenly out into desert sunlight, after their twisting and turning twenty-five mile passage. And now the travellers could pause thankfully on the shore to look back at the mountain from which they had escaped. They saw the east face of the Santa Elena—an escarpment of pale buff limestone with

hardly a break in its vertical thrust except for a shallow and sloping
bench about halfway up. Its horizon was flat and sharply cut, with great
nicks in it where waterless canyons bit into the rock to remain suspended
high up the cliff. As the mountain ended sharply, so the desert began
sharply, reaching far inland, and going with the river for the next forty
miles. The very rock of Santa Elena seen from the desert downstream
looked like a shimmering image of the heat. Sand, orange-colored foothills, blue haze in the canyon's mouth, all spoke of waste and heat, in
immense proportions. Such was its scale that for a week after leaving the
Santa Elena Hill's men could see its face from down the river. Hill could
proudly record that "as bold and extensive as is this mountain, it had
hitherto found no place or name on published maps."

Now entering the desert the Rio Grande in crossing the forty-
mile stretch wound for a hundred miles. Every variety of barren terrain
was visible on both sides of the river—level plains, deep terraces, arroyos,
lava-capped hills, summits and small mountain ranges. Hill said it was
the "hottest and most sterile region imaginable." In full summer the temperature often rose to one hundred and thirty or forty degrees by day,
and by night dropped close to freezing. Repeated enough, such violent
contrasts cracked rock, so that much of the wild and furious aspect of
the region could be traced to such earth action. Above the desert on the
north the range of Los Chisos mountains rose to a total altitude of nine
thousand feet, or sixty-five hundred above the river. "Wherever one
climbs out of the low stream groove these peaks stare him in the face like
white-cloud spirits rising from a base of misty gray shadow and vegetation," wrote Hill. Their name was said to be an Indian word for "ghosts."
The highest peak of the Chisos was named for Commissioner Emory.
Color was as extraordinary as form there—black, yellow, vermilion,
white, brown, buff, all altered by distance and heat, and, after cloudburst when the sweeping air held moisture suspended, all given mystery
by every variation of light—ray, burst, or curtain.

Hill saw almost no human life along the way, except for one small
band of cattle thieves "leisurely driving a herd of stolen cattle across the
river into Mexico," and an outlaw called Greasy Bill with a straggle of
followers who camped on the Mexican side. Surely the boats must be
nearing the apex of the Big Bend?—for each time the river turned northward Hill thought they had come to it. But five times they travelled
around southern bends of the river only to turn southeastward again on
the course by which they had left Presidio. And when at last they turned
northeastward to hold their new course beyond the apex, they saw

ahead of them another mountain barrier athwart the river. As they drew near to it they could see what looked in the face of the sierra like a heavy black line drawn from top to bottom. This was the slit into which the Rio Grande vanished; and they thought the river seemed to plunge into a "seething hole without visible outlet." Again it was a limestone canyon, with strata tilted and bent into odd formations. Here the river made many more turns and bends than in the Santa Elena, and its course was varied with many side-canyons entering through "pin-nacled and terraced cream-colored walls." It was the Little Mariscal Canyon, and was soon succeeded by Big Mariscal Canyon, of similar character. The voyagers saw in it "a Rocky Mountain sheep far above . . . upon an inaccessible ledge. Serafine took one shot at him, and he tum-bled back in a majestic leap." The trip through these canyons was unim-peded, and after a few hours, at noon, the party was out in the desert again, where they saw on the Mexican side the ruins of an old fort called the Presidio de San Vicente. The next day brought the boats to another canyon, through mountains like those of the day before, but not so big. Emerging from it, they soon came to "the village of Boquillas" where they "encountered the first and only American civilization upon our expedition."

Just east of Boquillas the longest and deepest of the Big Bend canyons appeared between the Dead Horse Mountains in Texas and directly opposite in Mexico, the Sierra del Carmen. Fifty miles long and five thousand feet deep, it was Boquillas Canyon—"little mouths," for the narrowness of the towering gateways cut in the mountain rock. The river, said Hill, "in approaching this mountain, first turns from side to side in short stretches, as if trying to avoid the mighty barrier above it, and then, as if realizing that it is constantly becoming involved in the maze of foot-hills, suddenly starts across it."

Once in the canyon the voyagers found even more extraordi-nary formations, colors and vagaries of the river than before. They made many right-angle bends, each producing startling new vistas. Im-mense caves hung empty in the cliffs. In many places the sheer yellow walls were cut from top to bottom by wonderful fissures gleaming with chalk white or vermilion minerals. Gigantic tributary canyons opened into the main course. During the passage of the Boquillas, which took several days, the moon was full, and night after night the men were awed by the coming and going of the moonlight which would first glow on the topmost pinnacles and then start down the western wall, "gently settling from stratum to stratum as the black shadows fled before it, until finally it reached the silent but rapid waters of the river, which became a belt of silver. . . . I could never sleep until the glorious light had ferreted out the shadows from every crevice and driven darkness from the canyon." And then the moonlight would creep up the other wall until all was darkness again.

They met no obstruction in the Boquillas, and one day never knowing which turn of the dark chasm would at last show them a vista not of another wall deep in shade but of open sky and horizon, they came out into the last of the desert basins in their course. At the canyon mouth there were a thousand goats with their shepherds and dogs. Startled, all ran away. The flat valley rose in terraces to the bases of mountains on either side. Hill observed, "The human mind is almost incapable of conceiving the vast quantity of boulders which in times past have poured out of these vertical canyons into such open plains."

Once again, having passed so much canyon and desert in which there was none, the travellers began to see animal life. A lizard; two immense ravens, "half-hopping, half-flying"; beaver slides on the banks; three deer; blue quail; a mockingbird—"only one who is accustomed to the animal life of the desert can imagine the joy with which we greeted these lowly friends."

After a twelve-mile desert stretch they entered another canyon with broken walls, the cliffs receded, and they passed the mouth of a dead river on the Texas side. It was Maravillas Creek, "a horrible desert arroyo, leading northward for one hundred miles or more. . . . It has a channel sufficient for the Hudson, but is utterly devoid of water. Now and then, in the intervals of years, great floods pour down its stony bottom, giving the boulders and other desert debris a further push toward the Rio Grande and the sea."

At this point the river turned due east, continuing in a narrow valley far below the complicated forms of a great limestone plateau. Would there be no end to these enclosures? Hill and his people were weary of them. "In the steep canyons there had always been a tense feeling of anxiety, accompanied by a longing to escape their dangers as soon as possible." Their first hint of comfort in those weeks came one Sunday noon. "Shortly after making the turn to the east, and in the depths of a beautifully terraced canyon, we came upon [a] copious hot spring running out of the bluff upon a low bench, where it made a large, clear pool of water. . . . Here we made our first and only stop for recreation. After lunch, most of the party proceeded to the warm pool, and, stripping, we literally soaked for hours in its delightful waters, stopping occasionally to soap and scrub our linen."

They speculated upon the height of the cliffs. Nobody guessed more than five hundred feet. Hill found "a good place for the first time in all our course to scale the canyon walls," went up and measured the exact height. Like all travellers in the southwest they had been fooled by the clear air which like a lens acted to bring distance near. The height was sixteen hundred and fifty feet. "The view from the summit was superb, revealing the panorama of the uplands, which is completely shut out while traversing the chasm below."

They went on eastward in their boats through curious formations. "In this eastern stretch the immediate gorge of the river is generally a canyon within a canyon." As it continued easterly, the river gradually surmounted the great limestone formation that had made its prison walls and tried to frustrate its course. But this relief was short. At the 102nd meridian the Rio Grande again vanished between the walls of a rocky trough whose color was no longer buff and orange, but white "which weathers into great curves rather than vertical ledges." The effects were handsome—hundred-foot pillars, immense overhanging gables under which the boatmen sailed for hours, finding wild game on the banks and wild honey in caves. But they were exhausted in temper and body, and "no longer appreciated the noble surroundings. We longed only to escape from the walls, upon which we now began to look as a prison."

Time itself must have seemed hostile.

They had rowed ten hours every day for over a month. More than once they had to drag the boats over dangerous rapids, getting ducked and soaked. The sunshine in the open stretches was pitiless. They were bored with their limited diet. Never out of mind were the dangers of river nature, and, if they had to abandon the river, the hopelessness of reaching safety overland through desert wilderness without water, on foot. They watched for a landmark that would tell them they had finished their hard journey. It was a sign known for decades to the few first travellers of the region—"a huge pile of sticks skilfully entwined into what is perhaps the largest bird's nest in America," which clung to the edge of a small cave in the yellow river bluff on the Mexican side. It was the home of a pair of eagles which every year produced their young in it.

The travellers finally saw it and knew they were done.

They landed on a little beach opposite the nest. The village of

Langtry was a mile and a half away, a station on the Southern Pacific Railroad. They sent for a packhorse and took their equipment to town, and were received by Judge Roy Bean under his sign which proclaimed him to be the Law West of the Pecos, a Justice of the Peace, a Notary Republic, and a purveyor of San Antonio Lager Beer. Locked in some crevice of cranky romance proper to his country and his character, Judge Bean kept a glowing image of the actress Lily Langtry, the Jersey Lily, for whose photograph he had conceived a passion. His village, first called Vinegaroon, Texas, he renamed in her honor. After his death she paused on a transcontinental tour in her private "palace car" to look wonderingly for a moment upon a reproduction of her portrait by Sir John Millais that hung over the bar in Judge Bean's Jersey Lily Saloon, and to accept as gifts from his successor Judge Bean's gavel and rifle.

Robert Hill and his men had navigated and mapped "three hundred and fifty miles of a portion of one of America's greatest rivers which hitherto had been considered impassable." To discover the last earth secrets of the Rio Grande they had lived for weeks in a lost world created through incalculable time. On reaching Langtry, Texas, and its transcontinental railroad, they were immediately restored to the modern world of technology in power and communication.

42.

Revolution and Reflex

It was a world by which the life of the United States Rio Grande was already much modified. Now beyond the river in Mexico, under the rule of President Porfirio Díaz, the first industrial techniques and systematic exploitations of Mexico's great natural wealth were being developed together. Mexican railroads came to the river at Matamoros, Nuevo Laredo, Piedras Negras and Juárez during the Díaz reign, and symbolized, if in their operation they did not fully demonstrate, that sense of order in communication by which the machine world and its society kept the promises implicit in timetables and other conventions of commercial accord. Much in the American nature enjoyed such order, for efficiency in the use of time and man power and machine materials was becoming a matter of the national faith. On the other hand, much in the Mexican nature was indifferent if not hostile to such order, for to many Mexicans time meant only that tomorrow would come, and as for man power, it could be shot to death, and machines would break down sooner or later. Still, the Mexican president, proudly striving to bring his country into the company of modern world powers, imposed upon it with the aid of tax revenues derived from huge investments by foreign capital his own vision of society. Díaz brought to Mexico a long period of political order, industrial development, economic stability, and even some broadening of public education. It was a program that had resemblances to the systems of life in the great world powers. Foreign statesmen regarded President Díaz as their peer. Foreign capitalists, investing in Mexican oil and mining and ranching properties, could talk with him, for he spoke their language. Where had he learned it, born of Indian blood in a poor Oaxacan family, this ex-seminarian, this law student under Benito Juárez, this revolutionary soldier and one-time land reformer? But what did it matter, for Mexican bankers and landowners spoke it too, and approved the presidential achievement, with all its years of growing prosperity and order.

But it was a prosperity and an order brought about at the expense of the individual independence and political freedom of the Mexican people—and even their ownership of property. For under laws passed during the Díaz regime Mexico's natural wealth rested in the hands of less than four per cent of the population. It required no special knowledge for Mexicans at large to know that if under their absolute ruler they were living an orderly life, they were also hungry for the lands that their fathers had owned even in the unsettled times of such a recurrent national chief as Santa Anna, and the wars of his various glories and disgraces. Mexico, with her leaders laboring to bring her into the modern world, at the same time suffered a relapse into feudal inequities in her social structure that could lead only to revolution, with both its sacrifices and its crimes, its visions and treacheries. President Díaz, coming to power after his own successful revolution launched across the lower Rio Grande in 1876, began to consider, by 1909, the possible consequences of his repressive and efficient rule. He was already hearing talk of candidates to oppose him in his next election, a discourteous threat.

But it was more than that, for popular support, with no reason to be loyal to the administration, was beginning to drift to those leaders who dared to breathe a promise of land reform on behalf of those millions who had no patch of earth on which to raise an ear of corn or a bean for themselves and the children who must follow them even as hungry and dispossessed.

President Díaz, at seventy-nine, had much experience of political gesture. It seemed to him that if he were to demonstrate before his nation how fully he enjoyed the confidence of the powerful republic above the Rio Grande, with all attendant implications of prestige and filtered wealth and perhaps even a hint of supporting force, then much opposition in the election of next year, 1910, might fade away. He wrote to President William Howard Taft of the United States to propose a public meeting between them; and with gratifying swiftness the proposal was accepted. President Taft in his first year of office was to make a great swing across the United States from coast to coast; and on his way back, would be pleased to stop over at El Paso to meet his colleague from Mexico City, and, as it were, shake hands with him across the Rio Grande.

Relations along the border had been generally good since the late 1880s when the last of the private bandit armies organized after the style of Canales and Cortina had been suppressed by General Don Ramon Treviño, to the satisfaction of President Díaz. True, there were still individual masters of the bravura style of lawlessness at work, like Old White Lip in the Big Bend, and Colonel Emory's remark of half a century before—"Property is very insecure all along the boundary"—was still applicable. But depredations from below the border were now frowned upon by Mexican authority, and the ruling temper above it was far different from that which, in all respectability, moved General Tom Green who like many Americans of his time was free in his thoughts about Mexican territory. In his published account of the Mier adventure he proposed that if the abolition of slavery should ever come—he shuddered to think of it—the United States should acquire all of Mexico as far south as the twentieth parallel, which amounted to about three fourths of the nation, and should deport all American Negroes to settle there.

With the new century, the terms of disagreement between border Mexicans and North Americans assumed new forms which had to do with social attitudes rather than with open crime. The Anglo-American technological society, with all its commercial originality, came to power over the old combination of Indian and Latin ways of life, and rapidly made a subject class of wage labor out of a population that for centuries had owned both sides of the river. The most easily recognized symbols of the respective positions of the North American and the Mexican peoples of the border were the white skin of the one and the brown of the other. The economic superiority of *white* over *brown* created corresponding social prejudice, until *brown* not only was dispossessed, but was made to feel inferior. It was a set of attitudes in which dwelt the seed of much trouble for later generations of the two Rio Grande peoples, one so heedless and energetic, the other so hapless and proud.

But as the two presidents approached their common frontier in 1909 all was courtesy and dignity, for good manners were easier to manage between heads of states than among simple citizens. President Taft was clear about what had occasioned the meeting. Díaz needed his public support, as the surge of liberal sentiment in Mexico might seem now to predict his overthrow. "I am glad to aid him," wrote President Taft to his wife as his special train trundled him dustily across the great spaces of Arizona toward the Rio Grande, "for the reason that we have two billions [of] American capital in Mexico that will be greatly endangered if Díaz were to die and his government go to pieces." It was an alarming prospect, for a turbulent Mexico would create in reflex agonizing problems for her neighboring government. "I can only hope and pray," added the corpulent American president, who thrived on comfort, "that his demise does not come until I am out of office. . . ."

The American presidential train came into the El Paso yards in the early forenoon of October sixteenth, while President Taft enfolded himself in his voluminous frock coat, as directed by State Department arrangements, which specified also that the Mexican president would appear in uniform. Waiting in the Tuscan-styled El Paso station was Colonel Pablo Escandón, the ADC to President Díaz, with greetings from his chief. Captain Archie Butt, the American ADC, descended from the private car with his president, and proceeded to the street where a cavalry escort from Fort Bliss was ready to conduct the commander-in-chief to the El Paso Chamber of Commerce. Once there, President Taft entered an empty back room, lay down on a black leather couch and went to sleep. But trumpets soon broke the distance with flourishes to announce that President José de la Cruz Porfirio Díaz was moving through the streets of Juárez. President Taft awoke to duty and rode to the international bridge. Advancing to the center over the cloacal drift of the shallow river the two presidents, while cannon salutes proclaimed their dignity, met and shook hands, as Captain Archie Butt did the honors: "The President of the United States—the President of Mexico!" President Taft, in English, said,

"I am very glad to welcome you, sir, here, I am very glad indeed," to which President Díaz, in Spanish, replied,

"I am very happy to meet you and to have the honor of being one of the first foreigners to come over and give you a hearty welcome."

The old Indian president was dazzling. His stocky figure was superbly uniformed and on his broad torso were spread the stars of a dozen orders. President Taft felt "quite outshone," and observed further that his aged colleague was "most remarkable in point of agility, quickness of perception and dignity of carriage." After preliminary courtesies the two chiefs moved to the American end of the bridge for a procession through the streets of El Paso. The United States Secret Service had put the city under augmented guard. An hour ago all citizens living along the line of march were obliged to close and lock their doors, and as the two presidents rode together to the Chamber of Commerce for a private conversation the Secret Service kept clear a running space in the crowds ahead and behind and on both sides of the state vehicle, and kept watching the populace for "sight of a drawn and set face," and, on seeing any such, at once arranged to search the suspect person. A member of the cortège reported that "over one hundred weapons were gathered in this way, although none of them may have been intended for purposes of assassination." Only one disorderly incident marred the day's arrangements—a dusty scuffle on the sidelines, a sob of passion, a flash of steel, and an American boy fell dead under the knife of a Mexican youth whose view of President Díaz he had obstructed. Amidst the cheers, who knew whether the great men bowing along the lane saw it happen?

Once in the Chamber of Commerce the presidents, with confidential aides and interpreters, retired to a private room to talk business—the business that had brought them both to the river. As it turned out, their interests were not, after all, identical. True, President Taft offered to President Díaz the benefits he had come to find; but there was now a provision attached. The price of "full friendship and support," as a Mexican who was present later told, was the renewal by Mexico of leases held by the United States Navy on basing facilities for the Pacific Fleet in Magdalena Bay, on the west coast of Lower California. The old Mexican's eyes were "dark, unblinking, bright, spirited," and now behind them moved thoughts that troubled him. He was already under hot fire at home from the increasingly bold critics of his whole policy, including the large concessions he had made to foreign powers. He was now forced to choose between a further concession to the United States and a gesture of independence on behalf of Mexico. He shook his head. It would be impossible to renew the naval leases. The decision may have been more costly than he could have anticipated, for the Mexican witness to the interview believed that it was "one of the chief reasons the American government later winked its eyes" at the works of Madero in opposing Díaz.

The incident may have seemed small, yet it dealt in costly failure, for by it neither president fully gained what he wanted. There remained two thirds of the day's ceremonial program to carry out, but there was a sense that the heart had gone out of it. Still, amenity must be preserved, and President Taft was famous for his jolly nature, and soon further compliments and expressions of satisfaction were flowing, and after twenty minutes champagne was brought in and toasts were exchanged, and then the President of Mexico withdrew to his own soil over the river. He was followed at noon by President Taft, who called on him in Juárez where the public courtesies were repeated. In the evening sixty guests sat down with the two presidents to a state dinner at which the Mexican was host. Both were in civilian evening dress, the one monumentally plain, the other wearing the red, white and green ribbon of Mexico over his breast, and a profuse garland of miniature medals. The table service was the silver and gold plate from the presidential palace of Mexico City. There were jokes—the presidents in inquiring after the health of each other's wife made amusing remarks about the duties and activities of a political consort; and there were speeches—the host said the occasion afforded "a happy precedent for Latin-American republics to cultivate constant and cordial relations among themselves, with us, and with all other countries of the continent," and the guest replied that "the aims and ideals of our two nations are identical, their sympathy is mutual and lasting, and the world can be assured of a vast neutral zone of peace in which the controlling aspirations of either nation is individual and human happiness. . . ." Under the sound of such decorous revelries already moved the forces that all too soon must bring Mexico to bleeding misery and the United States to anger against her.

Before the evening ended a photograph was taken of the presidents and their military aides together. It would be an important piece of evidence for President Díaz to scatter about to show how he stood with the Americans. "He thinks," noted President Taft, "and I believe rightly, that the knowledge throughout his country of the friendship of the United States for him and his government will strengthen him with his own people, and tend to discourage revolutionists' efforts to establish a different government . . ." The party was over. President Taft with his aides returned to his train at El Paso. Noticing how nervous they seemed to be, he proposed a highball. They all took one, and after a deep drink one of the company said to the president,

"Thank God we're all out of Mexico and the day's over. We've been half crazy for fear somebody would take a shot at you."

The president chuckled and made a joke about the target he presented with his great bulk. The train pulled out eastward across Texas, leaving the Rio Grande and the border city where in a matter of months the conspiracy against Díaz would be centered in the ideas and the acts of Francisco Madero.

For Taft as president was not after all to escape the trials that came with the overthrow of the Díaz government. Madero opposed Díaz in the election of 1910, but his campaign proposals became so popular that he was arrested for sedition. He escaped, fled to El Paso, and from there, in the long succession of revolutionists who used the left bank as asylum and platform, he cried out across the river his plans for reform—chiefly agrarian. The people heard him, he returned to Mexico to lead a revolution, and in 1911 Porfirio Díaz resigned to go into exile in Paris. Once in power Madero, hoping to achieve internal peace for Mexico, made compromises with the remnants of the Díaz faction, and in his turn faced revolutionary opposition from the agrarian party. In 1912 President Taft supported him to the extent of prohibiting the shipment of arms from the United States to his opponents. At the same time the United States government advised its citizens in Mexico to come home, in order to avoid the risk of involvement in the disorders that spread rapidly in the wake of the new phase of the revolution, while President Taft was abused at home for his "surrender" of American rights. He could not have been sorry to yield the Mexico problem, along with the Presidency, to Woodrow Wilson after the election of 1912.

Barely a fortnight before the new American president was to take office Madero was forced to resign in Mexico, on February 19, 1913, and three days later, after having been refused sanctuary in the United States Embassy in Mexico City, was assassinated, along with Suárez his vice-president, by the adherents of General Victoriano Huerta, who seized the Mexican presidency for himself. Huerta, as a conservative, received early recognition by Great Britain, with her huge oil interests in Mexico that had been developed under Díaz. But President Wilson, refusing from the first to be influenced by American capitalists who held even heavier investments in Mexico, regarded Huerta—"the unspeakable Huerta," as he called him—as one who had seized power illegally and through violence, and denied him recognition by the United States, so arousing enmities both at home and in Mexico. By 1913 American investments in Mexico amounted to approximately $1,200,000,000, and American miners, oilmen, engineers, agriculturists and their families to the number of about seventy-five thousand were living in Mexico as custodians of such wealth. Must all this be endangered by President Wilson's fastidiousness? And without the enpowering recognition of the United States must General Huerta face the perils that rose against him?

For within a month after assuming the presidency Huerta was in his turn the target of a revolutionary movement that gathered in the north, where old comrades of the beloved Madero were making an army and a policy. The north—it was there that Díaz himself had gathered his power, and again it was the vast northern deserts whose people, as so often before, bursting from their isolation and impassioned by their poverty, bore the seeds of revolution. *"Nordismo,"* they said, making a philosophy out of their bleak land for which they had nothing to lose but life, and for which anything gained must be a relief. Huerta, knowing that he must assure himself of northern loyalties, called the governors of the Rio Grande states of Coahuila and Chihuahua to his support. Chihuahua joined the Federal cause; but not Coahuila. On March 26, 1913, her governor, Venustiano Carranza, refused allegiance to Huerta, proclaimed a new revolution, announced himself as "First Chief" of all those who remained true to the Madero reforms, and took to the field with a large and ragged army. His principal command he gave to one of Madero's most ardent lieutenants—a certain Doroteo Arango, who was better known by the name he had adopted years ago out of respect for an admired bandit called Francisco Villa. Becoming popular as a bandit in his turn, the new Francisco Villa was spoken of everywhere by the diminutive of his first name—Pancho—and as his military adventures earned him his command, they brought him the rank of general of brigade—General Pancho Villa.

If in the rapid turns and overturns of power in Mexico following the fall of Díaz there seemed to be many separate revolutions during the ensuing decade, these were more truly seen as successive phases of one long struggle. For what Madero had launched was the Grand Revolution against the feudalism of Díaz, and what followed, with so many different personalities in the murderous tug of war between the adherents of absolutism and those of constitutionalism, really revived the political polarities that had divided Mexico from the time of the Emperor Augustín until the triumph of Díaz. In pain and barbarism Mexico resumed the long civil war through which for the better part of a century she sought to find her independent character.

First Chief Carranza's initial move must be against the neighboring state of Chihuahua if *nordismo* was to present a united front. General Pancho Villa marched against Chihuahua City and drove the Federal defenders all the way to the Rio Grande at Ojinaga, opposite Presidio, Texas. Out of ten thousand troops only thirty-five hundred remained there to defend the Federal idea against *nordismo*. In their ragged white uniforms they dug trenches before Ojinaga facing south, and Texans watched them from Presidio, and an American reporter told how "when the sun went down with the flare of a blast furnace, patrols of cavalry rode sharply across the skyline to the night outposts," and how "after dark mysterious fires burned in the town." Ojinaga was almost wholly in ruins, stirring with wounded, hungry, sick people, while Presidio on the American side knew a brisk trade in gambling and merchandising and conspiracy—for "you could not walk around a corner at night without stumbling over a plot or a counterplot." Two troops of the Ninth United States Cavalry patrolled the riverside, and now and then a Mexican sentry opposite fired a stray shot at them, and was fired on in turn. What all expected came to pass after about three months, when General Pancho Villa with his forces appeared through the mountains from the south and drove the Federal army over the river into Presidio. The fugitives were interned afterward behind barbed wire at Fort Bliss. General Pancho Villa seized Juárez, offering an absorbing spectacle to the citizens of El Paso who clustered on the tops of tall buildings to view through telescopes the bivouac fires by night, and by day, the drag of cannon and the wander of little columns of revolutionary troops. Chihuahua now belonged to the Constitutionalist Army—or, more properly, to Pancho Villa. There was little that Huerta could do about it.

His recognition by Great Britain made the American position more difficult. President Wilson, hoping that "a refusal to recognize any government founded upon violence" would prove instructive to Latin American republics, asked the British to withdraw their recognition of Huerta; and when this was not done, he sent a personal emissary to Mexico to persuade Huerta that for the good of Mexico he must resign and permit a new election to be held from which he must bar himself as a candidate. The *de facto* ruler of Mexico was not equal to such a display of ethical objectivity. It was a disappointment, but President

Wilson in reporting to the Congress on his failure urged patience in the face of Mexico's disorders which promised such trouble for American property holders in Mexico. "We shall triumph as Mexico's friends sooner than we could triumph as her enemies," he said, "—and how much more handsomely, with how much higher and finer satisfaction of conscience and honor!" If to many the accent here seemed like that of a proctor, and the manner superior and dry, and the vision too ideal in an uncloistered world where competition was ruthless and massacre an admitted technique of government in Mexico, there was yet an uneasy recognition that here the forces of goodness were working at large in the cause of humanity in general. President Wilson was a strong as well as a delicate man, even if he lacked the humor that might have kept him from saying to a British statesman in 1913, "I am going to teach the South American Republics to elect good men!", for all the world as if the Southern nations were seated before him in his lecture room on the top floor of Dickinson Hall at Princeton, where on Monday and Tuesday mornings he used to meet his class in Jurisprudence and Politics. In 1913 he was sure that Carranza and Villa were the best choices among Huerta's opponents. "Villa," he thought, was "not so bad as he had been painted." In any case, he had not recognized any of the three, and there was a charming tact in the little story his ambassador to Britain wrote him on October twenty-fourth. Mr. Walter Hines Page "ran across" Prime Minister Asquith at the wedding of Prince Arthur of Connaught to the Duchess of Fife and had a lively little exchange with him.

"What do you infer from the latest news from Mexico?" asked the Prime Minister.

"Several things," replied Ambassador Page.

"Tell me the most important inference you draw."

"Well, the danger of prematurely making up one's mind about a Mexican adventurer."

"Ah!" murmured the Prime Minister and walked off.

It did seem that the British were unable to feel the true significance of American forbearance and American determination that Mexico should learn to solve her own problems like a proper democracy. A few weeks later Ambassador Page reported another exchange, this time with Sir Edward Grey, the Foreign Minister.

"Suppose you have to intervene?" asked Grey.

"Make 'em vote and live by their decisions," said Page, wholly in accord with the President's view.

"But suppose they will not so live?"

"We'll go in again and make 'em vote again."

"And keep this up for 200 years?"

"Yes, the United States will be here two hundred years and it can continue to shoot men for that little space till they learn to vote and to rule themselves."

Sir Edward Grey laughed. "I have never seen him laugh so heartily," reported the Ambassador. "Shooting men into self-government! . . . he comprehends that. But that's as far as his habit of mind goes." If the British Foreign Minister could not grasp the point of the American policy, it was idle to expect Mexican bandit politicians to do so. Early in January, 1914, Ambassador Page detected signs of a new approach to the whole Mexican problem. If the British would not withdraw their recognition of Huerta, they might—it was hinted by the head of the British oil concessions in Mexico—they might undertake intervention jointly with the United States.

But the reality lay elsewhere, in a shift from the great quiet rooms of ministers and ambassadors and presidents where in every accent of education and wit the embroilments of Mexico were discussed, to the glaring plains where hard as the rocks of their concealment and irresponsible as the dust that blew past them General Pancho Villa and his band went about making carrion of all who disagreed with either their whims or their idea of revolution—which in itself was not wholly clear to themselves. In February, 1914, an Englishman, William S. Benton, was murdered at Juárez in the presence of Pancho Villa by one of his men. Britain cried out for revenge, and even threatened taking punitive steps, but was prevented by the terms of the Monroe Doctrine. Page wrote to the President that he was glad "for us and for the world that it is *our* job and not theirs. They would India-ize and Egypt-ize Mexico forever. . . ."

On April 9, 1914, the United States received an official affront at the hands of Mexican troops. Unarmed sailors from the U.S.S. *Dolphin* picking up supplies in a routine fashion at Tampico were arrested by Mexican soldiers. They were released in two hours, and General Huerta hastened to explain that the dock used by the American sailors was in a restricted area, and that as Tampico was under martial law, his soldiers had only done their duty. But clearly the Americans had not known the dock was out of bounds, and he expressed his regrets over the incident. These explanations were not satisfactory to Admiral Mayo, commanding the American Gulf squadron. He demanded that the United States flag receive a special salute from the Tampico garrison commander. The demand was referred to Mexico City. On April thirteenth General Huerta refused to order that the salute be given. Both countries had now taken steps which dignity would not permit them to retrace. President Wilson ordered naval reinforcements to Tampico and served Huerta with an ultimatum to require Mexico to salute the American flag by six in the evening of April nineteenth. The hour passed without a sign from Mexico. A day went by, and part of a night, and then at half past two in the morning of April twenty-first, the President was awakened at the White House by a telephone call from his Secretary of State, William Jennings Bryan. Also on the line were Josephus Daniels, Secretary of the Navy, and Joseph Tumulty, the secretary to the President. Bryan had alarming news. A German ship was reported by Admiral Mayo as due to arrive at Veracruz at ten o'clock the same morning. It carried "large supplies of munitions and arms for the Mexicans." The Secretary of State asked the President's judgment "as to how we shall handle the situation."

"Of course, Mr. Bryan," said the President, "you understand what drastic action in this matter might ultimately mean in our relations with Mexico?"

"I thoroughly appreciate this, Mr. President," answered Bryan, "and fully considered it before telephoning you. . . ."

The President fell silent in thought for a moment, and then asked Secretary Daniels his opinion. Daniels believed that the cargo must not be landed. The President "without a moment's delay" said to him,

"Daniels, send this message to Admiral Mayo: 'Take Veracruz at once.'"

The orders went out. "It's too bad, isn't it," said the President to Tumulty later, "but we could not allow that cargo to land. The Mexicans intend using those guns upon our own boys. It is hard to take action of this kind. . . ." Before the day was over American marines and sailors had captured Veracruz with a loss of four killed and twenty wounded, while Mexican casualties were reported "in hundreds." All Mexico was outraged—even Carranza, who opposed Huerta, demanded that the United States withdraw at once. But once committed, the President consolidated his position by ordering thirty-four hundred troops and twelve machine guns under Major General Frederick Funston from Texas to Veracruz. War was prevented from breaking out only by an offer of mediation on the part of Argentina, Brazil and Chile—the ABC Powers. Meeting at Niagara Falls they examined the whole Mexican state of affairs, hoping to find a solution in nominating a provisional president.

Meanwhile, the American garrisons of the Rio Grande border were under alert, and Brigadier General John J. Pershing was ordered to Fort Bliss, in April. He had won distinction and early promotion in the Philippine Islands fighting against insurgent Moros. His experience in putting down guerrilla fighters would surely be useful if war with Mexico should come. But in early summer there were signs that Huerta's position was growing precarious. President Wilson, seeing that Carranza and Villa made progress in their drive against Huerta, viewed them as "sincere patriots," and as for their British critics he said they were "radically mistaken. There has been less disorder and less danger to life where the Constitutionalists have gained control than there has been where Huerta is in control." In the face of the possibility that Villa might replace Huerta, Sir Edward Grey, with a nod to the moral position pre-empted for itself by the United States, thought that ". . . it was impossible to feel that morality was really to be secured by substituting him or his kind for Huerta. . . ."

If together Carranza and Villa had been successful in their drive against Huerta, now in the early summer of 1914 they began to fall out with each other. In June Carranza knew something that led him to write to Villa's supporters in the north, "I do not consider it advisable to promote Gen. Francisco Villa . . . excusing myself from giving the reasons which have determined this decision: I may add that at the proper time this promotion may be granted." Clearly, he was disciplining his military chief. Villa, though always ready with a fierce word in approval of loyalty, was used to having his own way. For the moment he was silent, while Carranza moved nearer to Mexico City. About Carranza there were at first glance all the signals of benevolence. He was a huge man, with an impressive head. His brow was open and broad. His white whiskers divided in the middle gave him a benign look. His eyes were shielded by blue-tinted glasses. His cheeks were ruddy and he had something of a paunch and he went about in modest and rumpled khakis. Mounted on a horse he sat like a bale of goods. A former senator and governor, he seemed at times diffident. But on closer acquaintance he showed a vanity so malignant and a nature so disagreeable that even his twinkling blue lenses could not conceal the hard black burn in his smallish eyes. A trancelike egotism seemed to inform many of his public acts. In July he had the satisfaction of seeing Huerta yield to him by fleeing Mexico City to seek sanctuary abroad.

After August 4, 1914, the affairs of Mexico became almost wholly a concern of the United States, for on that day the first World War began in Europe. On August twentieth Carranza made his entry as conqueror into Mexico City.

One of his early acts after assuming supreme control of the Mexican government was to demand the withdrawal of United States forces from Veracruz, where they had remained all summer. President Wilson found it possible to agree to the evacuation now that Huerta, the "unspeakable" wretch whose policies and actions had caused the occupation in the first place, was gone. The withdrawal was ordered on September fifteenth and was completed by November twenty-third. It was Carranza's first success in foreign affairs. Within his borders during the autumn he suffered a prompt demonstration of how the revolution, by a sort of cellular division, continued to perpetuate itself. On September thirtieth, in a manifesto issued from Chihuahua, the First Chief was repudiated by General Pancho Villa, who could not forbear to mention how he had been refused promotion to General of Division, while two others had been promoted over him. The manifesto then went on to declare a new revolution, with Villa pledging himself not to accept political office, and promising to establish a civilian *ad interim* president, and guaranteeing free elections. Calling on all to support him and his Division of the North, he cried, "Every Mexican citizen who does not contribute toward realising this freedom-bearing movement will feel remorse of conscience, in that he has not known how to love and how to serve his country." He signed it "Francisco Villa," and under that he promoted himself to "General-in-Chief."

Carranza answered him within a month, referring to the manifesto which he said was "written for Villa"—a sneer at the fact that Villa was illiterate. As for the promotion affair, the First Chief said "I did not deem it justified to recompense an insubordination with a promotion," for he had had evidence of Villa's disloyalty to him. Mentioning Villa's desire to refuse all political office for himself, Carranza remarked wryly, "we shall soon be able to ascertain whether or not he has this ambition." He knew his old comrade in arms, for within three months Villa proclaimed himself President of Mexico—though without seriously disturbing Carranza's claim to the position. Caught between the hatreds and rivalries of the two revoluntionary chiefs, and harried by the side-line activities of Zapata and others of his kind, Mexico entered upon the worst years of her internal struggles, of which Americans in growing numbers were victims.

President Wilson's Republican opposition and much of the press cried out for him to chastise Mexico. To what avail was the might of the United States if it must rest idle while her citizens were hurt, robbed, or killed by political bandits below the Rio Grande? Citizens bombarded their congressional delegations with offers to volunteer, to raise regiments of "Rough Riders" or of Negro soldiers, and many men proposed themselves for commisions in the Army or appointments in civilian war service. There was an outpouring of addresses to the President, printed in pamphlet form, that described the indignities and the horrors which Americans were suffering at the hands of Mexicans who were punished only with words from Washington. But he had supporters who though they made less outcry than his attackers outnumbered them greatly. "I have to pause and remind myself," reflected the President, "that I am President of the United States and not of a small group of Americans with vested interests in Mexico." But he did his utmost short of war for his countrymen beyond the border, continuing to bear upon Carranza with the pressures of world opinion and the weight of virtue. In March, 1915, he warned him against harming foreigners in Mexico, and "any apparent contempt for the rights and safety of those who respect religion—" for one of the revolutionary measures was to persecute the Church. "To warn you concerning such matters," wrote President Wilson to Carranza, "is an act of friendship. . . ." Such friendship seemed to mean nothing. Acts of depredation were continued, and at the end of March the President said "I am daily fearful that something imprudent may be done at Brownsville," and like his predecessor advised Americans in Mexico to come home. The advice was no more popular now than before.

United States Army garrisons along the border were augmented, chiefly by the cavalry in its last great service to the country. The lower river forts knew again some of the animation and importance of their first years, and bleak little stations of mounted troops were established in the Big Bend, and the border guard was intensified at Presidio, Fort Bliss, and Columbus, New Mexico, where the Thirteenth Cavalry watched over a vast plain that reached out of sight beyond the barbed wire fence of the boundary. President Wilson gave to the world a picture of what a wilderness Mexico had become by the acts of her own people. "Her crops are destroyed, her fields lie unseeded, her work cattle are confiscated for the use of the armed factions, her people flee to the mountains to escape being drawn into unending bloodshed, and no man seems to see or lead the way to peace and settled order. . . . Mexico is starving and without a government." One of her resources most ruined was the railroad system. Rebels used locomotives and chains to haul the railroad ties out of the ground, and to twist the rails into a tangle, and to make a heap of it all, which was then set on fire. All the railroad stations that could be reached were burned down. Rebel forces taking a town which had marshalling yards sent locomotives after freight cars on tracks in the near hundred miles. The cars were brought in and all burned. The destruction was so great that ten years would hardly suffice to set the lines operating again. Where trackage in parts of the north was allowed to survive, the army of Villa learned to use the railroad as a military instrument. The horses and cows of the army were put inside boxcars, the troopers in their huge hats and garlands of cartridge belts rode on top, and in time the signal of a rag of smoke on the distance came to mean terror and tribute in the hearts of the local people who could only snatch up a child, a chicken, a grandparent, and scratch their way to the mountains. "My poor Mexico," said Porfirio Díaz, in Paris, in that summer of 1915, and said no more, and died.

In midsummer one of Wilson's cabinet officers wrote of him, "These are times of terrible strain upon him. I saw him last night for a couple of hours, and the responsibility of the situation weighs terribly upon him." Now it was not only Mexico that heaped outrage upon insult, it was also Germany, for she was denying the open seas even to neutral shipping. On May seventh she had sunk the *Lusitania,* which—even if it was a legitimate target as a British ship—carried many American passengers; and war sentiment rose again in the United States. "How to keep us out of war and at the same time maintain our dignity—this is a task certainly large enough for the largest of men," concluded the secretary.

Carranza in his early acts of power had begun the restoration of certain land rights long taken from the communal villages by the Díaz laws. In consequence the Mexican revolutionary ranks closed behind him—excepting those commanded in the north by Villa. Carranza had, after all, a *de facto* government; and in the autumn of 1916 he was recognized by a conference of the United States and the other governments of the hemisphere as president of Mexico. The act of recognition sealed Villa's hostility to him. From now onward, the General-in-Chief of the northern deserts would go to any lengths to harass him. President Wilson, even though Carranza had refused to participate in the conference that had brought him respectability among the nations, saw the results in his own way: "The moral," he said to Congress, "the moral is that the states of America are not hostile rivals, but cooperating friends, and that their growing sense of community of interest, alike in matters political and alike in matters economic, is likely to give them a new significance as factors in international affairs and in the political history of the world." To the most thoughtful element of the Mexican people such words must have sounded reassuring; but the most thoughtful element was not in charge, and the ones that tore Mexico between them could only hear the message with imperfect comprehension of its generous humanity, and grow dull under its glow of high-mindedness.

A more understandable consequence, perhaps, of the new policy of recognition was an embargo declared on October twentieth on exportation of arms to Mexico, with the exception of territory controlled by Carranza. Villa and his other enemies were thus repudiated. It was a hard blow to General Pancho Villa and to the American arms manufacturers with whom he had been doing a great business. He was the lord of Chihuahua, now able to spend tens of thousands of dollars a month in purchasing American supplies. His agents and commissionaires swarmed in and out of El Paso. From now on if they wanted guns and bullets they would have to smuggle them—a duty they could manage with only a little bother. General-in-Chief Pancho Villa was well known in El Paso. Many men of business found it sensible to deal with him. At Fort Bliss his operations were watched. The cavalry drilled and trained against the day when they might be needed in action on the border.

General Pershing was a great believer in thorough training, and in the duty of example, down to the smallest details of an officer's bearing and deportment. He was himself a superb model of a soldier. If he seemed at times hard, he was fair, as he lived by the discipline which he required of others. He stood straight and his uniforms were cut in flat planes to fit the trimness of his figure. He spoke clearly in reflection of his clear thought, and so wrote. He was still too thin from the hardships suffered in the Philippine campaign, but he was gradually getting his full strength back, doing his job in command of his brigade with crisp respect for it and for himself. If he had feelings, few others, certainly none of his men, were permitted to know them. One morning in August, 1915, he met an occasion that called for all of his hardest self-discipline. He was told in a long distance telephone call that during the previous night his wife and three young daughters had lost their lives at San Francisco in a fire that destroyed their quarters. Of all his family only his infant son survived.

The young officer—young for a brigadier general—took leave to attend to matters that none could do for him. By midautumn he was again on duty at the Rio Grande. The training schedules went on as usual. He had been unable to bring himself to write even to close friends but this too he finally must do. On October fifth to one such he wrote, "I shall never be relieved of the poignancy of grief at the terrible loss. . . . It is too overwhelming!" He could not understand how he had lived through it all even thus far. He was trying to work and keep from thinking, but "Oh!" he confessed, "the desolation of Life! The emptiness of it all, after such fulness as I have had. . . ." He wrote again a month later. ". . . I cannot see that time makes the slightest difference. It is just as it was on the dreadful morning when the telephone message gave me the heartbreaking news." But he could see about him, and he saw how matters stood along the river. ". . . I shall be tied down with this border patrol indefinitely. I am working just as hard as possible and am really fortunate to have something to do." He was like a sword receiving through extremes of endurance its true temper.

Demands for national intervention in Mexico grew in volume throughout 1915. The hazards of intervention still seemed to President Wilson greater than the benefits, the injustice of it outweighing any possible material satisfactions. How, he considered, once having entered Mexico could the United States pull out? How ever convince Latin American neighbors that an invasion would be only a brief policing action? But many Americans did not want any such moderation. Citizens wrote to their congressmen and senators saying that the only way to make Mexico behave was to take her territory, whether only temporarily until quiet should be restored, or—why not?—in permanent annexation. And Mexico, hearing echoes of such sentiments, could remember what she had seen before across the Rio Grande, when North Americans came to live as Mexican colonists in Texas, and ended by owning Texas; and when soldiers singing "Green grow the lilacs, oh" came all along the Rio Grande and remained to own New Mexico, Arizona, and California. Would Mexico herself, like her northernmost states of yesterday, be turned now into a foreign land for her own people? President Wilson was a professional historian. He was not proud of the war of Mexican annexation of seventy years past. With all his sorrow and anger over Mexico's crimes, he could see some matters from her point of view.

Though it was true that she tried him sorely. In the late weeks of 1915 another hazard appeared out of Mexico. Secretary of State Lansing discovered that General Victoriano Huerta in El Paso was holding secret conversations with German agents, "looking toward the financing of a revolutionary expedition into northern Mexico." The Secretary declared that this "if it materialized" must end by involving the United States in active war "across the international boundary." It was clear, he said, that "the Germans were intriguing to cause trouble between this government and the *de facto* government of Carranza and also between the American authorities and the rebellious Villista generals. . . ."

There was an ominous quickening of affairs along the river. Mexicans were firing almost every day across the border at American patrols, among whom several were killed and wounded. In Carranza territory, down the river from Villa's empire, federal soldiers joined in outlaw raids on American settlements. On November twenty-sixth at Nogales, Villista troops fired into the American half of the town before withdrawing in a planned evacuation. After the New Year, General Pancho Villa, on January 10, 1916, threw an attack against a train on which American mining employees were riding near the Santa Isabel mines of Chihuahua, and murdered eighteen of them. If Villa had a policy that dictated his scattered pattern of outrages upon American citizens, it seemed to arise from his hatred of Carranza, and his desire at all costs to embarrass him, particularly by bringing down upon him, if he could, the full wrath of the United States. The most direct way to manage this—so Villa must think—was to continue his outrages upon American citizens. The work was congenial and he was a master at it, and so were many of his lieutenants, notably Fierro, "The Butcher," his greatest friend, who only made him sigh affectionately when he personally would shoot down a hundred prisoners for the simple pleasure of it.

The General-in-Chief was of medium height. He had the sort of figure that showed the baby in the body of the man, with thick shoulders, plump forward-hanging belly and short, light, curved legs. His face was deep-jowled. His short nose and wide nostrils and big lip suggested in a kind of good looks that nearness to the simian which was echoed also in his walk. When he walked, it was with a humped posture, and a somewhat pigeon-toed shamble. But like a Comanche Honey-Eater, the moment he was on a horse, he was a master of a physical style, whether to the sound of the shrill Mexican trumpet he rode at a smart walk along a troop-lined street in Juárez, or dirty and unshaven he picked his way at a gallop over the insecure footing of rocky foothills. It was his habit to say almost nothing, since he expressed his opinions in more direct ways, as so many dead men indicated. His mouth hung open under its thick mustache, and his expression was gentle but for his eyes, which an American journalist described as "never still and full of energy and brutality . . . intelligent as hell and as merciless." His bravery was famous. So was his short temper. He loved flattery and friendship, demanded loyalty and never gave it, except to Madero. He was the subject of many ballads which he could not hear often enough. He neither smoked nor drank, but—aside from killing—took his joys in venery and dancing. One time he danced steadily for thirty-six hours at a friend's wedding. In his savage infantilism he seemed to educated men who knew him more animal than man. "He is the most natural human being I ever saw," said one, "natural in the sense of being nearest to a wild animal." Another said ". . . he was as unmoral as a wolf." His general style was at least partly self-conscious, for like one of the frontier fantastics of early Western America, he once cried, "Qué chico se me hace el mar para hacer un buche de agua. . . ." In that boastful promise to use the ocean for a gargle there was a hint of the scale by which he measured himself. His land and people could measure him best by what he so often left behind him in his travels—a field full of dropped bundles of clothes that once had moved with the bodies inside them, or depending from a cottonwood tree clusters of hanged men like great bunches of gourds, and as hollow of life. Some of his countrymen saw him as the champion of the poor; others questioned the value of benefactions made possible by years of crime against humanity. As lord of Chihuahua he tried to make up a sensible government out of his own head. The effort was brave but erratic. Caged within the invisible bars of his ignorance he could escape them only through acts of violence upon others. This was the man who in January, 1916, was causing such grave concern to the United States, and to its officers on the Rio Grande border, including the young brigadier at Fort Bliss whose severe respect for life was to be measured by the sorrow he daily sought to overcome in acts of work.

In February the President told the United States Senate that seventy-six Americans had been killed in Mexico during the previous three years. Sixty-three of these had died in the last six weeks. In addition, thirty-six had been killed by Mexicans on American soil. For years feeling along the border had been against intervention, but now it shifted, and an American wrote, "As one striving to do business in the Republic of Mexico, I have been very hopeful that the next President of the United States might be a gentleman who did not hold such altruistic and ethical views as President Wilson. . . ."

General Pancho Villa continued to throw down his challenges. On March first an American family of ranchers south of the border in Mexico—their name was Wright—saw a band of horsemen ride up and identified them by their red saddle blankets as Villistas. In very little time the visitors did their work. They killed Wright, sent his infant son off with a squad riding to Juárez, put the mother, Maud Wright, up on a horse, took what they wanted of supplies, and circled off over the desert toward the international boundary. Mrs. Wright rode with the column for nine days on a forced march. She had nothing to eat but mule meat and once for thirty hours had to go without water. She understood Spanish and was startled to hear the bandits working out arrangements to raid Columbus, New Mexico, which lay two miles north of the border, and fifty west of El Paso. A town of four hundred people, it was the station of six troops of the Thirteenth United States Cavalry. She knew well enough what her captors liked to do to Americans. There was nothing she could do to give warning. On March eighth she saw go and return a squad of bandits and heard them report how they had crossed the border and spied upon Columbus. They said that most of the garrison were camping on guard near a ranch farther west, and that only a few American soldiers were at the Columbus post. She could only wait to witness further horrors.

On the same day a number of the officers of the Thirteenth were in El Paso, playing polo at Fort Bliss. There seemed no cause for alarm in the immediate situation at Columbus. The colonel of the regiment took what information he could get from Mexican residents, but he was prevented by orders from stepping an inch over the boundary to make personal surveys. He heard rumors that Villa was in the neighborhood, and was given the surprising, the even reassuring report that Villa was coming to give himself up as a prisoner of war. He was said to have very few men with him. The colonel continued his patrols along the American side of the barbed wire fence that marked the international line. There was a gate, of course, and the colonel stationed one troop there. Two others were at the ranch farther along the line. Three troops and the regimental machine gun were on post in Columbus. There was a late train that came out from El Paso on the Southern Pacific and passed through Columbus going west. Around midnight of March eighth-ninth, a young officer of the Thirteenth arrived on the train to go on duty as Officer of the Day. He had been at Bliss for the polo. It was a cold night, but he was wakeful, and once established in the Officer of the Day's shanty, he sat up reading. The rest of the post, and the town, were in darkness and quiet.

It was a quarter of four when he heard a muffled sound from a private on sentry post outside. He went to the door and saw a figure moving in the dim fall of light from the O.D. shack. There was a shot, the sentry fell dead, and the Officer of the Day shot the Mexican who had killed him. In another second there was rifle fire from two sides of the camp and the town. Families were awakened by what at first they "thought was hail on the roof." Then bullets broke against the walls of houses, and screams sounded, and wailing cheers from the Mexican attackers. Some of the residents thought they heard General Pancho Villa's voice "everywhere." The Officer of the Day, nearest the attacking fire, took charge of the awakened troops and directed their defense. The machine gun jammed after a few rounds and became useless. For a while the darkness made a blind fight of it, but when the Mexicans set some buildings to burning, the glare showed the scene to the cavalry, and their resistance turned into attack. The raiders were amongst the streets now, killing and burning noisily. Soldiers' wives took their children and ran under the protection of shadowing alleys to gather for safety in a sergeant's house that was defended by men of F Troop. The children were put under the beds and the women lay flat on the floor, while bullets swarmed above them through the walls. Everyone was quiet, even the children. Presently a sergeant of F Troop said to his soldiers outside, *"Pick your men,* there is hardly any more ammunition." In the wild firelight the battle hung for a little while longer at its peak, and then began to subside, for General Pancho Villa could not animate his men to another attack against such fire as they had finally faced. They began to fall away from the town. Dawn was near. Mrs. Wright, who had helplessly watched the battle from a ditch outside, saw General Pancho Villa as he retreated. She asked him to turn her free. He jerked his head toward Columbus and told her to go. She entered the town and went to the house of friends. She found them. The husband was lying dead face down on his steps, his wife was near-by, badly wounded. Mrs. Wright was helped by an officer who sent her to his wife. As the raiders disappeared into the early light of the desert, the officer's wife and all the others came out of the house where they had been safe. She saw "the dead and wounded everywhere." Nine townspeople and eight troopers had been killed, and many of Villa's men. She told later, "I did not know I could have such hate in my heart. I saw Mexicans horribly wounded and suffering terribly and did not care how much they suffered. . . ." She was soon "thankful to be busy" doing what she could for the wives, the children, of soldiers who had been killed or hurt that night. When Mrs. Wright came to her, she listened to her story, and judged her "a very strong intelligent ranch woman . . . a very remarkable person." Mrs.

Wright was able to give the officers much that was "valuable to know" about Villa and his band. She reported that he had between twenty-five hundred and three thousand men. Already convinced that she had lost everything, it would come as a great wonder when a few days later her baby would be restored to her.

In the growing daylight troops of the Thirteenth pursued Villa. They killed fifty of the raiders on the American side of the border, and following the rest over the line into Mexico, they killed another seventy in several little battles under the blazing sun. Lack of ammunition, food and water after eight hours forced the pursuers back to Columbus, while Villa and his men disappeared into their deserts, and decisions were taken in Washington and Mexico City.

Carranza made an immediate official apology for the Villa attack, promising to "use the most vigorous means to run this man to earth and avenge his horrible acts." Washington hoped he would indeed do so, but if Carranza's prompt apology was meant to prevent, or defer, American entry into Mexico, it failed of its purpose. The War Department ordered all garrisons on the Rio Grande to give chase into Mexico if attacked from over the border, and directed General Funston at Fort Sam Houston to send troops as soon as possible to overtake Villa and the raiders. "These troops will be withdrawn," commanded Secretary Baker, "as soon as the _de facto_ government of Mexico is able to relieve them of this work. . . ." In a further detail, the Secretary wrote ". . . you are instructed to make all practical use of the aeroplanes at San Antonio, Texas, for observation." A new military age was upon the nation.

On the day when the American orders were issued—March tenth—Carranza proposed that "armed forces of either country might freely cross into the territory of the other . . . if the raid effected at Columbus should unfortunately be repeated at any other point on the border." It was the only possible move for him to make if Mexico's dignity was to be upheld. President Wilson approved the proposal, and Secretary Lansing telegraphed the State Department's acceptance of it. On March fifteenth a United States cavalry column crossed into Mexico under the command of Brigadier General John J. Pershing in pursuit of Villa and his men. The act was a signal for Carranza to fly into one of his furies. The "reciprocal pursuit" agreement, he cried, was meant to apply only to _future_ raids—it was not to be applied retroactively to the Columbus raid. General Pancho Villa's policy of making trouble on an international plane was off to a good start. It effected corruption in simpler ways, too, for on the day after the attack, over a hundred thousand rounds of ammunition were sold in El Paso to Villa agents and taken across the river. "Fine doings," remarked the local citizen who reported the matter to Washington.

The American press expressed the rage felt by its readers. In New York, the *American* said "The American flag has indeed been saluted at last." The *Tribune* felt that "The Bryan-Wilson policy . . . has borne its perfect fruit," while the *Evening-Journal* demanded an immediate seizure of all Mexico and Central America: "What has been done in California and Texas by the United States can be done *all the way down to the southern bank of the Panama Canal and a few miles beyond.*" The *World* cried that "Nothing less than Villa's life can atone for the outrage," but the Chicago *Tribune* believed that in respect to the pacification of Mexico, "The death of Villa is a minor detail in such a program. . . . It is a condition—a chronic condition—of chaos, not a Villa, that confronts us." In another editorial, the New York *World* projected the real positions of the sovereignties involved: "So far as it is possible for a bandit to be at war, Villa is now at war with both Mexico and the United States. . . ." The hero of Chihuahua seemed really to feel like a sovereign power. His subjects had confidence in him, and said so in one of their songs, so touched with the acrid pathos of their land and its habits of life, death and war:

> Maybe they have guns and cannons,
> Maybe they are a lot stronger,
> We have only rocks and mountains—
> But we know how to last longer. . . .

President Wilson felt, at home, dangerous currents of opinion that if unchecked might bring war even closer. Two weeks after the Columbus disaster he said, "It is my duty to warn the people of the United States that persons along the border are engaged in giving currency to rumors of the most sensational sort, which are wholly unsupported by the facts. The object of this traffic in falsehood is obvious. It is to create friction between the United States and Mexico, to bring about intervention in the interest of the owners of Mexican properties. . . ." The Administration assured the country that the border was quiet; no preparations for war were necessary. This moved a businessman of the border to telegraph in a rage to a senator, ". . . I ask you to see that the Administration if it insists on being blind is forced to see the light and thereby stumble upon their duty. . . ."

The only note of satisfaction in the discussions of the hour came

from the German Ambassador to the United States. In early April Count
von Bernstorff reported to his government: "It seems to be increasingly
probable that the punitive expedition against Villa will lead to a full-
dress intervention. . . ." This suited Germany's plans precisely, for the
agitation of the Mexican issue owed much to German enterprise, and
"So long as the Mexican holds the stage here," continued Bernstorff, "we
are, I believe, safe from an act of aggression on the part of the American
government." This was a limited view of conditions that were seen in a
larger frame by President Wilson. The Mexican chaos, he said, represented "a revolution as profound as that which occurred in France," and
for his part he found that its aims were as valid, "no matter what the
excesses committed. . . ." The President's point of view was faced with
repeated challenges. General Pershing's command reached their point
of farthest penetration into Mexico as the town of Parral in southern
Chihuahua. There on April twelfth while buying supplies in town
American cavalrymen were fired upon by Mexican federal troops. The
attack was returned, and before it was over forty Mexicans and two
Americans had been killed. Acts of war had been exchanged now not
between a bandit and his pursuer but between the official forces of the
two nations. Once again a state of war seemed near. To dispel it by agreement, and to allow to Mexico her full sovereignty in affairs of internal
discipline, the United States proposed a conference between the military
chiefs of both nations, to be held at El Paso. Major General Hugh L.
Scott, chief of staff, and General Alvaro Obregón, Mexican secretary of
war, met for talks in late April and early May. General Funston was on
hand from Fort Sam Houston. The Mexican officer was received in
state. He reviewed guards of honor, conferred with his hosts on a private
car in the El Paso yards, and finally on May third agreed to a program—
though not until General Scott had kept him in a room at the Paso del
Norte Hotel for twelve hours of continuous, and secret, debate. It was
just past midnight when General Obregón signed the concordat, after
which General Scott, avoiding reporters, went out to telegraph his text
to Washington. It was entirely satisfactory to the President, who made
a public statement at once:

"The agreement drawn up and approved by officers of both governments contemplates the partial retirement of the American force
toward the border, the prosecution of the search for Villa, and the
dispersal of his remaining following by the Mexican forces, and the entire
withdrawal of the American expedition" eventually. For American
interventionists the formula gave too much respect to Mexico, for

Carranza, not enough. He refused to ratify the agreement because it fixed no date for the completion of the United States evacuation. And in the week of these discussions, Villa forces, striking in small and swift units, raided settlements in Texas near Dryden, and at Eagle Pass, and at Glen Springs and Boquillas in the Big Bend. The raids yielded the bandits little if anything in loot, and fewer than their usual captives or corpses, but were clearly intended to create further international mischief.

While Governor Ferguson of Texas urged the United States to "enter Mexico and assume control of that unfortunate country" for the purpose of establishing there a stable government "whether it takes 10 or 50 years to do it," troopers at Fort Bliss were called out to avenge the Glen Springs raid, where three American soldiers and three civilians had been killed on May fifth by a column of sixty raiders. On May sixth a second band of Villistas, twenty of whom were said to be residents of the American side of the Big Bend, galloped into Boquillas at dawn, looted a store and a neighboring mine, and captured eight men. News of the raids reached Bliss on Sunday, the seventh, while the officers were playing "an engrossing practice game of polo." By five in the afternoon two troops of the Eighth Cavalry were moving out by railroad for the Big Bend, and four days later, accompanied by two news correspondents and two motion picture cameramen in two Ford touring cars, and commanded by Major George T. Langhorne in his Cadillac "8"—his fellow officers knew he had "money on the outside"—crossed the Rio Grande at the old Spanish ford of San Vicente. The weather was fearfully hot and dusty. There was scarcely a road to follow. The motor cars made heavy going out of arroyos whose banks had to be dug away before they could be crossed on wheels, while the mounted cavalrymen chafed at the delays caused by their headquarters cars. Travelling at night the commander from his magnificent car would signal in an improvised code with a pocket flashlight to his soldiers following him—"good road," "bad road," "stop." When by day the pursuit force came upon Mexican settlements the cameramen took films of the residents, and "nearly frightened them to death by lining them up in front of their cameras. They had a pretty good idea," noted a young officer, "of what it meant to be stood up in a row and have a machine aimed at them. . . ." The cavalry sighted the bandits several times and gave chase, with "the Cadillac 8 bounding over the ditches and bushes like a steeplechase, to the tune of a cannonading." One time two American detachments manoeuvring unknown to each other in the same area nearly shot each other up in false dawn light. The chase lasted three weeks, and was called done when all prisoners had been retaken, the bandits dispersed, and several wounded and captured. Without having lost a man or a horse the Eighth Cavalry troopers returned to Fort Bliss on May twenty-eighth.

Meanwhile on May ninth the Carranzist forces in northern Mexico threatened to attack General Pershing's column. On the same day President Wilson called out the National Guard contingents of New Mexico, Arizona and Texas, even while he seemed to cling the more earnestly to his hope of avoiding a major contest with Mexico. On May eleventh he received Secretary of War Newton D. Baker and could not help speaking his innermost thoughts. "He said his Mexican policy," recorded the Secretary, "was based upon two of the most deeply seated convictions of his life. . . . First, his shame as an American over the first Mexican War, and his resolution that there should never be another such predatory enterprise. Second, . . . his belief in the principle laid down in the Virginia Bill of Rights that a people has the right to do as they damn please"—he really used the word "damn," said the Secretary—"with their own affairs. He wanted to give the Mexicans a chance to try. . . ." Furthermore, he seemed to see the country of Mexico in its vastness, and the vast effort needed to pacify it, for he said it would take "five hundred thousand men at least. . . ."

And there went Pershing, with a force that at its peak would not exceed fifteen thousand. An El Paso paper said that the pursuit of Villa was like turning a jackrabbit loose in Oklahoma and sending the El Paso police to hunt him. In the successive snows and winds, dusts and blasting sunlight of spring and early summer the Punitive Expedition creaked its way south on the plains beside the Sierra Madre. The General in order to travel rapidly between the scattered units of his widely deployed army went by motor. There were three light cars in his headquarters group. Early in the motor age desert travel was hard. Cars heated up and boiled over. Springs broke on the chucky roads. There was no roadside service. Keeping in touch with supplies of gasoline, oil, water and tires was difficult. The early movements southward were managed by rail—until Carranza denied the use of Mexican railroads to the American troops. Then an extended motor transport system had to be established with its base at Columbus, which became a boom town as the American source of all of Pershing's supply. In remarkably short time the quartermaster's motor truck supply lines were covering four thousand miles of Mexican trails, and penetrating to a distance of three hundred miles below the border. There were places where the trucks had to go as many as sixty miles in low gear. In all the strangeness of the country nothing was odder than the sudden appearance, along the motor lines, of little shops set up in booths by Chinese vendors who sold trifles and notions to American soldiers.

The Army brought many of its disadvantages with it. Equipment was inadequate, methods were all too often improvised. "Isn't this a great time," asked an officer, "for our cavalry to be going to war? No saddle and no drill regulations. . . ." He said that fifty-nine out of seventy-nine saddles in his troop were defective, and the trooper's regulation sabre was "an abomination," and ought to be thrown away. Others agreed with him, for a quartermaster later hauled two truckloads of discarded sabres all the way back to Columbus. The troops wore out their lariats and bandoliers. Shoe iron for the mounts was so scarce that the troop blacksmiths stopped to pick up a shoe cast anywhere along the road. The men carried horseshoe nails in a greasy rag to keep them from rusting. Troopers added kerchiefs to their uniforms against sweat and dust, and found "auto glasses" not a luxury but a necessity against the sun. Purchase of supply in the countryside was complicated. The colonel of the Tenth Cavalry had to resort to giving his personal cheques for purchases, and ran up a total of $1,680. Men grew so tired on the march that during short halts orders were given for "all to remain standing . . . otherwise men would immediately drop off to sleep, and there was much difficulty and delay in rousing them," and "horses . . . developed a hunger that caused them to chew the halter shanks," either of rope or leather. Was it the strange land itself that was trying to defeat these invaders? When the bandit trail led them into the Sierra Madre they found the temperature blazing hot by day, icy cold by night. "Men and animals had icicles hanging from their whiskers," and "canteens were frozen solid." In the canyons "darkness came on quickly. . . . The trails twisted and turned among the trees," and "a deceiving moonlight" changed all objects into fantastic shadows. But still, day after day, the packmaster rang his bell to call the animal train together, and the march would continue.

All along the extended line communications were all but impossible to maintain. The wireless and the telegraph were unreliable, and "the greatest deficiency," said an officer, "was the lack of an adequate air force." Eight open-seater biplanes from San Antonio were assigned to the expedition, and undertook a regular schedule of flights between the commanding general and his scattered units. A plane would fly in to a forward camp and land to deliver a message, and take one aboard, and rise off the scrubby desert to dwindle alone out of sight into the white sky. All too soon six of the planes cracked up, and the last two were left to cover the wilderness between Columbus and the commanding general's farthest station four hundred miles south of the river. And then those two gave out—one of them was fired at on the ground at Chihuahua City—and the air force was done in Mexico. Debate sounded throughout the service. Had the planes been properly employed? Should they be used to fly messages, or to conduct forward reconnaissance? A philosophy of the military air was being formed.

The ground troops remained. They persisted in their mission. They hardened. It was clear that the land was not defeating them. The United States continued its firm but mild pressure, and the National Guard began to appear on the border, though only after one or two false starts, for in Texas one hundred sixteen guardsmen refused to muster and were granted discharges, and in New Mexico certain guardsmen reported for duty in derby hats and certain others brought their feather beds. But still the border was strengthened and to Mexico the sight seemed menacing. On May thirty-first Carranza issued a demand to the United States for the instant removal of American troops from Mexico. The note insolently charged that General Pershing's men were being kept in Mexico to lend political value to President Wilson's campaign for renomination during the next few weeks. The President did not answer it until after the convention which renominated him had adjourned. Meanwhile, a number of scattered but possibly related acts gave emphasis to Mexico's policy. On June sixteenth, in a communication quickly ratified by Carranza, the Mexican commander of Federalist troops in the north notified General Pershing that any movement of United States troops further into the south, or to the east or west, or in any direction but north to the border, would be considered by Mexico a cause for war. On the next day bandits erupted near Brownsville and a detachment from Fort Brown crossed the river to chase them. One day later, across the great Mexican isthmus, two American naval officers of the gunboat *Annapolis* were arrested at Mazatlan, and their boat crew were fired on by Mexican troops on shore. On the following day, the commander of the *Annapolis* radioed his government that the Mexican state of Sinaloa had independently declared war on the United States. And along the line of General Pershing's march Federalist troops were gathering. Once more Carranza, having yet received no reply to his arrogant note of three weeks before, formally demanded that the Punitive Expedition retire from Mexico. On June twentieth his answer came: "The United States," it said, "cannot recede from its settled determination to maintain its national rights and perform its full duty in preventing further invasions of the territory of the United States. . . ." On the same day General Funston wired Washington to ask for sixty-five thousand more National Guardsmen. One day later Carranza's troops opened fire on two troops of the Tenth United States Cavalry at Carrizal, in the state of Chihuahua.

Word of the engagement in the field before the town went to the border command from a wounded cavalry captain who wrote at nine fifteen in the morning on June 21, 1916, "I am hiding in a hole two thousand yards from the field and have one other wounded man and three men with me." At half past six that morning, having marched since before dawn, the troops came to an open field southeast of town. They were on their way to Ahumada, to the east of Carrizal. The senior officer, Captain Boyd of C Troop, sent a note into Carrizal asking for permission to take his men through it on their way. The permission was refused, with the admonition that the American troops could proceed to the north, but not to the east. Presently word came from the Carranzist general commanding in Carrizal that Boyd could bring his men into town for a conference. By now there was a line of about one hundred and twenty Mexican troops on the edge of town facing the Americans. Captain Boyd "feared an ambush." He formed his troops as skirmishers and moved toward Carrizal. "When we were within three hundred yards the Mexicans opened fire," wrote the wounded captain, "and a strong one, before we fired a shot; then we opened up." A battle of an hour ensued. Captain Boyd was killed, along with six other cavalrymen, and twenty-three were taken prisoner.

Immediately the United States demanded the release of the Carrizal prisoners and seized the international bridges of the Rio Grande to secure them in case of a full-scale invasion of Mexico. General Pershing was ordered to hold his ground. The entire National Guard was sent to the boundary. People in the river cities of Matamoros, Juárez and other border towns began to flee to the interior. In the indignant if miniature Sinaloan war, Mexicans fired again on American bluejackets without provocation. General Obregón began to talk about taking San Antonio, Texas, in two weeks. The Guard poured across the United States by troop train until there were fifty thousand men stationed at each of three border defense positions—at Nogales, El Paso and Brownsville.

Now at last Carranza was impressed by the policy of the United States. In the face of such swift and heavy mobilization, he ordered within a week the release of the Carrizal prisoners, and promised to undertake the pursuit of bandits. An equilibrium was restored to affairs between the two governments, and orders were issued at Washington for the Punitive Expedition to pull back from aggressive pursuit to assume guard duty in Northern Mexico. There had been skirmishes with bandits—mounted men coming off their horses to take cover behind mesquite brush, and now and then a bloom and fade of cartridge smoke over sandy wastes, and then some fellow lying inert on his own shadow. One detachment was sure it had come upon Villa and had actually wounded him, and in any case, no further major assaults upon American settlements had taken place. The Expedition had not been wasted, though in back-country tales Mexicans told one another how Villa had played hide and seek with his pursuers, as he crouched in brush or cave to watch the hot, dirty and tired troopers ride past him. The commanding general calmly resolved the whole adventure afterward. "After we had penetrated about four hundred miles into Mexican territory," wrote General Pershing, "and overtaken Villa's band and others, and scattered them, wounding Villa himself, the increasing disapproval of the Mexican Government doubtless caused the administration to conclude that it would be better to rest content that the outlaw bands had been severely punished and generally dispersed, and that the people of northern Mexico had been taught a salutary lesson. . . ."

The Chief of Staff agreed that Pershing's mission had been accomplished. He "made a complete success . . ." said General Scott, "from the War Department's point of view." Now in late June of 1916 "activities in Mexico were discontinued," reported General Pershing, "the more advanced elements were withdrawn, and the expedition thereafter held a line of communications reaching only about one hundred fifty miles south of the border. As there was then little work to do except to protect this line, a systematic scheme of training was inaugurated throughout the command." Without the preoccupations of the field, he had to find other barriers against his own thoughts. He would still think now and then that he had only to go home to find them all there—and then he would remember, and confess to an old friend, "One *never, never* can get over it." But the new training program was something to cling to, and he wrote, "Work is the only possible relief and I work like a slave all the time. We have had some of the most valuable instruction here I have ever seen in the army and I have laid out and conducted the most of it myself—just to keep busy."

The crisis was eased. "Peace with Mexico," said the New York *Times*, "now seemingly well assured, will be most welcome to all Americans, save for those few plotters of mischief who, for personal interest, have desired intervention." A Brazilian paper had its own view of American policy, though it seemed never to have listened to President Wilson: "The severity and the contempt with which Washington looks upon the revolutions of the neighboring countries are neither just nor Christian," declared the *Gazeta de Noticias* of Rio de Janeiro. And once again, the President reached out to Mexico as to an equal and independent power. In July he asked that a joint commission composed of three representatives of the United States and three of Mexico be convened to arbitrate their difficulties for the two nations. From the perspective of Europe, the news struck an American ambassador as a "light in the universal darkness! What an example to civilization in the midst of anarchy!" The commission undertook its work at New London, Connecticut, and presently moved it to Atlantic City. Secretary of the Interior Franklin K. Lane was chairman of the American delegation. He was hopeful of the joint commission's purpose. "It ought," he said, "to indicate the line of political direction in the New World for the next thousand years." But he soon encountered a difficulty familiar to those who dealt with the First Chief of Mexico. "Carranza is obsessed with the idea that he is a real god and not a tin god, that he holds thunderbolts in his hands instead of confetti, and he won't let us help him. . . ." There lay the real trouble. "The hardest part of all is to convince a proud and obstinate people that they really need any help." Mexicans, discovered Secretary Lane, "distrust us. They will not believe that we do not want to take some of their territory. . . ." But the conference persisted in its work through the fall and early winter of 1916, while rumors of Villa flew across the border—he was raising a new army of eighteen thousand men, he was about to lose Chihuahua, he was about to take Chihuahua back again, he was hiding in the Sierra nursing his wound and getting about on crutches, he was on the verge of driving Carranza from the National Palace.

There were other alarms—the State Department had evidence of German attempts to persuade Mexico to grant permission for the establishment of submarine bases in Mexican territory. President Wilson had long been convinced that a great part of the border troubles could be traced to German propaganda. In the atmosphere of growing tension between the United States and Germany there seemed to be some indication that Germany took the Rio Grande to be her new frontier.

The border saw a great revolving system of training in its camps. When ten thousand newly mustered guardsmen were sent there for active duty, ten thousand already there were relieved and sent home. The lessons of General Pershing's training program told along the river, and gave a great proportion of the nation's man power its first exercises in modern warfare. They were lessons that would bear fruit within a very few months overseas. Meanwhile, in echoes of 1846, American young men wandered about in the river towns after duty, and ate scalding messes in chili parlors and dawdled under glaring lights that showed the way to darker indulgences, though *The Rio Grande Rattler,* a soldier paper published by the New York division of the Guard, reported that when saloons were closed and bordellos declared off-limits by the command, soldiers accepted these prohibitions loyally. General Funston had a brush with a revival sect when he declined to permit revival meetings to be held in the camps, where after all the usual services of chaplains of all denominations were available. He did not, he said, "wish the emotions of the soldiers stirred," and he "did not accept the view that because a man put on his country's uniform he was necessarily lost. . . ."

And suddenly the whole adventure drew to its close. In November the joint Mexican-American commission made its final recommendation, proposing as the only solution that full diplomatic relations be re-established and the troops withdrawn altogether from Mexico. The United States should retire to the border, patrol it, and hold Mexico responsible for any encroachments. On February 5, 1917, General Pershing began his retirement from the other side of the Rio Grande, after eleven months in Mexico. A veteran of the national guard on the border wondered why Pershing's command was called the Punitive Expedition, "since"— so it looked from McAllen, Texas—"nobody got punished." In the flyblown little bars of north Mexico, or by campfires, or amidst a column of horsemen crossing the desert, the song was still heard that could speak for Villa or any of his men.

> If some day I must die in a battle,
> If my body on the sierra must lie,
> Adelita, if God will allow it,
> You'll go to the sierra and cry. . . .

There, in the idea of the death that would bring to Villa and his men their first and all-claiming dignity, hovered the melancholy, the incurable lyricism of their harsh land.

For the United States, the Mexican involvement beyond the Rio Grande served a number of unforeseen but useful purposes. It steeled a commanding general and his citizen army for greater services in the first

World War. It gave the American air force its first trial at arms. In diplomatic co-operation between the sovereign nations of the hemisphere, it provided for the League of Nations and its chief architect a series of rehearsals that demonstrated a pattern of comity. Finally, it proved to Mexico that her neighbor above the river would suffer almost any lengths of indignity without resorting to an overwhelming retaliation whose aim would be acquisition of territory. Even though the time for it had not yet quite arrived, the way was open for full mutual respect between the countries of the Rio Grande.

All the old border troubles were resolved none too soon, if an unexpected new one was to be duly faced.

On February 27, 1917, the Secretary of State called at the White House to tell the President an astonishing story. As he listened to it, President Wilson several times exclaimed "Good Lord!", for it had become clear that the intentions of Germany—fantastic as it must seem—now included a plan to support Mexico in the seizure of the Rio Grande border states and Arizona if war should come between Germany and the United States. This was discovered through the interception of a telegram from Dr. Alfred Zimmermann, German foreign minister, to his minister to Mexico, Herr von Eckhardt. The telegram had come into the hands of the Allies through several channels. One copy was acquired by British agents in Mexico who sent it back to England where it was decoded—for the British had broken the German code months before, and were reading every official German dispatch that they could capture. Another transmission of the Zimmermann telegram, in partial form, was taken off the wireless. Another was intercepted out of Swedish diplomatic communication channels. And another, incredibly, was sent by telegraph attached to a telegram on a different, "open," subject, through the United States Embassy in Berlin, to Ambassador von Bernstorff in Washington, thus violating the diplomatic courtesy extended to the German Foreign Office by United States Ambassador James W. Gerard. "Good Lord!" exclaimed the President. This copy of the message had been forwarded by Bernstorff to Eckhardt on January nineteenth. As for what the message said, this was what it said:

"We intend to begin on the first of February unrestricted submarine warfare. We shall endeavour in spite of this to keep the United States of America neutral. In the event of not succeeding, we make Mexico a proposal of alliance on the following basis: make war together, make peace together, generous financial support and an understanding on our part that Mexico is to reconquer the lost territory in Texas, New

Mexico and Arizona. The settlement in detail is left to you. You will
inform the President [of Mexico] of the above most secretly as soon as
the outbreak of war with the United States of America is certain and add
the suggestion that he should, on his initiative, invite Japan to immediate adherence and at the same time mediate between Japan and ourselves. Please call the President's attention to the fact that the ruthless
employment of our submarines now offers the prospect of compelling in
a few months to make peace.—Zimmermann."

"Good Lord!"

But wait—there was more. In a second telegram Dr. Zimmermann
wanted his minister in Mexico to make it plain to Carranza that the
alliance he was being offered was intended to dispose forever of the
Monroe Doctrine, and that it represented Germany's long-range policy
for Mexican relations, rather than merely a wartime measure to be
repudiated with the end of hostilities. For the whole future, Mexico,
Germany and Japan would present a joint power against the United
States, who would have lost the old Spanish and Mexican provinces along
with their old boundary river.

The whole affair seemed so incredible that President Wilson took
extra steps to determine the authenticity of the messages. When this
was established, he instructed the State Department to release them to the
world as an example of German perfidy. Japan was horrified. She was
already a member of the Allied nations, and her foreign office declared
promptly, "Needless to say, Japan remains faithful to the Allies." To
those in the United States who sympathized with Germany, and to those
who prayed against American entry into the war, the messages could
not seem true, with their cynical assumption that as a result of unrestricted submarine warfare the United States would most likely be drawn
into the conflict; but the hopes of such citizens were punctured when
Dr. Alfred Zimmermann publicly confirmed the authorship of the tele-
grams and their official character. Germany was dismayed by the exposure of her most secret plans, and, said an American diplomat overseas,
"everybody is laughing at the frightful blunder the Germans made in
proposing to Mexico to become an ally . . . the annals of diplomacy, I
suppose, contain no filthier offer . . ." , and the scandal brought Dr.
Zimmermann's fall from his exalted post.

Still, whether in secret or in public, Carranza was amenable to
Germany's proposals. He asked if Germany could supply him with arms
and ammunition—he specified the Mauser 7mm.—and with money. In
the midst of talks with Germany he was constitutionally elected president

of Mexico on March 11, 1917, while the Mexican congress was dominated by the pro-German "military party." Relations with the United States sank again. The United States Cavalry watched the border not only for bandits but for saboteurs; and after April second, when President Wilson, meeting the challenge that a nation believing in the freedom of the seas could no longer ignore, went to the Capitol to ask the Congress to declare that a state of war existed between Germany and the United States, the border guard was intensified. General Pershing was still there. "With the declaration of war against Germany," he observed, "there was much excitement in the southwest and many were the demands for protection against sabotage. Our first concern was to guard government property and railways. Military detachments were sent to the most critical points. . . ." It was not long before he was called to Washington and given a division—he was now a major general—to take to Europe, where he would be raised to the supreme command of all United States forces. The cavalry remained behind on the border, for bandit alarms were not all done with. The secret service, too, was active there, for as Secretary Lansing said, "The Mexican border was especially watched to prevent the spies and agents of the Central Powers from crossing into Mexico. . . ."

So through the years of the first World War the status quo was preserved, despite Germany's best plans. President Carranza continued to be hospitable to German propaganda, but no formal alliance came of it. In 1918 German agents were said to be at work on arrangements with General Pancho Villa. They would give him money and arms if he would raise a revolt and seize the Mexican government, thereafter concluding a formal alliance with Germany. Villa seemed amenable—but it was another plot that did not thicken, and in the end, with the defeat of the Central Powers, the United States retained the old Rio Grande and boundary territories which a victorious Germany was pledged to throw to Mexico.

Mexico's cycle of fury was not yet spent. In 1920 President Carranza, fleeing a new revolution, was overtaken and assassinated. The turn of General Pancho Villa came three years later when old enemies shot him to death on his ranch where he had lived in retirement. Through the next decades their successors slowly brought into realization many of the reforms postulated in the Grand Revolution of Madero. Some of these gave further suffering to the people. Most of them were no official concerns of the United States. One that affected American landholders in Mexico was Article Thirty-three of a certain modern law

of Mexico. It was that one which regulated the conditions of expropria-
tion of foreign-owned property. A modern Rio Grande Mexican remarked
of it, "No, aquí en México hay no más dos artículos: el artículo treinta y
tres, y el artículo treinta-treinta—In Mexico there are but two articles:
article thirty-three, and article .30-30."

43.

Utility and Vision

1. utility

"Lot's things t'see," sang a character of youth in a twentieth
century folk opera of the Rio Grande Southwest,

> "Lot's things t'see,
> Gon' seem 'm all, and then some,
> Before I die.
> My granpa walked,
> My pappy rode,
> And me, I can fly."

It was an epitome of the cycle of change that came to the Rio
Grande with the machine, as it came to the rest of America and the
world. Previously, undergoing changes of predominant character with
each conquering race or nationality, the river societies had modified new
forms of social life with local circumstances and traditions—until the
coming of machine technics. And then, at a rate ever increasing, the addition of each machine technic in its turn made more swiftly certain the
domination of the environment through every technical means of the
modern age.

The difference of life along the Rio Grande from civilized human life elsewhere in the nation was at last only a matter of degree; for in kind, that life was established after the likeness of the corporate American character. In their various jobs and preoccupations the Rio Grande Americans—whether they passed by or stayed—revealed again their view of life through variations on the American theme—their materialism, their political vitality, their individuality, their passion for work, their tendency to make a recurrent frontier, and their devotion to an improved future on behalf of general humanity.

What remained to be seen of the river's past history were vestiges of its three old strains—those of the Indian epoch, the Latin centuries, and the American frontier—as they mingled with one another in forms often determined by commercial appeals addressed to residents and travellers moved by the local color. So in various places along the river were preserved together different illustrations of its earlier ways and times of society as if the river cut through the laminations of history as through those of the earth's crust. But finally all indigenous aspects of the river's three societies would be dissolved in the technological uniformity of the national life in the twentieth century.

The process was implicit in every step by which machine technics of energy and communication came to the river. It began when Captain Henry Austin brought the *Ariel* winding up to Matamoros in 1829 under its own steam power. It was furthered, at least in symbol, when in 1834 the printing press of Father Martínez produced for a few weeks at Taos the weekly newspaper *El Crepúsculo;* and when in 1865 General Sheridan brought the steam locomotive to the river at Brownsville. Electric telegraph lines reached Santa Fe from Denver in July, 1868, in what the acting territorial governor declared, in the first official telegram to be sent over the wires, addressed to President Andrew Johnson, to be "another advanced step of an enlightened age, bringing an old into instantaneous communication with newer though more advanced sections of our blessed Union, and with mankind in all civilized lands." The weekly Santa Fe *New Mexican* was immediately thereafter published as a daily, with wire service. Rail connections completed at Deming, New Mexico, in 1881 and at El Paso in 1882 brought the Rio Grande in the path of transcontinental commerce. The Rio Grande as the oldest vein of civilized life and communication in the area of the United States was unique in the settling of the West; for unlike other communities and areas of settlement, those of the Rio Grande were not born of the westward movement, but were already long established, with their own various patterns of life, when the recurrent American frontier

reached out and put over them a new complex of living ways. After
three and a half centuries of human life largely self-sustained the whole
river line was drawn into the pattern of American national life and its
material needs were increasingly met by distant sources.

The building of the railroads called for local labor; and a leading
effect of this was to take men of Indian and Latin heritage from their
little riverside farms and put them to work on the railroad right of way,
while their farms were either cultivated by workers whom they hired,
or were allowed to go untilled. And when the railroad work was done,
native laborers turned to jobs in mining, or hired out to large-scale farming operations whose produce was shipped to commercial markets far
away on the railroad lines. If in general the result of such change was a
new prosperity, occasional dreams of a rich future faded away when the
promises of a spellbinding promoter—the last frontier was full of the
type—came to nothing. More than one small Western town, after the
collapse of a railroad or land boom, celebrated the bitterness of disillu-
sion in a gesture of mass irony when citizens came together in funeral
style to bury the shovel that had been so hopefully used to break
ground for a set of new tracks that would lead to the world.

Santa Fe had gas for lighting in 1880; electricity came not long
afterward. The telephone was available in 1881, and ten years later in
a little mining town of central New Mexico a machine arrived on the
back of a burro to predict an industry devoted to the capture of the past
in its most immediate expression. The burro was brought to stand
before a mud-plastered log cabin while men, women and boys clustered
around, listening to what the burro's owner promised. If it seemed impossible to believe him, only let them wait while he gave them a demonstration, for a modest fee. Here—let four of the boys come forward, and let
him put into their ears the ends of small rubber tubes, and let them listen,
as he started a small motor fixed to a little platform on the burro's back.
The motor would turn a cylinder of black wax against which a stylus
would play. In a moment they would hear a voice start to speak through
the tubes, and then band music, and someone singing. He turned a
switch, a spring creaked, and then, amidst whirring and scratching
sounds, they were dazed to hear all that he had announced. Up a mountain trail the machine had come—it was a graphophone—bringing a
trapped voice, and a new time, and a whole new way of communicating
knowledge—the recording of sound. Motion pictures, radio and, finally,
television would bring to mass audiences in the river empire, as to others

the world over, a swift—often simultaneous—communication of images and ideas of experience that transcended the fixed limits of local traditions.

The last use of the river for water-borne travel ended early in the twentieth century. The last steamboat of the Rio Grande was the *Bessie,* a wood-burning sternwheeler, Captain Jesse Thornton commanding. She ran from the Gulf to the head of navigation at Roma. Like Captain Austin's *Ariel* and General Taylor's transports, she travelled only by day, tying up at night to the bank where piles of wood fuel awaited her at the end of a day's run. She carried freight and passengers— boys going to school at Brownsville, among others, and soldiers travelling between Ringgold Barracks and Fort Brown. In the summer of 1896 the commanding general of the Texas Department and his aide, a lieutenant, went on board to go downstream. Fifty years later, the aide, William J. Glasgow, then a retired general officer, remembered with musing joy how she was navigated through all the river's hooks and bends. It often happened that as the *Bessie* came to a bend, the wind would push her stern about in a grand arc until her bow was wedged into the bank. Then she would float free and sail on downstream stern first. At another bend a chance came to right matters. Captain Thornton let the leading stern take the bank, and the breeze and the current brought the bow around until the *Bessie* sailed once again like a proper ship, pointing her bow forward. The evolution was performed over and over, said General Glasgow, "and so she waltzed us all the way to Brownsville." She made her last trip in 1907, taking students from Roma to Brownsville, who when it was time to come home at the end of the school year, came overland; for the *Bessie,* worn out, was never replaced. Increased railroad and highway traffic on the littoral took the place of travel by river.

When the mechanization of private travel was made possible by the automobile, and the rapidly grown network of highways which it required across the nation, the great distances of the Rio Grande Southwest were contracted. With the interflow of increased personal traffic came a quickened interflow of local and national goods and experience and character. When mechanical flight—performing a myth fulfillment for mankind—was commercially established with an airport at every Rio Grande town of any consequence, the world's farthest reaches were only a couple of days away from the nation's oldest seats of civilized life. And when the demands of war required the development of a new release of energy—nuclear fission—the Rio Grande valley in New Mexico was the site of significant operations by the government's atomic scientists at Los Alamos and Albuquerque.

If all such discoveries in the age of mass technics created changes in material existence as great as those that came to the Indian with the development of corn; and to the Pueblo dweller with the arrival of the armored soldier with wheel, lever, gunpowder and horse; and to the Spaniard and Mexican with the arrival of the Anglo-American political system, then the American material triumph carried with it to the Rio Grande the same question that accompanied the machine, wherever, with all its implications, it was put to work.

The question was asked by a thoughtful American as he visited the Paris exposition of 1900. "I . . . go down," wrote Henry Adams, "down to the Champ de Mars and sit by the hour over the great dynamos, watching them run as noiselessly and as smoothly as the planets, and asking them—with infinite courtesy—where in the Hell they are going. . . ." The more he thought about the problem of where the development of mechanical power would lead, the more troubled he became. "I apprehend for the next hundred years an ultimate, colossal, cosmic collapse; but not on any of our old lines. My belief is that science is to wreck us, and that we are like monkeys monkeying with a loaded shell; we don't in the least know or care where our practically infinite energies come from or will bring us to." For himself, he did not, he said, care at all. "But the faintest disturbance of equilibrium is felt throughout the solar system, and I feel sure that our power over energy has now reached a point where it must sensibly affect the old adjustment. It is mathematically certain to me that another thirty years of energy-development at the rate of the last century, must reach an impasse."

ii. vision

But the answer that eluded Henry Adams seemed later to come clear out of the spirit of the nation most energetic in the use of the very technics that he questioned. "The useful, the mechanic arts are those which we have occasion for. . . .", John Adams had said long before his great-grandson felt such terrible doubts before the dynamos.

The old statesman, with his passionate belief in the American knack for utility, expressed the faith of his countrymen in their control over their powers. But the United States had no monopoly on the new social instruments of the age of mass technics. The world had them; and the world moved with them wherever they went. Among the implications of all new technics of communication and energy was the moral imperative to use them to serve rather than to destroy human society.

The Americans, westbound in the nineteenth century to fulfill their vision of a just society for their countrymen with the aid of their "mechanic arts," had once made a neighborhood of their continent.

Once again, in a process for which the American century on the Rio Grande was a typical western rehearsal, the spirit of the recurrent American frontier reached out; and halfway through the twentieth century the Americans, now with a vision of a just society for all the world's peoples, and with the aid of vastly expanded "mechanic arts," were trying to do their share to make a neighborhood of the world.

THE END

Roswell, New Mexico,
1940–1942;
1946–1954.

Sources for
Volume Two, by Chapters

APPENDIX B

Sources for
Volume Two, by Chapters

Each source is here noted in brief form which corresponds to its alphabetical position in the General Bibliography (Appendix C), where the reader will find full bibliographical particulars.

book three: the mexican rio grande

1. A Colony For Mexico: Barker, *Austin Papers,* and *Life of Stephen F. Austin;* Dougherty; Robertson.
2. A Wild Strain: Cleland; Ferris; Irving; Pattie; Pino; Twitchell, *Spanish Archives.*
3. The Twin Sisters: Bancroft; Barker, *Austin Papers;* Rives; Robertson; Santleben; Williams, O. W., *Pecos Country.*
4. Last Return: Robertson.
5. The Spark: *Antiques;* Bancroft; Barker, *Austin Papers;* Rives.
6. The "Ariel": Barker, *Austin Papers.*
7. Slavery: Bancroft; Barker, *Austin Papers,* and *Life of Stephen F. Austin;* Rives; Webb.
8. Bad Blood: Bancroft; Barker, *Austin Papers.*
9. The Mexico Trade: Barker, *Austin Papers;* Cleland; Dickey; Dunbar; Gregg, J., *Commerce of the Prairies;* Pino; Rives; U. S. Government, *Passport.*
10. Tormented Loyalties: *Antiques;* Barker, *Austin Papers,* and *Life of Stephen F. Austin;* James, M.; Rives.

11. "God and Texas": Bancroft; Barker, *Austin Papers,* and *Life of Stephen F. Austin;* Green; Rives.
12. From Mexico's Point of View: Bancroft; Barker, *Austin Papers,* and *Life of Stephen F. Austin;* Gregg, J., *Diary and Letters . . . Southwestern Enterprises;* James, M.; Rives; Wortham.
13. Fortunes of New Mexico: Dickey; Pattie; Pino; Read; Robertson; USDA, SCS, *Rio Grande Watershed in Colorado and New Mexico.*
14. Revolt Up River: Armijo, *Counter-pronouncement;* Pino; Read; Tannenbaum; Twitchell, *Leading Facts,* and *Spanish Archives;* Vigil, *Minutes.*
15. The River Republic: Bancroft; Smith, J. H.; Yoakum.
16. The Santa Fe Pioneers: Bancroft; Calderon de la Barca; Carroll; Falconer; Kendall; Read; Twitchell, *Leading Facts;* Yoakum.
17. Border Smoke: Bancroft; Dobie, *Longhorns,* and *Vaquero;* Dougherty; Emory, *Report;* Gregg, J., *Diary and Letters . . . Southwestern Enterprises;* Rives; Webb, Yoakum.
18. To Mier and Beyond: Bancroft; Green; Rives; Webb; Wilcox, *Laredo during the Texas Republic.*
19. Diplomacies: Bancroft; Bill; Grant, U. S.; Gregg, J., *Diary and Letters . . . Southwestern Enterprises;* Henry, R. S.; Henry, W. S.; Houston; Lewis, L.; Rives; Santleben; Yoakum.
20. The United States to the River: Grant, U. S.; Henry, W. S.; Lewis, L.; Smith, E. K.; Webb.

book four: the united states rio grande

1. "Way, You Rio": Downes; Wallace, L.
2. Collective Prophecy: Adams, H.; Adams, J., and J. Q.; Audubon; Botkin; Butterfield; Christensen; Crèvecoeur; Curti; Dunbar; Grassi; Gregg, J., *Commerce of the Prairies;* Handlin; Kouwenhoven; Lipman; McCoy, J. C.; Mencken, *American Language,* and *Supplement I;* Miller; Montlezun; Moreau de St. Méry; Moses; National Capital Sesquicentennial Commission; Parkman; Quinn; Rice; Rosenfeld; Rourke, *American Humor,* and *Roots of American Culture;* Smith, H. N.; Stone; Tocqueville; Trollope; Whitman, *Leaves of Grass,* and *Prose Works.*
3. Bivouac: Barbour; Downes; Lewis, L.; Thorpe.
4. The Army of the Rio Grande: Barbour; Emory, *Report;* Grant, U. S.; Gregg, J., *Diary and Letters . . . Excursions in Mexico;* Henry, R. S.; Henry, W. S.; Lewis, L.; Wallace, L.; Whitman, *Prose Works.*
5. The Cannonade: Barbour; Bill; Grant, U. S.; Henry, R. S.; Henry, W. S.; Thorpe.
6. Fort Texas: Thorpe.
7. The Listeners: Henry, W. S.
8. Palo Alto: Barbour; Grant, U. S.; Henry, R. S.; Henry, W. S.; Thorpe.

9. Resaca de la Palma: Barbour; Grant, U. S.; Hamilton; Henry, R. S.; Henry, W. S.; Thorpe.

10. The River Dead: Barbour; Emory, *Report;* Grant, U. S.; Hamilton; Henry, R. S.; Henry, W. S.; Lewis, L.; Thorpe.

11. The Nation's War: *Antiques;* Bill; Hamilton; Henry, R. S.; Lewis, L.; Polk; Strong; Whitman, *Leaves of Grass.*

12. Invasion Summer: Barbour; Bill; Giddings; Hamilton; Henry, R. S.; Henry, W. S.; Lewis, L.; Thorpe.

13. Recurrent Frontier: Barbour; Bill; Domenech; Giddings; Hamilton; Henry, R. S.; Henry, W. S.; Kenly; Lewis, L.; Smith, H. N.; Wallace, L.; Webb.

14. Upstream and Inland: Barbour; Bill; Dobie, *Vaquero;* Dougherty; Giddings; Grant, U. S.; Hamilton; Henry, R. S.; Henry, W. S.; Kenly; Lewis, L.; Polk; Thorpe.

15. The Army of the West: New Mexico, Citizens; Parkman; Read; Vigil, D., *Speech, May 16, 1846,* and *Speech, June 22, 1846;* Wislizenus.

16. The Secret Agent: Armijo, *Letter to Gen. Kearny;* Benton, T. H., in Connelley; Crane; Hughes; Keleher; Magoffin; New Mexico, Citizens; Pino; Read; Vigil y Alarid.

17. Bloodless Possession: Bill; Emory, *Notes of a Military Reconnoissance;* Gibson, G. R.; Henry, R. S.; Hughes; Keleher; Magoffin; Nelson; Read.

18. The Army of Chihuahua: Bill; Butterfield; Ehinger; Freeman; Gregg, J., *Diary and Letters: Southwestern Enterprises,* and *Excursions in Mexico;* Henry, R. S.; Wilcox, *Laredo.*

19. The Free Missourians: Bill; Gibson, G. R.; Gregg, J., *Diary and Letters . . . Excursions in Mexico;* Keleher; Magoffin; Robinson; Ruxton; Wade, in Parkman; Wislizenus.

20. Brazito and The Pass: Connelley; Drumm, in Magoffin; Gibson, G. R.; Hughes; Kribben, in Gibson, G. R.; Magoffin; Ruxton.

21. Counterdance: Bill; Hamilton; Henry, R. S.; Henry, W. S.; Hitchcock; Lewis, L.; Polk; Smith, A. D. H.; Strong; Wallace L.

22. The Avengers: Connelley; Garrard; Hughes; Keleher; Ruxton; Twitchell, *Leading Facts.*

23. Massacre at Taos: Benton, T. H., in Connelley; Dyer; Garrard; Henry, R. S.; Hughes; Keleher; Ruxton; Twitchell, *Leading Facts.*

24. Chihuahua: Gibson, G. R.; Magoffin; Polk.

25. Trial at Taos: Garrard.

26. All on the Plains of Mexico: Adams, H.; Bill; Edwards, in Gregg, *Diary and Letters . . . Excursions in Mexico;* Ehinger; Emory, *Report;* Gregg, J., *Diary and Letters: Southwestern Enterprises,* and *Excursions in Mexico;* Hamilton; Henry, W. S.; Hitchcock; Hughes; Lee; Lewis, L.; Lomax, *Folk Song USA;* Polk; Rives; Rourke, *American Humor;* Strong; Wallace, L.; Whitman, *Prose Works.*

27. El Dorado: Armijo, *Letter to Donaciano Vigil;* Bartlett; Bieber; Durivage, in Bieber; Eccleston; Polk; Robertson; Sumpter; Thoreau.

28. Contraband: Bancroft; Bartlett; Domenech; Durivage, in Bieber; Emory, *Report;* Gregg, J., *Diary and Letters . . . Excursions in Mexico;* Smith, J. H.; Webb.

29. A Thread of Spirit: Domenech; Emory, *Report;* USDA, SCS, *Rio Grande Watershed in Colorado and New Mexico.*
30. Boundaries: Bancroft; Bartlett; Bennett; Bill; Binkley; Burkholder; Jones; Twitchell, *Leading Facts.*
31. Flag and Lamplight: Bartlett; Bennett; Boyd, Mrs. O. B.; Cremony; Crimmins, *Col. J. F. K. Mansfield's Report,* and *Two Thousand Miles by Boat;* Cruse; Dickey; Dougherty; DuBois; Emory, *Report;* Hughes; Keleher; Plato; Santleben; Stanley; Sumpter; Thomlinson; Toulouse, J. H.; Toulouse, J. H., Jr.
32. The Rio Grande Divided: Crane; Dougherty; Fulton; Hollister; Keleher; McKee, J. C.; Richardson; Whitford; Williams, E.; Wortham.
33. The Desolate: Cremony; Keleher; Hollister; Ronquillo.
34. Confederate Border: Bancroft; Corti; Coulter; Dobie, *Vaquero;* Freeman; Gonzalez, *Folk-Lore;* Santleben; Soley; Sumpter; Wortham.
35. The Second Mexican Empire: Bancroft; Coulter; Dobie, *Vaquero;* Hergesheimer; Santleben; Sheridan; Simpich; Strong.
36. The Mexico Moon: Benedict; Bieber; Cremony; Davenport; Dobie, *Mustangs,* and *Vaquero;* Emory, *Report;* Parsons; Pino; Ruxton; Santleben; Sumpter; Thomas, *Plains Indians;* U. S. Congress, 43rd Congress, 1st Session, *Executive Document no. 257;* USDA, Field Flood Control Committee, *Survey Report;* Wallace, E.; Williams, O. W., *Baja el Sol,* and *Untitled Pamphlet.*
37. Bad Men and Good: Archdiocese, Santa Fe; Crane; Defouri, in Howlett; Dobie, *Vaquero;* Federal Writers Program, WPA, *Texas;* Fergusson, Mrs. C. M.; Fulton; Gibson, G. R.; Gregg, R. D.; Howlett; Keleher; Kerbey; Kohlberg; Kubler; Lavelle; McKee, I.; Pike; Pino; Richardson; Ritch; Salpointe; Santleben; Townsend, *Early border elections,* and *Rangers and Indians;* Twitchell, *Leading Facts,* and *Spanish Archives;* U. S. Congress, 43rd Congress, 1st Session, HR, *Executive Document no. 257,* and 44th Congress, 1st Session, HR, *Report no. 343,* and 45th Congress, 1st Session, HR, *Executive Document no. 13;* Ward; Warner.
38. The Last Wagons: Dobie, *Vaquero;* Santleben.
39. The Last Frontiersman: Abels; Botkin; Brown, D.; Dobie, *Longhorns,* and *Mustangs,* and *Vaquero;* Kohlberg; Lomax, *Cowboy Songs,* and *Folk Song, USA;* McCoy, J. G.; Richardson; Santleben; Siringo, *Riata and Spurs,* and *Texas Cowboy;* Smith, E. E.; U. S. Congress, 44th Congress, 1st Session, HR, *Report no. 343;* Wadleigh.
40. Treasure: Burkholder; Conkling; Davis; Federal Writers Program, WPA, *Colorado,* and *New Mexico;* Simpich; Tierney; USDA, SCS, Southwest Region, *Sociological Survey;* Wolle.
41. The Last Earth Secrets: Casey; Crimmins, *Two Thousand Miles by Boat;* Emory, *Report;* Hill; Townsend, *Rangers and Indians.*
42. Reflex and Revolution: Austin, M.; Baker; Beals; Borah; Brenner; Callahan; Carranza; *Cavalry Journal;* Cramer; Dallam; Emory, *Report;* Glasgow; Gonzalez, *America Invades;* Green; Grey; Hammond, J. H.; Hendrick; Hill; House; Lane, F. K.; Lansing; Lewis, M.; *Literary Digest;* Millis; *Motion picture film footage;* Outlook; Palmer, F.; Pershing, *Letters,* and *My Experiences;* Powell; Pringle; Reed; Richie; Rose; Scott, *Papers,* and *Some*

Memories; Sullivan; Tompkins; Toulmin; Troxel; Tumulty; Villa; Walsh; Whitlock; Wilson.

43. Utility and Vision: Adams, H.; Adams, J., and J. Q.; Dobie, *Vaquero;* Federal Writers Program, WPA, *New Mexico;* Glasgow; Horgan, *Tree on the Plains;* Keleher; USDA, SCS, *Rio Grande Watershed in Colorado and New Mexico,* and *Sociological Survey.*

APPENDIX C

General Bibliography

APPENDIX C
General Bibliography

For the convenience of the reader as he refers to this list from the brief entries of sources as listed by chapters in Appendices A and B, I have here grouped alphabetically all sources materials, whether manuscript, primary sources, general works, periodicals, motion picture film or conversations. If this course may overlook certain conventions of bibliographical technique, it may have, through its single alphabet, a compensatory value in bringing the inquirer as directly as possible to the reference he seeks.

Abels, Robert. *Early American firearms* (*The American arts library*). Cleveland and New York, The World Publishing Co., 1950.

Adams, Henry. *Selected letters of Henry Adams,* edited with an introduction by Newton Arvin. New York, Farrar, Straus and Young, Inc., 1951.

Adams, John, and John Quincy. *The selected writings* . . . edited and with an introduction by Adrienne Koch and William Peden. New York, Alfred A. Knopf, 1946.

Alessio Robles, Vito. *Coahuila y Texas en la época colonial.* Mexico, D. F., Editorial Cultura, 1938.

Alexander, Hartley Burr. *North American* [*mythology*]. V. 10, of Mythology of all races, edited by Louis Herbert Gray. Boston, Marshall Jones Co., 1916.

Altamira y Crevea, Rafael. *A history of Spain from the beginnings to the present day.* Translated by Muna Lee. New York, D. Van Nostrand Co., 1949.

. . . . . . *Antiques.* Texas Issue, June 1948.

Armijo, Manuel. *Counter-pronouncement, Sept. 8, 1837, by Manuel Armijo* [*et al.*] *at Tomé, New Mexico* . . . *appointing a commission to prepare*

957

and present an address to the Supreme [Mexican] Government. . . . Translated by Samuel C. Ellison, 1884. Original document. San Marino, California, Henry E. Huntington Library. (Excerpts quoted by permission of the Huntington Library.)

Armijo, Manuel. *Letter to General Kearny, written in Apache Canyon, August 16, 1846*. Translation. Original document. San Marino, California, Henry E. Huntington Library. (Excerpts quoted by permission of the Huntington Library.)

Armijo, Manuel. *Letter to Donaciano Vigil, written at Lemitar, New Mexico, July 16, 1850*. Translation. Original document. San Marino, California, Henry E. Huntington Library. (Excerpts quoted by permission of the Huntington Library.)

Armstrong, Edward. *The Emperor Charles V*. London, Macmillan and Co., 1910.

Artiñano, Pedro M. de. *Spanish art. The Burlington Magazine*, 1927.

Audubon, John James. *Audubon's America, the narratives and experiences of John James Audubon*, edited by Donald Culross Peattie . . . Boston, Houghton Mifflin Co., 1940.

Austin, Mary. *What the Mexican conference really means*. Reprint from *New York Times magazine*. New York, Latin American News Association, ND.

Baker, Ray Stannard. *Woodrow Wilson, life and letters*. V. 6. *Facing war, 1915–1917*. Garden City, Doubleday, Doran and Co., 1937.

Bancroft, Hubert Howe. *History of the North Mexican states and Texas*. 2 v. San Francisco, A. L. Bancroft and Co., 1884.

Bandelier, Adolph F. A. *The delight makers;* with an introduction by Charles F. Lummis. New York, Dodd, Mead and Co., 1916.

—— *Diaries, 1880–1890*. Ms. 10 v. Santa Fe, Museum of New Mexico.

—— *Documentary history of the Rio Grande pueblos*. Part two, of *Indians of the Rio Grande valley*, by Adolph F. A. Bandelier and Edgar L. Hewitt. Albuquerque, University of New Mexico Press, 1937.

—— *Final report of investigations among Indians of the southwestern United States, carried on mainly in the years from 1880 to 1885*. Part II. Papers of the Archaeological Institute of America. American series, IV. Cambridge, printed by John Wilson and Son, University Press, 1892.

—— *Hemenway southwestern expedition: Contributions to the history of the Southwestern portion of the United States*. Archaeological Institute of America. American series, V. Cambridge, printed by John Wilson and Son, 1890.

—— *Historical documents relating to New Mexico, Nueva Vizcaya, and approaches thereto, to 1773*. Collected by Adolph F. A. Bandelier and Fanny R. Bandelier. Spanish texts and English translations. 3 v. Edited . . . by Charles Wilson Hackett. Washington, Carnegie Institution, 1923.

—— *Historical introduction to studies among the sedentary Indians of New Mexico*. (In *Papers of the Archaeological Institute of America. American series. I.*) Boston, A. Williams and Co., 1881.

—— *Indians of the Rio Grande valley*, by Adolph F. A. Bandelier and Edgar L. Hewitt. Albuquerque, University of New Mexico Press, 1937.

Barbour, Philip Norbourne. *Journals of the late Philip Norbourne Barbour*, captain in the 3rd regiment, United States Infantry, and his wife, Martha Isabella Hopkins Barbour, written during the war with Mexico, 1846. Edited with foreword by Rhoda Van Bibber Tanner Doubleday. New York, G. P. Putnam's Sons, 1936.

Barker, Eugene C. *The Austin papers,* edited by Eugene C. Barker. *Annual Report of the American Historical Association, 1919.* 3 v. Washington, Government Printing Office, 1924.

—— *Life of Stephen F. Austin, founder of Texas, 1793–1836.* Nashville, Cokesbury Press, 1926.

Bartlett, John Russell *Personal narrative of explorations and incidents in Texas, New Mexico, California, Sonora, and Chihuahua, connected with the United States and Mexican Boundary Commission during the years 1850–1853.* 2 v. New York, D. Appleton Co., 1854.

Beals, Carleton. *Porfirio Diaz, dictator of Mexico.* Philadelphia, J. B. Lippincott Co., 1932.

Beazley, C. Raymond. *Voyages and travels mainly during the 16th and 17th centuries.* With an introduction by C. Raymond Beazley. "An English Garner." Westminster, Constable and Co., 1903.

Bell, Aubrey F. G. *Cervantes.* Norman, University of Oklahoma Press, 1947.

Benavides, Fray Alonso de. *Fray Alonso de Benavides' Revised Memorial of 1634* . . . edited by Frederick Webb Hodge, George P. Hammond and Agapito Rey. Albuquerque, University of New Mexico Press, 1945.

Benedict, Ruth. *Patterns of culture.* Boston, Houghton Mifflin Co., 1934.

Bennett, James A. *A dragoon in New Mexico, 1850–1856.* Edited by Clinton E. Brooks and Frank D. Reeves under the title, *Forts and Forays.* Albuquerque, University of New Mexico Press, 1948.

Beshoar, Barron B. *Western trails to Calvary.* Denver, The Westerners, Brand Book, 1949.

Bevan, Bernard. *Spanish art. The Burlington Magazine, 1927.*

Bieber, Ralph P. *Southern trails to California in 1849.* Glendale, The Arthur H. Clark Co., 1937.

Bill, Alfred Hoyt. *Rehearsal for conflict. The war with Mexico, 1846–1848.* New York, Alfred A. Knopf, 1947.

Binkley, William Campbell. *Reports from a Texan agent in New Mexico, 1849.* (In *New Spain and the Anglo-American west, historical contributions presented to Herbert Eugene Bolton.*) Los Angeles, privately printed, 1932.

Bishop, Morris. *The odyssey of Cabeza de Vaca.* New York, D. Appleton Co., 1933.

Bolton, Herbert Eugene. *Coronada, knight of pueblos and plains.* New York, Whittlesey House, 1949.

—— *The Spanish borderlands. A chronicle of Florida and the southwest.* New Haven, Yale University Press, 1921.

—— *Spanish exploration in the southwest, 1542–1706.* Edited by Herbert Eugene Bolton. *Original narratives of early American history.* New York, Charles Scribner's Sons, 1930.

Borah, William E. *Papers of Senator William E. Borah.* Mss. Washington, The Library of Congress.

Botkin, B. A. *A treasury of American folklore. Stories, ballads and traditions of the people,* edited by A. Botkin. New York, Crown Publishers, 1944.

Bourke, John G. *The folk-foods of the Rio Grande valley and of Northern Mexico.* (In *Southwestern Lore,* edited by J. Frank Dobie.) Publications of the Texas Folk-Lore Society Number 9. Dallas, The Southwest Press, 1931.

Boyd, E. *Saints and saint-makers of New Mexico.* Santa Fe, Laboratory of Anthropology, 1946.

Boyd, Mrs. Orsemus Bronson. *Cavalry life in tent and field.* New York, J. Selwin Tait and Sons, 1894.

Brand, Donald D. *Prehistoric trade in the southwest. New Mexico Business Review,* v. 4, No. 4, October, 1935.

Brenner, Anita. *Idols behind altars.* New York, Payson and Clarke, 1929.

Brown, Dee. *Trail driving days.* Text by Dee Brown; picture research by Martin F. Schmitt. New York, Charles Scribner's Sons, 1952.

Brown, Lloyd A. *Story of maps.* Boston, Little, Brown and Co., 1949.

Bryan, Kirk. *Pre-Columbian agriculture in the southwest, as conditioned by periods of alluviation. Annals of the Association of American Geographers,* v. 31, no. 4, December, 1941.

Buckle, Henry Thomas. *History of civilization in England.* 2 v. New York, D. Appleton Co., 1879.

Burkholder, Joseph L. *The middle Rio Grande conservancy district. Report of the chief engineer.* [State of New Mexico] 1928.

Butterfield, Roger. *The American past, a history of the United States from Concord to Hiroshima, 1775–1945.* New York, Simon and Schuster, 1947.

Calderón de la Barca, Frances Erskine Inglis. *Life in Mexico during a residence of two years in that country.* With an introduction by Henry Baerlein. New York, E. P. Dutton and Co., 1931.

Callahan, James Morton. *American foreign policy in Mexican relations.* New York, The Macmillan Co., 1932.

Carranza, Venustiano. *Reply of Don Venustiano Carranza to the chief of the Northern Division. The First Chief of the Constitutionalist Army, in charge of the Executive Power, to the Mexican people. Refutation of the manifest of General Francisco Villa.* Mexico, D. F., October 25, 1914.

Carroll, H. Bailey. *The Texan Santa Fe trail.* Canyon, Texas, Panhandle-Plains Historical Society, 1951.

Casey, Robert J. *The Texas border and some borderliners. A chronicle and a guide.* Indianapolis, Bobbs-Merrill Co., 1950.

Castañeda, Carlos E. *Our Catholic heritage in Texas, 1519–1936.* Prepared under the asupices of the Knights of Columbus of Texas, Paul J. Foik, editor. 7 v. Austin, Von Boeckmann-Jones Co., 1936.

Castañeda de Náxera, Pedro de. *Narrative of the expedition to Cibola, undertaken in 1540, in which are described all those settlements, ceremonies, and customs.* (In *Narratives of the Coronado Expedition, 1540–1542,* edited by George P. Hammond and Agapito Rey.) Albuquerque, University of New Mexico Press, 1940.

Castetter, Edward F. *The early utilization and the distribution of agave in the American southwest,* by Edward F. Castetter, Willis H. Bell and Alvin R.

Grove. Albuquerque, *University of New Mexico Bulletin,* Whole number 335, Dec. 1, 1939.

...... *Cavalry Journal,* July, 1916: *Notes on campaigning in Mexico;* November, 1916: *Cavalry equipment in Mexico; The cavalry fight at Columbus; Experiences in Mexico; Field notes from Mexico and the border.*

Céliz, Fray Francisco. *Diary of the Alarcón expedition into Texas, 1718–1719.* Translated by Fritz Leo Hoffman. Los Angeles, The Quivira Society, 1935.

Cervantes Saavedra, Miguel de. *Don Quixote de la Mancha.* Translated by Peter Motteux. New York, Illustrated Modern Library, 1946.

Chavez, Fray Angélico. *Our Lady of the Conquest.* Santa Fe, Historical Society of New Mexico, 1948.

Christensen, Erwin O. *The index of American design.* New York, Macmillan Co.; Washington, National Gallery of Art, Smithsonian Institution, 1950.

Cleland, Robert Glass. *This reckless breed of men, the trappers and fur traders of the southwest.* New York, Alfred A. Knopf, 1950.

Columbus, Christopher. *Discovery of the West Indies; journal of Columbus,* abridged by Las Casas. (In *Narratives of the discovery of America,* edited by A. W. Lawrence and Jean Young.) New York, Jonathan Cape and Harrison Smith, 1931.

Commager, Henry Steele. *America in perspective, the United States through foreign eyes,* edited by Henry Steele Commager. New York, Random House, 1947.

Conkling, Harold. *Water supply for possible development of irrigation and drainage projects on the Rio Grande river above El Paso, Texas.* Typescript, 1919. Albuquerque, Middle Rio Grande Conservancy District.

Connelley, William E. *Doniphan's expedition.* Topeka, Crane and Co., 1907.

Coolidge, Mary Roberts. *The rain-makers, Indians of Arizona and New Mexico.* Boston, Houghton Mifflin Co., 1929.

Cortés, Hernando, Marqués del Valle de Oaxaca. *Five letters, 1519–1526.* Translated by J. Bayard Morris. New York, Robert M. McBride Co., 1929.

Corti, Egon Caesar. *Maximilian and Charlotte of Mexico.* Translated from the German by Catherine Alison Phillips. 2 v. New York, Alfred A. Knopf, 1928.

Coulter, E. Merton. *The Confederate States of America, 1861–1865.* Baton Rouge, Louisiana State University Press; Austin, University of Texas, 1950.

Cox, Isaac Jolin. *Monroe and the early Mexican revolutionary agents.* (In *Annual Report, American Historical Association, 1911,* v. 1.) Washington, Government Printing Office.

Cramer, Stuart W. *Punitive expedition from Boquillas. Cavalry Journal,* November, 1916.

Crane, Leo. *Desert drums, the Pueblo Indians of New Mexico, 1540–1928.* Boston, Little, Brown and Co., 1928.

Cremony, John C. *Life among the Apaches.* Tucson, Arizona Silhouettes, 1951.

Crèvecoeur, Hector St. Jean de. *Letters from an American farmer* (extracts in *This was America,* edited by Oscar Handlin) . Cambridge, Harvard University Press, 1949.

Crimmins, Martin L. *Colonel J. K. F. Mansfield's report of the inspection of*

the department of Texas in 1856. Southwestern Historical Quarterly,
v. 42, nos. 2, 3 and 4.

—— Two thousand miles by boat in the Rio Grande in 1850. West Texas
and Scientific Society Bulletin, publication 5, bulletin 48, Dec. 1, 1933.

Croneis, Carey. *Down to earth, an introduction to geology,* by Cary Croneis,
William C. Krumbein and Chichi Lasley. Chicago, University of Chicago
Press, 1936.

Crow, John A. *The epic of Latin America.* Garden City, Doubleday and Co.,
1946.

Cruse, Thomas. *Apache days and after,* edited and with an introduction by
Eugene Cunningham. Caldwell, Idaho, The Caxton Printers, Ltd., 1941.

Curti, Merle. *The growth of American thought.* New York, Harper and Brothers,
1943.

Dallam, Samuel F. *The punitive expedition of 1916—some problems and experiences of a troop commander. Cavalry Journal,* July 1927.

Davenport, J. Walker. *Painted pebbles from the lower Pecos and Big Bend
regions of Texas,* by J. Walker Davenport and Carl Chelf. San Antonio,
Witte Memorial Museum, bulletin 5, ND.

Davis, Richard Harding. *The west from a car window.* New York, Harper and
Brothers, 1892.

Defouri, James H. *Historical sketch of the Catholic church in New Mexico.*
San Francisco, McCormick Brothers, Printers, 1887.

DeGolyer, E. M. *Across aboriginal America. The journey of three Englishmen
across Texas in 1568.* El Paso, The Peripatetic Press, 1947.

Denver Art Museum. *Leaflet series,* 1936; 1939; 1940.

DeVoto, Bernard. *The Year of Decision 1846.* Boston, Houghton Mifflin Co.,
1943.

Díaz del Castillo, Bernal. *True history of the conquest of Mexico, written in
the year 1568.* Translated by Maurice Keatinge. 2 v. New York, Robert M.
McBride, 1927.

Dickey, Roland F. *New Mexico village arts.* Drawings by Lloyd Lozes Goff.
Albuquerque, University of Mexico Press, 1949.

Dobie, J. Frank. *Ballads and songs of the frontier folk.* (In *Texas and southwestern lore,* edited by J. Frank Dobie.) Austin, Publications of the Texas
Folk-Lore Society, number 6, 1927.

—— *The longhorns.* Illustrated by Tom Lea. Boston, Little, Brown and Co.,
1941.

—— *The mustangs.* Illustrated by Charles Banks Wilson. Boston, Little,
Brown and Co., 1952.

—— *Tongues of the monte.* Garden City, Doubleday, Doran and Co., 1935.

—— *A vaquero of the brush country, partly from the reminiscences of John
Young.* New York, Grosset and Dunlap, 1929.

Domenech, Emmanuel. *Missionary adventures in Texas and Mexico. A personal
narrative of six years' sojourn in those regions.* Translated from the
French under the author's superintendence. London, Longsmans, Brown,
Green, Longmans and Roberts, 1858.

Dougherty, E. *The Rio Grande valley.* (In the *Magazine of History,* with notes and queries. Extra number, no. 138, 1867.) Tarrytown, New York, reprinted by William Abbatt, 1928.

Douglas, Frederic H. *Indian art of the United States,* by Frederic H. Douglas and Réné D'Harnoncourt. New York, the Museum of Modern Art, 1941.

Downes, Olin. *A treasury of American song,* by Olin Downes and Elie Siegmeister. New York, Howell, Soskin and Co., 1940.

DuBois, John Van Deusen. *Campaigns in the west, 1856–1861. The journals and letters of John Van Deusen DuBois,* edited by George P. Hammond. Tucson, Arizona Pioneers Historical Society, 1949.

Dunbar, Seymour. *A history of travel in America.* 4 v. in 1. New York, Tudor Publishing Co., 1937.

Dyer, Alexander Brydie. *Letter to Dr. Robert Johnston* [written at Santa Fe, New Mexico, February 14, 1847]. Ms. Santa Fe, Museum of New Mexico. (Excerpts quoted by permission of Museum of New Mexico.)

Eccleston, Robert. *Overland to California on the southwestern trail, 1849,* edited by George P. Hammond and Edward H. Howes. Berkeley and Los Angeles, University of California Press, 1950.

Ehinger, Augustus Frederick. *Diary of his travels from Illinois to Mexico and during his service as a member of Comp. H, Second Regiment Illinois Volunteers, July 1846–June 1847.* Ms. In the possession of Colonel Charles F. Ward, Roswell, New Mexico. (Excerpts quoted by permission of Col. Ward.)

Ellis, Havelock. *The soul of Spain.* Boston, Houghton Mifflin Co., 1924.

Emory, William H. *Notes of a military reconnoissance,* with introduction and notes by Ross Calvin. Albuquerque, University of New Mexico Press, 1951.

—— *Report of William H. Emory, Major First Cavalry and U.S. Commissioner, United States and Mexican Boundary Survey.* 34th Congress, 1st session, ex. doc. no. 135, Washington, Cornelius Wendell, printer, 1857.

Falconer, Thomas. *Letters and notes on the Texan Santa Fe expedition, 1841–1842 . . .* with introduction and notes by F. W. Hodge. New York, Dauber and Pine Bookshops, Inc., 1930.

Federal Writers Program, WPA. *Colorado, a guide to the highest state.* American Guide Series. New York, Hastings House, 1941.

—— *New Mexico, a guide to the colorful state.* American Guide Series. New York, Hastings House, 1940.

—— *Texas, a guide to the lone star state.* American Guide Series. New York, Hastings House, 1940.

Fergusson, Mrs. C. M. *Conversations,* at Albuquerque, New Mexico.

Fergusson, Erna. *Our southwest.* New York, Alfred A. Knopf, 1940.

Fergusson, Harvey. *Rio Grande.* New York, Alfred A. Knopf, 1933.

Ferris, W. A. *Life in the Rocky Mountains . . .* edited by Paul C. Phillips. Denver, Fred A. Rosenstock, Old West Publishing Co., 1940.

Fewkes, J. Walter. *The pueblo settlements near El Paso, Texas. American Anthropologist,* v. 4, 1902.

—— *Two types of southwestern cliff houses.* Washington, *Annual Report of the Smithsonian Institution,* 1921.

Fiock, L. R. *The functioning of a completed irrigation project as illustrated by the development and operation of the Rio Grande irrigation project.* Typescript. U. S. Department of Agriculture, Albuquerque, 1934.

Fisher, Reginald. *Notes on the relation of the Franciscans to the Penitentes.* Santa Fe, *El Palacio*, v. 48, December, 1944.

Fitzmaurice-Kelly, James. *New history of Spanish literature.* London, Humphrey Milford, 1926.

Forrest, Earle R. *Missions and pueblos of the old southwest.* Cleveland, Arthur H. Clarke Co., 1929.

Foscue, Edwin J. *The Mesilla valley of New Mexico: a study in aridity and irrigation. Economic Geography*, v. 7, no. 1, January 1931.

Frazer, James George. *The golden bough, a study in magic and religion.* New York, The Macmillan Co., 1935.

Freeman, Douglas Southall. *R. E. Lee, a biography.* New York, Charles Scribner's Sons, 1935.

Fulton, Maurice Garland. *New Mexico's own chronicle, three races in the writings of four hundred years,* adapted and edited by Maurice Garland Fulton and Paul Horgan. Dallas, Banks Upshaw and Co., 1937.

Garrard, Lewis H. *Wah-to-yah and the Taos trail.* Edited by Ralph P. Bieber. Glendale, The Arthur H. Clark Co., 1934.

Gautier, Théophile. *A romantic in Spain,* translated from the French by Catherine Alison Phillips. New York, Alfred A. Knopf, 1926.

Gibson, Charles E. *Story of the ship.* New York, Henry Schumann, 1948.

Gibson, George Rutledge. *Journal of a soldier under Kearny and Doniphan, 1846–1847.* Edited by Ralph P. Bieber. Glendale, The Arthur H. Clark Co., 1935.

Giddings, Luther. *Sketches of the campaign in northern Mexico in eighteen hundred forty-six and seven, by an officer of the First Regiment of Ohio volunteers.* New York, George P. Putnam and Co., 1853.

Gilpin, Laura. *The Pueblos, a camera chronicle.* New York, Hastings House, 1941.

—— *The Rio Grande, river of destiny. An interpretation of the river, the land, and the people.* New York, Duell, Sloan and Pearce, 1949.

Glasgow, Brig. Gen. William J. *Conversations* at El Paso, Texas.

Goldscheider, Ludwig. *El Greco.* New York, Phaidon Press—Oxford University Press, 1938.

Gonzáles de Mendoza, Juan. *A briefe relation of two notable voyages, the first made by frier Augustin Ruyz . . .; the second by Antonio de Espejo . . . taken out of the history of China written by Frier Juan Gonzales de Mendoça.* (In *The voyages, traffiques and discoveries of foreign voyagers . . .* by Richard Hakluyt, v. 10). London, J. M. Dent and Son, Ltd., 1928.

Gonzáles, Jovita. *America invades the border towns. Southwest Review,* v. 15, no. 4, summer 1940.

—— *Folk-lore of the Texas-Mexican vaquero.* (In *Texas and southwestern lore,* edited by J. Frank Dobie). Austin, Publications of the Texas Folk-Lore Society, number 6, 1927.

Grant, Blanche C. *When old trails were new, the story of Taos.* New York, Press of the Pioneers, 1934.

Grant, Ulysses Simpson. *Personal memoirs of U. S. Grant.* 2 v. New York, The Century Co., 1895.

Grassi, Giovanni Antonio. *Notizie varie sullo stato presente della repubblica degli Stati Uniti dell' America . . . (1819)* (Extracts in *This Was America,* edited by Oscar Handlin). Cambridge, Harvard University Press, 1949.

Green, Thomas J. *Journal of the Texian expedition against Mier . . .* [a facsimile reproduction of the original]. Austin, The Steck Co., 1935.

Gregg, Josiah. *Commerce of the prairies, the journal of a Santa Fe trader.* [Reprint from the edition of 1844.] Dallas, Southwest Press, 1933.

—— *Diary and letters of Josiah Gregg: Excursions in Mexico and California, 1847–1850,* edited by Maurice Garland Fulton, with an introduction by Paul Horgan. Norman, University of Oklahoma Press, 1944.

—— *Diary and letters of Josiah Gregg: Southwestern enterprises, 1840–1847,* edited by Maurice Garland Fulton, with an introduction by Paul Horgan. Norman, University of Oklahoma Press, 1941.

Gregg, Robert D. *The influence of border troubles on relations between the United States and Mexico, 1876–1910.* Baltimore, the Johns Hopkins Press, 1937.

Grey, Edward, Viscount Grey of Fallodon. *Twenty-five years, 1892–1916.* 2 v. New York, Frederick H. Stokes Co., 1926.

Gutierrez de Lara, José Bernardo. *Diary . . . 1811–1812.* Translated from the original Spanish by Elizabeth H. West. *American Historical Review,* v. 34, nos. 1 and 2.

Hackett, Charles Wilson. *Revolt of the Pueblo Indians of New Mexico and Otermin's attempted reconquest, 1680–1692.* Introduction and annotations by Charles Wilson Hackett. Translations of original documents by Charmion Clair Shelby. Coronado Cuarto Centennial Publications, 1540–1940, edited by George P. Hammond. V. 8 and 9. Albuquerque, University of New Mexico Press, 1942.

Hallenbeck, Cleve. *Álvar Nuñez Cabeza de Vaca, the journey and route of the first European to cross the continent of North America, 1534–1536.* Glendale, The Arthur H. Clarke Co., 1940.

—— *Land of the conquistadores.* Caldwell, Idaho, The Caxton Printers, 1950.

Hamilton, Holman. *Zachary Taylor, soldier of the republic.* Indianapolis, The Bobbs-Merrill Co., 1941.

Hammond, George P. *Narratives of the Coronado expedition, 1540–1542* [edited and annotated] by George P. Hammond and Agapito Rey. Coronado Cuarto Centennial Publications, edited by George P. Hammond. v. 2 Albuquerque, University of New Mexico Press, 1940.

Hammond, John Hays. *Autobiography.* 2 v. New York, Farrar and Rinehart, 1935.

Handlin, Oscar. *This was America,* edited by Oscar Handlin. Cambridge, Harvard University Press, 1949.

Hanke, Lewis. *The first social experiments in America, a study in the development of Spanish Indian Policy in the 16th century. Cambridge, Harvard University Press, 1935.

—— *Spanish struggle for justice in the conquest of America.* Philadelphia, University of Pennsylvania Press, 1949.

Harrington, J. P. *Old Indian geographical names around Santa Fe, New Mexico.* American Anthropologist, v. 22, 1920.

Hendrick, Burton J. *Life and letters of Walter H. Page.* 3 v. Garden City, Doubleday, Page and Co., 1922.

Henry, Robert Selph. *Story of the Mexican War.* Indianapolis, Bobbs-Merrill Co., 1950.

Henry, W. S. *Campaign sketches of the war with Mexico.* New York, Harper and Brothers, 1847.

Hergesheimer, Joseph. *Sheridan, a military narrative.* Boston, Houghton Mifflin Co., 1931.

Hewett, Edgar L. *Ancient life in the American southwest.* Indianapolis, Bobbs-Merrill Co., 1930.

—— *The Pueblo Indian world* . . . by Edgar L. Hewett and Bertha P. Dutton . . . Albuquerque, University of New Mexico; Santa Fe, School of American Research, 1945.

Hill, Robert L. *Running the canyons of the Rio Grande. A chapter of recent exploration.* Century Magazine, v. 61, no. 3, January 1901.

Hitchcock, Ethan Allen. *Fifty years in camp and field. Diary of Major General Ethan Allen Hitchcock, U.S.A.,* edited by W. A. Croffut, New York, G. P. Putnam's Sons, 1909.

Hodge, Frederick Webb. *Spanish explorers in the southwestern United States, 1528–1543,* edited by Frederick W. Hodge and Theodore H. Lewis. *Original narratives of early American history.* New York, Charles Scribner's Sons, 1925.

Hoffman, Fred L. *Why the Cliff Dwellers vanished. Scientific American,* v.123, 1920.

Hogan, William Ransom. *The Texas Republic.* Norman, University of Oklahoma Press, 1946.

Hollister, Ovando J. *Boldly they rode, a history of the First Colorado Regiment of Volunteers.* With an introduction by William McCleod Raine. Lakewood, Colorado, The Golden Press, 1949.

Hollon, W. Eugene. *The lost pathfinder, Zebulon Montgomery Pike.* Norman, University of Oklahoma Press, 1949.

Horgan, Paul. *Colonial Life in Latin America, an exhibition of history and art.* Roswell, New Mexico, Roswell Museum, 1949.

—— *The habit of empire* with landscapes by Peter Hurd. New York, Harper and Brothers, 1939.

—— *A tree on the plains,* Text for the opera by Ernst Bacon. Dallas, *Southwest Review,* v. 38, no. 4, 1943.

House, Edward M. *Intimate papers of Colonel House,* arranged as a narrative by Charles Seymour. 4 v. Boston, Houghton Mifflin Co., 1928.

Houston, Sam. *Proclamation by the President of Texas, announcing an armistice between Texas and Mexico, 29 July 1843.* Signed by Anson Jones, Secretary of state of Texas. Original document. San Marino, California,

Henry E. Huntington Library. (Excerpts quoted by permission of the Huntington Library.)

Howlett, W. J. *Life of the Right Reverend Joseph P. Machebeuf, D.D.* Pueblo, Colorado, 1908.

Hrdlička, Ales. *Physiological and medical observations among the Indians of the southwestern United States and northern Mexico.* Smithsonian Institution, Bureau of American Ethnology, *Bulletin 34,* Washington, Government Printing Office, 1908.

Hughes, John Taylor. *Diary* (in *Doniphan's expedition,* by William E. Connelley). Topeka, Crane and Co., 1907.

Hume, Martin A. S. *Phillip II of Spain.* London, The Macmillan Co., 1920.

Huntington, Ellsworth. *The red man's chronicle, a chronicle of aboriginal America. (Chronicles of America.)* New Haven, Yale University Press. 1921.

Irving, Washington. *The adventures of Captain Bonneville.* 2 v. New York, G. P. Putnam's Sons, 1895.

James, George Wharton. *New Mexico, land of the delight makers.* Boston, Page and Co., 1920.

James, Marquis. *The Raven, a biography of Sam Houston.* Indianapolis, Bobbs-Merrill Co., 1929.

Jaramillo, Cleofas M. *Shadows of the past (sombres del pasado).* Santa Fe, Seton Village Press, 1941.

Jeançon, Jean Allard. *Pueblo Indian clothing* by Jean Allard Jeançon and Frederic H. Douglas. Denver Art Museum, *Leaflet series 4,* 1930.

——*Pueblo Indian foods* by Jean Allard Jeançon and Frederic H. Douglas. Denver Art Museum, *Leaflet series 8,* 1930.

Jones, Stephen B. *Boundary-making; a handbook for statesmen, treaty editors and boundary commissioners.* Washington, Carnegie Endowment for International Peace, 1945.

Keleher, William A. *Turmoil in New Mexico, 1846–1868.* Santa Fe, The Rydal Press, 1952.

Kelley, J. Charles. *Association of archaeological materials with geological deposits in the Big Bend region of Texas,* by J. Charles Kelley, T. N. Campbell and Donald J. Lehmer. Alpine, Texas, *Sul Ross State Teachers College Bulletin,* v. 21, no. 3, September 1, 1940.

Kendall, George Wilkins. *Narrative of the Texan Santa Fe expedition . . .* 2 v. [facsimile reproduction of the original edition.] Austin, The Steck Co., 1935.

Kenly, John Reese. *Memoirs of a Maryland volunteer, war with Mexico, in the years 1846–7–8.* Philadelphia, J. B. Lippincott and Co., 1873.

Kerbey, McFall. *Texas delta of an American Nile. National Geographic Magazine,* v. 75, no. 1, January 1939.

Kidder, A. V. *An introduction to the study of southwestern archaeology with a preliminary account of the excavations at Pecos.* New Haven, Yale University Press, 1924.

Kincaid, Edgar B. *The Mexican pastor.* (In *Texas and southwestern lore,* edited by J. Frank Dobie.) Publications of the Texas Folk-Lore Society, no. 9. Dallas, the Southwest Press, 1931.

Kohlberg, Ernst. *Letters, 1875–1877.* Translated from the German. Original documents. El Paso Public Library. (Excerpts quoted by permission of El Paso Public Library.)

Kortwright, Francis H. *The ducks, geese and swans of North America.* Washington, American Wildlife Association, 1943.

Kouwenhoven, John A. *Made in America, the arts in modern civilization.* Garden City, Doubleday and Co., 1948.

Kroeber, A. L. *Pueblos* (in *Encyclopedia Britannica,* 14th edition).

Kubler, George. *The religious architecture of New Mexico in the colonial period and since the American occupation.* Colorado Springs, The Taylor Museum, 1940.

Lane, Ferdinand C. *Earth's grandest rivers.* Garden City, Doubleday and Co., 1949.

Lane, Franklin Knight. *Letters of Franklin K. Lane, personal and political,* edited by Anne Wintermute Lane and Louise Herrick Vail. Boston, Houghton Mifflin Co., 1922.

Lansing, Robert. *War memoirs.* Indianapolis, Bobbs-Merrill Co., 1935.

Lavelle, Francis. *Archbishop Lamy, of Santa Fe.* (In *Family Annual* for 1889.) New York, Catholic Publications Society Co., 1888.

Lee, Robert E. *Recollections and letters of General Robert E. Lee.* New York, Doubleday Page, 1904.

Leonard, Irving A. *Books of the brave, being an account of books and men in the Spanish conquest and settlement of the sixteenth-century new world.* Cambridge, Harvard University Press, 1949.

Lewis, Lloyd. *Captain Sam Grant.* Boston, Little, Brown and Co., 1950.

Lewis, Macmillan. *Woodrow Wilson of Princeton.* Narberth, Penna., Livingston Publishing Co., 1952.

Lipman, Jean. *American folk art in wood, metal and stone.* New York, Pantheon, 1948.

. . . . . . *Literary Digest,* March–December, 1916.

Lomax, John A. *Cowboy songs and other frontier ballads,* collected by John A. Lomax. With an introduction by Barrett Wendell. New York, The Macmillan Co., 1927.

———— *Folk song U S A, the 111 best American ballads,* collected, adapted and arranged by John A. Lomax and Alan Lomax; Alan Lomax, editor; Charles Seeger and Ruth Crawford Seeger, music editors. New York, Duell, Sloan and Pearce, 1947.

———— *Our singing country, a second volume of American ballads and folk songs,* collected and compiled by John A. Lomax and Alan Lomax; Ruth Crawford Seeger, music editor. New York, The Macmillan Co., 1941.

López de Gómara, Francisco. *General historie of the West Indies.* (Excerpts in Hakluyt's *Voyages, traffiques and discoveries of foreign voyagers.*) London, J. M. Dent, 1928.

Lowrie, Samuel Harman. *Culture conflict in Texas, 1821–1835.* New York, Columbia University Press, 1932.

Lummis, Charles F. *Land of poco tiempo.* New York, Charles Scribner's Sons, 1913.

———— *Mesa, canyon and pueblo.* New York, Century Co., 1925.

MacClary, John Stewart. *The first American farmers. Art and Archaeology,* v. 124, no. 3, September, 1927.

McCoy, John C. *Paper read before Old Settlers Historical Society, Jackson County, Missouri,* 1871.

McCoy, Joseph G. *Historic sketches of the cattle trade of the west and southwest.* [Facsimile reprint of the edition of 1874.] Washington, The Rare Book Shop, 1932.

McKee, Irving. *"Ben Hur" Wallace, the life of General Lew Wallace.* Berkeley and Los Angeles, University of California Press, 1947.

McKee, James Cooper. *Narrative of the surrender of a command of U.S. forces at Fort Fillmore, N.M., in July, A.D. 1861, at the breaking out of the Civil War* . . . second edition revised and corrected. New York, 1881.

McKellar, Mrs. S. B. *Conversations* at Eagle Pass, Texas.

Madariaga, Salvador de. *Fall of the Spanish American empire.* London, Hollis and Carter, 1948.

———— *Rise of the Spanish American empire.* London, Hollis and Carter, 1947.

———— *Spain.* New York, Creative Age Press, 1943.

Magoffin, Susan Shelby. *Down the Santa Fe Trail and into Mexico; the diary of Susan Shelby Magoffin, 1846–1847,* edited by Stella M. Drumm. New Haven, Yale University Press, 1926.

Martialis, Marcus Valerius. *Epigrams,* with an English translation by Walter C. A. Kerr. New York, G. P. Putnam's Sons, 1930.

Martin, George C. *Archaeological exploration of the Shumla caves. Report of the George C. Martin expedition, Southwest Texas Archaeological Society.* San Antonio, Witte Memorial Museum, 1933.

Martin, Paul S. *Indians before Columbus. Twenty thousand years of North American history revealed by archaeology,* by Paul S. Martin, George L. Quimby and Donald Collier. Chicago, University of Chicago Press, 1947.

Maugham, W. Somerset. *Don Fernando, or variations on some Spanish themes.* Garden City, Doubleday, Doran and Co., 1935.

May, Florence. *The Penitentes. Natural History,* v. 38, Dec. 1936.

Meier-Graefe, Julius. *The Spanish journey.* Translated by J. Holroyd Reece. New York, Harcourt, Brace and Co., ND.

Mencken, H. L. *The American language, an inquiry into the development of English in the United States.* Fourth edition. New York, Alfred A. Knopf, 1936.

———— Supplement I to the above, 1945.

Milham, Willis Isbister. *Meteorology.* New York, The Macmillan Co., 1929.

Miller, Alfred Jacob. *The west of Alfred Jacob Miller (1837),* from the notes and water colors in the Walters Art Gallery, with an account of the artist by Marvin C. Ross. Norman, University of Oklahoma Press, 1951.

Millis, Walter. *Road to war, America, 1914–1917.* Boston, Houghton Mifflin Co., 1935.

Montlezun, Baron de. *Voyage fait dans les années 1816 et 1817, de New-Yorck à la Nouvelle-Orléans et de l'Orénoque au Mississippi . . . (1818).* (Extracts in *This was America,* edited by Oscar Handlin.) Cambridge, Harvard University Press, 1949.

Montoya, Juan de. *New Mexico in 1602. Juan de Montoya's relation of the discovery of New Mexico.* Translated, edited, annotated, and with an introduction by George P. Hammond and Agapito Rey. Albuquerque, The Quivira Society, 1938.

Moreau de Saint-Méry, Méderic Louis Élie. *Voyage aux États-Unis de l'Amérique, 1793–1798.* (Extracts in *This was America,* edited by Oscar Handlin.) Cambridge, Harvard University Press, 1949.

Morfi, Fray Juan Agustín. *History of Texas, 1673–1779.* Translated, with biographical introduction and annotations by Carlos Eduardo Castañeda. In two parts. Albuquerque. The Quivira Society, 1935.

Moses, Montrose J. *The American dramatist.* Boston, Little, Brown and Co. 1925.

...... *Motion picture film footage,* showing Francisco Villa, General John J. Pershing, President Woodrow Wilson, President Venustiano Carranza, General Álvaro Obregón, General Frederick Funston, and desert fighting episode during the Punitive Expedition of 1916. New York, Lloyds Film Storage Co.

National Capital Sesquicentennial Commission. *American processional, 1492–1900.* Washington, The Corcoran Gallery of Art, 1950.

New Mexico, Citizens of. *Document addressed to President Santa Anna of Mexico, describing abandonment of New Mexico by Governor Manuel Armijo.* Signed by various citizens, Santa Fe, September 26, 1846. Translation. Original document. San Marino, Henry E. Huntington Library. (Excerpts quoted by permission of the Huntington Library.)

Nuñez Cabeza de Vaca, Alvar. *Narrative of Alvar Nuñez Cabeza de Vaca,* edited by Frederick W. Hodge. (In *Spanish explorers of the southern United States, 1528–1543.) Original narratives of early American history.* New York, Charles Scribner's Sons, 1907.

...... *Outlook,* 30 October 1909.

Palmer, Frederick. *Newton D. Baker, America at war.* 2 v. New York, Dodd, Mead and Co., 1931.

Palmer, Rose A. *The North American Indians. The Smithsonian Scientific series,* v. 4. New York, Smithsonian Institution Series, Inc., 1938.

Parkman, Francis. *The journals of Francis Parkman,* edited by Mason Wade. 2 v. New York, Harper and Brothers, 1947.

Parsons, Elsie Clews. *Pueblo Indian religion.* 2 v. Chicago, University of Chicago Press, 1939.

Pattie, James O. *Personal narrative of James O. Pattie of Kentucky . . .* edited by Reuben Gold Thwaites. *Early Western Travels.* Cleveland, Arthur H. Clark Co., 1905.

Percier. *Le sacre de S.M. l'empereur Napoléon dans l'église métropolitaine de Paris, le xi frimaire an XIII, dimanche 2 décembre 1804.*

Pérez de Lúxan, Diego. *Expedition into New Mexico made by Antonio de Espéjo, 1582–1583.* Translated with introduction and notes by George P. Hammond and Agapito Rey. Los Angeles, The Quivira Society, 1929.

Pérez de Villagrá, Gaspar. *History of New Mexico.* Translated by Gilberto Espinosa. Introduction and notes by Frederick W. Hodge. Los Angeles, The Quivira Society, 1933.

Pershing, John Joseph. *Letters* (unpublished). Mss. 1915–1917. Private collection, Washington, D.C. (Excerpts quoted by permission of Mr. F. W. Pershing.)

—— *My experiences in the world war.* 2 v. New York, Frederick H. Stokes Co., 1931.

Peyton, Green. *America's heartland: the southwest.* Norman, University of Oklahoma Press, 1948.

Pike, Zebulon Montgomery. *The expeditions of Zebulon Montgomery Pike . . . during the years 1805–6–7,* edited by Elliott Coues. 3 v. New York, Francis P. Harper, 1895.

Pino, Pedro Bautista, *et al. Three New Mexico chronicles; the Exposición of Don Pedro Bautista Pino, 1812; the Ojeada of Lic. Antonio Barreiro, 1832; and the additions of Don José Agustín de Escudero, 1849.* Translated with introduction and notes by H. Bailey Carroll and J. Villasana Haggard. Albuquerque, The Quivira Society, 1942.

Plato. *Dialogues.* Selections from the translation of Benjamin Jowett . . . edited with an introduction by William Chase Greene. New York, Boni and Liveright, 1927.

Polk, James K. *Polk, the diary of a president, 1845–1849,* edited by Allan Nevins. New York, Longmans, Green, 1929.

Powell, Fred Wilbur. *The railroads of Mexico.* Boston, The Stratford Co., 1921.

Prescott, William H. *History of the reign of Philip the second, king of Spain.* Boston, Phillips, Sampson and Co., 1855.

Priestley, Herbert Ingram. *The coming of the white man, 1492–1848.* New York, The Macmillan Co., 1929.

Pringle, Henry F. *Life and times of William Howard Taft.* 2 v. New York, Farrar and Rinehart, 1939.

Quinn, Arthur Hobson. *A history of the American drama from the beginning to the Civil War.* New York, Harper and Brothers, 1923.

Read, Benjamin N. *Illustrated history of New Mexico.* [Santa Fe, New Mexican Printing Co., c. 1912.]

Reagan, Albert B. *Evidences of migration in ancient Pueblo times. American Anthropologist,* v. 35, 1933.

Reed, John. *Insurgent Mexico.* New York, D. Appleton Co., 1914.

Renaud, Etienne B. *Evolution of population and dwelling in the Indian southwest. Social Forces,* v. 7, 1928–1929.

Rice, Martin. *Old timers' poem,* read by the author Martin Rice at Old Settlers' meeting, Jackson County, Missouri, 1880.

Richardson, Rupert Norval. *The greater southwest . . .* by Richard Norval Richardson and Carl Coke Rister. Glendale, The Arthur H. Clark Co., 1934.

Richie, Ed. *Conversations* at Eagle Pass, Texas.

Ritch, William Gillet. *Article addressed to Editor, New York Herald, concerning establishment of archbishopric of Santa Fe. June 21, 1875.* Original document, ms. San Marino, Henry E. Huntington Library.

Rives, George Lockhart. *The United States and Mexico, 1821–1848.* 2 v. New York, Charles Scribner's Sons, 1913.

Robertson, William Spence. *Iturbide of Mexico.* Durham, Duke University Press, 1952.

Robinson, Jacob S. *A journal of the Santa Fe expedition under Colonel Doniphan.* Reprinted, with an historical introduction and notes by Carl L. Cannon, from the edition of 1848. *Narratives of the Trans-Mississippi Frontier.* Princeton, Princeton University Press, 1932.

Ronquillo, E. W. *Notes on "Rio Grande dry" in 1851 and 1863.* Written August 23, 1877. Original document. San Marino, Henry E. Huntington Library. (Excerpts quoted by permission of the Huntington Library.)

Rose, Stuart. *Conversations* at Philadelphia, Pennsylvania.

Rosenfeld, Paul. *An hour with American music. The One Hour Series.* Philadelphia, J. B. Lippincott Co., 1929.

Rourke, Constance. *American humor, a study of the national character.* New York, Harcourt, Brace and Co., 1931.

—— *The roots of American culture, and other essays.* Edited with a preface by Van Wyck Brooks. New York, Harcourt, Brace and Co., 1942.

Ruxton, George Frederick. *Ruxton of the Rockies.* Collected by Clyde and Mae Reed Porter, edited by LeRoy R. Hafen. Norman, University of Oklahoma Press, 1950.

Salpointe, Jean Baptiste. *Soldiers of the cross. Notes on the ecclesiastical history of New Mexico, Arizona and Colorado.* Banning, California, St. Boniface's Industrial School, 1898.

Sanford, Trent E. *The architecture of the southwest: Indian, Spanish, American.* New York, W. W. Norton and Co., 1950.

Santa Fe, Archdiocese of. *The old faith and Old Glory, 1846–1946, [the] story of the Church in New Mexico since the American occupation.* Santa Fe, New Mexico, 1946.

Santleben, August. *A Texas pioneer. Early staging and overland freighting days on the frontiers of Texas and Mexico.* New York and Washington, The Neale Publishing Co., c. 1910.

Scott, Hugh Lennox. *Papers of Major General Hugh L. Scott.* Mss. Washington, The Library of Congress.

—— *Some memories of a soldier.* New York, The Century Co., 1928.

Segale, Sister Blandina. *At the end of the Santa Fe Trail.* Milwaukee, Bruce Publishing Co., 1948.

Sheridan, Philip H. *Personal memoirs.* New York, Charles L. Webster Co., 1888.

Sibley, George Champlin. *The road to Santa Fe. The journal and diaries of George Champlin Sibley and others pertaining to the surveying and marking of a road from the Missouri frontier to the settlements of New Mexico, 1825–1827.* Edited by Kate L. Gregg. Albuquerque. The University of New Mexico Press, 1952.

Sigüenza y Góngora, Carlos de. *The Mercurio volante of Don Carlos de Sigüenza y Góngora. An account of the first expedition of Don Diego de Vargas into New Mexico in 1692.* Translated, with an introduction and notes, by Irving Albert Leonard. Los Angeles, The Quivira Society, 1932.

Simpich, Frederick. *Down the Rio Grande. National Geographic Magazine,* v. 76, no. 4, Oct., 1939.

Siringo, Charles A. *Riata and spurs.* Boston, Houghton Mifflin and Co., 1931.

—— *A Texas cowboy, or fifteen years on the hurricane deck of a Spanish pony, taken from real life* . . . with bibliographical study and introduction by J. Frank Dobie and drawings by Tom Lea. New York, William Sloane Associates, 1950.

Sitwell, Osbert. *Winters of content, and other discursions on Mediterranean art and travel.* London, Gerald Duckworth and Co., Ltd., 1950.

Smith, Arthur D. Howden. *Old Fuss and Feathers* . . . *the life and exploits of Lt. General Winfield Scott.* New York, The Greystone Press, 1937.

Smith, Ephraim Kirby. *To Mexico with Scott; letters of Captain E. Kirby Smith to his wife,* prepared for the press by his daughter, Emma Jeanne Blackwood. . . Cambridge, Harvard University Press, 1917.

Smith, Erwin E. *Life on the Texas range.* Photographs by Erwin E. Smith; text by J. Evetts Haley. Austin, University of Texas Press, 1952.

Smith, Henry Nash. *Virgin land, the American west as symbol and myth.* Cambridge, Harvard University Press, 1950.

Smith, Justin H. *La república del Rio Grande. American Historical Review,* v. 25, Oct. 1919–July 1920.

Smith, Victor J. *A survey of Indian life in Texas.* Alpine, Texas, *West Texas Historical and Scientific Society, Circular no. 5,* 1941.

Soley, James Russell. *The blockade and the cruisers. (The navy in the Civil War.)* New York, Charles Scribner's Sons, 1903.

Stanley, F. *Fort Union [New Mexico].* Denver? [World Press], 1953.

Stone, John Augustus. *Matamora and other plays,* edited by Eugene R. Page. Princeton, Princeton University Press, 1941.

Strong, George Templeton. *The diary of George Templeton Strong,* edited by Allan Nevins and Milton Halsey Thomas. 4 v. New York, The Macmillan Co., 1952.

Sullivan, Mark. *Our times. v. 4 and 5. The United States, 1900–1925.* New York, Charles Scribner's Sons, 1933.

Sumpter, Jesse. *Life of Jesse Sumpter, oldest citizen of Eagle Pass, Texas, commenced to be written down May 30, 1902. Taken down by Harry Warren. Finished June 14, 1906.* Original document. Typescript. Eagle Pass, Texas, private collection. (Excerpts quoted by permission of owner.)

Talman, Charles Fitzhugh. *The realm of the air.* Indianapolis, Bobbs-Merrill Co., 1931.

Tannenbaum, Frank. *Mexico, the struggle for peace and bread.* New York, Alfred A. Knopf, 1950.

Thoburn, Joseph B. *Ancient irrigation ditches of the plains. Chronicles of Oklahoma,* Oklahoma Historical Society, v. 6, 1931.

Thomas, Alfred B. *The first Santa Fe expedition, 1792–93.* Chronicles of Oklahoma, Oklahoma Historical Society, v. 6, 1931.

—— *The plains Indians and New Mexico, 1751–1778.* Albuquerque, University of New Mexico Press, 1940.

Thomlinson, Matthew H. *The garrison at Fort Bliss.* El Paso, Hertzog and Resler, 1945.

Thoreau, Henry David. *Journal.* Edited by Bradford Torrey [In collected edition of] *The writings of Henry David Thoreau.* Boston, Houghton Mifflin Co., 1906.

Thorpe, T. B. *Our army on the Rio Grande.* Philadelphia, Carey and Harte, 1846.

Tierney, Luke. *Pike's Peak gold rush guidebooks of 1859,* by Luke Tierney, William B. Parsons *et al.* Edited by Leroy R. Hafen. Glendale, Arthur H. Clarke Co., 1941.

Tocqueville, Alexis de. *Democracy in America.* The Henry Reeve text . . . edited . . . by Phillips Bradley. 2 v. New York, Alfred A. Knopf, 1945.

Tompkins, Frank. *Chasing Villa, the story behind the story of Pershing's expedition into Mexico.* Harrisburg, Military Service Publishing Co., 1934.

Toulmin, Harry A. *With Pershing in Mexico.* Harrisburg, Military Service Publishing Co., 1935.

Toulouse, Joseph H., Jr. *The mission of San Gregorio de Abó. A report on the excavation and repair of a seventeenth-century New Mexico mission.* Albuquerque, University of New Mexico Press, 1949.

Toulouse, Joseph H. *Pioneer posts of Texas,* by Joseph H. and James H. Toulouse. San Antonio, Naylor Publishing Co., 1936.

Towne, Charles Wayland. *Shepherd's empire,* by Charles Wayland Towne and Edward Norris Wentworth. Norman, University of Oklahoma Press, 1945.

Townsend, E. E. *Early border elections. Bulletin 44,* West Texas Historical and Scientific Society: Publications No. 4. Alpine, Texas, Sul Ross State Teachers College, 1932.

——— *Rangers and Indians in the Big Bend region. Bulletin 56,* West Texas Historical and Scientific Society: Publications No. 6. Alpine, Texas, Sul Ross State Teachers College, 1935.

Trend, J. B. *The civilization of Spain.* London, Oxford University Press, 1944.

Trollope, Frances. *Domestic manners of the Americans.* Edited . . . by Donald Smalley. New York, Alfred A. Knopf, 1949.

Troxel, O. C. *The Tenth Cavalry in Mexico. Cavalry Journal,* July, 1927.

Tumulty, Joseph P. *Woodrow Wilson as I knew him.* Garden City, Doubleday Page and Co., 1921.

Twitchell, Ralph Emerson. *The leading facts of New Mexican history.* V. 1 and 2. Cedar Rapids, The Torch Press, 1911.

——— *Old Santa Fe, the story of New Mexico's ancient capital.* Santa Fe New Mexican Publishing Corp., 1925.

——— *The Spanish archives of New Mexico.* 2 v. Cedar Rapids, The Torch Press, 1914.

Underhill, Ruth. *Work-a-day life of the Pueblos.* United States Indian service, *Indian life and customs, no. 4.* U. S. Department of the Interior. Phoenix, Phoenix Indian School Printing Dept., 1946.

United States Congress. 43rd Congress, 1st session. House of Representatives. *Executive document no. 257. Depredations on the frontiers of Texas. Message from the President of the United States, transmitting a communication from the Secretary of State, and a copy of the report of the commissioners to inquire into depredations on the frontiers of Texas.* May 26, 1874.

—— 44th Congress. 1st session. House of Representatives. *Report no. 343. Texas frontier troubles.* February 29, 1876.

—— 45th Congress. 1st session. House of Representatives. *Executive document no. 13. Mexican border troubles. Message from the President of the United States* . . . 1877.

United States Department of Agriculture. Field flood control co-ordinating committee. *Survey report. Run-off and water-flow retardation and soil-erosion prevention for flood-control purposes. Rio Puerco watershed, tributary of the upper Rio Grande.* Signed Hugh G. Calkins, Arthur Upson, Millard Peck. 1940.

United States Department of Agriculture. Soil Conservation Service, Region 8. *A description of the lands contiguous to the Elephant Butte Irrigation District of Southern New Mexico.* Typescript. Albuquerque, 1938.

—— *Reconnaissance survey of human dependency on resources in the Rio Grande watershed.* Regional bulletin no. 33, Conservation economics series no. 6. Albuquerque, December, 1936.

—— *A report on the Rio Grande watershed with special reference to soil conservation problems.* Prepared by Rio Grande District staff in collaboration with the staff of the regional office. Signed E. R. Smith, District manager, Rio Grande District. Albuquerque, November 22, 1936.

—— *Rio Grande watershed in Colorado and New Mexico. A report on the condition and use of the land and water resources together with a general program for soil and water conservation.* Albuquerque, August, 1939.

—— *The sociological survey of the Rio Grande watershed.* Typescript. Albuquerque, 1936.

—— *Tewa Basin study. v. 1, The Indian pueblos; v. 2, The Spanish-American villages; v. 3, Physical surveys and other studies.* Mimeographed. Albuquerque, April, 1935.

United States Department of the Interior. Bureau of Reclamation. *Reclamation Handbook.* Washington, Superintendent of Documents, 1942.

United States Department of the Interior. Bureau of Reclamation, Region 5. *Brief descriptions of irrigation and multiple-purpose projects proposed for construction in the post-war period. June 1, 1945.*

United States Department of the Interior. National Park Service. *San Buenaventura Mission, Gran Quivira National Monument.* Santa Fe, Southwestern Monuments Association, ND.

United States [government] Office of the Superintendent of Indian Affairs. *Passport issued to a party of prairie travelers; signed by William Clark, Superintendent of Indian Affairs, July 23, 1820.* Original document. San Marino, Henry E. Huntington Library. (Excerpt quoted by permission of the Huntington Library.)

Vargas Zapata Luján Ponce de León, Diego de. *First expedition of Vargas into New Mexico, 1692.* Translated, with introduction and notes, by J. Manuel Espinosa. Albuquerque, University of New Mexico Press, 1940.

Vásquez de Coronado, Francisco. *Letter to the King of Spain from the province of Tiguex, Oct. 20, 1541.* (In *Narratives of the Coronado Expedition, 1540–1542,* edited by George P. Hammond and Agapito Rey.) Albuquerque, University of New Mexico Press, 1940.

Vega, Garcilaso de la. *The Florida of the Inca.* Translated and edited by John Grier and Jeanette Johnson Varner. Austin, University of Texas Press, 1951.

Vigil, Donaciano. *Minutes of a meeting held at Santa Fe, 27 August, 1837, by supporters of Governor Gonzáles . . . signed by Donaciano Vigil, acting secretary-sergeant.* Translation. Original document. San Marino, Henry E. Huntington Library. (Excerpts quoted by permission of the Huntington Library.)

—— *Speech made before New Mexico Assembly, May 16, 1846.* Original document. San Marino, Henry E. Huntington Library. (Excerpts quoted by permission of the Huntington Library.)

—— *Speech made before the New Mexico Assembly, June 22, 1846.* Original document. San Marino, Henry E. Huntington Library. (Excerpts quoted by permission of the Huntington Library.)

Vigil y Alarid, Juan Bautista. *Proclamation by Acting Governor Vigil y Alarid, Santa Fe, August 1846, to the citizens of Santa Fe, publishing General Kearny's proclamation of reassurances to the New Mexicans.* Original document. San Marino, Henry E. Huntington Library. (Excerpts quoted by permission of the Huntington Library.)

Villa, Francisco. *Manifesto addressed by General Francisco Villa to the nation, and documents justifying the disavowal of Venustiano Carranza as first chief of the revolution.* Chihuahua, Constitutionalist Army, headquarters, Division of the North, 1914.

Wadleigh, A. B. *Ranching in New Mexico, 1886–1890. New Mexico Historical Review,* v. 27, no. 1, January, 1952.

Wallace, Ernest. *The Comanches, lords of the south plains,* by Ernest Wallace and E. Adamson Hoebel. Norman, University of Oklahoma Press, 1952.

Wallace, Lew. *An autobiography.* New York, Harper and Brothers, 1906.

Wallace, Susan E. *Among the pueblos. Atlantic Monthly,* v. 46, August, 1880.

Walsh, Thomas J. *Papers of Senator Thomas J. Walsh.* Mss. Washington, The Library of Congress.

Ward, Charles Francis. *The Salt War of San Elizario (1877).* Thesis presented to the faculty of the graduate school of the University of Texas . . . Unpublished. Austin, 1932.

Warner, Louis H. *Archbishop Lamy, an epoch maker.* Sante Fe New Mexican Publishing Corp., 1936.

Watson, Don. *Cliff palace, the story of an ancient city.* Ann Arbor, Michigan, 1947.

Webb, Walter Prescott. *The Texas Rangers; a century of frontier defense.* Boston, Houghton Mifflin Co., 1935.

White, Leslie A. *The pueblo of Santo Domingo, New Mexico. Memoirs of the American Anthropological Assn.,* No. 43. Menasha, Wisconsin, 1935.

Whitford, William Clarke. *Colorado volunteers in the Civil War; the New Mexico campaign in 1862.* Denver, The State Historical and Natural History Society, 1906.

Whitlock, Brand. *Journal.* Chosen and edited . . . by Allan Nevins. New York, Appleton-Century Co., 1936.

Whitman, Walt. *Leaves of grass.* New York, Heritage Press, ND.

——— *Prose works.* Philadelphia, David McKay, ND.

Wilcox, Seb. B. *Conversations* at Laredo, Texas.

——— *Laredo during the Texas Republic. Southwestern Historical Quarterly,* v. 42, no. 2, October, 1938.

Wilder, Mitchell A. *Santos, the religious folk art of New Mexico,* by Mitchell A. Wilder and Edgar Breitenbach. With a foreword by Rudolf A. Gerken, Archbishop of Santa Fe. Colorado Springs, The Taylor Museum, 1943.

Williams, Ellen. *Three years and a half in the army; or, History of the Second Colorados.* New York, Fowler and Wells, 1885.

Williams, O. W. *Baja el sol.* Pamphlet. Undated.

——— *Pecos county—its history.* Pamphlet. Undated.

——— *Untitled pamphlet in form of a letter, dated Alpine, Texas, March 16th, 1902, addressed to "My dear children."*

Wilson, Thomas Woodrow. *The public papers of Woodrow Wilson. The New Democracy. Presidential messages, addresses, and other papers (1913–1917).* 2 v. Edited by Ray Stannard Baker and William E. Dodd. New York, Harper and Brothers, 1926.

Wislizenus, A. *Memoir of a tour through northern Mexico, connected with Colonel Doniphan's expedition, 1846–47.* 30th Congress, 1st session. *Senate, Miscellaneous no. 26.* Washington, Tippin and Streepen, Printers, 1848.

Wissler, Clark. *The American Indian.* New York, Oxford University Press, 1922.

Wolle, Muriel Sibell. *Stampede to timberline, the ghost towns and mining camps of Colorado.* Boulder, Colorado, The Author, 1949.

Wortham, Louis J. *A history of Texas from wilderness to commonwealth.* Fort Worth, Wortham-Molyneaux Co., 1924.

Wright, R. R. *Negro companions of the Spanish explorers. American Anthropologist,* v. 4, 1902.

Yoakum, H. *History of Texas from its first settlement in 1685 to its annexation to the United States in 1846.* 2 v. New York, Redfield, 1856.

APPENDIX D

The Names of the Rio Grande

APPENDIX D

The Names of the Rio Grande

The Rio Grande has borne various names during different periods and along several different reaches of its course. These are the names I encountered in my study of the river:

Grand River (General Wilkinson, 1806).
P'osoge (modern Tewa—"big river").
Rio Bravo (Castaño de Sosa, 1590, and Oñate, 1598).
Rio Bravo del Norte.
Rio Caudaloso ("carrying much water").
Rio de la Concepción (Rodríguez expedition, 1581).
Rio de las Palmas (Pineda, 1519).
Rio de Nuestra Señora (Alvarado, 1540).
Rio de San Buenaventura del Norte (Fernando del Bosque, 1675).
Rio del Norte (Pérez de Luxán, 1582).
Rio del Norte y de Nuevo Mexico (Map, in Sigüenza y Góngora, 1700).
Rio Grande.
Rio Grande del Norte.
Rio Guadalquivir (Rodríguez, 1581).
Rio Turbio (Pérez de Luxán, 1581).
River of May (David Ingram, 1568).
Tiguex River (Jaramillo, 1540).

Index

Index

VOLUME I: *pages 3 through 440*

VOLUME II: *pages 453 through 945*